Viscount Halifax and Mr. Anthony Eden

THE IMPACT OF HITLER

BRITISH POLITICS AND BRITISH POLICY

1933 – 1940

MAURICE COWLING

Fellow of Peterhouse, Cambridge

CAMBRIDGE UNIVERSITY PRESS

Published by the Syndics of the Cambridge University Press
Bentley House, 200 Euston Road, London NW1 2DB
American Branch: 32 East 57th Street, New York, N.Y. 10022

© Cambridge University Press 1975

Library of Congress Catalogue Card Number: 74–12968

ISBN: 0 521 20582 4

First published 1975

Printed in The Netherlands

CONTENTS

PREFACE

This volume is the third in a sequence about *The Politics of British Democracy*. In the future there will be an introduction bearing the sequence-title which will deal in its widest aspects with the period from 1850 to 1940 and will assess the methods used in the volumes which have now been published. Whether there will be anything more is uncertain. For that period an abundance of material is already available or will be shortly. For later periods there is a problem. It can be only a hope that a volume entitled *The Development of the Class Struggle 1924-1935* will be followed by *The Impact of Inflation* (from 1936 onwards).

For this volume no general introduction is needed. Readers who want one should read the first twelve and last forty-seven pages of *The Impact of Labour* or pages 287-340 of *Disraeli, Gladstone and Revolution*. All it is necessary to say here is that no attack is intended. The sole aim is to remove misunderstandings based on an implied contradiction between expediency and principle, and to present democratic politicians in a multi-dimensional context where they display on the fragmented nature of God's handiwork the only rational way of acting politically.

'Rational' here means what politicians can understand. It means working through contingency and accident, not rising above them. It means that principles are manifestations of personality no less than interests and passions and that all three form the context of political consciousness.

Politicians understand as much as they need to of the situations in which they work. This need not be much. But their actions follow from the solipsisms in which they are located. In locating them and in imputing right to no one in relation to the rest, history need not deny that conflict can be good or its outcome better than its parts.

What political history can do is to dissect solipsisms. What it can also do is to show them in conflict. What it can do most of all is to show them conflicting in face of perpetual envelopment in a prudent, necessary and corporate venality.

For access to material which they own or control, the author is grateful to Mr and Mrs Stephen Lloyd, Mr John Grigg, Viscount Bridgeman, Captain Stephen Roskill, Mr William Rees-Mogg, Lord Keyes, Mr Patrick Attlee, Lord Croft, Mr Julian Amery MP, Mr David Marquand MP, Mr Martin Gilbert, Mr Philip Goodhart MP, Lady Beatrix Levison, Viscount Simon, Mr Michael Dawson, Mr John Hull, Mr David Watt, Mr Guy Paget, Sir O. O'Malley, Lady Vansittart, Mr Robert Rhodes James, Mr Alan Beattie and Professor David Dilks.

He is grateful to the Controller of H.M. Stationery Office for permission to quote from Crown-Copyright records. He is grateful also to other owners of copyright material for permission to use it, and he apologises to any whom he has failed to consult. He has been helped by innumerable librarians and archivists — and especially in the Public Record Office and by the staffs of the Beaverbrook, Churchill College, Bodleian, Birmingham University and Cambridge University libraries.

The author has incurred debts to the Faculty of History at Cambridge for a grant from its Political Science Fund; to Messrs Peter Baker, J. McNee, M. Ramsay and T.A. Woolley for checking references; to Mrs M.J. Anderson for making the index; and to Mrs E.D. Beebe, Mrs O.G. Page, Mrs J. Ratcliffe and Mrs H. Stephens for typing. To Mrs H.M. Dunn his debt in these respects is especially great.

Professor F.H. Hinsley, Professor J.R. Vincent and Mrs Zara Steiner very kindly read the typescript and made many valuable suggestions. Dr C.M. Andrew, Lord Blake, Dr Fraser Cameron, Mr Alistair Cooke, Dr Patrick Cosgrave, Professor J.A. Gallagher, Mr C. Howard, Professor E. Kedourie, Dr Andrew Jones, Mr J.J. Lee, Dr E.R. Norman, Dr Anil Seal and Mr I.R. Willison made suggestions or gave advice. Dr P. Byrd kindly lent his Ph D thesis. Mr Paul Addison, Mr Martin Ceadel and Dr Daniel Waley made helpful remarks or read helpful papers at Mr A.J.P. Taylor's seminar. The Master and Fellows of Peterhouse provided conditions which were both helpful and agreeable.

April 1974   Maurice Cowling

'I doubt whether the absolutely unparalleled series of diplomatic blunders in the last four months can ever be sufficiently repaired. They may quite easily end by destroying all that you and I have worked for. For Baldwin doesn't know and cánnot act, and is well fitted by virtues, dilettantism and inertia to become the Lord North of a far greater catastrophe.' Garvin to Amery, October 2 1935

'No supporter of the Government should ever again without shame lift up the Union Jack at a public meeting or on an election platform. The Labour party is alone entitled to lift not only the Union Jack which stands for Britain, but the Red Flag, which stands for Socialism and democracy. The "old man of Munich" and the rest could only raise the white flag of the coward on the one hand and the black flag of the traitor and the robber on the other.' Dalton at Southport, May 28 1939, *The Times*, May 29

'I feel that our world, or all that remains of it, is committing suicide, whilst Stalin laughs and the Kremlin triumphs.' Henry Channon MP, Parliamentary Private Secretary to the Under-Secretary for Foreign Affairs, in his diary, September 3 1939

INTRODUCTION

In 1933 Europe was governed by innumerable politicians presiding over the many pockets of insecure power which constituted the régime in each particular state. On all these régimes the impact of Hitler was profound. In all the geography of politics was transformed as the danger of war raised problems so acute that all other problems were affected. By 1939 few régimes had escaped a transformation. By 1945 many had been swept away.

In Britain the problem was defined psephologically. Though a general election in 1940 might have returned a Labour government with greater power than Labour had in the Churchill Coalition, the possibility was important not just because it might have occurred but because the thought that it might be prevented affected policy when Hitler had been made central, not just by himself but by publicists and the party leaders.

In these years foreign policy became central not only because it was but because politicians could fit it into the political battle which had begun in the twenties. To the Labour party it gave a respectability it might not otherwise have regained so quickly after 1931. By others the domestic appeasement of the twenties was assumed in order to attack the international appeasement of the thirties. The result was an alliance between a class-conflict programme in the Labour party and an international-conflict programme in parts of the Liberal and Conservative parties.

In 1939 the effect was devastating. In the first nine months of the war, Chamberlain tried to circumvent it. In May 1940 he was discredited and his coalition replaced.

The displacement of Chamberlain was a victory for Conservatives who, in disputing his leadership, had developed links over the whole range of opinion. In reducing him from being leader of a party into being leader of a group, Churchill had abandoned the anti-socialist rôle he had played since 1919. In the process he had assisted at the event at which Labour was in office not as minor partner, not as pathetic

remnant and not on Liberal sufferance, but as a major element in a centre government.

As a centre coalition, the government of May 1940 realised
the hopes which many politicians had had since the 1931
régime had first cracked electorally six years before. It survived the fall of France, the threat to Egypt and the loss of
Singapore, developing in office the consensual relationship
established in opposition and leaving it uncertain whether it
was a Lib-Lab trap for Conservatives or a Conservative trap in
which Attlee was the victim. Its continuation into the period
of Russo-American victory established the post-war illusion
that a régime which had been on the 'right side' in relation to
Hitler must have embodied an indefeasible centrality for the
future. Through Churchill, Sinclair, Attlee and Eden (who
were its founders) and through Butskellism (which was invented by Hoare in 1934) it lasted until Macmillan's retirement, establishing inflation, disestablishing the Empire and
permitting a receptivity in which the central features of
Labour thinking became entrenched as normal.

For historical writing the régime's success had two consequences. It made it possible to see the foreign-policy conflict of the thirties as anticipating the egalitarian patriotism
of the forties rather than as continuing the class conflict of
the twenties. And it produced a built-in negativity about the
régime which had been defeated. Though neither normally
deliberate nor always self-conscious, identification with the
régime that 'won the war' made writing about its enthrone-
ment an act of self-congratulation.

This obstacle to understanding was supplemented by another. The most accessible material, being designed for publication (to the public or other governments), enabled policy
to be equated with diplomatic statement and the half-truths
of democratic reassurance with the intentions behind acts of
state. Since the intentions of critics were similarly lost in
their public appearances, policy conflict was presented in the
single-dimensional terms in which it had been discussed publicly in the first place.

The result was neglect of the fact that the public statements of politicians were functional, not 'true', and were
about other politicians as much as about policy. This was
strengthened by the reticence of Feiling's *Chamberlain*

(which was completed in 1944)[1] and by the sale and scale of the first volume of Churchill's *Second World War*.

Churchill's report of his encounter with destiny embodied more genuine recollection and more impressive documentation than Lloyd George's report of his. But both were coloured by the needs of their post-war situations and by their desire to stand above the post-war conflict of the parties. How far the 'saviour of the nation' was the suppliant leader of a defeated party is not clear. What is clear is that Churchill established a view by catching a mood which so deepened the contrast between himself and what went before him that even defenders of Chamberlain thereafter assumed that the differences were as he had described them.

A similar conviction that the policies differed, and that Munich reflected the difference, was enshrined in Wheeler-Bennett's *Munich* and in the crude memorials to his fellow Jews erected by a great historian of British aristocracy.[2] It was confirmed by denigration of Chamberlain's civic origins and by shrill nonsense from a great thinker. It was deepened by the assumption that Chamberlain had emasculated parliament and deceived the people, and had caused Britain to stand alone after commitments had been given that he never really wanted. It was condoned historically when Rowse discerned a 'deep ... propriety' in the 'coming together' in May 1940 of the 'old ruling class ... and the solid representatives of the working class'. It achieved immortality when the self-inflicted wounds of June were seen as permitting a 'happy breed' to make a 'contribution to the world...even greater than that of our ancestors'.[3]

This assumed that 'liberty' was being defended, not an empire being lost, and that Churchill was Pericles, Marlborough, Elizabeth and Drake. It did not ask whether he was implicated in the situation he inherited and how far his relations with Baldwin affected the positions he adopted.

Churchill need not be blamed for climbing Olympus. Nor need his Lib-Lab laureates like Rowse, who had spent the thirties as laureate to Keynes and Morrison.[4] Nor even should Bryant, who had been Chamberlain's editor and a Baldwinian defender of the Chiefs of Staff, and who might have been expected to know better.[5] But assumptions generated in malice and gratitude between Dunkirk and Abadan established a living interest which will survive the most zealous attempts at reinterpretation.

Reinterpretation began in the mid-fifties with the memoirs of Hoare. They were followed by works from Medlicott, Watt, Taylor, Thompson, Gilbert, Robbins, Lammers, Wendt and Gannon, and by the slow unearthing of a City and Whitehall-based suspicion of the economic power of the United States.

Hoare gave a retrospective coherence and did considerable injustice to his own positions. Lammers established that neither Chamberlain nor the Foreign Office thought 'ideologically': he also questioned the belief that Chamberlain wanted to set Hitler on to Stalin.[6] Gilbert's *Roots of Appeasement* (1966) recanted much of *The Appeasers* of 1963. Without either Chamberlain's papers or the Public Records, Watt had intuitions which in policy respect were right.[7]

Taylor's book was an isolationist landmark which implied the need to explain why Chamberlain felt obliged to intervene in Eastern Europe. Robbins saw that the explanation would be complicated. Wendt emphasized economic policy, Howard the Empire. Thompson and Gannon gave differing twists to Medlicott's view that the difference between Chamberlain and his critics was insignificant. Before and after the government archives were opened in 1970, all of these differed from Taylor in assuming — what Middlemass, Aster, Parkinson and Barnett assumed also — that 'the notables outside the government, most backbench MP's, the Parliamentary Opposition and the Press... made little impact on decisions during the Chamberlain government.'[8]

Whether foreign policy can be understood from governmental archives depends, however, on its place in party conflict. In the past hundred and fifty years, though often important, it has seldom been central. From the beginning of 1936, it was as central as Protection in 1846 or Ireland in 1886, and as the Turkish question had been in the 1870s.

In these circumstances, policy-making was a complicated matter. Ministers were informed by Foreign Office, Treasury and Defence staff advice. And they reacted to an indictment. But advisers were listened to or not as the indictment connected 'manifest truths' about the international order with the controversial 'truths' of party conflict, and decisions were taken in face of other politicians who, like ministers themselves, were artificial persons made up of the assessments they made about the advice that they were given.

For party leaders, some ex-ministers and a few back-benchers, advice came from a parallel bureaucracy. For most backbenchers on most questions, it came from newspapers, White papers and discussion with one another. For everyone it involved an implicit understanding that policy-making was inseparable from the spectrum of conflict which had been established when Baldwin and MacDonald stabilised the class struggle ten years before.

Whatever the legacy of the past, the future was unknown. Churchill, Eden and Sinclair helped the Labour leaders to become central. But they did not know that they would do so, and the 'truths' they established about the régime they replaced must be seen, initially, as merely instruments for replacing it.

When foreign policy is marginal, it is possible to neglect the total situation and still show how policy was conducted. In the late thirties, foreign policy was the form that party conflict took. Politicians conducted it in the light of party considerations; it can only be understood if these considerations are reconstructed. It is for this reason that the Prologue sketches the party situation of the early thirties. Part I then presents foreign policy as an extension of its function from the Hoare-Laval pact to the occupation of Prague in March 1939. Part II describes the attacks made on Chamberlain, Part III their effect between Prague and the Russo-German pact in August. Chamberlain then resumes control (Part IV), fighting a politician's war and expecting a political victory until brought down (the sketchiest part of the book documentarily) by defeat in Scandinavia.

The theme is the relationship between the objectives of politicians and their decisions about policy. The claim is that this is the way in which foreign policy must be understood.

To make this claim, and write in this way, is misleading since the obvious context was the international system. This, however, whatever else it was, was a register of opinion in national capitals. If it is to be understood, the politics of the Powers must be seen through the filtering effected by the politics of the parties. Until they are seen — and seen in detail, in most of the states concerned — it will be impossible to give a real account of the development of events.

Parties performed different functions in different places and registered differing relationships between politicians and public. Though all reacted to Hitler (who was also reacting), their reactions reflected pre-existing functions, as well as considered conclusions about the international situation. These functions must be established in depth. Establishing them may take a long time. In some cases it may be impossible. For the moment British policy may be seen emerging from the situation in which Hitler became a problem.

This situation was dominated by the class struggle, which had been defined in the early twenties, won (by the forces of resistance) in 1931 and renewed with the electoral dilapidation of 1934. In 'the following six years, it was dominated (and the class struggle transformed) by Hitler's challenge to the double-talk which surrounded nearly all discussion of Imperial defence.

The realisation that the world would not be as it had been was the essence of the situation to which politicians had responded in the decade before 1914. Whether 'peace' was 'threatened' by 'violence' or 'the Empire' by 'rivals', this was the need to which relevant thinking responded. On the one hand, it produced the internationalism which became the norm when the war was over. On the other, it produced demands for autarky, Imperial unity and renovation of the national and Imperial defences.

Though pre-1914 Imperialism had an expanding and jingoistic rhetoric, its essence was the realisation that the Empire was in danger. To some extent it assumed that defensive impregnability was possible so long as Isolation was ended. To some extent, it assumed that sentiment could make up for financial deficiency. The system of sentiment lasted the war which, however, eroded the financial base on which military power depended. In the indebtedness of post-war Britain, the League of Nations on the one hand, the Statute of Westminster on the other, and Locarno — the type of non-alliance guarantee of peace — provided new sentiments and altruistic clothing to deal with the fact that air power had placed Imperial frontiers on the Rhine.

Both the sentiments and the clothing were impermanent. The peace settlement was denounced in England as soon as it was made and had lost moral force long before Hitler began to dismantle it. Though victory brought entanglements which had not been there before, the governments of the twenties undermined them by leaving it uncertain at what point British intervention in Europe could become effective. With the rejection of the Geneva Protocol and the refusal to make Locarno an alliance, financial, imperial and isolationist considerations became important.

In spite of this, the nakedness of the Empire created a vested interest in the *status quo* and contradictory desires both to restore the pre-war economic system and to anticipate its erosion. Moreover, the importance of liberal opinion in a class-polarised politics made a power-political justification unsuitable, so foreign policy was presented in terms which the League of Nations Union would approve. *Laissez-faire*, however, was dead, and was buried in 1933. 'Collective Security' was a bluff which had only to be called. When Hitler, Mussolini and the Japanese called it, politicians created new aligments among themselves in the course of wrestling with the discovery that this had happened.

The effect was as striking as the discovery of the Labour party in the twenties. It produced the same reactions and provided similar opportunities for reputations to be made. Where MacDonald had played according to the rules, however, Hitler did not, and did much damage in the course of establishing that he would not do so. All but one of the foreign secretaries and prime ministers who dealt with foreign policy were destroyed, as well as a number of soldiers and officials. But it was neither depravity which determined policy up to September 1939 nor a reign of virtue that began in May 1940, and Chamberlain merely fumbled when faced with a contradiction between the desire to maintain peace by being detached from central and eastern Europe and the desire to be involved strenuously in it.

Central and eastern Europe had never been areas of British interest; except at the Peace Conferences, they had not been primary subjects for British action. Though the Turkish collapse had produced conflict with Russia and Greece and the beginning of a Middle Eastern empire, both conflict and empire had been confined. In the post-war decades, British interests followed the thin line of oil and trade through the

Mediterranean, Red Sea and Persian Gulf to India, Malaya, Hong Kong and Australasia.

This was the 'Empire' as the Services saw it — and the hard core of the strategic problem. It required acquiescence from Italy, Turkey, Greece and Egypt and a want of interest in central and eastern Europe. Politically, however, central and eastern Europe became the crux. Not because of direct interests and commitments but because French governments regarded a second front as crucial if the Rhine was to be defended. It was for this reason that the British desire to keep out was thwarted by the French need to keep in, and why policy had to be conducted on the assumption that detachment was impracticable.

Whether, in these circumstance, Britain should help or halt German influence in central and eastern Europe depended on whether this was seen as a guarantee of peace or a prelude to world domination, and on whether an anti-German alliance would give undue assistance to the Russians.

The East European commitments of 1939 were, of course, primarily about Hitler. But to say this is to beg the question. For, if Hitler's 'object' was to 'hurl his armies against Russia' (rather than to secure relations with the army and the German public), then the decision to obstruct him would have done Stalin's work for him if the French collapse in 1940 had not prevented it being done, and this would have been so unless Stalin wanted to co-operate with France and Britain more than he wanted to involve them in war against Germany.

Hitler may have wanted to destroy the British Empire. But this was not obvious then and is far from obvious now. It is at least as likely that he aimed primarily to fulfil promises about Germany's economic and world rôle and was compelled to attack Britain only by British action in May and September 1938.[9] Even if it is assumed that his aims from the start were to 'purify' Germany, destroy Russia and colonise the Ukraine, that suggests nothing about his attitude to Britain.

It may be that Hitler was the 'beast from the abyss' whom Britain had a duty to destroy.[10] It may be that victory over Russia would have been followed by an attack in the West. It is possible to deny the duty, to question the sequence or to believe that success, or failure to succeed against Russia, would have affected the character of the régime in Germany.

Why Hitler wanted to destroy Russia and what he would have done afterwards are questions to which many answers can be given. This book gives none. All it does is to display the problem and the curious thinking that lay behind the British decision to resolve it.

The final solution was a succession of commitments between the Runciman mission in August 1938 and the guarantee to Poland eight months later. At each point in the approach to involvement, however, detachment was the objective. That it turned into an attempt at alliance with Russia was the work of Halifax who was the chief cause of the events which made Chamberlain a ghost in the machine between the occupation of Prague and the Russo-German pact in August.

To history, until yesterday, Halifax was the arch-appeaser. This, it is now recognised, was a mistake. His rôle, however, was complicated. In these pages he is not the man who stopped the rot, but the embodiment of Conservative wisdom who decided that Hitler must be obstructed because Labour could not otherwise be resisted.

Why Britain should have chosen to obstruct Hitler except in France or the Low Countries was not obvious. Until September 1938 it had been out of the question. The change was made possible by the decision then to underwrite an international guarantee of a dismembered Czechoslovakia.

However ambiguous, the guarantee was crucial. If Chamberlain erred (as, given his intentions, he did), one element in the error consisted in the decision to give it when he had previously assumed that Britain's only commitment beyond Locarno should be in the defunct mechanics of the League. Up to September 1938 his policy was exactly that; he abandoned it then the better to pursue it, and his failure thereafter was a result of political pressures imprisoning him in a policy he had no intention of adopting.

Chamberlain knew that war would be damaging to Britain, to the Empire, and in terms of human suffering. He had, therefore, been performing a balancing act in which the threat to intervene was designed to make intervention unnecessary and where commitments to France had been stepped up, beyond the formal need, in order to prevent the

French intervening. After Berchtesgaden this failed; he lost balance, gave a guarantee he did not expect to honour and, after Prague, gave himself a retrospective firmness when he needed to establish that he had meant it.

The negative calculations of 1938 thus initiated the commitments of 1939. But these, too, were made so that the threat of war would prevent war being declared, just as the declaration of war would make it unnecessary to fight it, and because, after Prague, the policy of avoiding war could only be pursued in terms which the political climate would permit.

This was determined by the reactions of politicians which themselves were a function of the conceptions they had of the rôles they should play in the system they were working. For some (not only in the Labour party) the leading rôle was a class-war one. For others, it involved adopting positions designed to conceal the class war. For many Conservatives, it involved sensitive responses to what was conceived of as the opinion of the Centre.

As an object of pursuit, the Centre was a moving fixture. With the crumbling of the Centre established in 1931, it had meant primarily economic flexibility (and criticism of Chamberlain for being inflexible) until it came to mean criticism of Chamberlain for being inflexible about foreign policy.

No more than in office were changes in opposition dictated solely by the merits of questions. For Chamberlain's critics, as much as for him, the conclusions reached resulted from the situations in which they reached them and the effect they had from the situations to which they applied them. Whether as genuine belief or as 'an instrumentality' necessary for removing a prime minister, the 'Centre' was central both in developing criticism after 1936 and in affecting policy in 1939.

The 'central' position in foreign policy in the early thirties was a League and disarmament one, but, until 1935, foreign policy was not central. The Peace Ballot and Abyssinia then became the chief focus of discussion and the issue through which Baldwin re-established his 'centrality' at the election. It was the lead Chamberlain gave against the League after the defeat of the Abyssinians which initiated a division about himself and the foreign policy his party position had led him into representing.

On the one hand, the Labour party, Sinclair, Churchill and the League of Nations Union emphasised the need to rescue the League and moved, when this failed, towards demanding 'collective' resistance to dictators. On the other, Chamberlain and most Conservatives contested the League's 'centrality' and asserted the significance of other methods of maintaining peace.

Chamberlain implied a contrast with what had gone before, but the differences were verbal. The new policy involved the same aim as the old and the same search for issues with which to bring France and Germany together. Even when the language was different, it pursued the same combination of rearmament and reconciliation as had been pursued since 1933 and maintained the same hope for agreement about treaty revision, disarmament and a German return to Geneva.

By March 1939 Chamberlain had been pursuing this for two and a half years. He had also been opposed for two and a half years for doing so. The objection, however, was not so much to 'appeasement' (which was not an accurate description of his policy) as to his insistence on asserting that 'Collective' Security was dead. When the occupation of Prague showed that *'détente'* was dead too, it came to seem that it had died because 'dictators' could not be 'resisted' while the League was disregarded.

Whether Churchill (or Eden) would have been more successful it is difficult to know, since their policies (except about Russia) were much the same as his. The similarity, however, did not stop them seeming to be different or prevent the 'difference' having an effect. The effect was the commitments of 1939 which were given because a climate had been created which made it dishonourable not to give them.

Since the climate which established the relationship dominated most subsequent accounts of the pre-war party situation, a peculiar self-denial is needed if Chamberlain is to be understood in his functioning context, where he was the new embodiment of a realistic version of average wisdom, and where his actions were contested and dismissed because contest and dismissal were the normal modes of procedure in the system on which his power depended.

In the thirties the system contained heavy deposits of Conservative opinion. These included Chamberlainite Unionism, as well as innumerable droppings from the resistance situations of the twenties, the coalition situations of 1916 and 1921 and the soothing streams of Cecilian, Whig, Young England and suburban idealism which had persisted throughout.

The deposits cannot easily be separated; together they created a coherence as effective as the coherence of the Liberal Left. But whereas the foreign-policy coherence of the Left has found its place in history, the Conservative coherence has suffered the oblivion of defeat. If it is to be recovered, disbelief will have to be suspended.

This is not the same as believing that Chamberlain 'had a case' for delaying an 'inevitable' confrontation or did 'the right thing' in going to war when he did. It involves asking (heuristically) why 'inevitability' should be assumed and why Conservatives recognised that more options were open than were taken. It demands as dispassionate a language in writing about Chamberlain (and Nevile Henderson) as in writing about Churchill (or Vansittart). Above all it demands the assumption that it was neither morally obligatory nor prudentially self-evident that Hitler should be obstructed in Eastern Europe.

Inevitably, these demands will make it seem that Chamberlain is being defended. But, in fact, no defence has been given; nor would *defence* be an historical undertaking. What is required, alike by inherent probability and the historical duty, is a dramatic detachment which presents all equal actors equally and imputes logical equality to all the positions with which it deals. If this reduces Chamberlain's responsibility, it does so only by seeing him in the context of the system of which he was a part.

Whether Britain would have obstructed Hitler or gone to war under a different system, régime or form of government cannot be known. What this book does is to show in what sense the decision to do so was a facet of the way in which 'politics' were conducted in the shadow of 'British democracy'.

PROLOGUE

THE UNFOLDING OF THE PROBLEM

1

THE RECOVERY OF THE LABOUR PARTY

'If Simon is a catastrophe, as I agree that he is, the Prime Minister seems me to be a cataclysm. If only there were an alternative government, I think it would be the duty of all of us to say so.'
Cecil of Chelwode to Lloyd George, April 27 1934.

'At the last general election the Government had immense support in popular journalism. Now the *Daily Herald* and the *News Chronicle* together give the Socialist opposition all the pull in the Press for the millions. For different reasons, and pointing their guns from divergent angles, the *Daily Mail* and the *Daily Express* batter National Government from the other side. Nothing can correct this enormous disadvantage but some new and vivid organisation for propaganda directly organised by the Government itself.' Garvin in the *Observer*, May 6 1934.

'The National government in 1934 is certainly not as strong as it was in 1931 ... Yet the alliance between different schools of political thought which brought it into being, has become quietly and steadily stronger, in spite of a Liberal recession. The allies at first regarded the emergency which brought them together as a mere interruption of normal conditions; they are beginning to recognise it now as the end of an era. Old policies which they had been willing to suspend as temporarily inapplicable, they are now inclined to write off as fundamentally obsolete. They are no longer content with the "doctor's mandate"; they want a new school of medicine. And if any of them feel some doubt whether the National Government, as at present constituted, can found such a new school, they are at least sure that it cannot be founded by any of the old political parties acting on the old lines.
'All these considerations are obvious enough ...' Lord Eustace Percy, *Government in Transition* (1934), pp. 2–3.

At the general election of 1931 MacDonald, Baldwin and Samuel received over 14 million votes, won 554 seats and had a majority of almost 500 in the House of Commons. Three years later the 'National government' seemed likely to lose the next election. During the electoral dilapidation of 1934 it was under attack from Lloyd George, the Labour party and the Samuelite Liberals (who had resigned in 1932), and from Cripps and the Socialist League, Cecil and the League of Nations Union, Mosley and the British Union of Fascists and a broad span of Conservative critics who clustered round

Garvin, Amery, Churchill, Salisbury, Rothermere and Austen Chamberlain.

These oppositions opposed in the shadow of the belief that the general election had been a fluke and that the by-elections supplied a more adequate guide to the future. The questions they raised were whether the Conservative party would stay in one piece, whether the government could keep hold of its Liberal vote and what changes (if any) would be needed if a Labour victory was to be avoided.

Of the oppositions about which ministers had to think, the least significant was that led by Mosley, who was thought to have such bad judgment that there was nothing to fear.[1] This may have been a mistake. It might have been more accurate to say that Mosley was unlucky in the timing of his major acts as a politician. There was room for the broad-based Centre lead he had aimed to give on resigning from the Labour Cabinet in 1930. But the formation of the National government followed closely on the formation of his New party, which might have gone far if the election of 1931 had been indecisive. Nor is it certain what would have happened if he had still been a Labour MP after the Labour party had been massacred. It was only after the election (when the prospects for unemployment seemed limitless) that he staked his future on the presumption that the régime would collapse.

Mosley came from a family of Conservative squires who had become rich with the development of Manchester. Politically he was a Young Englander ex-service MP who had worked with Salisbury and Cecil and had married Curzon's daughter. From both angles he was well placed to understand the uncertainties felt by Conservative politicians in face of an unknown electorate.

Mosley intended to be a demagogue. But, in being one, he was trying, like Baldwin, Salisbury and Cecil, to translate the politics of judgment and decision into terms which an uneducated electorate would understand. Being an opportunist and seeking an opportunity where none existed so obviously in the Conservative party, his membership of the Labour party from 1923 onwards involved him in another approach to the problem which all politicians faced equally. It was only when that failed in 1930, after coming near to success, and after he had failed with the New party, that he tried the British Union of Fascists.

It is easy to say that Mosley stood no chance of getting anywhere as a Fascist. Certainly he got nowhere. He provided something for Labour politicians to be solemn about. He worried the government when Rothermere supported him at the point of electoral recession. His followers fought a few seats on local councils. But Hitler's violence on June 30 1934 did him no good; his own violence at Olympia did him less. Association with Randolph Churchill did nothing to restore him.[2]

Apart from Carson, no serious modern parliamentarian had called the régime in question. But where Ulster escalated at Carson's touch, unemployment did the opposite to Mosley. In the four years after the British Union of Fascists was formed, unemployment halved as the restrained demagoguery of the parliamentary leaders and the relationship between newspapers and the parliamentary parties destroyed him. The rise in unemployment in 1938 did him no good. Nor did Jewish immigration and the prospect of a war 'on behalf of Jewish interests'. By 1939, he mattered as little as the Communist party, and had less effect. In his early forties, his only hope was a German occupation. Once he is put into the Cecilian context from which he emerged, there is no Mosley problem except to explain why a Cecilian should have expected the politics of Limehouse to become the politics of the nation.

Where Mosley and the British Union of Fascists fought elections Cecil and the League of Nations Union did not. They, however, did not need to, since the Union had for long been established as a respectable statement of the desire for peace. Though many of its active supporters were Liberals, Cecil expected the Union to seek support in all parties and expected all parties to support it. Until he resigned from the Baldwin government in 1927, he was Austen Chamberlain's ministerial assistant. Having been Henderson's adviser during the second Labour government, he accepted membership of the Geneva delegation after the formation of the National government.

Cecil was an uncomfortable colleague and natural resigner: in office he was seldom decisive. Yet, through persistent propaganda, a nation-wide organisation and association with politicians who mattered, the Union contributed to the frame of mind which established that 'alliances' were bad and League and Locarno 'mutuality' the remedy for the power-politics by which war situations were supposed to have been created.

In the 1930s the leaders of the Union were Cecil himself, Gilbert Murray, who was an Asquithean, and Noel-Baker, who was a member of the Labour party. Apart from Lansbury and MacDonald, the party leaders were all presidents (with Grey as distinguished figure-head until his death in 1933). The Conservative contingent included Austen Chamberlain, Lytton, Cranborne, Crookshank, Lord Eustace Percy and Mrs Dugdale (until she joined the National Labour party in 1937).

Cecil's object remained what it had been ten years before — a 'complete transformation of international relations' and the 'abolition of war'. Success in inserting this into the political vocabulary had not been paralleled by success in Whitehall. Resistance there had been paralleled by failure at Geneva where the League machinery reflected the absence of the United States. When the Japanese rubbed the point home in 1931 and the Disarmament Conference collapsed two years later, the problem became acute.

To Cecil the events of the next two years were a struggle between the Union, backed by the 'whole force of public opinion' and the instinct of ministers and civil servants for circumventing it.[3] In these years experience at Geneva convinced him that the League was being endangered by two major defects in British thinking.

The first was 'Hankeyism' — the belief that the balance of power and interests of states were the only basis for international relations and that 'war' was 'the right and proper process by which things move in this world'.[4] Cecil had for long believed that Hankey was 'not in favour of the abolition of war'.[5] In the years when the Disarmament Conference was broken, Hankey, his 'technical advisers' and the dominance of the Services over the Service ministers were seen as major obstacles to British support for the League.

This would not have mattered if Cecil had believed that

the government intended to be firm. Its ambiguity towards Japan convinced him that it did not. He admired Eden[6] and Halifax[7] and had high regard for Baldwin's intentions. But Baldwin was not Prime Minister and had no grip where foreign policy was concerned. MacDonald was an enemy of the League and Eden was not in the Cabinet, which included Simon as Foreign Secretary, Londonderry as Air Minister and Hailsham, who did not conceal his 'contempt and disapproval of the disarmament movement and all that led up to it'.[8]

What Cecil and his followers wanted was 'courage ... sincerity' and moral leadership at Geneva.[9] What they got was a clever lawyer who believed in secret diplomacy where 'everything that ha[d] been hopeful in the Disarmament Conference ha[d] been achieved by public discussion'[10] and whom 'foreigners at Geneva, Americans in the United States, officials in the Foreign Office [and] may I add, colleagues in the Cabinet' dismissed as 'the worst Foreign Secretary since Derby in 1876'.[11]

Cecil wanted a disarmament agreement as an end itself, and because the Versailles settlement had assumed that other states would reduce their armaments at the same time as disarmament was imposed on Germany. Having supported the attempt to make one with Brüning, he continued to want one when Hitler arrived in office. In March 1933 he favoured 'the total abolition of naval and military aircraft, plus the creation of an international air force' (for civil aviation), believing that 'if we fail to secure substantial air disarmament and to give the Germans equality there ... [there would be] little hope [of] doing anything anywhere'.[12] Even after setbacks later in the year he advocated 'the abolition of aggressive arms' since 'the power of the defensive' would be such that 'France and the smaller countries would be safer than ... in any other way'.[13]

Hitler, however, presented a problem. Though 'much disturbed by [his] educational policy', Cecil and Murray were not sure that 'militarism' had come to stay or was 'quite as dangerous or ... deep-rooted as it would be ... in France or America'.[14] On hearing that 'Goebbels [had] made rather a favourable impression at Geneva and [was] said to be quite pleased with the League', Cecil explained on the wireless a month before the German withdrawal that the 'rules govern-

ing [German] disarmament' should be 'the same in principle
as those governing the armaments of any other civilised
power'. [15]

Uncertainty did not survive the events of 1934. Barthou, it
is true, was 'a bad man' and Herriot a 'dangerous' one, and
the Germans were 'seriously frightened of ... a preventive
war'. [16] But the manifest fact of 'German youth ... being
trained to ... idealise war' made it difficult to believe 'the
peaceful professions made by German statesmen for foreign
consumption'.[17] An Anglo-French *alliance* was as undesirable
as it had been before, but Russian membership of the League
was highly desirable. By the end of the year, Cecil was much
less sure about the opinion he expressed six months earlier
that 'if [the French] made an attack on Germany after Germany had expressed her willingness to accept some reasonable settlement of the disarmament question, England would
not support France, and we should have to consider what our
duty was under the Locarno Treaty'.[18]

1934 was decisive for Cecil's judgment of the government
which missed the opportunity provided by the election victory of the French Radicals to get French co-operation and
entered the disarmament conference with so little conception of a policy that, when asked, he was even more unwilling
to join the delegation than he had been the year before. [19]
When even Baldwin cited the 'arch-militarist F.S. Oliver' in
declaring that Britain's frontier was on the Rhine, it was
obvious to Cecil, for whom Collective Security knew no
limits, that he was a very long way from a League frame of
mind. [20] He decided that the government 'ought to go', in
spite of 'the intellectual nonentity of the Labour party'.[21]

1934 was the first of Cecil's years of ultimate anguish. The
world-wide spread of 'nationalism' had been matched by 'isolationism' at home. Yet 'the truth was' that isolation was a
'principle of anarchy' and that 'in modern conditions' nations
could 'no more live alone than individuals'. [22] It was in this
situation, when both government and Union were at their
nadir, and when 'blind tradition and bewildered selfishness'
were resuming their sway, that the Peace Ballot was invented.

The Peace Ballot, or National Declaration, was designed to
give members of the Union a sense of participation between

crises. By getting them to distribute a nationwide question-naire, it was hoped to restore the 'waning faith' in the League, rehabilitate the Union as a public force and combat Beaverbrook's and Rothermere's 'mischievous campaign of isolationism'. [23] Cecil did not anticipate the attention the Ballot received when it was completed in 1935. Nor did he anticipate the conflict it produced between himself, Murray, Noel-Baker and their supporters in the Union on the one hand and Austen Chamberlain, Percy, Cranborne and most Conservative members of the Executive on the other.

As the Foreign Secretary who negotiated Locarno, Austen Chamberlain embodied an average Conservative commitment to the League. In that rôle and at the request of Conservative Central Office, he had joined the Executive of the Union in 1932 after Manchuria had undermined Simon's credibility. When he got there, he found 'some of the worst cranks [he] had ever known [24] and spent the next two years 'immobilis-ing' (Cecil's word) their attempts to 'dictate to the govern-ment the exact method it shall employ' at each particular crisis. [25] The outcome was a prolonged argument in 1934 about the wording and presentation of the Ballot, in the course of which he threatened to resign and left Cecil the impression that he had called him 'a liar' in a letter to The Times. [26] The Ballot arrangements, as eventually adopted, met Cecil's rather than his requirements. [27]

Murray was a prolific publicist with political access and liberal beliefs that cut across the politics of the classes. Cecil was an experienced politician who had played an important part in Conservative politics between 1906 and 1927. Despite the blows struck at the League by both Germany and Japan, both believed from some time in 1933 that the government was so vulnerable electorally that it could be compelled to resume the policies Simon seemed to have abandoned in 1932. [28]

Cecil was treated respectfully by Baldwin, but also re-proachfully; he was conscious of the malice displayed by Garvin, Rothermere and Beaverbrook in reflecting Conserva-tive feelings about the League, even when they failed to make them effective. He had no relations with Lansbury who did not like the League. On deciding that the government was so 'anti-League' that he should 'sever' his Conservative 'connection',[29] he began to play up relations with Attlee and Ponsonby.

This had some effect. Despite Conservative objections to the loaded nature of the Ballot,[30] Baldwin eventually allowed it to be said that he did not object to it being held.[31] When its findings were presented, he welcomed them.

The 'National Declaration' was supported by an unusual collection of public figures, including Sir Cedric Hardwicke, Dame Sybil Thorndike, Miles Malleson, A.A. Milne, Rose Macaulay, Sir Norman Angell, H.A.L. Fisher, Dick Sheppard and Jack Hobbs. It received *imprimatur* from Archbishops Lang and Temple, from the Chief Rabbi and the Roman Catholic Archbishop of Liverpool and from a variety of surgeons, physicians and Free Church leaders. On July 23, Cecil took Baldwin a deputation to present it. In the presence of representatives from the British League of Unitarian Women, the National Sisterhood and Brotherhood Movement, the National Union of Soroptimists and the Woodcraft Folk, as well as more obviously political manifestations of the power of fragmented Liberalism, he explained how much he hoped to be a help to the government. For the rest of the year, with eleven million signatories behind him, he was a presence to which both the government and the Labour party responded.[32]

For the Labour party, the events of 1931 were a shock. From being the largest party in the House of Commons, it became a Rump, with no prospect of power, no certainty of survival and an obvious leader — Henderson — who was not even an MP. Some of the most important Labour leaders of the previous decade had left — MacDonald, Snowden and Thomas in one direction, Mosley in another.

However, although only about fifty MPs were returned, five million voters voted Labour, including a large part of the Trade Union movement and major parts of the whole community in areas of South Wales, Scotland and Northumberland. This sort of die-hard support was not adequate if Labour was to be a governing party. But it promised a social indestructibility which the Liberal party lacked.

One by-product of MacDonaldite participation in the

National government was the loss of the leaders who invented the accommodation with which Labour had covered itself in the twenties. Another was a refusal to be frightened when central opinion seemed to have gone for good. From both viewpoints the primary question was how best to convince its members that the movement had a future.[33] To Lansbury, Attlee and Cripps, who ran what was left of the parliamentary party, and to all three equally, the answer was to exclude compromise with any of the other parties. In the aftermath of betrayal, Lansbury, at seventy-four, was a popular figure in the House of Commons. Brotherly love (except for capitalists) and community politics (in Poplar) supplied a harmless, and mindless, basis for a platform which was not really a legislative programme.

What the platform said was that Capitalism had failed not just because of the unemployment of the twenties but because the Great Crash had highlighted its incapacity to control its own inner workings. In this sense the economic crisis widened the area of discussion and propaganda. It was in the light of manifest disaster that the claim was made not only that Capitalism was evil but that there was so much 'muddle and chaos' in the international economic system that 'the Capitalist system was breaking down under its own weight, and this state of affairs [was] recognized not only by Socialists but by the Capitalists themselves'.[34]

The feeling that Capitalism could no longer be justified economically made it easy to justify state action in furtherance of 'the rational organisation of economic life'.[35] It did not mean, however, that Capitalism was dead politically. On the contrary, so many interests were involved in maintaining it that it was unlikely to collapse without a struggle. In this context the National government — 'the most reactionary...of modern times'[36] was seen as Capitalism's attempt to prop itself up in defence of that vast body of private profits which were all that was left of its justification.

After the counter-revolution of 1931, therefore, it was Labour's duty to defend the *status quo* created by the changes which had been effected in the 'political privileges of wealth' during the previous half-century in face of anything the City of London or the House of Lords might do to prevent 'the abolition of private profit-making' in the future.[37]

One of the chief things that had been effective in 1931 had been the 'parliamentary dictatorship' which, it was proposed, should be controlled by defining the relations between party and Prime Ministerial decisions and by taking Emergency Powers to deal with 'vested interests', 'reactionary mono-polists' and 'money-lords' whose 'nefarious conduct...had manoevred Labour...out of office...by international juggling with gold and credits'. [38]

These accusations were made generally. They were also made in detail. In detail the targets were the housing and rent policies of Young, the police reorganisation of Gilmour and Trenchard, the damage done to trade with Russia by Simon's handling of the Metro-Vickers case and the contrast between Chamberlain's 'tariffs...fiscal policy, restriction of public works and cutting down of social services' and the socialist and technocratic policies pursued by Roosevelt in the United States. [39]

Trenchard's reorganisation was an attempt to 'turn the police into a middle-class force' which could be 'used against the workers'.[40] The government's housing policy would do nothing to meet the 'wretchedness and...degradation' of the slums. [41] Chamberlain's protectionism would restrict trade and employment and increase import duties at the expense of the working-class consumer. [42] His deflationary 'packages' were dictated by Norman and the Bank of England and aimed to reduce taxation, increase unemployment and im-prove the position of the 'well-to-do'. [43] The 'economies' he was imposing on the social services were 'undermining...phy-sical and mental health' and perpetuating 'the monstrous paradox of poverty in the midst of plenty'. [44]

These claims remained constant. From the position reach-ed at the end of 1933, there were no significant changes in the content of the domestic programme, despite changes in the tone. In relation to foreign policy, the changes were sig-nificant.

The new aspect of the foreign policy platform which emerged in the next two years was a result of the demolition of German Social Democracy, the setbacks suffered by inter-national socialism [45] and the difficulties which stood in the way of European disarmament. The attempt to absorb these experiences coincided with a change in the leadership as the removal of Henderson, Cripps and Lansbury completed the process which the removal of Mosley and the MacDonaldites had begun.

Under the new leadership the Labour party developed the intimation that pacifism was not enough. This, however, came slowly and without premeditation. Though it produced no systematic rejection of the positions which had gone before, it made a perceptible difference as Dalton, Morrison, Bevin, Alexander and Citrine were projected by Stevenson, Williams and a *Daily Herald* circulation of around two million.

When disarmament was still a possibility in 1933, Angell's attacks on patriotism were the ordinary staple of political diet, and it was possible for the Labour party, the League of Nations Union and the pacifist movement to feel that they were moving in a common direction. Nor was sentiment divided by the response to Sheppard's Peace post-card in 1934. So long as there was no occasion to use League-based force as an instrument of peace, issues could be blurred in face of a government which was hindering Henderson's efforts on behalf of 'peace, disarmament and international co-operation'. [46]

The nearest the Labour party came to wanting an active international policy came through its support for China against Japan. Even there, however, it had confined itself to demanding a trade boycott. In general its view was that Labour should strike if the government neglected its League or Kellogg duties [47] and that 'international anarchy' was the result of 'international monopoly' which 'Socialism' would cure. [48]

In the sense that peace remained the priority, the Labour attitude was unaffected by Hitler's arrival. In relation to the Versailles settlement, it produced a change.

One aspect of Labour belief in the twenties had been that Versailles was tyrannical and oppressive and should be speedily and thoroughly overhauled. What Hitler did was induce a doubt. This was not exactly a belief that Versailles was right or that the Germans deserved the treatment they had received. Rather it was a feeling that explanations of his appeal ought not to be allowed to excuse it.

The earliest Labour reactions were mixed. At first Hitler

was a 'clown' who would be defeated by inflation and rearmament on the one hand or by the Junkers and Hindenberg
on the other.[49] Soon, however, it was clear that there had
been a brutal revolution which had established his paranoids
and perverts for a long time to come.[50] Once this was understood, the Labour attitude was both shocked and accommodating, distressed by the fate of comrades who had been
killed, determined to help the German people condemn
bestiality[51] and yet moved by the comfortable hopes that
Hitler would not last[52] and that his reassuring noises might
be genuine expressions of a desire for peace.[53]

The belief that Hitler might genuinely want peace was not
strong. But its weakness did not kill the peace-policy which,
though compatible in principle with rearmament, was assumed to be incompatible in fact. For this, and for many other
uncertainties, there were two chief reasons.[54]

The first was that the leader of the parliamentary party
was Lansbury whose pacifism was religious and whose object
was a disarmed Britain, an unarmed Germany and a weapon-
less world.[55]

The second was that Henderson, much more than Lansbury, was the architect of the Labour movement and carried
it with him as Chairman of the World Disarmament Conference. The government mistrusted Henderson not because
he was pacific but because he encouraged the public to be
optimistic[56] and was too much in France's pocket. The Conference ended in failure, and the contrast which he implied
between his own commitment and the government's evasions
was misleading. But its proceedings confirmed the belief that
Labour had a practical peace rôle which support for rearmament would obscure.

Even, therefore, in face of Hitler's treatment of their German comrades, Labour responded by attacking rearmament
profiteers, demanding a state monopoly of arms manufacture[57] and placing an emphasis on the League which grew
greater as Simon discovered how difficult it was to use it.

From the viewpoint of the Labour leadership, 'Geneva'
embodied both a genuine belief and a convenient symbol. It
had not attracted the ILP: nor did it recommend itself to the
Socialist League. But when Hitler replaced disarmament as an
issue and Germany and Japan had left, the demand to involve

Stalin and Roosevelt instead became a focus through which
the party responded.

It did not, however, respond militarily. So far from credit-
ing the League with a military capability, the claim was that
it could cope with aggression provided 'courageous leadership' mobilised 'the moral forces of the world' in 'acceptance
of higher loyalty to the world community of mankind'.[58] It
was only the events of 1934 which established that Collective
Security might involve 'the government of Great Britain [in
using] its military and naval forces in support of the League
of Nations to restrain an aggressor nation which refused to
submit to the authority of the League'. [59]

This did not involve approval of national armaments which
were to be abolished by a 'Peace Act binding the government
...to abandon force as an instrument of national policy'.
There was a promise that 'the immediate short-term measures
of the next Labour government 'would be [taken] with reference to the...establishment...of a Cooperative World Commonwealth'. But there was also a statement that 'Labour' was
prepared to 'fight against any nation which breaks the Collective Peace'. [60]

At the same time as this shift was occurring in the thinking
of some, at least, of the Labour leaders, attempts were made
to meet the accusation that Labour was a party of revolution.
This took shape in the Programme of Action of July 1934.

The Programme of Action was intended for use in case an
election took place. In publishing it, the leaders were aiming
to restore 'respectable Socialism'. They were also preparing
to meet, and pre-empt, the criticisms which Cripps and the
Socialist League were expected to make, and made, at the
Party Conference in October.

From 1933 onwards the Labour leadership faced a Cripps
problem. Or rather, Cripps attached himself to the problem
which Lansbury, Smillie, Hodges and the Clydesiders had invented — whether Labour should establish governing credentials by liberal accommodation or doctrinal integrity.

The prophets who denounced accommodation during
Labour's rise to power had not been effective in face of
MacDonald's desire to display a governing capability. It was
only when the MacDonaldites were left stranded in office in

1931 that virtue became an option.

After the landslide in November, virtue became dominant. For the next two years there was no prospect of an election, so a ghetto propaganda was suited to the situation. The prophetic position, therefore, became official as the ILP broke off and suffered a relapse while the parliamentary leaders offered not 'gradualism and palliatives' but 'the pure milk of the word'. [61]

This situation did not last long. The electoral improvement of 1933 and the LCC elections of March 1934 opened prospects which the failure of the Samuelites made real. The Labour leaders did not make a dead set at the support the government was losing. But there was an instinct that some statements of policy were too stark and that some 'worthwhile...things' could be done without promising to 'abolish Capitalism'. [62] It was in this setting that the Cripps problem became acute.

Cripps's father had been a member of the first Labour Cabinet, but in the thirties Cripps was a new recruit. His father was not a socialist but a High Church Conservative. His first political mentor was H.P. Macmillan, who, though also a member of that government, was also a Conservative. Cripps, so far from responding to offers of Labour seats [63], had spent the twenties establishing a lucrative practice at the commercial Bar. It was not until MacDonald offered him the chance to be Solicitor-General in 1930 that he yielded. [64] In August 1931 he may just possibly have thought of joining the National government. [65] His success in keeping his seat when nearly all the Labour leaders lost theirs then gave him a position he could not have expected two years earlier.

Cripps was forty-two, rich, well-educated and a member of a highly respectable family. His attitudes were paternal (after the manner of the Webbs and Sir Charles Trevelyan); he aimed to give elevated leadership by identifying himself with the 'interests' of those he wished to lead.

Descending thus from a height to help, many things influenced him towards becoming the Labour party's conscience. A Christian sensitivity, a sense that prophecy was needed as power approached and a belief that good men would leave if prophecy was abandoned — all helped him into the niche which the ILP had vacated. In the next six years he worked through a variety of organisations which provided platforms as effective and audiences as captive as the League of Nations Union to Cecil, the Disarmament Conference to Henderson, the TUC to Citrine, the Council of Action to Lloyd George, the National Executive to Dalton and the LCC to Morrison. Of Cripps's platforms, the first in time was the Socialist League.

Unlike the ILP out of which it grew, the League was not intended to be an extraparty group. When it was founded, Cripps was part of the parliamentary leadership and wished to make his 'influence within the party as effective as possible'. [66] Nor did he differ from the rest of the triumvirate. With Lansbury, who was his pensioner and an early member, he had 'revolutionary' Christian affinities, while Attlee, without the Christian affinity, for a time saw nothing odd in the opinions he was expressing. [67]

Cripps's quarrel was with Citrine and Dalton, and with the party and trade union 'bureaucracy', which disliked the grandeur of his manner, the intermittent nature of his attention and his attacks on its management. The censure passed by the Executive Committee in January 1934 [68] made the League step up its attacks. It increased the impression, which Cripps 'seemed...unable to see', that he was 'damaging the party electorally' [69] by using newspaper coverage to dramatise a conflict between 'socialism', as embodied in conference resolutions proposed by a handful of constituency parties, and the 'compromises' embedded in the 25-page programme which the National Executive presented to the Southport Conference. [70]

Cripps, Pritt, Laski, Mitchison and their allies presented Britain as a battlefield on which Fascism — not only Mosley's — was advancing and it was necessary to take extreme steps to resist it. It was the 'spiritual' and 'world-wide' nature of the struggle and the extremity of the situation as they saw it which was taken to justify the proposal to set up a virtual dictatorship in the first days of a Labour government.

The Socialist League's programme included abolition of the House of Lords, extensive reform of the House of Commons and the socialisation of land, banks and industry without compensation. It included attacks on the League of Nations as a 'Capitalist institution' and demands for a foreign policy based on alliance with the Soviet Union and any other socialist states which happened to emerge. [71]

In describing the boundaries of a position, Crippsians were offering the details of a 'busy scene — the building of a new Socialist State...instinct with life and reality'. [72] This did not make Cripps more popular among his equals.

The objection was to a degree personal; Dalton — who was also in his forties — disliked Cripps who had done nothing for the Labour party until Dalton had fought half-a-dozen by-elections and had kept a seat at the election of 1931 when Dalton had lost his. Primarily, however, it was practical; his critics thought Cripps lacking in experience and common sense and insensitive to trade union and central opinion. [73] Like Laski and Strachey, he saw Fascists under every bed and forgot, they thought, that Britain had a well-established legal and parliamentary system which Baldwin and MacDonald were not planning to subvert, and which Mosley would not succeed in subverting.[74] In the event Morrison — his would-be patron — conducted the platform attack. No trade union supported the League, whose amendments were defeated, though its major objective was achieved with Cripps's election to the National Executive.

In 1934 Cripps established himself as a late arrival. But his chief significance for the Labour party lay in the opportunity he gave for Citrine, Dalton and others to highlight themselves by adopting a 'responsible' position against him. So far as he was significant over the political spectrum as a whole, he was so because politicians and newspapers of all opinions, and particularly anti-socialist opinions, fixed collusively on him as a Labour leader for the future.

In spite of Cripps, the Labour party had re-established itself. Henderson had been removed from the party secretary-ship, much against his will. [75] Lansbury had become a well-loved parliamentary booby. But in the various satrapies that individuals had built up, public reputations had been made. Henderson had played a world rôle at Geneva. At London County Hall, Morrison had been a well-publicised success. In newspapers, at Party Conferences and the National Executive and through *Practical Socialism for Britain*, Dalton had become the important figure that Bevin had been for fifteen years. In the person of Citrine, trade union power had been identified with the Peace Ballot. [76] The 1934 local government and by-elections had been considerably more favourable than those of 1933. Optimism about a general election was not as great in the first half of 1935. [77] But manifest recovery gave the same sort of purchase as in 1921.

2

THE REJECTION OF LLOYD GEORGE

'This afternoon the PM called Baldwin, Chamberlain, Thomas, Runciman and myself together and told us formally that he was, on grounds of health, giving up the Premiership. He spoke with manly dignity and one felt it was a historic moment. We all expressed our sympathy and devotion in sincere and unstudied terms. I could not help contrasting the scene with the satirical, not to say malignant, description which Rosebery once gave me of Gladstone's leavetaking – "William Harcourt, blubbering like a child,-produced from an inner pocket a much correct-ed manuscript, *yellow with age*, from which he read a valedictory address". Today all was simple and between real friends and comrades'.
Simon, diary, May 28 1935

'If S.B. offers the deputy leadership in the Commons to Simon until the end of this Parliament in order to soften his fall, he is not proposing to give the post any increased importance...I am quite aware that Simon likes the idea of being deputy leader because he thinks it would bring him back into touch and sympathy with the House of Commons and might enable him possibly to become PM on the ground that a minority leader was required to preserve the character of the National Government.

'In this Simon deceives himself and I need never be jealous of him because I know now that he lacks certain qualities essential to a leader ...The fact is the House detests him; he hasn't a friend even in his own party and the reason is that, quite wrongly, they distrust his sincerity'.
Chamberlain to Hilda, May 22 1935.

'I had never seen him before, and in his photographs his face had always seemed to be chiefly amiable and a little whimsical, just as his speeches sound simple, honest and ingenuous. Actually he is not like that at all. His face is rugged and knobbly; his right eye is either going wrong or has some sort of a cast in it and was mostly half shut. But the character-istic of his face is its determination and shrewdness — or rather, because it is much more than shrewdness, a sort of deep rustic craftiness. More than any other politician he reminded me of Lloyd George in this, but while L.G. is gleefully and maliciously cunning, Baldwin seemed to me to look shrewd and crafty in a rather hard and grim way. I got quite a new idea of him and for the first time understood how he had come to be leader of the Tory party and Prime Minister'. W.P. Crozier, editor of the *Manchester Guardian*, interview with Baldwin on June 12 1934.

By 1935 Labour was the major party of opposition. Cecil, Murray and Noel-Baker had carried their followers farther

away from the Conservative party than at any time since the
League of Nations Union was founded. In addition, there was
a Liberal opposition which consisted not just of Lloyd
George and his family but of Samuel, Sinclair and their followers.

Under Lloyd George and Samuel, the Liberals campaigned
at the 1929 election as the only party with a policy for
unemployment. Despite a marked increase in their vote, the
failure to gain more than twenty seats was a major setback.
The decision to support Labour in office then produced
strains and splits which centred on Lloyd George's belief that
the Liberal party had a future as the brain and money behind
the reluctant radicalism of MacDonald, Snowden and their
followers. By the time of the government's collapse in August
1931, Runciman had virtually withdrawn from day-to-day
politics. Simon and Brown led parliamentary groups which
saw no future in alliance with Labour and had Conservative
links through positions of carefully defined support for
Protection. Lloyd George had had a serious illness and a
major operation, and had transferred effective leadership to
Samuel who, however, had only a handful of supporters to
lead.

From a position of gloom and despondency extreme even
in the experience of twentieth-century Liberals, Samuel rescued them by playing a crucial part in forming the National
government. He became Home Secretary and was leader of a
major constituent which included Reading, Maclean, Sinclair,
Crewe and Lothian. In the measures which were taken to save
the pound and to leave the Gold Standard, Samuel and Reading — the Samuelite members of the Cabinet — were involved intimately.

At the general election the Samuelites differed from the
Conservative party about Protection, but probably gained a
few more seats than they would have done if they had not
been part of the National government. Fighting separately
both from Lloyd George and from the Simon group (which won
35 of the 40 seats it contested), they had thirty-three seats in
the new House of Commons. After the election Maclean and
Sinclair entered the Cabinet when Reading and Crewe left.
Maclean died, unexpectedly, in June 1932. In September all
but one of the Samuelite ministers[1] joined Snowden in re-

signing when Chamberlain and Baldwin gave effect to the
Imperial Preference policy on which the body of the Conservative party had fought the election.

Once Snowden left the government, he did not think of
going back. As a pensioner of Beaverbrook and Lloyd
George,[2] he despised MacDonald's 'ignorance and incapacity'
even more than he despised Labour. For him the future lay in
'Radicalism'. After supporting the anti-government freetrader
at the East Fife by-election in February 1933, he was an
active supporter of the New Deal. In 1935 he and his wife
watched rancorously as the National Liberal party became a
'laughing stock', as Brown disgraced himself at first appearance on the government front bench and as 'slimy Simon'
was humiliated by being removed from the Foreign Office.[3]

The Samuelites, on the other hand, were by no means certain that opposition was their natural position. They were
not sure what the government would do at the World Economic Conference,[4] and they put off a decision when they
resigned because it would not have been unanimous if it had
been made.[5] The votes polled by the anti-government candidates at East Fife,[6] however, made a decision inevitable.
Half a dozen Welsh MPs joined Lloyd George in opposition.[7]
When the party conference passed a resolution,[8] the decision
began to press. By mid-1933 Samuel was looking for an excuse. He would have found one if a reduction in unemployment and a measure of economic recovery had not made the
moment seem inappropriate.[9]

When they went into opposition, the Samuelite leaders
were conscious that the breakdown of the World Economic
Conference had taken the stuffing out of 'Free Trade'. In its
place, they needed 'a large issue of [their] own choosing'.
When they first thought of moving, the 'demand in the country' and among 'newspapers of all shades of opinion' had
been for a positive policy to deal with unemployment. 'A
moderate policy of expansion', however, was less helpful
when unemployment began to fall, so it was supplemented
by 'the Conservative party's hatred of the League' as the
reason why the Disarmament Conference had collapsed.

In 1934 Liberal policy was a system of 'truths' about the
politico-economic system, in which a third way was suggested
between Conservative 'tariffs' and socialist 'planning'. It gave

extended attention to the need for treaty-revision and presented rearmament as a consequence of economic error. It is
doubtful whether the leaders believed in the world they had
lost or expected to get very far until Protection had had time
to get hung. In any case, none of this succeeded. [10]

What Samuel hoped when he found opposition thrust
upon him was to beat the Labour party to that part of the
non-Conservative vote which had been lost in 1929 and had
been decisive on behalf of the National government in 1931.
In 1933 the Labour failure to pick up the votes the government was losing made this seem possible. By the end of 1934
it was still only a possibility. There had been no public response and no real support from the *News Chronicle*. There
was no reason to believe that Labour could be reduced to
insignificance in the two or three years before the election.

Between 1933 and 1935 Samuel's Liberals showed that
they could not stand up by themselves. When they went into
opposition, they lost a number of supporters. At by-elections
they suffered heavily. At the LCC elections in 1934 they
were wiped out. At the 1935 election they polled one and a
half million votes and were returned in twenty-one seats.

From 1935 onwards, the Samuelites had hoped that the
Conservative preponderance could be destroyed. It was not
destroyed. In 1935 it was partially restored when Cecil and
the League of Nations Union half-returned part of the Liberal
support which they had intended to remove. In retrospect,
one must say that the Samuelites under-estimated both
Labour and Conservative flexibility. So did Lloyd George,
but it took six months of Cabinet negotiation and a general
election to make him see that this was what he had done.

For Lloyd George in his early seventies, the years from 1933
to 1935 were much like most other years since he left office
in 1922. Volumes three and four of his *War Memoirs* were
published in the autumn of 1934; the rest were nearly finished. Most of his time was spent with Frances Stevenson at
Churt where he was a small-scale farmer. Despite occasional
depression, he was in better health than at any time in the
previous ten years and was positively looking for something
to do. [11] What he found was the fourth opportunity to regain
the importance he had lost ten years before.

In these years the pattern of the past was repeated. There was the same shifting from position to position as circumstances and possibilities changed and the same ambiguity of intention as he left it uncertain, even probably to himself, whether Radical Conservatism or a Radical Labour party would provide the better instrument for making use of the government's failure.

To Samuelite Liberalism he was hostile, even while leaving the impression of wishing to be reconciled to it. [12] He despised the official leaders whose distinguishing characteristic was that they were anti-Labour, 'provide[d] the sort of "slop" that Tory voters would accept' and 'were not likely to get more than a dozen seats at the next election'. He made it clear that he disliked the National Liberal Federation and did not think the Liberal party worth leading. [13]

For his successors as the Conservative party's Radical allies, he expressed his customary contempt which grew as their reputations grew weaker. The weaker their reputations, the less 'national' he thought it likely that the National government would become. The more this happened, the more it would become apparent that the Conservative party did not have a majority and would not win an election without a new infusion of Radical blood to replace Simon who was 'a world catastrophe', Runciman, about whom the *War Memoirs* repeated a nasty remark Kitchener was supposed to have made before he died, and MacDonald, under whom he would 'never...serve' and who would have to resign shortly because he was 'nine-tenths gaga'. [14]

The thought that he might once more become the Conservative party's ally occupied only one part of Lloyd George's mind. In others he was conscious of the difficulty of removing MacDonald against his will [15] and the probability that the government would survive unless all its opponents worked together. [16]

Lloyd George would have liked the government to collapse. In early 1933 he was hoping that Chamberlain's economic policy would provide the occasion. [17] For a short time in late 1934 it seemed possible that India might. In general it seemed likely that nothing would, so he had to prepare for an election at a time of the government's choosing. Since neither he nor Samuel was going to have a majority, he convinced himself that either of two courses was open to him. He could persuade one or other of the parties that neither could win without him, in which case a coalition situation might arise before the election. Or, by backing 'any candidate of any party who [would] support his programme' he might emerge from the election at the head of a block of 'progressive' MPs in which case 1929 would be repeated if neither party had a majority of its own. [18]

The first policy was pursued, largely in relation to the Conservative party, up to July 1935. The second, pursued concurrently with it, came to an end when the Conservative majority at the election removed the opportunity to play a part.

In relation to the Labour party Lloyd George had no great expectation. After the LCC elections of 1934, he was thinking of a merger between the *News Chronicle* and the *Daily Herald*. He supported Addison when he won Swindon for Labour. He had discussions with Lansbury about electoral co-operation between the Liberal and Labour parties and the 'growing body of able young men on the government side who would go along with an...effort to lift the poor out of the mire and the needy from the dunghill'. [19]

By the end of the year these hopes had collapsed. Layton would not allow the *News Chronicle* to become a Labour newspaper. [20] Lansbury's view was that Labour was 'the second party in the State' and that there could be no 'mutilation of the socialist programme'. He added not unreasonably that, whatever might be possible after an election, it was unreasonable to expect to 'come to terms *before* the election with both parties at once'. [21]

Though he let it be known that he was up for auction in early 1933, Lloyd George found no Conservative bidders until, at various points of electoral difficulty in the following year, approaches came from Boothby, Macmillan and the Oliver Stanleys who disliked Chamberlain's economic policy and wanted a repetition of what they had wanted Mosley to do in 1930. They also came from Rothermere, Astor, Jones, Horne, Smuts, Grigg and Wood. [22] After the municipal elections at the end of the year there were nibblings from Baldwin.

In order to be worth nibbling at, Lloyd George needed an

'issue' about which to establish a 'position'. Which issue to take and which position to adopt were dictated by his understanding of the opportunities that were open. In early 1934, with a Free Church audience in mind, he tried a 'great appeal for Peace'. This had proved that no such audience was available[23] and had been followed, as India difficulties became acute, by support for Churchill's Air Defence campaign through which Conservative credentials were presented.[24]

Until Lothian persuaded him that it did, Lloyd George had assumed that foreign policy did not matter. For much the same reasons as Rothermere, he had a fellow-feeling for Hitler — 'a very great man'[25] and the German equivalent of a Welsh Radical leading the Conservative party on the way to becoming a world statesman. Since Britain had no 'special interest in the racial conflicts of Europe', he spent the winter of 1934 taking economic advice and preparing a set piece to match the professorial set pieces of the twenties.

In making unemployment the centre of the New Deal he launched at Bangor in January 1935, Lloyd George was doing six things. He was contrasting the Chamberlain policy of 'waiting for a trade recovery' with the Roosevelt policy of providing the 'workless' with 'work'. By his willingness to use tariffs 'ruthlessly and to the full', he was showing that he had finished with the Liberal party except in Wales and was standing above party as the mouthpiece of Wales's contribution to the nation's life. By rejecting nationalisation of the Bank of England, he was distinguishing himself from Labour. By being agreeable about Eden and Macmillan and by attacking the financial policy of the Bank, he was fishing for support in the higher reaches of the government. And he was claiming to embody practical, non-partisan sanity without prejudice to ultimate decisions for or against 'Individualism, Capitalism or Socialism, Fascism or Communism or even the old "isms" of Conservatism or Liberalism'.[26]

It is an open question whether he wanted to join the government and expected to be invited, or was trying to show Frances Stevenson that she had a future. She, on the whole, was sceptical. His feelings varied. Sometimes he was 'not going to pull tory chestnuts out of the fire' and 'wanted the existing government to be beaten at the next election' since the defeat any government would suffer 'would be a tragedy for the new blood that joined it'. On other occasions he was 'worth a million votes to the government' and willing to take charge of slum housing or unemployment, but did not believe that Chamberlain would let him even if Baldwin wanted to. [27]

Lloyd George had no reason to doubt that Baldwin was 'as crafty as the craftiest of politicians'. But he had been flattered by him in public, allowed himself to be convinced and started talking about forming a government with him (and Churchill) if the India bill had to be abandoned. [28]

At this time Baldwin allowed Grigg to promise that he would have a talk. When the India bill was saved in December, he decided that a talk would be 'premature'. [29] In the New Year Lloyd George was excited by the newspaper reception of the New Deal and by the by-election results. [30] When the Cabinet decided to interview him, the New Deal seemed to have more than justified the effort. Knowing that he had admirers among Conservatives, he recalled that he was 'instinctively drawn towards [them] for his friendships', 'hate[d] the sanctimonious humbug which...characterised the majority of successful Liberals' and had always said that 'there are no Liberals who would make a jolly dinner party such as we used to have in the days of the old coalition'. [31]

In May (probably without Simon's knowledge), his agents were co-operating with the Scottish Simonites to seize control of the Scottish Liberal Federation. By mid-May, having been outmanoeuvred both there and in the Cabinet, he began to threaten. [32] When Baldwin formed a government without him, he decided that Conservatives were neither interested in him as an asset nor intended to do anything about his programme. By mid-July, he had reverted to being a Radical who would get enough seats at an election 'to form a government with Lansbury as nominal Prime Minister' so that, between them, they could 'formulate a devastating progressive programme' and get 'a majority of 150' at a second election. [33]

In the course of the summer, Lloyd George had been in close touch with Allen's *Next Five Years* group. They, however, had found him a demanding collaborator and had declined to be taken over. [34] When he had failed there too, he published his own manifesto, called a Convention and set up a Council of Action for Peace and Reconstruction. [35]

In respect of its main target — unemployment — his campaign suffered when Abyssinia pushed it off the head-lines. [36] About foreign policy his followers were divided. [37] For him, as for the Samuelites, the election was a catastrophe. It rubbed home the fact that, except in Wales — and really there too — he no longer mattered.

Between 1933 and 1935, then, five armies were advancing. They had neither a common language, common aims nor a common policy. For the government the danger was that an election might produce a Labour majority in the House of Commons (without any vast increase in the Labour vote) if Cecil, Samuel and Lloyd George between them stuck Liberal pins in the broad-based balloon that had taken off in 1931. [38]

The non-Conservative leaders of the government were Mac-Donald, Simon, Runciman and Thomas. About Runciman there is little to say except that he was a distinguished Liberal who happened to have been converted to the need for import duties. Having remained in office when Samuel resigned, he spent the subsequent years as President of the Board of Trade justifying 'tariffs' on the ground he claimed Grey had approved before he died — that they would facilitate negotiated reductions in the 'foreign tariffs to which [British] goods were subjected'. [39] Runciman was a silent member of the Cabinet, but he hated Lloyd George, his presence was a symbol of Liberal support and he may, for a moment, have been a possible successor to MacDonald. [40] In general, however, he did not present a problem. The National Labour party and the Simonites did.

The most important fact about Simon, MacDonald and their followers after 1932 was that they were political prisoners. They complained about the treatment they received and threatened to go on strike, and they effected an undefined erosion of Conservative thinking. But they were so lacking in public or party support that they had nowhere to go if the government collapsed and no audience to appeal to if Conservatives decided that they had had enough. Though the government was run by what were known to themselves as the 'Big Six' — only two of whom were Conservatives — it was true from the start, and became truer in the course of

1934, that the major domestic decisions were made by Baldwin and Chamberlain.

The Big Six were these two, along with MacDonald, Thomas, Simon and Runciman. Between Runciman and Chamberlain, Chamberlain and Thomas, Thomas and MacDonald and MacDonald and Baldwin, there were close relations. But otherwise each would quite happily have got rid of any of the rest. This may not have been so at the start, but it was so by the middle of 1933 as mutual execution plans were made in the sections into which they were divided.

This permeated down, as similar feelings permeated up, with the result that in both non-Conservative groups there was almost total demoralisation. This was, perhaps, greater in the National Labour group, since animosity between Simon's and Samuel's Liberals was not as deep as the animosity which the Labour party felt for MacDonald. But both were conscious of the overwhelming weight of the Conservative party. [41]

So were Conservatives. Despite the knowledge that they were dominant, they assumed that the price to be paid was so small that coalition should continue. This assumption, once made, produced four sorts of consequence — a search for symbols to prove that something more than a Conservative government existed; an attempt to provide it with a *raison d'être*; an attempt to show that illiberal (divisive) Conservative policies had been abandoned; and efforts to square such critics as were willing to be squared on the assumption that a 'national government' would continue.

What needs to be said about Conservative criticism can be said briefly. MPs from Depressed Areas ran campaigns. But except in three respects, criticism centred on the housing, [42] debt settlement, incitement to disaffection, [43] and betting bill questions [44] or on the figures of German aircraft production about which, by April 1935, Churchill made the government look extremely foolish. All of these were important. None presented a serious threat. Unemployment assistance and India did.

The chief elements in Chamberlain's economic policy were the lowering of interest rates, the raising of prices, the balancing of the budget, the establishment of an Imperial Trade bloc, a reciprocal lowering of tariffs and an overriding determination to avoid governmentally-created inflation. These policies, intellectually conceived (if not by Chamberlain) and professionally secured, were ambiguous in terms of political credit. Whether because of their character or because of the movement of world trade, there was, by late 1933, a distinct drop in unemployment. At the same time, there remained a core of $2\frac{1}{2}$ million unemployed which seemed unlikely to disappear.

Whether the policy was presented as a success or a failure depended on the response which Chamberlain aroused. The Labour party accused him of being obsessed by inflation. Its criticisms were echoed in the Cabinet, in the City and among economists. Among the leaders of Conservative opinion, it was an important consideration in the minds of those who wanted to remove Baldwin and MacDonald in 1933 [45] and among the Lloyd George collaborators of 1935.

In Chamberlain's mind there were two feelings — that the reduction in unemployment was a result of his policies and that the refractory nature of the residual problem was something that no government could control. This double standard was necessary in preparing for an election; it meant that the electoral aspect of unemployment depended on the course of international trade. It meant too that, unless the trade recovery was startling, unemployment would have to be given a wide berth at a general election.

Unemployment, however local in incidence, would have been sensitive in any circumstances. It became doubly so when complicated by the Means Test.

For the Labour party, the unemployment assistance problem had been made symbolic by MacDonald's betrayal. Whether, and how much, unemployment assistance should be reduced had been a main source of conflict in his Cabinet and the breaking-point with those who left him. Since, however, the cuts introduced by the National government were not very much different from those accepted by the defectors before they resigned, it was a matter of importance for Labour, but for no one else, that they attacked them when they were made. [46] Given the government's invincibility in its first two years of office, their attack had little effect. In 1933, though an important element in the by-election platform, it cut no ice with serious politicians. When a radical reorganisation of unemployment assistance was instituted, it did.

The Unemployment Act of 1934 was the work of Chamberlain and Betterton, the Minister of Labour. Its object was to put unemployment insurance on a firm footing after existing deficits had been funded and to remove unemployment assistance from the hands of local authorities by laying down uniform rates which would apply nationally. By establishing a statutory commission (the Unemployment Assistance Board) to administer whatever money was voted by parliament, and by appointing a national figure to run it (after others had refused, Betterton, on retiring from the House of Commons), Chamberlain hoped that the question could be 'removed from party politics'.

Though the bill was fought by the parliamentary Labour party on the ground that working-class welfare was a proper subject for democratic discussion, its criticisms were politically insignificant. They remained so until the Act came into force and the Board laid down, and paid, the new scales of benefit.

While the Act was being passed, the government's supporters, and indeed members of the Cabinet, believed that the new scales would not be lower than the old. When the Board's regulations were presented to the Cabinet Committee in November 1934, Chamberlain found them so strict that he had them revised. [47] Even so, when given effect in early 1935, many rates of benefit were lower than they had been before. This produced a great deal of complaint, a widespread feeling of alarm at a time of psephological disintegration and parliamentary attacks from so many sides at once that Chamberlain had no time to consult the Cabinet or the Cabinet Committee when allowing Stanley (the new Minister of Labour) to announce a standstill on their operation. [48]

What followed was a battle between Chamberlain and Betterton to maintain the UAB's powers and Stanley and the Ministry of Labour to reduce them. Stanley had expected criticism before the regulations were published; [49] having to bear the brunt of the Labour attack, he was 'rattled' and thought of resigning. [50] He asked for drastic changes, including a restoration of some of their powers to local authorities. [51] Chamberlain resisted this but agreed that the regulations should be revised. After a Cabinet decision to withdraw them temporarily, he persuaded Baldwin to put off further decisions until Stanley and his Under-Secretary [52] had been found new departments. When they were moved in June, he and Brown defused the situation. [53]

The UAB problem arose from administrative mistakes and became a political issue when Labour took the opportunity to show that it had been right in 1931. Once the political issue arose, its impact was so great that the government seemed, not only to its opponents, as though it was *intending* to be mean. When combined with everything else that had happened in the previous two years, it inflicted the deepest damage on the morale of the Conservative party [54] and precipitated a Cabinet conflict between Chamberlain and the 'compassionate' friends of Lloyd George at a time when Lloyd George was offering a 'compassionate' programme of public works. It convinced Baldwin that the Conservative party needed reassurance if a 'National' government were to survive. It destroyed the impression, which the India bill had left, that Chamberlain alone could provide it.

The India bill was a continuation of the long-term policy of implicating a larger part of the Indian educated and propertied classes in the ostensible aspects of British rule and was presented in terms which suggested that, so far from destroying the Indian Empire, 'there [was] more chance of losing India' if it was defeated. [55] Though tailored to meet Conservative criticism, it had little genuine support in the parliamentary party and was widely disliked in the constituencies. In the Cabinet until a late stage, Simon, Hailsham and Chamberlain were prepared to move either way. But for Hoare's determination, it might well have been abandoned. [56]

The campaign against it was run by Churchill, Lloyd, Croft, Wolmer and Salisbury. It began in constituency associations (especially in Lancashire) and at area and national meetings of the Conservative party. It was then continued (with much heat, without Opposition support and with personal animus against Hoare) [57] in the Conservative party in the House of Commons. The major failures were with Derby, Amery and Austen Chamberlain. The major successes were at the Bristol Conference in October 1934, in Parliament in December and on the second reading the following February, [58] a few days after Randolph Churchill had ensured a

Labour victory by standing as an 'Independent Conservative' in the Wavertree by-election.

The passage of the bill had four sorts of significance. It established Hoare as a major figure. It gave Rothermere and Beaverbrook something to complain about. It eroded Baldwin's authority. And it compelled the government to appease critics in other directions.

This last compulsion became pressing when Conservative mistrust of the bill was strengthened by Samuelite and, eventually, Simonite, approval. [59] It was one of the factors the party chairman had in mind when opposing the attempt to turn the government into a national party. [60] It was why MacDonald was pressed to take steps about House of Lords reform and to defer to the Conservative campaign against the land tax which Snowden had introduced in the Labour government. [61] It had some importance in making it necessary to be agreeable to Beaverbrook and Rothermere.

The fact that Beaverbrook and Rothermere were journalists whom ministers wanted to ignore did not remove the difficulty they felt in ignoring them. They had been effective through high-tension efforts for short periods in the past — against Lloyd George in 1921 and against Baldwin in 1930, when Baldwin had had to attack them in order to deal with them. Neither was a conventional Conservative but between them they had created a popular politics which could be mistaken for 'Conservatism' by those who thought they were. That a large part of the electorate, including the Conservative electorate, got its view of the National government from them was important. It was extremely important at a time when the government had to prepare for elections with no other support from the large-circulation newspapers. [62]

Although it was assumed that both were dangerous, it was not assumed that both were equally approachable. Rothermere had for long been treated as an oddity. In the thirties this impression was confirmed. Having supported the National government in 1931, he had then decided that it should be brought to an end. [63] Having been scared by Cripps, he gave public support to Mosley and the British Union of Fascists. After dropping Mosley in July 1934, he reconciled himself to Labour succeeding and looked forward to paying Conservatives back for what they had done in India. [64] Along with everyone else, he played a part in the baiting of Simon. He then supported the New Deal and urged Lloyd George to take up India and air defence so that 'at the end of a couple of years' he could become 'leader of the Conservative party and...Prime Minister'. [65] When Lloyd George went on stressing unemployment instead, Rothermere started to support the government. He was hoping that it would scrape home at an election when its League position about Abyssinia drove him away again. [66]

Rothermere's closest acquaintances in the government were Thomas and MacDonald who succeeded, from time to time, in scaring him about the consequences if the coalition collapsed. In general, however, he had no friends there. In this respect Beaverbrook's position was rather different.

Like Rothermere's, Beaverbrook's connections were loose. At the 1931 election he gave highly detached support on an Empire Free Trade basis. When the election was over, he became more detached still, criticising Norman's economic policy and advocating the need for 'inflation'. He had views about agriculture, including higher wages for agricultural workers, which were expressed by the candidate he ran, unsuccessfully, at the East Fife by-election. He spent a good deal of time with Lloyd George whose views about domestic policy coincided with his own. Unlike Rothermere, however, he did not support the New Deal. Again, unlike Rothermere, he supported the India bill (and was against Churchill). He was prepared to 'smash' the British Union of Fascists. [67]

Over the years Beaverbrook had accumulated four friends who happened to be in the Cabinet. With Hailsham relations seem to have been intermittent. [68] With Hoare his relationship grew out of their friendship with Law. With Thomas it started in the early twenties when Thomas was offering himself, almost licentiously, as a central figure. Through Wood, and directly, he had links with Chamberlain for whom a highly synthetic regard fed on the hope that he believed in Imperial preference and could be used to show up Baldwin for what he was. The last three were all involved in the negotiations which Thomas started in February 1934. [69]

When Thomas asked why Beaverbrook was not supporting the government, Beaverbrook offered to do so 'until the day

after the next election' provided there was a protection
policy for wheat and a 'Customs Union' with 'such of the
Crown Colonies as were not controlled by Treaty'. [70] Negotiations, thereafter, were conducted through Hoare who arranged conversations, correspondence and a dinner with
Chamberlain. [71] They were punctuated by requests (from
the Conservative chairman) for a newspaper campaign to make
the Junior Imperial League the spearhead of resistance to
Mosley.[72] They came to a head when Beaverbrook sent a
memorandum about the Customs Union in June.

This plan was abandoned when the Colonial Office shot it
to pieces. [73] The following January [74] it was revived (by
Thomas). A couple of months later Chamberlain asked for a
further statement [75] during the Norwood by-election [76] and
replied in a way which made Beaverbrook expect the Colonial Office if he became Prime Minister. [77] It was Baldwin's
failure in this, as well as in policy directions, which freed Beaverbrook to attack Eden's influence on Hoare, whose Abyssinia policy he disliked even when he recognised its electoral
effectiveness.[78] His newspapers, while technically supporting
the government at the election, were unenthusiastic and at
times 'intolerable'.[79]

Although, in other words, there was contact with Rothermere and Beaverbrook, it did not affect policy thinking. This,
so far as it had a political content, aimed at restoring the
impression of 'progress' which had been brought in 1931 and
lost since.

This need was met in the first place negatively — by
dropping controversial legislation, pressing reassuring legislation and resisting Conservative causes. The Tithe bill, [80] for
example, was withdrawn as an irritant to both farmers and
Nonconformists. [81] The Committee and Royal Commission
on the Private Manufacture of Armaments, on which Mac-
Donald and Thomas insisted, were substitutes for a Disarmament Convention. [82] The India bill did not please Simon
but was welcomed as an application of Liberal principles and
a proof that the National government was not 'an instrument
of Toryism'. The same could have been said about House of
Lords reform.

'Reform of the Lords' was a pre-war reaction to Liberal

attacks. For the wartime Coalitions, it had been delicate and
divisive. By 1922, nothing had been agreed. In the decade
which followed, Conservative governments were no more active than Lloyd George. The idea of an enlarged and, in part,
elected Chamber, would have died if it had not been kept
alive at Conservative Conferences and in Parliament by Salisbury, by his relatives, Selborne and Rockley, and by Midleton, Steel-Maitland, Linlithgow and Rankeillour. [83]

The arguments varied; in 1934 Salisbury was trying to
'make democracy safe against Mosley, Cripps and Co'. [84] He
found little support among the Conservative managers [85] and
none in the Cabinet, except from Ormsby-Gore (who was his
son-in-law) [86] and from Hailsham who had to threaten to
resign before Baldwin and MacDonald would agree to appoint
a Committee. [87] A point was gained in May when the Lords
gave a decisive majority to the second reading of his private
member's bill. In the Liberal and Labour parts of the government, however, this was so unpopular that Sankey and de la
Warr, who had voted against the first reading, had to be
restrained from doing so again by a Cabinet decision that
ministers should not vote at all. [88] When Baldwin told a large
deputation of Conservative MPs that there would be 'no time'
to deal with it in the House of Commons, Hailsham again
threatened to resign, withdrawing only when Baldwin explained (after Chamberlain had intervened), that his remarks
referred to 'the present session'. [89] Even if he was hampered
by Salisbury's disregard of popular opinion, it is unlikely that
he wanted to do much. [90] In the course of 1935, it was
decided that the bill introduced by Rankeillour should be
opposed and no opinion expressed about Rockley's. The
ministers who drafted the election manifesto decided that the
question should not be mentioned. [91] The public did not
know of Chamberlain's assurance that this would not 'debar'
the government from 'introducing a measure...in the next
Parliament'. [92]

These were negative actions designed to remove obstacles to
reassurance. They did nothing to provide a *raison d'être*.

In this respect, nothing systematic existed when the
government was formed in 1931. Then the purpose was to
save the pound. When the pound fell and the Gold Standard

was abandoned, it was still 'responsibility in crisis' which provided the justification. No single policy was produced to justify the mandate at the election in October, when protection and free trade were both offered as crucial aspects of economic strategy in the future. One aspect of the contradiction was resolved when Chamberlain replaced Snowden as Chancellor in November and it was decided to give protection to domestic industry, in this respect confirming what many Conservatives had said was necessary at the election. It was not until the Ottawa policy began that Snowden and the Samuelites resigned.

There were, then, two stages in the acceptance of protection which was supported by Simon's and Brown's Liberals and advocated by Runciman in terms which made it so uncontroversial (except to Protectionists[93]) that it ceased to be a serious slogan.

As Protection receded, Baldwin hoped that disarmament and economic recovery would replace it. In 1933 it was possible to believe this. In the following year international tension seemed about to threaten economic recovery[94] at the same time as India threatened the government. By the end of 1934 events in Europe had not only made disarmament problematical but had made rearmament necessary on an extensive scale in the not very distant future.

Baldwin recognised this but was unwilling to say so in public. As a basis of policy, rearmament was as unpopular among the Simonites and MacDonaldites as among the leaders of the Opposition. It underlined the need for a platform which would do more than MacDonald had done to create a unity of sentiment between the Conservative party, the non-Conservative support of 1931 and the non-Conservative parts of the Coalition.

This is not to say that MacDonald had not tried. He had tried hard. There was nothing apologetic about his contempt for the 'cowards' who had 'sneaked away' in 1931 or the asinine vacuity of Lansbury's platform. Nor did he conceal the duty to wean the people from their 'willingness to...get... something for nothing...and make claims...of right...upon incomes...they had never earned'.[95] By inserting a 'fine, proud spirit' into the 'national character', he was aiming to prepare it for foreign competition 'the like of which we have never known'. [96]

In marrying 'voluntary effort and government action' (especially about housing) [97] and in injecting both with a new moral vigour, MacDonald was not 'abandoning socialism'. On the contrary, he was imitating Mussolini in defending it against the 'sentimentalities' of Poplar. [98] But where Mussolini was young and in control, MacDonald was harassed by Conservative vigilance, to which his only answer was the double-edged threat of dissolution. [99] Though he battled with his critics and threatened where that seemed helpful [100], his failure reflected a wider failure to establish parity of esteem between the Conservative party and its allies.

From early 1932, mechanical relations had been managed by a committee whose main function was to receive Simonite and MacDonaldite demands for more seats. This, however, was made difficult by the reluctance of Conservative associations. Difficulty was increased by Simonite reluctance to support non-Liberal candidates against sitting Samuelites and by the failure of the National Labour party to gain constituency existence in face of the 'unpleasantness' that would be created in relations with 'fellow Trade Unionists' if they stood against them. [101]

There was, therefore, in organisational terms, an even greater Conservative preponderance than in 1921 and the same problem as then about the desirability of converting the coalition into a party. At one point a hundred Conservative MPs supported the idea. On the other hand, a great many others — especially opponents of the India bill — threatened to secede if it was adopted. [102] Simon and MacDonald also opposed it, believing, doubtless, that they had a position in a coalition of equals which they were much less certain to keep under any other arrangement.

The 'National party' did not get off the ground, so the problem of a 'National policy' did not arise in that connection. Since, however, the Coalition was to continue, the policy question became urgent when by-elections made it unsafe to rely on the claims which had served two years before. At this point in some quarters there were varying versions of a desire for a move towards an *étatisme* of the Right.

The belief that *'laissez-faire'* was as dead as the 'slave trade',[103] that the state would "become associated...more and more...with the industrial life of the country'[104] and that it was desirable to 'drop' one's 'Toryism on...public ownership of land and land taxes'[105] had an extensive existence in the higher reaches of the party. There was a widespread feeling that 'capitalism' was 'finished' and that a 'national' programme on this basis was the most plausible response to the re-emergence of the Labour party.[106] This was an important element in the Amery/Lloyd movement.[107] It existed on the Garvin/Astor front, and among those who wanted Lloyd George in the government.[108] On the basis of what Elliot had done at the Ministry of Agriculture (and Mussolini in Italy), it was a strand in the propaganda conducted by Lord Eustace Percy.

Percy had been a junior minister and high-level League propagandist in the twenties. After the 1935 election he presumed on a côterie reputation to use National Labour to make the Conservative party a 'Tory Socialist' party of the Centre.[109] He probably tried too hard. The following April he left the Cabinet when Baldwin neglected to make him minister for the co-ordination of defence[110] after making it clear that he would not give him serious office at all.[111] His period of significance covered the eighteen months before the election when *Government in Transition*, *The Modern State*, *Conservatism and the Future* and a well-publicised period as 'Minister of Thought' attempted to recommend the government to the intelligentsia in the same way as Allen's *Next Five Years* group recommended positions slightly further to the Left.

From being the tied exponent of the National Labour position in 1931, Allen had been alienated by the distance of MacDonald's manner. MacDonald's failure to promote National Labour ministers when the Samuelites resigned and his inability to make much of the 'National Labour' idea showed that an opportunity had been 'missed'.[112] In loosening ties and resuming his independence, Allen hoped to give leads MacDonald ought to have given towards 'reconstruction' at home and peace, disarmament and the amicable settlement of disputes abroad.[113]

This produced the Liberty and Democratic Leadership and

Next Five Years groups, which, beginning from League-based pacifism, shifted internationally as circumstances changed and developed domestically a non-marxist demand for a 'new social order', based on a recognition that neither competitive capitalism nor state control provided the answer for the future.

Allen's object was to mobilise opinion, not to form a party. He had no real organisation (apart from Macmillan's publishing house) and made no real public appeal. By themselves, his activities were of little significance, except to the liberal intelligentsia who signed his manifestos and to the National Labour party (which he refused to support at the general election). [114] But they implied the same needs as were implied elsewhere and contributed to the climate to which the government felt obliged to respond.

So far as the League was concerned, Hoare responded gracefully. So far as planning was concerned, Chamberlain did not.

In theory Chamberlain had no objection to state activity. But he had no contact with Allen, had no time for Percy and equated 'planning' with Lloyd George whom he wished particularly to avoid. Moreover, from an electoral point of view, he was more interested in the future course of international trade. The result of discussion with Conservative ministers and the other parties to the Coalition was, therefore, a programme of safe progress involving changes in the school-leaving age, the five-day week, workers' holidays, land settlement, unemployment insurance for agricultural workers, the organisation of leisure and the unification of coal-mining royalties. [115]

The third method of appeasing modern opinion involved evaluation of existing members of the government for the 'national' purposes to which they were being put and the possibility of replacing them by others. Addison and Bevin were mentioned as reinforcements, as well as Lloyd George. Simon, Young and MacDonald were the chief candidates for replacement. [116]

Simon's inadequacy was obvious; the newspaper attacks he suffered in 1934 were the result of his being a weak link about whom ministers' judgments stimulated the judgments of public critics. [117] MacDonald would almost certainly have removed him from the Foreign Office but for unwillingness to weaken the non-Conservative element in the Cabinet. [118] Towards the end of the year plans were made to remove him by creating a policy Cabinet of overlords, or by giving the Foreign Office (according to the needs of the situation) to Baldwin, to Chamberlain, Halifax and Eden (in order to guarantee that the government was) or to Chamberlain and Hailsham (as a guarantee that it was not) internationalist. [119]

In the case of Young, another Liberal problem, there was a similar difficulty. Housing was as sensitive a subject as unemployment and one to which the Labour party gave much attention. It was also one on which Chamberlain had made his reputation. The policy — of ending the Wheatley subsidies, allowing private enterprise to build for letting and developing a local authority programme for slum clearance — was under constant attack. But it was approved by the government majority[120] and would have presented no problem if the slum clearance proposals had included adequate compensation for owners of slum properties. There was, however, a coincidence between by-election criticism, Young's sensitiveness about it and the feeling that property (often the property of not very wealthy Conservatives) was being expropriated. It was this that produced the decision that Young should go to the War Office unless Housing was detached from Health and given to another minister to look after. [121]

The first plan failed because Sankey, when asked to vacate the Lord Chancellorship so that Hailsham might vacate the War Office, 'made a terrible scene' with MacDonald about the injustice of 'promoting...the source of the trouble' (i.e. Young) while he was to be 'sacrificed'. [122] The second was dropped when it became known that Chamberlain wanted to replace Young, not by a Liberal, doubting, as he did 'whether Shakespeare' (the obvious Liberal) 'was the right man', [123] but by a Conservative of his own. [124] This gave MacDonald a shock [125] and raised difficulties perhaps, as Chamberlain was told, on account of the 'jealousies' it would create, [126] possibly because it would represent an undue strengthening of his influence in the Cabinet. Success in keeping office did not reduce Young's demoralisation or make him less critical of MacDonald for allowing him to feel it. [127]

In Baldwin's attitude three things were important. The first was the possibility that the India bill would be defeated. The second was that Chamberlain's credit seemed to have survived it better than his own.

The third was that his advisers did not believe that electors who were shifting their votes were either socialists or sympathisers with a socialist programme. What they thought had been lost since 1931 was 'youth', 'virtue' and 'progressive Liberalism'. They discerned a non-socialist radicalism which was waiting to be fed and would do them damage, especially in the north of England, unless they fed it. They had no idea how to present rearmament, unemployment or the Means Test. Cecil and his followers were unpopular in the Conservative party, weak in the country and antagonistic to the government, so there was no point in running after them. From alliance with Lloyd George, one major gain was expected in relation to the difficulties which lay ahead.

This was that Lloyd George was not only Joseph Chamberlain's chief successor as responsible Radical — and a more vigorous example than MacDonald and Simon — but was a coalition of opinions in himself. He had no commitment to one way of conducting India policy rather than another. [128] He was not necessarily an admirer of the League of Nations. He believed in associating in the Concert of Europe but did not object to armaments or to rearming. His admirers included Garvin, Astor, Beaverbrook and Rothermere; if an answer was needed, he was an answer to Mosley. In the course of a pragmatic career, he had acquired many principles and some friends, who could be used to associate the Conservative party with his un-socialist concern for the 'future of the underdog'. From some time in 1934 Baldwin was brooding on the mechanics of bargaining. He mentioned them in a speech in May. [129] Between the Putney by-election and MacDonald's retirement from the Prime Ministership, they were a major preoccupation.

So far as Chamberlain was concerned, the position remained the same throughout. The Bangor proposals were 'the poorest stuff imaginable, vague, rhetorical and containing not a single new idea'. [130] The document of mid-March, on which Lloyd George had sweated blood, was 'sketchy...full of padding and without details or estimates'. [131] To sit with him in Cabinet would involve the 'demolition of all [Chamberlain] had worked for as Chancellor'. [132]

By this Chamberlain meant that he believed in his own handling of the financial problem, did not believe in the handling to be expected from anyone else and would have nothing to do with deficit financing or inflation. Since becoming Chancellor, he had aimed to restore international confidence and reduce taxation in time for a general election. When tempted with the Foreign Office at the end of 1934, it was for this reason that he thought Baldwin and Runciman the only tolerable successors, though he ruled the first out by reason of his laziness and assumed that the second was ruled out because he was a Liberal. [133]

The Foreign Office was suggested by Margesson: it is not certain that Baldwin had agreed. Even if he had, it is not certain why the suggestion was made. It may have been made in order, as Margesson claimed, to get rid of Simon. It may have been made in order to facilitate co-operation with Lloyd George by giving the Treasury to Cunliffe-Lister. [134] Probably the situation was not so far advanced. What is certain is that Chamberlain's hatred halted any moves there might have been in that direction.

The hatred Lloyd George had earned he had earned by the treatment Chamberlain was given as Director of National Service in the third year of the war. Neither subsequent success nor Lloyd George's failure had softened it. It was as strong in 1934 as in 1917; between November, when Chamberlain first heard of the Lloyd George idea, and the following June when it was finally dropped, he let Baldwin know that he would resign if it happened and persuaded the rest of the Big Six to do the same. [135]

Chamberlain treated the problem as a personal conflict in which it was his enemy's dearest wish 'to hit out at the Chancellor, "cold, narrow, hard, unimaginative", as the *News Chronicle* describes him'. [136] In the first month of negotiation, when Lloyd George was given newspaper coverage, he was unhappy. Instead of responding directly, however, he let him 'develop his ideas' before beginning 'to attack in earnest'. [137] Eventually he was rewarded. 'I have', he wrote to one of his sisters in late February, 'thought of such a lot of really nasty things to say about him that I am almost sorry I have no more speeches to make. But I am not sure that it doesn't hurt him more to have no notice taken of him. Today he does not appear on the notice-board of any of the Sunday papers.' [138]

The Bangor speech and newspaper reception of the New Deal had two main consequences — assurances of attention from the Cabinet and a Cabinet discussion about 'financial policy in relation to public works' (at which younger ministers were represented). [139] It also produced statements from MacDonald, Runciman and Simon that they would resign if he was offered office. Since this would have destroyed the government and might have split the Conservative party as well, [140] Baldwin assured Chamberlain that he would not serve with Lloyd George either. [141] Even if his own, Simon's and Thomas's real feelings were more ambiguous, [142] the real decisions were made before the Cabinet charade began. On February 7 the Big Six agreed that they would all resign rather than work with Lloyd George. [143]

In ignorance, and with an optimism which the newspapers encouraged, Lloyd George began, nevertheless, to believe that he had them where he wanted them. When nothing had been done to honour the 'assurances', he complained about a speech in which Chamberlain had implied that public works were not a remedy for unemployment. [144] After an article on these lines in the *Daily Mail*, he had a further 'assurance' from MacDonald and a request that the Cabinet might see his plans. [145]

Lloyd George answered on the assumption that Chamberlain was isolated and on the run. [146] In this he was mistaken. It was certainly a Cabinet decision that MacDonald should write, and Chamberlain might not have written if the decision had been left to him. But he converted the letter into a request to see 'estimates and calculations' which he believed did not exist. [147] He had no doubt that the 'bluff' could be 'called' [148] by showing that the New Deal consisted of projects which the Cabinet was undertaking, was in process of investigating or had already, for the best of reasons, turned down. [149]

When MacDonald asked to see Lloyd George's plans, there was a fortnight's delay before they arrived. [150] In the fortnight following they were studied by the General Purposes

Committee of the Cabinet. [151] The Committee, which contained none of Lloyd George's admirers, invited him to a
special meeting on April 18. Chamberlain, believing that most
of his colleagues [152] were afraid, devised a procedure which
would prevent a general discussion taking place. [153] He encouraged an appearance of friendliness — by which Lloyd
George was surprised [154] — but insisted that the object of the
meeting was 'elucidation'. He wrote out 'in CAPITALS' a list
of questions for MacDonald to ask. In reply to Lloyd
George's suggestion that the Cabinet should send investiga-
tors to see how continental countries dealt with 'bacon-
curing, training camps, housing in suburbs, cooperative farm-
ing etc., [he] suggested that possibly it might be found that
we already had the information in Whitehall'. [155]

Lloyd George's impression of the meeting, and of his meetings with individual ministers in the afternoon, was that 'they
want to make terms', though 'of course, as cheap terms as
possible'. [156] Chamberlain's opinion was that Lloyd George
was 'kept guessing' and weakened his case by 'stat[ing] that
the unemployment problem would...be solved if work were
found for 550,000'. [157] The 'very long and wasteful' [158]
meetings which followed were designed to ensure that Lloyd
George went away a lesser man than he arrived. [159]

By the middle of 1935 Baldwin had been playing Lloyd
George along for a year. He was still afraid of him [160] but
knew that nothing could be done. When Cecil provided an
alternative, he took it. In the week in which the breakdown
of the Lloyd George negotiations was announced, [161] he gave
a warm welcome to the Peace Ballot. Acton might well have
claimed that 'he did not know the difference'. It would be
better to say that he did not mind.

From before the discussion about Lloyd George, Conservatives were clear that the rebellions about India and unemployment assistance were symptoms of a positive hatred of
MacDonald. Just, however, as Simon did not realise how
much he was despised even after the Putney by-election, so it
took time to make MacDonald see that all the disasters —
from the LCC elections to Wavertree — were being blamed on
him. [162]

From early in 1933, the National Labour ministers were

conscious of difficulty — about their party organisation, about the impression the Labour party left that they had sold out to reaction and about Conservative disloyalty to the extinct volcano by which they were led. [163] They were embarrassed by the contrast between themselves and the New Deal in America which was damaging their 'moral influence' and making it difficult 'to return to...and bring the [Labour] party back to its old principles and political conceptions'. [164]

Over the land tax, the House of Lords and Chamberlain's plans for taxing Co-operative Societies, they had inconvenient commitments. In face of the Conservative newspapers, the agricultural lobby and the difficulties of the housing question (in which MacDonald invested much energy), they found it difficult to establish a continuity with what they had been doing in the past. They were sensitive about their difficulty and greatly discouraged by deterioration in the European situation. Even a striking by-election at Kilmarnock in November, wiping away the Conservative failure at East Fulham in October, did not help them much. [165]

In mid-1934 MacDonald's eyesight was so bad that he was expected to resign. [166] At various points of extreme irritation, he or Thomas threatened to do so. [167] When he went to Canada to recuperate in the summer, it seemed unlikely that the party would survive. [168] His health was better when he returned, but not the political situation. [169] On one or two occasions Thomas, probably hoping to be told to stay, suggested that he and MacDonald should go. In a condition of mental depression MacDonald, from time to time, threatened to go. [170] In February 1935 Baldwin suggested that he and MacDonald should go together when the India bill was out of the way.[171] After a rumour-laden week, in which Baldwin stated publicly that the 'government was not breaking up', MacDonald promised to go before Whitsun. [172]

Between the point at which MacDonald agreed to go eventually and the point at which his going became imminent, Baldwin changed his mind about the succession. In February, he more or less told Chamberlain that Chamberlain would succeed. In mid-May he left him in no doubt that he proposed to become Prime Minister himself. On June 7 he did so. [173]

MacDonald's removal (to be Lord President of the Council) and the subsequent reconstruction were designed to achieve two sorts of objective. These were to have a Conservative Prime Minister, and to provide symbolic assurance of the fact that Stanley and Hudson had left the Ministry of Labour, Londonderry the Air Ministry, Gilmour the Home Office and Young the Ministry of Health and that Simon had been removed from the Foreign Office.

There were difficulties. As Derby's son and an intelligent holder of 'humanitarian views', [174] Stanley had to be given something. Despite Chamberlain's feeling that he was too weak to deal with the teachers' unions, he was given the Ministry of Education. Londonderry was closely connected with MacDonald, a great Conservative host and a makeweight to Salisbury among peers. Hailsham and MacDonald both pressed Baldwin to keep him. When Cunliffe-Lister replaced him as Air Minister, he was made leader of the House of Lords. [175]

Young was removed summarily, despite an offer to stay until the election, [176] and replaced by Chamberlain's candidate, Sir Kingsley Wood. When Eden was not made Foreign Secretary, which some hoped he would be, he and Percy were added to the Cabinet as reassurance. Simon was reassured first by being told that Hoare would not be Foreign Secretary if he moved, then by the promise that the Cabinet would include an extra Simonite, [177] finally by being made deputy leader of the House of Commons and Home Secretary instead of Lord President of the Council (with MacDonald-like oversight of foreign policy) which had been suggested when negotiations began. [178] After declining another suggestion that he should leave the Treasury, [179] Chamberlain was left where he was, nursing suspicions of the price Simon had got for accepting the demotion he deserved and not altogether trusting Baldwin's promise to let *him* become deputy leader in the House of Commons if the election was won. [180] On hearing that *he* might be made Minister without Portfolio, Hoare renewed claims to be Foreign Secretary. [181] Apart from these, the chief difficulties centred around MacDonald and the National Labour party.

As soon as MacDonald saw that his days as Prime Minister were numbered, he began to state his price for moving. Apart from an outside wish to become Viceroy, [182] this had three elements — a desire to keep oversight of foreign policy (which was met when he became chairman of the Defence Policy Requirements Committee after the election); insistence on keeping Thomas in the Cabinet, despite heavy drinking and a reputation for newspaper leaks;[183] and pressure (which Conservatives expected[184]) to be joined there by his son, Malcolm, who was thirty-four. This made it necessary to remove Sankey, the Cabinet's third National Labour member.

Sankey was an elderly and extremely morbid Puseyite who lived with his sister. After his father's death when he was young, his mother had scraped to send him to Lancing, Oxford and the Bar, where he had a successful practice until, in 1914, at the age of forty-eight, he became a High Court judge. Thereafter his career was a triumph of situation over opinion.

Sankey had begun legal life in South Wales where he made his name on workmen's compensation. Up to 1919, however, his political reputation, so far as he had one, was as a Conservative opponent of Welsh Church disestablishment and a moderate member of the LCC. Then Lloyd George made him chairman of the Coal Commission in order to get impartial support for a sell-out to the miners. This turned him into a miners' hero. He would have been offered the Lord Chancellorship in the first Labour government if Haldane had not insisted on being Lord Chancellor himself. In 1929 he was made Lord Chancellor because no adequate Labour lawyer was available. He followed MacDonald into the National government in 1931 after trying hard to bring the rest of the Cabinet with him. Since then his chief interest had been in the passage of the India bill.

Being, as he put it, both 'a public school' and a 'university man', though, as he also believed, a man who had made his way,[185] Sankey liked working with Conservative and Liberal ministers. He had, however, little contact with MacDonald, except through Thomas. With Thomas he had only such contact as Thomas encouraged when difficulties loomed. He was, in fact, a cipher. His appointment as Lord Chancellor had 'astonished both bench and bar'.[186] He had a rough passage when the National Economy Act was applied to judges' salaries and was publicly censured by the Lord Chief Justice over the Judicature bill.[187]

Sankey's sole claim to consideration was his one-time

membership of a Labour government. Having assured him that he would resign rather than let him go, MacDonald tried to get him to go in March 1934.[188] Sankey knew — and Thomas hinted — that MacDonald would try again. In subsequent months he was in touch, perhaps innocently, with Snowden, Laski and the Secretary of the Labour party.[189] When eventually asked to go (by Thomas and Baldwin) because his place was needed for Malcolm MacDonald,[190] he consulted an old friend who was a friend of Baldwin. The friend, having told him to stand firm, suddenly told him that he would have to go. Sankey then refused the earldom he was offered on the ground that he would not connive at nepotism.[191] When MacDonald failed to mention Malcolm Mac-Donald in a talk they had after his resignation, Sankey added himself to the members of the 1929 Cabinet with whom MacDonald's parting was unfriendly.[192]

When Baldwin became Prime Minister, he did so knowing that he would have to fight an election before November 1936. He did not know when the election should take place or how it could be conducted. Least of all had he solved the problem of providing an alibi for unemployment. When he went on holiday in August, he had been thinking of October but had made no decision.[193] The decision was made with the Labour party's demand for military sanctions against Mussolini and the opportunity this gave to play peaceful support for a League policy in Abyssinia in place of uneasy support for the New Deal which Lloyd George had hoped might be used as the guarantee of Conservative centrality.

3

THE FUNCTION OF THE LEAGUE OF NATIONS

'I know that Henderson has a convention worked out and which he intends to put before the Conference when it is at its last gasp. This would not suit us at all (i) because of political reaction at home (ii) because from what little I hear his Convention would prove unacceptable to us. We should then be on the defensive, the victim and not the hero'. Eden to Baldwin, February 24 1933

'I am glad to know that I correctly interpret your sentiments when I say that the object of the Ballot was by no means to criticise the Government...but rather to show the Government that we have a large volume of public opinion behind us in the efforts which we are today making to maintain the authority of the League of Nations...The League of Nations remains, as I said in a speech in Yorkshire, "the best sheet-anchor of British policy".' Baldwin, at meeting with the National Declaration Committee to present the result of the Peace Ballot and the Resolution passed at the Albert Hall on June 27, July 23 1935. *The Times*, July 24

'I am bound to recognise that, if I supply the policy and the drive, S.B. does also supply something that is perhaps even more valuable in retaining the floating vote'. Chamberlain to Hilda, November 9 1935

(i)

When Foch turned the German offensive of 1918 into a rout, he destroyed the power-balance which had operated in Europe before the war. Despite a vacuum in Russia, the withdrawal of America and the balkanisation of the Danube, an Anglo-French alliance had a potentiality for dominance which it had never had before.

In fact, the reality in the 1920's was not an Anglo-French alliance but French predominance. British disarmament was more rapid and thorough than that of any of the Powers apart from Germany. Russia was not the power she had been in 1914. The United States had declined to take her place. Though French connections in central and eastern Europe to some extend had, the security of France depended on the powerlessness of Germany and France's willingness to make use of it.

In using it to protect themselves against future German predominance, French statesmen insisted on French predominance in the present. In Britain this produced suspicion of France as great as the pre-war suspicion of Germany. The Locarno Treaty guaranteed Germany against France as well as France against Germany, but the disarming of Germany and the occupation of the Ruhr remained formidable warnings.

Within ten years of Locarno French predominance had been destroyed. In withdrawing from the League, agitating in Austria and announcing conscription, Hitler started to do what previously he had promised. In these years he re-established Germany as a major power.

At the same time he played a political, as well as a military, rôle, aiming in the course of destroying the Versailles settlement, to appease Poland, isolate France and establish that Germany had no quarrel with Britain. If his object was to provide reassurance, he was unsuccessful.

The British reaction had two aspects and produced two sorts of policy which, however, interacted. Though diplomacy was affected by considerations of financial and military power, it was conducted on the assumption that it could do, without force, what force could not do by itself to ensure the peace of Europe and the stability of the world.

In attacking the post-war settlement before he came to power, Hitler had singled out reparations, the demilitarisation of the Rhineland, the restriction on German rearmament (together with the failure of the other powers to disarm) and the steps which had been taken to divide Polish and Czech Germans from Germany and reduce Austria to insignificance.

So far as reparations were concerned, the German criticisms had been recognised and accepted at the Lausanne Conference in 1932. After Lausanne, the centre of interest was disarmament and the Disarmament Conference at Geneva where Eden, as Foreign Under-Secretary, got the first of his Geneva enthusiasms[1] (for the abolition of military aircraft). In Whitehall, he aroused little enthusiasm as Hankey established, among the ministers and departments concerned, that an arms, or arms manufacture, agreement was crucial and improbable, and should not be accepted if likely to damage the armaments industry or leave Britain more vulnerable than she was already.

Ministerial discussions about poison gas, police bombing, international supervision and the internationalisation of civil aviation were overshadowed by Hankey's insistence and by the fact that, in reflecting departmental suspicions, the Service ministers embodied a Conservative reluctance to permit other states, or international bodies, to control, or view, Britain's defences.[2]

Whatever hope had been left by Lausanne disappeared in the course of 1933. Thereafter, breakdown was expected because the French demand for guaranteed assistance in case of German infringement of an agreement was incompatible with any conditions which Hitler was in a position to accept. Increased British involvement was not something the Cabinet would have offered, even if its military power had been greater. Establishing a scale of equality between France and her overseas empire on the one hand and Germany with her East European frontiers on the other would have been difficult in any circumstances. Since general reassurance was unlikely, the French were unlikely to agree.

Even before Hitler's arrival, depression had dominated Geneva. In early 1933 the French proposed a disarmament plan which, in many respects, went too far for the British. The British proposals of January 31 and the draft convention of March 16 were answers.[3] But these were proposed less in order to produce agreement than because it was as undesirable, if the conference broke down, that Britain should be blamed for the breakdown as that she should be blamed for the breakdown of the Economic Conference.[4] Until Germany withdrew in October, the fear of blame was equalled only by a refusal to give even tactical support to proposals that were thought objectionable.[5]

Fear took three forms — fear of Hitler, fear of France and fear of Arthur Henderson. Hitler, for example, might demand equality in rearmament as a preliminary to disarmament.[6] If this was challenged, he might leave the Conference and rearm illegally, while blaming Britain for lining up behind the French.[7] Or he might 'manoeuvre' Britain into conceding 'a measure of rearmament' before security arrangements had been agreed, thus exacerbating relations with the French. The French, on the other hand, might make impossible conditions about 'equality' and involve Britain in resisting German rearmament.[8] In either case the government would suffer if French jumpiness and German clumsiness produced an 'incident' leading to a 'flare-up'.[9]

In some ways Henderson was feared most of all. As President of the Conference, he was well placed to cover his own failure by implying the need for unacceptable advances towards the French[10] and to use his position as an election platform (which he did when he won the Clay Cross by-election in August). Fear was strongest at the end of 1933. But it was present when he produced his programme of work for the Conference in January and was one of the chief reasons why Eden and the Geneva delegation produced the plan which MacDonald took on his European tour in March.[11]

The tour was a failure. In Rome MacDonald resumed long-standing socialist cordiality with Mussolini.[12] But in Paris there was a frame of mind which was thinking in terms of 1914. Though the British plan was accepted in principle, the Conference was not expected to survive.[13]

In proposing the plan, ministers had gone as far as they thought safe. Though willing to go further at a late stage if agreement would otherwise be impossible, they believed that Hitler's only object was to strengthen himself against his neighbours.[14] They were not surprised, and may well have been relieved, that it was his withdrawal which broke up the Conference.[15]

In the following six months, they wanted, and to some extent expected, an agreement. To some extent, they went through the motions because Henderson had caught them on the hop by producing a Convention which the French liked, the Germans would reject and contained points 'considerably embarrassing' to themselves.[16]

In the winter of 1933 Simon, MacDonald and Eden worked hard. But the reality behind their professions was the realisation that Hitler intended to rearm, whether by agreement or not and that his 'tactical position' was 'strong' because he had 'nothing to lose either way'.

This meant that France was expected to move forward. It meant that, unless she did so, and did so quickly, German rearmament would become formidable.[17] And it imposed a strain on France during the early stages of a revolutionary situation. [18]

What a French government could have done without 'Stavisky' is uncertain. Probably no government would have done much. In the circumstances of early 1934, it seemed obvious that no government would be stable enough to carry through a policy.

In 1933 the British attitude had not been sympathetic. In the course of 1934, it became unsympathetic in face of French insistence on negotiating at Geneva, to which Hitler had said that he would not return, and the 'fallacious' opinion, which was held in Paris, that the Nazi régime was 'tottering'. [19] Mutual suspicions developed as British ministers emasculated French control proposals and the French excluded any increase in the accepted level of German armaments. There was also a suspicion that France and Germany might do a deal to Britain's disadvantage.

In these circumstances, the British attitude was one of ostentatious impartiality. There was no French alliance and no suggestion, even when withdrawal from the League cast doubts on Germany's participation in Locarno, that Locarno had been turned into an alliance with France and Belgium. [20]

Although French policy was disliked, [21] it was not supposed that Germany could be relied on. In the first six months of 1934 almost everything that was to be said about Hitler in the next six years was said for the first time. Doubts were expressed about his good faith and about the perceptiveness of some of his British visitors. [22] It was said that he 'trail[ed] his coat' and 'raise[d] his bids' as soon as he was given anything he wanted, and that he was trying to divide Britain from the French. [23] He was thought of as a 'racial... idealist...like Hess' [24] who led a 'reforming' element [25] and (before the killing of Roehm) was encountering opposition from the Junkers who would be much less accommodating than he was. It was thought that, if he *wanted* to expand, he might go east and south-east rather than west. [26] It was hoped that he would be reasonable and autarky modest, and that Schacht would find grounds for economic co-operation. [27] Baldwin thought about a visit; the chief visitor (Eden) described Hitler as having 'charm', having too much

to do 'internally' to be planning to go to war and seeming
much 'more like Dollfuss on a larger and rougher scale than
like the Hindenberg type or the von Bulows' who were 'the
sinister beings' in Berlin, having 'learnt and forgotten
nothing' in their hatred of Britain. [28]

Once German rearmament was accepted as a fact, the Service departments saw the point of a disarmament agreement to
keep it under control. In early 1934 Hankey had a positive
enthusiasm [29] as a new optimism produced discussion about
the extent to which Britain could help it forward.

So far as Germany was concerned, there were doubts
about the size of the army and the predominance which
equality with France would establish in relation to Austria
and Czechoslovakia. But the demand for equality was regarded as a requirement which could not reasonably be contested.

To French requirements, the attitude was more complicated. Though French insistence on supervision reflected an
'outmoded' assumption of superiority, reassurance was regarded as important. Throughout the winter of 1933, the
public objective of ministers was to do whatever was possible
to secure French co-operation. [30]

In fact, very little was possible; the concessions that were
made were limited, and designed much more for English than
for continental consumption. In April the French made it
clear that they wanted something more binding than 'consultation' in the event of aggression or the breakdown of an
agreement.

Despite the hopes of 1934, ministers were going through
the motions. The British Memorandum of January 26, and
Eden's visits to Paris, Rome and Berlin were earnests of intention. But all that emerged was the certainty that the Germans
wanted a scale of rearmament which the French were unlikely to accept, and that the Conference would break down
unless the British attitude changed radically.

This led to two conclusions — that Britain would support
whatever economic sanctions the United States would agree
to impose in the event of aggression or the breach of an
agreement, and that efforts should be made to establish a
world-wide system of regional pacts to supplement the general obligations imposed by Kellogg and the Covenant. [31]
Since no other changes were acceptable, the ministerial dis-

cussions of April and May were conducted in the belief that France must be made to take the initiative which led to breakdown. [32]

Breakdown was then made more certain by French attempts to approach 'security' outside a disarmament convention. Barthou's 'Eastern Locarno' and luridly-expressed objections to disarmament and treaty revision raised Anglo-French tension. [33] It was not reduced until his visit to London in July, when the Cabinet accepted an East European pact as a guarantee of German security and a method of limiting Germany's claims to agreed rearmament. [34]

'Encirclement' was unpopular. But the events of 1934 (especially in Austria) showed that Germany was a major power which, under Hitler (or other, less amenable, management) might make a systematic attempt to dominate Europe. [35] There was no *conviction* that this would happen. But the basis of discussion was the possibility that it might and the prospect of the same threat as had been faced in 1914 to the peace of Europe and the existence of the Empire.

With territories as vast and co-ordination as limited as in the Empire of 1933, it was impossible to be impregnable against all contingencies at once. This had not mattered in the twenties when few contingencies seemed likely to arise. From the beginning of the Japanese action on the mainland of China, it did.

Up to this point, the assumption had been that an equilibrium had been established in both Europe and the Far East and that Middle Eastern oil — the new factor in the post-war Empire — would be safeguarded if the Middle Eastern garrisons operated in the shadow of Mediterranean peace. India was seen as a guarantor of Middle Eastern power, as much as the other way round. But it was assumed that financial effort to create a more decisive superiority was impossible and that relations within the Empire put unified defences out of the question.

The Empire, therefore, was a mass of plunder which could not be protected by force, and whose existence was bound up with the sword-settlement, practical idealism and naval bargaining embodied in the Versailles, Locarno, League and Washington Treaties. It depended on naval power. But it also depended on Collective Security, which depended on the unwillingness of other powers to change the *status quo*.

The Japanese invasion of Manchuria threatened the *status quo* in the Far East and made it uncertain whether diplomacy, shoe-string defences (in relation to world responsibilities) and political policies in Europe, India and the Middle East were sufficient. It also made the Far East the most probable area of conflict and Japan the most probable enemy. With the dropping of the ten-year rule and the restarting of the Singapore base (which had been set back in the twenties), this was the assumption until Hitler's arrival in office. In the course of 1933, it disappeared. By the time the Cabinet initiated an investigation of the defence position in late 1933, different assumptions had prevailed.

The Defence Requirements Committee, set up after Germany left the Disarmament Conference, consisted of Hankey, Fisher, Vansittart and the Chiefs of Staff. [36] Assuming a present 'menace to our position in the Far East' and that the 'German menace will grow to formidable proportions within the next few years', its report stated that war with France, Italy or the United States were not contingencies that needed to be faced, that naval power was crucial and that a deficiency programme was needed to get back to the position that had been abandoned in the twenties. [37] Despite being edited in anticipation, [38] this was given critical analysis by the Ministerial Committee on Disarmament which issued two reports — an interim report on air defence, [39] and a report on defence and finance which the Cabinet accepted in July 1934. [40]

The Ministerial Committee and the Cabinet confirmed the Hankey Committee's analysis. While confirming it as an analysis, however, it modified its recommendations. Basing itself on the view that financial recovery was too fragile to sustain the proposed expenditure without deficit financing (which it was the object of policy to avoid), it decided that the naval and military programmes should be smaller and the air programme considerably larger. [41]

These decisions assumed that Japan or Germany could be dealt with separately but not together, that Japan had to be dealt with by diplomacy, and that military attention should be concentrated on Germany. They made no provision for action under the Covenant of the League. Recognising that air power had made isolation impossible, they took Locarno seriously, not least because they took more seriously still the public fear of air attack from the Low Countries under hostile occupation. [42] But they allowed for only a token expeditionary force on the Continent in honouring it, and they decided against a special guarantee to Belgium as 'lead[ing]... logically...to a tripartite alliance with France'. [43] They assumed that the size of the Empire made further entanglements undesirable unless very much more money was to be spent. They took it as axiomatic that none would be. They issued in Baldwin's declaration of November 28 that 'in air strength and air power, this country' could 'no longer' be 'in a position inferior to any country within striking distance of these shores'. [44]

Defence decisions, made first in order to remedy deficiencies, and then, after the announcement of German rearmament, to step up the size of the defence effort, did not assume that war was inevitable. They assumed that rearmament, once effected, would make war less likely and that a strengthened Britain would be in a better position to handle Hitler and bring France and Germany together.

Execution of this policy involved Treaty revision. In the next four years there were many points at which it seemed possible that this might start. Until the Munich Conference in September 1938, no agreed revision took place.

For this, at different times, there were differing reasons. Difficulties began with the attempt to develop a special Locarno relationship with France and Italy.

The essence of the Locarno Treaty of 1925 was the mutual obligation, established under League auspices, between Germany, France, Italy, Belgium and Britain. In the twenties it had worked unproblematically. In 1933 it ceased to, as Franco-German relations deteriorated. In attempting to restore them as a prelude to disarmament, Simon fixed on Italy as the central factor.

For this there were two reasons — that, except in Memel, [45] the most dangerous threat to peace, once Polish-German relations were settled, was in Austria [46] and that French security in relation to Germany could not be guaranteed unless Italian relations with France were as cordial as those with Germany. Mussolini's special relationship with Hitler and his special interest in Austria, therefore, gave him dual status as earpiece and barrier against expansion, and made it possible to hope that he might bring Germany back to the League. With Britain it established a common interest in Locarno as a 'buttress' to 'sustain the *status quo* without pressing on one side more than the other'. [47] Even in face of doubts about his connection with Hitler and his complacency in face of Nazi influence in Austria, Mussolini was treated, after MacDonald's visit to Rome, as holding 'the key to European peace' when manifest rearmament made it a matter of time before Hitler repudiated the 'Versailles limitations' he was 'secretly disregarding'. [48]

Although it had been known for some time that the Treaty had been violated, there was reluctance to say so in public. At MacDonald's insistence [49] the air programme of July 1934 had been presented in terms of a general threat of air bombardment. Despite explicit accusations from Churchill, Garvin and Austen Chamberlain, it was not until November that accusations were made specific.

The Cabinet responded then by gearing defence requirements to the possibility of a German war before 1939 [50] and by coupling announcement of the air parity policy with the news that it knew about German rearmament. [51]

In doing this, it was not shifting ground. It was rearming, but it was in favour of conciliation too. On November 28 Baldwin stated that Germany had a military air force of between 600 and 1,000 and would shortly have an army of 300,000 (with more in reserve). But he did not say what could be done to remove 'apprehension' or restore 'the Concert of Europe'. [52] The function of the speech was to establish (against critics) that Britain had air superiority, to pull Hitler up short (so as to get a better negotiating position about disarmament) and to edge the French towards negotiating on the basis that Germany had rearmed. Simon was explicit about the 'wisdom' of 'get[ting Germany] back to Geneva on the basis that these violations of Part V are condoned'. At the end of the debate, he spoke of 'an opportunity based not on the prescriptions of the post-war period, but on a new effort to establish more firmly a secure prospect of peace in the world'. [53]

In talking in this way, Simon was anticipating the next step. This was expected to be a German announcement, after the Saar plebiscite the following January, that rearmament had been proceeding in violation of the Treaty. He was certain that the French would not punish the violation. He believed that the alternative to legalisation would be further illegal rearmament and that it was desirable to 'keep the initiative' by beginning Four-Power discussions before the conclusion of the Saar plebiscite relieved Hitler of the need to be agreeable. [54]

What Simon intended was to deny France the chance to arraign Germany at Geneva and to prevent a polarisation between a Franco-Soviet *bloc* on the one hand and Germany on the other. At the same time he thought that Hitler would be more dangerous outside the League than in it and might be pushed, by threat of a tripartite alliance, into returning to Geneva in order to obstruct it. He expected prolonged bargaining about the future level of armaments once agreement had been reached about the past and proposed, as Britain's contribution, a reaffirmation of the obligation to Belgium, a new statement of interest in the independence of Holland (which the Cabinet rejected) and further expressions of indirect support for a pact in eastern Europe. Despite a German landslide in the Saar plebiscite, a new phase seemed about to begin with Britain, France and Italy making concerted approaches to negotiation. [55]

In the next two months, France and Italy moved closer together. During Simon's Paris visit, the Barthou position was abandoned. When Flandin and Laval came to London, the Cabinet agreed to a Locarno-style mutual guarantee against air attack [56] and a declaration of interest in Belgian independence. [57] A strong Anglo-French statement during Simon's second visit to Paris a few days later [58] was followed by German agreement to the Air Pact and a German request for a British visit to Berlin. [59]

The Simon/Eden visit was called in question when the much-rewritten wording of the Defence White Paper of March 1935 [60] caused a good deal of offence in Germany. When eventually made (after German violations of the Treaty had been admitted) it convinced Simon that, though Hitler wanted an 'understanding' (especially about naval rearmament), his methods were likely to divide Europe and drive Britain and Russia together. [61]

From the Berlin visit onwards, policy ran along tightropes. On the one hand, it had to make sure that firmness did not make Hitler recalcitrant. On the other, it aimed to develop relations with France and Italy and to imply the prospect of closer relations with Russia so as to make him accept an East European treaty. [62] Yet again, while aiming to support both an East European treaty and the independence of Austria, it had to avoid action which might increase the range of British commitments. [63]

After the Berlin visit, Eden visited Moscow, Warsaw and Prague. At the Stresa conference in April, 'solidarity' showed Hitler that he could not do to Locarno what he had done to Versailles. [64] Between April and June German air strength became the central subject of political discussion and the cause of a further air programme, [65] as the government and the Conservative party developed the opinion [66] that France, Italy and Russia might have to come very close together if Hitler would not negotiate reasonably. By the end of May, it seemed possible that he might. [67] On June 7, Simon was removed from the Foreign Office, just before the signature of the Naval Agreement with Germany.

Simon's removal was not exactly the result of disagreements about policy. Though an instinctive isolationist, [68] he saw, as well as anyone else, that with '$2\frac{1}{2}$ million people enrolled in the forces...Hitler...*might* be menacing'. [69] Nor did sympathy for Germany distinguish him from most of the Cabinet who would have been much less certain than Vansittart whether to see 'Joan of Arc' or 'the bottomless pit' in Hitler's 'simple bearing', and 'dangerous' but 'sincere' 'conviction' that 'he [was] destined to bring about the moral rehabilitation of the German people'. [70]

Part of Simon's difficulty arose from a want of warmth, an appearance of insincerity (particularly at Geneva) and a humourless rigidity that irritated such diverse figures as Thomas, Chamberlain and Ormsby-Gore. Part of it arose from a failure to express generous sentiments, [71] a deep uncertainty about the presentation of policy and a failure to convince his equals that he knew what it was. [72] There was also a suspicion, which time confirmed, that he was trying to dodge the blame about defence weakness [73] and rearmament, for both of which he was as much responsible as any other member of the Cabinet. [74]

Like MacDonald, Simon felt the lack of newspaper support where, before Manchuria and the resignation of the Samuelites, he had had some. [75] This made him sensitive to appearances and unwilling to expose himself in public. It also made him anxious to be liked by those he did not know, including 'Youth' with whom he was conscious that he was a failure where Eden was a success. The result was that he dressed Eden down too often for his own safety and was blackguarded, not only behind his back, [76] by Ormsby-Gore, Tyrrell (from the Paris embassy) and Eden himself, who had all become Baldwin's listening-posts on (and off) the Continent. [77]

So far as rhetoric was concerned, Simon's language was impeccable. The 'disease of fear', [78] the 'barriers of memory' [79] and the 'character of the people' [80] were prominent. He made the usual noises about 'mutuality' and disarmament and made few attempts to resolve the unavoidable contradiction between detachment from Europe and an 'unshaken purpose' in relation to the League. [81]

Unfortunately for him, success was impossible within the framework of expectation which the public was encouraged to entertain. 'The League', 'disarmament' and 'Collective Security' had not had very much in them, even before Hitler came to power. Hitler destroyed them, and Simon with them.

In some respects Simon was more pro-German than *The Times*; in others he stood somewhere between *The Times*'s 'understanding' and Vansittart's dislike of Germany. He was, however, identified with neither and was not involved in the campaigns each waged against the other. If he seemed publicly cautious, that was at least partly because of the diplomatic danger involved in 'speaking out'. [82]

In this, he was in the same position as other ministers who were tougher in Cabinet and committee than they wished to seem, talked the same language as he did in public while feeling the same doubts in private and differed only in avoiding over-exposure when manifest contradictions made this dangerous.

Knowing that his future was at stake, Simon tried hard to

prevent contradictious occurring. But, though aware of the power struggle and the need for rearmament, he was aware of the unpopularity of both, and regarded emollient altruism as the best guarantee that his future would be assured. [83]

Simon did not conduct foreign policy by himself. It was processed by Vansittart and the Foreign Office on the one hand and by the Disarmament Committee on the other. What emerged from the Foreign Office ran the gauntlet of the Committee and was then put to the Cabinet. Though the Cabinet added criticisms of its own, the main sifting occurred in committee where MacDonald, Baldwin, Hankey, Hoare, Monsell, Hailsham, Londonderry, Thomas, Chamberlain, Runciman and Cunliffe-Lister were the chief performers.

Of these, Thomas talked chiefly about tactics except when he talked about the need for disarmament. When Londonderry spoke, he did so with little effect. Monsell was prepared to abandon the Disarmament Conference and wanted chiefly to improve relations with Japan in order to negotiate renewal of the Naval Treaty. Hailsham disliked Geneva [84] and mistrusted Germans. [85] He regarded the Economic and Disarmament Conferences as 'mistakes' and believed that the government had 'acted with a courage almost amounting to foolhardiness' in 'disarm[ing] itself in the hope of persuading other people to do the same'. [86]

Hoare, too, by and large, expounded a negative line about Geneva. [87] Cunliffe-Lister spoke, almost invariably, in an isolationist sense standing, it is true, on Locarno but being willing to sympathise with Hitler's point of view, unwilling to extend commitments, and anxious to abolish military aircraft as the best defence against the bombing of London. [88] Against this background Chamberlain was an internationalist hawk with a firm grasp of the importance of France and the interconnectedness of European peace.

Simon's policy was accepted by all his colleagues more or less equally. Despite reluctance to support Dollfuss, who was unpopular on the Left, [89] he wanted to be on good terms with Mussolini. He was irritated by the French, unenthusiastic about Russia and overwhelmed by the whiphand he thought the Germans had about disarmament. [90] Even when being criticised for the Eastern Security pact [91] or being taken apart by Chamberlain and Hailsham (for neglecting

France [92] or assisting German rearmament [93]), he was really being attacked for incompetence in execution rather than for the wrongness of his opinions. [94]

Until Barthou's assassination, Simon hedged approval of an East European pact with stipulations about 'mutuality' being 'to the fore' and Germany regarding it as 'helpful'. [95] Afterwards, he was much more forthcoming. In the winter of 1934, he was congratulating himself on the 'steadiness' of his policies. He continued to believe in success until Hitler gave him a kick in the teeth after the publication of the Defence White Paper on March 1. [96]

By the middle of 1935, Simon was trusted as little as Curzon, had had his telegrams redrafted as much and left the impression of having been 'led up the garden' when he met Hitler. [97] Vansittart and Eden were both trying to get rid of him. [98] He had been attacked by name on more than one occasion at Conservative backbench meetings. [99] Above all, he had been at the receiving end of a great deal of criticism from MacDonald.

Signs of age and peculiarities of public performance did not prevent MacDonald playing an important rôle in foreign policy in his last three years as Prime Minister. He went to Lausanne, made the European tour of 1933 and led the British delegation to Stresa. He presided at both the Cabinet and the Disarmament Committee and gave leads which Simon's inadequacy made it doubly easy to give.

MacDonald had thought deeply about diplomacy and had strong views about how it should be conducted. He recognised the nature of the German threat and that 'peace itself ... was in jeopardy'. [100] His long-term identity and dislike of Henderson brought home to him, more acutely than to other members of the Cabinet, the importance of ensuring that rearmament could be avoided.

MacDonald disliked the League and 'military alliances' and believed in something like secret diplomacy. He accepted Locarno (as a non-alliance). But he objected to extending it and was adamant about retaining the power to determine the 'automatic' nature of its 'obligations'. [101] While conscious that Britain lacked friends, he mistrusted the French and treated Barthou as a menace who might make Hitler into an 'aggressor'. [102] Having visited America in 1930, he believed in a 'special relationship'. For this reason he wanted no special relationship with Japan and regarded the Washington Treaty as the sole guarantee that the Far East could be stabilised without an unacceptable measure of rearmament. He felt no confidence that rearmament could be avoided. Even at his most optimistic, he felt a deep pessimism about the future and from a mature, disillusioned, pacifist practicality reached conclusions not very different from those of Hailsham, Londonderry and Monsell. [103]

MacDonald wanted a bipartisan policy and objected when party politics intruded. [104] He was irritated by idealists [105] and contemptuous of their failure to understand the difficulties of situations. But he kept in touch, even when suggesting that the world had moved on. While confident that his German policy had been right in the twenties, [106] he made no bones about the 'dangerous unsettlement' Hitler was causing by rearming secretly. [107]

Nor, at first, did he avoid the real problem. Even if his Canadian recuperation coincided with its adoption, he did not really oppose the deficiency programme of 1934. Much as he disliked it, and much as he complained about rearmament a year later, [108] he took the unusual step of signing the Defence White Paper which caused so much offence in Germany in 1935.

MacDonald was not alone in wanting 'a security agreement' rather than 'inferiority for Germany'. But he knew that Hitler would have to be pressed if he was to behave reasonably. He opposed the Simon/Eden visit to Berlin as a sign of weakness [109] and allowed himself to be overruled, in the week in which he agreed to renounce the Prime Ministership, only when the Cabinet Committee insisted. [110] He was generally regarded as the best person to lead the delegation to Stresa when an Eden illness made it unsafe to send Simon by himself. [111]

Simon understood the significance of Mussolini and knew that he had to put up with the 'stiffness and intransigence' of the French. He agreed too (when pressed) that tripartite firmness was essential. But where MacDonald treated diplomacy as a game at which he was rather good, he merely went through the motions with little sense of execution, both eyes on the public and no conception of the unity of the European situation.

By the time MacDonald and Simon had been replaced, differences had been small and concerned the mode of execution of policies that were agreed. Hitler had been identified as a threat to peace and a possible enemy in war. A policy of pressure had been developed in company with France and Italy. There was no certainty that pressure would be needed. It was thought, however, that it might be, and that it might have to be heavier than Simon could manage if Hitler was to be made co-operative.

How, if at all, it would operate was not clear. But it was clear that the public would have to be educated. It was at least partly with a view to maintaining 'the facade of national unity' [112] as an aid to educating it that Simon and MacDonald were kept in the government. It was with a view to ironing out differences in the Foreign Office that Hoare replaced them. [113]

(ii)

Baldwin had made himself Prime Minister in order to win the next election. In approaching it, he had a programme (which Chamberlain had written) but he lacked a theme. It was doubtful whether a theme could be invented. It was certain that invention would be important if the election was not to be dominated by the Means Test, unemployment and disarmament, about which little could be said that was thought convincing.

The Abyssinia problem emerged from circumstances which the government regretted and could not control. As soon as the contours were identified, reactions were controllable. One control-element which came to be increasingly important was the opportunity the Peace Ballot provided to hold an election after the blowing out of the storm from Lloyd George and his replacement by Cecil as leading evaluator of Conservative liberality.

Cecil was not aiming to stand by Baldwin. Nor was his support constant or secure. The doubts of 1934 persisted and it remained uncertain whether support would be earned. But he had no doubt that the electoral power the Ballot had created could be used to make the government rescue the League from disintegration.

That disintegration was in sight had not been doubted. Russia, it was true, had joined, and the government (no thanks to Simon) had proposed an international force for the Saar. [114] But Hitler was an enemy. The Disarmament Conference was in ruins and Simon 'minimize[d] the extent' to which he was willing to 'enter into a system of Collective Security'. [115]

From Cecil's point of view, Stresa was objectionable because it looked like an *alliance* from which Germany was excluded[116] and condoned the other powers' failure to fulfil their part of the Versailles bargain by disarming. It was desirable, therefore, even after the admission that Germany had rearmed illegally, that Hitler should be given the chance to sign a treaty 'for the limitation and reduction of armaments'. [117]

This was the first priority, but Cecil did not expect it to be effective. Everything Hitler had done, and everything that had been done by Prussia in the last two hundred years, suggested that it would not be. The sole object in proposing it was to reach a position in which, after it failed, the League would have grounds for thinking about the 'economic and financial measures which might be applied to a state endangering peace by unilateral repudiation of its international obligations'. [118]

This mention of sanctions was made in relation to Germany against which it was assumed that they might have to be applied. Nor did Cecil want either a quarrel with Mussolini or unilateral British action to stop him. He wanted him stopped, but assumed that he would back down in face of 'a collective threat from the League or a breach of British friendship'. [119] He approved of the attempt to buy him off by ceding part of Somaliland. When Mussolini began to act like 'the mad Mullah', [120] he was clear that even a madman would not take on France, Britain and the Little Entente if he knew that they would be against him. He did not feel sure, however, that he would take the point unless Britain compelled the League to make a stand, and he spent a good part of late 1935 using the Union to remind the government that this was so. When Mussolini refused to respond, he wanted oil sanctions and the closing of the Suez Canal (even to the point of infringing international law). [121]

In 1934 Cecil had threatened to attack the government for betraying the League. Nothing done by Simon or MacDonald in the New Year made him alter his opinion. [122] In May he was 'in entire agreement with the Labour party' and wanted an 'arrangement' by which it would 'accept the assistance of Liberals or others on [the foreign policy] issue'. [123] At the end of August he was talking about joining the Labour party. [124] It was an indication of the standing the Union had regained as a result of the Peace Ballot that he was called to the Foreign Office along with Churchill, Austen Chamberlain, Lloyd George and the official party leaders at the beginning of the third week of August.

When approached, Cecil agreed to talk about foreign policy at Lloyd George's Convention. [125] At the same time he refused to support the New Deal and was cautious about getting involved generally. His caution was increased by the 'excellence' of a speech Eden made at Fulham in May and by Eden's inclusion in the Cabinet in June. Instead, therefore, of getting closer to Lloyd George, he brought pressure to bear on MPs to strengthen the 'Eden wing of the Cabinet' (among whom, at this time, Hoare was numbered). [126] On September 10 the Executive Committee of the Union offered 'unwavering support in the country for any action necessary to prevent Italian aggression in Abyssinia'.[127]

As the situation developed, Cecil felt revived suspicion of Hankey and Vansittart behind the scenes. [128] For Herbert Morrison, on the other hand, when he appeared with him at a public meeting, he felt extraordinary admiration. [129] There can be no doubt that he was much impressed by the Labour party's change of mood.

The Union position at the election was that electors should vote for the candidate most likely to support the League. [130] Even while Cecil wondered whether ministers meant what Eden had been saying, there was a swing towards the government at the same time as Labour suffered an upheaval.

Between August and October there were four indications of upheaval. There was Ponsonby's resignation from the leadership of the Labour peers. There was Lansbury's resignation from the leadership of the parliamentary party. There was Cripps's withdrawal from the National Executive. And there were commitments from the Trade Union Congress and the Labour Party Conference to support a sanctions policy, including military sanctions, if Mussolini invaded Abyssinia. By the time the invasion began Lansbury had resigned and Citrine, Henderson, Bevin, Morrison, Dalton, Attlee and Noel-Baker had put the party on one rather than the other of the foreign-policy forks over which it had been hovering in the previous year.

It is not clear whether the removal of Lansbury was designed from the start or was the fortuitous result of the embarrassment caused by senility, sympathy for Cripps or longstanding pacifism in a situation very different from the one in which he had been elected. Nor, probably, was there a plot, however strong the desire, to reduce Cripps's influence (and if there was, Attlee's election was not part of it). But the coincidence of two Conferences with a foreign-policy crisis increased the effectiveness of Dalton, Morrison, Bevin and Citrine and produced an impression, which far outweighed the impression of disunity, that the Labour party had become more belligerent internationally.

In 1934 Lansbury had reluctantly accepted both the flight from Cripps and the shift from pacifism. In 1935 his reaction to the Abyssinian problem had two faces. In parliament and in official conversation he reported the party's position. In public speeches he explained his own.

Like Hoare's, the party position envisaged a League crisis in two stages. In the first it was necessary to 'state publicly [Britain's] adherence to [her] obligations', which the government had been none too quick in doing, [131] and to show that Labour favoured 'collective' (by which was meant 'Anglo-French') action on the ground that 'it was...essential that the League machinery should be tried out'. If, however, 'there proved to be the basis for collective action and...collective action then failed, the time would have arrived for scrapping [it]...and for attempting some new plan of international cooperation', [132] perhaps in the form of a 'world economic conference' to 'discuss and organise plans for a sharing of raw material'. [133]

Alongside this official view that 'the causes of war are economic', Lansbury's own became more personal the closer other Labour leaders came to demanding action. Eventually the differences became striking. Few, if any, of the others believed that the alternatives were 'to abandon the whole idea of war...or to try and dominate the world by overwhelming force'. [134] There was no affinity between their language and the idea Lansbury repeatedly expressed that 'now is the time to say that in the name of God we shall have no more fighting'. [135] Citrine and Bevin would not have been happy, if they had been asked, to approve the call for 'a truce of God'. [136] Far less were they in tune with the claim that

it is the duty of the Christian Church to stand forth, whether from Mount Calvary, from Rome or from Geneva, and tell the nations that it is blasphemy both against God and Nature to endeavour to find means to destroy one another rather than sitting down to discover how better they can use the gifts God and Nature have given us. [137]

By the time Lansbury appeared as fraternal delegate, Citrine had sewn up the Trade Union Congress behind the view that 'pious declarations on the need of preserving peace were wasted on Mussolini', [138] that League-based coercion would be needed if he invaded Abyssinia and that the acceptable means of coercion would be 'economic and financial sanctions', 'closing the Suez Canal to Italian ships' or war. [139]

In proposing a resolution on these lines, Citrine urged delegates 'not to let George Lansbury down by voting against it'. [140] When Lansbury told him that he would have to explain his position, Citrine replied that the fraternal delegate could only explain the position of the Labour party. For this reason Lansbury made a noncommittal speech which, when interpreted as a sell-out, was followed by a public statement.

During the whole period I have been serving as Leader of the Labour party [he said on September 8], I have made it quite clear that under no circumstances could I support the use of armed force, either by the League of Nations or by individual nations...My own view remains if anything, stronger than ever and...I should quite loyally and cheerfully make way for someone who would be able to voice [the] views...of my colleagues...on this matter better than it is possible for me to do. [141]

Between this announcement and the Labour Party Conference a month later, attempts were made to persuade Lansbury to stay. They were accompanied by public statements of his own opinion [142] and by counter-statements from Morrison against 'unilateral British disarmament'. [143] The ILP had expressed its 'deep horror' at the attitude of the Party Executive and the TUC towards a 'capitalist quarrel' which was 'not worth the life of a single British soldier'. [144] On September 17 Ponsonby, who had been thinking of resigning because of the expense, resigned the leadership in the Lords because of the 'jingoism' of the trade unions, the impossibility of unanimous sanctions and his long-term position as 'an extremist in favour of disarmament'.[145] Cripps resigned from the National Executive and announced that he would not stand for re-election at the Party Conference. On October 1 Lansbury told the Conference that the movement was 'making a terrible mistake'. [146] He resigned when it gave overwhelming support to the advice it received from Dalton, Bevin, Clynes, Dallas, Marchbanks and Morrison [147] two days later.

By October 9, there had been an uncontested election. The parliamentary Labour party was led for the rest of the session by Attlee and Snell and was committed, where the government was not, to supporting military sanctions. On October 19 Baldwin decided that the general election should be held in three and a half weeks' time.

(iii)

By the summer of 1935 Hitler seemed to be potentially so strong and politically so ruthless that collective restraint might have to be threatened. There was no alliance against Germany, nor any extension of Britain's commitments. But there was a distinct hope that the League might get teeth, particularly since Russia had joined in 1934. The next year was spent in a shattering and unsuccessful attempt to show them to Hitler by showing them to Mussolini.

When Hoare succeeded Simon, there was every prospect of a change of mood. Hoare intended to go on working with Italy and France in order to press Germany to come to terms. But he intended to be more active in carrying Mussolini and to show a good deal more warmth toward the Soviet Union.

At this time Hoare was a register of Conservative opinion and intended to give the lead he thought it wanted. Unlike Simon and MacDonald, he had been rejecting 'pseudo-disarmament' from an early stage [148] and had wanted a tripartite *bloc* with France and Italy to resist the 'menace' which Germany 'present[ed]...to the peace of Europe'. [149] Even if a 'strong' attitude was a way of outbidding Churchill over the India bill, [150] he did not exclude a military alliance with France and treated Stresa as the beginning of something very much more formidable. His 'Conservative instincts' were 'rather outraged' by the thought of Simon and Eden 'runn[ing] around' after Hitler. [151]

Before June 1935, however, Hoare was advocate of a position rather than executor of a policy. The policy he inherited was the restoration of Locarno, which was neither an alliance against Germany nor an alliance with France [152] and the pursuit of which was designed less to restrain Hitler than to reassure France by keeping Mussolini out of his arms. [153] Both the East European and Stresa policies had been recommended on the ground that it was the 'mutual' reciprocity of Locarno that 'constituted its essential feature and made it so valuable a guarantee of European security as a whole'. [154]

Although Hoare would have been happy to build a system of 'alliances', he was in no position to do so. The unreality of the League position had in no way diminished its rhetorical force. Even when its professional proponents were most conscious of its weakness, politicians continued to make their genuflections.

So long as aggression was unlikely, this had few consequences. When the imminence of aggression coincided with Cecil's rescue-operation on the League of Nations Union, Hoare faced a body of organised opinion such as few Foreign Secretaries had faced before.

Hoare had no reputation as a friend of the League [155] and had been actively critical. Knowing that League opinion wanted Eden to be foreign secretary, he insisted on him staying at the Foreign Office when he went there. [156] In responding to what turned out to be the death-rattle of the Union, he anticipated 'the kind of movement that Gladstone started over the Bulgarian atrocities'. [157]

Hoare was conscious that an Italian conquest of Abyssinia could be represented as a threat to India and Egypt, and would diminish the prospect of collective resistance to Hitler in Europe. From this point of view he could not let Mussolini succeed in face of open British opposition. Far less, after the Peace Ballot, could he connive at a breach of Italy's (or Britain's) obligations under the Covenant. At the same time, he shared the Cabinet belief that Italian co-operation was crucial to Franco-German agreement and was willing to do a lot to get it.

It is not certain that Hoare would have raised the Abyssinia question at Stresa, where Simon and MacDonald did not. Nor is it clear that an understanding would have been reached if he had. The opportunity, in any case, was missed; by the time the Peace Ballot was completed, Mussolini was not talking in terms of agreement. In these circumstances Hoare had to seem to want to stop him and was compelled, both by previous undertakings and by judgments of public feeling, to appear to be acting through the League.

Individual League members, however, had no obligation to resist aggression unless the League asked them to and, in the British view, were under no automatic obligation even then. There had been little enthusiasm when the Cabinet discussed sanctions as a guarantee of French security the year before. There was no reason to expect greater enthusiasm now.

The prospect of Italy invading Abyssinia when the summer rains stopped in October first became actual in May. At this point Simon was conscious, chiefly, of difficulty; while willing to support the League if compelled to make a choice, he hoped, by conciliation at Geneva, to avoid having to do so. [158]   One of Hoare's first actions was to send Eden to Rome to buy off Mussolini by compensating Hailé Selassie out of British Somaliland.

When Mussolini rejected this, the second phase of policy aimed to persuade the French government to join in conciliation, on the understanding that there would be Anglo-French resistance if it failed. [159]   This was put cautiously in respect both of Anglo-French and of League action, [160]   and was qualified by the view that the objection was not to 'Italian expansion' (the 'need' for which was 'admitted') but to the proposal to 'achieve' it 'by war'.[161] It, too, failed because Laval failed to respond. [162]

Before parliament dispersed in August, Hoare made a strong League speech which, however, did not explain what Britain and France would do if Mussolini defied them. Nor was it clear that Britain and France would act together. [163] Eden saw Laval in late July and was in Paris for three-cornered discussions with the Italians in mid-August. [164] By August 21 it was obvious that the French would not promise to co-operate before it was necessary [165] and that Mussolini was unimpressed by British threats.[166] It was for this reason that Hoare had the Cabinet brought back from their holidays in order to decide what to do if something happened in September.

This was a prelude to the third phase, in which Hoare, anxious to avoid the odium which would come from 'repudiating the Covenant' but sensitive to the effect of Italian retaliation, [167] tried to set up a position which would meet all eventualities. He saw Lansbury, Austen Chamberlain, Lloyd George, Samuel and Churchill separately on August 20 and 21 and had Cecil interviewed by Eden. The position (which all accepted [168]) was that, though military action was out of the question, economic sanctions were unavoidable, provided Britain and France acted together and received 'collective' support. [169] During Baldwin's flying visit from Aix on August 22 [170] the Cabinet decided to investigate the sort of sanctions that might be suitable.

Throughout this series of half-decisions taken in a slow-motion run-up to an anticipated invasion, the Cabinet was both cautious and reluctant. Not all ministers objected to economic sanctions. [171] But it was well understood that French support was problematical and that the naval and air position in the Mediterranean would remain weak unless the Home defences were weakened in order to strengthen them. There was overriding knowledge that isolated action might 'exhibit our weakness' to Japan, and there was a resolute determination to prevent Eden and the Geneva delegation committing the Cabinet without its knowledge. It was as clear in June as in October that the Cabinet would not impose sanctions unless other governments did the same, and would do everything possible to avoid them until other members, and the non-League powers, had made up their minds about co-operation. [172]

At some points the Italians seemed likely to do so badly if they invaded Abyssinia that time would solve the problem. [173] At others Mussolini seemed to have been so effectively isolated that he would think twice before allowing anything to be done. [174] On the other hand, both he and the Italians were in such an 'abnormal' frame of mind that he might do something regardless. Even when hoping that he would not, ministers assumed that a response would be necessary if he did. [175]

This was as true of those who did, as of those who did not, share Eden's belief that sanctions were desirable. [176] At his one brief appearance in August, Baldwin said only that he agreed with Chamberlain and 'was going to catch the 8 p.m. train' back to Aix. But MacDonald, who wanted only a 'completely pacific method of applying economic sanctions', was certain that the public would expect action of some sort. [177] It is evident that Hoare and Chamberlain felt the same. [178]

In Baldwin's absence, Chamberlain was Hoare's collaborator and was in the closest touch. Neither was sure that Laval would co-operate, or that other League members would do so if he did. Even if the League agreed that sanctious should be imposed, they would not be effective unless Germany, Japan and the United States — the non-members — co-operated. It might even turn out, they thought, that there was 'no collective basis for sanctions', in which case the world would have to 'face the fact that sanctions were impracticable'. [179] The 'general feeling of the country, fully reflected in the Cabinet', was to combine the 'self-contradictory...feelings' of 'determination to stick to the Covenant and anxiety to keep out of war', and this had been met by the decisions of August 22 which made it 'impossible to criticize us on the ground that we were deserting the League'. [180] The one essential now was 'to play out the League hand'.

We must [Hoare wrote to the Ambassador in Paris on August 24] on no account assume the impracticability of sanctions until the League had made [its] investigations. It must be the League and not the British government that declares that sanctions are impracticable and the British government must on no account lay itself open to the charge that we have not done our utmost to make them practicable. [181]

The next major event, short of an Italian attack, was assumed to be the Council of the League meeting at which
Hoare intended to speak on September 11. There was no
Cabinet before this. But Hoare 'took a great deal of trouble'
about what he was to say, [182] consulted Eden and Chamberlain continuously, and thought of having Parliament recalled
in order to go with unanimous support. [183] When Baldwin
returned from Aix, he had him to dinner [184] (along with
Chamberlain) in order to tell him what had been agreed. [185]
Though warned by the Rome embassy that Mussolini would
not back down, [186] he made his speech in the belief that
'things' could be 'made unpleasant' for him without giving an
excuse to attack Britain in return.

The speech had three sorts of significance. In Cobdenite
fashion, it fixed on economic dislocation as the cause of war.
It singled out access to raw materials as the most important
aspect of the Colonial question, about which 'certain Powers'
had a right to be 'satisfied'. And it stated that 'the attitude of
His Majesty's Government has been one of unwavering fidelity to the League and all that it stands for'.

In conformity with its precise and explicit obligations the League
stands, and my country stands with it [Hoare said], for the collective
maintenance of the Covenant in its entirety and particularly for steady
and collective resistance to all acts of unprovoked aggression. The attitude of the British nation in the last few weeks has clearly demonstrated the fact that this is no variable and unreliable sentiment, but a
principle of international conduct to which they and their Government
hold with firm, enduring and universal persistence. [187]

This was received as a 'terrific' commitment and was applauded as a 'resounding' success. [188] It struck oil in liberal
areas where the Conservative party felt particularly vulnerable and where its managers wished to generate support. It
sprang, nevertheless, from as little expectation as the decisions of August 22.

Though Hoare had declared his belief in Collective Security, he was not sure that it could be made effective. Even
when Laval was most co-operative, he seems almost to have
expected the opposite. When Mussolini failed to respond, his
policy was to 'strengthen our weak points in the Mediterranean' and take steps to 'avoid the risk of Geneva going on
talking for weeks'. But this was designed to stop Mussolini

fighting, not to fight him, and 'if the League breaks down
under the test, the sooner we know this the better'. [189]
Chamberlain, on holiday in Scotland, had the same idea when
he wrote, after talking to Hoare on the telephone from Geneva, that, though Mussolini could not now draw back, 'I cannot help feeling that he must be worried over the unanimity
among other countries and maybe, if he can claim something
like a success when he advances to Adowa, he may be prepared to call a halt and open discussions'. [190]

One difficulty about economic sanctions was that, if applied, they might provoke military sanctions in return. This
made ministers cautious about enforcing them alone. It made
their viability depend on the reactions of other states in general and of France in particular, including especially Laval,
who, 'with his very cunning peasant mind, was determined
not to commit himself until the last possible moment'. [191]
There were moments when Hoare thought that he could be
relied on. [192] There were many others at which it was clear
that he could not be.

Nor was there greater confidence elsewhere. The Chiefs of
Staff, the Defence Requirements Committee and the Cabinet
all expressed fears about Laval's 'elusiveness'. [193] They all
sensed that public opinion, which had supported Hoare so
far, was 'a very long way behind feeling at Geneva' and would
be deeply divided 'if it came to a question of war'. They were
quite clear that there could be no sanctions without 'an un-
mistakeable announcement that an attack on one meant an
attack on all'. [194]

Even this limited measure of belligerence had to be pressed
by Chamberlain before the Cabinet would accept it. [195] At
subsequent meetings, on October 2 (before the invasion began) and October 9 (after it) and in the week that followed,
it disappeared in face of the realisation that Laval would not
take military action and was trying to get out of economic
action, [196] and that the door must be kept open for territorial adjustments leading to a settlement. [197] After two months
of impenetrability, [198] Baldwin assured the Conservative
Conference on October 4 that he wanted friendship with Italy, that the government 'have not, and have never had, any
intention of taking isolated action' and that 'Collective Security and the League of Nations' provided 'the best means of

preserving peace or of exercising some measure of control over events'. [199]

Unwillingness to quarrel with Italy was a general back-bench and party feeling of which a deputation on October 15 was only a marginal die-hard expression. [200] In the Foreign Office it was felt, by 'everybody of importance' apart from Eden that 'we ha[d] beaten the drum too vigorously in response to the demands of the ignorant public'. [201] On Hoare's part this produced scrupulous attention to any aspect of sanctions which might offer 'provocations' to Mussolini. [202] It produced sharp words at the Cabinet of the 16th, 'a considerable feeling', however unjust, [203] that [Eden] had recently taken the initiative too much at 'Geneva' and 'a unanimous desire that [he] should go as slowly as possible and take the initiative as little as possible...whilst we are still running the risk of being stabbed in the back'. [204] Caution remained the keynote when Baldwin decided to hold an election. [205]

The person who had prepared most effectively for an election was Chamberlain. He had turned Baldwin's mind to the problem in 1934, had consulted Conservative ministers and had produced a programme. On the other hand, he had kept Lloyd George out and, while believing that prospects had been improved by the new Cabinet, was not convinced that it had solved the problem. He was worried by the Labour assault on the Unemployment Assistance bill and the continuing level of unemployment, and was troubled in a personal way by the electoral relationship between rearmament and taxation.

By origin, Chamberlain was a Chamberlainite – a believer, that is to say, in the significance of Imperial Defence in the spectrum of duty. But he had belonged for far too long to the ruling cadre to be part of a faction; his *record* was much like that of anyone else. Nor had the movement to replace the National by a Conservative government in 1933 looked to him as a probable leader. In the course of time, however, it did, and Chamberlain came to think rearmament a central issue. When Mussolini exposed the weakness of Britain's defences, he decided that this was the subject about which an election could be fought.

Before leaving for Aix in early August, Baldwin had made no decision about an election and had left the impression that unemployment could be dealt with by existing schemes for the depressed areas. [206] Chamberlain thought Baldwin did not understand the depressed areas or how much had been done for them [207] and that the schemes to which he referred, though useful 'for a debate in the House when we come back', were things upon which 'we can never win an election'. He decided that an issue was needed 'that will put them in the background and, if possible, substitute for the hope of future benefits a fear in the public mind'. He found this in Cripps's social programme, Hitler's armaments programme and the government's programme for rearming Britain.

This platform was thought to have two advantages, apart from the enthusiasm he expected it to arouse among Conservatives. It would bring help to Tyneside and the Clyde – in the form of shipbuilding orders – more effectively than existing plans for the depressed areas. And it would stymie the most damaging facet of Labour propaganda.

The Labour Party, [Chamberlain wrote] obviously intends to fasten upon our backs the accusation of being 'warmongers' and they are suggesting that we have 'hush hush' plans for rearmament which we are concealing from the people. As a matter of fact we are working on plans for rearmament at an early date for the situation in Europe is most alarming...We are not sufficiently advanced to reveal our ideas to the public, but of course we cannot deny the general charge of rearmament and no doubt if we try to keep our ideas secret till after the election, we should either fail, or if we succeeded, lay ourselves open to the far more damaging accusation that we had deliberately deceived the people...I have therefore suggested that we should take the bold course of actually appealing to the country on a defence programme, thus turning the Labour party's dishonest weapon into a boomerang. [208]

Chamberlain had a favourable reception when he tried this on Simon, Runciman and Hoare. He also tried it on Rothermere who 'approved' and promised to 'help with his papers'. [209] Others [210] hesitated, perhaps because of the 'heavy weather' MacDonald and Thomas had made during the latest rearmament discussions and the possibility that the National Labour ministers might think it necessary to break up the government as a consequence. [211] When Chamberlain tried it on Baldwin, he was told that it would be 'something to think over at Aix but...he would prefer not to express an opinion now'. [212]

In the month which followed, Chamberlain had only one

period of contact with Baldwin — on August 21/22 — and then strictly for the business in hand. Baldwin was in Aix the whole time where, however, he had visitors from Geneva. Chamberlain was also away for part of the time — in Switzerland briefly and then in Scotland. But everything that happened in these weeks, including an approach from Garvin and Lloyd, [213] 'emphasize[d] the wisdom of the conclusion at which I was the first to arrive viz. that we ought to fight the election on a defence programme'. [214] In Scotland on September 21 he made a rearmament speech which was intended to be 'the preliminary to the election campaign'. [215] He repeated its substance at the Mansion House, in Glasgow and at the Conservative Conference where 'the party showed great enthusiasm'. [216] There was no doubt in his mind that the election should be held soon and on this issue. [217] He was surprised when Baldwin decided that it would not be the leading issue. [218]

The prospect of an election by the end of 1936 had dominated Baldwin's politics since the first run of by-election defeats in 1933. The obvious steps had been taken and the obvious instruments brought into play. Despite a marked improvement at the by-elections of 1935, [219] it was still felt at high levels that the government majority could be lost, without a large Labour advance, if the Liberal vote which had supported the government in 1931 declined to do so again. The Chief Publicity Officer expressed this view to Baldwin in August:

Even if the Socialist party did not obtain the support of a largely increased section of the electorate we could still lose the next election or at any rate arrive at a stale-mate position if the bulk of the Liberal vote went over to them. From that point of view the Liberal vote is vital and no political issue is likely to influence them more than the question of peace and war and the future of the League of Nations. [220]

In the course of the summer and after Baldwin's return from his holiday, Chamberlain had more than his usual difficulty in getting decisions out of him. About the election his difficulty was even greater. Whether because he was sensing the belligerence of the new Labour position, wanted to avoid identification with 'the theory of large armaments' [221] or was hoping that 'an emergency' would absorb the issues about which he felt uncertain, [222] Baldwin's intentions were veiled.

Eventually he decided that, though rearmament on Collective Security grounds should play a part, Labour belligerence had made it possible to emphasise the League as guarantor of a peaceful outcome in Abyssinia. [223]

PART I

THE NEW DEPARTURE

4

THE FAILURE OF THE LEAGUE OF NATIONS

'I have never known anyone in anything like Eden's position who has achieved such universal approval'.
Cecil to Baldwin, June 6 1935

'I was sitting next to Neville as hostess of the 1900 Club and was chuckling with delight at his pronouncement. I do hope it will achieve the desired result, though I confess I should like it to do even more, as for some time past I have thought that Anthony is a great danger to European peace'.
Lady Londonderry to Hailsham, June 18 1936, Londonderry MSS.

'Eden ha[s] put his country in a position where she sustained the greatest diplomatic reverse since Bismarck in similar circumstances had called Palmerston's bluff in the matter of Schleswig-Holstein...Further damage was done when Russia proved by her action in Spain, that she was not a good European as Mr Eden had assured the world was the case'.
Petrie, *Lords of the Inland Sea* (1937) pp. 272–6

(i)

The election of 1935 restored much that the government had lost in 1934. Labour did well in London and parts of the North but realised none of its larger expectations. Liberals, except when supported by the Conservative party, did badly. Even Conservative support could not rescue Malcolm and Ramsay Macdonald who lost Bassetlaw and Seaham respectively. Though only a third of the qualified electors voted Conservative, there was a bigger majority than had been expected[1] and the prospect of a simple struggle between Labour on the one hand and a thinly disguised Conservative party on the other.

Within six weeks Conservative 'centrality' had been destroyed as the 'betrayal' of the League became the government's 'failure' and the occasion for onslaughts on its integrity. These onslaughts, and the Conservative reaction, established the foreign-policy polarisation which constituted the centre of high politics in the three years that followed.

Whatever the effect of Abyssinia on the election, it is certain that Hoare raised expectations of a League policy to resist Mussolini. In spite of campaign rumours to the contrary,[2] these expectations were in no way reduced when the election was over. 'The government', he told the editor of the *Manchester Guardian* on November 21, 'is going to move rather more towards the Left' and, in relation to the League, 'there is not going to be any change in any way. ...With regard to the chances of settling the war I have at present no hopes. Mussolini's terms are too far from anything that either this country or the League could accept'.[3]

The decision to support economic sanctions, made when the war began, was not expected to involve military sanctions, unless an extension (in the direction of oil sanctions) made Mussolini attack the nations responsible for enforcing it. Hoare wanted an oil sanction because it was 'politically impossible' not to. He threatened to resign if he did not get it and was willing to be held back only so far as the Cabinet wanted the situation to develop without Britain making it.[4]

Oil sanctions, though accepted in principle on October 9, were not to be supported at Geneva unless non-League as well as League producers agreed to co-operate. Agreeing to co-operate, however, would not involve enforcement at sea, let alone action against Italian retaliation, which it was assumed would be directed against France or Britain rather than against Russia, Rumania or the United States. The American decision (towards the end of November) that American co-operation would be forthcoming, so far, therefore, from solving the problem, merely made French co-operation vital.[5] On December 2 Hoare told the Cabinet that Britain might find herself at war alone if retaliation occurred.

At this meeting the Cabinet agreed to support oil sanctions if the other League members did the same, provided the French were willing to co-operate militarily, but decided to ask for a postponement in case settlement-terms emerged from discussions which had been going on between British and French officials.[6] It was explicitly stated that the problem should be brought back if the peace talks offered no prospect of a settlement or if 'the military conversations showed that France was not willing to co-operate effectively'.[7] Ministers almost certainly expected to discuss proposals for a settlement before they were published as statements of policy.

They had not expected, therefore, to read in *The Times* on

December 9 that Hoare had reached agreement with Laval and was 'satisfied' with the agreement that they had reached. They were surprised to find the terms laid out in a French newspaper later in the day. They were even more surprised to find, at a Cabinet meeting called hurriedly that evening, that these envisaged only the vaguest disclosure to the Abyssinian government of what the Italians were to be told in detail.[8]

Hoare did not propose that the settlement terms should be imposed on Abyssinia. All he was doing was to 'bring back the League into the front of the picture'.[9] This was not convincing.

After sending an account of his discussions to London, Hoare had gone to Switzerland for a holiday. He was not, therefore, present when Simon made difficulties and Eden proposed modifications, including one, which the Cabinet, in 'supporting' Hoare's policy, approved — that Laval should be told that the plan must be shown to the Abyssinians as well as the Italians.[10] Laval, when consulted, asked for a declaration that Britain would not agree to an oil sanction.[11] Baldwin, Chamberlain and Eden, meeting together next morning, proposed, and the Cabinet accepted, a declaration that, though oil sanctions could not be imposed now, they were not to be dismissed from consideration.[12] Eden was authorised to speak in the House of Commons that afternoon, defining the principles on which a settlement could be based but leaving it uncertain whether the Hoare-Laval proposals had the government's backing.[13]

These 'principles'[14] were discussed at the Cabinet next morning when Eden was reluctant to 'champion' Hoare's proposals 'in detail' at Geneva. Chamberlain proposed that Eden be given the principles as instructions, but Baldwin refused, so he went off free to use his discretion.[15]

By the time Hoare returned to England on the 14th, Baldwin had talked to him reassuringly on the telephone.[16] Eden had seemed to be suspicious and, with the help of the head of the Abyssinian department of the Foreign Office (who spoke at the Cabinet of the 10th), had left the impression that the proposals were more favourable to Italy than they should have been.[17] The criticism they had attracted in the Foreign Office, the newspapers and the House of Commons (even among Hoare's own admirers[18]) had ensured that

they were dead. Hoare recognised this. He prepared to abandon them, while also defending them, when he spoke in the
House of Commons on the 19th. By the 19th he had been
forced to resign.

During his stay in Switzerland, he had broken his nose in a
skating accident. On returning, therefore, he let it be known
that he would stay indoors until he made his speech. Baldwin
called to repeat that everything was all right, and Chamberlain
to discuss the line of defence. [19] After Chamberlain had
sketched this to the Cabinet on the morning of the 17th,
Baldwin and Eden were sent with him to tell Hoare what was
wrong. [20] Hoare then redrafted the speech and sent Chamberlain a copy that evening in preparation for the Cabinet next
morning. [21]

During the 18th Dawson told Hoare that he should resign. [22] The same conclusion had been reached by MacDonald, by a wide range of newspapers and by Simon and the
National Liberal party. [23] Among Conservative backbenchers
it was felt that, even if Hoare's object was tolerable, it was
intolerable to reverse the policy immediately after it had won
an election. After receiving criticism of Baldwin's slackness,
and after the Foreign Policy Committee had instructed its
chairman [24] to tell Baldwin that Hoare must go, the Chief
Whip had formally asked Baldwin to make him. [25]

At the Cabinet on the morning of the 18th Chamberlain
explained that Hoare's line when he spoke next day would be
that the terms he had negotiated were better than those Mussolini had demanded in the summer and included some points
which the Abyssinians and the League had already accepted.

He would be able to say that there were many of the proposals that he
had not much liked, but that they were the best that he could at the
time get the French to agree to with a reasonable chance that Signor
Mussolini would discuss them. That would bring him to a point which
the public ought to be made to grasp.

There were only two methods of making peace: either (1) a negotiated peace, or (2) a dictated peace. Force could only be exercised if
either we were strong enough to exert it alone or had a definite and
concrete arrangement with other Powers. The Foreign Secretary would
be able to say that we might try and try for a negotiated peace at the
present time, but it would be impracticable to get it without giving
something to the aggressor. That was the fault in the alternative to a
dictated peace. The Foreign Secretary would admit that the peace pro-

posals were dead, but would say that they were the best that he could be got in the form of a negotiated peace — though, admittedly, they were not acceptable.

We had therefore to fall back on sanctions. This was very dangerous. The effect of sanctions was cumulative, and that was equally true of the existing relatively mild sanctions. As they approached the point of becoming effective there was always the danger of an act of aggression. The Foreign Secretary would probably speak with the utmost frankness as to the position M. Laval had taken up in the event of sanctions. Sanctions might mean war. We were not prepared to engage in war alone and had to look round and assure ourselves on the position. The actual situation was that no ship, no aeroplane or gun had been moved by any nation except ourselves. We alone had done all that we could. The future, therefore, lay in the hands of the League. Unless it was prepared to implement its action in putting on sanctions, success could not be expected. So the whole position must be cleared up. [26]

To all this Chamberlain found an unwelcoming and perhaps a concerted response. Only Zetland said anything in its favour. Wood was 'apprehensive'. Stanley said that the speech would be 'disastrous'. Hailsham thought it looked like an announcement that sanctions were impossible. For Percy it was 'tragic' but clear that anyone who took the line that we were 'afraid of Signor Mussolini...could only do so if he resigned first'. Elliot felt that the speech would have 'a shattering effect in Europe' and should not be delivered, even from the back benches. Duff Cooper questioned the claim that France was not ready to fight. Swinton feared that the speech could only be made by Hoare speaking personally. Thomas wanted him to resign before he spoke because, if he did, 'the whole thing...would be dead'. Ormsby-Gore was clear that Hoare had been 'caught' by Laval and would have to go. [27] Halifax agreed. When asked (by Chamberlain) whether Hoare might offer to go and go only if the debate went badly, he said that what was 'at stake' was 'the whole moral position of the government before the world' and 'if the Prime Minister were to lose his personal position, one of our national anchors would have been dragged'. [28]

After Baldwin had closed the meeting without commitment, Chamberlain went to Hoare's house to explain what had happened. Hoare was upset, but promised to resign at the end of his speech. Seeing Austen Chamberlain (the chairman of the Foreign Policy Committee) on the way back, Chamberlain was told that he should resign at the beginning. Baldwin then completed the salvaging of the position by going to tell him that he must resign at once. [29] It is not surprising that, when Neville Chamberlain went to 'say goodbye' on Friday, he found Hoare 'more emotional than usual and, as I thought, a little inclined to bitterness'. [30]

Hoare's last wish was that he should be succeeded by Austen Chamberlain, [31] whose age and status would ease his fall and who agreed that Germany, not Italy, was the central problem. Baldwin however, preferred Eden not just as the brighter symbol of the League, but also, perhaps, because his firmness in German directions was smaller.

At an interview on December 21, he told Austen Chamberlain that his health ruled him out and asked what he would think of Eden, who had been Chamberlain's private secretary ten years before. [32] Getting veiled warnings about Eden's health and stability, he sent for Chamberlain again next day. [33] After explaining that Eden was to be appointed, he asked him to join the Cabinet with undefined defence responsibilities and the possibility of becoming Lord President if Macdonald failed to find a seat. After establishing that the salary could be £5,000 p.a. (rather that the £3,000 Baldwin was offering), Chamberlain promised to consult his wife. Her negative confirmed his instinct. 'You laid so much emphasis on my age and health', he wrote, 'that I am compelled to add that anxiety about my health has played no part in my decision'. In a memorandum, like the one he wrote in a similar situation in 1923, [34] he explained that Baldwin's

repeated reference to Ramsay MacDonald's condition and to the danger of men becoming senile without being aware of it were offensive in their iterations. I could perceive no prospect of public usefulness in the acceptance of such an offer so conveyed and I came to the conclusion that what he wanted was not my advice or experience but the use of my name to help patch up the damaged prestige of his government. [35]

(ii)

With Hoare's resignation, two foreign secretaries had been broken. Another casualty now occurred as Eden identified himself with the view that the League could stop Mussolini if Abyssinian resistance gave sanctions time to bite.

When Eden became Foreign Secretary, he had been in of-

fice for four years, all of them at the Foreign Office, as
Under-Secretary, Lord Privy Seal and Minister for League of
Nations affairs. From his prolonged residence at Geneva in
1933 he had been greatly admired by the leaders of the
Left. [36] Admiration was increased by his attacks on Isolationism and the *Daily Express* [37] (which did not 'grace or dis-
grace' his 'breakfast table' [38]), by the assertion that there was
no Russian threat to Germany [39] and by repeated reiteration
of commitments to 'the Covenant, the whole Covenant and
nothing but the Covenant'. [40] His visit to Moscow in 1935,
his promotion to the Cabinet and his appointment in Hoare's
place were all designed to reassure that broad band of enlightened opinion to which he was responding when he deviated
from the foreign secretaries he was serving. [41]

In attempting to stop Mussolini Eden had advantages over
Hoare. He had positive support from Baldwin who had been
shaken by the uproar of late December and told the Cabinet
that 'a refusal to impose an oil sanction...would have a disastrous effect both now and at the next general election'. [42] He
had the benefit of a feeling that the defence programme required trade union support which would not be given if the
Defence White Paper was published at the same time as 'our
representative at Geneva had just declined to co-operate in an
oil sanction'. [43]

In spite of this he was 'under no illusions' about the difficulties. He hoped that Mussolini would have difficulties of his
own and proposed to 'go slow' in bringing pressure on him.
In any case he expected Cabinet resistance; he accompanied
his oil sanction proposal of February 26 with alternatives
which the Cabinet might prefer. [44]

Only Runciman and Monsell recorded their dissent. [45] But
Eden was told to avoid the initiative at Geneva since there
could be 'no question' of 'applying' an oil sanction 'unless
the oil-producing or exporting countries co-operated'. [46]

At Geneva, Flandin suggested a further attempt at mediation. When Eden agreed, because he did not see how he could
refuse, French support was made conditional on a British
undertaking to resist a German occupation of the Rhineland. [47] A decision of this sort required Cabinet authorisation
which Eden did not have. It would have taken time to get it,
so he made a speech which took the lead about sanctions

much more than the Cabinet had intended. [48]

This speech was made for public consumption at a point at which there was little danger that an oil sanction would be imposed. The Cabinet of March 5 refused Flandin's conditions. It would have precipitated discussion about Locarno if the prospect of French co-operation in Abyssinia had not disappeared with the German occupation of the Rhineland two days later. From then on, the Rhineland occupied the centre of the stage. Despite continuous affirmations of the possibility of defeating Mussolini, [49] Eden had not imposed an oil sanction by the time Hailé Selaisse fled to Palestine in May.

The 'débacle' of May 1936 imposed a strain on Eden personally. [50] But it was not the central problem in British policy during his first year as Foreign Secretary. The central problem was Germany, about which he was at least a common denominator and was, if anything, at times an advocate of the soothing touch.

When he became Foreign Secretary, Eden had three sorts of reputation. Through age, looks and dress, he had become a symbol of 'Youth'. Through service in the trenches and at Geneva, he embodied the heartfelt desire for reconciliation through the League. He had been a guarantor of Russia's suitability to be a member and, when Russia joined, had aimed to complete its rôle as guarantor of peace by persuading Germany to return as well.

Eden's attitude to Germany was a continuation of the attitude he had had acquired when Hitler had behaved, on first meeting, like an ex-serviceman [51] and the French desire for ' "Locarnos" in various parts of Europe' seemed 'a foolish' contribution to 'encirclement'. [52] In early 1936 he was blaming French insensitivity then for the difficulties which Hitler was creating now. [53] His Cabinet paper on 'The German Danger', like Hoare's on German rearmament two months before [54], explained Hitler's aims as being 'the destruction of the peace settlement and re-establishment of Germany as the dominant Power in Europe'. He proposed to do this, Eden told the Cabinet, by acquiring 'new markets for German industry', 'new fields for German migration' and new 'sources of...raw material', and by 'absorbing all those of German race who are at present citizens of neighbouring states'. [55]

Eden had no wish to quarrel with Hitler. While half-expecting 'foreign adventures' as a way of 'distracting attention from...[economic] failures at home', he regarded them as 'an additional reason for coming to terms quickly'. [56]

Eden's appeasement raised a finely-aimed combination of expectations. His long-term objective was League-based disarmament. But this would only be possible if short-term rearmament was effected first. Short-term rearmament was necessary in order to prevent Hitler taking steps to make *détente* or disarmament possible. Since this would be greatly disliked 'by an important section of British opinion' it was essential, therefore, 'so far as the home front is concerned', to make a 'renewed attempt at a political settlement'. [57]

Eden was not aiming to resist any particular act of aggression. He had wanted to defeat Mussolini because a victory for 'the League principle' would facilitate 'a political settlement in Europe'. [58] But he did not want Anglo-French, or British, involvement in a Franco-Russian alliance against Germany, [59] and he resented the Abyssinian somersaults of the French as much as he resented those of his critics in the Cabinet. One reason why oil sanctions receded in the New Year was his refusal to promise Flandin reciprocal co-operation in Europe. One reason why he was unwilling to do this was his belief that it would be unnecessary if Mussolini could be checked in Abyssinia.

What Eden had to do was to recognise that Stresa was dead. What he wanted instead was a return to the normality of the twenties and the creation of conditions in which Hitler could behave like Stresemann. This would involve major adjustments and a major effort to bring institutional arrangements in line with the realities of power. It would remove the impression which Hoare had created and confirm the moral centrality of the Conservative position. By the time of the next election (in 1940), success might be in sight, he thought, after a three-year haul [60] in the course of which Hitler would remilitarise the Rhineland, have 'one or more' of the ex-German colonies and benefit from economic priority along the Danube in return for signing a disarmament convention, joining a reconstructed League and renouncing further territorial claims in Africa and Europe. [61]

Nor was this affected by March 7. That Hitler would put

armies into the demilitarised Rhineland had been expected for
a long time before he did it. When the Cabinet had discussed
the possibility after Flandin asked it to, it agreed that, since
'neither France nor England was...in a position to take effective military action', [62] its Locarno obligations should be
swallowed up in discussion of a general settlement. This was
swallowed up by Hitler's action two days later.

Eden described the *coup* as discrediting Hitler's peaceful
protestations. But he said that 'good' might come out of 'evil',
that the Rhineland might have been conceded in negotiation
and that it was desirable to promote a 'far-reaching settlement'. [63]

When faced with the occupation, the Cabinet talked in a
way which frightened Baldwin. But the outcome was an earlier opportunity of discussing a settlement than there would
otherwise have been. Eden was sent, at Flandin's request, to a
meeting of the Locarno powers in Paris, where he was asked
to support a public demand for withdrawal on pain of war.
On his return to London, the Cabinet allowed him to approach Hitler secretly with a view to persuading him to withdraw pending discussions about the future. When this was
leaked to the newspapers, his main object at the League and
Locarno meetings in London was to defuse the conflict. [64]

Eden had no desire to go to war. His policy was the Cabinet's policy of avoiding war while trying to 'avoid a repudiation of Locarno'. [65] Such firmness as he displayed [66] was
designed to anticipate Flandin's demands for more; none of it
was intended to be turned into action.

The question was not, in fact, put in terms of action; the
French claim was that the threat to act would be enough to
be effective. But, whereas he was prepared to push the Cabinet where his own threats were concerned (in Abyssinia),
Eden did nothing to press it about the Rhineland.

In restraining Flandin, Eden was conditioned by defence
deficiencies, by the damage a German crisis would do to
sanctions against Italy and by the Conservative party's refusal
to go to war. He was also moved by the belief, which Flandin
sometimes confirmed, that French firmness was designed for
public consumption in France. [67]

After his isolated approach to Hitler, Eden aimed to persuade Belgium to restrain Flandin, whose position at the be-

ginning of the London meeting was that troops sent to the Rhineland since March 7 'should be withdrawn before negotiations for a settlement were begun'. [68] Though van Zeeland wanted Locarno procedures activated if Hitler refused guarantees for the future, his demands were a great deal less extensive. He and Flandin were both pulled back when Eden 'insisted on the importance of constructive negotiations for the new Europe' and 'could not agree to fight a war to drive Germany out of the demilitarized zone' if it was to be handed back as part of a settlement. [69]

This first erosion was followed by a French proposal that the Hague Court should be asked to decide whether Locarno and the Franco-Soviet pact were incompatible. This was accompanied by a Cabinet decision that Hitler should be asked[70] to send a senior person to London to be on hand while the other powers discussed the German action. [71]

From March 13 British policy was conducted by Eden, Halifax and Chamberlain in the shadow of brooding negatives from Baldwin and unsuccessful attempts by MacDonald to 'thrust himself into [the] team'. [72] By March 16 they had sold Flandin and van Zeeland the idea of an international force on both sides of the French and German frontiers. [73] Though Flandin was told that a German refusal would 'harden British opinion' against Hitler, [74] the point was not to harden British opinion but to remove any excuse for verbal belligerence and 'get the 5 Locarno Powers (including Germany) round the table'. [75]

In spite of Flandin, the British government emerged a fortnight after the occupation of the Rhineland without having honoured existing commitments, without having gained new ones and having 'rather limited than extended our commitments under Locarno'. [76] When Hitler then restored tension by rejecting all short-term proposals about the demilitarised zone, Eden aimed to postpone discussion of the major issues until the French elections relieved Flandin, or his successor, of the need to yield to pressure. [77]

In aiming once more at restraint, Eden asked the Cabinet to reaffirm the Locarno position and propose staff talks with France and Belgium about the 'technical conditions' necessary to meeting it. [78] Despite doubts about the public's reaction, the Cabinet agreed. On March 26, there was a successful

parliamentary debate in which, for the first time since
March 7, by being firm themselves Eden and Chamberlain
elicited a demonstration of conciliatory firmness towards
Germany. [79]

These acts of reassurance did nothing to satisfy the French
who fixed on the fortification of the demilitarised zone (if
that occurred) as a ground for Locarno sanctions against Germany. Eden denied the Locarno powers' authority to impose
sanctions and questioned their ability to enforce them. On
April 22 he persuaded Flandin that there should be no further Locarno meeting until the French elections were over.

By this time Hitler had made no concessions about the
Rhineland and had justified the occupation on the ground
that the Franco-Soviet alliance was a threat to German security. [80] In response to the British suggestion, he had sent both
Ribbentrop and a *Peace Plan* to London. Their arrival (on
April 1) [81] enabled Eden to claim that conciliation was going
on when sanctions were rejected. It was his promise to send a
probing reply which enabled Flandin to agree that the Locarno meeting should be postponed. [82]

The defusing of the Rhineland situation without an Anglo-
French confrontation [83] was, doubtless, a triumph for British
diplomacy. But the occupation had not been, and nothing
that had been done had improved the credit of the League.
When it was further damaged by the Italian victory in Abyssinia, collapse was complete.

(iii)

While the government's reputation was thus being damaged,
Baldwin's retirement was becoming fixed. From the beginning of the year, when retirement was first mentioned for
1938, until Margesson and Chamberlain were allowed to arrange a date, [84] Chamberlain became certain that he would
hold the position for which he had first been suggested thir-
teen years before. [85]

Not that the final approach was easy, or was eased by
Baldwin who talked about retiring with nods and winks rather than with open statements of intention. Having been disappointed in 1935, Chamberlain was anxious about rivals. He
was nervous about *The Times* (until a visit to Dawson in

Yorkshire) and afraid that it might be left to the newspapers to 'run alternative candidates'. [86]

Nor was co-operation closer than in the past. Baldwin at seventy, slightly deaf, depressed mentally and suffering from low blood pressure, lumbago and insomnia, increasingly irritated Chamberlain by his failure to work, by his apparent aimlessness when he did work and by the extent to which the public was encouraged to believe that he was working hard where Chamberlain did much of his work for him. [87] At the 1935 election, over Abyssinia, over the Rhineland, over defence and even over the abdication, when Baldwin recovered the ground he had lost in the previous year, Chamberlain thought he was working at least as hard — and probably harder. [88]

In this year of waiting, he was conscious of a change in Conservative thinking about foreign policy. He did not believe in the things the initiators of change believed in; in responding, he was behaving politically. Nor did he say as much as some of his admirers heard. Even when his novelty seemed most striking, he reflected a great deal more of the Cecil and Foreign Office frameworks than he might have cared to admit. It is important, nevertheless, that he did not admit it and that the atmosphere imposed, as he thought, both a conflict and a duty to impose his will. If we are to understand his policies as Prime Minister and the support and opposition they aroused, this atmosphere must be understood, including, in the first place, the Opposition atmosphere after Abyssinia.

The salient feature of the propaganda conducted by the enemies of the National government in the two years before Chamberlain became Prime Minister was an emphasis on foreign policy as the head and front of the attack. There was a sense that important events were occurring in Europe and that there was advantage to be gained from discussing them. The shift made by Labour was paralleled in the Liberal party and in the large body of liberal opinion over which Cecil and Murray presided from one end and Layton and the *News Chronicle* from the other.

Although the directions ran parallel, they were also competitive. This was so at the start of the Abyssinian crisis when

the government had adopted Liberal policies where Labour
was confused and divided. [89] It would have been so during
the Hoare-Laval episode if the Liberal party had not suffered
so heavily at the election.

Even before their clothes were stolen, a general election
was the last thing the Liberal leaders had wanted. Baldwin's
decision to exploit the consensus was 'monstrous'. Despite
Samuel's last-minute reconciliation with Lloyd George, the
results were disastrous. [90] Samuel lost his seat. Seven candidates out of every eight were defeated. In the new Parliament
there were about twenty Liberals, of whom three were members of the Lloyd George family. Though the Council of
Action had named the candidates of which it approved, the
result made its approval irrelevant. The size of the government majority and the strength of the Labour party made it
impossible for a Lloyd George *bloc* to emerge. [91] The Council
remained in existence as a personal secretariat and in the next
few years endorsed (chiefly Labour) candidates at by-elections. But it suffered a distinct recession as Lloyd George
entered into loose co-operation with the Liberal leadership.

When Lloyd George proposed Sinclair as parliamentary
leader after the election, [92] the position, as Liberals understood it, was that 'the country no longer regards us as a
competitor for office'. [93] Unless the Labour vote frightened
the government into reforming the electoral system to the
Liberal party's advantage, [94] they had, therefore, two alternatives — to 'encourage liberally-minded people to join the
other two parties' or to find a new rôle for the Liberal party
itself. [95] In either case, they assumed that the future would
revolve around the relationship between the Liberal electorate and the Conservative and Labour leaders.

The Labour party, they believed, was a thread-bare coalition between Marxists and liberal socialists which might well
break up in approaching power as it had nearly done in 1921.
The Conservative party was also a coalition, which Baldwin
had created, between Imperialists and Liberals, and this too
might break up as soon as he retired. If it did, and if the
Conservative party became so 'Tory as to drive its liberal
section out' at the same time as Labour was 'torn by conflict', then even a small group of parliamentary Liberals
might provide 'an...influence over the liberal vote' which

would make it an indispensable ally for either of the other parties. [96]

These were, initially, hopes for the future. They became present realities when the Hoare-Laval pact 'destroy[ed] the...illusion that Baldwin...could be trusted' [97] and subsequent events showed that Eden could not uphold the League. To Johnstone, Harris, Meston, Muir, Mander, Lothian, Acland and, above all, Sinclair, they showed that a new future was around the corner.

Sinclair was a Scottish landowner who had begun life as a professional soldier. He had been Churchill's second-in-command in the trenches in the War and had been his private secretary at the War and Colonial Offices afterwards. Since entering Parliament as an Asquithean in 1922, he had sat continuously and been Chairman of Committees and a Liberal Whip. In the National government, he had been Secretary for Scotland until resigning with Samuel and Snowden in 1932. When elected Chairman of the parliamentary party after the 1935 election, he was standing in (at the age of forty-five) until Samuel found a seat (which he had not done by the time he accepted a peerage in 1937 [98]).

Sinclair's chief aim was to bring 'Liberalism' out into the open and Liberals out of their hibernations elsewhere. Though cautious about attacking Protection until the gilt had worn off, he was clear that the attack should begin. [99] He had been civil towards the New Deal and had prodded Samuel into making it up with Lloyd George before the election. [100] When the leadership was suggested afterwards, he made it a condition that Harris, Acland and Lloyd George should be given the reversion if they wanted it. [101]

About defence and foreign policy, he had been cautiously firm: Liberal pacifism could not survive if Germany meant business [102] and international forces were projects for the future. [103] He was responsible for much of the vigour with which the Liberal party spoke about Abyssinia. He expected the access-to-raw-materials and colonial aspects of Hoare's Geneva policy to create tensions inside the government.

With the fall of Hoare, these tensions were exploited. In the New Year of 1936, Sinclair was contrasting 'Liberalism' with the 'true-blue creed of Sir Henry Page Croft and the Duchess of Atholl'. [104] He opposed 'exclusive Imperialism' to 'world co-operation' and 'failed to see' how Simonites could prefer a 'closed Colonial Empire' to the 'Liberal conception of the Open Door'. [105]

In addition to rejecting 'conservatism', Sinclair rejected the doctrines of Labour, which issued in 'public' rather than popular ownership and nationalization rather than redistribution of wealth, and which 'so far as [it] advocated social reform... was following in the footsteps of the Liberal party, but, when it attacked private property...was pointing the way to the totalitarian state'. [106]

Sinclair may not have meant much by this. But he saw no point in making exorbitant proposals for public expenditure when Attlee could easily outbid him. [107]

In adopting these positions, Sinclair was not meaning to exclude co-operation. He would have liked co-operation with Conservatives and Simonites (as well as with members of the Labour party) in a popular front on an economic and foreign policy, rather than a class, basis. Co-operation, however, especially with Labour, was likely to divide the Liberal party. [108] It was impossible without a fully-developed public demand and was difficult to envisage while Baldwin had more Liberal MPs than he had. [109] Since Baldwin was well supplied with mugwumps to affirm the Liberal character of his government, Sinclair's public position remained that an 'aggressive Radicalism' [110] and a strong Liberal party were essential if a 'natural' alternative to the National government was ever to be developed. [111]

In preparing for eventual co-operation, he gave new twists to old doctrines. Freedom remained the keyword, not *laissez-faire* which 'was never a doctrine of the Liberal party'. By freedom was meant not just 'social improvement' within the framework of 'private property' or 'laws which restrict the rights of the individual so far as was necessary to advance the general good', but free trade as a cure for the conflict which Imperialism had generated. [112]

For Imperialism, he was saying, 'socialism' was not a remedy. Nor was 'isolation' or a policy of 'alliances'. [113] Neither was it reasonable to think that the Tory party would reverse what had been done at Ottawa. [114] It was, indeed, only if a new government was allowed to 'moralise' the Empire by allowing 'liberal principles' to do their work that armaments would be reduced, taxation diminished and an end put to the 'frenzy of...economic despair' which had driven Germany and Japan into a state of nationalistic hostility. [115]

If [the government] were to secure world peace [he told the Eighty Club] they must free trade from shackles...abolish Imperialism and re-establish the old Liberal principle of trusteeship...for the natives and civilization...as the only moral justification for British possession. [116]

Sir Eyre Crowe [he told the National Liberal Club] had pointed out that Britain could not have hoped to retain undisturbed a quarter of the world's surface except on principles of trusteeship and the open door. That was the safety valve, and at Ottawa we had jammed it. If we want peace, we must loosen it. [117]

As father of a family and leader of a party which was short of money, Sinclair rationed appearances both in parliament and by-elections. As leader of a coalition of generations and opinions he compromised. [118] What, nevertheless, he developed was a platform which could lead, 'by natural stages', as tension escalated, into emphasising 'freedom' rather than 'free trade'. In identifying 'Liberalism' with the League, Eden and the Commonwealth, in presenting the occupation of the Rhineland as a consequence of the Hoare-Laval pact and in demanding increased sanctions after the Italian victory in Abyssinia, he aimed eventually to divide liberals from protectionists in the government. [119]

The government [he wrote to an academic correspondent on June 29] have allowed themselves to be blown about from one course to another by every change of wind — at Stresa, by the fear of German re-armament, then by the Peace Ballot, then by the chance of exploiting Hoare's September speech at a general election, then by Laval, then by the public reaction...to the Hoare/Laval negotiations, till they have finally relapsed into their original mood of cynical scepticism, having injured both the League and the prestige of Britain by their vacillations. [120]

In many of these respects his platform resembled that of Cecil and the League of Nations Union.

To Cecil, Murray and the League of Nations Union the Hoare-Laval pact was objectionable because, if put into practice, it would mean that 'as between the League of Nations and Mussolini, Mussolini ha[d] won'.[121] It did not matter that, without it, Britain might have to conduct sanctions by herself, which it had never been Union policy to propose. [122]

The 'only thing that matter[ed]' was the affront to the 'authority of the League'[123] and the fact that Hoare had done more even than Simon to set back the only hope of showing that aggression would not pay.

This meant that Hoare was a bad thing who should not be allowed to return to office.[124] It meant that Eden's promotion was a good one which stimulated a demand for oil sanctions.[125] At the same time there was discussion about the need for disarmament, limited rearmament and co-operation with the Soviet Union, which had been a feature of Union policy since Germany and Japan had turned against the League two years before.[126]

Cecil treated the French obsession with Germany as the main cause of backsliding over Abyssinia and wanted to bargain British co-operation against Germany for French co-operation against Mussolini. His sharpness survived the occupation of the Rhineland which, though the 'most dangerous crisis since 1914', would not be resolved by 'letting off Italy', since 'the security of France, of Russia and indeed of every country in Europe would now be greater had the League already proved by its defeat of Italian aggression that the organised community as a whole could stifle war'.[127]

Cecil did not question the Italian desire for colonies. Nor did he doubt that Abyssinia was a backward state. His interest was in the League and Britain's chance to rise to the level of her 'greatness'.[128] He saw no use for 'kid gloves' since Italy was not a formidable power and was 'as much afraid' of Hitler 'as any of us'. Even when aiming to restore peace by saving Mussolini's face, he was clear that Abyssinia had to be treated 'not less well than she would have been before the war'.[129]

In April 1936 Cecil wrote that, since the Italians were 'in a very bad way' and needed to 'smash' the Abyssinians quickly, 'we ought...to press...not only for the existing sanctions but for increased sanctions'.[130] When Abyssinian resistance collapsed a few weeks later, Italy was 'out for control of the Mediterranean and Egypt' and should be expelled from the League in order to establish that 'an effective system of collective security' was possible.[131] Unless it was, it would become obvious, he thought, not only to those who believed it already, that the League was·'a...failure', the Union 'bankrupt' and Collective Security 'a farce'. [132]

The belligerence of the Union's response stimulated resistance among its Conservative members and the resignation of Austen Chamberlain.[133] Though Lytton and others remained, the Union became more partisan than in the past. Noel-Baker's campaign as Labour candidate at the Derby by-election was not 'a turning-point in the history of this country or even of the world'.[134] But the first occasion on which Cecil gave a Labour candidate official support as President of the Union was the prelude to a leftward shift in the years that followed.

For the Labour party, too, Abyssinia was a crux. Overnight its foreign policy was transformed. Once the new course had been embarked on, there was a raising of stakes as the policy it advocated was fudged by the government, then failed and was finally dropped in May 1936. Thereafter, Labour credited the League with potentialities it had not always attributed before. It was not until Henderson was dead (in October 1935) that this aspect of his policy became unequivocally central.

This is not to say that Labour was warlike at the 1935 election. In emphasising the government's failure to resist aggression, it emphasised the peaceful possibilities of the League. Nor did the emphasis on military sanctions, which had been given at the two Conferences, become a salient feature of Labour policy in the year that followed. Despite Dalton and Citrine,[135] the line for most of 1936 was that the Defence White Paper would produce a boom in the armaments industry and 'six new Millionaires'[136] and was the result of the marked 'decline of the world's position' for which the government had been responsible since 'Labour was in office in 1931'.[137] It was not until Spain transformed the situation that a speech from Bevin,[138] two National Executive meetings[139] and Baldwin's unfortunate admission[140] gave the 'instruments of death'[141] a respectable place in Labour policy.

The National Executive resolution of October 6[142] was a cautiously-hedged statement that the 'armed strength of the countries loyal to the League of Nations must be conditioned by the armed strength of the potential aggressors'. The ac-

companying discussion established that Labour would not
support the rearmament programme until it reflected the requirements of an intelligible policy abroad. [143]

The assertion that the government had no policy had begun when the Hoare-Laval pact was presented as evidence of
Tory hostility to the League. Hoare's resignation had shown
this sort of Toryism defeated and a rift in Tory thinking,
which had been resolved when Eden was promoted. From
Eden's promotion a great deal had been expected, including
victory for the Abyssinian resistance whose collapse at a time
when Hoare seemed to be on his way back shocked the
Labour movement as much as it shocked the League of Nations Union. [144]

By then, moreover, the failure in Abyssinia had been anticipated in the Rhineland where the abrogation of Locarno
might seem to leave Britain *allied* with France and Belgium.
The decision to hold staff talks with the French was presented as a preference for 'alliances' over 'the League'.[145] The
belief that the Defence White Paper marked 'a return' to the
policy of attaining 'security' by 'national armaments'[146] became the occasion for highlighting the relevance of the Geneva Protocol to the 'socialist principle' that the world must
'co-operate or perish'. [147]

These statements were expressions of the view that the
causes of war are economic and that 'civilization' could be
'saved' by 'a new world order' based on the 'language of
humanity' and 'the brotherhood of man'. [148] Redemptive socialism thus aimed to provide reassurance as the Labour leaders moved grudgingly through a series of peace demonstrations to the view that 'this country [should] make its proper
contribution to the collective forces which are necessary for
the preservation...of peace' until such time as all 'national
forces' are merged into an international force. [149] With the
outbreak of the Spanish war in July a policy which aimed to
maintain sanctions against Mussolini in order to protect the
League was absorbed in the general demand that good should
be protected against evil.

The positions developed by the Labour party in the course
of reacting to Spain had already been reached in relation to
Manchuria, the Rhineland and Abyssinia.[150] But Manchuria
was a far-away country and Hailé Selassie an ideological em-

barrassment. It took Blum's victory in France[151] and the 'threat to democracy' in Spain to turn dislike of Hitler and Mussolini and a reluctant emphasis on the Franco-Soviet alliance into a systematic affirmation that a world struggle called Labour to an historic destiny.

This was as true of those who supported non-intervention as of those, like Morrison, who did not. When non-intervention was dropped in 1937, it was true of everyone.[152] When a 'Great Crusade', the 'Immediate Programme' and a membership drive were launched in June,[153] the League lessons taught by Abyssinia and the Rhineland had been transformed. The Republic 'was creating a new Spanish nation after... years of hopelessness'. Collective Security could now be equated with 'socialist reconstruction'.[154] Both condemned a government which allowed the 'class' interests of its members to override Britain's 'historic' interest in keeping 'strong continental powers out of the Iberian peninsula'.[155]

(iv)

Between 1933 and 1935 the Labour party had been thought a dangerous threat, even when its progress was not positive. After the election Baldwin thought that its intellectual leaders might be finished off for good.[156] If this ever seemed likely, it seemed much less likely after the Hoare-Laval pact. It was not until the League position had been destroyed by Mussolini's victory six months later that Conservative opinion shifted the initiative as foreign-policy truths which had previously been unfashionable were given relevance by events.

In the 1931 Parliament the Conservative party had been comparatively quiescent about foreign policy. In the midst of quiescence, however, dissent had existed. Doubt about the League had been expressed by Hailsham and others in Cabinet. It was expressed most clearly in the *Observer* and the *Morning Post* (until its death in 1937), in the *National Review*, the *English Review* and the *Saturday Review* (under Lady Houston's proprietorship), in Wilson's *Nineteenth Century and After*, in the Beaverbook and Rothermere newspapers, in the writings and speeches of Amery and Croft, in Lloyd's attempt, with Carson's blessing,[157] to remove Mac-Donald and Baldwin[158] and in the efforts which Grigg made,

first with and then without Lloyd, to replace the feeble Radicalism of Simon by the national Radicalism of Lloyd George.

This was a movement among politicians and publicists who
regarded themselves as leaders of opinion or makers of an
alternative 'when the present government collapses'. [159] It
was paralleled by fringe organisations dedicated to rescuing
the Conservative party from 'Socialism', 'Pacifism' and Coalition. Its effect was to revive a 'realistic' way of talking which
showed that the League was 'futile' [160] and the Empire 'central' and that 'our foreign policy during the last thirty years
ha[d] been beneath contempt because we simply would not
face "hard facts" '. [161]

These were the assumptions which Hankey and the Chiefs
of Staff had always made. But their political expression had
seemed reactionary, and their exponents eccentric, through
lack of major leaders to put the point of view. Nor had unity
of action made up for lack of authority. On the contrary,
there was so little organisation that, until events transformed
them, they were (and must be seen as) random attempts to
control the parameters of discussion by defending Unionist
principles against enemies on the Liberal-left.

Rothermere's interest in foreign policy was affected by his
interest in Hungary which had begun with a signed article in
the *Daily Mail* in 1927. In this he had called for revision of
the Treaty of Trianon on the ground that Hungary had got
rid of the Communist tyranny of 1919. This had given him a
Hungarian reputation and enabled him to pay visits over the
next ten years in conditions of almost royal splendour. As a
result, he developed the Hungarian dislike of France and admiration for the German Right, and decided, after Hitler's
arrival, that disarmament was doomed. [162]

From 1933 onwards, he ran rearmament campaigns. In the
course of 1934 he decided that the 'world' was going to be
'ruled' by 'right-wing politics'. One aspect of this was that
Hitler — 'one of those gallant men of the trenches' [163] —
wanted British friendship and, if he did not get it, would
compel 'our political mandarins' to choose between 'abject...
surrender' and 'destruction by aerial bombing'. [164]

This now became the centre of Rothermere's politics. He
gave repeated and exaggerated warnings about France's weak-

ness [165] and the growth of German air and submarine power. [166] Throughout the next three years, he was talking about
the imminence of war, the irrelevance of the League and the
importance of meeting the Nazi desire to be on good terms
with Britain. [167] In some respects Beaverbrook agreed. But
not in all.

For Beaverbrook, Britain was an Imperial power and in
that rôle impregnable. This meant not only that a whole-
hogging League policy would have been a mistake if it had
ever been adopted but that Locarno was a 'menace' which
'enacts' that 'we must go to war for the defence of France or
Germany when the League of Nations Council directs it'. [168]

Having first despised and then admired the Nazi régime, he
had been alienated by its violence, and had come to dislike it
for 'regimenting' opinion, supporting the aristocracy and per-
secuting the Lutheran Church. This, however, did not reduce
his desire to destroy the League. Even when Hitler had become a 'danger', 'Isolation' was the object. [169]

As an isolationist, Beaverbrook knew himself to be a ma-
verick in relation to effective politics and politicians. In
1933/4 he had felt this strongly. In 1935, he hoped to move
into orbit if the Franco-Soviet alignment made Conservatives
see that the choice lay between 'alliance with France and
Russia on the one hand...and the Empire on the other'. [170]

Beaverbrook disliked Hoare's Abyssinia policy and the part
played by Eden ('that misguided gentleman') in creating it.
But he was a supporter of Hoare personally and was in close
touch with him, even when taking pains to make it seem that
he was not. [171] The reaction against the League in June 1936
gave him his first real sense that the public was on his side. In
November he was pleased to believe that the government,
while talking the language of Collective Security, was about
to pursue a policy of 'undiluted...isolationism'. [172]

When Beaverbrook began to be optimistic, he made a distinction between the public who agreed with him and politicians who had not yet been persuaded. It is not clear that he
tried very hard with politicians or was in touch with politicians who mattered. He had supported Randolph Churchill
against Malcolm MacDonald in the Ross and Cromarty by-
election earlier in the year. Like Rothermere, and as improb-
ably, he had run Horne to succeed Baldwin. His relations

with Lloyd George and Churchill were intermittent. In terms of policy he was probably closest to Amery.

When the National government was formed in 1931, Amery was on holiday in Switzerland. Nobody seems to have minded. It is easy to see why so relentless a protectionist was omitted from a coalition which included equally relentness Liberals and the leading Socialist Free Trader, and why it was not thought necessary to invite him when Snowden and the Samuelites resigned.

In 1932, at the age of fifty-eight, Amery settled into a regime as company director, publicist and backbencher who made it his business, as a supporter of the National government, to run parliamentary and public campaigns in criticism of its failures. Simon was an old and, for a time, close friend. Halifax too was an Oxford friend and a member of the 1924 government. Chamberlain in addition, was a fellow-Birmingham member. Amery had access to all of these, and also to Baldwin. With Hoare he had sympathy and contact which increased when he supported the India bill as the best hope for the Empire. [173] But those to whom he talked 'agreed' without necessarily being persuaded, while the vigour of his politics became less plausible the further he found himself from power and office.

Amery came from a semi-professional, middle-class family and had made his way, by academic effort, through Harrow, All Souls, *The Times* and the South African war into a Birmingham seat. Unlike many Conservatives, therefore, he had no social position from which to lead. Since he was an intellectual, he had a doctrine instead. This included a comprehensive interpretation which asserted the irrelevance to the twentieth century of the methods suitable to dealing with the 'international society' of the nineteenth. It also included the belief that 'nationalism had come to stay' [174] and that it was desirable to give up the 'silly make-believe that the future of civilization depends on our running round with our fussy well-intentioned efforts to mediate' when what was needed (instead of Simon) was 'a Foreign Minister who could say frankly that his main duty is to defend British interests'. [175]

These criticisms were present at most periods in Amery's career; in the thirties his targets included Chamberlain's failure to go far enough at Ottawa (and Runciman for being insufficiently protectionist), the world Economic Conference (as an attempt to re-establish a nineteenth-century international order) and Salter's *Recovery* — the 'vain effort of an amiable nineteenth-century liberal to restore a world on the nineteenth-century pattern'. [176]

As the government's standing dropped, Amery prepared for a situation in which it would drop to rock bottom, criticising over a wide range of policy from the inadequacy of defence preparations, [177] through Chamberlain's 'pure Treasury budget', [178] to a demand for a Policy Cabinet to provide a 'clear point of view'. [179] The break-up of the Disarmament Conference marked 'the end of the era of Wilsonism' and a chance to 'get back to the more elastic methods of the old diplomacy'. At the beginning of 1934 he wanted Germany told that 'she can now rearm as she likes' because the removal of the 'psychological grievance' would enable Hitler to 'counsel moderation' in using the rights that he would gain. [180] When he met him in 1935, though much less bewitched than others, he thought him 'intellectually better equipped than is commonly supposed'. [181]

Amery was an Imperialist, not an Isolationist; he favoured limited Continental commitments ('no commitment beyond Locarno') [182] and none that would endanger the interests of the Empire. It was for this reason that he opposed both the Abyssinia policy and any sort of alliance with the Soviet Union.

His objection to a Soviet alliance was not so much to the character of the régime as to the danger of making Japan an enemy and driving Germany and Japan together. [183] In relation to Abyssinia he was the leader of Conservative dissent.

For this there may have been more than one reason. He had hoped for office in 1933 and may well have expected it two years later. [184] However, he was passed over when Baldwin became Prime Minister and, though encouraged (by Hoare) to expect something after the election, [185] thought he had waited long enough. He was as unwilling to quarrel with Hoare as Hoare was with him, [186] but saw no reason to restrain indefinitely the expression of opinions he would have held in any case. [187]

Amery's objection, from Hoare's Geneva speech onwards,

was that, 'for electioneering purposes' and 'largely through Eden's insistence', Italy was being made an enemy where the German problem demanded that she remain a friend, and that Britain was being committed to new League obligations which might 'shake the Empire to pieces'. [188] His first public criticism was made in a speech in his constituency three days after the invasion of Abyssinia. [189] It was followed by a letter and deputation he took to Baldwin on behalf of about forty MPs and peers who wanted a declaration that Britain would not support sanctions at Geneva. [190]

When Amery first understood the strength of his own feelings, his chief hope was that Laval would get Hoare off the hook. [191] Everything that happened thereafter, including everything he found in his postbag,[192] confirmed his instinct. Far, therefore, from being shocked by the Hoare-Laval plan, he supported it, approved of the defence Hoare made of it and blamed the occupation of the Rhineland on the government's failure to support it. [193] In 1936, as a well-established critic of the League, he merged into a movement of which Garvin was the symbol.

In the nineteen thirties Garvin was the intellectual Chamberlainite. Far more than Amery (who had been originally) and more effectively than the *Round Table*, he was the organ of the message which Joseph Chamberlain had left. It was Garvin who wrote the official life (of which three volumes were published between 1932 and 1934). It was Garvin — and Astor, his proprietor — who made the middle page of the *Observer* an event which politicians and an important part of the educated public read most Sundays of the year.

Astor was a transatlantic millionaire whose (American) wife was the first Conservative woman MP. Like Lothian, he was both a Milnerite and a Christian Scientist. He was also an H.A.L. Fisher Conservative, with a rich man's concern for social causes, a viewy interest in agricultural rationalisation and a desire to be in touch with the best that was thought by the English intelligentsia. Though a disappointed member of the Garden Suburb, he remained an admirer after Lloyd George had refused to become a prohibitionist. [194]

Like Londonderry and his wife, the Astors were major Conservative hosts. Again like the Londonderries, they made a great deal of Ribbentrop (both before he became German ambassador in 1936 and afterwards). Their salon included Inskip, Hoare, Dawson, Grigg and Jones.

About the League, Astor was a disillusioned idealist who hoped, eventually, for World Federation. As patron of Chatham House, he was against France's East European entanglements; he worked with Angell, Bartlett, Toynbee and Noel-Buxton in the 1937 campaign to restore colonies to Germany. [195] As owner of Cliveden, he was much disturbed by the immortality it was given in the course of that year. [196]

Garvin's *Observer* stood for the Unionist transformation of the Conservative party. While assuming that capitalism (in the ownership sense) was beyond question, it had none of that fear of state activity which 'Liberalism' in some respects had made its own. Whether social welfare was Danegeld to keep the poor happy or the outcome of positive protectionist idealism, its combination of Empire, welfare and defence had enabled a large part of the Conservative party to find its way towards a conception of political duty in the first third of the century.

Before the war Garvin had been anti-German. After the war he was interested in Europe so far as the peace settlement would affect the Empire. At the beginning of the thirties he held orthodox opinions in favour of the League and Locarno. He was a strong advocate of 'National Government' and admired MacDonald for making it a possibility. [197]

Garvin's 'Empire' was an expanding confederation in which men of goodwill and all colours and creeds co-operated in pursuit of common ideals. It embraced a self-governing South Africa, which it had been the experience of his generation to tame, as well as something approaching a self-governing India. He did not, however, suppose that the Empire could be preserved merely by showing that it had been moralised. Remembering the pre-war situation, he conceived it as being based ultimately on military power. From 1933 onwards, along with Rothermere, he was the most insistent advocate of a large-scale rearmament programme as the unavoidable reaction to 'the new barbarism in the centre of Europe'. [198]

Garvin's initial judgment of Hitler was not favourable, but it was not unfavourable either. He grasped the unexpected nature of the phenomenon, regarding him as an unknown quantity who might, or might not, settle down under the weight of the economic problems he would have to face. The licensed teaching of a war gospel, so much at variance with Goethean Germany, was deplored, and also the persecution of the Jews. The suppression of communism was seen as an excusable benefit and a valuable contribution to the stabilisation of Europe. But it soon became obvious (more so, perhaps, in private than in the *Observer*) that 'the absolute suppression...of all advocacy of peace and the organized glorification of the spirit of war must lead to war itself'. [199]

This led to three conclusions. The first was that the 'sword-drawn settlements of 1919' were 'the cancer of Europe'. The second was that German inequality could no longer be sustained and that the Versailles frontiers would have to be revised. Garvin did not, therefore, conclude that the 'excited and vehement temper rampant in the Reich' should be 'appeased'. Not would peace be preserved by 'the methods... pursued at Geneva'. Disarmament by itself might 'facilitate war'. If revision was to be effective, Britain must make it clear that illegal revision would be resisted. [200]

Garvin did not move willingly into a position of detachment from Europe. Before Barthou made him change his mind, he was willing that France should be given 'solid guarantees'. He was suspicious of Hitler's assurances and treated an Anglo-French defensive alliance as more essential even for British than for French security. [201]

This did not mean that Britain should take sides in a tribal quarrel. All that was necessary was a 'defensive' air alliance and rejection of any 'mental' involvement the government might have slipped into so far. [202]

It was in this context that the Abyssinia policy was objectionable. The objection was to the nature of the Abyssinian régime, the loss of Italian friendship and the fact that Baldwin's neglect had made it impossible to stop Mussolini, even if that was desirable. The supreme facts were the danger from Germany, Hoare's failure to make Eden see it and the fact that Laval saw it only too well. [203]

Garvin believed that Laval was as right from a French point of view as the Cabinet was wrong from an Imperial one. Between Laval's 'common sense' and the Imperial viewpoint, there was a consonance which the League should not be allowed to destroy. Its 'rabid jingoes', he wrote a fortnight after the war had started,

already clamour for the economic stifling of the Italian people; for a total interruption of the communications between that people and its armies in East Africa; for the closing of the Suez Canal; for a naval blockade in the Mediterranean and the Adriatic.

It is a course that would lead not only to desperate war between Britain and Italy, but to long convulsions in Europe and the world, such as will assuredly bring the British Empire to its doom, whatever happened to the others. [204]

Between August and December Garvin argued that Stresa was better than the League and that a bargain with Mussolini was essential in face of Germany. [205] Above all, he was clear that oil sanctions must be avoided.

Garvin had no notice of the Hoare-Laval agreement (which became public on a Monday). The following Sunday it had saved peace from 'insane destruction by an Abyssinian mania'. [206] Hoare's defence (on December 19) was 'a classic document...in the history of the League'. [207] His resignation showed (innocently) that

without reproach to his colleagues but without hesitation in his own duty, [he had] decided that neither with integrity nor usefulness...could he consent through his own mouth to stultify his position, policy and character; or to continue in office without the willing support of his colleagues and the decisive confidence of the nation. [208]

Between Hoare's resignation and the defeat of the Abyssinians a gale blew among Conservative publicists and politicians against the new policy which the government was supposed to have adopted. Until Abyssinia changed it, British support for the League had been based, it was alleged, on rejection of the Geneva Protocol and a 'tolerably well-defined policy...directed towards the organization of peace through interlocking pacts...of which the Western Locarno Treaty was the model'. [209] More recently, the government had moved into a position 'as rigid and pedantic as anything Bob Cecil might have asked for', the danger of which was that Article XVI of the Covenant might 'involve us later all over the world, perhaps even in supporting Russia against Germany'.[210]

The sole consequence of Eden's policy, therefore, had been to damage Anglo-Italian relations (where Britain's 'only hope of maintaining [her] Empire was to have Italy as an ally'[211]) and to 'invoke the logic of the League as a reason for [the] vast disaster which the older statesmanship...would assuredly have prevented'.[212]

This 'older statesmanship' would have returned to 'alliances and the balance of power' as soon as it was realised that the existing League included 'some nations not all'.[213] Even when the ultimate objective was World Union,[214] it was felt that the coercive clauses should be dropped, that the Empire was 'the only successful experiment in international government' and that there would be no improvement in Europe or the Far East until Britain was 'extricated' from 'the egregious entanglement of sanctions'.[215]

'Reform of the League', though a central concern in all these quarters in mid-1936, was not, however, thought an adequate guarantee for the future. Three further things were required — the development of a 'British' as distinct from an 'international' point of view, a comprehension (which the Foreign Office lacked) of the ability and popularity of totalitarian régimes,[216] and a policy, especially about Germany.

About Germany there was a spectrum of agreement, incorporating a variety of positions, few of which were occupied by supporters of France. On the whole (except in the *Morning Post*), there was a lack of sympathy for France and positive hatred of the Soviet alliance which had 'brought war to Europe once' and could easily do so again.[217] Even when there were doubts about the skill of Nazi diplomacy, allowances were made in face of German sensitivity to the belief that Collective Security without her was a form of 'encirclement'.[218]

In some senses Germany was seen as resembling Britain. For the Nazi leaders 'were not anxious to promote paganism' and wanted only to 'put the German churches into the same position as the Church of England'.[219] Their need for expansion was matched by the British need for peace which was 'vital' to the Commonwealth's 'scattered world-wide interests' and, as the Aga Khan testified after talking to Hitler and Goering, could be met if a modest colonial deal was followed by a settlement that would 'once and for all bury the hatchet and make all the great European race fellow-workers for world-prosperity'.[220]

From some points of view, indeed, it seemed that 'Germany was seek[ing] our...friendship'. [221] From others — Londonderry's for example — British policy since 1918 consisted of 'slavish subservience' to France which was 'a less dependable ally' since the Germans 'at least knew what they were trying to do', and Hitler 'dread[ed] war'. [222]

As Air Minister and a member of the Disarmament Committee, Londonderry had been stiff and negative about air disarmament in 1933, and had made a fuss about German rearmament. At first he had supported the other Service Ministers in making a fuss about *British* rearmament. Then, he began to deplore it as a Rothermere stunt, preferring instead to 'pull' Hitler 'up short' by having his violations of Versailles 'out with him' in the hope of bartering 'equality' for an arms limitation agreement. In 1935 he objected to Simon going to Berlin since the Germans 'ought to be made to come here'. [223]

Londonderry disliked Geneva, mistrusted Eden and complained about Simon's failure to control him. He sensed connections between the Foreign Office which had 'always apologised for our having an Air Force' and 'the Ormsby-Gores of the Cabinet who look[ed] on the services as the playthings of politicians'. He found Thomas's pacifism jocular and offensive. [224]

As social link between National Labour and the House of Lords, Londonderry's standing was high in the early years of the National government. By the end of 1934 he was a lightweight who kept office because MacDonald was a member of his household. Speeches about air disarmament and the League, [225] difficulties about the estimates of German air strength and signs that he would become a major target once India was out of the way, [226] ensured his removal to the leadership of the House of Lords and a banishment from policy-making so complete [227] that he was thinking of resigning[228] when Baldwin compelled him to after the election had made MacDonald's feelings irrelevant. [229]

Like Rothermere, Londonderry had seen much of the Nazi leaders. He admired them as self-made men and was impressed by their successes with communism. While sensing hostility and opposing 'grovelling', he believed that they need not turn against Britain.[230] From different assumptions and by

different routes *The Times* eventually reached the same conclusion.

The identity was accidental. Until they began to stand
behind Halifax and Chamberlain in early 1938, Dawson and
Barrington-Ward had stood firmly behind Eden.

Barrington-Ward was a young mandarin who, having been
marked by the trenches, believed profoundly in the League
of Nations. Though he had been made by Garvin on the
Observer, he felt as strong a revulsion against Mussolini's 'militarism' in Abyssinia as he felt against 'Hitlerism' in Germany.

Dawson came from a middle-county family in Yorkshire.
After Eton, Magdalen and All Souls, he was taken to South
Africa by Milner, where his reputation was made in a situation of violence and conciliation. In his early thirties he was
editor of the Johannesburg *Star*. His arrival as editor of *The
Times* in 1912 marked its affirmation of the modern Conservatism of his generation.

Though socially Conservative, Dawson was also a Milne-
rian. In his hands in the thirties Modern Conservatism meant
administrative efficiency, popular Imperialism, land disarmament and *détente* with Germany. [231]

About Europe Dawson knew no more than most other
leading Conservatives. What he knew was South Africa and
England. His life moved between Printing House Square,
Eton, All Souls and the moorland estate he inherited from an
aunt in 1917. His affections were engaged in the last three as
much as in the first. *The Times* made a brilliant deployment
of the average opinions of his age and station.

As a party Conservative, Dawson saw Baldwin often and
advised him regularly. He was a close friend of Halifax and
was on easy terms with Ormsby-Gore, Hoare, Wood, Inskip
and Eden (as well as with Jones and the Cliveden Astors). In
1936 he took the view that reactionary Conservatism no
longer existed.

Dawson supported both the National government and its
non-Conservative components. But he had more time for
Eden than for Simon (and perhaps also than for Hoare). [232]
He treated Thomas as a music-hall turn. He saw through Mac-
Donald — the 'weary Titan' — and failed to respond to at-
tempts to gain his sympathy. [233] To him Rothermere seemed

a joke and Cecil a 'menace to the League'. Lloyd George had
'nothing to suggest', and the Labour party was saved from
absurdity by the hair's breath which made Greenwood a better man than Attlee. [234]

Dawson did not believe that Conservative intellect should
be peremptory. Like his 'Empire', his *Times* was 'bound up...
with social reform'. [235] Both stood for 'liberal magnanimity'
of which Smuts, both by presence and doctrine, was the
embodiment.

Like Smuts, *The Times* had picked up most of the nos-
trums of the post-war world. It stood for Collective Security
as the only way to carry the Empire through an 'era of suspicious nationalisms'.[236] It saw the Empire and the United
States as guarantors of law and freedom and liberal-Conservative centrality as the answer to socialism. Detachment, information and rejection of Isolation distinguished it from
Garvin, Rothermere and the rest. [237]

Dawson shared Garvin's uncertainty about Hitler, sensing a
portent and fearing that his 'methods' would destroy confidence in France. He did not mince words about debt repudiation, Church persecution or brutality in Austria which was
'making the name of Nazi stink in the nostrils of the world'.[238]
In criticising the imprisonment (after acquittal) of the
Communist suspects in the Reichstag's fire-trial, *The Times*
doubted 'whether Germany can...be treated on the same basis
as other nations...in...the difficult political problems of the
moment'. [239]

Nevertheless, *The Times*'s policy in 1933/4 was to keep
the Disarmament Conference going and to make the League a
reality. [240] While denouncing the savagery, it interpreted the
Roehm *putsch* as Hitler's way of transforming 'revolutionary
fervour into moderate and constructive effort'. [241] Dawson
may not have been taken in by the 'impeccable pacifism' of
Hitler's early speeches, but he interpreted German rearmament as restoring 'self-respect' by acquiring a defensive army.
Provided offensive rearmament was avoided, he accepted the
German claim to equality among the nations. [242]

The Times wrote of a 'prison of the mind' being built
'from Strasbourg to Vladivostok'. [243] It recorded the violence of Hitler's language and the 'militancy' of Mussolini's
doctrine. But it interpreted both cynically. In 1934 Mussolini

was seen as wanting to avoid 'a common frontier with the Germans', Hitler as turning on the Nazis as soon as the army insisted. [244] It was then hoped that he would respond to generosity as Smuts and Botha had responded before the war.

The Times associated Hitler with the 'stern discipline of the Prussian code' and the 'fervour and idealism of South Germany'. [245] But it did not identify him as a Prussian nor suggest that his aims were those of the Junkers. So far was it from sharing the Vansittart view that it sensed the chance to do what Haldane and Joseph Chamberlain might have done if the Germans had been willing. [246] It showed British policy aiming 'impartially' at reconciling the irreconcilables in France and Germany. [247]

Until some time in 1937, The Times's position was that peace would only be kept through the League. Having supported Hoare's League policy, having attacked the Hoare-Laval plan and having expressed Eden's suspicions of Mussolini after sanctions had been dropped, it gave bitter reminders of the 'immorality' of successful aggression. [248] Throughout these years Barrington-Ward believed that 'alliances' had failed and that the public would willingly make sacrifices for 'Collective Security'. [249]

Nor was The Times unsympathetic towards the French. It did not criticise Barthou; after initial doubts, [250] it praised Blum for keeping France out of Spain. It approved of the Franco-Soviet pact for leaving it open to Hitler to turn an alliance into a Locarno-type pact of mutual security. [251] After broadcasting Eden's position that the occupation of the Rhineland might herald a 'return to peace', it spent the following year reminding Hitler that it would be his fault if it did not. [252]

The Times was as suspicious of the Comintern as Dawson of 'the Bolshies'. But it liked Litvinoff (even if he was only a frontman against Germany and Japan). [253] The liquidation of the brutalities of the twenties registered a shift towards 'normality', just as the Purges were significant in case a Red Army counter-revolution reversed it. [254]

Up to late 1936, The Times was judicious about the Russians and criticised Hitler for criticising the Franco-Soviet pact. [255] It rejected anti-Bolshevism both as an attack on Czechoslovakia and because the Berlin-Tokyo axis would divert Japanese attention towards South-East Asia. [256]

In supporting Eden's search for 'a new world order', Dawson said that Britain should take a lead. It was on this ground that he justified the rearmament programme of 1936. [257] Though *The Times* became cautious after Abyssinia had shown it up, it criticised Chamberlain for criticising the League and reflected Eden's (and Baldwin's) resentment at his interventions. [258] It was not until Spain joined Abyssinia as a 'failure' that *The Times* slipped slowly via 'regional pacts' [259] towards the League as an 'organ of conciliation'.

In Barrington-Ward's version, the position was that 'no great country' could be kept indefinitely 'in an inferior position'; he believed that Germans, emerging from the 'valley of humiliation', might be induced to 'prefer the self-respecting to the thuggish elements in Nazism' if they could be given a 'vested interest in a peacefully evolving world' by relieving the League of its obligations to Versailles. [260] This was not, he thought, a matter for 'power politics', 'alliances' or the 'balance of power' which was 'no longer a British doctrine'. [261] Even when it thought that Hitler wanted to go East, *The Times* would do nothing to encourage him. It rejected the Garvin doctrine of a 'free hand' [262] since so 'cynical and shortsighted' a conception fell short of the challenge, which was to 'secure by negotiation the removal of the causes of war'. [263]

Though negotiation would involve concessions, *The Times* was opposed to any concessions outside a general settlement. When the Nazi leaders took up Hoare's point about colonies and raw materials, Dawson almost always mentioned the Empire's duty towards its subjects and the insignificance of colonies to the German economy. [264]

In 1937, there was a shift. Not only was Britain's rôle increasingly perceived in terms of 'interest', [265] but Stalin was criticised for his actions in Spain. [266] Though a 'Holy Alliance' against Bolshevism would make 'Europe safe for Bolshevism in the future', the German attitude was increasingly 'understood'. 'No Englishman in German shoes', *The Times* wrote on January 28, 'could consent to...a new treaty while the Franco-Soviet pact and the Russian pact with Czechoslovakia are in force'. [267]

In 1935/6 *The Times* had wanted strong ministerial contact with Berlin. In 1937, it was still doing so. But it was increasingly conscious of German reluctance. The line did not change (even after its correspondent's expulsion in August [268]). But it began to say that, though agreement was essential, 'the threads' were 'not in Britain's hands'. It reflected Eden's irritation at German intervention in Spain. [269]

About Spain Dawson was so scrupulously neutral that Conservatives attacked him. [270] In addition, he shared much of Eden's vexation with Mussolini. He was a strong supporter of the cordon policy of January and of the Nyon policy in September 1937, and wrote approvingly about Eden's concern for British interests. [271]

By mid-1937 Dawson's position was that disarmament had failed 'because too much was attempted all at once' [272] and that any attempt at military action by the League would divide Europe into *blocs*. It was the fear of 'alliances for and against the *status quo*' [273] that made 'economic appeasement' the only suitable area for League activity. [274]

In 1937 *The Times* took up van Zeeland's plan for economic co-operation. But it said little about treaty revision in Europe. It was not until the Halifax mission that it began to talk urgently about the German desire for colonies. [275]

What Dawson felt about the League is obscure. What *The Times* said was that an ailing League 'was no guarantee against aggression', and that it was urgent to do something to restore it. [276] What was meant was what Barrington-Ward had meant before — that 'the road to peace lies through Berlin'. When Halifax set off on November 13 'world peace' required 'a solid understanding between the British and the German peoples'. [277]

Where the *Observer* was explicit about German predominance in Eastern Europe, *The Times* was explicit only about colonies. Where Garvin's positions veered off towards the Imperial Right, Dawson allowed Barrington-Ward to write about 'appeasement'.

Dawson thought of *The Times* (rightly) as a world power; his journalism up to a point was tactical. The object, on *The Times* no less than with Eden, was to lead Hitler towards a settlement. There can be no doubt that, in Barrington-Ward, this hope flowed from feelings as genuine as they were absurd, that power politics were evil.

In 1937 Chamberlain had to work hard to convince Dawson that he was moving fast enough towards Hitler. [278] In 1938 Dawson kept close to the government, moving when it moved and imposing increasing restraint upon his staff. [279] After the Anschluss, he wanted 'no wild measures';[280] he was heavily attacked (on the Liberal Left) for wanting Czechoslovakia dismembered in September. [281] For him the Anglo-German declaration was 'a great achievement' and a 'set-back to the Nazi extremists'. [282] At the time of the pogroms, he renewed demands for a deal with Hitler about colonies.

Dawson saw Chamberlain off to Godesberg. But he had little contact with Halifax between Berchtesgaden and Munich. In the winter of 1938 he watched gloomily as Halifax fell into the hands of the Foreign Office. [283] After the Polish guarantee in March 1939, *The Times* (like Beaverbrook) gave a narrow definition of its scope. For this, and for other attempts to restrict the continental commitment, it was the object of bitter assault. [284]

In 1939 *The Times* was blown off centre as the 'anti-appeasers' advanced towards political credibility. [285] In 1937 it had seemed to be reviving the Peace Movement of the early thirties as Dawson carried in his wake a boatload of Liberal, *Round Table*, Oxford, Chatham House and even pacifist opinion whose most plausible exponent was Lothian. [286]

Though more important than Lady Astor (with whom he was caricatured), Lothian was not of first importance. But he was listened to. As a Milnerite young man, he had been one of Dawson's friends. As a Lloyd George secretary, he had been at the top of Coalition politics and, as an active Samuelite, had joined the National government when it was formed in 1931. Before Ottawa, he was the least willing of the resigners; he had not allowed his friendship with Lloyd George and an assured place among the Samuelite leaders to prevent him keeping in touch with Baldwin and Simon afterwards.

Lothian had a highly-developed capacity for theoretical statement. His statements mattered because he was a prominent Liberal who believed that the Liberal era had ended.

About Germany, he made three assumptions — that National Socialism did not want to 'incorporate other races into itself', that it was a 'national movement against internal disunity' and that, without Austria-Hungary, the Polish corridor and many of her pre-war fortresses, she was strategically so weak and the Franco-Soviet treaty so obviously a threat that Hitler had had good reason to rearm contrary to Versailles and reoccupy the Rhineland contrary to Locarno. [287]

From this, further conclusions followed — that 'pro-French timidity' must stop, that there must be a summit meeting between Baldwin and Hitler [288] and that the only way to restore the League was by giving Germany 'a square deal in Central Europe'. [289]

From this point of view, German co-operation was the best way of preserving the Empire. It was the only way of dealing with Mussolini who presented a threat to Egypt and Kenya and whose tail could not be twisted until Germany was 'on the Brenner'. [290] 'If we join or drift into the anti-German group, we shall have world war' Lothian wrote in May 1936. 'The only way to peace is justice for Germany', including 'a German solution of the Austrian problem'. [291] 'Personally', he wrote to Eden early in June, 'I believe that, if we assist Germany to escape from encirclement to a position of balance in Europe, there is a good chance of the 25 years of peace of which Hitler spoke and that we shall then be able to deal with Mussolini.' [292]

In 1936 this seemed a possible position to adopt. In 1937 he woke up to the difficulties. In Berlin (like Henderson later), he found an 'ominous' suspicion of British policy and a feeling that it might be necessary to 'threaten London with bombing'. [293]

I am sure [he wrote to Chamberlain on his return] that the idea that by strengthening the military combination against Germany and continuing relentlessly the economic pressure against her, the régime in Germany can be moderated or upset is an entire mistake...

The German people are determined by some means or other to recover their natural rights and position in the world equal to that of the great powers. If they feel driven to use force in power-diplomacy or war, they will do so with a terrifying strength, decision and vehemence. Moreover, because they are now beginning to think that England is the barrier in the way, they are already playing with the idea that...they may have to look for support...to Italy and Japan, if they are to achieve their aims. [294]

With much of this Garvin agreed. He too thought that Hitler was right to be obsessed by encirclement, and that

Litvinoff's aim in supporting the League was to 'draw...Britain into commitments' in Russia's favour. [295] In these circumstances he thought it was idle to expect Germans to put up with 'any kind of military restrictions' from which Russia was free, and dangerous to connive at a French policy which might compel 'Britain and Germany [to] destroy each other' in order to 'establish Bolshevist supremacy over Europe and Asia'. [296]

These judgments were strengthened by Russian intervention in Spain and by Benes's 'suicidal' policy of allowing Prague to become Moscow's 'open door' into central Europe. [297] They made it important to avoid mistaking the military preparations Hitler was making against Russia for threats against Britain. [298]

Garvin blamed Eden for Abyssinia and gave a cool reception to his appointment as Foreign Secretary; he disliked the Egyptian treaty as a 'fatal example to India'.[299] Coolness was increased by the 'self-righteous temper' of the 'questionnaire', [300] and when Eden seemed to imply a British 'commitment...to Paris, Moscow and their clients'. [301]

These criticisms were indications. But they implied the need to remove Baldwin and Eden [302] so as to see whether Chamberlain was 'deep enough' to solve the problem. 'Especially' they implied a duty to 'scrutinize the melodramatic theory that any and every expansion of German scope in the East must be an automatic menace to the West'. [303]

In early 1937 Garvin saw relations between Britain and Germany — 'natural allies...through many generations' — as the crux for peace which would best be approached by a German attempt to create an East European and Danubian federation as makeweight to Russia.

Such a federated system [he wrote on March 14 1937] would contain at least 150,000,000 of people with an equal wealth of industrial and agricultural resources. It would be able to hold its own in all ways and circumstances — thus removing one of Herr Hitler's chief anxieties for the future against the Soviet power which...within a few years will number 200,000,000 of people.

If we are for world peace in earnest we must refresh our imaginations, broaden our minds, and brace our moral courage. No jealous nor frightened motives should daunt us or deter us. Let the German race, in its turn, have a mission and a task and a scope corresponding to its greatness and given a peaceable outlet to its incomparable organising energies. [304]

In the thinking of many Unionists, this combination of altruism, 'realism' and rejection of 'collective lunacy' was a central feature. The defeat of the Abyssinians had proved it 'triumphantly right'. [305] When the Austen Chamberlain faction [306] questioned it, they were being distinctly old-fashioned.

Although Austen Chamberlain was old-fashioned, he had the natural importance of an ex-foreign Secretary who had propounded the policy which was under consideration and had predicted Hitler's responses in 1935.

Up to then, moreover, he had had no major conflict with the government. Over the housing and slum clearance programmes, his co-operation had been important. Over India, his refusal to co-operate with Churchill had given him an influence he had previously had only through office. [307] As the Hitler problem emerged, he had brought authoritative support against Attlee, Samuel, Sinclair and Lloyd George.

Nevertheless, differences existed about German and British air strengths, about an Expeditionary force for the Continent [308] and about the extent to which 'hostility to the League' would place Britain and the Dominions 'in antagonism to any other country which felt it'. [309]

Chamberlain's criticisms of Hitler were put at first cautiously, as queries about the extent to which Nazi propaganda contradicted his assurances. [310] He denied that the Versailles frontiers were unjust or that Germany was being encircled. He underlined the extent to which the economic clauses had been revised, and was clear that further revision would be problematical. [311] He gave a warm welcome to the French decision to develop closer relations with Russia. [312]

Chamberlain anticipated 'a time...when some nation will make war...of set purpose'. He concluded that 'the only way' to prevent this was 'by overwhelming force',[313] which, however, was not available, because the military aspect of the League had been neglected. [314] In May 1935, when 'the situation in Europe [was] graver than...at any time since 1914', [315] this was crucial. [316]

Chamberlain was scathing about the Labour and Liberal oppositions, the League of Nations Union and *The Times* which was 'entirely under Lothian's influence...and might have been written in Berlin'. [317] He thought Simon 'basically wrong' about Hitler, a danger to relations with France and Italy and a handicap to MacDonald who had 'the root of the matter' in him. He shared MacDonald's desire to avoid war against Italy and made direct attempts to dissuade Mussolini from invading Abyssinia. [318] But he approved of Hoare's League policy and praised the vigour of Hoare's public statements. Despite doubts about French reliability and an Imperial contempt for the Abyssinian state, he supported him because the League could not fail in Africa 'without...destroying the value of collective security...for Europe.' [319]

On this view Germany, not Italy, was the problem and Austrian, not Abyssinian, independence the key to peace. Abyssinia, however, had consequences in Europe, where the League machinery would have to be strengthened if it was to be effective in the future. [320] Its failure there made him insist on the Locarno obligation in the Rhineland in March.

Chamberlain did not want war. [321] He wanted a symbolic German withdrawal while the International Court discussed the Franco-Soviet treaty [322] and a stronger affirmation of Collective Security than Eden at first appeared to offer. [323] After initial doubts, however, Eden was supported, and Chamberlain moved through Locarno-based rearmament and a refusal to return colonies [324] towards a division between 'those who take a short view of what lies in front of us and those who...cannot feel it in their conscience to accept an easy settlement if they know that it will bring disaster to their children in a few years time'. [325]

I wonder how many members [he asked the House of Commons on May 6] can realise what [the remilitarization of the Rhineland] means not merely to the excited politicians in Paris, but to the French peasant in his hovel, to the mother who feels that once again the...peril has come near and that once again her children will be mowed down by the scythe of war.[326]

These were statements of hostility to Hitler. They were also hostile to Baldwin against whom Chamberlain retained the animus of 1922 as much as Neville Chamberlain retained the animus of 1917 against Lloyd George. In early 1936 he made a bitter personal attack about the air programme in the House of Commons. [327] As the foreign policy 'sheet-anchor' was dragged, chronological intemperance waited resentfully

for Baldwin's ignorance, arrogance and incompetence to be
rewarded. [328]

(v)

In early 1936, then, there were two movements of Conservative criticism, one complaining because Hitler had been
trusted and Collective Security neglected, the other complaining because pursuit of the wrong sort of League had
made it impossible to trust him. As Baldwin's decrepitude
increased, their importance was illustrated by the fact that,
for a time, it looked as though both might be led by Hoare.

When compelled to make him resign, Baldwin had left
Hoare the impression that he would have him back soon.
Margesson, however, had told him that he should not return,
too soon, so, when pressed for a decision, Baldwin had been
vague.

During the six weeks he spent in Switzerland after his
resignation, Hoare thought a great deal about his future. The
situation, as he understood it, was that he had been let down.
Though the Cabinet's reasons were reasons he would have
approved of in September, they could be used to imply a lack
of interest in the German problem. From whichever angle
foreign policy was looked at, Germany could be made to
seem central, and this applied whether one agreed with
Churchill and Austen Chamberlain, who were unsympathetic
to Hitler, or with Amery and Garvin, who were not. As a
senior politician, Hoare needed less to adopt a point of view
than to pinpoint a problem. He was as well placed for an
anti-sanctions as for a rearmament line and for using the
freedom he had been given to restore the Conservative credentials he had lost over India. [329] When Baldwin delayed, he
used 'the advances of discontented factions' as a way of ensuring his return to office.

Hoare said that he had no wish to be 'a captious critic of
the government' but might need to prepare for 'a new line of
life' in 'literature', 'business' or 'politics'. He said, too, that
the coalition could not last, that a 1922 situation was on the
way and that his 'future' might lie in 'a more Conservative
government'. [330] The impression he left was that 'he hoped
to be taken into the Cabinet very shortly' and meant to be

'disagreeable if he was kept waiting'. [331]

In early February, Neville Chamberlain persuaded Baldwin to make Hoare minister for the co-ordination of defence when the office was established. [332] Having discussed the possibility with Hoare, [333] Baldwin then spent a month brooding over alternatives. [334] After backbench criticism, [335] complaints from Eden, Elliot and MacDonald [336] and a tastelessly ingratiating speech from Hoare, [337] he decided to send him to the Admiralty instead. [338]

In mentioning the Admiralty as an alternative, Baldwin had told Hoare that, if he went there, he would do so before Whitsun 'at the latest'. [339] When Hoare accepted in March, the offer was to be effective between Easter and Whitsun. [340] In early April he was 'disappointed' at having to wait but promised to do so provided Baldwin would make the change when Parliament adjourned. [341] When he returned on June 5, he was saying that the flight of the Emperor had justified his attitude the previous December and that the real blame should be laid on Simon and MacDonald for failing to mention Abyssinia at Stresa. [342]

Hoare had been able to threaten because Baldwin had seemed to be slipping. Chamberlain sensed a similar opportunity when the Rhineland and Abyssinia made him slip further.

In the first four years of the National government, Neville Chamberlain had succeeded far better than Baldwin in retaining his credentials as a guarantor of Conservatist principle. His involvement in the India policy had been marginal.[343] His financial policy had been 'sound'. He had left the impression that he understood the need to rearm. Even when seeming to favour a new party to 'look at...new problems with unprejudiced eyes', [344] he had gained a reputation as an enemy of both MacDonaldite pacifism and the 'internationalism' of the League of Nations.

This reputation was an illusion. Chamberlain objected not to the League but to the 'cranks', 'fanatics' and 'Anti-Japs' who ran the League of Nations Union. [345] He had no objection to Collective Security so long as it worked, and was the prime advocate of an international force to deal with breaches of a disarmament agreement and the Saar in 1934 and the

Rhineland problem in 1936. In between he had been heavily implicated in Hoare's League policy when the Peace Ballot made this desirable and was only thinking of a 'reconstructed League to deal with European affairs' if it failed. [346] He was pleased when the election result showed that the Beaverbrook-Rothermere foreign-policy campaign had made no difference. [347] After the last Cabinet before the Hoare-Laval meeting, he thought that 'by putting his great army on the other side of the Suez Canal, Mussolini [had] tied a noose round his own neck and left the end hanging out for anyone with a navy to pull'. [348]

At this time, Chamberlain did not express doubts about the League, support for which was an essential element in justification of the rearmament programme. Even after the Rhineland made sanctions questionable, and Mussolini established that they had failed, he was unwilling to have this said publicly. [349]

Nevertheless, Abyssinia had made the League a problem. In early April, Eden asked the Cabinet to think about closing the Suez Canal. [350] When Baldwin, 'without contradiction', gave an emphatic negative, [351] he was still hoping that the Italians might be beaten by the rain. [352] Soundings at Geneva, [353] however, convinced him that collective support no longer existed and that the war was over. By the end of April, the Cabinet had agreed to have a committee to discuss the League's future. [354]

From April 22 onwards, these discussions centred around Article XVI of the Covenant and the automatic duty to cooperate in imposing sanctions on an aggressor. No decisions were reached, and a Baldwin speech on May 14 implied the need for a League to which all the great powers belonged.

In saying this, Baldwin reflected the reluctance which ministers felt about handling the subject in public and the danger they anticipated if they said too strongly that the League had been a failure. The League had, nevertheless, received extensive attention (even if no conclusions had been reached [355]) before the speech of June 10 in which Chamberlain stated that a policy of alliances or isolation was as reasonable as 'Collective Security based on sanctions', and that the League of Nations Union demand for increased sanctions was 'the very midsummer of madness'. [356]

Chamberlain did not make this speech in May, because he doubted the public's willingness to be told that Mussolini had won. [357] He made it in June because the Labour, Liberal and League of Nations Union demand for increased sanctions made it safe to say negatively what it was unsafe to say positively. The speech was made because 'the party and the country needed a lead' which others were failing to give. Eden was not consulted because he would have asked Chamberlain not to make it; Baldwin was not consulted because it was his neglect that was being repaired. [358] Its effect, and the effect of subsequent speeches, [359] was to bruise Cecil as effectively as Hankey had been bruised earlier in the year, to show Chamberlain off to Eden's disadvantage at a moment when he was thinking about his future [360] and to make the point, which Hoare had bungled in December, that there were ways of talking about foreign policy at least as sane, and quite as realistic, as those favoured on the Left.

Chamberlain was not attacking the ideals on which the League was based. He left the impression that he wanted it strengthened [361] and said, what Baldwin said also, that 'we should...devise...more effectual means of achieving the objects for which [it] was founded'. [362] His real feelings are difficult to intuit; he probably wanted to seem ambiguous even when appealing to the Right. It is likely that he fudged his points in order to avoid too abrasive an impression when the Prime Ministership was in sight.

5

CHAMBERLAIN AND EDEN

'There seems to be a certain difference between Italian and German positions in that an agreement with the latter might have a chance of a reasonable life especially if Hitler's own position were engaged whereas Mussolini is, I fear, the complete gangster and his pledged word means nothing'. Eden to Chamberlain, January 9 1938, PREM 1/276

(i)

With the defusing of the Rhineland crisis on April 22 and the collapse of Abyssinian resistance in the week following, the foundations of British policy had been destroyed. Collective Security had failed, and it was necessary to find something to replace it. From mid-April onwards a major element in Eden's policy was the search for an alternative.

So far as the League was concerned, he was clear that it could not be restored to its pre-Abyssinia position.[1] However unwilling to abandon it and however insistent on the need to revitalise it,[2] he saw that it would be a long time before it was revived. Germany was not a member. Since German and Italian intentions were the problem, it could only be restored if Hitler turned out to be a reliable European. He had left no reason for supposing that he would be.

Towards Italy Eden had been consistent and unequivocal. It had been essential, in the first place, that Mussolini should be beaten. When he won, it had been essential to do nothing to condone his victory. In both cases Eden had refused to buy co-operation against Germany,[3] since an Italian success, following Hitler's success in the Rhineland, would so much discredit the League that there would be Rhinelands elsewhere.[4]

This policy was a paper-tiger. In the first place, because Eden had no more power to contest German action in Austria than he had had to contest it in the Rhineland. Secondly, because it was doubtful whether he had the power to damage Mussolini once Flandin made it clear that French support would not be forthcoming. Without French support, he had no Cabinet support; he received repeated warnings[5] that naval defence against Germany could not be guaranteed so long as the navy was preparing for sanctions against Italy.[6] When the Abyssinian rains had failed to help him, his only object had been to reduce the Italian economy to a point at which Mussolini would have to negotiate before Hailé Selassie was beaten.

There had, then, been a close connection in his mind between his inability to do anything about the Rhineland and his wish, and inability, to keep on doing what he had failed to do about Abyssinia. This was so for one set of reasons when Hitler and Mussolini seemed to be working together. It was so for another set when the prospect of a German *coup* in Austria seemed likely to frighten the Italians.

From the position thus reached at the end of April, disentanglement was rapid. By mid-June the Cabinet and opinion at Geneva had compelled him to agree that sanctions should be lifted.

In the process, Eden's calculations changed. Having originally expected Italian failure in Abyssinia to make Hitler think twice about intervening in Austria, he now decided that intervention was more likely if Mussolini continued to be under pressure, and would be much less likely if he returned to the League.[7] Eden had no more intention of asking the Cabinet to fight over Austria than he had over the Rhineland. But he was led, reluctantly and suspiciously, to three conclusions — that Locarno[8] would have to be reconstructed, that Italy's position would be crucial and that it would be easier to carry the French towards a European settlement if Mussolini had not been forced to come to terms with Hitler. For these reasons he asked the Cabinet to agree that sanctions should be raised and secured the face-saving assurances with which Mussolini rescued him in the closing part of the Abyssinian chapter.[9]

The liquidation of the Abyssinian problem did not mean that Eden wanted an alliance with Mussolini. His object continued to be the MacDonald policy of reassurance to France in preparation for negotiation with Germany.[10] In this respect he was both active and unsuccessful.

In announcing the occupation of the Rhineland on March 7, Hitler had given assurances of peaceful intentions.

When asked what he intended for the future, he had edged away. By the time Ribbentrop brought a Peace Plan to London on April 1 (after the German elections), Hitler and Eden were both trying to swallow the Rhineland in discussion of a general settlement

The *Peace Plan* of March 31 deplored 'the tendency to involve Europe in a network of military alliances' and repeated that the Rhineland had been occupied because of the Franco-Soviet alliance. It announced Hitler's willingness to contribute to a 'lasting and secure peace' through an air treaty, extended naval agreements, a colonial settlement, a return to the League and the replacement of Locarno by a twenty-five year non-aggression pact.

The document affirmed the German government's 'confident belief' that it had 'opened the way...to European understanding'. [11] But it did not 'take into account' the 'shock' caused by the occupation, and it failed to meet the points the Powers had made. [12] When the French recognised that negotiation was unavoidable, Eden prepared questions which Hitler was to be asked to answer.

Before presenting the questions to the Cabinet, Eden reported Phipps's belief that German expansion would go east *and* west and that there was no longer a moderate party in Germany. He also reported his own belief that probing of Hitler's intentions should continue notwithstanding. [13]

The questionaire was drafted in the Foreign Office and discussed at three Cabinet meetings between April 30 and May 6.[14] After criticism and redrafting,[15] and after the removal of phrases likely to be offensive to the Germans, it was sent to Berlin.

In sending it, Eden had three objects — to register doubt about Hitler's manner, to keep negotiations going and to find common ground between the British and German understandings of the future. There was a Cabinet decision that the colonial question should not be mentioned. The League's position was put interrogatively, because it had not been decided how it was to be reformed. [16] But Eden was hoping to find out on what terms Hitler would rejoin, whether he was willing to renegotiate Locarno and how far he 'claimed to speak...for Germans outside the Fatherland'. [17]

From this point onwards, virtually nothing happened. Hitler let it be known informally that he would not guarantee to leave the Rhineland unfortified. When Eden wanted to press him to say so formally (so as to be free to talk to France and Belgium), the Cabinet refused to let him.[18] When he telegraphed from Geneva six weeks later for approval of a meeting of the Locarno powers (without Germany), he was brought back to explain why he wanted it. [19]

When he returned, ministers were suspicious. They became even more suspicious when it was made clear that the meeting would be held without Italy. [20] They agreed only when Eden convinced them that the French would impose impossible conditions unless he and van Zeeland persuaded them not to, and that there could be no question of a five-power meeting with Germany unless the preliminary meeting was held first. Even so, he was compelled to negotiate the final communiqué before the meeting was held and had to submit it to the Cabinet before it was agreed to. [21]

What Eden expected from abandoning the questionnaire is not clear. He would have liked, doubtless, to negotiate a new Locarno but was far from certain that he could do it. He now believed that a conflict was going on between 'moderate' and 'extreme' elements in Germany, which it was far from clear that the moderate elements were winning, and that the fragility of German economic recovery might make Hitler do something desperate in order to conceal it. He half-thought that the questionnaire had had the wrong effect and was looking for ways of producing the right one. [22]

Eden had no illusions about small powers supporting collective resistance unless Britain and France supplied teeth. [23] Nor did he want to quarrel with Hitler until teeth had been grown. [24] He feared, however, that the League would be lost in 'humiliation' if an attack took place. [25] It was with a view to saving it that he thought of sending Halifax to Berlin in order to arrange a conference whenever Hitler and Mussolini might agree to have one. [26]

By 'saving the League' Eden meant the Geneva protocol and a strengthening of the machinery of coercion, not a watering down of the Covenant. While expecting it to be a long time before the public or the Cabinet would accept the first, [27] he wanted to avoid a decision in favour of the second in order to give the first a chance. [28]

Whether there could be a revived League depended on Hitler and Mussolini being willing to talk. Early in the winter both agreed to. [29] In the following six months, the prospect of agreement receded. Though the Spanish interventions of late 1936 made a conference more necessary, [30] they also made it impossible. By the time Baldwin retired, no conference had been held.

Of Baldwin, alternative things may be said. It may be said that he was hoping to 'get alongside Germany' [31] in order to 'see some agreement' [32] in his last year as Prime Minister and was considering a meeting with Hitler in order to lay the foundations. Or he may have been 'tired and discouraged', unwilling to make up his mind and 'disinclined' to make a 'sustained effort'. [33]

Baldwin played an important part in the defence programme of 1936. But he was conscious of the difficulty in making it acceptable 'in a democratic country'. He steered clear of Chamberlain's negativity about the League, but felt as deep repugnance for French belligerence over the Rhineland as he had for League belligerence over Abyssinia, and had a die-hard fear that a diplomacy which aimed at resisting Hitler might establish Bolshevism in Berlin.[34] He was no more willing to prejudge German policy than to prejudge Italian policy six months before, and he was as suspicious of 'automatic' Locarno obligations as of automatic League ones then. [35] Hitler and Mussolini were 'lunatics'. But he found the mood of the Cabinet unintelligible and insisted on involving Halifax in the Rhineland negotiations because he was the one minister who seemed to understand how dangerous it was. [36]

In the summer of 1936 Baldwin's temper was unrelievedly pacifist. He coupled the decision to rearm with reminders about the horrors of war and an 'appalling frankness' about his reluctance in 1933. [37] Even if he used them to justify rearmament, there can be little doubt that these feelings were real and were conveyed when Jones saw Hitler in May.

Nor, despite differences of mood, did Baldwin differ radically from the body of the Cabinet. Everyone could see that Hitler wanted something, but it was no clearer than in 1934 whether it was colonies, economic supremacy and war against France and Britain or whether his main object was 'a western pact...that would permit him to attack Russia while...prohibiting France from coming to Russia's aid'. [38] Nor could they tell whether he would conduct himself as part of the European Concert once the servility of Versailles had been removed. The difficulty he would face in getting Germany through another winter might 'impose a restraining influence' 'at any rate for a year or two'; it might compel him to aim at 'foreign adventure'. [39] British rearmament was so determined that, 'if he waits too long', he *might* find that 'he had missed the bus' [40] or might decide that he had to take up the challenge.

In these circumstances policy was based on the conflicting beliefs that Britain must keep out of war, must be willing to 'go a long way...to get...a real settlement' and, while trying to deal with [Germany] on the basis that she means what she says', must recognise that she might be 'seeing how far [she] can exploit our weakness' or 'playing for time until she feels herself strong enough to make her next spring'. [41]

By the time Baldwin retired, Eden had been as unsuccessful as Simon. There had been discussion about the relationship between a colonial deal in Africa, an air pact or new Locarno for western Europe, the willingness of Germany to return to a reformed League and the possibility of an Eastern Security treaty. [42] But the League had not been revived; there had been no Locarno conference, and there was no sign of one taking place.

In the months before Chamberlain became Prime Minister, Eden was increasingly announcing the possibility of economic break-down in Germany. He expected Hitler to deal with it by war (if the Nazi party had its way) or by trade liberalisation if it did not. [43] In attempting to encourage the latter, publicly-proclaimed rearmament was one factor. [44] Another was the threat of intimacy with Russia if Stalin allowed Litvinoff to liquidate the Comintern. [45]

Whereas in 1935 a tripartite alliance had received a good deal of Conservative support, now it was highly controversial. Not only among Conservatives at large but also in the Cabinet, adhesion to a Franco-Soviet alliance was interpreted as certain to precipitate division between Britain on the one hand and the enemies of Russia on the other.

The Berlin-Tokyo axis was based ostensibly on fear of Russia. From that point of view it had no significance for Britain which was neither allied with Russia nor ideologically connected with her. Nor did Eden want an alliance. [46] But he wanted to be liked by the opposition (which admired the Popular Front in France)[47] and needed to keep close to Blum (so as to help him resist French pressure to abandon non-intervention in Spain). This combination of needs, and anxiety to be disconnected from Hitler's crusade against Bolshevism, made it easy to identify him as a 'crusader against Fascism'. The result was an increase in the fear that war with Germany and Japan was being brought closer by an ideological conflict which had nothing to do with the danger they presented.

Eden was aware of this. He said repeatedly that he wanted to involve states in the benefits of 'freer trade, freer speech [and] freer thought across the frontiers of Europe' and to induce recognition that, 'in the modern world', where 'war' was the 'merciless begetter of poverty', nations were all 'members one of another'. [48]

In relation to public opinion, Eden thought he was succeeding. But his claim to speak on behalf of 'the democracies' and his identification as Litvinoff's friend did not always cohere with his objective. By the time Chamberlain became Prime Minister, the ideological division was the most delicate of his problems.

(ii)

In the six months after Baldwin decided to retire, the irritation with which Chamberlain had watched him in the previous two years issued in two sorts of practical intention. It issued in a determination to shake up the machinery of government. And it produced a desire to show that he could 'get more done in a month than he could in six when SB was on top'. [49]

Chamberlain did not send Hore-Belisha to the War Office in order to give lessons to the General Staff. His object was to remove Duff Cooper, who had been 'lazy' and had disagreed with Chamberlain about the Army's rôle in war. The need for competence was established by Inskip and the C.I.G.S. [50] and was nearly abandoned when the Cabinet jigsaw presented difficulties. [51] The appointment meant, however, that the War Office was being run by a minister who shared Chamberlain's belief that it must 'renounce all idea of a Continental army on the scale of 1914-1918'. [52] It meant, also, that a radical 'trouble-shooter' could behave as Joseph Chamberlain might have pretended to behave in an entrenched institution. [53] This sense of movement was then confirmed as Chamberlain discovered that he himself was a national figure[54] and by 'a sense of the wonderful power' induced by the knowledge that he had become a world statesman.[55]

The discovery that there was a public willing to respect him came as he toured the country in the summer of 1937, making speeches to establish the key-note of his approach and staying in the houses of his richer supporters. Public acclamation was a new experience to one whose contempt for the public that he knew had been considerable. Spontaneous greetings in the streets created a sense of affinity which his apparent distaste for ordinary press publicity convinced him must be real. This feeling was increased by the intimacy of the acquaintance which many of his correspondents claimed to have got from his broadcast talks and by the response he received from the King, from Baldwin, from the Commonwealth Prime Ministers, from functionaries like Perth and Grandi whose profession it was to keep their hearers happy, and from those who were closest to him whenever he made a speech.[56]

By the end of June Chamberlain felt free of the Baldwinian incubus. He was admired, as he understood, in the House of Commons. At the Imperial Conference, he had been popular. His few attempts to take a grip on government had sent ripples of activity through it. His wife had been a success, not least by contrast with her predecessor, and the confetti had been showered not only on the junior ministers whom he had appointed but also on the 'older hands' who were 'show[ing] a new confidence which is being remarked on a good deal'. Conscious of having established himself in the hearts of the people and feeling a great sense of success, he turned his attention to foreign policy. [57]

In doing this, Chamberlain did not know that he was to

spend the rest of his Prime Ministership, indeed, the rest of his life, on it. At first he hoped for a quick success so as to return to domestic questions in time for the next election. [58] His understanding was based, nevertheless, on extensive experience.

By 1937 Chamberlain had been involved for six years in the high-level web of professional calculation in which all politicians were engaged with the Chiefs of Staff, the Service departments, the Treasury, the Foreign Office and the Board of Trade. He knew which parts of the analysis and which persons he trusted, and which he did not trust. He had given twists and emphases of his own in Cabinet, on the committees and as financial controller of the defence programme, and had been present at the Lausanne and Ottawa Conferences in 1932 and at the World Economic Conference a year later.

Having watched the hopes of Lausanne fade, he had seen that nothing would happen at Geneva unless Britain eased the way for France. He had had full experience of the difficulties surrounding Collective Security. But he had had no time for the 'older diplomacy' and had wanted chiefly to make the Collective System manageable by limiting its operation.

In 1934 Chamberlain shared the Cabinet desire to revise the treaties. But he was clear that this must be done by 'agreement' and that 'the only thing which would make Germany hold her engagements was...force'. He wanted the closest collaboration with France and believed that Britain's continental interests could not easily be limited. He wanted the French to take German fears seriously but believed that it would be Hitler's fault if they did not. [59]

Chamberlain was closely concerned in the Defence White Paper of 1935. When Simon's visit was put off in retaliation, his reaction was that 'Hitler's Germany' was 'a bully' and that Eden's visit to Moscow must go on. He wanted the Germans told that 'we only saw two ways of attaining security — a system of Locarno pacts or a system of alliances' and, if denied the first, would be forced into the second. [60]

While willing to hold out Russia as a threat, [61] he wanted to avoid the impression that France, Britain and Italy had lined up against Hitler. [62] Having been irritated by Simon's failure to press the Eastern security pact when his German visit eventually took place, he thought that *he* should have led the delegation to Stresa. The press briefing he gave (while MacDonald was on his way to the Conference) included so striking an affirmation of Collective Security that the delegation had to play it down. [63]

In May 1935 Chamberlain was talking about Hitler's attempt to 'drive a wedge' between France and Britain. But he was impressed by his proposals for a settlement. [64] Though the Rhineland made him write about the 'mad dictator', [65] it no more relieved him of the desire to keep contact than gloom about disarmament had made the Cabinet wind up the Conference in 1933. On both electoral and public grounds and because talking did not exclude rearming, he thought it necessary to do decisively what had not been done by Baldwin.

From his close-up position, Chamberlain had watched Eden and Vansittart being damaged and Hoare and Simon being destroyed. He had formed a low opinion of Foreign Office 'lethargy' [66] and believed that Baldwin had survived only because he was too lazy to be involved.

Although Chamberlain had exerted himself about foreign policy, it had not been his central interest. His central interest had been economic reconstruction. Fear of a crushing arms programme dislocating confidence had dominated his view both of defence and of foreign policy and had produced effective and distinctive interventions to reduce the scale of military risk to which Britain might be subject in the future.

During defence discussions Chamberlain had combined support for rearmament with a determination to stop Hankey rearming too heavily for health. Egged on by Fisher he was primarily responsible for the Cabinet's treatment of the Defence Requirements Committee programme in 1934. He then developed an animus against Hankey [67] who had defeated his proposal for an international force and was overruled in his turn when the Cabinet accepted the French proposal for a Locarno Air Convention.

In the discussions which followed Hitler's announcements of rearmament, Chamberlain had protracted arguments with the Service ministers. He questioned the meaning of the Baldwin pledge and attacked the view that it meant parity of numbers. He was responsible for deferring part of the naval programme and for rejecting the Continental Field Force. He was an effective opponent when Hankey used the Defence Requirements Committee to revive plans for a Field Force and a major naval expansion after ministers had been scared by Abyssinia. [68]

Though Baldwin was chairman of the Ministerial Committee, Chamberlain was a leading member, played a leading part in drafting the Defence White Paper of 1936 and increased taxation in the Budget as a way of educating the public. [69] He had Weir added to the Committee and tried to persuade Baldwin to get Hoare or Austen Chamberlain to conduct an investigation of the defence position. [70] When Hankey resisted, he damaged his control of defence policy by establishing that a minister would be in control. [71] While refusing to take control himself, [72] he was responsible for establishing that air defence was the 'best' and 'cheapest' way of dealing with Germany, and that 'if war ever c[a]me...our resources [would] be more profitably employed in the air and on the sea than in building up great armies'. [73] He had no time for the War Office view that the French would 'refuse to defend the Low Countries' unless the British army was prepared for Continental service. [74] By the end of 1936 an expeditionary force was a way of preparing for the next war 'from the point of view of the last'. [75]

Chamberlain, then, had proposed economic strength as an element in defence and had pared down the Hankey programme accordingly. But he did not question the analysis on which it was based or the need to deal with the dangers that it suggested. Where he differed was in thinking that enough of them could be dealt with by air power and diplomacy to make the Hankey level of rearmament unnecessary.

Before failure in Abyssinia added a third, this took two forms — pressure to restore relations with Japan and a desire to help Germany acquire a stable economy. By 1937 neither had got very far. There was no prospect of Anglo-Japanese understanding, let alone a restoration of the alliance, abandonment of which, under American pressure in 1922, Chamberlain had greatly regretted. Nor had the military threat been reduced by developing Hitler's taste for economic progress.

For doctrinal purposes Chamberlain was an Imperialist: he was also apprehensive about American economic power. In practice, his doctrinal component was thin. Though responsible for Ottawa, he did not regard the agreements as autarkic and presented them as negotiable bases for a co-operative World System.

Moreover, the Imperial Conference confirmed what Abyssinia and the Rhineland had suggested — that Dominions statesmen were suspicious of the League. It became clear that Canada and South Africa were allergic, that the primary Australian interest was in Japan and that the British interest in the Low Countries and France aroused no enthusiasm for France's alliance-system in eastern Europe.[76]

Though the Imperial connection was valued, there was reluctance to anticipate difficulties and no sentiment in favour of a unified Treasury. Not only was the Royal Navy the chief line of defence, the British taxpayer was the chief source of revenue. It was, therefore, the coincidence between Chamberlain's desire to keep down taxation and the Dominions' dislike of limitless commitments which produced the feeling that a 'general interest' might be developed by reconciling the non-imperial Powers to the Powers of the *status quo*.

Chamberlain shared the contradictory feelings that economic dislocation was a cause of war and that Hitler might be restrained if his economic difficulties became acute.[77] He did not, however, draw simple conclusions. Nor did he fall into Sinclair's trap.[78] While borrowing the Hoare idea that access-to-raw-materials was the most important aspect of the colonial problem, he made it clear (for the benefit of Imperial Conservatives) that economic agreement would be impossible unless there was political agreement first.[79]

Political agreement, however, did not depend, as economic agreement did, on 'the German moderates'. Politically Hitler was the problem; Chamberlain's fundamental task was to find out what could be done with him.[80]

Once involved in the details of negotiation, Chamberlain dramatised his rôle into one of feeling and principle. When attacked by critics he deployed arguments which were not present to his mind at the beginning. But his reactions under pressure, and the anxious peacefulness of his speeches, should not obscure the fact that his interventions began at a point of tension rather than crisis in intelligent pursuit of the lessons he had learnt in the past.

Chamberlain believed that there was no necessary identity between the aims of Hitler and those of Mussolini, and that their ideological solidarity was thin. His object was to detach one from the other in order to involve both in a general negotiation, but in both directions his expectations were limited. Germany was the bigger bait as well as the bigger danger and, 'if we could only get on terms' with her, he would not 'care a rap for Mussolini'. [81] At first, too, Germany appeared the more promising prospect. [82] It remained the more important one, even after the lack of response made it less promising. [83] In July 1937 he made Mussolini the first priority when an Italian military build-up synchronised with the development of an anti-British propaganda by the Italian broadcasting services in the Middle East.

Chamberlain's first reaction had been to think of improving relations with Germany.[84] When Eden proposed the reinforcing of the Mediterranean fleet, he referred the question to the Chiefs of Staff who replied that this would only be done by dangerously weakening the Home Fleet. Hankey then made it his business to ask for an effort to improve relations with Italy 'in any event during the completion of our defence programme'. [85]

In 1936 Chamberlain had beaten Hankey about control of defence policy and the Continental Field Force. Once this had happened, they collaborated to work out the implications of the policy he had imposed. Until his retirement in July 1938, Hankey not only recognised 'sound finance' as a strategic asset [86] but, as Secretary to the Cabinet and spokesman of the Chiefs of Staff, was Chamberlain's chief check on the Foreign Office.

The belief that a check was needed arose from the realisation that post-war foreign policy had been a failure. Baldwin understood this and had talked about cleaning up the Foreign Office before he retired. [87] In fact he had not done so; all he had done was to allow Vansittart to refuse to go to Paris.

About Hitler Vansittart had been clear from the start. Any-thing he said was 'for foreign consumption'. He would need time before he took on Poland but might win in Austria without a blow and, once he had done so, would 'loose off another European war just as soon as [he] feels strong enough'. [88]

Vansittart was not an advocate of the *status quo*. Like everyone else he believed that treaty revision was desirable. What he believed Hitler had done was to defer it indefinite-ly. [89]

Vansittart was not looking for barriers against Bolshevism. He was unenthusiastic about negotiations and believed that 'the collapse of Hitlerism' was essential. His fears gained point when the Roehm *putsch* 'handed Hitler over' to 'the Junkers', who were much more likely to move towards rap-prochement with Russia. [90] It was for this reason that he advocated a Russian alliance with France, British co-opera-tion with Litvinoff and tripartite firmness towards Germa-ny. [91]

Like Hankey, Vansittart was urgent about rearmament. He regarded the Austrian struggle as the beginning of a crisis. But he had no proposal for resistance and was troubled chiefly by the fear that Simon had isolated Britain by his incapacity to effect tripartite cordiality. [92]

Vansittart disliked Germans who 'cringed' when 'down' and had a 'superiority complex' when 'up'. [93] In this he dif-fered from Simon.

In 1934 ministers had well understood that there were differences of emphasis between Simon's German, and Van-sittart's French, orientations. These had been resolved and transcended in the short term by Cabinet decisions; for the long term they were supposed to be resolved when Hoare and Eden took over the Foreign Office.

Before Abyssinia Vansittart saw no similarity between Nazism and Fascism or between Hitler and Mussolini (who was 'the bigger and wiser' of the two [94]). At the beginning of the crisis, he was in favour of resistance. Once seized of Laval's reluctance, he could tell as little as Hoare or Chamberlain whether resistance would succeed. [95] The Hoare-Laval plan involved only incompetent adoption of one rather than the other of the options they all thought they were keeping open in the summer.

From the subsequent outcry, Vansittart suffered as much as Hoare, and felt the same need for self-justification. [96] In the course of 1936 he was under continuous fire from Wilson, Hankey and Fisher and was increasingly discredited with both Baldwin and Chamberlain. [97] He was heavily criticised in the Foreign Office, and, though closer to Eden than to Simon, seems still to have been breathing unwelcome fumes down an unwelcoming neck.

The decision to remove him has been seen as a reply to the rightness of his warnings about Germany. His warning, however, had been matched by Hankey and Fisher and had more than registered with Chamberlain and Hoare, with whom he had then been implicated in encouraging Hitler by failing to halt Mussolini.

Vansittart had for long doubted whether Hitler 'meant business in our sense of the word'. But once the League and Stresa had collapsed, 'the policy of waiting' would be 'dangerous'. 'Collective security' would become 'encirclement... unless...combined with an elastic policy of settlement', so it was essential that the Czechs should be flexible. Though reluctant to negotiate without prior decisions about objectives, he was willing to start so long as German expansion in Europe was excluded. [98]

In the summer of 1936, moreover, Vansittart visited Germany. There he found a climate which 'the ghost of Barthou would hardly have recognised' and where, since 'the people in authority' wanted 'an understanding' and 'perhaps, even something closer', he decided that negotiation should be pursued.

Vansittart treated the Franco-Soviet alliance as non-negotiable. But he assumed that a settlement would have to provide for German expansion. This he was willing to contemplate. What he rejected was the 'immoral' desire to 'satisfy' Hitler's 'land hunger at Russia's expense'. It was because Germany had equality in Europe already that he wanted Britain to facilitate expansion in Africa. [99]

While talking tactically in terms of 'democracy', [100] Vansittart wished to avoid an ideological policy. But by late 1936 he was clear that Hitler was not conducting one. Whatever he had been doing before the *putsch*, Hitler was now a successor of the Prussians. The 'Bolshevist menace' was a cover for 'expansion in Central and South-Eastern Europe'. [101] His attacks on 'Semitic Marxism' were neither directed at the Soviet Union nor excluded a deal with Stalin, which would certainly be made if it became necessary to isolate the French, just as the Berlin-Tokyo axis had anticipated the British desire to improve relations with Japan. [102]

Like Hankey, Vansittart thought in real-power terms. He saw Hitler brooding on the historic options of Prussian policy. But he did not know whether he would follow Goebbels (and Tirpitz) in viewing Britain as 'the ultimate enemy', or whether he would adopt the Ribbentrop policy of appeasing Britain in order to engage in military expansion in the East. In either case the 'position' had to be 'stabilised' and 'time bought for rearmament' by pursuing economic agreement, meeting the 'genuine grievance' about colonies and giving 'moderates and moderation' a chance in Germany. [103]

In 1936 this was as central a position as the belief that war between Germany, France and Britain would destroy the 'social order as we know it'. [104] So, too, was his defence of Non-Intervention (as a political necessity in England), even after the communisation of Republican Spain. [105]

Despite scepticism about Hitler's intentions, Vansittart did not deviate until late 1937. Then, like Eden, he objected to Chamberlain's precipitancy with Mussolini and to the Halifax visit to Berlin. At the same time he moved sharply towards the belief that Germany was 'not ready for action on a large scale' and that Britain could 'contemplate' her 'own position...without the panic and precipitation that seem to animate some of our publicists'. [106]

About Mussolini Vansittart blew hot and cold. But he wanted to detach him from Hitler if that should be possible. While doubting the outcome, he supported the idea of German negotiations, even when Schacht's influence was moving towards its close. The real difference between his position on the one hand and the Cabinet's on the other was that, since Conservatives might resist concessions about colonies, Chamberlain, Halifax and Eden assumed that there might have to be unspecified adjustments in Europe.

Vansittart thought the Empire an 'incubus'. [107] He regarded 'Europe' as the central British interest and doubted whether agreement would be possible there. His doubt hinged on
the claim that the object (if Nazi attention turned eastward)
would be a military Empire between the Baltic, the Adriatic
and the Black Sea. [108] Even at his most forthcoming, he was
vigorously contemptuous of those who disagreed.

Vansittart felt persecuted by Lothian, Londonderry and
The Times and tried to persecute them in return. [109] He
evidently believed in 'Cliveden' and claimed to be an object
of concerned assault. [110] There is no need to adopt this explanation of his removal.

Vansittart's prose and prognostications were dramatic
(and, as it turned out, accurate in respect of German expansion). They also implied that 'Collective Security' should be
submerged into 'national interests'.

It is likely that Eden found him an inconvenient adviser. In
any case, he may well have been tired of a situation in which
he had to mediate as nervously as Simon between the Foreign
Office and the Cabinet.

Eden's uncertainties reflected his own inexperience and
differences among his advisers. As his grip tightened, his preferences prevailed, with the result that he stubbed his toes not
only on the 'power-politics' of Vansittart (who did not believe in the Empire) but on the 'power politics' of the Chiefs
of Staff, who did.

Throughout the twenties the Chiefs of Staff had deplored
disarmament, while recognising that nothing could be done
to check it. It was not until the Japanese action in 1931 that
they sensed a chance. When the Japanese danger was supplemented by the German, they expected the chance to be taken.

What they wanted was an attempt to educate the public —
an attack by 'statesmen' on 'the false teachings' of 'pacifists'
and 'politicians'. [111] Occasionally they made public statements themselves; [112] more often they assumed that ministers would do it better. In any case, they felt called to battle.

By 1935 it had been made clear that the battle would be
lost. However preferable to what had gone before, [113] the
National government had its limitations. They did not need

to be told that conscription was impossible, that money would be limited and that the 'Empire in arms' was not a conception to which the Cabinet would respond.

Up to a point, no doubt, their reactions were tactical, exaggerating the dangers in order to make the Cabinet afraid. To some extent, they were worried about differences among themselves as scarce resources were competed for by conflicting Services. From both angles, they were driven to an important conclusion about foreign policy.

This was that Britain had either to arm sufficiently for a world rôle, or to reduce the world rôle to the measure of her power. From early 1935 these were the lessons they began to teach. They taught them over Abyssinia, the Rhineland and in considering the European situation thereafter. In doing so, their most important agent was Hankey.

Throughout the twenties Hankey had tried to resist disarmament. After 1931 he had made himself the spearhead of assault on the 'pacifists' in the Cabinet. He had done his best to begin naval rearmament in face of Chamberlain's Treasury scrutiny and had defended the munitions industry against liberal and socialist attacks on its independence.

In this last respect (by 1937) he had succeeded. [114] In other respects he had not. Chamberlain had restricted rearmament and affected its direction, and had wanted a forward policy in Europe and Africa notwithstanding.

Hankey's view of Hitler was conditioned by the 'moral disarmament' created by the peace movement of the twenties. By 1933 he knew that Germany was rearming and might eventually have to be resisted. [115] He knew, too, that a preventive war was the answer. [116] But he knew that it was impossible politically. He knew, also, that it would be strategically dubious in view of his longstanding mistrust of France which Chanak had established and the French connection with Russia now greatly increased.

Hankey's mistrust of France did nothing to reduce his fear of Germany; if massive rearmament had been possible in 1933, fear would have become a policy. The rearmament programme, however, by his standards, was niggardly. It necessitated a chronological priority, in which the build-up against Germany had to be long term in case the danger ever became imminent. [117]

This did not stop him feeling that danger existed. But the immediate danger came less from foreign enemies than from the enemy within, and much more from Cecil and Eden than from anything that was being planned in Berlin.

The danger was that moral sympathies, League requirements or unlimited obligations would land the Empire in difficulties which disarmament made it incapable of facing, and would produce disasters so manifest that it would have to be dismembered, whether the Powers wanted to dismember it or not. The danger was implicit in the loss of the pre-war alliances with Italy and Japan. It would have been brought closer by the proposed Japanese trade embargo in 1932, by Chamberlain's International Police Force two years later and by the air pact of early 1935. [118]

Hankey's preference was for naval superiority in all the seas at once. This was politically difficult, and became impossible when the German naval agreement was not accompanied by renewal of the agreement with Japan. In these, and other respects, he expected the pace of rearmament to be slow and the period of danger protracted.

Hankey was no respecter of politicians [119] who reflected the 'era of shame' which Cecil had imposed upon them. [120] He treated the League as merely an 'organ of conciliation', and regarded the break-up of the Disarmament Conference as a chance to return to the 'balance of power'. From his point of view, the Empire, France and the Low Countries were the real limits of British commitment; [121] he saw a great maritime Empire being turned by defects of prudence and imagination into the Sick Man of the World. [122]

These feelings, strongly entrenched by the beginning of the Abyssinia crisis, were confirmed by it [123] and became acute as Spain divided Eden from the Cabinet. In 1937 they provided the ballast for Cabinet resistance.

What was feared was 'foreign policy...carry[ing] us into war when we are not ready for it'. [124] What was also feared was military, or naval, defeat in a war fought without allies. [125] What was feared, after Blum's victory in 1936, was a war fought in company with the French ('half-riddled with discontent and Communism') and in indirect alliance with the Russians, whose object was 'to...force Bolshevism on a shattered Europe. [126]

Neither Hankey nor the Chiefs of Staff saw any reason to bring this about. They saw 'the sentimentalists' dragging them into war against Japan. They felt the same about Spain and had no interest in propping up the Republic. They had no objection to Mussolini ('however untrustworthy') and wanted to repair the breach which Spain and Abyssinia had been causing. [127]

In urging negotiations, they were not assuming that 'an enemy' was to be 'appeased'. They believed that the Italian people were friendly and that there was no need for enmity between the governments. [128] They discerned an Anglo-Italian interest in 'a free Mediterranean and Red Sea' and believed that the only obstacle was Eden's dislike of Mussolini. [129]

About Germany they were apprehensive. But they were also cautious. Sometimes they treated German colonies as a threat; at others they thought them likely to disperse German naval power. [130] They thought the German economy inadequate to dominate Europe, and they did not expect Hitler to attack the Empire. So long as there was no evidence that he would do so, they were willing to accept German expansion in south-eastern Europe. [131] They were quite clear that the Russians were 'foul'. They were equally clear that Britain had a duty to 'stave off war...and strengthen ourselves in case one day we can stave it off no longer'. [132]

In the first half of 1937 Hankey did not need to exert himself since the Cabinet had its own reasons for holding Eden back. When he undertook his special intervention in July, he was much more worried.

It was, therefore, [133] in the hope of better relations 'carry[ing] us' through a 'danger period' that Chamberlain was acting when he opened negotiations. It was in order to buy the 'necessary time' for rearmament that he sent Mussolini a letter hoping that relations would be better in the future. [134]

At first, he wanted a bargain — with Mussolini promising to withdraw volunteers from Spain if Britain undertook to initiate recognition of the Abyssinian Empire at Geneva. He thought, however, even then, that recognition, though something the Italians wanted, would become less valuable as time went on and that Italy could best be excluded 'from the list of possible enemies' by not making conditions. [135] By the end of August he believed that his correspondence with Mussolini had so completely blunted Italian propaganda that he should take the initiative regardless. [136] In this, as Eden warned him, he was taking a risk. [137] But he took it with his eyes open in the hope that success would 'weaken' the 'artificial' ties between Germany and Italy and be of 'immense value...if we had any disagreement with Germany'. [138]

In approaching Mussolini, Chamberlain aimed to set an example to the Foreign Office. [139] Its hesitations increased his determination to conduct policy himself, largely through the regular machinery but occasionally through intermediaries like Ball and Ivy Chamberlain. [140] Though these were intended to be supplementary, rather than central, they ensured that major questions were discussed with Wilson, Hankey and Halifax as much as with Vansittart and Eden.

During the attempt to talk Mussolini out of war in 1935 Chamberlain had formed a favourable opinion of Eden's diplomatic skill. [141] During his period as Mayor of the Palace, his view was that Eden had a 'genius' for 'personal contacts',[142] was good at listening to advice and showed 'courage and statesmanship' over the Rhineland. [143] Eden, however, was forty, he was sixty-eight and there was no affinity of sympathy or background between them. The League position he had adopted in June 1936 had been implicitly critical. Eden, for his part, feared that Chamberlain would destroy his bipartisan position by intensifying party conflict. [144] In the months of waiting, he had threatened to resign if he could not remain Foreign Secretary. Within ten days of Baldwin's retirement he had annoyed Chamberlain and upset the Imperial Conference by trying to get the Dominions Prime Ministers to make a strong statement of support for the League. [145]

On both sides, therefore, there had been difficulties. On both there was a predisposition to prickliness — on Eden's at Chamberlain's conception of the relationship between party and foreign policy, on Chamberlain's at the feeling that Eden had had too much limelight under Baldwin for reasons, and in defence of causes, that were bogus.

Except in the sense that it was an achievement to have

become Foreign Secretary at thirty-eight and to have implied
the possibility of further advancement in the future, Eden's
period at the Foreign Office had not been either a technical
success or punctuated by successes. No four-power conference had been held. Germany and Italy had, in effect, withdrawn from Locarno, as had Belgium after the party crisis of
1936 and the French alignment with Russia. [146] In Spain
Russia had behaved badly. Mussolini's capacity for failure
had been over-estimated, not only in Abyssinia (even after he
had won [147]), but also in Spain where non-intervention, if
considered as a contribution to a Republican victory or the
emergence of a 'middle government', was self-defeating, and
where increasing Communist control of the contracting Republic made it extremely unpopular among Conservatives. [148]

For Eden Anglo-Italian relations were delicate. Mussolini
was not only the Fascist who had committed atrocities in
Abyssinia. He was also the man who had stood up to the
League and beaten it. When deciding on conciliation, therefore, he took pains to avoid enthusiasm. He had done so,
even when contemplating a Mediterranean Locarno [149] and
would have had great difficulty in doing anything else in view
of the tenuousness of the connection between the Embassy
in Rome and the highest reaches of the Italian government. [150]

How long Eden would have persisted with virtue is uncertain. In the early winter of 1936 he was under Cabinet pressure [151] to move faster than he liked, and tried to use Austen and Ivy Chamberlain as intermediaries with Mussolini. [152]
After the conclusion of the 'gentleman's agreement' in January 1937, however, Italian intervention in Spain was stepped
up.

The Spanish war had begun at a time when Eden was
interested primarily in renegotiating Locarno. Since, therefore, it came inopportunely, he had wished, so far as possible,
to contain it. This was the object when he and Blum proposed, and the Powers agreed, that none of them should intervene. Despite the establishment of a Non-Intervention Committee in London, it became clear by October that Russia,
Italy and Germany were intervening in strength and that the

Labour party proposed to turn 'Spain' into a test of merit. [153]

Eden's chief aim was to limit intervention (including interventions from organised Italian volunteers). He had not been very successful. When Italian intervention was stepped up in early January, he confronted first Baldwin and then a hastily summoned meeting of ministers with a plan to ask for international agreement to the establishment of a British naval cordon round the Spanish coast. [154]

In excusing his haste, Eden explained the need to prevent 'an international war between the Fascist and Bolshevist states' and the danger, if the dictators got away with it, of the 'moderate influences in Germany' being 'silenced' and the Germans 'undertak[ing] other adventures, for example, in Czechoslovakia'.

If he was trying to rush the Cabinet, he was disappointed. Hardly anyone spoke in his favour. Wood and Inskip told him that the plan did not amount to much and would, in any case, be rejected by the governments concerned. Stanhope disliked 'this country playing the role' of 'unpaid policeman to the world'. Simon did not see how the world could agree to it being judge as well. Hoare said that the plan amounted to an attempt to 'stop...Franco winning' where 'some members of the Cabinet were much more interested in stopping the Soviet Union winning'. When Eden replied that 'there would be a great deal of complaint in this country...if Madrid was captured by the Insurgents', he was told [155] that 'many people...would be equally troubled if the Bolshevists achieved a victory'.

Hoare pointed out that the Admiralty had not been consulted, was not in favour and regarded land control at ports of embarkation as the only feasible way of proceeding. Some ministers disliked even this, and it eventually became clear that most of them wanted the Germans and Italians to make proposals of their own. When Baldwin ruled out the blockade, Eden suggested a conference of the Powers in London. He dropped this (after the Cabinet had agreed) in favour of an attempt to collect 'views' and refer them to the Non-Intervention Committee. They emerged from there a month later as a plan for a joint naval patrol by all the leading Powers, which was not put into operation until the beginning of April. [156]

In deciding, early in the war, that the Republic ought to win, [157] Eden was thinking strategically (in terms of the Mediterranean) and politically (in terms of the liberal Left in England). He stuck to non-intervention, which the Cabinet and Conservative party would not have agreed to abandon and which gave a negotiating hold through the French threat to open the Spanish frontier. But he was against an agreement with Mussolini so long as Italian troops were fighting for Franco and was conscious of a difference between his own desire to prop up the Republic and the feelings of many other members of the Cabinet. From his point of view, the war went the wrong way.

For Chamberlain, on the other hand, it went the right way. Though in no sense a partisan, he had no desire to see Franco, or anyone else, 'messed up' by 'the Bolshies' who were 'the limit'. [158] For him 'Spain' meant the possibility of war between France and Italy and a cementing of Mussolini's alliance with Hitler. He did not believe that a Franco victory would establish 'a third dictator State', give France 'a third frontier...to be defended' or 'increase the likelihood of some early advance elsewhere' by Hitler and Mussolini. Nor did he expect Italy to get 'submarine bases...for bargaining purposes...in case of war'. [159] He, therefore, minded less than Eden about the presence of Italian troops and was much more concerned with playing Spain down in order to negotiate elsewhere. He did not agree that 'the only way to make any impression on the Italians' was 'to hit back at them'. [160]

In 1937 Chamberlain went a long way with Eden against Cabinet pressure to grant belligerent status to Franco. Until late in the summer he agreed that a *quid pro quo* would be needed from Mussolini. Eventually, however, a point was reached at which the Mussolini problem seemed to be too urgent for bargaining. [161]

From the beginning of negotiations, Chamberlain believed that Mussolini need not be an enemy and could be made a friend. He knew that Eden was sensitive and that negotiations would be difficult. Instead, therefore, of getting him to conduct them, he conducted them himself. His first sense of success, and the first quarrel, came when Halifax was his link with the Foreign Office while Eden was on holiday. [162]

On August 10 Halifax held a meeting of Foreign Office officials in order to write Chamberlain a programme.[163] When Eden saw it, he spent a great deal of time chewing it over. Having made up his mind that he 'really...could...not... bring [him]self to any kind of approval of what Italy had done', he asked Halifax to spend a night with him in his holiday house on the Solent.[164]

Halifax brought back the news that Eden, though 'very sensitive' about getting 'advantages...for ourselves' from recognising the conquest of Abyssinia, was 'probably willing' to 'contemplate' action at Geneva provided 'the French and as many others as possible [were] willing to co-operate'. He feared, however, that, 'having once given Mussolini the thing that he principally wanted' Britain might get nothing in return. He thought it best therefore to begin by encouraging the newspapers to anticipate recognition so that, when other League members had taken the initiative, he would be in a position to tackle the Italians about their naval build-up, their propaganda and their forces in Spain.[165]

Halifax also brought back the news that Eden wanted Chamberlain to come back from his holiday. The result was that Chamberlain insisted on having his way, while leaving it uncertain at what point recognition would be given. The dispute was not resolved before the submarine attacks which led up to the Nyon Conference in September.[166]

Eden had been put down in January and had had prolonged disagreement with the Admiralty about the blockading of Bilbao three months later.[167] When German warships[168] were attacked on naval patrol by Republican submarines, he refused the German request for a naval demonstration in front of Valencia.[169] On both occasions he left his critics the impression of being insensitive to the German position,[170] of acting on behalf of the Republic[171] and of wishing to avoid even minimum recognition of Franco's status.[172]

Eden had no ideological preferences. But he was sensitive to those who had and was anxious to prevent the Labour party making Spain a ground for challenge. He was embarrassed by the Insurgent sympathies of other ministers and the Conservative mistrust of the Republic.[173] When he appealed to 'the governments of Europe' to turn 'the Spanish tragedy' into an 'occasion for co-operation',[174] he was hoping to undermine

Franco's supporters. The bombing of Guernica at the end of April and Italian attacks on Republican ships produced additional reasons for demonstrating his liberality.

From this point of view, attacks on British ships at the end of August were damaging. At first he was shrill and nervous. [175] In the following fortnight he began to sound like Palmerston. [176] When the Nyon Conference agreed to 'set up a police force' and '80 Anglo-French destroyers patroll[ed] the Mediterranean' in late September, he believed that 'a profound impression' had been made. [177]

At Nyon Eden recovered from the gloom of January. He, however, was not the only person who was pleased. Chamberlain was pleased too, because the demonstration of strength would make it reasonable to resume negotiations. Even so, he tried to stop Eden addressing a Conservative rally, ostensibly because he would 'tire himself out', [178] in fact because he would present the agreement as a victory over Mussolini. [179] Only the danger of the Blum government opening the frontier when Mussolini announced involvement in Franco's victories compelled him to drop talks for the time being. [180]

The concurrent switch to German appeasement produced disputes about which Chamberlain proposed to 'sav[e] Eden from himself'[181] while praising him in public in view of German newspaper claims 'that there were fundamental differences between them'. [182] The decision that Halifax should go to Germany was settled as a result of a newspaper leak while Eden was at the China Conference in Brussels. [183] It produced an Eden tantrum [184] on the ground that Anglo-German relations would suffer from 'exaggerated expectations'. [185]

Chamberlain's response was that he should 'go back to bed and take an aspirin'. [186] His comment, when the visit was over, was that Halifax would not be reporting to him until 'honour had been satisfied' by a visit to the Foreign Office. [187] He was amiably contemptuous when Eden's followers took pains to establish that Eden's authority had not been damaged. [188]

Although Eden irritated Chamberlain, there was a measure of agreement. Eden raised no objection to Halifax's visit when it was first suggested [189] and eventually came to support it. [190] He supported the removal of Vansittart whom he had presssed Baldwin to send to Paris in 1936 and was able to shunt sideways a year later, because Chamberlain wanted a 'sane, slow man' like Cadogan to have a steadying effect on his own 'natural vibrations'. [191]

Nevertheless, there were differences. Eden preferred Hitler to Mussolini and had for long believed that the 'moderate elements' in Germany deserved help in their attempt to prevent the Nazi party capturing his mind. [192] He took Italy less seriously than the Chiefs of Staff whose sense of weakness rationalised an instinctive desire to 'clamber on the bandwagon with the dictators'. [193] In November, he began to say that negotiations with Germany should be deferred until rearmament had been completed. [194] After the defence review in December, he talked about the need to hurry it up and denied that Britain could find herself at war alone against Germany, Italy and Japan. [195]

Eden was not alone in thinking the Mediterranean important and Turkish, Arab and Egyptian collaboration central. But, where others expected this to be matched by collaboration with Spain and Italy, he assumed that Spain and Italy were certain to be hostile.

So far as Chamberlain could see, Eden did not understand the danger from the anti-Comintern powers or the urgency of the need to keep them apart. He 'deserved' the rebuke he was given for attacking Mussolini in reply to an attack on the 'democracies' a few days after Ciano had refused to come to Brussels for a meeting during the Conference on China. [196]

The Brussels Conference was attended by most of the signatories of the 1922 Treaty. It marked a definitive rejection of the idea that international action would be taken to stop the Sino-Japanese war. [197] With its failure, a problem which had haunted British diplomacy for four years became a reality.

Fear of war against Germany and Japan had been a central feature of the defence discussions of 1934. It had not, however, become critical, because it had been assumed that diplomacy could deal with Japan. [198] Diplomacy had then made Italy hostile.

By mid-1937, the attempt to restore Anglo-Italian relations had failed; by the end of the year, relations with Mussolini were as difficult as in 1935. Russian intervention in Spain and the Franco-Russian alliance had produced the Anti-Comintern pact which, though aimed at France and Russia, was the greatest danger the Empire could face. The problem then escalated when the Japanese attack on China in late July was followed by incidents in the international settlements.

The British interest in the Sino-Japanese war was that limits should be placed on Japanese expansion. But it was not obvious whether this should be done by restoring peace, by propping up the Chinese or by encouraging the Japanese to become over-committed. Nor was it obvious what could be done by way of retaliation, so long as it was impossible to send an adequate fleet, dangerous to send an inadequate one and essential to avoid a direct Japanese attack on the Empire.

In these circumstances, the Japanese action increased the importance of appeasement in Europe at the same time as the danger in Europe made it 'suicidal...to pick a quarrel' in the Far East. [199] At first this did not affect relations with Italy since the Blum government's domestic difficulties would hold up Abyssinian recognition so long as Mussolini was openly announcing his support for Franco. [200] But it was a material factor in Chamberlain's enthusiasm for the Halifax visit to Germany. The Yangtse incident in December merely highlighted the difficulty. [201]

The escalation of tension in all three areas in late 1937 presented, therefore, in an acute way, the simmering conflict between Eden on the one hand and Hankey and the Chiefs of Staff on the other.

Hankey's reaction was a sharp escalation of pressure as the Chiefs of Staff were persuaded that war with Italy was being made inevitable by Eden whose 'perspective' was 'wrong' and who was 'play[ing] to the gallery of the extreme Left'. [202] It was in the belief that coolness towards 'dictators' was no longer supported in the Foreign Office and was becoming unpopular in the Conservative party that Hankey pressed Chamberlain to the view that improved relations with Italy were 'vital' to the Empire's existence...as a first-class power'. [203]

Eden's reaction was subtler than the Palmerstonian reaction of September. Now he took the view that, though negotiation was desirable because action was impossible, agreement should be avoided while Britain was weak. In relation to Italy, he believed that the weakness was not serious. Elsewhere, he believed that nothing should be decided until there could be agreement from strength.

So long as agreement with Germany was unlikely, this was not different from Chamberlain's point of view. It became very different when Chamberlain moved on from the tactical aim of 'detaching one dictator from the other' towards 'far-reaching plans for the appeasement of Europe and Asia'. [204]

Chamberlain talked about 'checking' the 'mad armaments race' [205] and 'bringing about European peace', [206] but he did not think that this would be easy. On the contrary, peculiarities of character and the nature of the régimes would make it difficult. [207] His consciousness of the odds made him sensitive when Eden seemed to be sabotaging the policy he was adopting.

In these circumstances he came increasingly to rely on Halifax — 'the most important statesman...England ha[s] at the present time' [208] — who had convinced Hitler of Britain's sincerity and brought closer the time when discussion of the colonial question might produce conditions in which 'we' say to Germany 'give us satisfactory assurances that you won't use force to deal with the Austrians and Czechoslovakians and we will give you similar assurances that we won't use force to prevent the changes you want, if you can get them by peaceful means'. [209]

Eden was relieved that the Halifax talks had been more or less a failure. Chamberlain believed that they had not been [210] and looked forward to talks about air disarmament, Locarno and Eastern Europe in the future. He was willing to go 'a long way' about Colonies if that seemed likely to produce agreement in Europe. [211]

Chamberlain was conscious of backsliding in the Foreign Office. He knew that he had to set the pace and make constructive suggestions. Eventually, he and Eden settled down to consulting the French and making preliminary approaches to Hitler. [212]

There were differences of emphasis. [213] Eden wanted a strong League, Chamberlain agreed with Hitler that the League 'should not impose its views by force'. [214] Eden did not share Chamberlain's urgency after the January flare-up in the Far East. [215] But he shifted when a statement he made about arms limitation attracted favourable attention in England [216] and seems then to have accepted the Chamberlain time-table for negotiations with Italy. [217]

Having accepted, he interfered with a Grandi/Chamberlain meeting on February 4 and tried to stop Ivy Chamberlain talking to Mussolini. When the Schuschnigg/Hitler meeting of February 11 made Italy crucial, he 'horrified' Chamberlain by imposing delays and conditions, and then, after agreeing that talks should go on, asked him to postpone them until Mussolini had agreed that Italian troops would be withdrawn from Spain. [218]

Eden alleged that Hitler's Austrian policy had been cleared with Mussolini and that the Germans were claiming that it had been cleared with Halifax too. [219] In any case he had no intention of resisting and differed from Chamberlain only in doubting whether the prospect of German armies on the Brenner had produced conditions in which Mussolini could be detached. [220]

After a sharp exchange the day before, [221] Chamberlain's impression on February 9 was that he and Eden were 'in... more complete...agreement' than at any time in the past. [222] On February 12 Eden more or less said so in public. [223] On the 16th he asked that Grandi be allowed to see him at the Foreign Office instead of with Chamberlain in Downing Street, giving, however, as his reason the 'sharp reaction' a Chamberlain/Grandi meeting would cause in Berlin 'where it may be regarded as taking advantage of the Austrian situation in order to seek to break the Berlin-Rome Axis'. [224]

From Chamberlain's point of view, crucial events occurred on February 17 and 18 when Ciano used Ivy Chamberlain to send a request for talks to begin and Eden, having claimed, inaccurately as it turned out, that Vansittart objected, edged Cadogan forward at luncheon to press the view that he should see Grandi alone. [225] The argument they had after their joint meeting with Grandi on the morning of the 18th confirmed Chamberlain in the view that after losing 'chance after chance with Italy' Eden was so obstinately determined to repeat his performance that they could 'never work together'. [226]

Even before this meeting Chamberlain had made up his mind that talks must begin at once. [227] Having made the decision, he explained the dispute to the Cabinet on the 19th. No one supported Eden. It was not until after the discussion, when he said that he would have to resign, [228] that he received any support of substance. Though ministers were greatly worried when they thought about the consequences, the one constant factor at the two Cabinets before his resignation next day was Chamberlain's determination not to stop him. [229]

In the week after the resignation, Chamberlain decided that 'at bottom Anthony did not want to talk either with Hitler or Mussolini and, as I did, he was right to go'. [230] It is unlikely that Eden would have admitted this, even if it was true. It is not likely that it was true, in the form in which Chamberlain put it, since one of Eden's objectives was to prevent Mussolini driving a wedge between Chamberlain and himself. [231] For this reason he attached great importance to procedure and believed, as he said more than once, that 'we have nothing to gain by showing ourselves over-eager' as 'it always pays to be firm with the Italians'. [232]

Eden gave three reasons for refusing to run after Mussolini — his breach of the 'gentlemen's agreement',[233] his insignificance in relation to the 'big issues' of the year[234] and the certainty that the anti-Comintern powers would quarrel among themselves 'unless we gravely mishandle the international situation in the near future'. [235]

These judgments assumed that Hitler would not go to war 'at the behest of Japan and Italy' and was so 'sincere' about the 'racial business' that he would dissociate himself from the anti-white crusade being run from Tokyo. They assumed that Mussolini had to chose between 'going deeper into the mire' and 'cutting his losses' after Franco's failure to take Madrid, and that his appeal to Hitler had provoked disagreement in the German government, the removal of 'the moderates' (i.e. von Neurath) on February 4 and the establishment of the Ribbentrop policy in Austria. [236] Mussolini would dislike this, Eden thought, even if he had promised Hitler a free hand, [237] but could do nothing about it in face of military set-backs in Spain where Chamberlain's negotiations would merely help him 'rally his...disgruntled fellow-countrymen...to a further expedition'.[238]

The judgments were genuine, but it may still have been the

case that Eden wanted to resign as much as Chamberlain wanted him to. There is much reason to suppose that he sensed support on the government back benches, expected Chamberlain to fail (for the new reason that Hitler and Mussolini were in league) and thought it wise to present the negotiations as 'another surrender' which would cause 'panic' among 'our friends' in Europe and the United States and leave an impression of 'scuttle' in England. [239]

Recognition of the conquest of Abyssinia was a reminder of the extent to which the purposes implied by Eden's tenure of the Foreign Office were being abandoned. It was the challenge presented to 'liberal hopefulness' which made Mussolini seem like 'anti-Christ'. [240] It was the damage he would suffer if he remained in office while the League failed in Austria which justified the claim Eden made after his resignation that he could not have supported the Anglo-Italian agreement if he had stayed. [241]

It is true that Hitler had not occupied Austria (which he did not do until March). But Eden had already talked about the danger of negotiating with Germany while rearmament was incomplete [242] and thought of resigning both at the time of the Halifax visit to Berlin and in the course of the argument he had had about Roosevelt's 'initiative' in January 1938. [243] At a moment at which Hitler had bullied Schuschnigg, the negotiations with Germany, which he had been involved in starting, were about to become indefensible to the moral constituency he represented.

On the two earlier occasions, Eden had got his way but he had not really tried to stop negotiations with Hitler. After initial support and subsequent doubt, he had begun to be critical only when the German government made negative noises about returning to the League. Even then, he left it an open question whether to abandon the League element in a settlement. [244] At the point of maximum reluctance over Mussolini, he agreed once more that relations with Hitler should be developed. [245] Over the Roosevelt problem, he and Cranborne had got their way.

The disagreement then was a continuation of differences of opinion about Roosevelt's interventions in general. Eden and Chamberlain agreed that American involvement was desirable and recognised that it would be reluctant. [246] But where Eden found the few steps Roosevelt had taken 'the most important thing that had happened for years', [247] Chamberlain found American policy 'incredibly slow', even in the Far East. [248]

Roosevelt wanted to resist Japanese expansion, but American opinion did not. Therefore, he had to move cautiously. He did not move cautiously enough. [249] In the Cabinet it was well understood that this was so and that action might not be forthcoming. [250] It was also understood (by Eden as well as Chamberlain) that sanctions could not be enforced without the risk of war [251] and should not be imposed unless 'the United States and the other signatories of the China Treaty' agreed to support them 'by the use of force if need be'. [252]

Chamberlain had learned 'from experience' that the chief effect of Roosevelt's interventions had been that Britain bore 'the blame and the odium' while Japan was driven towards Italy and Germany. This made him cautious in public and much more pacific than he felt. Even when hoping for a 'steadying influence' from an Anglo-American demonstration of force after the *Panay* incident in late 1937, he did not believe that the United States would make one. His doubts survived the American naval mission to Britain in the New Year. [253]

By the Labour leaders and the League of Nations Union, on the other hand, every attempt to edge the American public towards recognising the danger was interpreted as support for sanctions and every hint at American action against Japan interpreted as a challenge to the British failure to resist dictators. It was Eden's sensitiveness in these directions which determined his response to Chamberlain's treatment of the Roosevelt 'initiative'.

This began in January 1938 when Roosevelt asked the ambassador in Washington to find out whether the Cabinet would welcome a small-power conference to discuss the world situation and define possible areas of agreement about arms limitation, access to raw materials and the laws-of-war aspects of international tension.

This was intended to look like a contribution to appeasement. When Chamberlain replied (while Eden was abroad), he so much emphasised the importance of his own negotiations that Roosevelt was put off. [254] When Eden returned, he treated it as so much the most important step that had been taken for a long time that he raised strong objections to Chamberlain's failure to respond gracefully.

Chamberlain described the initiative as a 'preposterous effusion'. His judgment was confirmed, as he believed, by the embassy in Washington, despite Eden's attempts at concealment. He gave way after the event, when Eden insisted on the question being taken to the Cabinet Committee. [255]

Eden and his entourage misunderstood Chamberlain's opinions and made the wrong accusations. The accused him, for example, of being anti-American (which was only true economically). But they did not make the serious point that he was over-optimistic. They also thought that he allowed Hoare and Simon to flatter him where he seems to have been much less dependent on his intimates than Eden on his. The policy differences they discerned certainly existed. But it is difficult to avoid the feeling that their real objection was that Chamberlain was undervaluing the Foreign Office and was leading the Conservative party. [256]

Although, then, policy was a cause of disagreement, it is difficult to see it as the only cause of resignation. Eden had not only got his way in January; by the time he resigned on February 20, Chamberlain had (perhaps disingenuously) bridged the gap by accepting his formula about volunteers. [257]

Halifax and others offered this as a basis for agreement, but Eden refused to be trapped. It is not clear how far he was thinking about the Cadman report [258] or the Ipswich by-election of February 11 [259] (when a boyhood friend of Crookshank and Macmillan could not save a Conservative seat, despite his obvious ability). Nor is it clear to what extent he was tired and ill, [260] hoping for other resignations or trying to catch up with that liberal stage-army of the good of which his 'World Free From Fear' had become a symbol. [261] What is clear is that six years in office were ending in ignominy (in Austria) when resignation enabled him to turn an unsuccessful stewardship into a claim to the Prime Ministership when Chamberlain retired.

6

CHAMBERLAIN AND HITLER

'Czechoslovakian rule in the Sudeten areas for the last twenty years has been marked by tactlessness, intolerance and discrimination'.
Runciman to Chamberlain, September 21 1938 PREM 1/266A

'Neville annoys me by mouthing the arguments of complete pacifism while piling up armaments'.
Attlee to Tom Attlee, February 22 1939

'The principal trouble, of course, remains that we cannot possibly tell... what is going on inside the brains of the one man who matters'.
Halifax to Runciman, September 6 1938, FO 800/309

Chamberlain did not try to get rid of Eden and Cranborne, but he felt a great sense of relief at their going.[1] Now that they had gone, the Foreign Office could be run as he wanted it run, secure in the knowledge that Halifax and Butler[2] were enthusiastic proponents of his own point of view who would be less sensitive to Opposition opinion and more willing to take the steps needed 'to avoid another Great War'. In particular they would help him to rid himself of 'Collective Security' of which Eden had been the symbol[3] and Chamberlain's attack on which was thought of by those who heard it in the House of Commons to be 'a scrapping of the ideas which had been built up since the war' and a reversion to 'good old Tory doctrines'.[4]

In this, those who heard him were mistaken. In preferring 'national strength' to an 'international police force' (which previously he had wanted) Chamberlain took a politician's view of Tory opinion. Though willing to use them as threats he took a moralistic attitude towards 'power politics'. He had two views about 'alliances' and had made it his chief object in 1937 to break up the ideological alliance by which he was confronted.

Chamberlain was innocently jealous of the contrast between democracies which made governments 'lay their cards on the table' and dictatorships which would 'keep them in their hands'.[5] But he had no admiration for dictators in general or for Hitler and Mussolini in particular; he hovered between believing that Russia had shown her strength in Spain and that she had been weakened by the purges. He was anti-Bolshevik. But he had as little desire to join the anti-Comintern pact as to 'defend democracy' against 'the dictators'. He thought ideological conflict dangerous because it would push Britain into alliance with France and Russia and cement the connection between Germany, Italy and Japan.[6]

By the beginning of 1938, he had acquired two leading ideas — that the division of the world into ideological *blocs* would damage Britain and the Empire and that Britain could not resist attack in both Europe and the Far East. He had reached three conclusions — that France was politically unreliable, that the United States would do nothing anywhere and that the national interest required a policy of positive, pacific, international amicability. He had a conviction of the connection between the maintenance of peace on the one hand and the preservation of the Empire on the other, and a calculation that a national interest was involved in the systematic attempt to prevent the division of the world on ideological lines.

By this time, moreover, the defence review of late 1937 had abandoned bomber parity and the bomber deterrent (as providing no guarantee against a knockout blow) and had decided that the main effort should be defensive. With an increased fighter programme, it came to be assumed that, given time, Germany would be unable to win an air offensive against Great Britain.

These emphases were designed to ensure that, if war came, it would last long enough to allow naval blockade to reveal the weakness of the German economy. It was because economic weakness would prevent Hitler winning and because the 'staying power' of the British economy was an 'essential element in our strength' that rigid control was exercised over every form of military expenditure.[7]

For foreign policy this provided an assurance, quite different from the bomber deterrent, that a German victory would be impossible once the air programme had been completed. It proved that a German war could be won if delayed long enough. It convinced Chamberlain that Hitler and the German General Staff knew this as well as he did and, unless tempted by an early knockout blow, would do their best to avoid it.

Chamberlain was worried by the 'knockout blow' and allowed it to affect him at points of crisis — to some extent, probably, at Munich, more notably during the occupation of Memel. In general, however, he did not believe until early 1939 that Hitler was even thinking of attacking Britain and, by the middle of the year, believed that a knockout blow could no longer be effective. Although, therefore, defence expenditure was controlled, he thought that he and Hitler understood that *he* would shortly have the advantage. It was the desirability, from a British point of view, of avoiding war in the near future and the hope that Hitler would understand the danger he would face in going to war at all (unless he could win quickly) that formed the strategic basis from which he operated in the next eighteen months.

How far, and at what point, Chamberlain believed that he had a mission to prevent war, how far, and at what point, his policy was tactical, must be matters for guesswork. What cannot reasonably be doubted is that he brought a consistent range of thought and calculation to the shocks and surprises he experienced in the months which followed the Anschluss.

One reason Chamberlain had given for pressing the Italian negotiations in mid-February was that they provided the only hope for preserving 'the last shreds of Austrian independence'.[8] But neither he nor Halifax regarded Austria as more than a counter for negotiating the general agreement which Halifax's visit had hinted at. On Eden's advice, and after he resigned, there had been caution about warning Hitler in case that forced him to turn Schuschnigg's capitulation into an Anschluss.[9] It did not hold up the decision to present proposals for settling the colonial question. [10]

Like Eden, Halifax and Chamberlain believed that the Austrians could not resist and should not be helped if they did. They took differing views of Mussolini but agreed that he was the person whose reaction mattered most. Schuschnigg's decision to hold a plebiscite was treated as a mistake, about which they had not been consulted and for which they felt no responsibility. [11] But, since they were assuming that the Berchtesgaden meeting was itself the *coup*, they were greatly shaken a month later by news of the occupation.

This arrived in the middle of a luncheon at which Chamberlain was telling Ribbentrop about his plans for improving relations. His reaction was that the Italian conversations should have started earlier, that Roosevelt would have looked foolish if his 'initiative' had been pursued and that what Hitler had done was a 'typical illustration of Power politics'. [12] He decided to 'announce some increase or acceleration in air and anti-aircraft rearmament' and to stop the conversations which Henderson had started ten days earlier. [13]

His aim in doing this was not, however, to abandon the conversations but to prevent a *coup* in Czechoslovakia so that they could eventually be resumed. [14] It was in order to keep open relations with Hitler and to reassure him that he thought of giving the Czechs a guarantee or promising to support France if France went to war in honouring the Czech Treaty. [15]

The Czech guarantee was dropped because nothing could be done to make it effective. So also was alliance with France and the Little Entente in deference to the view that it would extend commitments while adding nothing to strength. An alliance with Russia was rejected on the ground that Russia's chief aim was to get Britain involved in fighting her war against Hitler for her. [16]

These produced subsidiary decisions which constituted policy for the future. There was an attempt to persuade Yugoslavia and Turkey to anticipate anything Hitler might do in the Balkans. There was the agreement with Italy which, though emasculated in order to forestall criticism in Parliament, was effected in April to the accompaniment of a warm exchange of letters with Mussolini. [17]

From Chamberlain's point of view, the Anschluss was important as confirming that no country could 'appeal to Collective Security with any prospect of success'. [18] While cooperation with France in Locarno remained the kernel, there was, however, to be no 'alliance'. There was reluctance to underwrite French commitments [19] and a refusal to be involved in central Europe, where it was as desirable to take the Sudeten question out of Anglo-French relations with Germany as it was to take the Abyssinian question out of relations with Italy. [20]

Three decisions, therefore, were made. One, approved by the Cabinet on March 23 and announced by Chamberlain in Parliament next day, [21] was that no guarantee could be given of British support for a French attack on Germany if Germany attacked Czechoslovakia. The second, announced at the same time, was that, though there could be no guarantee that support would be given, it nevertheless might be. The third was that the Czech government should be 'induced...to apply themselves' to producing a Sudeten settlement [22] so that 'it might presently be possible to start again in Berlin'. [23]

In the next two months, this combination of positions was designed to show the Germans that 'they could get say, 75% of what...they wanted by peaceful means', to ensure that the French pressed Benes as the price for British support in war and 'to keep Hitler guessing' so that the reasonable assumption that Britain would not fight for Czechoslovakia could not be turned into the presumption — fatal to *détente* — that he could use force without Britain doing so too. [24]

At Anglo-French meetings in London in April, Chamberlain intended to explain that Britain's land forces were so small that military staff talks were unnecessary. [25] Eventually, he decided that talks were the best guarantee of French pressure being brought to bear on Benes. [26] But it was made clear that, though the Sudeten Germans must be satisfied 'while this was still possible', Britain would express no opinion about the terms and give no guarantee of action in the event of breakdown. [27]

It was in this frame of mind that he responded to the war scare of May 21 when troop movements on the Czech frontier and expectations of a German invasion were reported throughout the world. Believing these reports, he acted out the scenario that had been anticipated in March. Benes was told to be generous, the French to be careful and Hitler given the impression that a French response to a German invasion might involve Britain in open intervention. [28] This was, in fact, a bluff, [29] which the Germans could not call since they had not been preparing to invade and could neither make, nor halt, an invasion. Their denials, when made public, were

not believed. When no invasion took place, Chamberlain saw
how easy it was to restrain Hitler when the League was not
involved. [30]

His conduct, thereafter, was overshadowed by the twin
beliefs that British firmness had worked and that the Franco-
Czech alliance had nearly caused a war. [31] British pressure on
Benes, and the assurances Hitler was given that pressure was
being brought, were coloured by 'success', by the 'nasty
shock' supposed to have been given to the Rome-Berlin Axis
by the Italian treaty and by the Anglo-Turkish financial
agreement which proved that 'in central and south-eastern
Europe...Hitler had missed the bus'. [32]

It was from a position of 'strength', therefore, that Chamberlain took pains to prevent marginal difficulties dominating
the situation. He imposed iron control on anything likely to
produce conflict with Japan and persuaded the Cabinet to
reject Halifax's proposal to make a loan to China. [33] He for-
bade any sort of intervention in Spain, even when British
ships were attacked, [34] and did his best to damp down both
the Foreign Office and the French desire to retaliate whenever Mussolini behaved disagreeably. [35]

About Germany he had no illusions; any that had survived
the Anschluss were dispelled by May 21 which proved that
Germans were 'bullies by nature' and would keep Europe in a
state of 'chronic anxiety' so long as they had the advantage. [36] *Détente* continued to be the objective (and one which
the German people wanted [37]), but it did not seem to be
urgent so long as Britain had a long way to go militarily.

Chamberlain, therefore, behaved cautiously. He mentioned
the resumption of negotiations at a press conference in
June [38] and to the German Ambassador in July. But he did
not take the initiative. Contact, begun as a German initiative, [39] culminated in a visit by one of Hitler's staff and a
proposal that Goering should come to London. Chamberlain
'welcome[ed]' the idea of a Goering visit provided there was
'adequate preparation' and a 'favourable...atmosphere...parti-
cularly in connection with Czechoslovakia'. But he emphasised that no amount of provocation would justify the use of
force [40] and erected a peaceful settlement of the Sudeten
question into a hurdle before a general negotiation could
begin. [41]

Since Chamberlain and Halifax were not pressing, there was no real motion in the summer of 1938. May 21, however, had nearly produced a 'wholly unprofitable' war[42] which might well happen unless the Sudeten question was settled. This convinced them that something must be done. They thought of three possibilities.

The first[43] was that Benes should couple the best terms he could offer the Sudeten Germans with a choice between an immediate plebiscite and a plebiscite about joining Germany after the new offer had been in operation for five years. The second, which Chamberlain preferred, was to help France abandon the Czech treaty by giving Czechoslovakia a Swiss status under international guarantee, provided the Sudeten Germans could be made a 'contented people' within the existing state.[44]

The third was to send a Foreign Office official[45] to Prague and Berlin. When he decided that the Germans were worried primarily by 'encirclement', an opportunity was discerned to bring together their fears with the French desire to renounce the treaty. It then became the object of policy to find ways of doing this, while repeating warnings about the need to produce concessions striking enough to satisfy Henlein.[46]

When Benes seemed to be stalling and Hitler to be thinking of a *coup*[47], this merged into the plan, conceived by Chamberlain in the last week in June, that an independent arbitrator might work for agreement between the Czechs and the Sudeten Germans. This was the mission that Runciman accepted, reluctantly and without expectation and agreed to formally when the Benes/Henlein talks broke down in late July.[48]

By the time Runciman arrived in Prague with a British staff on August 3, it seemed so likely that the German government would be unco-operative that Chamberlain and Halifax wrote Hitler a letter.[49] After repeating that a Czech settlement was a pre-requisite to negotiation, this repeated the formula which had been used in May — that his present attitude might involve all the Great Powers in war.[50]

When Hitler side-stepped by getting Ribbentrop to answer,[51] there was a plan to send a special ambassador to Berlin with proposals for a settlement.[52] By August 30 this

had developed into the idea that Chamberlain should visit
Hitler.

Chamberlain's difficulty was that he had no feel for the
situation in the German Government. [53] Hitler had little contact with ministers and officials, imposed secrecy on his staff
and 'lived in a state of exaltation' unusual among English
politicians. He was almost certainly at least 'half mad', but
'the fate of hundreds of millions depend[ed] on him, [54] so it
was as essential to understand him as it was difficult to do so
without meeting him.

It was essential, in particular, to know whether he was
determined to invade Czechoslovakia. Chamberlain had
floods of Intelligence reports and a good deal of unsolicited
warning from anti-Nazis on the army staffs. But he could not
evaluate the reports, and he compared the anti-Nazis to the
Jacobites. Invasion, however, would make *détente* impossible
so he needed to know — what he could not know indirectly
— whether invasion was intended. As it came to seem likely
in the last week of August that invasion *was* intended, pre-
vention became the essence of policy. [55]

In order that the policy should have a chance, it was necessary that Hitler should do nothing to stop it. This made the
'warning' of March 24 important. It was repeated by Simon
at Lanark on August 27. [56] It was the main subject when
Chamberlain recalled ministers from their holidays three days
later. [57]

The problem, as he and Halifax explained it, was to evaluate Henderson's analysis of Hitler's intentions. [58] They pointed out how difficult this was. They laid out what they knew
about opinion in the German army and recorded the claims
registered by Churchill, Boothby and the German opposition
that an early statement of intention to declare war in the
event of invasion would enable Goerdeler and the generals to
get rid of Hitler. [59]

Since they did not feel sure that the Goerdeler plot existed, their advice was that a statement of this sort would be
resented in Britain and the Empire and, if carried into effect
after an invasion, would neither prevent Czechoslovakia being
overrun nor lead to a restoration of the 'existing' Czech state
after an Anglo-French victory. Though there was more to the
problem than the continued existence of Czechoslovakia,

they doubted 'whether it [was] justifiable to fight a certain war now in order to forestall a possible war later'.[60] The practical question therefore was whether the Simon warning was 'innocent' enough to puzzle Hitler, while 'strengthen[ing] the hands of the generals' in case the reports about them were 'really true'.[61]

About the warning they made no false claims. Its sole purpose was to keep Hitler guessing, but if he had already decided to invade, then it was redundant. It was only if his mind was not made up that it might be effective. It was on this assumption that they urged the importance of handling him more gingerly than in May and persuaded the Cabinet to agree that no further warnings should be given for the moment.[62]

What Chamberlain was doing between August 21 and September 14 was to prevent a deteriorating situation deteriorating so far that he could play no part in it, and to prevent action likely to 'bring about exactly what we want to avoid — namely Hitler, faced with no choice save war or humiliation', invading Czechoslovakia or mounting an air attack on London and Paris.[63] The refusal to mobilise the fleet, evacuate the cities or give commitments to the French,[64] and his reluctance to repeat the warning, all reflected a determination to persist until he had got beyond Henderson, Ribbentrop, the Foreign Office and the German Foreign Ministry to real knowledge of Hitler.[65]

The idea of a visit was conceived of as a *coup* which needed surprise in order to be effective. It was not proceeded with at the end of August because invasion did not seem to be imminent. In early September Chamberlain was not sure that it would be needed. It was only when the Sudeten Germans threatened to break off negotiations and Intelligence sources predicted an early invasion that the Cabinet Committee decided (late on the evening of September 13) that it should be put into operation.[66]

Between conceiving the visit and deciding to propose it, Chamberlain had tried it on Henderson, Cadogan, Vansittart, Wood, Runciman, Wilson and MacDonald in addition to Simon, Hoare and Halifax (the members of the Cabinet Committee). All had been told to keep it secret from the Cabinet, which knew nothing as a body until the morning of September 14, after Henderson had been told to ask whether Hitler would see Chamberlain if he came. [67]

In the first week of September Halifax had come to the conclusion that the Sudeten situation could not be controlled by any of the proposals which had been made so far. When the Sudeten Germans twice rejected Benes's proposals, [68] he decided that they might have to be given the chance to become German citizens. He also decided that Britain might propose a rectification of frontiers and offer a loan to facilitate the transfer of populations if that seemed likely to be helpful. [69]

The idea of transferring Czech territory had been considered after the Anschluss and mentioned by Chamberlain at a press conference before the May crisis. [70] It had not, however, become part of policy. In deciding that it should be, Halifax may have been thinking about 'self-determination' as a genuine solution; he may have wanted the Czechs to accept it in order to ensure that the Cabinet could not abandon them. [71] Whatever his reason, it was at this point that a shift occurred from the federal and cantonal aspects of a solution (which Benes had virtually accepted [72]) to the idea of detaching the Sudeten areas, which Hitler did not raise until his speech at the Nuremberg Rally on September 12.

This speech hinted at it and Chamberlain picked up the hint. [73] When the Cabinet Committee approved Plan Z next day, it agreed that, though a plebiscite should not be discussed unless Hitler mentioned it first, it would be wrong to 'involve the country in war' if 'a plebiscite on fair and reasonable terms' was the alternative. [74] At the Cabinet meeting next morning one of Chamberlain's chief objects was to establish that a transfer of Czech territory was not to be ruled out of consideration. [75]

In the fortnight before he went to Germany, Chamberlain had thought a great deal about what to say when he got there. He hoped that Hitler would be flattered by the visit and moved by the prospect of making 'Germany and England the twin pillars of European peace and barriers against Communism'. Having held out 'the inducement...of...better relations', he proposed to say that these would only be possible if the Sudeten question was settled first. When Hitler replied with his customary 'tirade' against Benes, he would then suggest that the Czechs and Sudeten Germans should 'put their views before Lord Runciman — who had reluctantly agreed — and 'accept [him] as the final arbitrator' with an 'international body to supervise any agreement that was reached'. It would only be if Hitler asked for a plebiscite that he proposed to discuss dismembering Czechoslovakia and only if dismemberment seemed likely to occur that he would mention a guarantee. [76]

The Cabinet of September 14 congratulated Chamberlain on the decision to fly to Germany. The plebiscite, however, aroused suspicion, and seven ministers expressed doubts. [77] Four or five supported the proposals as a whole, but there was general agreement that the conditions must be defined carefully and that the ideal solution was the plan Halifax had mentioned in May, and which Simon now made his own, for the Sudeten Germans to have five years autonomy within Czechoslovakia before a plebiscite took place. [78]

Chamberlain left for Berchtesgaden on the morning of the 15th, intending, when he got there, to talk about *détente* in the future and to put off the Czechoslovak discussion until next morning. On arrival, he began according to plan but found that Hitler put the Sudeten problem so urgently that he had to talk about it straight away. [79]

Chamberlain's account of the preliminaries was as follows. Adopting the attitude of a 'practical man' who had to take account of British opinion, he began by saying:

Since I have been Prime Minister I have been anxious to improve Anglo-German relations...but during the last few weeks events have occurred which aroused such feelings of apprehension that I saw the whole prospect of a renewal of these Anglo-German relations disappearing... Many people in England thought that [the Führer] was not sincere, that his words in respect to Peace were only words and that he had behind them a plan which was not at all consistent with what he was saying... I do not myself accept that view but I welcome an opportunity of a frank talk with him to see where he stood.

He then said that however desirable it might be to explore one another's views on general questions between the two countries, there was a question which was very urgent and could not wait. According to today's information three hundred Sudeten Germans had been killed and many more injured and that produced a situation which demanded instant solution, so that it would be better if we started at once on it to which I said 'All right: go ahead'.

The Führer then began a long account of what he had done; how he had made an agreement with Poland which finally settled territorial questions so far as himself and Poland were concerned... He had publicly disclaimed any idea of attempting to recover Alsace and Lorraine. As far as we were concerned he had made a naval treaty under which he had limited his strength in regard to ours but that treaty was made on the understanding that we would not go to war...and if people talked as they had been doing lately of the possibility of England coming into a war against Germany, then it would be better to denounce that treaty.

When I reached that point in the translation...I interrupted and said 'Does the Führer mean that he might denounce the treaty before we go to war?' He replied that, unless there was an understanding on both sides that in no circumstances would we go to war with one another, in his opinion it would be impossible that the treaty could stand... He said that from his youth he had been obsessed with the racial theory and he felt that Germans were one, but he had drawn a distinction between the possible and the impossible and he recognised that there are places where Germans are where it is impossible to bring them into the Reich; but where they are on the frontier it is a different matter, and he is himself concerned with ten millions of Germans, three millions of whom are in Czechoslovakia. He felt therefore that those Germans should come into the Reich. They wanted to and he was determined that they should come in. Apart from what he said, there was no other place where frontiers made any territorial difficulty. He spoke of Memel and said as far as that was concerned he was glad to leave that as it was as long as the Lithuanians followed the Memel Statute. It was impossible that Czechoslovakia should remain like a spearhead in the side of Germany.

So I said 'Hold on a minute; there is one point on which I want to be clear and I will explain why: you say that the three million Sudeten Germans must be included in the Reich; would you be satisfied with that and is there nothing more that you want? I ask because there are many people who think that is not all; that you wish to dismember Czechoslovakia'.

He then launched into a long speech: he was out for a racial unity and he did not want a lot of Czechs, all he wanted was Sudeten Germans. As regards the 'spearhead in his side'...he could not feel he had got rid of the danger until the abolition of the treaty between Russia and Czechoslovakia.

I said 'Supposing it were modified, so that Czechoslovakia were no longer bound to go to the assistance of Russia if Russia were attacked, and on the other hand Czechoslovakia were debarred from giving asylum to Russian forces in her aerodromes or elsewhere; would that remove your difficulty?'

To that his reply was that if the Sudeten Germans came into the Reich, then the Hungarian minority would secede, the Polish minority would secede, the Slovak minority would secede — and what was left would be so small that he would not bother his head about it.

I then said: 'Well, you have stated pretty clearly what your view is and I will restate it to show that I have got it right'. I did so and he confirmed it.

I said that...I saw considerable practical difficulties about the secession of the Sudeten Germans... Even if, for example, the areas containing 80% of Germans were taken into the Reich, there would still be a very considerable number of Germans left outside, and moreover there would be a considerable number of Czechoslovakians in the German area and, therefore, it looks as though, for a solution of the problem in your sense, it would require more than a change of boundaries; it would also require a transfer of population: have you any ideas about that?

He said that percentages of Germans could not come into this. Where the Germans are in a majority, the territory ought to pass to Germany, and for the rest, the Czechoslovaks in German Sudetenland should be allowed to pass out and the Germans in the other parts to pass in; or alternatively each minority could remain where it was under suitable safeguards.

I was then going on to some further inquiries on the subject when he said 'But all this seems to be academic; I want to get down to realities. Three hundred Sudetens have been killed and things of that kind cannot go on; the thing has got to be settled at once:... I am determined to settle it and settle it soon and I am prepared to risk a world war rather than allow this to drag on'.

To that I replied 'If the Führer is determined to settle this matter by force without waiting even for a discussion between ourselves to take place, what did he let me come here for? I have wasted my time. If on the other hand he is prepared to discuss the question with me as to whether he is prepared to find a peaceful solution, why does he not make a joint appeal, to be signed by both of us perhaps, to both sides to refrain from incidents and to keep quiet while we have time to converse'.

He replied 'I could not appeal to the victims: how could I accuse them while they are flocking across the German frontier because their homes and villages are being burnt. It is imposssible for me to do that because the German people would not understand me and I cannot do it'.

I said 'I do not see then how we can make any further progress unless the Führer has got anything further to suggest'. [80]

This brought discussion to the crux — whether Britain would agree to...secession...and an alteration in the present constitution of Czechoslovakia...[for as Hitler explained] if Britain could assent to a separation of this kind and this could be announced to the world as a fundamental decision of principle, then, no doubt, it would be possible by this means to bring about a large degree of pacification in the regions in question. [81]

According to his own accounts, Chamberlain's reply was that, so far as he personally was concerned, he 'didn't care two hoots whether the Sudetens were in the Reich or out of it'. He added, however, that he 'was not in a position to give...an assurance on behalf of the British Government who had not authorised [him] to say anything of the kind, and moreover [he] could not possibly make such a declaration without consulting the French Government and Lord Runciman'. [82] According to the minute of Schmidt, Hitler's interpreter, the only other person present, Chamberlain stated that 'he...personally...recognised the principle of the detachment of the Sudeten areas' but saw 'difficulty...in the implementation of this principle' and 'in these circumstances...wished to return to England' in order to consult Runciman and the French and 'to report to the Government and secure their approval of his personal attitude'. [83]

Neither Hitler nor Chamberlain mentioned a plebiscite, but Chamberlain assured the Cabinet that that was what Hitler meant by secession and self-determination. [84] He believed, therefore, that Hitler was asking for something he had already persuaded the Cabinet was possible and had promised in return, 'even at the risk of this being interpreted as weakness, as perhaps the British Press would interpret it', that he 'would not give the order to set the military machine in motion during the next few days, unless a completely impossible situation should arise'. [85]

Armed with his first success in keeping Hitler's triggerfinger still, Chamberlain returned to England next day prepared to sell his opinion to the Foreign Policy Committee, the Cabinet and the French government. Runciman was brought home from Czechoslovakia. He attended the Cabinet Committee on the evening of the 16th and the Cabinet on the morning of the 17th. At the Committee he reported Benes as telling him that the Czech army would prevent a plebiscite being held and himself as telling Benes that he had 'done more than anybody else to sacrifice his country'. [86] After giving the Cabinet a further criticism of Benes, he told it that none of the plans he had considered stood any chance of acceptance. 'Something' nevertheless 'would have to be done' and 'the only solution' was 'a plebiscite'. [87]

At the Cabinet Committee on the 16th Chamberlain was 'satisfied that it was impossible to go to war to prevent self-determination' and that 'there was no longer any solution except by self-determination'. [88] On some parts of the Cabinet next morning he left a 'painful impression' of having been 'blackmailed', of having 'failed to mention' the 'elaborate schemes' he had taken with him and that he had been 'made to listen to a boast that the German military machine was a terrible instrument'. [89] This did not stop ministers accepting his proposals in principle. But it produced a feeling that the method of effecting self-determination and the nature of the international guarantee would be crucial, and that Hitler must not seem to be getting 'everything he wanted' without 'our' getting 'some concession' in return. [90] It was stated more than once that 'if we reached a settlement which looks like a surrender to force, it was doubtful whether the Government would carry the policy in the House of Commons or... the country'. [91]

At this stage this had no effect on Chamberlain who refused to take back preliminary conditions since, if he did, Hitler would simply invade. When, however, he promised to ask Hitler to behave reasonably once self-determination had been approved, it turned out that even those whose misgivings were strongest about the method would not say that they disagreed with the policy. The result was that he received approval in principle on the understanding that formal agreement would be given after the visit Daladier and Bonnet had proposed for next day.

The uncertainties of the French government belong to the politics of France. French reluctance to face war, however, and French suspicion of the Berchtesgaden visit were turned at meetings on September 18 into support for an initiative which Daladier and Bonnet hoped might save them from obligations they thought it impossible to fulfil. In this they eased Chamberlain's task with the Cabinet.

They did this in two ways. In the first place, because their reluctance weakened any British obligation to fight if Hitler invaded Czechoslovakia. And, secondly, because, if they were reluctant, there was no reason why Benes should receive special consideration.

Benes was France's ally, not Britain's, but the obstacle he presented arose from the dangers the French government would face in France if it took the lead in forcing him to 'capitulate'. French ministers were better placed, and more willing, to follow a British lead than to propose one of their own; they allowed Chamberlain to press the Cabinet to agree to the Czechs being made to do what they had been slow to do so far.

Nor is there reason to doubt that British participation in a guarantee to Czechoslovakia and willingness to associate with Russia in giving it — both major departures in policy — were thought of as temporary aids in solving the immediate problem which would provide bargaining counters in subsequent negotiation with Germany and be abandoned once *détente* had been achieved.

The possibility of guaranteeing a neutralised Czechoslovakia had been discussed by the Cabinet before the Anglo-French meetings. At long meetings on the 18th, the Cabinet Committee and the French agreed to tell the Czechs that, unless they preferred a plebiscite, an International Commission should decide which areas were to be transferred to Germany. Provided this was done peacefully and according to an agreed schedule, Britain would provide a loan to ease the transfer of populations, and the new state would receive a guarantee 'against aggression' from France, Russia, Britain and (possibly) Germany. [92]

These 'Anglo-French proposals' were the detailed formulation of policy for which the Cabinet had asked. After being approved in Paris, they were sent to Prague next day while the Cabinet was discussing them. [93]

The discussion of the 19th registered dislike of the guarantee (as a new entanglement) and acceptance of its inevitability, [94] along with a determination that it should bind the guarantors together but not separately and concern unprovoked aggression, not the preservation of a particular frontier. Though Chamberlain still refused to ask Hitler to define the conditions before self-determination was accepted, there was a wide measure of agreement about what the conditions ought to be. [95]

When the proposals were sent to Prague, the Czech government was asked to reply in time for Chamberlain to return to Germany on Wednesday. [96] Since it took a long time to make up its mind, Chamberlain's return was delayed. A negative reply arrived at 8 p.m. on Tuesday, accompanied by the British Minister's opinion that the Czechs would probably bow to an ultimatum. An ultimatum was then sent in the early hours of Wednesday morning after Halifax had come back to the Foreign Office at eleven o'clock at night to consult Chamberlain about it. By the time the Cabinet met at three o'clock on Wednesday afternoon, the Czechs had, 'sadly' and under pressure, 'accepted'. [97]

At the Cabinet on the 19th, Chamberlain had reacted stiffly to the suggestion that Britain should go to war if the Czechs decided that they would prefer to. [98] At the Cabinet Committee on the 21st, he refused to discuss the question but had to listen when told that the press and the public would expect him 'to show that he had obtained some concession from Herr Hitler'. [99] At the Cabinet that afternoon he promised to refer back or send for Halifax if Hitler wanted anything done about Hungarian or Polish Czechs, or objected to the Russians being associated with the guarantee. He also proposed that in the predominantly German parts of the Sudetenland, the Czech army and police should be replaced at once by units of the German army. [100]

This proposal, made deliberately and fudged only when opposed, was much what Hitler asked for next day. When ministers heard it they responded so sharply, and from so many angles, that Chamberlain was obliged to withdraw. He promised not to propose a German occupation in advance of a plebiscite or international control and not to accept it without consulting the Cabinet. He also agreed not to mention an international force unless Hitler claimed that the withdrawal of the Czech forces was insufficient. [101]

Chamberlain went back to Germany on the 22nd not expecting to succeed. [102] On arriving at Godesberg, he told Hitler that self-determination could be applied to 'all Germans in Czechoslovakia' and made 'practical proposals for putting [it] into effect'. After rejecting a plebiscite because 'it would mean...delay...and disorders', he explained that

the simplest method...would...be...to agree on a cession of territory by Czechoslovakia...There were no difficulties to be overcome in the cession to Germany of districts where there was a preponderant German majority. But in districts where there was a mixed population...the frontier could not be systematically laid down as a rigid line, but a commission must be set up [consisting of a German, a Czech and a neutral] and provided with guiding principles... As a guiding principle for the decision of the commission he proposed the establishment of a

given % of Germans in relation to the total population... In all districts
where the German population reached 80% the decision presented no
difficulty at all. Where, however, the proportion of Germans was
smaller an average figure must be taken as a guiding principle. He had in
mind 65%.

In addition to this major condition, Chamberlain made
suggestions about government property and the national
debt, the protection of minorities and enclaves and the guaranteeing of the new state.

Although...the Führer had told him in his first conversation at Berchtesgaden that, apart from the Sudeten German question, Germany would
make no further territorial demands, it could be understood if the
Czechoslovak government, after giving up part of their territory and the
fortifications situated within it, demanded a substitute for the security
which they had lost...He recalled that in their first conversation the
Führer had spoken of Czechoslovakia as a spearhead directed against
Germany's flank. The objections expressed by the Führer and the desire
of the Czech government...could be satisfied by replacing Czechoslovakia's existing treaty alliances [and] military obligations by a guarantee
of security against unprovoked agression. The British government were
prepared to join in an International guarantee against an unprovoked
attack on Czechoslovakia whereby this guarantee would replace existing
treaty alliances, involving military obligations.

Having thus discharged his duty to the Cabinet, Chamberlain found that Hitler had moved on. At Berchtesgaden, he
told him, 'he was naturally speaking in the first place for the
Germans'. But he sympathised with the other minorities and
could not guarantee the dismembered state until their claims
had been dealt with too. When Chamberlain pointed out that
he had confined himself to the Germans because that was
what Hitler had talked about, he was told that their problem
must be 'finally and completely solved by October 1'.

Hitler's conception of a solution — immediate occupation
of the whole of the disputed area and a plebiscite afterwards
— was more or less the proposal the Cabinet had turned down
the day before. Chamberlain, however, did not reject it. He
explained that 'he was being accused' at home of 'having...be-
trayed Czechoslovakia' and that the public would dislike a
plebiscite under military occupation. But he asked for a map
of the areas that Hitler wanted. After a certain amount of
grumbling, he went back to his hotel where he sat up with
Wilson for a good part of the night making up his mind what
to do. [103]

What he decided was to write Hitler a letter, offering to put his proposals to the Czechs but holding out no hope that they would be accepted. The letter repeated what he had said in conversation – that a plebiscite was unnecessary for the bulk of the areas of occupation, where both sides agreed on the size of the German population. But he was 'sure that an attempt to occupy forthwith by German troops areas which will become part of the Reich at once in principle and very shortly afterwards by formal delimitation, would be condemned as an unnecessary display of force' which the Czechs would 'order their forces to resist...in the event of German troops moving into the areas as you propose'. [104]

In the course of the letter Chamberlain suggested that the Czechs might be asked to allow the *Sudeten* Germans to take control of the areas that were to be evacuated. Hitler rejected this and, in paragraphs of his oldest propaganda, left no doubt that he would go to war if pressed to abandon his proposals.

When this reached Chamberlain on the afternoon of the 23rd, he was in a difficulty. He did not want to go home since this would leave Hitler free to invade, but he could not accept the proposals, nearly all of which the Cabinet had rejected. He decided, therefore, to ask for a written statement which he was given at the final meeting with Hitler late that evening. [105]

Before leaving his hotel to go to it, Chamberlain had a telephone call from Halifax about the need to end his visit on a note that the public would like. In the course of the meeting, he was told about Czech mobilisation, which he had asked Halifax to put off and which greatly shook him when he heard about it.

Chamberlain did not, however, speak as sharply as Halifax had suggested. When Hitler said that Czech mobilisation meant the end of negotiations, he described it as a 'defensive measure' and stated that the Czechs would not go back on their assurance about the 'cession of territory'. It was only when Hitler repeated that 'the memorandum was really his last word' that Chamberlain made it clear that 'there was no point in continuing the conversation'.

At this point it was kept going by the Germans who asked Chamberlain to read the memorandum. When Wilson and

Henderson had done so, he replied that it was an 'ultimatum' which, when published (as it would be, if sent to Prague), would 'have a very bad effect on opinion in Great Britian and other countries'. After getting one concession (a common date—October 1—for the transfer of territory), he failed to persuade Hitler to distinguish areas of obvious German predominance from areas where occupation should be deferred until after a plebiscite.

During this talk, Chamberlain became aware of a 'gulf' between Hitler's demands and the conditions the Cabinet would be likely to accept. He neither exceeded his authority nor suggested that the Cabinet would agree. Whenever he mentioned the Czechs or the French, however, he meant the Cabinet; it was the Cabinet he had to carry with him when he promised to forward the proposals to Prague. [106]

By the time he arrived in England — at lunch-time on the 24th — ministers were in a strong frame of mind. In his absence there had been four meetings of the Cabinet Committee and almost continuous consultation. There had been rebukes to Hungary and Poland for mentioning their minorities. There had been discussion of the procedure to be followed if negotiations broke down, and a decision that the best issue to stand on would be the German determination to use force. The occupation of Sudeten towns by the German Freikorps had become the occasion for reopening the decision that Czech mobilisation should be halted. The French government, when asked, had replied that it should begin. When Halifax telephoned Godesberg on the 22nd that the Committee agreed, he had been told that Chamberlain wanted to leave it till next morning before making up his mind.[107]

When the ministers met at three o'clock next day, Halifax reported both the French view and Chamberlain's request for a delay until Hitler had replied to the letter he had been sent that morning.[108] After the letter had been read out, it was decided to tell the Czechs that the ban had been withdrawn.[109]

At this meeting Simon was authorised to give background briefings to other ministers, which he did in a critical and belligerent frame of mind. He also carried a proposal to ask Chamberlain whether British mobilisation could begin [110]

By the time of the next meeting — at nine-thirty that

evening — Chamberlain had said that mobilisation must be put off until he returned. Halifax, however, had decided, after talking to Wilson on the telephone, that the visit 'should end on some simpler and stronger statement than...the Prime Minister seemed to contemplate'. He produced a draft which the Committee agreed should be sent to Chamberlain unciphered by telephone ·'in view of the urgency of getting a message to [him] before [he] left...for his final talks'. [111]

Chamberlain intended originally to fly on from Godesberg when the talks were over in order to tie up the plebiscite and transfer arrangements in Prague. In the new situation, he flew back to England to tie up the Cabinet.

On the morning of the 24th his last action in Godesberg was to transmit Hitler's proposals to the Czechs. [112] His first on returning to England in the afternoon was to tell the Cabinet Committee that 'there was not much difference between the Franco-British proposals and Herr Hitler's', that Hitler 'would fight...if [his terms] were rejected' and that, 'having once agreed to cession, the sooner the transfer took place the better'. [113]

At the Cabinet afterwards, he explained that Hitler 'had certain standards', which were 'racial', and that his object was 'racial unity, and not the domination of Europe'. He thought that Hitler 'trusted him' and would 'work with him', and 'would not deliberately deceive a man whom he respected'. In the course of the conversations he had left the impression of being 'extremely anxious to secure the friendship of Great Britain' and had said that 'if the present question could be settled peaceably, it might be a turning point in Anglo-German relations' and the end of his 'territorial ambitions'. There was every reason, Chamberlain thought, to assume that Hitler meant this, and 'it would be a great tragedy if we lost this opportunity of reaching an understanding'.

The only way of taking the opportunity, however, was to work on the lines of Hitler's proposals. These were not the proposals the Cabinet had accepted the previous Sunday. The differences were extensive but it was, Chamberlain suggested, an open question whether they 'justified us in going to war'. In pressing ministers to face the question, he urged them to bear three things in mind.

The first was that, if the Czechs decided to fight, 'there

would...in future...be no Czechoslavakia as it existed today
or...might exist if the...proposals were accepted'. The second
was that 'if we now possessed a superior force to Germany,
we should probably be considering these proposals in a very
different spirit'. The third was put as follows:

> This morning I...flew up the river over London. I imagined a German
> bomber flying the same course. I asked myself what degree of protec-
> tion we could afford to the thousands of homes...stretched out below...
> and...felt that we were in no position to justify waging a war today in
> order to prevent a war hereafter. [114]

Chamberlain probably believed these arguments. He was
also using them to edge the Cabinet towards the conclusion
that he wanted. In this he was by no means successful. He
established that a decision of principle would be made before
mobilisation was considered. But the Cabinet refused to be
rushed; when ministers returned after dinner to look at the
maps, they saw that he was proposing a 'capitulation'. That
evening at least six of them were thinking of resigning. [115]

At the Cabinet of the 24th it was decided to transmit
Hitler's proposals to the French government. [116] After this
had been done in the course of the day, Daladier and Bonnet
announced that they would be coming to England next
morning.

On the 25th there were two meetings of the Cabinet — one
all-day one and another at eleven-thirty at night after the
Cabinet Committee had met the French. At the first there
was widespread dissent, not only from the usual dissenters
but also from Hailsham, Hoare and Dorman-Smith who complained variously about the absence of a guarantee, the lack
of proposals for international control and the moral defeat
the Czechs would suffer if they had to accept. It also became
clear that Halifax saw 'a distinction...between orderly and
disorderly transfer' (with Hitler apparently 'dictating terms')
and wanted 'to lay the case before the Czechs' so that 'if they
rejected it [and] France...joined in...we should join in with
them'. This opened up a difference which survived Chamberlain's attempts to play it down. The Cabinet was held together only by deferring decisions until the French ministers
had arrived. [117]

At the Cabinet at eleven-thirty that night Chamberlain,
looking 'absolutely worn out', [118] stated that the Czechs

would almost certainly reject the German terms. After considerable disagreement, he prevented more by announcing that he was sending Wilson to Berlin. There he would see Hitler and tell him that, though a settlement could be reached by accepting a Three-Power Commission to supervise execution of the Anglo-French proposals, it 'seemed certain' that, 'if this appeal was refused, France would go to war... and...we should be drawn in'. [119]

This statement was an advance on anything that had been said so far. It was followed next morning by further Anglo-French meetings in the course of which Gamelin, who had been sent for the night before, explained in what sense he would attack Germany on land if she attacked Czechoslovakia. The Cabinet immediately afterwards decided that Parliament should be re-called and that mobilisation should begin whenever it seemed suitable. [120] At the Committee of Imperial Defence meeting on the afternoon of the 26th, 'dozens of decisions' were taken 'which would have taken months or years to get through in peacetime'. [121]

These events marked the end of the attempt to keep Hitler guessing. They left no room for doubt about Anglo-French intentions, even while leaving it uncertain how they would be carried out. There is no record of Chamberlain's opinion; there is evidence that he tried to soften their effect. A denial that the Czech rejection was the 'last word' [122] and the claim that Britain had not approved of Czech mobilisation [123] — both suggest a reliance on Hitler to keep control of the Cabinet and a wish to keep in touch in case Hitler needed help in getting off the hook his bluff had put him on. [124] This impression is strengthened by Sir Frederick Maurice's visit to Berlin on September 26, by a press communiqué appealing to Hitler to play the game [125] and by a request that he should ignore statements from anyone but Chamberlain, whose position should not be made difficult by 'false moves' likely to upset his control of British policy. [126]

When Wilson saw Hitler on the evening of the 26th, Hitler was rehearsing a speech and behaved so hysterically that Wilson did not transmit the warning. [127] The speech, on the other hand, left the impression that Hitler did not intend to go to war. Though the Cabinet Committee discussed mobilisation after reports had arrived, it decided that nothing should be done until the warning had been delivered. [128]

When Wilson saw Hitler again before flying back next morning, he delivered Chamberlain's letter. He also stated that, although the French had not said that they would attack Germany if Czechoslovakia was invaded, they would 'fulfil their treaty obligations' and, if this involved 'their forces...in hostilities against Germany, then...Britain would feel obliged to support them'. [129] At four-thirty that afternoon, the Cabinet Committee decided that the Fleet should be mobilised next morning. When Wilson told it that war could only be avoided by immediate evacuation of the undisputedly Sudeten territories, Chamberlain insisted on a Cabinet meeting to consider his opinion. [130]

The Cabinet at nine-thirty on the evening of the 27th saw the first rejection of a Chamberlain proposal since the Cabinet of September 21. And on this occasion as then, the proposal involved German occupation of parts of the Sudetenland before agreed procedures had been established. Chamberlain did not take the initiative in making the proposal. But he introduced Wilson's statement with a survey which showed that the Dominions wanted peace, that the Poles would support Hitler and that the Czechs were facing the fate of Abyssinia.

As an official, Wilson did not make proposals. But he put the position in the following way:

Assuming that Czechoslovakia would not accept Herr Hitler's terms, the only plan which could prevent the country from being overrun would be for the Czechoslovak Government to withdraw their troops...and allow Germany to occupy them without loss of life. When this had been done, the determination of the areas to be ceded permanently could be carried out by an international commission, with a plebiscite. If this happened, the Czechoslovak Government would have the benefit of Herr Hitler's public declaration that Sudeten German territory represented the last of his territorial aims in Europe. They would also have the Franco-British guarantee, as proposed in the joint Franco-British memorandum.

Chamberlain did not ask the Cabinet to press the Czechs to accept this. But he wanted it conveyed with a statement of the consequences if they refused. It was this proposal that Halifax squashed.

Halifax was unequivocal. What Chamberlain was asking involved 'so complete' a 'capitulation' that the Czechs could not be pressed to accept it. The House of Commons would not approve it and 'we could not adopt [it] unless we assured...Czechoslovakia', which he would find difficulty in doing, that the Germans would 'stop' where they were supposed to. [131]

Halifax was not thinking of resigning. But his statement was so formidable that Chamberlain at once offered to withdraw. When Simon supported Halifax, and no one disputed what they said, the plan was dropped.

This negative decision was a decision to go to war if Hitler fulfilled his promises. But war did not happen, because Chamberlain and Hitler took steps to prevent it.

In the course of the speech he was preparing when Wilson interrupted him on the 26th, and during their conversation next day, Hitler had said that he would not attack France or Britain and did not want them to attack him. This was interpreted as a wish to be rescued and was confirmed, as it seemed, by the friendly tone of his reply to the letter which Wilson had left. This reached Chamberlain during the Cabinet of the 27th. On the 28th he asked Mussolini to mediate at the same time as the French moved significantly towards Hitler's position about the area of occupation. In reply to Mussolini's request, Hitler sent invitations to a Four-Power Conference at Munich next day.

In the fortnight since his first visit to Germany, Chamberlain had not found it difficult to persuade the Cabinet to agree to a cession of Czech territory. After establishing that this was unavoidable, he had confined discussion to the small print. Godesberg, however, had provided the only procedural discussion he had had with Hitler which, though discouraging, he had no reason to believe could not be repeated more profitably. On the 28th Wilson told Ribbentrop's London representative that it was essential to remove the appearance of 'forceful occupation'. With this in mind Chamberlain went to Munich on the 29th.

In announcing the Conference, the German government had referred helpfully to the French proposals of September 28. When Hitler opened it, he wished to 'absolve' the occupation from the 'character of violence', proposed six, seven or ten days for evacuation to take place and offered to 'leave open the question whether Germany would...march into the territory in which the plebiscite was to be held...in order to conciliate public opinion in England and France'. This move towards the Anglo-French position was taken further in a detailed Italian plan, which had been drafted in Berlin.

This plan, to which all four governments agreed, went a long way to meet Anglo-French views about procedure. It provided for a ten-day occupation, an international commission to supervise the transfer of territory (together with a plebiscite in areas of greatest uncertainty) and a Four-Power guarantee of the dismembered state to replace the Franco-Czech Treaty once the Polish and Hungarian questions had been settled. [132] It was followed by a conversation in Hitler's flat at which Hitler and Chamberlain talked amicably about Spain, south-eastern Europe and disarmament, and signed a statement, which Chamberlain had brought with him, about Germany and Britain 'never go[ing] to war with one another again'. It was this *détente* afterthought — the real object of his visits — which made Chamberlain speak on his return to England of 'peace for our time'. [133]

Opinions differed about what Chamberlain had accomplished, but he did not think that he had failed. Nor had his actions been either weak or dishonourable. He had pushed himself to the limit of endurance, but in the end 'all the prayers of all the peoples of the world including Germany' had prevailed 'against the fanatical obstinacy of one man'.[134] Hitler had backed down. He had not gone to war. What he had gained was that Chamberlain thought he was entitled to. He had gained it in the shadow of a British undertaking to support France if Czechoslovakia was invaded and in the light of far-reaching decisions to contribute to an international guarantee to relieve France of her burden. An acute sense of national solidarity and relief at saving the world from war confirmed the belief that honour, duty and dramatic success 'had laid the foundations of a stable peace'. [135]

Nor had Chamberlain been subjected to criticism that mattered. He had had the usual business in the House of Commons. He had been attacked in the Opposition newspapers. He had heard Halifax and others dissent in Cabinet. But political criticism was what politicians were trained to ignore. He had no respect for the Opposition and disliked Attlee.

Halifax's dissent proved, what Eden had proved before, that the Foreign Office was unreliable. By the Right, by Garvinian Unionists, by the provincial press, by the Royal family, by innumerable functionaries and by Baldwin — his 'old friend and trusted colleague' — he had been supported. [136] Above all, he had sensed 'a gratitude' so 'universal' [137] as to leave no doubt about his standing as a public figure.

At this time Chamberlain talked chiefly to Wilson, from whom he received not criticism but confirmation. This would not have been a problem if Chamberlain's policies had been successful, but it led Wilson to write things which, with retrospective historians in mind, it would have been prudent to leave unwritten. Once it is assumed that the policy was wrong, Wilson's minutes and memoranda show not only that he connived at it, but that he was the genius behind it.

Yet the policy was a communal work. All Wilson did was advance towards the objectives which Chamberlain had chosen. In this he was acting as a chef de cabinet, not as a 'statesman in disguise'. There was an affinity of experience and competence between Chamberlain and himself, and a sympathy which enabled them to work together against the unscrupulousness of critics and the recalcitrance of events. If their touch had been lighter, or their success greater, they could easily have been 'Happy Warriors'.

Since what Chamberlain had done had been widely acclaimed, he felt free to criticise his critics and to pursue his policy despite their criticisms. He also felt it right to ignore disappointments like the Anglo-German newspaper war, [138] Hitler's failure to mention the joint statement in his first speech after Munich and 'horrif[ying]' things, like the pogroms, which showed that there was a 'fatality about Anglo-German relations which invariably blocks every effort to improve them'. [139]

A more formidable difficulty emerged with Intelligence reports which Halifax brought to an urgent session of the Foreign Policy Committee on November 14. These showed that Hitler was treating Munich as a defeat; they connected the Goering-Ribbentrop power-struggle with attempts to press Hitler to turn anti-Semitism to account by enlisting Arab (and Italian) aid in driving Britain out of the Middle

East. They were followed by hints that he was irritated by
Chamberlain's popularity in Germany, was allowing Ribbentrop to make up to the French in order to break up the
Anglo-French alliance and was thinking of invading the Low
Countries in order to mount an air attack on London. After
Schacht's dismissal, the German economy seemed so shaky
that he might do almost anything, including the constructing
of a Russo-German alliance, whether by overthrowing Stalin
or by doing a deal with him. [140]

Whether this was true (or, as Henderson thought, false)
and whether British Intelligence ever knew anything about
Hitler's court, is a question for its historian. Whether true or
false, it had an effect.

Chamberlain did not believe everything Halifax told him.
At the November meeting of the Cabinet Committee he quer-
ied his sources and questioned their reliability, and persuaded
the Committee to reject the demand to replace the voluntary
national register with a compulsory one. [141] In January, however, he took a lead in deciding that the invasion of Holland
would involve war against Germany and was led on into accepting a Continental Field Force and Anglo-French staff
talks on a scale and intimacy characteristic of an 'alliance'. [142]

Neither in November nor in January did Chamberlain deny
that his earlier expectations had been disappointed. This,
however, necessitated not only a heightened scale of military
preparations and the introduction of Chatfield to the Cabinet
but also a new attempt to move forward with Mussolini, who
had contrasted favourably with Hitler at Munich, had invited
Chamberlain to Italy and, after a 'heart-to-heart' talk,...
might...feel that our friendship would...help him...to escape
from the German toils'. [143]

The decision to go to Rome entailed a preliminary visit of
reassurance to Paris; [144] neither there at the end of November nor in Italy in January did Chamberlain receive the impression that France and Italy would be likely to co-operate
with one another. In Rome he talked about the benefits of
disarmament. [145] But Mussolini took none of the opportunities he was given 'to express his real feelings' about Hitler or
to facilitate talks with Germany. [146] The visit was followed
by Italian abuse of France so striking that Chamberlain had

to make a major declaration of Anglo-French co-operation on his return. [147]

These setbacks showed 'what fools' dictators were in their dealings with 'democratic states'. [148] But Chamberlain neither abandoned the hope for *détente* nor wavered in the desire to prevent the Foreign Office expressing its 'dislike...of the totalitarian states'. [149] Munich had made war less likely. [150] Doors should be kept open, therefore (and none slammed in response to the pogroms, which had had more effect in America than in England). [151] Neither should rearmament escalate so much as to make a political policy impossible. [152]

For Chamberlain's residual confidence, there were three reasons — the prospect of peace in Spain (as reducing Franco-Italian friction), [153] improvements in the Anglo-French defences which meant that the Germans could 'not make...such a mess of us' as at the time of Munich, [154] and the certainty, born of the family contribution to political science, that the Italian people wanted peace, 'loathed Germans' and could have an effect on Mussolini. [155] Even in relation to Germany, he read the reverse side of the coin Halifax presented, believing — what, according to Halifax's information, Hitler believed too — that he rivalled Hitler as a hero and emphasising not the 'jealousy' Hitler felt but the prospect of a second Munich provoking popular acclamation or military revolution in favour of himself as 'a nice, kind old gentleman who would not ever want to treat Germans roughly and unfairly'. [156]

About *détente*, Chamberlain was as inactive in the winter of 1938 as he had been in the early summer. He emphasised that Munich had been a matter of 'treaty revision' and that rearmament was not directed against Germany. [157] But he took no steps to resume talks. Until well into the New Year his policy consisted of decisions to step up wireless propaganda, [158] accelerate rearmament [159] and declare war if Germany invaded Holland. Such discussions as went on with the German government were almost exclusively economic and, though designed to lead to political discussions later, had no material effect on the situation.

In the summer Chamberlain had refused to take the initiative until war was imminent because he believed that Hitler might do so if he did not. Now there was much less reason to believe that Hitler would do anything unless he did some-

thing first. In order, therefore, to prevent Franco-Italian conflict doing what the Sudeten conflict had nearly done six
months before, he took the initiative himself. From a position of 'firmness' and 'strength', [160] he let Hitler know that
he would welcome a 'reassuring' statement about the situation. [161]

When this was given, [162] he called for deeds in addition to
words. [163] He then waited for a response, believing, as he
waited, that Hitler was 'searching round' to 'approach...us
without the danger of a snub'. [164] The response came in a
conciliatory passage which Henderson was told that Hitler
had inserted into a speech by the Duke of Coburg at an
Anglo-German Fellowship dinner in Berlin. When Chamberlain read it, he knew that his policy was alive. [165]

For the next three weeks he went about 'with a lighter
heart...than for many a long day'. Confirmed in his instincts,
he began to believe that 'we have at last got on top of the
dictators' [166] and looked forward to a period of 'disarmament' and 'gradually increasing peacefulness' in the course of
which, if 'given three or four more years, [he] might retire
with a quiet mind'. [167] At Blackburn on February 22 'the
reward of our foreign policy' was to be an 'increase of employment among our people'. [168] At a meeting of backbenchers on March 7, he was 'jolly...open and confiding' and saw
'the dangers of a German war' receding 'as our rearmament
expands'. [169] On the evening of March 9, he gave a talk to
Lobby correspondents in which he again mentioned disarmament. [170] When Czechoslovakia was dismembered during the
night of March 14, his reaction was not very much different.
This phase of thought ended with the talking-to he was given
by Halifax between the Cabinet meeting and his parliamentary statement on the 15th and the sternness and firmness of
his Birmingham speech two days later. [171]

PART II

THE OPPOSITION

7

THE LABOUR PARTY

'Only by a firm adherence to righteous principles sustained by all the necessary instrumentalities...can the dangers which close in so steadily upon us and upon the peace of Europe be warded off and overcome. That they can be overcome must be our hope and our faith.' Churchill in House of Commons, November 5 1936, *Hansard* (317) cols. 312—13

'It is a very melancholy thing to find that one is a true prophet. The Labour movement has warned the country ever since 1932 that yielding to aggression in one part of the world meant an increase of aggression in another. We are now paying in anxiety for a wrong foreign policy assumed since Labour was thrown out of office. I pray heaven that we may not have to pay in blood.' Attlee at Limehouse Town Hall, September 18 1938, *The Times*, September 19

'Our proposal is the building up of a League not only of peace and security, but on the principle of social justice. You cannot preach the brotherhood of man abroad and practise the Means Test at home.' Attlee at Old Kent Road Baths, March 7 1938, *Daily Herald*, March 8

Between 1936 and 1939 the Labour movement found that the positions it had reached doctrinally in the previous three years acquired practical point. This happened as foreign policy moved from being a matter of report to being a matter of threat, and hostility to dictators on ideological grounds was supplemented by hostility on behalf of the British Empire. Even though the threat to Empire was not as prominent as the threat to Collective Security, a propaganda was developed which identified the abandonment of the League and the threat to freedom with the tendency to put the interests of class and capital above the interests of Britain.

This composite position assumed that Britain had a rôle to play and that Labour had a part to play in choosing it. It presupposed the rejection of both 'Isolation' and 'Alliances' and of the 'white flag' the government had shown in face of Hitler and Mussolini.[1] In attempting to remove humiliation, it squared the circle between socialist internationalism on the one hand and the silent jingoism of the trade union movement on the other. As the existing foreign policy consensus was replaced by a nasty type of Capitalistic Toryism, it tried to establish that this could have been avoided if

Arthur Henderson had been at the Foreign Office to establish for the benefit of Germany, Italy and Japan that 'one could not buy peace in one corner of the globe by conniving at war in another'.[2]

The 'indivisibility of peace' was thus an important element in the conflict between the democratic states and the dictatorships which was occurring because world politics was a manifestation of Capitalism. This explained the failure to check Hitler. Since 'Imperialism' was a 'stage of Capitalism', it explained the failure to check Italy and was the reason for non-intervention in Spain. Chamberlain's pussyfooting with Japan where there ought to be a trade embargo and his attempts to get onto terms with Hitler and Mussolini made purposeful and self-conscious what the nature of Capitalism had made inevitable.[3]

Where, therefore, Chamberlain wanted to end the ideological conflict with which he thought he was confronted, the Labour leaders claimed that the 'there was a fundamental conflict between the Aggressors and the...Empire' which turned on an identification between the 'democratic principles' which lay at the root of British politics and the duty (or interest) to co-operate with democratic sentiment elsewhere.[4]

This was supplemented by Cockburn's invention of 'Clivedenism' which suggested a false identification between Chamberlain, Halifax, Garvin, Dawson and the Astor family on the one hand and Hitler and Mussolini on the other, and imputed a Conservative desire to thwart democracy by attempts at mutual co-operation. When taken up as a staple of anti-Chamberlain propaganda, this enabled recognition of the need for rearmament and a distinctive dislike of it to combine in withholding support from a government which 'had betrayed both democracy and the security of the British Commonwealth of Nations' and bore a 'terrific responsibility for the...cruel slaughter which is afflicting China, Abyssinia and Spain'.[5]

This did not mean that there could not be a settlement with Germany. Both publicly and in private, the Labour leaders said that the causes of war were economic and could be dealt with in part by a colonial settlement. They also said that they wanted a disarmament agreement because arma-

ments expenditure was depressing living standards throughout the world.[6] These, however, were long-term features of
Chamberlain's thinking. The fact that Chamberlain said them
made it difficult for the Labour leaders to repeat them, but
the fact that they believed them did not reduce the need to
say something which gave them the advantage. In early 1938
it seemed possible that the Eden problem would bring considerable advantage.

Before Eden resigned, he was beginning to be criticised;[7]
afterwards he was praised at the expense of Halifax — 'the
servile instrument of an ignorant and reckless Prime Minister'[8] who 'did not take his stand on a moral basis'[9] and had
'returned to the old policy of alliances'.[10] Since this was
'dividing the nation' and bringing war closer, and since Labour would play a crucial rôle in war, an election should be
held about the opening of negotiations with Italy, the plight
of the Spanish people and the 'sacrifice' of Austria on 'the
altar of power politics'.[11]

It is possible that the setbacks in Spain and the peace
position which Chamberlain had carved out made the Labour
leaders more belligerent than they would otherwise have
been. If so, they fell into a trap. It was a feeling that the trap
might be sprung, as at the election of 1935, which made
them cautious in the early days of the September crisis.[12]

In the summer of 1938, they were saying that Chamberlain
was 'spineless' and 'immoral', had lost touch with public feeling and was blinded by 'class prejudice' to the duty to organise the 'democratic powers' to resist the dictators. This, it was
claimed, was what Henderson would have done; it was the
'inept and evil policy' pursued since 1931 that had transformed the peaceful world he left into the 'barbarism' that was
'now upon us'.[13]

Mr Chamberlain and his colleagues [wrote Morrison on July 9] talk
peace not because they mean [it] but because the language of pacifism is
the new political technique of the Tory Central Office. On the Prime
Minister's own admission, we are living under more disturbed international conditions than at any time since the outbreak of the Great War.
And I charge that the British government by its betrayal of the League
of Nations, its sabotaging of the Disarmament Conference and its rejection of the policy of the collective organisation of peace has made a
major contribution to the wars taking place and to the unsettlement of
Europe.[14]

At the Trade Union Congress in early September, there were resolutions in favour of accelerated rearmament. [15] The National Council of Labour repudiated the government's right to use diplomatic or other pressure to compel the Czech government 'to yield its democracy to force' and called for 'positive' action to convince Hitler that Britain would 'unite with the French and Soviet governments to resist'. [16] By Morrison, Attlee and Greenwood the crisis was seen in terms of a battle for 'freedom' in which 'the Fascist dictators' must 'be given to understand that...if they went into war, they risked defeat and revolution at home'. On September 18 Attlee hoped that 'peace might be preserved without yielding to... threats of military force and...the sacrifice of the rights and liberties of the people of Czechoslovakia'. [17]

This was one side of the Labour face. The other was Attlee hoping that Runciman could solve the problem by agreement [18] and Morrison suggesting a transfer of populations. When Halifax asked whether they wished to declare war 'if there were aggression in Czechoslovakia', Attlee and Greenwood hesitated before replying that, if France honoured her obligations, 'we should immediately declare ourselves in support of France'. [19] When told by French socialists and by Snell, who had just been to Paris, that even Blum was not certain that France should fight, Dalton talked privately about dissuading the Czechs from a heroic battle against overwhelming odds. [20]

When told by Chamberlain on the 19th that the Czechs should transfer territory rather than population, [21] the Labour leaders decided to turn on the heat. That evening, the National Council of Labour announced its 'dismay'. [22] On the 20th Attlee asked Chamberlain to recall Parliament in view of the 'reported proposals submitted to the government of Czechoslovakia which contemplate the dismemberment of a sovereign state at the dictation of the ruler of Germany and involve this country in giving a guarantee in the future of continental frontiers'. [23]

The attack was then developed with a new vigour. On the 21st Chamberlain was visited by Attlee and Greenwood; the National Council of Labour sent Dalton, Citrine and Morrison to see Halifax. In both interviews the tone was sharper than before. [24] There was no demand for a declaration of war, but a campaign was launched against the 'shameful surrender' of Britain's tradition of democracy and justice. 'Hitler's ambitions', the Joint Labour statement of September 21 concluded, 'do not stop short at Czechoslovakia...His present triumph will be a new starting-point for further warlike adventures which in the end must lead to a general conflict.' [25]

The Labour leaders may have called on the government to 'stand fast for peace and freedom' because they thought Hitler would back down if it did. Or, expecting war, they may have wanted to establish that they were not responsible. [26] In whichever mood they were acting, they filled the gap between Godesberg and Munich proclaiming a 'moral obligation' the betrayal of which had produced 'a general feeling of shame and humiliation throughout the nation'. The same idea was pursued when Attlee and Greenwood visited the Czech Ambassador to express 'deep sympathy...with the people of Czechoslovakia in their tragic plight'. [27]

After Godesberg, the imminence of war produced a claim that the government could have taken steps to prevent it. Co-operation with Russia was one. A clear warning to Hitler was another. There was, however, no demand that Britain should go to war. All there was was a restatement of the view that 'a strong and united stand by...France, Britain and the Soviet Union...could prevent war'. A letter which Attlee wrote to Chamberlain, unwillingly at Dalton's insistence on September 26, alleged that 'the terms of Herr Hitler's memorandum which you agreed to submit to the Czechoslovakian government' had 'profoundly shocked British opinion' and that 'the only means by which peace could be preserved' was through the Labour policy of a tripartite declaration of intention 'to resist any attack upon Czechoslovakia'. [28]

For a moment after Chamberlain's return from Munich, the Labour party was uncertain. Very soon it adopted the position that 'several million people' had been 'sacrificed for peace' and another 'blow' struck at the League of Nations. Hitler's Saarbrücken speech showed that 'talk of a Tory peace in our time' was 'humbug' since 'what had happened...had not averted war but merely postponed it'. War would not be averted by a Prime Minister who 'did not understand the conditions of the modern world' and had failed to stop Axis penetration of British markets. Chamberlain had 'tricked' the

Labour party 'again and again', truckled to the dictators because he 'liked their principles' and made it impossible to
support National Service so long as he was Prime Minister. [29]

The demand for a new government anticipated the changes
that would be needed if war began and Labour support was
needed, or if Conservative doubts were translated into a major
erosion of Chamberlain's authority. [30] It was not certain how
erosion would occur; in a sense, it depended on Hitler's co-
operation. Yet there was a distinct hope in late 1938 that
Chamberlain might come a cropper. This raised the usual
question about the future.

This was the question, which had been asked in 1921,
1923, 1929 and 1934 — whether Labour should ally itself
with other parties if alliance seemed likely to bring it into
office. After the 1935 election, there had been no need to
take the Liberal party seriously, however seriously some Labour leaders took 'Liberal opinion'. [31] In 1935/6 a Left-Wing
Popular Front had been rejected. [32] After the Anschluss and
in 1939, the problem centred on the possibility of a Popular
Front with the Right as well as the Left. In both cases a
leading part was played by Cripps.

In the year following the defeat of the Socialist League at the
party conference in 1934, Cripps stood out as the leading
critic of two aspects of the compromises inherent in 'gradual'
socialism. On the one hand, he attacked the blurring of intention which left it uncertain whether a Labour government
would give priority to the 'abolition of capitalism'. On the
other, he attacked the assumption that Collective Security
through the League was a policy which would help the working classes.

Of these aspects of his platform, the first remained un-
changed through all the changes of emphasis it underwent in
the following five years. When he was expelled from the Labour party in 1939, Cripps's position was what it had been in
1934 — that the party had 'lost its spiritual and moral background' [33] and ought to split (as in 1914) so that 'one part
of it' could 'do what it can to protect the workers while the
war is...being fought' and the other could be 'ready to step in
when the workers are disillusioned by the result'. [34] Throughout his subsequent treatment of the war as harbinger of a

'change' in 'our civilisation' and a 'ferment in social living', [35] this continued to be the case up to the point at which he joined the Churchill government, after Russia had become an ally, in 1942.

At the same time Cripps developed an emphasis on foreign policy. This became the basis for a new view of the party situation which his Labour critics treated as itself a capitulation. [36]

In 1935 he had begun by supporting the policy from which Lansbury dissented. When Lansbury's resignation seemed likely to result, he resigned from the Party Executive on the ground that the League was an Imperialist organisation which it could not be a 'working-class' interest to support. As the Labour party emphasised the League in the years that followed, Cripps rejected it, along with rearmament, in favour of a socialist foreign policy based on alliance with the Soviet Union. Spain merely strengthened and deepened the ideological obligation from which the Popular Front emerged.

Cripps's support for the Popular Front became an issue in 1936 when Labour setbacks in the municipal elections coincided with Baldwin's prospective retirement, the hints dropped by Sinclair in favour of a Popular Front and the Labour and TUC decisions to support rearmament. It coincided also with a self-styled 'jingo-Imperialist' declaration from Citrine in favour of a non-Communist People's (as opposed to the Popular) Front and the National Executive's decision to dissociate itself from a speech in which Cripps 'did not believe it would be a bad thing for the British working class if Germany defeated us'. [37]

It was at this time that *Tribune* was founded in order to put Cripps's point of view and to establish the viability of a Front between the Labour, Communist and Independent Labour parties. His first calls for a United Front were then rejected by the National Executive, which disaffiliated the Socialist League early in 1937. However, he neither resigned from the Labour party nor dissociated himself from it. Instead, he became chairman of the Committee of Constituency Labour parties which, along with *Tribune*, was his chief platform for the next eighteen months and helped to elect him, Laski and Pritt to the National Executive at the same time as the rejection of the United Front was confirmed at the Party Conference in October. [38]

In the eighteen months following, his position was that, though the decision was mistaken, he had no intention of resigning so long as Labour had the only organisation capable of opposing Chamberlain. [39] Along with Pritt, Laski, Strauss, Gollancz and Bevan, he used *Tribune* and the Left Book Club to create the impression that, by supporting rearmament, the Labour leaders were producing a consensus situation by default.

This campaign was an attempt to play on two Labour sentiments — of friendship for Russia and fear of a 1931. [40] It produced a decision, not very effectively pursued, that Morrison should be put in Attlee's place. [41] It issued in demands for alliance not only with the Communist and Independent Labour parties but also with Sinclair, Amery and the dissentient Conservatives, with whom Cripps thought agreement was possible about a programme for 'the preservation of our democratic liberties, reconstituting Collective Security and national control of...economic life'. [42]

In this respect, he was a dissenter. Despite backstairs negotiation in October 1938, Attlee and others believed that Conservatives would not co-operate unless they had to, and that Liberals and Communists would do so only in order to steal, or divide, the Labour vote. The National Executive withheld official approval of Bartlett, to whom Cripps, like others, sent a letter when he stood at Bridgewater (with support from the Labour association).[43] Cripps, in his turn, despite his own co-operation with anti-Chamberlain Tories and anti-government Liberals, attacked Labour co-operation in government war preparations. [44]

By the time the National Executive expelled him from the Labour party in January 1939 (on a technicality), Cripps had been under attack for advocating the sort of accommodation which in 1934 it had been one of his chief objects to prevent. Where previously he had regarded a Lib-Lab alliance as involving opportunistic compromise, he was now hooking himself on to the main chance. 'In the light of our experience, and bearing in mind especially the difficulty of winning over large numbers of the middle class and all classes in the rural areas,' he and his supporters wrote after the Anschluss, 'we have come to the conclusion that an effective victory by the Labour party alone is highly improbable at the next election'.[45] On January 3 1939 after a detailed analysis of Labour's prospects he wrote to Middleton:

I certainly should not desire to encourage the Party to any combination with other non-socialist elements in normal political times [but] the growth of strength of the Labour party...is not such as to warrant the belief that the Party can defeat the national government single-handed at a general election within the next eighteen months.... . A progressive democratic block dominated by a numerically strong Labour nucleus would be vastly preferable to the continuance of the National government...and, if the Labour party were to come out boldly as the leader of the combined opposition to the National government...and...support combined opposition candidates in such of those constituencies not at present held by any opposition member, as could offer no reasonable chance of success in a straight fight between any single party opposition candidate and the National government...such a step would, I am sure, enormously increase its prestige and popularity...and...bring within its ranks many who are not at present ready to join up because they are not convinced of its power and capacity to defeat the National government.[46]

Cripps claimed that an alliance of this sort was necessary to meet the 'certain use by the National Government' at the next election 'of the call for National Unity against the foreign enemy'.[47] He asserted that any government which emerged would be likely to improve old age pensions, raise the school-leaving age, expand secondary and university education, nationalise mining, transport and the Bank of England and build up an alliance with France and Russia.

The socialist element in the programme raised doubts in the Liberal party. After his expulsion, Cripps tried to organise a monster petition (in company with Strauss and Gollancz). He then tried to tempt Lloyd George, Baldwin, Churchill, Roberts, Richard Acland, Halifax, Wood, Stanley and others (including Dean Johnson of Canterbury) into a broad-based front to deal with the international situation.[48]

In 1938/9 Cripps's theatre was a versatile piece of hedge-hopping, an attempt — entirely unsuccessful — to make a 'Left-wing' foreign policy the centre of power in a positively constructed coalition. In this respect Attlee was right to see him as the successor of Mosley and MacDonald.

The idea of electoral alliance with Liberals and dissentient Conservatives had begun after Eden's resignation.[49] It had not survived his conduct out of office. The Labour leaders were not interested in assisting dissentients unless they would damage the Conservative party in the process. They needed to be sure of a major secession. Until Munich, none seemed to be in sight.

It was probably Macmillan, Sandys and Cartland rather than the Labour leaders who made the first approaches. There were then meetings with Dalton and limited co-operation about procedure in the House of Commons. There was, however, no co-operation at by-elections.

At the Oxford by-election, Liberals and Conservatives had worked with the Labour association in support of A.D. Lindsay, the independent candidate. Oxford, however, was an untypical constituency. The working arrangment was not regarded as a precedent[50] and Lindsay had, in any case, been defeated. Even the support of the Co-operative party and the letter sent by thirty-nine Labour MPs when Bartlett fought the Bridgewater by-election as a progressive Independent did not indicate that the Labour party was prepared for electoral co-operation.

The Executive's decision of November 24 may have been designed to leave open the possibility of an anti-government alliance at or after a general election.[51] So far as the immediate future was concerned, it concluded that 'coalition would be a grievous discouragement to those holding Socialist convictions' and that a 'combination of parties was...politically unsound, electorally disadvantageous and governmentally impossible'.[52]

The Popular Front was rejected because it would raise the 'Red Bogy'.[53] The 'National Opposition' was rejected because Labour would be the beneficiary of the government's difficulties without it.[54] Rejection was also connected with Labour's Immediate Programme which was 'a coherent whole' where 'the workers' movement', 'social reconstruction' and an attack on luxury would do more than a 'bourgeois...government' to 'save the world from the abyss'.[55]

The object of national reorganisation was that Britain should 'take the van in the cause of peace'.[56] This meant a Britain where the Immediate Programme had been carried out. 'I would ask those who are dissatisfied with the Government's handling of international affairs', said Greenwood on December 4, 'whether they hate Socialism more than they hate Fascism or whether they are prepared, in the interests of democracy and freedom, to sacrifice some of their ancient prejudices in order that Labour may have the opportunity to blaze the path of peace abroad and prosperity at home'. [57] 'Only in Socialism', Williams wrote on December 9, 'is there to be found any true resolving of the conflicts which present us with the threat of war abroad and the reality of poverty and distress at home'. [58]

What the Labour leaders were saying in the six months after Munich was that 'the very foundation of our Western civilisation' was 'imperilled' [59] and that the government had 'allowed the peace forces of the world to be dissipated'. [60] The world's 'one strong voice' was Roosevelt's [61] but both Russia and America had been neglected. In Britain Labour was the only embodiment of progress and the only party that had the nerve to stop the rot. For this reason it had a right to Liberal support and had no need to depend on a Popular Front. By the time the decision to expel Cripps had been confirmed by the Southport Conference on May 29, [62] the disappearance of Czechoslovakia seemed to have shown that Chamberlain was finished.

To the Labour leaders the events of March 1939 had come as 'no surprise'. Hitler-based appeasement had always been an 'illusion'. A 'peace pact with France or Russia' was the only way of checking German aggression and facilitating 'a world conference...to deal with the fundamental causes of war'.[63] 'Labour's foreign policy had been right' and 'now, in far less favourable circumstances', with Czechoslovakia and Austria lost, 'the government had come round to the views which we had so long been pressing upon them'. [64]

The claim that it was following Labour's lead did not produce support for the government. For Chamberlain 'hatred' was as 'passionate' as it had been six months before.[65] When Greenwood went out of his way to contrast him with Hitler, he was unusual. Behind the public moves towards France and Russia and the continental guarantees, the government's chief characteristic was still said to be 'Simonism — in other words casuistry'. [66] After the occupation of Albania, it became once more an important point that 'Chamberlain Must Go'. [67]

Although the Labour leaders were pushing at an open door so far as Halifax was concerned, they left no doubt that they would reject 'appeals...to rally behind the government in the interests of national unity'. [68] They made aggressive demands for advances towards Russia which became more pressing the clearer it was that Chamberlain's feet were being dragged. [69] They also objected to Conscription.

Conscription was an industrial as well as a political issue; the reaction of the trade union leaders mattered more even than those of the party leaders. It is at least possible that many of both were 'happy in their hearts' when it was introduced. Nevertheless, they protested and, in doing so, made two claims. They claimed to know what war would be like if it came. And they claimed that foreign policy must be right if industrial co-operation was to be given.

The two claims were connected. On the one hand, there was the view that in war Britain would keep sea-lanes open, deploy the largest air force in Europe and develop a munitions industry for her allies (while having no spare capacity for a large continental army). On the other hand, in the modern forces 'highly skilled men' would be operating expensive machinery where the continually rising ratio between the size of the Services and 'the far greater numbers engaged on munitions and supply services' would make 'national service' mean 'in effect...industrial Conscription...a demand that the whole nation should be regimented and particular jobs allocated to every individual'.[70]

To this the objection was that it would be a step on the road to fascism. Under a Capitalist government, Conscription would do nothing to ensure that essential goods were produced. The national debt would be increased by deficit financing and almost anything done to keep purchasing power out of the hands of the state. An increase in state power was essential, however, if as much was to be done as in the first war to 'produce...the right things', 'conscript wealth' and 'impose equality of sacrifice' in order to 'maintain the standard of life and morale of the people'. [71]

In the summer of 1939 the Labour Leaders had to face in two directions. If there was to be a general election, the domestic programme of 1937 had to be deployed constructively. If there was to be a war, they had to state the terms on which they would offer co-operation. The common factor was the removal of Chamberlain.

With these eventualities in mind, Labour was 'ready for an election' whenever one might come. If war came instead, equality and public ownership would ensure a 'strong nation' and socialism success. The Immediate Programme would be as relevant as when it was devised; it would be specially relevant in turning the Services into a 'citizen army' where trade unionism would be permitted, where promotion would be from the ranks and where the distance between the ranks would be diminished. [72] Labour was not, as its enemies claimed, a war-mongering party. But in face of 'war more catastrophic than the last', the only sane reaction was the twin policy of economic accommodation for states with a grievance and a strong group of states pledged to 'mutual aid against aggression'. [73] 'The banks', Bevin told the Labour Conference on May 30, 'are responsible for the policy of appeasement of Germany...I don't want us to fight for them...but for the common people throughout the world.' 'This country', said Attlee on May 15, 'is not organised as it should be because at every point the interests of private profit and the interests of property and class are put before the interest of the country as a whole...You will only get first things put first when you have a government that stands for the whole nation.' [74]

8

EDEN, CHURCHILL AND THEIR ALLIES

'Let our first thought be of our duty to England. Let it be our desire
and determination...that we shall so acquit ourselves that the name of
England shall be honoured and respected. ...England would wish, I
believe, to see prevail throughout the world those conditions which she
has tried and is trying to create in her own land, an equal opportunity
for all to develop to the full their own individuality without let or
hindrance. We have found that one essential condition of such progress
is the rule of law. This being so, what must be our aim? We must first
wish to see the rule of law between nations acknowledged. We must
wish this because it is a condition of civilized life between countries. We
must, therefore, also wish justice to be done by just means. This must
make us readily accept, as trustees of a great part of the earth's surface,
the duties of trusteeship, the need of understanding, of toleration, and
of generosity. The England of to-day stands for something positive, the
creation at last of a comity of nations in which each can develop and
flourish and give to their uttermost their own special contribution to
the diversity of life'. Eden at annual dinner of the Royal Society of
St George, Grosvenor House, April 26 1938, *The Times*, April 27

'I venture to send you a little book I have just published on much the
same subject as your St. George's day speech, though you call it England and I call it Liberality'. Murray to Eden, June 1 1938

'I am not sure what your line would be in the present crisis. I found it
this week quite easy to make a class analysis of the situation and leave
it at that, but I felt that it would be cowardly. If it is true that there is
half a chance of preventing war by the Winston sort of policy, I feel I
ought to say so...As you know I have always tried to make a distinction
between a war we ought to risk which would genuinely be in the
interests of Socialism in Spain and a war for the British Empire. It is
now, I am afraid, obvious that they would be the same thing...'. Martin
to Cripps, March 18 1938

The Labour opposition to Chamberlain was bitter but its
power to change policy was small, and what power it had
came from the need for trade union support in war. Chamberlain, however, was not aiming to go to war. He was aiming
to persuade Hitler to keep the peace. In doing so, he needed
less rather than more of the belligerence which some of the
Labour leaders were offering. The Labour party affected his
policy, chiefly through a change in climate in which the non-
Labour opposition was more important.

At its fullest extent, the non-Labour opposition was the work of Churchill, Sinclair, Eden, Amery and Cecil, assisted by twenty or so Conservative or National MPs inside Parliament and a handful of publicists outside. For the development of policy, the crucial points were the Anschluss, Munich and Prague. In the development of expectations, the resignations of Eden and Cranborne were crucial.

The resignations, however, were less important than they seemed at the time.[1] The Conservative party turned out to be a hard nut to crack. Easy victories were not available. No sudden sweep of feeling restored the critics to the centre of the scene. A raising of stakes, a heightening of tension and much searching of hearts was to go on before events fell out as Churchill and Eden wished. A prolonged, complicated and devastating experience turned out to be necessary before either could make his way back.

Of the five leaders under discussion, Amery was the least important. In the first place, because of his comparative isolation. Secondly, because, after the disagreements of 1935, he agreed with a good deal of what Chamberlain did in 1937. Thirdly, because, having been a founder-member of the régime in 1922, being close, though none too friendly, to Chamberlain and always imagining that he might be needed, he did not, until a late stage, regard himself as part of a regular opposition.

When it became clear that Chamberlain was going to be Prime Minister, Amery called 'to inform [him] quite unasked, which of the great offices of State he would be prepared to accept'.[2] Believing, 'now...Austen [Chamberlain] had gone', that he had 'more influence and authority in the party than anyone', he did not 'consider [himself] an ordinary candidate for office'. When Chamberlain apologised for failing to fit him in,[3] he received a dignified note which pointed out 'what a difference' Amery would have made to his government both in fact and in public estimation...had he intended a real Imperial policy'.[4] His view of the government was that it had emerged from

a mere reshuffle dominated by no other consideration apparently than of giving the appropriate number of places to the representatives of the so-called parties. That...de la Warr is made Privy Seal and a member of the Cabinet and bouncing Hore-Belisha put into the War Office. The Admiralty is inflicted with Duff Cooper while Sam [Hoare] moves on to the Home Office of all places...Worst of all, Oliver Stanley is put at the Board of Trade. That Neville should not only put a Liberal at the Exchequer but a very partially converted Free Trader at the Board of Trade at a time like this shows a complete disregard not only of the feelings of the party but an even more complete lack of any real interest or understanding in his father's policy.[5]

From this position, Amery developed an indictment. It was not just, he was saying, that Chamberlain had constructed a 'one-man cabinet', for that obviously was what he had wanted to do.[6] It was much more that he was failing to give it a 'national character'.

By 'national character' Amery did not mean what Baldwin had meant. Nor did he mean the inclusion of all parties in a national government. He meant, on the contrary, a policy in the mould of Milner and Joseph Chamberlain and an attempt to re-do what they had done 'for those of us who were young men before the war'. He meant a repetition of his own campaign in the Boer War, a revival of Roberts's defence campaign and 'convert[ing]...the...negative *rationale* of the coalition into a positive...creed based on social welfare and...Empire unity'.[7]

Amery did not object to appeasement. He thought it important to prevent Europe being divided into ideological *blocs* and was willing to recognise Germany's 'natural economic predominance' in central Europe. He regarded Mussolini as a good European and hoped that encirclement could be 'eliminated' by making him France's ally in place of Russia.[8]

On the other hand, he was cautious about any particular step to ease relations with Germany. He had strong views about the Colonial campaign (which he thought had been set off by Hoare's Geneva speech in 1935) and founded a Colonial Defence League (with help from Sandys) in order to oppose it. Above all, he took the view that the best policy was to approach Italy first because Mussolini was more amenable than Hitler.[9]

Over Eden's resignation, Amery supported Chamberlain, whose criticism of the League was 'the first breath of fresh air on the Government front bench for many a long year'.[10] He refused to support Churchill in exploiting it[11] and, when told about Hitler's brutality to Schuschnigg, recalled his 'tragic apprehension [at] Eden's performances and those of the

Cabinet in launching the Abyssinian campaign at Geneva in 1935'. [12]

For Amery the Anschluss meant 'facing realities and, much as I dislike it from an Empire point of view,...Continental entanglements'. [13] He believed, however, that the government's policy and his own were 'identical' and rejected Churchill's 'Grand Alliance' because one of the allies, Czechoslovakia, was surrounded, Hungary was an enemy and 'we have got to fall back on holding Yugoslavia and the Balkans and giving Germany...plenty to occupy her in the rest of the Danubian and Eastern European area'. [14]

In the summer of 1938 Amery was asking for a policy Cabinet to include the Opposition and a National Register as a first step towards Conscription. He wanted a Ministry of Supply (which Churchill did not understand), a policy for food supplies (which Chamberlain did not understand) and an attempt to use Italy as a barrier against Germany (which was one object of the visit he paid to Rome in April). [15] On these, and other matters, he expressed his opinions in Parliament, in the newspapers, at public meetings, through the organisations he helped to run and at committees of the parliamentary Conservative party, which he found more congenial platforms than the floor of the House of Commons.

During the early days of the Munich crisis, he was terrified by the sound of Hitler's voice, [16] unable to believe that France could 'do...nothing if the Czechs fight' [17] and convinced that the government had 'to avoid...Grey's mistake and leave [the Germans] in no doubt where we stand'. [18] Believing that a settlement was 'almost impossible' but hoping for a solution if the Czechs offered 'a corner of Czechoslovakia', he regarded the Berchtesgaden visit as 'a bold stroke...which might just conceivably save the situation'. [19] He wrote to Chamberlain and told Halifax that this was his opinion. [20]

This did not mean that he was happy. On September 20 he refused to propose a pro-Chamberlain resolution at the party conference in October. [21] When Eden told him, while Chamberlain was at Godesberg, that the British plan was 'quite vague as to who is to be handed over', he began to anticipate 'a general mutilation...that would...make our guarantee of [Czech] neutrality very different from what [he] had contemplated'. [22]

The fear that the Cabinet might press proposals of this sort was so worrying that he wrote both to Halifax and *The Times*, and got up at six o'clock on the morning of September 25 to write to Chamberlain in anticipation of the Cabinet meeting that day. To Halifax he wrote that 'almost everyone I have met has been horrified at the so-called Peace Plan' and that it was unlikely that the House of Commons 'would stand any more surrender'.[23] The letter to Chamberlain expressed the opinion that 'we could not shirk the responsibility of expressing our own views about Hitler's ultimatum, namely that it was unreasonable and that we should not ask the Czechs to accept it'.[24]

On September 23 Amery attended a meeting of MPs in Spears's house. On the 26th he went to a meeting in Spears's office at which his main contribution was to refuse to sign a statement in favour of co-operation with Russia.[25] From there he was taken, with the rest of the meeting, to Churchill's flat where he found a 'queer collection' consisting, among others, of Cecil, Lytton, Lindemann and Lloyd.

Amery had had no special contact with Churchill, none with Cecil, of whom he was not an admirer, and very little with Eden, of whom he was intellectually contemptuous. It was not until Spears took him to Churchill's flat that he was anywhere near the centre of the anti-Chamberlain movement. He went to another Spears meeting on September 27 and to meetings of Churchill's on September 28, October 3 and October 5. Thereafter, he had little direct contact with the Churchill group, which probably found him wooden about Collective Security and Russia and too willing to hedge his bets about Chamberlain.[26] He tried, unsuccessfully, to involve Attlee and Lloyd George in supporting Conscription[27] and to construct a joint programme with the Sinclair Liberals.[28] From late October he was a regular member of a group which included Eden, Cranborne, Duff Cooper and Nicolson.

Amery was an enemy of the League of Nations, a hammer of pacifist, 'leftish' or woolly-minded internationalism and a critic of Cecil's understanding of the needs and nature of Collective Security. As recently as September 25, he had written that the real origin of the crisis was to be found in the 'years of self-deception...when, refusing to reason, we thought that we could interfere anywhere...on behalf of

Peace through the League'.[29] Nevertheless, the alliance he had joined included Cecil who believed that 'the old attitude about power and imperialism...was as dead as Queen Anne'.[30]

The high point of the influence exercised by Cecil and the League of Nations Union was in 1935. 1936 was a bad year for the League; the Union lost the central position it had regained the year before. Thereafter the decline was sharp, as Cecil and Murray had a developed experience of being in their seventies, as the Peace Pledge Union emphasised peace rather than the League and as both Chamberlains turned official Conservative opinion against them.[31]

It is true that they tried to stop the Conservative withdrawal by dodging the colonial question[32] and presenting the League as 'an almost ideal machinery' for the 'preservation' of the Empire.[33] It is true also that, at times, they expected the German and Italian problems to go away or be solved if 'peaceful Change' was taken as seriously as Collective Security.[34] In company with Lytton, they held meetings, issued statements and used a long-standing entrée to Downing Street to support Eden and Cranborne in February and the Czechs in September 1938. But it was clear that something was missing as the breach with Chamberlain produced conditions in which, for the first time since the war, the Union lost its standing as a sacred cow.[35]

Despite Eden's and then Halifax's presence at the Foreign Office and the restraint they would impose on 'the anti-League party in the government',[36] the result was a further swing to the Left and an increase in the number of embarrassing bedfellows. This showed itself in a heightened desire for association with Russia, support for Republican Spain and the development of relations with the International Peace Campaign which Cecil hoped might do what the National Declaration had done in 1935.[37]

This followed a wrangle which had begun at an office Christmas party (in 1936) when one of the Union's senior officials, who was a Roman Catholic, gave imitations of Cecil, Noel-Baker and other Union leaders expressing admiration of the IPC. In the next two years Cecil and Murray were much pre-occupied with the subsequent argument in which Catho-

lic, trade union and most Conservative members of the Executive opposed amalgamation on the ground that the IPC was
a Communist front. When settled in favour of Cecil's view
that relations should be close — he had said in 1936 that
'Communism [was] not a danger' [38] — it was followed by the
resignation of Archbishop Hinsley, the dismissal of Garnett,
the Union Secretary, and complaints from Chamberlain and
Conservative Central Office about the Left-wing tone of
Union propaganda.

Except for a brief period after the false alarm of May 21,
Cecil spent 1938 'struggling for the survival of the work' to
which he had 'given the last twenty years of his life'. [39] The
government had 'allowed the League to disintegrate'. [40] The
Union was suffering a 'psychological slough' such as had been
experienced in 1934 and a 'general loss of faith in League
principles'. Churchill was beginning to provide one substitute,
Eden a more 'central' one. But the government's 'ambiguities
and timidities' were failing to make Hitler understand that
further aggression would be a breach of even Chamberlain's
conception of international relations. [41] Right into 1940
Cecil was complaining about the failure to resist aggression in
the Far East. [42]

By the winter of 1938 his party connection had disappeared. Halifax had been written off. [43] Chamberlain's activities
before Godesberg had been 'disastrous to British interests and
fatal to British honour'. [44] Munich was an 'abdication' and
necessitated 'a great effort to try and organise a joint opposition to the government of all those who are really terrified by
their foreign policy'. [45]

If war had come before Munich, Cecil would have wanted
Churchill at the head of a Conservative government. At the
Oxford by-election he wanted Lindsay to win (when Murray
decided not to stand himself). [46] After Prague he wanted
Eden to stay out of office because 'any strengthening' of
Chamberlain would be 'a disaster'. [47] But except for Cripps
and Noel-Baker, he had lost regard for the Labour party
which he thought doctrinaire and unpractical and to join
which 'at [his] age seem[ed] ridiculous'. [48] He had no time
for Attlee who was 'not a leader' and would have to be
removed if it was to become effective. [49]

What Cecil wanted was what Eden was trying to make his

own — a liberal-minded, post-Imperialist centrality leading to intimations that Collective Security was an aspect of the British way of life, that freedom and democracy required resistance to dictators and that the post-war world should include a 'closer union between European states' against 'nationalism'. [50] In presenting these sentiments for the benefit of the young, he offended a great many of the Union rank and file. [51] When he appeared with Lytton at Churchill's flat in September 1938, he was not the man he had been three years before. In these directions Sinclair was the effective leader.

Sometime in 1936 Sinclair had seen that foreign policy might help him to effect a Liberal revival. In the following two years, however, his position remained what it was then — that Liberals had a part to play in 'construct[ing] a platform on which the parties of the Left would come together' but would not 'go grovelling to the Labour party' or 'exhibit [themselves] in the guise of a weak applicant' to anyone else. [52]

Though electoral alliance was 'impossible' and 'undesirable', [53] he saw scope for advance, as Lloyd George had in 1935, in face of all those on both sides who advocated 'trade wars' or 'class wars'.[54] This might happen as the result of a Labour split. [55] It might happen, in the absence of Labour electoral success, as it came to be seen that 'Liberal candidates, supported by active organisations, would do far more' in many constituencies 'to weaken the government vote' than the Labour party could do by itself. [56] There was a greater chance in this way, he thought, of a general election producing an anti-Conservative majority pledged to reform the electoral system to the Liberal party's advantage. [57]

Encouraged by the Labour failure to follow Cripps, Sinclair played a part in the League of Nations Union, the New Commonwealth and Churchill's Focus of which he was an unpublicised member from an early stage. He had hopes of both Parmoor and Snowden (before his death in 1937) [58] and through White and Mander, had a certain amount of cautious contact with the New Five Year group. [59] In addition to Lloyd George (who also helped Nathan win Wandsworth for Labour), at least one of his sixteen MPs — Mander — supported Noel-Baker when he won the National Labour seat for

Labour on Thomas's retirement from Derby.[60] Another —
Dingle Foot — was deputed to liaise with Macmillan's plans
for a Popular Front.[61] Harris and Sinclair talked frequently
to Bernays, and Meston to the National Labour Party.[62] Formal support was withheld from Salter at the Oxford University by-election only because of the uncertain temper of the
electorate.[63]

In facing the future, Sinclair thought primarily about the
young, the universities and the communicators. Much was
said about being 'radical and imaginative' and something
about Simon's 'smugness'.[64] Though technical objection was
raised to the Defence White Paper of 1936, Liberal pacifism
was rejected. In preparing against a possible threat to 'the
people of these islands', League-based co-operation with
France was the only way of 'sharing the risks' entailed by the
'world-wide' character of the Empire. 'I am', Sinclair wrote in
April 1935, 'entirely opposed to the conception of the Rhine
as the frontier of Great Britain...It would be as sensible to
describe the Vistula as our frontier. If we want to preserve
peace in this country, we must prevent war from breaking
out in Europe.'[65]

Peace, however, would be preserved only by removing the
causes of war, which were not to be found in the character of
Nazism or the idiosyncrasies of Hitler. The cause was the
Ottawa policy of erecting tariff walls against German and
Japanese goods. This was why the Samuelites had resigned in
1932, and why their resignation freed them from responsibility for armaments expenditure. It was why Chamberlain was
primarily to blame for the situation in which

Japan [would] seize by force...what is denied her by peaceful trade,
Italy [would] take Abyssinia and Germany [would] prepare to break
the ring which holds the economic life of her people in a vice...and you
will have to pay in direct...and indirect taxes on the necessities and
luxuries of daily life, 1 million pounds every weekday for the next five
years to arm yourselves against the resentments and designs of foreign
countries.[66]

In mid-1936 Sinclair expected the 'betrayal' of election
pledges to create conditions in which, 'among those who
[had] voted for the government' there were 'tens of thousands' who would not vote Conservative again.[67] As Abyssinia and the Rhineland receded and Baldwin was restored by

the abdication, expectations then waned. Even when Chamberlain presented a rawer target after Baldwin had retired, Sinclair was much less confident than the year before. [68] It was not until the Ipswich by-election in February 1938 that opportunities seemed to knock.

Ipswich taught Sinclair two lessons — that the Simonites, even in their strongest area, could no longer deliver the Liberal vote, and that a Labour candidate — standing on a Liberal programme — had done infinitely better than Labour candidates had done when they stood on a socialist programme. It seemed, therefore, that the prospect for a Liberal revival was not dead. When followed by Eden's resignation, it seemed certain that it was very much alive. [69]

In the previous eighteen months Eden had been acclaimed as much by Liberals as by Cecil and the Labour party. For Sinclair, he was a man of 'sincerity...in a Cabinet of agnostics'. In an 'Imperialistic and isolationist' government, he was the one supporter of the League and had quarrelled with Chamberlain against whom the Liberal understanding of international relations had been established in 1936. [70]

Up to Eden's resignation, Liberals had been active — about food prices and the damage Protection had done to the economy. [71] Sinclair shared Eden's reluctance to recognise the conquest of Abyssinia. [72] But, so far from prejudging Hitler, he had blamed Conservatives for suppressing discussion of the colonial question and criticised Labour for wanting a line-up — at variance with League universality — between Britain, France and Russia on the one hand and the Rome-Berlin axis on the other. [73] While half-anticipating a crooked deal, he had welcomed Halifax's visit to Germany and the attempt to make friends with Italy. [74] Despite contrary pressure inside the party, [75] he had supported non-intervention in Spain. [76] His demand for sanctions against Japan had co-existed with the policy of the Open Door. [77] He had criticised Conscription as an 'encroachment on civil liberty' [78] and, when Hitler was established in Vienna, wanted 'moderation' and 'generosity' in Prague. [79]

With Eden's resignation the plans Sinclair had made in 1936 had become relevant. The 'determination' to have a League policy including Russia, was not new. What was new was the Conference decision to co-operate with other parties and groups, [80] the attack on non-intervention in Spain [81] and the assertion that, if peace was to be kept, it was not Swinton but 'the architect of Ottawa' who must be removed. [82]

In the summer of 1938, Sinclair sensed a shift as Eden's position took root on the Left. Until Munich proved otherwise, he expected Mussolini to transform the party situation. In early September he wrote:

The Prime Minister's failures are obscured by the crisis in Central Europe, and the edge of criticism is naturally blunted by its seriousness... Nevertheless, if the Central European cloud does pass, the criticism of the Prime Minister's failure in Spain and in Italy will be renewed with full force, and Eden may yet get his opportunity if he has the strength and agility to take it. [83]

These policies were challenged in the Liberal party. [84] So was Sinclair's urgency. [85] Samuel was sceptical about the League. [86] Crewe, who was eighty, and Spender, at seventy-six, tried to establish collective leadership. [87] All three supported the Munich settlement, though Crewe (like Sinclair) supported Lindsay (where Samuel criticised him) at the Oxford by-election. [88]

From Sinclair's shift, Spender's Imperial 'pacifism' suffered as much as Hirst's Cobdenism had begun to suffer from the attempt to have a social policy. [89] Having no wish to have anything to do with the Labour party, Spender offered to resign the presidency of the Liberal Council. He then echoed the Hankey view that 'the League of Nations Union...wishes us to face another war, with Italy and Japan as well as Germany hostile'. [90]

In relation to the Liberal party, Sinclair and Johnstone were in control. But Johnstone was not an MP and the party scarcely functioned in the House of Commons. [91] In developing public positions, the greatest difficulty was with the *News Chronicle*.

The *Chronicle* had been formed in 1930 by amalgamation between the *Daily News* and the *Daily Chronicle*. Since then, to a rising circulation, it had brought Radicalism up to date. Under Vallance, Barry, Cummings and Layton (the presiding mind), it had pinpointed the choices that lay between Radical Liberalism on the one hand and the revived Labour party on the other. In 1934 it hovered cautiously between Lansbury and Lloyd George. In 1935 Layton was a go-between

between the Peace Ballot and the Left. [92]

Layton was a Cambridge economist. He stood, politically, where Keynes and Beveridge stood, exposing the position more contentiously and antagonising Conservatives more obviously; but expressing, through his journalism, the mediating uncertainties of unbeneficed Liberalism. [93]

As editor of *The Economist* and in the *Chronicle*, Layton was a 'rational' Radical who equated 'reason' with the mixed economy and the League of Nations Union. In 1933 his formula consisted of political disarmament, economic appeasement and that it was a matter of 'expediency' whether there was to be 'socialisation' or not. [94]

As the Lothian of the Liberal-Left, Layton gave economic body to vague aspirations towards an 'international order'. [95] He also supplied vague aspirations towards 'a new vision built up on...understanding...private office [as] a public trust'. [96] After supporting the New Deal, he supported the Council of Action and Reconstruction at the 1935 election. [97]

Layton's foreign-policy language was a negation of Chamberlain's; Chamberlain's 'confession of disbelief in the League' gave *The Economist* a handle. [98] In 1938 it criticised the appeasement of Italy and the failure to support democracy in Spain. It presented early war as likely to be more favourable than a war later. Chamberlain's attempt to replace 'the international democracy of Geneva by a Four Power Pact' should be rejected, it said, since there was 'no common ground...between the democracies and...the liberty-destroying régimes... and...no assurance that...the...desire for economic betterment...in totalitarian states [would] put a check on imperialist designs fostered by mass propaganda'. [99]

Like Cripps, Layton intended, from a height, to provide something for the people to believe in. He wanted them to believe that Imperialism was wrong and that autarky would fail. He implied an ideological identity between a liberal economic system, League commitments and the defence of 'civilization'. [100]

In all these respects, his support was valuable. Samuel had treated him as a colleague. When Sinclair became leader, he had hoped to do the same. [101]

This turned out to be impossible. [102] Though Layton was a Liberal (and an associate of Allen as well as Lloyd George),

the *Cronicle* aimed to be a mass-circulation newspaper at a
time when the election had shown that mass-circulation Liberalism was dead. The 'combination of progressive forces' [103]
which Layton wanted in 1936 (when Sinclair was tactically
cautious) was presented, therefore, as something the Labour
party might bring about, [104] while the Popular Front of 1939
(which Sinclair supported) was played down because it was
Cripps who was leading it. [105]

Like the Liberal party, the *Chronicle* was a coalition of
generations (between ownership and staff). It produced a similar combination of antagonism to 'power politics', 'collective' resistance to aggression and the half-hope that economic
appeasement might turn Hitler into the world statesman Layton had hoped for in 1933. [106] Even after Munich, it did not
give up. The point was, however, that appeasement was impossible without the Soviet Union, that 'inspiring leadership'
was needed and that 'unity of purpose' could only be achieved under 'a new government formed on the broadest possible
basis of opinion'. [107]

Layton's *Chronicle* highlighted divisions in the government
and implied that Chamberlain had lost his following. It was
virulently nasty about the Nazis and was the newspaper of
which the Nazi leaders complained most regularly. But it did
not exclude a peaceful outcome. After Munich it was winded
(though it soon recovered). Its celebrations of Benes, Russia
and the League got under Chamberlain's skin, even when its
line (like his) combined resistance (if necessary) with reconciliation (if that should be possible). If Crowther's *Economist*
reflected Layton's frame of mind, Layton may still just possibly have had hopes in the summer of 1939. [108]

In addition to being close to Labour, Layton was closer to
Churchill than to Eden. So was Sinclair, [109] and it may be
that 'Eden' was his way of saying 'Churchill'. Certainly it was
later. Until well into 1939, however, Eden was the more
credible symbol of Conservative division and more likely to
make the Liberal party look central by association.

When he resigned, Eden faced alternatives as problematical as
those he had faced when Foreign Secretary. Having climbed
faster than anyone in the twentieth century and having expectations of a further climb into the highest place of all, he

had, now that he had taken off, to take care not to kick away the ladder he had been climbing.

The problem, which neither the Anschluss, May 21 nor Munich resolved, was whether to keep to a Conservative line, or whether he should put himself at the head of an eclectic movement of public protest in order to establish that between him and Chamberlain there was 'a difference of outlook' which was 'deep and real'. [110]

Churchill had chosen the second course, which, however, involved association with the Labour party. This Eden wanted to avoid, not least because an essential feature of his progressive reputation was that he was a Conservative. Moreover, the door back into the Cabinet was being kept open. Simon said so. [111] Chamberlain did not say so and was happy that he had left. But Chamberlain did not want Eden stumping the country and did his best to play down the disagreement. [112] Even if he did this as much in order to keep Eden quiet as because he meant it, it had an effect. [113]

After a mild resignation speech (which he had cleared with Hankey [114]), Eden's first step was to have a holiday. His second was to consult, not Churchill (whose threat of a Midlothian campaign he found as embarrassing as the Labour embrace), but first Halifax, to whom he wrote and talked in Yorkshire, [115] and then Baldwin, whom he visited in the South of France. [116]

Baldwin had not seen Chamberlain much since May 1937 but there is no reason to believe that he disliked his foreign policy or admired Eden as Foreign Secretary. [117] What he believed, or was reported as believing, was that Chamberlain had destroyed the central position it had been his own life's work to establish, had alienated the 'floating vote' and 'liberal opinion' and, at a time when trade union support was essential, was making the government look reactionary by conducting it on 'party lines' and 'splitting the country'. [118]

After Swinton's resignation, Baldwin was 'proud' to be his 'friend' and did not expect 'the country' to 'stand' Chamberlain 'much longer'; [119] his advice thereafter was that Eden should go around, showing himself off and performing the manifold functions which a Conservative politician had to perform if he was to look like a prime minister. 'Studying the

depressed areas and unemployment', 'the danger of democracy ending if allowed to deviate to Left or Right' and 'a revival
of Disraelian Tory Democracy' were the slogans he suggested
in the course of repaying Chamberlain for the criticisms he had
been given in their twenty years of uneasy collaboration.[120]
    Eden did this. He exposed the danger of the country being
'split into two camps on foreign policy'. He called for 'national unity', talked about the moral and physical 're-equip-
ment of the nation' and promised to 'attack' the government
if it 'could not secure TUC co-operation' for a 'drastic regi-
mentation of industry and labour'.[121] He advised his supporters in the House of Commons to 'keep the flag flying'
above the 'reactionary' backbenches while he 'stood for post-
war England against the old men'. [122] He offered youth, patriotism and service in the trenches in justification of the claim
that liberty, equality and moral regeneration were necessary to
the establishment of a 'lasting peace'. [123]
    In the midst of this synthetic Jacobinism, there was not
very much about the League of Nations. There was a great
deal more about Anglo-American liberty and the rule of law,
and about the League dream not having become a reality. [124]
    In his constituency on June 11 Eden announced that 'mo-
dern Conservatism' was a 'virile, progressive force' which
would not forever identify 'retreat' with 'the path of
peace'.[125] He then decided to make each of his speeches 'hotter'
than the last. [126] He made factory visits to Durham (in July)
and Tyneside (in August), the outcome of which were statements about the increase in unemployment [127] and essays for
Baldwin at Aix announcing further visits to South Wales and
Lancashire and the commonplace reflections that any young
politician might offer to a mentor. [128]
    If Eden expected his resignation to trigger off others and
bring down the government, [129] he was disappointed. Labour
won government seats at Lichfield and West Fulham, and
Swinton was allowed to resign. But no one else did. Chamberlain reacted strongly on May 21. The Stafford by-election [130]
in early June was a good one for the government which looked no weaker in July than it had been in January.
    Whether Eden expected to be the next Prime Minister is
not certain. His entourage talked about the possibility; [131] he

said that he was not going to be used by the present one and
had ruled out a return to office in the present Parliament. [132]

From this position he acted cautiously. He made no
complaint when the Runciman mission was appointed. [133]
When Czechoslovakia seemed likely to produce a crisis, he
said that Hitler should be warned. When the Lanark warning
was not repeated, he wrote a letter to *The Times* which Halifax suggested and Chamberlain approved before it was
sent. [134] While sharing Halifax's fear that the government
might 'run away if it came to a show-down', he did not
support Churchill's demand for a declaration of willingness to
go to war. [135] On September 18 he was going to 'go for the
government' when Parliament reassembled but, in a mood of
considerable depression, wanted neither resignations nor a
Cabinet revolt. On September 21 he made a public call for a
'stand'. [136] He found the idea of recommending the Godesberg terms 'incredible' and wrote to Halifax to say so. On the
28th he wished Chamberlain God speed in Munich. Next
day he refused to sign a Churchill telegram because he would
not be party to a 'vendetta against Chamberlain'. [137]

After March Eden telephoned Halifax to object to the fact
that Britain had presented Hitler's ultimatum for him. [138] At
the same time he began to say that it would 'give us time to
reconstruct'. By 'reconstruction' he meant nothing hostile to
Chamberlain who deserved 'deep sympathy...in [his] unparalleled ordeal', [139] but the use of special wartime powers to
increase industrial production and, if Chamberlain could invite
Labour and Liberal cooperation, he would become personally
impregnable and impress the world with Britain's resolute
intentions. [140]

Until the settlement was reached, Eden's chief ally was
Halifax; he played no part in the Churchill group meetings in
late September. He was present on October 3 when Churchill
and Dalton drafted a Labour motion for which Conservatives
could vote, but, like the rest of the dissentients and against
Churchill's advice, abstained in the division three days later. [141] He told Amery that Chamberlain's speech had almost
persuaded him to support the government. [142] He told Halifax that he had 'agreed with 90%' of it 'and would have voted
with the government had it not been for his feeling of obligation to those with whom he had been working'. [143]

Eden was leader of a parliamentary group which had been meeting secretly. It consisted of about twenty-five MPs. He was careful to distinguish it from the Churchill group.

Apart from Eden, Churchill was the most formidable leader of Conservative opposition. And in his case, more even than in Eden's, ambiguity was important. He had had a period on a sort of Left before 1914 and had picked up the language of reaction as the Liberal party had fallen away under him. From then onwards this was the language he used. By 1932 he had cast himself as an anti-Bolshevik, pro-Japanese admirer of Mussolini with a well-established reputation for fiscal backwardness.

In the course of the next couple of years, this rôle was confirmed as the enemy of the India bill (with a semi-Mosleyite son and connections with Lady Houston) developed an articulated distaste for universal suffrage. It was only when Chamberlain made a dead set at the Conservative Right in June 1936 that Churchill tried to form a miscellaneous orchestra out of the Labour party, a broad span of Liberal and Conservative politicians and the League of Nations Union where his name had previously 'st[u]nk in the nostrils of [its] warmest supporters'. [144]

For Churchill the thirties so far had been a period of extensive activity and total failure. His first attempt to challenge Baldwin (in January 1931) had been followed by the formation of the National government and its attempt to exclude him at the general election. He was in a relationship of critical hostility as his sixties heaved into sight, when it obtained the largest parliamentary majority any government had had since 1832. The result was an intensification of literary effort of which the completion of *Marlborough* (with its account of British leadership in Europe) and the beginning of the *History of the English-Speaking Peoples* were the fruit.

Though Randolph Churchill did, [145] Churchill did not intervene in the by-elections of the early thirties. Nor did he attempt to emulate Mosley. Though fishing for a position on the Right, it was the parliamentary Right that was the object of his attention.

In the course of the thirties Churchill took up four causes and, from a position of formal independence from the government, used them as ways of attacking it. The first — the Betting bill — was a rehearsal for the India bill. [146] India failed him and divided him from natural allies like Derby and Austen Chamberlain; in 1935 he dropped it. The third — the uselessness and over-promotion of the MacDonalds — lasted a long time and touched sensitive areas. [147]

The fourth — air defence — was an admirable subject for parliamentary warfare, combining, as it did, a major public fear, an unavoidable reticence on the part of the government and a minister who was both a childhood friend and close to MacDonald. By April 1935 he had cast doubt on the government's figures for British and German air strengths and was primarily responsible for Londonderry's removal from the Air Ministry. From the middle of 1936 his interest in air parity with Germany turned into an invigilation of the execution of the air programme, the chief effect of which in 1938 seemed, somewhat misleadingly, to be the removal of Swinton and Winterton.

In the cases of Londonderry, Winterton, and perhaps Swinton, Churchill was shooting at targets he did not really want to hit. It is not clear when he saw that foreign policy might restore him to the centre of the scene. Even after Hitler's arrival in office, he had thought India more important. In reacting to the murder of Dollfuss, the invasion of Abyssinia and the occupation of the Rhineland, he was still, despite dim forebodings, acting as an ex-minister who was laying bets both ways. It was not until 1938 that 'destiny' began to come through, alcoholically, at the same time as Chamberlain experienced the feeling without alcohol.

One of Baldwin's first acts as Prime Minister in 1935 was to invite Churchill to join the Air Defence Research sub-committee of the Committee of Imperial Defence. [148] Churchill accompanied acceptance with the announcement that he would be on good terms in view of the 'period of strain' which lay ahead. Having supported Lloyd George in January, he now changed direction, supporting the League line in Abyssinia, expecting Hoare to make Mussolini 'climb down' and thrusting his help onto Baldwin at the election. [149]

Chamberlain thought this Churchill's way of easing himself into office, [150] but it is likely that Baldwin wanted only to take defence and rearmament out of public argument. Even if he wanted to have Churchill in the government, Chamberlain would have objected (as he had to Lloyd George eighteen months before); Baldwin did not want to, not least in view of the nuisance Churchill would make of himself if he was there when Baldwin retired. [151]

During the search for a minister to co-ordinate defence, Austen Chamberlain and others wanted Churchill. Churchill agreed with them and made the mistake of offering to suppress criticism 'if there were any chance' of being appointed. [152] After Inskip's appointment, Chamberlain and Churchill built up a heavy-weight body of defence critics who caused Baldwin a great deal of trouble. [153]

In pressing the defence question, Austen Chamberlain hoped to remove Baldwin. By mid-1936 Churchill had virtually resumed hostilities and was having a measure of success. No less than Hoare and Neville Chamberlain, he was preparing to take hold as Baldwin's grip loosened. In speaking powerfully about defence deficiencies, he was speaking to the Right. Through connections with Cecil, Citrine and the League of Nations Union, and by emphasising the League (which he had first hooked on to in 1933), he was showing how well he would wear liberal clothes when Baldwin removed his. [154]

At the turn of the year Churchill's clothes were removed. The attempt to form a King's Party during the abdication proved that he was as erratic as the worst interpretations suggested. Austen Chamberlain's unexpected death four months later removed his strongest supporter. With the beginning of Neville Chamberlain's Prime Ministership, the prospect of office disappeared.

Though Churchill may have offered himself, [155] his prevailing expectation was that office was impossible unless the situation changed. The best way of changing it was to develop an opposition.

This meant finding policy dilemmas that would ring bells in quarters which were ready to criticise the government in the first place. About the Rhineland it meant the estrangement of Mussolini as Hitler's opportunity and Britain as the real cause of Laval's failure. [156] It also meant 'national honour' versus 'funk', 'encircling' Germany 'through the League' and 'organis[ing] the merciful tolerant forces in the world' against the 'heavily armed, immoral dictatorships'. [157] Later, in spite of

Spain, it meant restoring relations with Mussolini and recognising that 'we are...not in position to go to war without very active Russian assistance'. [158] As Chamberlain dissociated himself from the League, it meant 'stand[ing] by the Covenant' and the French, and 'gather[ing] together...the largest number...of well-armed peace-seeking Powers'. In suitable company it meant the 'preservation' of 'the British Empire... for a few more generations in its strength and splendour'. [159]

By the beginning of 1938, Churchill had got nowhere. After the excitement of 1936, nothing had happened. Blum, whom he professed to admire, [160] had been removed (along with the Popular Front). His League position, though tailored to meet Conservative dislike, was a passport to Cecil; [161] during the abdication Cecilian goodwill had disappeared. What he had left was not very much. He had a German (and unusually reactionary) scientific adviser — Lindemann — who was treated as a nuisance when he joined the Air Defence Research Sub-Committee, [162] was resisted when he tried to become Conservative candidate for Oxford University and had been defeated when he stood against the official Conservative notwithstanding. [163] In the House of Lords his only supporter was Lloyd, who, even if he hoped (mistakenly) for office from Chamberlain, had been ostracised (by Baldwin) as a 'die-hard extremist' after his Egyptian performance in the twenties. [164]

Otherwise, Churchill's support was random. He was close to Sinclair and, at his request, had become President of Lord Davies's New Commonwealth Group. [165] He had a loose friendship with Lloyd George, who was old, and had nibbled at Crewe, who was even older. [166] He had taken trouble with Kenneth Lindsay (of the National Labour party). He had had something to do with Citrine and Dalton and had praised the 'great trade unions' for the new interest being taken 'by the Left-wing forces' in 'questions of Imperial defence'. [167] He had formed the 'Peace with Freedom' movement which held lunches and meetings with a view to applying 'Liberal principles' to foreign policy. [168] This had merged into *The Focus* through which Spier's money enabled him to meet a broad range of conspirator, some of whom were concerned primarily about Jewish persecution, one of whom (Steed) was in the pay of the Czech government, and another of whom (Angell)

believed that 'patriotism was a menace to civilisation'. [169]
When Eden began to quarrel with Chamberlain, Churchill
took trouble with him — over the Halifax visit, in the South
of France during a holiday in late 1937 and in Parliament
throughout. [170] But his only real successes were with non-
Conservatives with whom his leads had, on the whole, been
surreptitious. Until Eden and Cranborne resigned, only Vansittart's demotion suggested [171] that anything was moving in
the monolith over which Chamberlain presided.

The resignations were promising in themselves and made it
possible to identify a change of direction. Since Chamberlain
had 'dismissed the Liberal, Labour and non-party voters
whom Mr. Baldwin had painstakingly gathered', Churchill did
his best to break in from the Centre, praising Cranborne as a
Cecil, Eden as a 'memorable' Foreign Secretary and anticipating in 'millions of cottage homes throughout this country...a pang of bitter humiliation' if Britain made a pact 'involving the recognition of the conquest of Abyssinia'. [172]

In presenting the resignations as a victory for Mussolini,
Churchill still hoped for Italian co-operation in Austria. [173]
When Austria was occupied, the 'nation' had to be 'roused' if
'catastrophe' was to be avoided. But Chamberlain's statement
of March 24 went a long way. Churchill did not expect an
immediate attack on Czechoslovakia, wanted only a temporary pledge against invasion and spoke mainly of the need for
a Franco-British alliance to provide stiffening in the Balkans. [174] He went to Paris to advocate staff talks and 'bring
the...democratic European countries into combination with a
view to resisting the dictator countries'. [175] When waving the
prospect of fifty rebels under Margesson's nose, he threatened a rearmament campaign through the League of Nations
Union if Chamberlain really did intend to 'throw over the
League'. [176]

The League campaign began with meetings at Bristol and
Manchester [177] and Randolph Churchill began editing his recent speeches. [178] But no real rebels materialised in Parliament. The attack on the Irish Treaty was a failure. Demands for an enquiry into the administration of the Air Ministry were refused. It was not only Churchill's criticisms which
made Chamberlain appoint a committee. Its demolition of
Swinton was the work of Cadman, Wilson and Fisher, and

perhaps, even of Garvin and the *Observer*. [179]

Although Churchill had established himself as a well-informed critic, [180] he recognised that air deficiencies imposed restraints on policy. When Wood succeeded Swinton, he half-threatened to resign from the Air Defence Research Sub-Committee. [181] During Henlein's visit to London in May he was as much bamboozled as anyone else. [182]

About Germany Churchill was a monarchist who hoped that Hitler could be removed. After a visit from an agent of the German General Staff, he believed that the 'German people' were against war and that the army might do something to stop it. He consulted Halifax before sending a reply which told Beck and his colleagues that an invasion of Czechoslovakia would produce a 'world war' which the Empire would fight to the 'bitter end'. [183]

In telling Halifax that a demonstration of naval power, an appeal to the League or an Anglo-French approach to Russia would be ways of activiating the 'peaceful elements in Germany', [184] Churchill was not intending to 'irritate' Hitler 'if his mind was really turning towards a peaceful solution'. [185] But the 'old Germany' was anti-Nazi and wanted to be rescued. Anglo-French land superiority would disappear by 1940; and Chamberlain was not doing his 'utmost to avert war'. [186]

At the beginning of the second week of September, Churchill asked for a declaration that the government 'would go to war in the event of a German invasion of Czechoslovakia'. He described Chamberlain's decision to go to Berchtesgaden as 'the stupidest thing he ha[d] ever done'. [187] Afterwards, he is said to have said that 'having chosen shame' he would nevertheless 'get war'. [188]

Having been to Paris in order to repeat the incitements of March, [189] Churchill's view was that the issue was 'not...self-determination but...[the] murder by a great state of a small one'. [190] He interpreted Hitler's speech of September 26 as a 'climb-down'. [191]

As the situation developed, Churchill held meetings of friends and allies, including Sinclair, Cecil, Lloyd, Lytton, Wolmer, Bracken, Lindemann, Amery, Grigg, Boothby, Macmillan, Horne and Nicolson. The first decided that, if Chamberlain came back from Godesberg carrying 'peace with dishonour', they would 'go all out against him', the second that it was essential 'to take Russia into our confidence'. These decisions set the tone for the effort which most of the critics were to make between Munich and Prague. [192]

Between September 20 and 29 all the forces of opposition came together to make identical noises at Chamberlain and Halifax. In these days of uneasy collaboration the embryo began which was born eighteen months later as a new coalition.

However, although it began, it was not very strong. In relation to Churchill, Attlee was less forthcoming than Dalton. Such warmth in contact as there was came largely from Churchill. There is no sign of Attlee believing that Conservatives would dissent on any widespread scale or that the Labour party should co-operate unless they did.

Attlee was right. On the Conservative side, conceptions of co-operation varied. In some cases, it was limited to specified subjects. In others it arose from fear of an election at which constituency associations might withhold readoption. [193] In general, Conservatives avoided open entanglement once their constituency associations had been squared. [194]

It is true that Churchill, when challenged, prepared for a by-election with Liberal and League of Nations Union support, and had discussions with Muir and Sinclair about it. [195] His victory in the Association vote in early November, [196] however, made open co-operation unnecessary. When the Duchess of Atholl resigned her seat and re-fought it as an anti-appeaser (after her Association had adopted a new candidate for the next election) he supported her on the ground that she 'adher[ed] to the first principles of the Conservative party'. [197] But he refused to support Lindsay [198] and Bartlett. [199] Despite much Liberal support, some of it unsolicited, [200] he was so far from expecting a transformation of parties that Macmillan seems to have been alone in doing so.

In 1938 Macmillan was forty-four and had been in Parliament for fourteen years. In spite of wealth, marriage and intellectual respectability, he had been outdistanced by his contemporaries. Where Stanley, Eden and Duff Cooper had succeeded, he had failed and had allowed infatuation with

Mosley to be converted into hysterical dislike of Baldwin and Chamberlain.

As member for a vulnerable seat where Liberal and Labour votes mattered, [201] he had wanted a 'National party' in 1933. In 1934 he was hesitating between Churchill and MacDonald (who was 'deeper than any of us imagines') and hoping that the government might fall as a result of the India bill (which he did not himself oppose). [202] Then he had worked with Allen's *Next Five Years* group before the 1935 election [203] and through *The New Outlook* (on edging Allen out of the group) after it. [204] After resigning the Conservative Whip (over the raising of sanctions in mid 1936), he developed contact with Sinclair and renewed the Lloyd George contact which the group had broken off the year before. [205] After Baldwin's retirement he resumed the Whip. [206] 1938 provided the third opportunity to persuade Conservative dissentients and the Sinclair Liberals to work with Labour in preparing for a reverse-version of 1931.

Macmillan aimed to liberate political thinking from the 'class war'. He stood for the fact that 'the free play of the market' had never ensured 'that the right things [are] produced in the right quantities'. He wanted 'Socialism' reconciled with 'Capitalism' and was against the 'diehards on both sides' who would produce a 'trial of strength by...ballot-box...strike or lockout...and (if the problem of poverty is too long neglected) by Civil War'. [207] In sketching plans for the next stage in 'social progress', he aimed at a high-tensioned fusion between the liberal intelligentsia and the progressive Conservatism which was the chief aspect of Eden's theatre.

In the thirties Macmillan's later manner had not yet been perfected. He was thought of as odd, way-out and bookish and would have been no more significant than Boothby (with whom he worked) if publishing had not provided a platform. He was the only Conservative MP who supported Lindsay at the Oxford by-election. [208]

During the September crisis, the Conservative critics were hampered by the fact that Parliament was not sitting. Before the final visit to Munich, the arrival of war was expected to damage Chamberlain permanently. The visit and, even more, the agreement had a dampening and cautionary effect on those who had decided to oppose him. [209]

Churchill's speech of October 5 was an indictment of the past, not a plan for the future. It presented the settlement as a defeat, predicted the early destruction of the Czech state and implied that Anglo-French co-operation with Russia could have had a striking effect on opinion in the German government. But he neither called for a new Cabinet nor suggested a policy. In face of the dominance which Hitler had gained and the threat he presented to France and Britain, the only way of avoiding further humiliation was to 'acquire that supremacy in the air which we [had been] assured [that] we had' and which would alone 'make ourselves an island once again'. [210]

On October 6 about twenty-five MPs [211] abstained in the House of Commons division on Munich. Thereafter they formed the nucleus for two dissenting groups.

Churchill's group consisted of Bracken, Boothby, Sandys and Keyes (with Lloyd in the House of Lords). Boothy, however, was erratic; Bracken was a personal aide and Sandys a relative. All three of these were in their thirties. Though Bracken used reactionary language and Sandys's version of the Percy line had a reactionary component, neither embodied influential Conservative opinion. [212] Keyes, so far from being an experienced politician, was a war-time hero and die-hard admiral who had taken up politics after being passed over for the post of First Sea Lord. Having known Churchill at the Admiralty and Lloyd in Egypt in the twenties, he had been supported by the India Defence League when he won the Portsmouth by-election in 1934. Though much neglected when he arrived in Parliament, he had for long identified himself with 'the restoration of Sea-Power' and the overwhelming nature of Churchill's merits. [213]

Keyes sensed an 'all-round slackening of the nation's fibre';[214] he stood for 'St George and England', 'English liberties' and the 'fight against the enemies within our gates'. [215] He 'despised parliamentary government' [216] and went out of his way to attack Cecil and the League of Nations Union. [217] Though a cruder version of Lloyd, who had the mind and opinions of an authoritarian proconsul, he was not very much like Sandys, Bracken, Boothby or Randolph Churchill.

Lloyd had an unpleasing manner and made little impact. Keyes was an appalling speaker and carried little weight. [218]

Towards Chamberlain, Boothby was as ingratiating as Simon. [219] Bracken's fantasies about 'the Coroner's' 'bleak character' did not help; nor did 'shame' and 'danger' get Churchill any further. [220] The most significant die-hards supported Chamberlain. Sandys's attempt to flatter Amery into forming an Amery group was a failure. [221] Even when Conservatives responded, Churchill succeeded much more in extending the non-Conservative support he had picked up in the previous three years. If McKenna, at seventy-six was merely an answer to Runciman, [222] Sinclair was a very great deal more.

To what extent Sinclair and Johnstone were acting as Churchill's agents is uncertain. The answer is, probably, not at all. But just as it is difficult to believe that Sandys was acting innocently with Amery, so Sinclair may have been a rallying-point for elements on the Centre-Left where Churchill was neither particularly acceptable nor wished publicly to be thought so.

The methods of stealth, if they were used, [223] would have been dropped if Churchill had fought a by-election in his constituency. In the end, he did not have to. For Sinclair, however, stealth was unnecessary (except in contact with Hannington, the Communist). [224] He supported Lindsay and Bartlett and praised Cripps (without actively supporting him). [225] He persuaded the Liberal candidate to stand down as part of the Liberal and League of Nations Union campaign to rescue the Duchess of Atholl at the West Perth by-election. [226]

Lindsay, Cripps and the Duchess failed in their immediate objectives. The Conservative dissentients were reluctant to co-operate with Sinclair while their numbers were small. [227] Approaches to the Labour party were received with as much coolness as Attlee had shown towards Churchill. [228] Angell's support for the Liberal candidate at Holderness was not important. [229] Even Bartlett's success at Bridgewater [230] was a disappointment since he did not stand as a liberal (though he was one) and did not ask Sinclair to appear on his platform because Attlee would not join him. [231]

The Liberal party began to do better at the elections of 1939 at the same time as the Labour party began to do worse. Though this made the 'democratic Conservatives' important, Sinclair got little attention from the Conservative newspapers and was virtually ignored by the *Telegraph*. [232]

Nevertheless, he was important. He said reputably, and bitterly, what Conservatives could not say about Chamberlain being the 'dupe' of 'dictators' and the government no longer being 'national'. [233] He said what some parts of the Labour party believed about the need for a Popular Front. In offering to abandon controversial policies in order to create a 'national opposition', he was basing himself on the Liberal, League of Nations Union and IPC policy of defending 'the moral principles of our civilisation against the principle of force'. In advocating a Russian alliance, praising Halifax and Eden and demanding Conscription as an aid to the German opposition, he was close to Churchill to whom, in return, the Liberal party 'represent[ed]...the heart and soil of the British nation'. [234]

Eden's group — which met in the houses of Tree, Thomas or Patrick — was a more influential body than the one over which Churchill presided. It was also more broad-based. Alongside Amery, there were two ex-Liberals — Spears (who was part-French and had close contact with Mandel, Reynaud and the war-party in Paris) and Hopkinson, protesting against the treatment he saw Chamberlain giving Inskip when he was his Private Secretary. [235] And there was Nicolson — an ex-Mosleyite and National Labour MP, who had been a successful diplomatist and written a trendy book about Versailles and who, as protagonist of the League of Nations Union and regular columnist in Harris's *Spectator*, embodied more brashly than anyone else the group's desire to square circles with the Liberal Left. [236]

Most members of the group, however, were both Conservative and comparatively young, and left an impression of being smart officers or 'old school tie men' (i.e. the Glamour Boys). This included progressive amiability of which Eden was the embodiment. Law, the son of Bonar Law, ran Federal Union. Crossley had been part of the Percy conspiracy in 1935. Tree (who had a lot of Liberals in his constituency) had wanted a National party in 1934 and had had a certain amount to do with the National Labour party thereafter; as a 'Christian idealist', Cartland had thought of joining it. [237]

Cranborne and Wolmer were also Christian idealists. Duff Cooper regarded the group as a protest by Baldwin's 'most loyal supporters in evil days' against 'all that element in the party' which was once 'so false' to him; he wanted an 'ideological' foreign policy to attract American support in the future in the same way as Baldwinian virtue had attracted Liberal support in the past. [238]

Even if some of them were friends of Noël Coward, the body of the group consisted of intellectually industrious MPs who, on personal or public grounds, were discontented with existing arrangements. They laboured the point that the Conservative party must appeal to the body of the people who, while not Conservatives (however conservative by instinct and inclination), would respond to a programme of 'social reform and national regeneration'.

What Eden claimed was that, if the group did not contain all the 'best' elements in the Conservative party (since some of these — like Halifax and Stanley — were in the government), it represented them where the Prime Minister had handed over to 'businessmen'. [239] By this he meant that Wood and Simon were nonconformist lawyers who lacked charm and League idealism, and would have made unconvincing Young Englanders. He meant also that, apart from Halifax and a single Stanley after Lord Stanley's death, the Cabinet lacked that paternalistic compassion which the various Percies, Stanleys, Cavendishes and Cecils were supposed to have given to all Conservative governments up to 1929. In this respect he was claiming not only that the Cabinet was socially defective, but that the only two of its members who were not agreed with the policy criticisms he was making. [240]

There may have been a point after Munich when he thought of leading a Left-Centre government consisting of the dissentient Conservatives, the Sinclair Liberals and the Labour party. If so, he decided not to. [241] The demands, [242] even threats, [243] he made for Labour and Trade union participation in a government of national unity were not pointers towards the radical democratic party of the future. If meant seriously at all, they envisaged nothing more radical than the existing Conservative leadership plus himself and a Labour contingent pursuing egalitarian policies which Labour would not accept from Chamberlain.

It is true that he stated that he was 'fed up with Parliament and the politicians', and might oppose Chamberlain at by-elections unless an All-Party reconstruction occurred. It is true, too, that he said that Baldwin and Halifax should be given the opportunity to effect one. But those were threats. He at no point voted against the government, in which he would find many admirers if he was given the chance to return. Baldwin's opinion was that Churchill's and Lloyd George's attempts to 'use' him had failed, and that he could return if Chamberlain wanted him to. Eden was probably hoping for a situation in which Chamberlain would need him at an election. [244]

Unless he was expecting Chamberlain to crack up as suddenly as his father and half-brother had done, [245] it is likely that Eden's desire to get back increased the clearer it became that the expectations of February had been false ones. After a visit to America, he was playing down his disagreement in the New Year [246] and dropping hints about accepting office. [247] After Prague he made emollient calls for a government of national unity [248] and discouraged the group from supporting Conscription when Chamberlain refused to accept it. [249] The group's newspaper conspiracies embarrassed him visibly. [250] On at least two occasions he offered to join the government — after Albania, and in August 1939, by undertaking special missions to Turkey and Russia. [251]

Nor was Eden the only person who hoped to be recalled. Duff Cooper (despite ferocity towards Chamberlain) and even Amery, after eight years of waiting, half-hoped that they might be brought back. [252] Nor did the group as a whole join Churchill, Bracken and Macmillan when (for the first time) they voted against the government on November 17 (over Chamberlain's refusal to set up a Ministry of Supply). [253]

Though the increase in its expectations was not continuous, the group was encouraged by the feeling that Chamberlain had lost touch with the House of Commons, that the government (especially the National Liberal element) was weak and that Baldwin would have got Labour to agree before introducing Conscription. [254] It kept up running demands for a firm policy in the Far East, for a National government and a National Register and for a genuine attempt to reach agreement with the Russians. In July it was involved in a major press campaign.

This was set off by a German staff officer's claim, which Tree brought to a group meeting on June 29, that a German occupation of Danzig could only be stopped by mobilising the Fleet, sending the air force to France and putting Churchill in the Cabinet. [255] One result was that Amery wrote to Halifax, spoke to Margesson and Hoare and made a speech at Birmingham, praising Halifax and demanding a War Cabinet. [256] Another was that Macmillan drafted a letter which he and Nicolson were deputed to get printed in the *Daily Telegraph*.

The *Telegraph* was chosen because Camrose — its proprietor — admired Halifax and had said that Chamberlain could not form an All-Party government 'as Labour did not trust him'. [257] On June 30 he was visited in his office by Eden, Nicolson and Macmillan. Efforts were also made with other newspapers, [258] and with Sinclair who then made a series of speeches praising Halifax's 'liberal spirit' and demanding office for Churchill and Eden. [259]

At the same time the same feelings were being felt by Garvin, whom Prague had turned into a guilt-ridden anti-Chamberlainite, and by Astor, who, having turned round with him, wanted to declare war when Mussolini invaded Albania. [260] In the summer of 1939 they wanted Conscription and a Russian alliance. [261] From the end of June, with Halifax's approval and Trenchard's help, Astor was negotiating with Churchill, Eden, Sinclair and the Labour leaders for a public warning to Hitler. [262] He not only went with Eden to see Camrose but was in touch with a group of Conservative backbenchers who sent an observer to the meeting.

Though Camrose and Astor pulled their punches (in case denigration of Chamberlain encouraged Hitler unduly), they made it plain that Halifax was important and Churchill vital. About Churchill there were numerous newspaper articles. They were punctuated by statements from Salisbury and Selborne — whose sons were members of the Eden group — and by a public wrangle about *The Times*'s refusal to print a Churchill letter from Layton, Meston, Smuts and Lady Violet Bonham-Carter. On July 9 the *Telegraph* had a leading article

explaining why Churchill's admission was a necessary act of
state. [263]

This campaign was in no way decisive. It irritated the
Edenites who did not understand why there was so little
mention of Eden. [264] It confirmed not only Camrose's brother, Kemsley, [265] but also Chamberlain in a determination not
to be 'bounced' into giving way to agitation. [266] Even after a
good Liberal by-election in North Cornwall, [267] Chamberlain
seemed as secure as before. For the effect of criticism, it is
necessary to look at the inner history of the Cabinet.

PART III

THE EFFECT

9

HALIFAX

'Reverence for the old, dislike of things new, made it indubitable that
his sympathies in matters of religion would be Catholic, and cast him
back in the middle of contemporary difficulties upon what he regarded
as his sheet anchor – the ancient consent of the Universal Church. At
the same time allowance must be made, in the cause of charity, for past
mistakes. "Dissenters" he used to say "should be dealt with lovingly
and forbearingly" '. Halifax (Irwin), *John Keble*, 1932 (new edition of
work first published in 1909) p. 233

'When I heard your wireless address to the young some weeks ago I felt
it was saying in more measured language exactly what I had been saying
to the students at Aberystwyth a few weeks before. It is not worth your
while to read my remarks, but I think it is rather interesting to see how
you from your Conservatism and I from my Liberalism come to so
much the same conclusion about the present dangers of the world'.
Murray to Baldwin, April 9 1934

'Have you really quite decided to go? If you go the country will be
plunged back into party politics and union will vanish and our enemies
rejoice. There is no member of the House *on either side* who wants you
to go, who would not rather have you than Neville. I believe every
member of your Cabinet feels the same – I have better means of
knowing than you have'. Wedgwood to Baldwin, March 12 1937

(i)

A striking feature of Chamberlain's first twenty months as
Prime Minister was his feeling that he need have so little fear
of opposition that he could do more or less as he liked. There
was the battle with Eden, which he won. There were backbench revolts – over the National Defence Contribution (as
'a tremendous instrument in the hands of the Left') and over
the unification (or 'nationalisation') of coal-mining royalties.[1] There were major upheavals because of his speeches
about agriculture,[2] the agricultural implications of the Irish
treaty and the bill for rationalising (or 'socialising') the distri-
bution of milk, which resulted in the replacement of the
Minister of Agriculture.[3] There were moments of difficulty –
after the Anschluss, about Franco's bombarding of British
ships and over air production in May 1938, when Swinton
was removed in order to save the government.[4] On the second

day of the Munich debate, criticism was so strong that a general election began to seem unavoidable. [5] At the turn of the year there was a period of 'anguish' and 'isolation' when Chamberlain first wanted and then threatened to call an election but was compelled, by the prospect of losing it, to sacrifice Inskip and Winterton instead.[6] In general, however, whatever others felt, he felt untroubled by criticism and capable of meeting it whenever it was made.

One reason for this was a certain pride in his own capability which reacted gratefully to praise and answered criticism by showing that it resulted from the ignorance, demagoguery or self-seeking of his critics. Another was that he was lucky in his relations with public opinion and was encouraged by this, as the international situation became more complicated, to develop a conviction of rectitude and indispensability.[7]

Chamberlain was attacked by the *Daily Herald*, the *News Chronicle* and the *New Statesman*. After Eden's resignation, he had only uncertain support from Mann and the *Yorkshire Post*.[8] He had a difficult time with the *Daily Telegraph* where Camrose allowed criticism a free hand. After Rothermere's retirement, the Rothermere newspapers were controlled by Esmond Harmsworth, whose enthusiasms were less helpful than his father's. But (except about agriculture), Beaverbrook on the whole supported him.[9] So did Kemsley, Hadley and Sidebotham — the proprietor, editor and columnist of the *Sunday Times* — who believed, more simply and far later than he did, that Hitler could be made a friend. [10] So too did Garvin and the *Observer* and Dawson and *The Times*, and a wide range of provincial newspapers. There was enough newspaper support for Chamberlain to feel that his position was being put and more than enough response when millions of listeners heard his voice. [11] Despite psychological recessions in May [12] and November 1938, there was no run of by-election disasters to compare with the by-elections of the previous Parliament.

If it had been simply temperamental seriousness which stopped Chamberlain responding to alternative points of view, the silence would have been broken by other ministers. In these months they did not really bark. Where they seemed likely to, except immediately before Munich, he was able to silence them because there was neither unity among the possible oppositions nor sufficient confirmation from events to make their understanding of policy more credible than his own.

Nor had Conservative MPs any reason to doubt his credibility. The Baldwin/Chamberlain management of the Conservative party had been highly successful. Protection had been established; the era of revolutionary danger had passed. The defeat of 1929 had been turned, almost casually, into the landslide of 1931 and the jettisoning of Snowden and the Samuelites who had helped to make it possible. The Liberal accessions, both before 1931 and afterwards, had provoked social tension and varying responses in the Conservative party. But the more prominent recruits belonged to the comfortable classes or the respectable professions. Though occasionally Jewish, nonconformist or too obviously ideological, they accepted Protection, opposed socialism and did not seem out of place.

Baldwin's methods had been slow. He avoided detail; critics said that he avoided thought. [13] He did not avoid thought about the major problem of the time. He assumed that, since constitutional safeguards would not stop socialism 'if the Socialists [were] determined', [14] persuasion had to work instead.

Considering that he was a reactionary Tory, his achievement was remarkable. By the time he began his third period as Prime Minister, no politician doubted that his freedom from 'high and dry Toryism' made him 'totally acceptable' to his non-Conservative colleagues, to the 'mugwumps', 'clericals' and earnest, theoretical 'liberals' [15] who were to be found in all parties [16] and to the many Labour politicians for whom his 'quintessentially English' combination of peaceful intentions and a 'modern outlook' [17] provided a social reassurance which no other Conservative could provide.

Baldwin aimed to demonstrate the humanity, responsibility and social edgelessness of industrial wealth. So far, however, from showing that his message was different from the message of Hatfield, he had shown that it was very much the same. As the protectionist overtone receded, his speeches became statements of decency and law in face of the 'wild menace of totalitarianism'. He talked about England and the English and did not 'hesitate to speak in plain terms of

Christianity'. [18] His address to the Peace Society during the
1935 election was 'the most beautiful and sonorous' he had
'ever delivered', [19] proved that 'one' could 'remain' an Englishman and yet back the League' [20] and seemed, even to an
unfriendly critic, to be more 'packed with wisdom and
humanity' than anything he had 'ever read'. [21]

Baldwin presented the working-class movement as created
by average men who were very much like himself and would
respond to a message of conciliation. In implying the existence of a strong, gentle and happy people who had not been
perverted by 'intellectuals' and 'press-lords', he held up a re-
pertoire of social heroes, none of whom resembled Beaverbrook or Layton and most of whom reflected, in sometimes
eccentric ways, the qualities which the English were supposed
to admire. [22]

The context was pre-industrial. Though 'rural society' had
'disappeared' in Baldwin's lifetime, [23] his rhetoric implied an
admiration of its virtues. His newspaper appearances confirmed this, and his speech writers articulated it. 'I enclose for
what it is worth a draft of my very introductory talk', wrote
one of them, when asked to prepare a broadcast on the
National Character.

After that I go to an historical survey which will be more interesting on
national types like the Squire, the Parson, the Yeoman, the Craftsman,
the Merchant, the Adventurer and the Housewife... But I believe that
what people would like most, and what you, above everyone else could
give them, [is] a few sketches of the English men and women whom
you have encountered both in life and books and who, though one
could never explain why, reveal that they are English from the very
moment that one meets them: I mean people like Falstaff and Sarah
Gamp and Lord Radnor and old squire Askhurst of Waterstock and
almost any middle-aged working man you can think of. [24]

Was Baldwin creating a myth? Probably not. Jones, who
wrote some of his prose, may have been. But Bryant probably meant what he wrote. Davidson almost certainly did. It is
likely that Baldwin felt as he spoke, meant what he said and
really thought, like his admirers, that he was 'recalling' them
to 'the fundamentals of life'. 'It isn't easy', he wrote in 1933,
'it isn't easy... There is so much I hate in this age. But there is
a lot of good, and one must hold to it and have Faith.' [25]

Baldwin had moral, social and aesthetic beliefs, and also a
religion, but few of his beliefs were political. He was pessi-

mistic about purpose and felt an instinctive resistance to it. [26]
Though he succeeded, where necessary, in mastering the reluctance that he felt, his interests were spiritual and at-
mospheric, his instrument of demonstration the wand rather
than the baton.

What he wanted to express were the feelings of a 'decent
Englishman'. In imagination he lived a version of what these
were and created a teaching about what they should be. In
doing so, he did something that no twentieth-century politician, except Grey, had quite done before. In doing it he
implied a consonance between the politics of the public-
school gentleman of middle rank, literary interests and rural
tastes and the reticence of the body of the people as a whole.
'Englishmen', he wrote in 1935, 'may appear to take [their]
mutual loyalities for granted: we don't talk about them. But
it is good once and again to break the silence of our instinctive reserve and say to each other what we might regret never
having said if death came to one of us unexpectedly.' [27]

All this, however moving, was also misleading. Baldwin was
a tough operator of long experience and high accomplish-
ment; he had beaten everyone who had challenged him. By
the middle thirties his scalps included Lloyd George, Birkenhead, Beaverbrook, Rothermere, Cecil, Salisbury, Churchill,
MacDonald and Austen and Neville Chamberlain.

In the 1931 Parliament there had been difficulties and, in
relation to India, a major problem. Over unemployment assistance there had been a full-scale loss of nerve. In the new
Parliament the same thing had happened over Abyssinia,
where backbench Conservatives were expected in the course
of six months to believe that League support for Abyssinia
would be forthcoming, that the Hoare/Laval policy was
necessary because it would not be, that sanctions could be
effective and then that sanctions should be dropped.

This produced the realisation that Cecil was a 'highly
dangerous man', [28] that it would be dangerous to do anything
about the Rhineland [29] and that there was a defence crisis
which the Defence White Paper had done little to resolve. It
produced argument about the 'liberal or semi-socialist' nature
of the Coalition, back-biting about the use of 'Conservative'
funds for 'national' propaganda and a nasty spirit of Tory
hostility towards the retention of the MacDonalds. [30]

Baldwin's followers counter-attacked but the period of difficulty lasted throughout the autumn. It was only the abdication that ended it. The abdication, however, ended it decisively. By the time Chamberlain became Prime Minister, the prevailing fact was success with Chamberlain as one of its engi-
neers.

Chamberlain was a Midland Unionist who came to Parliament late in life after failing, when given a chance, as an
administrator during the Lloyd George Coalition. Like Baldwin he had spent a long time in business. Like Baldwin, too,
he was public schoolboy who believed in the decency and
modesty of all good men. Moreover, he was a tough (and
quietly rough) manipulator who represented the marriage
between Left and Right that Baldwin had made his own.

There, the similarities ended. Though they had the same
social objective, Chamberlain lacked the external embodiment which Baldwin, or Jones, had created. Where Baldwin's
prose was distinguished, Chamberlain's was serviceable (and
his slang juvenile). [31] Baldwin had a relaxed perspective about
effort and social contact and a Leibnizian security about the
providential order. Chamberlain was 'shy' and 'bottled', [32]
with a temperamental will to succeed and a Unitarian conviction of infallibility. Where Baldwin's father was a Tory,
Chamberlain's was a civic Radical first and a Unionist second,
the creator of the Unionist doctrine and one of the tributa-
ries by which civic Radicalism became conservative. Where
Baldwin had long holidays in an inaccessible place and had to
be 'shamed' [33] into shortening them, Chamberlain and his
wife accepted invitations to the discomfort of other people's
homes, was usually available for consultation and was always
ready to come back if he was not.

Chamberlain had strong opinions about policy and intended to assert them. He had even stronger opinions about
persons and showed no false tolerance for those he disliked.
Baldwin had spent fifteen years 'suffering fools' [34] and shuf-
fling the pack between leading politicians. Chamberlain deployed narrower sympathies and was well aware of the contrast which others drew between himself on the one hand and
'that good grey head that all men knew' on the other.

Chamberlain believed that Unionism was radical and comprehensive enough to be right. He had the thinking Radical's

contempt for the unthinking Radicalism of the Labour party and the practical Liberal's contempt for the theoretical Liberalism of the Liberal party. Where Baldwin believed little, and put up with those who believed more, he expressed his own feelings, had no time for sentimental resonances between working-class politicians and the aristocracy and allowed 'sarcasm' to raise the bristles which Baldwin went out of his way to smooth. [35]

Chamberlain disliked Mrs Simpson ('a heartless adventuress') and admired King George VI and his Queen. He attached spiritual significance to the nation's physique; until evacuation showed that it was bad, he was pleased when Conscription showed that it was good. He believed in separated peoples rather than our common humanity and in the nation as the centre of political virtue. But his 'patriotism' was as quiet as his 'decency' and as unlike Kipling's as Kipling's was unlike Mill's. Indeed, he was much more like Mill than he was like Kipling, and much more like him than his father who admired Mill much more. [36]

Chamberlain thought of himself as a typical Englishman, upright and honourable and honouring honour and uprightness in others. He believed in 'ordinary people' who were 'patriotic, progressive [and] sympathetic with the underdog' [37] and shared his mistrust of political posturing, even when he was good at providing it. He was a 'stiff' man. [38] He was a man of 'brains and common sense'. [39] He would allow neither 'sloppy sentiment' nor 'personal considerations' to obstruct the 'causes' to which he had become committed, [40] and he had a burning belief that any policy which had been objectively conceived could be effectively sold to Parliament and the public. He admired the younger Pitt more than any other Prime Minister. He thought popularity 'a very ephemeral thing' by the side of the one thing '[t]hat mattered' — which was 'to do the job'. [41]

In doing their 'jobs', Chamberlain expected ministers to know their subjects. In Chatfield (who was an admiral), in Wilson, Hankey and Anderson (who were civil servants), in Zetland, in W.S. Morrison (for a time), in Burgin and Hore-Belisha (whom he had disliked as Financial Secretary to the Treasury), [42] in Butler, Geoffrey Lloyd and Malcolm Mac-Donald (whom he much preferred to his father) and in Sir

Reginald Dorman-Smith (who brought professional knowledge to the Ministry of Agriculture), he found what he wanted. He found it, most of all, in Sir Kingsley Wood.

Wood was a Methodist solicitor who had graduated through LCC politics into the lowest reaches of the Lloyd George Coalition. Throughout the 1924 government, he was Chamberlain's Under-Secretary at the Ministry of Health. By 1933 he had established himself as an efficient manipulator of the party system.

In the thirties Chamberlain was closer to him than to any politician. He brought him into the Cabinet and the Conservative machine and had him as Chief of Staff during the 1935 election. He consulted him regularly and allowed him to be influential at the major turning points — when forming his Cabinet, removing Inskip, [43] declaring war, and in relation to newspapers throughout.

Wood's constituency was in Woolwich; his home was a large house in Tunbridge Wells. He was writer of legal textbooks. But he had been to neither a public school nor a university. Much more than Chamberlain (who fished and shot, and whose interests as a naturalist were so attractive to his hosts), he was rurally tone-deaf. If his critics spoke of him as a 'cynical professional', [44] that meant merely that he registered the civic mind and was the successful propagator of a reactionary reassurance foreign to the elevating half-truths of aristocratic idealism.

As the only politician who had made anything of the Post Office [45] and one of the few ministers whom Chamberlain would trust at the Treasury, [46] he was a possible, if socially unusual, War Minister in 1937. [47] As the minister responsible for the three millionth post-war house, he was a natural successor when Swinton left the Air Ministry in 1938. [48] Chamberlain may have been clearing the way when he put Inskip out of political circulation in September 1939. [49]

If so, he was disappointed. By mid-winter Wood was doing badly. [50] He was worried when Chamberlain abandoned Hore-Belisha with whom his relations had been almost as close; [51] his removal in 1940 recorded a failure which Chamberlain had not anticipated.

In addition to being close to Chamberlain, Wood recognised the potentialities of Lloyd George, whose advocate he was

in 1935. Eventually, too, he recognised the importance of
Churchill to whom, after inducements, he transferred in May
1940.

It was not, however, for these connections that Chamberlain valued him, nor for any striking originality of mind, but
for 'competence' without abrasiveness, fertility and shrewdness in advice and the certainty (until damaged by the war)
that he would exercise sensitive control over any of the departments of state. [52]

Wood was efficient. In this he was unusual; Chamberlain
complained as continuously about government backbenchers
as he had about Baldwin's inefficiency before he retired. [53]

Chamberlain was not the only person who drew the contrast with Baldwin. But, so long as he was waiting to succeed,
criticism was confined to colleagues and rivals. The trouble
he had over unemployment assistance [54] and Lloyd George
did him no permanent damage with the parliamentary party
which shared none of the distaste felt by his Cabinet critics
for his clarity of mind about inflation.

Nor had Chamberlain done anything untoward on Baldwin's retirement. He had got rid of Runciman and Mac-
Donald but had allowed Simon to get rid of the National
Defence Contribution (through which, as Chancellor, he had
himself upset Conservatives). But he was so far from constructing a Conservative government that the Simonites and the
Labour party were reassured. It was some time before it
seemed that a Baldwin-type government would be used to
lend respectability to the foreign policy of the Right.

In the Conservative attitude to post-war Europe, there had
been many shifts, all of which were reflected in the Cabinet.
Even after the occupation of the Ruhr, Conservative feeling
was anti-German. The stubbornness of the French then modified it. German rearmament, the assassination of Dollfuss and
Hitler's repudiation of Versailles modified it in the other direction and produced a period, after Russia's accession to the
League, when Germany was regarded as the danger and
League-based co-operation with Russia a guarantee of stability. [55] The Franco-Soviet pact, on the other hand, was disliked and was a source of sympathy for German action in the
Rhineland. Disillusionment about the League, the Russian
intervention in Spain and Labour hysteria against Franco

then turned the coin over. [56] From 1937 there was a feeling, as strong as the anti-Russian feeling of the twenties, that Russia was a bad thing and the Franco-Russian alliance worse.

Though most Conservative MPs sympathised with Franco from the start, the Spanish war did not become significant until Communist infiltration highlighted the connection which the Left increasingly made between the ideological correctness of the Republic and the need to activate the League in order to resist dictators. Conservatives did not regard Franco as a Fascist or his rebellion as a Fascist revolution. [57] They spoke of him as a 'Christian gentleman' and did not expect British interests to suffer if he won. [58] They believed that the 'Socialists' were being 'wagged by their Communist tail' in trying to turn the League into an anti-Fascist 'War Office' which would bring Britain into conflict with Germany, Italy and Japan when it was not even certain that the public would fight for France and Belgium. [59]

Though they lacked the clarity of the Chiefs of Staff (who had not spent the previous decade making League noises to their constituents), they were afraid of blundering into war. They did not want war. They did not want avoidable escalations of public expenditure. [60] The knew that there were commercial reasons for working with the Japanese and that, about communism, Japan was the 'one outstandingly realistic power in the Far East'. [61]

They were not, therefore, impressed by eulogies of the League (even from Eden) [62] and were quite prepared to listen to criticism. Their willingness was greatly increased when it came from the top.

By 1937 Chamberlain had been at the top for a very long time. He seemed efficient, could make up his mind [63] and could present anything that was decided as a development of party principle. He pulled the party together when faction-fighting broke out in 1936 and, by criticising the League, had given it something to believe in. He was not identified with the Foreign Office and shared none of Eden's liking for Litvinoff. There was no hint of him cutting a dash, leading fashion or corsetting himself in the sunburnt romanticism of the Riviera. [64] His deviations from Eden could be seen as rejections of encirclement, communism and (quite wrongly) Blum.

Eden's resignation was a problem. But it was not obviously about anything in particular and was not supported by particular criticisms in the future. So far as it had a policy content at all, it was about Italy (where the major problem was to be German).

Chamberlain's German policy seemed as much like the Peace movement's as MacDonald's had seemed like Monsell's in 1934. But he had previously been typecast as a 'fire-eater' (like Amery and Churchill) [65] and remained convincing about defence even after Baldwin had ceased to. There was every reason to admire the creative imagination which had blurred the issue between those who were against war and those who wanted to avoid war over central Europe.

It was not only that Chamberlain had blurred the issue but that his natural critics had been undermined. The peace movement of the early thirties had been broad-based. After Abyssinia, the Peace Pledge Union divided it by pin-pointing the prospect of Collective Security entailing war. Over Eden's resignation and at Munich, Chamberlain was supported by Ponsonby, Lansbury and the Union and by McGovern, Maxton and the ILP.

Even in the Labour party, antagonism was not as universal as it was made to seem. At the time of the Runciman mission, Noel-Buxton went to Czechoslovakia to give a hand with 'treaty revision'. MacDonald's Arnold and a blind ex-member of the Executive resigned from the party out of sympathy with Chamberlain. Among non-pacifists, Greenwood and Alexander (until a late stage) showed considerable understanding. Citrine seems to have liked Chamberlain as much as Wilson and Hankey did. He coached him for meetings to attract TUC co-operation for the defence programmes and left the impression, at many points up to the beginning of the war, that his policies were not as depraved as Dalton and Attlee were suggesting. [66]

In spite of Ottawa Chamberlain received friendly attention from Cobdenites who believed in economic appeasement as the cure for war. [67] Though an emphatic advocate of a League policy, Allen gave support on these grounds and joined Noel-Buxton in supporting the transfer of the Sudeten Germans at the time of Munich. [68] Among party Liberals, Lothian praised Chamberlain (after Munich) as 'the only per-

son' who refused to believe that 'Hitler and the Nazis are
incorrigible'. [69] So did Samuel, who had described Hitler as 'a
mystic' with a 'conscience' and told Chamberlain that he had
done the right thing since 'any fool can go to war'. [70]

Conservatives who supported Chamberlain by their votes
or acquiescence did not all claim to know about Europe. Nor
were they consistent or predictable in their reactions. [71] But
they knew that the Opposition was dishonest and its views 'a
menace to the peace of the world'. [72] They believed that
Chamberlain preferred 'facts to exploded theories'. [73] They
were impressed by the 'build-up' he was given as the guarantor of European security and they saw no one who was as convincing. [74] The more monstrously Hitler behaved, the easier it
was to claim that what had happened was 'bound to happen'
and that, thanks 'mainly to the Prime Minister's visits...we
can now fight, if we have to...with...clean hands...and the
advantage...that the peoples of Germany and Italy know him
...to be a just man and lover of peace'. [75]

This applied not just to admirers of Hitler, of whom there
were a few, [76] but to the body of average MPs who had no
interest in German politics, were impressed by Chamberlain
personally and would not think of upsetting him unless compelled to by contradictions between policy and events.

About defence policy, contradictions had been easy to
establish. What foreign policy dissentients tried to do, from
Austen Chamberlain onwards, was to establish that there
were contradictions in foreign policy too.

The difficulty was that, while still Chancellor, Chamberlain
had given a foreign-policy lead which informed opinion had
then followed. In acting out the assumption that the League
was finished, he seemed only to have reacted sensibly in a
disappointing situation.

In Chamberlain's mind, the objective was 'peace'. In the
minds of others, it was a disciplined and stable Germany.
Whether heartfelt (as with him and the Peace Pledge Union),
prudential (as with him and his military advisers) or ideologically anti-Bolshevik (as among those who saw the point of
Hitler), the outcome was a feeling that the lines on which he
was working were right.

For a long time, MPs found the feeling reflected among

their constituents. They found contradictions easier to discern in the Opposition view than in Chamberlain's and accepted his because he had been the first to point them out. It
was not easy to think that an industrial power like Germany
could be kept down permanently. There was a strong wish to
believe that no nation could ' "unalterably be the enemy of
another" '.[77] Beaverbrook was not the only person who
sensed connections between dislike of Continental entanglements, the prospect of war and the feeling that there were
'already far too many Jews in London'.[78]

Conservatives did not believe that Chamberlain's object
was 'alliance with dictators' at the expense of 'democracy'.
The policy they were supporting was the Eden policy of
getting France and Germany to create a regional pact in place
of the limitless commitment which had been discredited by
Abyssinia. 'Rearmament and reconciliation' seemed as realistic
as any alternative and much more reasonable than 'Arms and
the Covenant'. It was much more reassuring than the critics'
claim, so much at variance with Hitler's assurances, that
Hitler's ambitions were Napoleonic.

There were Cecils (on grounds of Church persecution) and
long-term anti-Germans who believed that Hitler was as evil
as the Prussians. To others he was merely confusing. He had
attacked Versailles and aimed to upset the victory of 1918.
But he was a racial patriot, an enemy of communism and an
ex-serviceman who, like them, had seen through the cobweb
of illusion which surrounded the League of Nations. Some
did, most did not, believe in the international Jewish conspiracy (of which, where necessary, Blum could be represented as a leader). Hitler often seemed mad, odd or idealistic.
But he expressed sentiments which some shared and had expressed forcibly in the early twenties,[79] and had made a
point of wishing to be allied with Britain.

These judgments did not exclude the belief that German
rearmament was a threat and that colonies ought not to be
bartered. Nor did they remove the impression — which the
wireless confirmed — that Hitler was violent, dangerous and
hysterical. But they made it difficult to believe that he would
attack the Empire. They made it impossible to forget — what
many of them knew from boardrooms, bank parlours or the

Empire Economic Union — that Britain and Germany had interests in common while America's interests were often antagonistic. [80]

These assumptions died hard, buttressed as they were by the belief that 'the British people' 'would not willingly go to war except in the defence of interests [that were] vital'. After Prague a young Conservative MP stated that Britain's interests would best be served by Germany having central Europe. [81] Even Bracken thought 'the fear of war negligible if we push on with our rearmament programme and avoid internal political quarrels' since the 'real hope for peace' lay in the 'Nazi gangsters'' sense of 'weakness in the event of a war in which first-class powers engage'. [82]

These assumptions had not really been destroyed in September 1938 when Britain threatened Hitler and the Blum rôle was played by Benes — the pin-up of the League of Nations Union [83] — who ruled a country 'half of [whose] people could not be relied on to give it loyal support'.

The objections to Benes were ample — that he had been Arthur Henderson's assistant at Geneva, that he was doing nothing about treaty revision and that his 'diabolical cunning' was perpetuating the 'disastrous artificialities' of the French 'system' by letting the Russians into central Europe. They were deepened by a widespread assumption that the consequence of fighting on September 27 might well have been 'the triumph of Communism in Europe'. [84]

Though most backbenchers believed that treaty revision was unavoidable, they wanted Britain to avoid the responsibility. [85]   From this angle the Runciman mission was a 'danger' and the Anglo-French guarantee a mistake; the Czechs, therefore, should be grateful to Chamberlain for averting their 'annihilation'. [86] It was the 'midsummer of madness' to fight once it had been decided that territory would be transferred, and 'the maddest war...a reluctant people...ever faced — to fight over a method of implementing an agreement that had already been agreed by all concerned'. [87] So far from apologising for refusing to 'go meddling in distant parts of Central Europe', they saw 'right triumphing over might', 'God's will' being done and Chamberlain emerging as 'a great leader' and the 'greatest statesman of his generation'. [88] Even those who doubted whether Hitler meant what Chamberlain had said did not expect to be 'worse off' if he broke his word 'in six months or a year's time'. [89]

Chamberlain did not repeat to the House of Commons what he had said about 'peace for our time'; he told it, on the contrary, that 'the superstructure' was 'not even begun'. [90] His credibility depended, however, on Hitler meaning what *he* had said; he had said that his territorial demands had ended. It was in this context that the occupation of Prague and his Commons statement of March 15 made Chamberlain look incredible. Even so, he might have got away with it if he had not changed direction at Birmingham two days later. It is far from clear that he made the change willingly.

Since Chamberlain believed that he had overwhelming public support even when the occupation of Prague had made him look foolish, he was not really interested in the pressure brought by the Labour and Liberal parties and by the Conservative dissentients. So far as they were concerned, his view was that he knew where he was going, and they did not.

Nevertheless, their pressures had an effect. They sank, or seeped, into the minds of publicists and MPs. They were reported, and repeated, in the Cabinet. They came slowly, as events appeared to confirm them, to create an indefeasibility which no politician could ignore. In making them effective, the chief instrument of mediation was Halifax.

In the course of 1938 Halifax developed doubts about Chamberlain's policy which he had not felt when he became Foreign Secretary. This happened, however, not just because he acquired a new view of Nazism, but because of the damage he imagined Chamberlain to be doing to the Conservative party.

In public life, before everything else, Halifax was a pin-up, or symbol, of the twentieth-century Conservative alliance between education, wealth and social standing. In his context 'Conservatism' was a flexible, even porous, container which various Cecils and Stanleys had constructed and into which (though not a Conservative) Grey had poured much Whig water immediately after the war. In their cases, decency, idealism and landed virtue had been offered as bandages to industrial society. Halifax's contribution was a tone and manner which Tractarian benevolence had established, which implied a Whig attitude to dissent and which was connected with conceptions about the duties and instincts of a 'gentleman'. [91]

Halifax's father had been the lay brain behind the most successful failure to unite Canterbury to Rome. His paternal grandfather was Gladstone's Halifax. From his early years he shared Gladstone's regret at the Church of England's failure to remain the centre of the nation's life. An interest in *moral* solidarity followed and developed, with experience, into the belief that any point of view could contribute, provided it was meant sincerely and was not meant to be revolutionary.

Like Baldwin, Halifax talked about the 'character' of the British 'race'. He sensed an instinctive desire to subordinate 'theory' to 'practice' and a resistance to 'promises' which politicians had no intention of redeeming. He presented democracy as an 'endless adventure' towards an 'ideal social order' where 'the Christian personality' could be 'developed' and necessary extensions of State power mitigated by a Mill-like conception of rational freedom. [92]

Halifax disliked communism as a doctrine and Russia as a state, and was reluctant to have anything to do with either. For this reason (among others), he had been a minor Die-Hard hero in the early twenties. Since 1925 his career had been built on conciliation (especially in India); it had produced a Conservatism which, though neither reactionary nor Machiavellian, was socially impregnable and assumed that existing society was good. Though he believed this, and was relaxed about it, Halifax was anxious that no one should do anything to shake it. [93] In fearing that it might be shaken by class conflict or international tension, and in approaching it with a religious dimension, he had long-standing affinities with Baldwin who treated him as though he was a younger Bridgeman. [94]

Chamberlain also admired Halifax, as he had done when he got to know him in the twenties, and intended a compliment when suggesting that he might be the first Chairman of the Unemployment Assistance Board. [95] He regarded him as a desirable Foreign Secretary in the period of Simon's disintegration.

Confidence, therefore, was long-standing before he was inherited as leader of the House of Lords. It increased in the next nine months when Eden was on holiday or at Geneva, Brussels or elsewhere. Nor was Halifax devious in using the opportunities this gave him. Eden's supporters in the Foreign Office were suspicious, [96] but it is fairer to say that he did not share Eden's feelings about the League of Nations, of which he had had little direct experience, was less dependent on the approval of Cecil, with whom his relations were closer, and felt no objection to being a 'realist' when Eden had pre-empted his usual rôle as practical idealist. [97]

As Fellow of All Souls, MP, infantry officer, Viceroy, Churchman and working landowner, Halifax had touched life at many points. He made use of his versatility and treated himself as a leading member of the government. He may well have thought that Chamberlain would find him a more congenial Foreign Secretary than Eden, who was fifteen years younger.

Halifax's 'soul' had 'risen in indignation' against Mussolini's 'crimes' in Abyssinia. He had done the same about the League's inability to stop them, and had reached the same conclusions as Chamberlain about the illusions by which it was surrounded. He disliked involvement beyond the Rhine and wanted only a defensive arrangement with France. He wanted the French alliance-system dropped (in return for 'tight commitments from us') because of the danger of being dragged into an east-European war if it continued. [98]

The Germanies he assumed were the Germany of the Oxford of the nineties, the Germany of Anglo-Saxon mythology and the Germany that had fought bravely in the war. He assumed that communism would destroy them, that Nazism might not and that Hitler had restored Germany's 'self-respect'. He thought Eden at fault in having better contact with Blum's government than with Hitler's and that British opinion was 'biassed' against the German attitude to Spain. [99] Before his visit to Hitler in 1937, he thought 'sympathy' suitable and that 'Britain should go as far as...possible' about Austria and Czechoslovakia. He expected 'a great many questions' to become 'less intractable' if it could be established that 'we wanted to be friends'. [100]

Halifax did not like the impression he received of 'barracks' and a 'regimented people' or the evidence he found of 'a different set of values'. [101] But Hitler 'struck' him, though 'dangerous', as 'very sincere' and the régime as 'absolutely fantastic'. He 'liked all the Nazi leaders' and 'could not doubt' that they were 'genuine haters of Communism'. Unless 'these fellows' were 'kidding', immediate aggression was unlikely 'if only' because they had 'constructive work to do at home'.[102] After talking to Hitler, Goering and Goebbels, he felt 'more than ever [the] tragedy [of] Versailles' and that it was 'essential for us to get on with them'.[103] On returning to London, he mounted a campaign to persuade their proprietors to stop Low and Dyson drawing 'cruel' cartoons of Hitler.[104]

Halifax agreed with Chamberlain and Hankey that avoiding a three-cornered war against the anti-Comintern powers would place an 'immense...burden' on diplomacy. He took a low view of Roosevelt's power. Having 'ridiculed' his 'initiative',[105] he moved into reverse only when it seemed possible that Eden would resign.

In relations with Eden, there was no animosity, though he undermined Eden's position and his tone was that of one who was equal in the Prime Minister's sight.[106] He wanted to take Abyssinia out of Anglo-Italian relations, even if 'many good people' would oppose 'a bargain...with the aggressor'.[107] But the difference between Eden and Chamberlain was 'a comparatively small one'.[108] Public disagreement would be damaging, so, when Eden threatened to resign, he took the lead in working for a 'compromise'. When Eden resigned after getting his way, his comment, said to be an angry one, was that he had 'put us in a most impossible position'.[109] His summary afterwards was that 'Anthony was over-strained and tired and...his judgement was not at its best', partly because of 'his excessive sensitiveness to the criticism of the Left' and partly because of 'his natural revulsion from Dictators, which I have always told him is too strong inasmuch as you have got to live with the devils whether you like them or not'.[110]

Halifax may, or may not, have had doubts about taking Eden's place.[111] From February 21 he worked harmoniously with Chamberlain in negotiating with Mussolini, preparing for conversations with Hitler[112] and adapting League 'ideals' to the facts of life. It was Halifax who faced Hailé Selassie at Geneva when the League was asked to recognize Italian rule. He told

the Cabinet that the Anglo-Italian agreement had 'made a
deep impression in Italy'. [113]

Halifax's view of the Italian problem was that, since the
Italians 'want to make friends', they should be encouraged;
he encouraged politicians who wanted to go to Rome. [114]
He believed that reconciliation would be helped by a Franco
victory in Spain, as enabling Mussolini to withdraw.

About Spain which was an 'excrescence' he carried no
ideological lumber. He supported non-intervention and tried
to avoid all but verbal retaliation when British ships were
torpedoed. [115] Mediation (to avoid a direct clash between
France and Italy) [116] was held back only by the rebuff he
received from Ciano when he tried it. [117] He was more
'ashamed' when women and children were bombed in China
where, after all, it was not a 'Civil War that was raging'. [118]
His view of the German problem was as distinctive.

Halifax did not assume that Hitler had an 'international
power-lust' since his policy was 'based on race'. He was greatly impressed by Anglo-French weakness, and had no desire to
convert Locarno into an alliance. In case Anglo-French talks
implied the opposite, he spoke 'with obvious emotion' about
'the kindred nations, Germany, Britain and the U.S. unit [ing]
in joint work for peace'. [119]

Halifax knew that the German Churches were being harassed. He was not sure why and was quite sure that they would
be harassed more if harassment was denounced publicly. He
did as much to keep English Churchmen quiet as he had done
to quieten the press. [120]

After his visit to Germany, he had discovered that Hitler
was less accommodating than he had supposed. [121] He half-
expected an Anschluss but thought it would be done 'in a
manner which did not enable any other country to interfere'. [122] When it happened he was 'somewhat excited' and
gave Ribbentrop a lecture about the 'rude...shock' it had
given to 'European confidence'. [123] According to Cadogan he
was 'calm and sensible' about the fact the Britain could do
nothing about it. [124] According to his private secretary, he
talked about 'highwaymen's methods' and the 'situation'
being 'bloody'. [125]

It was not, however, in his view, 'a new situation' and

provided no reason for new commitments. He rejected the Grand Alliance (while recognising the danger of Anglo-French isolation) and was not yet persuaded that Hitler would end by attacking the Empire. His advice to the Cabinet was that the British obligation to Austria was minimal and that the dictators should be spoken to sharply lest the public decide to follow Eden's 'lead about Mussolini. [126]

Like Chamberlain, Halifax's resting-place was the 'guessing game'. He justified this on the ground that dictatorships would not last indefinitely since '*hubris* in international affairs brought its own revenge'. [127] After the May crisis, he was willing to talk to Hitler about Colonies. But he was against German hegemony and wanted to stiffen resistance in the Balkans. He wanted Benes to offer a plebiscite in five years' time and the French to 'liquidate' their Czech commitment which had been 'entered into many years ago' at a time when they had a backdoor approach to Germany through the Rhineland. [128]

In preparing for *détente*, Halifax thought seriously about the neutralisation of Czechoslovakia. [129] He agreed that Danzig and the Corridor were 'an absurdity' and was prepared to mediate between Germany and the Poles. [130] He thought it a good idea to invite Goering to Sandringham and was 'rather startled' when told that it was a bad one. [131] He thought it possible that Hitler feared France and Britain as much as they feared him, and that his military demonstrations were a reaction to Intelligence predictions of a preventive war against Germany. [132]

As he understood it, Chamberlain's policy was to show Hitler that he could get much of what he wanted provided he would not go to war. [133] He believed in this and thought it viable, so long as France and Britain avoided the details of negotiation. [134] He had, however, a number of reservations.

In the first place, pursuit of *détente* in Europe need not, he thought, immobilise Britain in the Far East, where the need to appease Japan did not reduce the need to boost British influence in Asia by containing Russian influence in China. [135] Secondly, German relations with Franco and the Arabs were important, Italian policy was opportunistic and 'the stronger we can show ourselves in the Mediterranean', the more likely events were to 'swing...in our direction'. [136]

Thirdly, although the French should be discouraged from going to war over Czechoslovakia, it was clear that, if they did, 'we could not stay out' [137] and that, although Czechoslovakia ought to become a Switzerland, the Little Entente should not be destroyed[138] or the French, Czech or Russian governments asked to denounce their alliances. [139] Finally, while believing that Benes had been 'slow with his reforms' [140] and that a plebiscite might eventually be necessary, he complained when *The Times* discussed it because he doubted whether Benes could accept it and survive. [141]

These were differences of emphasis; none of them conflicted with Chamberlain's understanding of policy. On Chamberlain's part there was relief at having an 'unruffled Foreign Secretary' who liked having him around, 'never cause[d him] any worry' and might have prevented the Anschluss if he had been at the Foreign Office at the start of negotiations with Mussolini. [142] Where differences existed, they resulted from Chamberlain's abrasiveness about 'internationalist woolliness', his contempt for the Liberal and Labour leaders and the impression Eden was trying to create that he was out of touch with modern feeling. [143]

This did not amount to much, but it reminded Halifax that anti-dictator feeling was strong [144] and that 'harm' was being done 'by hitting up the Opposition' at a time when trade union co-operation was essential. [145] He pressed Eden to return to office on the grounds that Chamberlain's 'methods' were 'unlikely to retrieve the floating vote' and that Baldwin regarded him as his 'successor'.[146] After an offensive speech from Mussolini in May, he said that, after all, Eden 'had been right'.[147] In the summer of 1938 he was closer to Eden than Churchill was and closer to Churchill than Eden was, and was very more effective than either.

Halifax may not have believed that he could be Prime Minister while Eden was trained up. But he found his resignation speech 'awfully good', [148] paid close attention to what the Labour leaders said and reminded them of the co-operation he had received as Viceroy during the second Labour government. [149]

From Halifax's point of view, in one sense, Munich was a non-event. Between September 13 and 30, Chamberlain was his own Foreign Secretary and had his own adviser — Sir Horace

Wilson. Halifax was neither part of the team which went to Germany nor carried the interim message between Godesberg and Munich. At all these points he was an onlooker with no more control than any other member of the inner ring of the Cabinet.

This is not to say that he had no opinions about what was done or failed to express them, or that there was nothing for which he was responsible. He was an important presence at the committees to which Chamberlain explained himself before explaining himself to the Cabinet, and was one of the dozen or so people who knew about Plan Z before it was put into operation. His preliminary surveys set the tone and structure of Cabinet discussion. They helped to establish that France was unwilling to fight and that Britain had no obligation to Czechoslovakia whose 'thousand year old' problem would lead to war unless the Czechs and Sudeten Germans were 'separated and divided up'.[150] In discussion with critics, he deployed a casuistry and 'commonsense' which issued in claims that it was difficult to know the mind of a 'mystical politician', that 'we had "lectured" everybody too much... during the past few years', and that 'those who spoke for this country should not place themselves in a position of using language which, in the last resort, they might not be prepared fully to implement'.[151]

Halifax did not overplay the merits of the policy he was supporting. Neither did he allow the Cabinet to have illusions. He sketched the risks and the dangers and laid out the odds. The odds were that Hitler was mad, wanted to use force and intended to chloroform Britain until he had done so. In that case no outside action would have an effect, so it was easy to justify a policy to which only irrational calculations were relevant. When put in his 'languid, weary' manner, these were important aids without which Chamberlain could not have gone as far as he did.[152]

Nevertheless, the Munich fortnight marked a parting of the ways. It was Halifax[153] who wanted the BBC to repeat the Lanark warning, had been worried when Chamberlain disagreed[154] and had been greatly upset when Henderson protested against the warning he was allowed to send notwithstanding.[155] On September 9 he was 'very much afraid' that the government might 'yet run away and let the Czechs down'. [156] He was staggered by Chamberlain's decision to fly to Germany. [157]

Halifax had anticipated, and accepted, most of the Berchtesgaden conditions. [158] He then sent Butler and de la Warr to Geneva to ask Litvinoff what Stalin would do in the event of war. During Godesberg week he turned round. [159] At the first Cabinet afterwards he was sensitive to suggestions of an Anglo-French plot. [160] After a sleepless night thinking over a talking-to from Cadogan, he 'was not sure' next day 'whether he and the Prime Minister were quite together' since 'he could not rid his mind of the fact that Hitler...was dictating terms...as though he had won a war without having...to fight'. [161] After telling the last Cabinet before Munich that there would be no peace until Nazidom was destroyed, he sabotaged Chamberlain's attempt to carry the 'capitulation' which Wilson was proposing. He was responsible for the decision that Britain should go to war, [162] in spite of the fact that she was not equipped to fight it. [163]

Like everyone else, he was exhausted by strain and tension in the fortnight of constant brinkmanship. [164] He had seen how near Chamberlain had come to failure; he saw how easily the failure could be repeated. He made an effective defence in the House of Lords, [165] but the impression he left on those to whom he talked was that he was tired and wanted to quit, [166] that the whole thing 'had been a horrid business... there was no use blinking the fact' [167] and that he had come to 'loathe Nazism' and regarded Hitler as 'a criminal lunatic'. [168] 'He put up such defence as he could', wrote Amery on meeting him the day after the Four-Power Agreement was signed, 'excusing Hitler on the ground that no revision could ever have come about without the threat of force ...but he obviously wasn't proud of the result'. [169] 'All the credit', he told a young minister, 'is Neville's and my admiration for him surpasses all bounds but I see political troubles ahead both in parliament and in the country.' [170]

For Halifax's gloom at the moment of Chamberlain's triumph, there were three reasons. The first was that he had come to believe that the sincerity which Chamberlain intuited in Hitler, even when he saw and recorded the opposite, simply did not exist. The second was that, where Chamberlain talked daily to Wilson, he talked to Cadogan and Sargent

who believed, and said, that Chamberlain was being con-
ned. [171] The third was that it was Halifax who bore the
burden of dissent while Chamberlain was involved in the
negotiations.

This was not just the Cabinet dissent, nor the 'dishonour'
and 'humiliation' discerned by the Labour and Sinclairite leaders, [172] but a moral disturbance which fixed on the 'shame'
involved when a small democracy was bullied and the bully
being helped by the British government. This was put in a
variety of ways and at the highest of levels. The King's private secretary was 'horrified' and 'disgusted' and let it be
known that he was consulting Eden. [173] Eden and Churchill
were in 'the depths of despair'. [174] Cecil 'had not felt so
bitterly on any public question since the fall of Khar-
toum'. [175] Lloyd, though a collaborator of Churchill, was
one of Halifax's oldest political friends.

It would be worse than war [he wrote to him with Anglo-Catholic fervour
on September 12] to be unwilling to be the champions of weak peoples,
or that we should, through a shrinking from suffering, fail in a task
surely set us by Providence. This is the moment to play the man, to
face clearly what is coming, confident that we are capable of drinking
the cup and that we shall not be left without the power to do so. [176]

The feeling was put more emotionally still by George Dallas,
the leader of the agricultural workers and chairman of the
Labour Conference, who, when Halifax met a Labour deputation before Godesberg, half-rose from his chair at one stage
to say that 'Lord Halifax, after listening to you, we are
ashamed to be Britishers'. [177]

What these experiences taught Halifax was the need for
political reconstruction. Since *détente* would be intolerable
unless Hitler changed, there would be difficulty if Chamberlain persisted regardless. Not only would the policy fail if
Hitler was as evil as he believed, but Chamberlain would look
incredible as his failure to avoid war, or his surrender, if that
was the outcome, were attributed to rejection of consensual
positions about the League.

Halifax believed in consensual government which Chamberlain seemed to have abandoned and which Labour would
pick up if Munich was established as a 'capitulation'. This was
a dangerous possibility, requiring a restoration of the sort of
unity which would be needed if industry was to be mobilized

for war or the Conservative party to retain its moral supremacy in peace. It meant, as he told Chamberlain after Munich, that he should resist the temptation to snatch a cheap advantage by holding an election. It meant also, as he told him more than once in the three weeks following, that he should invite Eden and the Labour and trade union leaders to join the government, if only for the reason that much would be gained from an offer that was rejected. [178]

The only effect was an attempt at 1931-style unity and a strengthening of Chamberlain's control when the death of Lord Stanley, Duff Cooper's resignation and the removal of Hailsham enabled Anderson and Runciman to join the Cabinet at the same time as Samuel refused to. [179]

Halifax did not doubt that bankers and industrialists should prepare for economic agreement. But he was reluctant about ministerial contact with Germany. In the winter of 1938, the most important aspects of his thinking, behind the advocacy of policies he only half-approved, were the linked beliefs that 'Hitler [was] much more dangerous than Mussolini' and that for him there were going to be 'no more Munichs'. [180]

Halifax saw Munich confirming — what he had long thought inevitable — a 'German predominance in Central Europe'. He expected France to withdraw while Poland drifted permanently into the German camp. Russia could not be allied with Germany ('so long as Hitler lives'); she might well be attacked. Though the French should take care to keep out if she was, he wanted the Soviet pact kept going since 'for good or evil', Russia was 'part of Europe'. His conclusion was that France and Britain should 'uphold' their position in 'Western Europe', keep a 'tight hold' on their Empires and maintain their existing positions in the Mediterranean and Middle East.

This involved rearmament 'sufficient for strength' and 'the closest co-operation with the United States'. It did not exclude *détente* (given French co-operation). But it necessitated a sensitive effort to counter defeatism in France as the French government bit hard over the unpalatable truth that Franco was going to win in Spain. [181]

During his visit to Rome with Chamberlain in January, Halifax found Mussolini 'calm and unaggressive' and unlikely to go to war. [182] But he warned the Cabinet before he went against giving him anything unless he would help positively towards *détente*. [183] He told Chamberlain when he got there to keep a written record of the conversations and was responsible for the affirmation of an Anglo-French 'alliance' which made Chamberlain so popular in early February. [184] He thought Chamberlain unduly optimistic about the prospect of reconciliation between France and Italy. [185]

About Hitler Halifax thought that not very much could be done, except to ask what he wanted, [186] keep in touch with Russia [187] and use charity to refugees as reassurance to American opinion after the pogroms had made appeasement unpopular. [188] In mid-November he gave the Cabinet Committee a lurid account of Hitler's determination to destroy the Empire and the need to encourage 'moderate elements' in Germany by correcting the 'false impression that we were... spineless'. [189] Having failed then to persuade Chamberlain to accept the first steps towards Conscription, he tried again in January with accounts of the extent to which 'the financial and economic condition of Germany was...compelling the mad Dictator...to insane adventures'.[190] In early February he told the Cabinet that he would 'sooner be bankrupt in peace than beaten in a war against Germany'. [191] On February 20 he told Henderson that 'smooth words' in Berlin did not guarantee the existence of 'friendly hearts'. [192]

It is unlikely that Halifax responded to the general run of anti-appeasement propaganda. He probably did not read the *Chronicle* or the *Herald* (though it would be surprising if he did not see the *Telegraph*). He may not have read Gedye, Voigt, Rauschning or Reed or been affected (except by Rauschning) if he did. But he did not need to examine Penguin Books or the Left Book Club to know what was going on. He knew that a propaganda was being accomplished and that a new climate was being created.

Halifax had never been a pacifist; he was remembered on the Right for being 'at heart...a warrior'. [193] When the issue was presented he had little doubt.

In these months he hardened, both because he had new policies to propose (in relation to France and Holland) and because he was responding to a climate very different from Chamberlain's. It would be wrong to say that he had lost confidence in Chamberlain, though he may have been under

the impression that Chamberlain had lost confidence in
him.[194] But there was a sharpening of tone flowing from a
sense that doubt and disaffection were spreading among
junior ministers, 'the young' and 'the best traditional elements' in the Foreign Office and Conservative party of which
Eden was claiming that Halifax alone had not turned against
Chamberlain.[195]

(ii)

Up to the end of 1937, for most ministers, the Foreign
Office meant Vansittart. He, however, had been damaged by
the Hoare-Laval pact and by his conduct of his office. As his
standing dropped, the Foreign Office's dropped too. By the
end of 1937, its influence had been greatly reduced, as
Fisher, Hankey, Leith-Ross and Wilson helped Chamberlain
tackle the foreign-policy failures of the previous four years.

To some extent, no doubt, Vansittart was a scape-goat.
But it was primarily a judgment of competence by Chamberlain and of compatibility by Eden that made them agree that
he should be replaced. It was because he would not take an
embassy and would be dangerous if pushed out altogether
that he was pushed downstairs to be Chief Diplomatic Adviser at the beginning of 1938.[196]

Though Cadogan was Eden's choice as successor, he had
only six weeks with him. From the end of February, it was
Halifax with whom he dealt.

Where Vansittart had conducted himself as a politician and
thought of standing for Parliament after his demotion,[197]
Cadogan acted as an official, advising Halifax but not cajoling
him, and avoiding a conspiracy-conception of his function.
There is no sign that he dissented from the Cabinet's policy
in the summer of 1938. It was only a general dislike of the
'surrender' and 'gullibility' involved in Chamberlain's attitude
after meeting Hitler that made him press his opinions on
Halifax in September.

Though the Foreign Office felt the 'ignominy' of Munich
and the abandonment of professional diplomacy, Cadogan
accepted it as a consequence of the failure to make concessions in the twenties. He recognised that Britain could not go
on policing Europe and must give first attention to the Medi-

terranean. He interpreted Munich as showing the German people that they could get what they wanted without war. He was in favour of a colonial deal. 'Even at this late date', he wanted Britain to propose an 'examination of the difficulties, fears and suspicions that seem likely to make Europe shortly uninhabitable'. [198] It was not until the beginning of 1939 that he responded to the Intelligence assessment that what Hitler would 'like best, if he could do it, would be to smash the British Empire'. [199]

This was what Vansittart had been saying, but, since he had been saying a lot of other (contradictory) things besides, Cadogan was no more willing to take him seriously than he had been in the past. [200]

In 1938 Vansittart had mattered very little. He had a room in the Foreign Office and kept up a high output of memoranda. He retained contact with Intelligence sources, and developed contact with Churchill and Dalton. He made himself an alternative source of briefing for the press. He tried to stir up feeling against Phipps (his brother-in-law) in Paris and against Henderson in Berlin and was responsible for much of the contempt which Chamberlain aroused in the lower reaches of the Foreign Office. [201] But his memoranda were not important. Halifax treated him as a foil and Cadogan barred the way. Phipps was indestructible and Henderson had not yet been destroyed.

Just as the Foreign Office and the Chiefs of Staff conveyed opinions to the highest quarters, so did ambassadors in the most important capitals. These were not necessarily the opinions of those who made policy at home. But even if (as is unlikely) Loraine's Ciano, Phipps's Bonnet and Henderson's Goering were systematically misleading to their auditors, they conveyed as adequately as Vansittart's sources an important set of possibilities.

As Ambassador in Berlin, Phipps had had no more time for the Nazis than his predecessor (Rumbold). Nor did he think much better of French politicians after moving to Paris in 1937. There, however, he had a ladder of reputability on which believers in the Entente came top and the advocates of 'ideology' bottom. For this reason he was glad when Blum fell in 1938 and did his best to keep Boncour out of the Daladier government on the ground of his 'idiocy about Mussolini' and hankerings after intervention in Spain. [202] He regarded the Daladier/Bonnet combination as the best possible in the circumstances and suggested more than once that Halifax or Chamberlain should 'fortify' it 'by a visit'. [203]

Phipps presented Halifax a version of his rôle which showed him aiming to restrain the 'war-mongers' in and out of the new government. In addition to the Communists, these included Reynaud and Herriot who, in spite of believing in the Entente, 'revel[led] in the Soviet bloodbaths' as 'increasing the efficiency of the Soviet army'. [204] Above all, they included Mandel, the only incurable in the Cabinet whose 'real name' was 'Rothschild' and who, like most French Jews, had his own reasons for 'tightening up the Soviet connection. [205]

In relation to Italy, Phipps's object was to circumvent Léger — the permanent head of the Quai d'Orsay, who encouraged Daladier to be obstinate about Mussolini. He had no time for Kemsley's brother-in-law, Flandin, whom he regarded as a defeatist. Nor was he a defeatist himself. But he reported Bonnet's doubts during the September crisis and stated that Daladier 'always talks bigger than he acts'. He recorded the belief that they would not go to war over Czechoslovakia unless Hitler made them; he expected them to accept 'any plan' advocated by Chamberlain and Runciman and to 'disinterest' themselves if the Czechs rejected it. [206] It was at least partly on Phipps's advice that Bonnet and Daladier were treated brutally when they came to London on September 18. [207]

Phipps assumed that Bonnet was 'prudent' about Germany and 'well-meaning' about Italy, and, in a delicate situation, would be more resistant than Boncour to the 'extreme elements of the Popular Front'. [208] In the middle of 1938 he invented a triangle on which he pressed Halifax (on Bonnet's behalf) to neutralise the pressures Daladier received from Mandel, Reynaud and Herriot. [209] In 1939 the triangle was developed to include François-Poncet, the Ambassador in Rome, when Chamberlain made his unsuccessful attempts to get Daladier to come to terms with Mussolini. If war had not begun when it did, Halifax and the King would have made further attempts on Daladier during his visit for army manoeuvres in Yorkshire in September. [210]

As well as being Vansittart's brother-in-law, Phipps was a

friend of Hankey. He was unhappy about Henderson's view of Berlin. He knew that Vansittart (who had supported him in Berlin) was unhappy about his own view of Paris, [211] and he helped Hankey and Wilson against him. He described Cadett (*The Times* correspondent) as a 'red' and Bartlett and Scott of the *News Chronicle* as 'feather-brains'; he spent a great deal of time attempting to thwart the conspiracies he expected when Pertinax came to England. [212]

Phipps's aim was to persuade the French government to pursue British policies; he reported what he knew within these limits. What he saw, on the one hand, was a 'criminal' war party stoked up, during visits to Paris, by Spears, Churchill, Duff Cooper and Lloyd George.[213] What he saw, on the other, was that 'the French' would 'fight like tigers' for the 'independence...of metropolitan France'. [214] In Berlin, Henderson had the same feelings about 'the Germans'.

Henderson was not sent to Berlin because of any belief he may have had in the significance of Anglo-German amity. Nor did he think of his mission as urgent until Chamberlain talked to him in October. [215]

What Henderson felt (when called upon to feel) was that Britain was an 'island' rather than a 'continental' people and that the centre of her interest was the Empire. Between the Empire and the Reich there need be no incompatibility and should, he thought, ideally, be a positive identity based on the fact that both embodied the principle of national, or racial, self-determination. It was belief in self-determination as a 'principle' for world organisation which sustained the claim that 'the British Empire was...infinitely too valuable to be risked' in a situation where principle had not yet issued in 'real practice'. [216]

Before the Anschluss Henderson was not optimistic. Nor did he want it to be the Nazis who brought it about. But he had no sympathy for the Austrians who, he had 'always believed', would have to join Germany once the Hapsburgs had been removed. He thought that they should be abandoned gracefully so as to give Czechoslovakia a chance of survival. [217]

Henderson's view was that Benes would have to concede if conflict was to be avoided. He made more of neutralising Czechoslovakia than Halifax liked. But his solution was cantonal; he did not advocate dismemberment, which he believed that the Germans did not want. [218] Benes's failure to do anything made him extremely upset.

Henderson shared the Conservative and Chiefs of Staff view of the League, and Garvin's view of Germany's rôle in central Europe. [219] He was as much relieved when Eden resigned as when Duff Cooper resigned after Munich. [220] But he liked neither the balance of power nor the 'narrow' pursuit of British interests. The 'truest...interest was the highest... principle', and the principle of the twentieth century was nationalism. It was because Czechoslovakia was polyglot and anachronistic (like the Hapsburg Empire) that the Sudeten Germans had 'a moral right' to 'self-determination'. [221]

Henderson's principles would have been less exigent if the danger had been less urgent. As the danger of war became acute, long-standing judgments became effective. From early May 1938, he was telling Halifax that Hitler would not let the Sudeten question slide. [222] But he 'could not bear the thought of losing a single British life for either Sudetens or Czechs'. [223] Whether by Czech concessions or a Runciman award, he wanted the question settled. [224] He regarded May 21 as wholly deplorable. His advice was that Benes was courting disaster and that May 21's must be avoided. [225]

Henderson liked Goering. But he held no brief for the Nazi system. He disliked Ribbentrop who was 'as vain as he is stupid and as stupid as he is vain', and was a dangerous influence on Hitler because he did not know when to stop. [226]

On the spot, ill, in close touch and overworked, Henderson could not make up his mind whether the Germans would behave reasonably if given the chance. Up to early September, he was saying that Hitler should be handled carefully since he had not yet decided to go to war. [227] In the next three weeks he was disabused. Though he wrote (to Chamberlain) about the 'moral rightness' of the Munich agreement, he told Halifax that he 'never wanted to work with Germans again'. [228]

Before returning to London for a cancer operation, Henderson aimed to dispel optimism. Though the German public admired Chamberlain for Munich, there was no point trying to divide it from Hitler. It was ridiculous to clutch at the idea

that Germany was 'short of food, personnel and oil'. Hitler
had won at Munich because of air superiority. Even if he did
not intend to attack Britain, he intended to enforce a 'Pax
Germanica' on Europe. [229]

Between his return to Berlin and the occupation of Prague,
Henderson's agnosticism was restored. He exonerated Hitler
from responsibility for the pogroms. [230] In late February he
wrote that the 'Germans want peace' and that 'all would be
well' so long as the defence programme was continued in
Britain. To this frame of mind Prague came as a shock. [231]

After Prague, more even than after the Anschluss, Henderson's object was to persuade Halifax of Hitler's determination
about Danzig, and to make it clear that much needed to be
said if he was to be convinced that Britain and France would
fight a world war to stop him. [232] Polish concessions were
essential. But a Russian Alliance was essential too. It was
only when he sensed that 'the Germans were getting at Stalin'
that he began to be urgent about the need for British agreement with Germany.

From his special position, Henderson decided that parliamentary belligerence was bringing war closer. He discounted
Vansittart's fears and refused to examine the Intelligence reports on which they were based. [233] 'Public Enemy No 1'
was 'the Press'; he sensed the situation he had long foreseen
in which Jews, journalists and the London intelligentsia
would envelop diplomacy in a 'conflict of philosophies'
which had nothing to do with British interests. [234]

Henderson's concern was with the effect of newspapers
and political speeches on the Nazi leaders. But he also believed that the Foreign Office had been infected. He made it
his business to mediate between it on the one hand and Hitler
on the other, just as Chamberlain had mediated with the
Cabinet the previous September.

In face of criticism from the Embassy in Warsaw, Henderson received little sympathy from Halifax. [235] He was increasingly operating at the limits of physical tolerance. His
letters became increasingly intense as he discerned increasing
insensitivity to the central fact that 'hundreds of thousands
of British lives' were being risked 'in order to free Germany
from Hitler', where prudence required a renunciation of 'Vic-
torian' assumptions and a recognition that 'the sooner...we...

cut our coat to the measure of our cloth, the better it will be
for the British Empire'. [236]

What Henderson was saying was what Halifax believed until he turned round. Henderson can scarcely be derided for
crying painfully in a wilderness from which an active imagination saw Halifax's capitulation making war certain by giving
'a blank cheque to Poland'. [237]

Henderson did not conceal Hitler's determination to incorporate Danzig into the Reich. But he believed that war
could be prevented [238] by showing both that Britain meant
business and that there was no desire to attack Germany in
the future. [239] With the Russo-German pact, he expected the
Poles to get what they deserved. [240] 'If the British public
cannot stand Hitler's fidgetiness any longer', he wrote on
August 24, 'there is nothing more to be said'. [241]

When Henderson's reports were circulated in the Foreign
Office, Vansittart presented his own understanding of the
situation. [242] Cadogan, Sargent and the Intelligence Services
presented theirs. From early 1939 all contributed to the view
that Hitler might be intending to 'strike an overwhelming
blow at the Western powers'. [243]

Halifax was not run by Cadogan. Far less was he run by
Vansittart. As elsewhere, so in the Foreign Office, he listened.
Having come to believe that Munich had made Hitler antagonistic to Britain, he groped slowly towards prudential conclusions very similar to the ideological ones which had been
reached on the Left.

By mid-February Halifax had come to grips with his office
and used the power this gave to exercise the skills he had
learnt during thirty years at the top of Conservative politics. [244] Where Chamberlain had made a divisive departure,
he aimed to restore the atmosphere in which Baldwin had
been enveloped. Where Eden seemed to be floundering, his
touch was sure, responding to the need to confront evil, even
when nothing could be done about it, and leaving an impression on Eden's followers, on the followers of Cecil, Sinclair and Churchill, in the Labour party and among his own
advisers, that he understood the need for a line so stiff that
he was in fact 'very close to Eden'. [245]

The outward signs were sparse — an address to the 1922

Committee, a talk to Churchill's *Focus* and a speech in the House of Lords on February 23. But they were accompanied by an extreme fussiness about what he said and an insistence that Cadogan should help him to say it. They issued in a firm incantation and a warning that the British were not only not 'decadent' but would be 'not less tenacious in defence of their liberty than they had ever been before'. [246]

Apart from the rebuke he administered on the occasion of a Chamberlain talk to Lobby correspondents in early March, [247] there was a continuing loyalty, even when he may not quite have felt it. In talking to Eden and other politicians, and in talking to his private secretary, who talked in his turn to members of the Eden group, there were many occasions on which he made clear the identity between the drift of his own thinking and the drift of theirs.

With a manner as offhand as Halifax's, it is impossible to know whether he thought he could be Prime Minister or, indeed, whether he would have wanted to if he had thought he could be. It is probably best to make a positive assumption, while not suggesting that he wanted to do more than get the government back on course after Chamberlain had blown it off. He did not exactly put himself at the head of the movement which Eden and Churchill had created. But he absorbed what he was told and had decided, long before Prague, that his major priority was to persuade them to renew support for the government.

How he, or anyone else, was to do this given that Chamberlain had no desire either to give up being Prime Minister or to have them in the Cabinet, [248] was not a question to which anyone gave an answer. Probably it did not need to be asked since a mood was being created not, at this stage, a *coup* being planned. Halifax was not thinking of removing Chamberlain, even when he doubted Eden being 'tough enough' and spoke of the impossibility of Hoare, Simon or Inskip succeeding. [249] He was thinking aloud, as were Eden and Stanley [250] when they said that the ideal solution would be a Halifax government with Eden as leader of the House of Commons.

The idea of a Halifax (or Baldwin) government may have been put about by Eden and his followers because Halifax was the weak link and the one valuable minister who might be detached from Chamberlain. Or it may have emerged from a considered judgment that he and Baldwin were the only leaders who could restore the Conservative position. Whatever the origin or reason and whether Chamberlain realised this or not, the dominating fact as Hitler occupied Prague was Halifax's belief that the policy would have to be changed if the party was to be saved.

10

CHAMBERLAIN, CHURCHILL AND HITLER

'The Government has to take seriously the fact that the two Oppositions are now appealing over its head to a certain amount of latent jingoism in the country'.
Spender to Simon, August 1 1939

'I often think to myself that it's not I but someone else who is P.M. and is the recipient of those continuous marks of respect and affection from the general public who called in Downing Street or at the station to take off their hats and cheer. And then I go back to the House of Commons and listen to the unending stream of abuse of the P.M., his faithlessness, his weakness, his wickedness, his innate sympathy with Fascism and his obstinate hatred of the working classes'.
Chamberlain to Hilda, May 28 1939

'All our information points to a quiet time until about the third week in August when it is suggested a "crisis" might begin to boil up. But nearly always it is the predicted crisis that never materialises and I expect it will be so again. The curious accident by which we shall have a gigantic fleet exercising in the North Sea all August and September may possibly have some influence in this direction. There are more ways of killing a cat than strangling it and if I refuse to take Winston into the Cabinet to please those who say it would frighten Hitler, it doesn't follow that the idea of frightening Hitler, or rather of convincing him that it would not pay him to use force, need be abandoned'.
Chamberlain to Hilda, July 15 1939

(i)

The barrage of critical testimony with which Chamberlain was confronted — from the Sinclairites, the Labour party, the Collective Security and League of Nations lobby and two sorts of Conservative dissentient — did not at first make much impact on him. Before Berchtesgaden, there was no problem. After Munich his position was so strong that he was a free agent. Nothing Hitler had done had destroyed it; the public really supported it. With a good by-election in mid-February, a strong statement of Anglo-French unity and the divisions created by Cripps's expulsion from the Labour party,[1] the future seemed boundless.

Like Chatham [he wrote on March 12] I know that I can save this country and I do not believe that anyone else can...Barring accidents...I ought to be good for at least one more Parliament after this to exasperate and infuriate the *Gilbert Murrays* of this world...

Meanwhile all the Prodigal Sons are fairly besieging the parental door. You may have seen *Winston's* eulogies as reported in the Saturday press. *Anthony* loses no opportunity of letting me know how cordially he approves the government policy. *Duff Cooper* is loud in his praises. *Young Jim Thomas* wants to be a Whip(!) *Wolmer* speaks in the country in the warmest and most admiring terms of the P.M. *Duncan Sandys* is a reformed character and makes moving speeches in support of the government. *Vernon Bartlett* says the P.M. is going to win and *Harold Nicolson* declares he is 'dead right'! ... *Even poor Leo Amery* is eating humble pie.[2]

Of the prognostications of doom which these critics had uttered, the German occupation of Prague two days later gave apparently decisive confirmation. It marked the end of the period in which Chamberlain was confident that policy would respond to his touch. From then onwards, he ceased to be confident — because Hitler was not responding and Halifax moved into an independent and potentially commanding position from which, in September, Simon exercised command.

Halifax and his advisers treated the occupation as proof that Hitler was not the racialist they had been willing to believe in and was seeking European or world domination. The conclusion they drew was that Western Europe was not safe, that *every* act of expansion must be contested and that a new policy was needed, including a systematic attempt to activate Russia. Chamberlain's practice was not exactly different, except so far as Russia was concerned, but it was a balancing act that he began to perform, not a collapse on one side of the policy fence or the other. He recognised, as before, that Hitler was a 'mad dog' and was now convinced that he was untrustworthy. But he did not accept the view that his aim was European or world domination. Neither did he draw the conclusion until a little later — and then perhaps disingenuously — that 'Collective Security' was the answer.

After Munich, there was prolonged discussion, but no decision, about the Four-Power guarantee to replace the temporary guarantee which the British and French governments had given in order to facilitate dismemberment of Czechoslovakia. There was a pronounced fear of Britain and France being pledged to provide protection by themselves (as France had been before Munich)[3] or being 'asked to take action with...Russia against Germany and Italy on behalf of a State which we were unable effectively to defend'.[4] Despite the 'moral obligation' announced in Parliament on October 5, Chamberlain was hoping that the guarantee would 'fade out'; it had been decided, before March 14, that the secession of Slovakia would annul it even if it had come into operation.[5] Since nothing could be done to give effect to the temporary one and since the advantages of delay were now a leading feature of policy, the question of war was excluded from consideration.

The exclusion of war, however, left a difficulty. This was not just that Hitler had broken his promises but, as the new duke of Devonshire (a significant junior minister) explained in public on March 16, that Chamberlain's policy was 'not bearing fruit'.[6] It soon became obvious that the optimism and involvement of the previous September had made it difficult for even isolationist supporters to pretend that the occupation did not matter. It was at least partly with a view to his own credibility that Chamberlain asked the Cabinet to cancel Stanley's and Hudson's visits to Berlin and to recall Henderson for consultation.

At Birmingham on the 17th — the day before his seventieth birthday — Chamberlain announced a new determination.

Germany [he told the City's Unionist association] under her present régime has sprung a series of unpleasant surprises upon the world. The Rhineland, the Austrian Anschluss, the severance of the Sudetenland — all these things shocked and affronted public opinion throughout the world. Yet, however much we might take exception to the methods which were adopted in each of those cases, there was something to be said, whether on account of racial affinity or of just claims too long resisted, for the necessity of a change in the existing situation.

But the events which have taken place this week in complete disregard of the principles laid down by the German government itself seem to fall into a different category, and they must cause us all to be asking ourselves 'Is this the end of an old adventure, or is it the beginning of a new? Is this the last attack upon a small State, or is it to be followed by others? Is this, in fact, a step in the direction of an attempt to dominate the world by force?'

It is only six weeks ago [he went on, in tactful explanation of more recent optimism] that...I alluded to rumours and suspicions which I said

ought to be swept away. I pointed out that any demand to dominate
the world by force was one which the democracies must resist, and I
added that I could not believe that such a challenge was intended,
because no government with the interests of its own people at heart
could expose them for such a claim to the horrors of world war.

And, indeed, with the lessons of history for all to read, it seems
incredible that we should see such a challenge. I feel bound to repeat
that, while I am not prepared to engage this country by new unspecified commitments, operating under conditions which cannot now be
foreseen, yet no greater mistake could be made than to suppose that,
because it believes war to be a senseless and cruel thing, this nation has
so lost its fibre that it will not take part to the utmost of its power
resisting such a challenge if it ever were made.[7]

This speech, important as it was in English politics, did not
say what would be done if Hitler went on. Nor was a decision
made as a result of the disintegration of Czechoslovakia. The
first Cabinet, on March 15, merely reduced contact with Germany.[8] The second was called at short notice three days later
to deal with a similar situation in Rumania.[9]

The information on which the Cabinet was called was that
Hitler had threatened to invade unless the Rumanian government gave Germany a stranglehold on the Rumanian economy. This was false, as Halifax had discovered by the time
the Cabinet met. It seemed, however, so possible that it
might be true that the Cabinet acted on that assumption.[10]
It decided that Rumania was important strategically and that
the French, the Dominions and the public were so determined that it was possible to have a policy of resistance.

This policy was intended primarily to deter. It was also
designed to make sure that Hitler would have to fight on two
fronts if the deterrent failed. At the meeting on the 18th it
was decided to ask Russia, Poland, Yugoslavia, Turkey,
Greece and Rumania to announce their intention of resisting
German aggression in south-eastern Europe.[11]

Like the Birmingham speech, this decision was the symbol
of a change, but it had no consequences. It was recognised as
a slow and extended commitment which few of the states
concerned would be likely to accept. The day after it was
approved, it was abandoned in favour of an attempt to persuade Russia, Poland and France to give a formal promise to
'consult together' in the event of 'any action which con-

stitutes a threat to the political independence of any European state'.[12]

This 'not very heroic'[13] proposal got no further than the one before. It was criticised in Cabinet as a 'limitless' commitment. When made known to governments throughout the world, the prospect of association with the Soviet Union was disliked, not only in Portugal, Spain, Japan, Italy, Canada and South America but in Rumania and Poland as well.[14]

Despite this second failure, it was still intended to threaten a war on two fronts. This was the object of the reciprocal defence pact with France, Poland and Rumania which was proposed after the occupation of Memel.[15] When a Generals' plot in Germany and an invasion of Poland seemed imminent three days later it was why Chamberlain and Halifax decided on a British guarantee of Polish independence.[16]

In Chamberlain's actions between March and September, there was a conflation of responsibilities. Once his personal credibility had been restored with the guarantee to Poland and the 'check' which Hitler had been given,[17] the object was to prevent war by delaying it until Britain's defences were complete and a European defence system had redoubled the certainty that Hitler could not win quickly.

Chamberlain assumed that short-term war to free a German-occupied state would be ineffective, even if a declaration of war had repercussions in Germany.[18] To that extent the attempt to construct an alliance-system was a bluff predicated on Hitler (or other Germans) believing that, in the long run, Germany would be defeated or a German victory prevented, provided the blockading power of the British and French navies was supported by an unbeatable defence system in the air.

Chamberlain assumed that Anglo-French defensive capability was unbreakable or would become so if enough time was bought. His conception of his function was, therefore, more clearly than in 1938, to avoid action likely to enable Hitler to rally Germans behind him[19] and to hold off war for as long as possible so that the situation would eventually be created in which Hitler died, something happened to the Nazi régime or Germans who believed that war was 'not worthwhile *yet*' would suddenly come to see 'that it never will be worthwhile'.[20]

There was therefore, both a stick and a carrot. The stick, bent from the beginning, consisted of Conscription, the isolation of Germany and guarantees to Poland, Greece, Denmark, Holland and Switzerland.[21] The carrot continued to be frontier revision in Poland and elsewhere and economic agreement once Hitler had come to see that nothing would be gained by force which might not be gained more securely by negotiation.

Chamberlain did not rely on good intentions. He imputed few good intentions to Hitler, whom he thought 'fanatical' and unreliable and unlikely to behave decently in a situation he could control. He believed that *he* had snatched control at Munich with the result that Hitler had 'missed the bus'.[22] At various points he began to think that firmness was beginning to bite.[23] After the first Danzig scare in May, he thought that Germans might drop it 'perhaps...because they realise this time that they can't get what they want without fighting'.[24]

Chamberlain did not intend the Polish guarantee to exclude frontier revision. On the contrary, he wanted the Poles to be reasonable.[25] While hoping that they would be,[26] he felt more confident than the Foreign Office that Hitler knew that Britain would go to war if they were attacked.[27] He thought even Ribbentrop understood this, and that Hitler, who 'was not such a fool as some hysterical people make out', would be willing to compromise 'if he could do so without what he would feel to be humiliation'.[28]

On this basis Chamberlain flew kites (which the Foreign Office shot down) in favour of Scandinavian mediation and tried, also without success, to get Mussolini to propose a twelve-month truce in preparation for a general discussion.[29] When the ending of a second Danzig scare made it seem that Hitler had dropped the question in late July, he 'could not imagine [him] living to be an old man'.[30] He told the Cabinet of July 5 that there would be large-scale naval exercises in the North Sea if that seemed to be desirable.[31] His chief comment on recurrent Intelligence predictions of a Russo-German pact was that it 'shed a sinister light on *Russia*'s intentions'.

Despite half-hearted efforts to keep *détente* open,[33] Chamberlain was not really expecting to do anything about it. He was hoping that nothing would happen to rule it out and that Hitler would not choose to rule it out by unavoidable aggression. It was in order both to be flexible and to make Hitler flexible that he permitted a renewal of the economic discussions which Prague had halted.

From the point in 1933 at which economic discussions were first taken seriously, the United States had been a major economic problem and Germany a possible makeweight to it. At times with, at times without, Foreign Office support, an analysis had been developed which (after 1936) explained Hitler's decision to take up the Colonial question as a function of the relationship between economic development, the openness of world markets and the access-to-raw-materials aspect of the Colonial question. When a Colonial deal became politically difficult (in England), an eastern and central European one was seen as bait with which to buy a modification of autarky in the unlikely event of it not being essential to resist German economic expansion.

These were, at various times, the staples of departmental thinking in the Treasury, Foreign Office and Board of Trade. Through prolonged collaboration with Fisher and Leith-Ross, they supplied an element in Chamberlain's thinking and fitted into the policies which he and Eden adopted. They adopted them, however, for political reasons, not because economic appeasement was the pivot on which policy had to turn. Indeed, they assumed the opposite and argued with each other on this basis. They knew that any opportunities that existed for economic agreement (before Schacht's dismissal) depended on political decisions which Baldwin had avoided, and this was so even when Eden and Vansittart aimed to help the 'moderates' against the 'Nazis' in the German government.

A decision that it was desirable to reach political agreement with Hitler involved a great many imponderables, including the prospect of reducing British dependence on the United States. These may, in Chamberlain's case, have been verbal hopes rather than real ones, however real the fear of American power after Munich. In any case, the discussions which went on up to Prague [34] were abortive precisely because of uncertainty about the extent to which the Munich declaration could be made effective. [35]

The decision to stop discussions did not mean that Chamberlain no longer wanted an agreement. On the contrary, he saw positive advantages, just as (negatively) he wanted to avoid war because *détente* and co-operation would iron out economic recession, create an outlet for heavy industry and provide a secure basis for a general election. [36] By mid-1939, his fear of war *against* Germany in alliance with Russia was so much greater than before that he was actively hoping that the Anglo-Russian negotiations would break down. He was initiating a great deal more than a contingency programme when he allowed economic negotiations to start again secretly in Berlin in May. [37]

After a general statement by Halifax at Chatham House in June, the talks were transferred to London, where they were conducted by Wilson, Hudson and Ball. All that was mentioned publicly, however, was the desirability of agreement; nothing was said about talks until Hudson leaked them to the newspapers. Hitler stopped them immediately before the signature of the Russo-German pact (ostensibly because of the publicity they were attracting), but held out the hope of resuming them if the Danzig question could be settled. [38]

These talks, which were not discussed in Cabinet, were not designed to supersede the guarantee to Poland. They were designed to remind Hitler, or Goering, of the advantages to be gained from allowing a *détente* situation to develop, but Chamberlain understood that *détente* was dead unless Hitler could be convinced that Britain meant business militarily. However, since it would be dangerous to 'quarrel with all the strongest military powers at once', it was necessary to show extreme caution in the Far East, to make a serious attempt to remove the causes of Arab violence in Palestine [39] and to begin a further appeasement of Mussolini. [40]

The problem about Mussolini was whether he was in Hitler's pocket and, if he was not, whether he could be persuaded to keep out of it. Chamberlain was told, and Halifax believed, that he had treated the occupation of Prague as a prelude to further German penetration of the Balkans. This was encouraging, even when his actions were not; the turning points in policy were explained to him. [41] After the Polish guarantee, there were Intelligence predictions of an occupation of Albania, which Chamberlain expected to be presented as 'an agreed arrangement' and, which, since nothing could be done to stop it, he treated as 'strengthen[ing] Italy against Germany' rather than as a *coup* against Greece. It was, however, hunch rather than knowledge which persuaded him that Mussolini was no longer to be trusted. [42]

The idea that 'any further chance of a rapprochement...had been blocked' did not last. A guarantee was given to Turkey which had been excluded from the Four-Power proposals of March 20 because of the offence inclusion would cause in Italy. [43] Guarantees were given to Greece and Rumania and an attempt made to get the Turks to create a Balkan *bloc*. [44] But, instead of denouncing the Italian agreement, which would have been popular in parliament, Chamberlain accepted Conscription and a Ministry of Supply. By April 23 Mussolini was 'friendly and cordial' about accepting excuses for the fact — which embodied a Cabinet decision [45] — that the new British Ambassador's credentials did not mention the Kingdom of Albania. [46]

In the lull which followed, Chamberlain pressed the French to 'smooth...out their difficulties with Italy'. [47] When told what Mussolini wanted, he decided that 'it might be possible to give the Axis another twist...and this might be the best way of keeping Master Hitler quiet'. [48] His optimism was not dimmed by Mussolini's decision to join in military alliance with the Germans.

By 1939 Chamberlain's view of Italy had prevailed; neither Halifax nor the Foreign Office doubted that it was essential 'not...to drive [her] into greater reliance on Germany'. [49] Loraine wished to be tough; until the Russo-German pact, he was far from optimistic. It was because Chamberlain regarded Daladier as the chief obstacle that Bonnet was persuaded to press him to approach Mussolini; it was, Chamberlain thought, Daladier's reluctance which made Mussolini unresponsive. Loraine's ambiguous prognostications were interpreted as suggesting that in Rome the prospect of war was 'looked upon with terror'. [50]

Except in distributing unenforceable guarantees, Chamberlain was less active in the summer of 1939 than at any time since he had taken control of foreign policy. Believing that

Hitler had to be deterred meant various acts of rearmament and, after Albania, Conscription, a Ministry of Supply and a doubling of the Territorial Army. But his objection to a Ministry of Supply the previous October had been tactical and technical;[51] he had already accepted the doubling of the Territorial Army as an alternative to Conscription and had to accept it in addition when Halifax and Simon agreed that Hore-Belisha was right to want it. [52] The international significance of the Ministry of Supply was neutralised by appointing as its head not Eden or Churchill but Burgin. It did not exclude the belief that, given British rearmament, 'every month that passes without war makes war more unlikely'. [53]

In the summer of 1939, Chamberlain no longer controlled foreign policy. But he did not capitulate to his critics. His objectives had to be sought deviously but he refused to rule *détente* out of consideration. In any case he wanted to delay war as long as possible and had an almost physical sense of the fact that 'the ultimate decision, the Yes or No which may decide the fate not only of all this generation but of the British Empire itself rests with me'. [54]

Nor was he unsuccessful about Russia. While accepting the political need for 'association', [55] he had no wish to enter into an 'alliance', since she had no 'offensive' capability and her main object was to meet the German and Japanese threats by 'egging' the ' "capitalist" Powers' 'on' to 'tear each other to pieces' in fighting her battles for her. [56] When Litvinoff resigned, he was greatly relieved. He described an alliance as a provocation which might 'unite Germany' and play into the hands of the 'many influential persons who have been trying to persuade [Hitler] that the time...to strike was when the Three-Power Pact was concluded'. [57]

Halifax's Russian policy was not based on liking or trust. He had had nothing to do with Eden's Litvinoff spectaculars and was well aware that 'the Bolshies' were deceitful.[58] He believed that peace would be kept, if at all, only by establishing that aggression could not succeed. [59] He gave due weight to intelligence predictions of a Russo-German pact and thought the Chiefs of Staff right in thinking that the damage Hitler would suffer if he made an alliance with Russia would be outweighed by the freedom he would gain in relation to Poland. [60] Up to mid-May he was trying to interest the

Russians in East European guarantees which the guaranteed states would be likely to accept. He was forced to go further when the Russians made it clear that they wanted an alliance or nothing. [61]

Halifax was willing to agree, not just because it would enable the Poles to resist Hitler but because the certainty of Polish resistance would reduce the French fear of encirclement between Germany and Spain. This would reduce Daladier's dependence on the war-party and enable him to talk to Mussolini. Once Bonnet had developed French relations with Franco, it might even lead, he thought, to French agreement with Italy and a return to a Stresa attitude to Hitler. [62]

Halifax did not assume that war was inevitable. But he recognised that it was likely and that the only way to avoid it was by leading towards firmness and strength. It was because the domestic situation required them and because peace would be unlikely without them that he looked on the Russians as indispensable.

If Chamberlain had had his way, there would have been no Russian negotiations after the beginning of May. Hoare, Simon and Inskip, however, supported Halifax and Chatfield, or thought it impossible to follow Chamberlain; so, after a long struggle in Committee, he allowed them to continue. Even then, he objected to being forced to prefer Stalin to Hitler and was compelled to only because the Cabinet insisted. [63] A month's negotiation with Molotov showed that 'we had made concession after concession'. After two months, it was doubtful whether the 'Soviet government really desired any agreement'. [64] Though surprised by the Russo-German pact, he was much less worried than his colleagues. [65]

Chamberlain was trying to prevent Europe boiling over and finding it difficult to rely on those whose co-operation he needed. About the public and the electorate, he was confident. But about politicians, he was not. Hitler, Mussolini and the Japanese were not as co-operative as they should have been. The contrast they created between his (necessarily tactical) words and reality lent weight to the criticisms of his critics. His critics' desire to 'weaken' his 'authority' by 'mocking' him shortened the odds, 'stifl[ed]' his attempt 'to prevent a war' and produced a feeling of gloom and isolation that he had not felt before. [66]

For the Labour party he felt total contempt. Its leaders were as 'pathetic' when they demanded arms for Spain after the Republic had been defeated as in demanding increased sanctions after Hailé Selassie had fled. Over Conscription they were divided. Over Russia they had no sense of the damage an alliance could do. Much more than the Londonderries and Astors in relation to Ribbentrop, they behaved, he thought (like Churchill and Lloyd George), as agents of Maisky and the Russian embassy. [67]

With a few of the Labour leaders, Chamberlain's relations were good. [68] But he found it difficult to do business with Attlee who was a 'cowardly cur' and whose 'aggressiveness' was a reaction to the 'dissatisfaction' his leadership was causing 'in his own party'. [69] In general he not only despised Labour politicians (who could face facts as little as Sir Walter Layton) but wished constantly to remind them how despicable they were. [70]

About the body of opinion which focussed on the *News Chronicle*, the Liberal party and the League of Nations Union, his feelings were even less restrained. Layton had made the *Chronicle* 'the most dangerous British newspaper'; [71] he was punished by being given 'what must have been the most unpleasant quarter of an hour he ever had in his life' when it reported, quite wrongly (after Albania), that Chamberlain was negotiating a security pact with Mussolini. [72] Sinclair's 'fatuous and imbecile propositions' and his 'uplift' and 'hypocritical cant' induced feelings so strong that Samuel (whom Chamberlain did not really like) was invited to rejoin the Cabinet in order to spite him. [73] About Lloyd George and his advocacy of a Russian alliance he felt 'as [he] looked down at his red face and white hair' in the course of the first meeting they had had alone for twenty years 'all my bitterness...pass away for I despised him and felt myself the better man'. [74]

To Eden Chamberlain's attitude was subtler but not less determined. There was an appearance of cordiality; there were messages of mutual appreciation, and there was considerable caution, before Munich, so long as it seemed possible that Eden might come out on top. But Chamberlain did not want him in the Cabinet; he watched contemptuously as he responded to the success and ambiguity of his policy. Between Munich and Prague he was not only pleased by his uncertainty but was confirmed in the belief that 'the mere announcement that he had been taken back...might... tempt...[the dictators] to break out now before the democracies had...strengthened their position'. [75]

Neither the occupation of Prague nor Halifax's wishes made any difference. The advantage to be gained by splitting Eden from Churchill would be lost, Chamberlain thought, if the chief consequence was to link Eden and Halifax in a Cabinet combination. After Albania Eden made an approach, which was rejected and followed it up with one 'disloyal' step after another until he not only made a 'foolish' offer to go to Moscow to settle the Russian alliance but also got Lloyd George to support him. [76]

To Churchill Chamberlain was as discouraging, feeling, as he had since at least 1936, the contempt of the office-holder for the office-seeker. [77] On the one hand he resented the certainty of the attack and the challenge it offered to his own certainty vis-à-vis the Foreign Office and the Labour party. On the other, he did not take it seriously and implied that Churchill did not take it seriously either. [78] 'The nearer we get to war', he thought, 'the more [Churchill's] chances improve', [79] but, since his object was to put off war, that strengthened the need to keep him out.

Churchill's offences were continuous — a 'foolish' broadcast to the United States about 'their duty to come to the assistance of the British Empire', an expression of the view, that Britain should occupy Corfu (in retaliation for the invasion of Albania) and a nasty speech in a subsequent debate when 'smarting under the disappointment' of not being made Minister of Supply. [80] His strategic insights included a playing down of the Japanese threat (as a distraction from the threat from Germany) and dismissal of the idea that Singapore could be taken. [81] He maintained close relations and engaged in obvious conspiracies with Masaryk and Maisky. [82] When explained in telephone calls and letters designed, as Chamberlain thought, for posterity or in 'orations' which interested, without persuading, the House of Commons, these activities did not matter. [83] When Halifax and the *Daily Telegraph* responded, they did. [84]

The threat Chamberlain feared in the summer of 1939 was that Churchill and Eden in office would be party to a plot to produce 'a more amenable Prime Minister' [85] who would do Maisky's work by involving Britain, France and Germany in war. In order to avoid this, it was necessary not just to refuse Churchill when he offered himself [86] or when newspapers made offers on his behalf. It was also necessary to believe that there could be no 'real alliance between Russia and Germany', that Hitler would 'not in cold blood start...a world war for Danzig' and that Chamberlain 'alone...could steer this country through the next four years out of the war zone into peace and reconstruction'. [87]

When Chamberlain left London for a holiday in Scotland in the second week of August, he was not sure that there would be a crisis. The messages he got soon afterwards did not enable him to know much better. [88] On the last day of his holiday he received a Halifax letter containing Intelligence predictions of a German attack on Poland and of Mussolini's unwillingness to support it. [89] On arriving in London he approved Loraine's (and Halifax's) request to involve Mussolini in negotiation and agreed to a proposal, transmitted secretly from Goering, that Goering should come to England. [90]

(ii)

When Chamberlain returned to London, he expected to replay the rôle he had played in May and September 1938. He did not know whether it would be as successful, but he was afraid that it would be as painful. Whether he would keep control or whether Hitler would run out of control was not something that could be known in advance. All he knew was that, even if Hitler was not rational, it was necessary to act as though he was. [91]

This was done by recalling Parliament, signing the Polish treaty [92] and rejecting the request to send a high-ranking mission to Berlin. [93] In case Hitler 'believe[d] that we do not mean to fight', Henderson and Halifax proposed, and Chamberlain and the Cabinet agreed, that a warning should be sent. [94]

The warning, delivered by Henderson on the 22nd, [95] produced a rough interview [96] and belligerent reply [97] in which Hitler stated that, if British mobilisation began, German mobilisation would follow. To the Cabinet of the 24th, this seemed uncompromising, even if it left open a shade of a loophole. [98]

On the 24th two other things had happened. Goering had explained that he could not come to England unless real negotiations were likely to follow; [99] Mussolini had been invited to involve himself in mediation. [100] It was not, however, decided that general mobilisation should begin, though Chamberlain explained, when asked, that he would decide after Henderson had paid the further call which Hitler had suggested for the 25th. [101]

Whether or not Hitler intended 'a war of nerves', [102] his meeting with Henderson was its start. Henderson had been told to come at 1.30 p.m. On enquiring what to say three-quarters of an hour before, he was told to say nothing until he had sent an account of the interview to London. In London, Chamberlain, half-expecting an ultimatum, waited with his wife in his Downing Street drawing-room 'unable to read, unable to talk, just sitting with folded hands and a gnawing pain in the stomach'. [103]

Henderson, however, was given not an ultimatum but the news that Hitler, having 'turned things over in his mind... desired...to make a move towards England...and...after the solution of the German-Polish question...would approach the British government with an offer'[104] — in other words that, if he got his way in Poland, he would move towards *détente*.

When, therefore, the Cabinet met at 6.30 p.m. on the 26th (with Henderson present after flying from Berlin), its members were not clear that war was imminent or that they were playing from weakness. Henderson did not know whether Danzig, the Corridor or the minority question was foremost in Hitler's mind. Halifax could not say whether he 'wanted a settlement with Poland on his own terms more than he wanted to avoid war with the British Empire'. Chamberlain's contributions were an emphasis on caution [105] and a draft reply which was sent to a committee after being 'practically torn to pieces' by the Cabinet. [106]

In the course of this meeting on Saturday evening, at the

meeting on Sunday afternoon [107] and at the Cabinet on Monday the 28th which approved the reply, the assumption was that Britain was ready (as she had not been in 1939), that Hitler was 'hesitating' in face of British readiness and that Mussolini would not support him because of the danger of 'revolution' if he did. It was believed that the German High Command feared that the Axis was breaking up. This general analysis was confirmed by the fact that, in negotiating an agreed text of Henderson's interview, the Germans had drawn attention to something Henderson did not remember Hitler saying about his willingness to be generous to the Poles. [108]

These hopes were deepened by the announcement that Dahlerus (about whom the body of the Cabinet knew nothing until Sunday afternoon) had been conducting parallel discussions with Goering. His arrival with a message from Hitler showed that Goering had 're-established his influence' and was willing to come to England after all. [109] Telephone calls when he returned to Germany next day confirmed the impression that Hitler, having failed to 'divide Britain from Poland', [110] might, just possibly, have 'got cold feet'. [111] When Hoare was deputed to conduct a press briefing on the 28th, he said that, since there were 'two views' about whether Hitler wanted to 'break with England', it was best to 'go quietly' and not assume that he had 'said his last word'. [112]

This assessment assumed that the Russo-German pact had not damaged Britain's position. Those who had made an Anglo-Soviet alliance the centre of their complaint maintained that it had. To those who had not, it was no more than a serious incident in Hitler's progress — even 'a measure of desperation', [113] which would not help him keep together the supporters of the anti-Comintern pact. Spain and Portugal had been alienated. The Japanese were 'puzzled and irritated' and the Japanese government was falling. [114] It seemed certain that Italy would not go to war and that American opinion had been shocked 'profoundly'. [115]

Hitler's 'cynical' alliance with the Bolsheviks[116] did not, therefore, dismiss the policy Chamberlain thought he was pursuing — of combining firmness and clarity of menace with a willingness to consider grievances where these existed. Indeed, it seemed to have been strengthened as Hitler faced war alone while Britain avoided a three-cornered war against his allies.[117] 'Surprising',[118] in other words, as the pact was, it was not expected to enable Hitler to win a short war. In relation to a long one, it continued to be assumed that he knew himself to be highly vulnerable.[119]

From this understanding of the situation, three conclusions were drawn. The first was to establish that Britain meant business by stiffening the draft reply and telling Dahlerus that there should be no 'Diktat to the Poles'.[120] The second was to handle Mussolini carefully by rejecting Eden's offer to go to Ankara to negotiate a treaty with the Turks,[121] and by responding gracefully when Ciano telephoned to say that Britain should talk to Hitler.[122] The third was to carry the Poles along, which accounts for the care taken to get Beck's authority before assuring Hitler that they would have early talks with the German government.

The British reply, approved in principle by the Cabinet of the 28th and touched up by Halifax afterwards, was taken by Henderson to Berlin and delivered to Hitler at 10.30 that night.[123] Hitler's reply was conveyed in conversation at once and developed in a letter which Henderson was given when he saw him again at 7.15 p.m. next day.[124]

When a summary of the letter arrived in London late that night,[125] it 'looked' so 'bad' that Chamberlain asked Halifax to draft a stiff reply.[126] When Halifax looked at the full text with Cadogan, however, he saw 'a man...trying to extricate himself from a difficult situation'.[127] So far as it accepted the international guarantee, an independent Poland and direct discussion with the Poles, it represented an advance. So far as it made negotiations depend on the Poles sending an ambassador to Berlin during August 30, it proposed conditions which could not be accepted.[128]

By the time the Cabinet met at 11.30 a.m. on the 30th with a revised version of the reply, it was felt that Hitler was in an 'awful fix'.[129] This feeling was strengthened by a further visit from Dahlerus, who arrived three-quarters of an hour before with the news that Goering was suggesting a plebiscite in the Corridor and the return of Danzig as the basis for a settlement.[130] That Hitler had been 'beaten' was then confirmed by a fresh batch of Intelligence reports of unrest in Germany and a broadcast announcement that Goering's powers were being strengthened. [131]

From a position of 'strength', therefore, it was decided that Warsaw should be spared the indignities of Prague. The Poles were to be told that mobilisation should begin. The Germans were to be told that negotiation could not begin under threat of invasion and must be conducted in a neutral country later. [132]

When Henderson delivered the reply, Ribbentrop explained that Hitler's proposals had been withdrawn. [133] On August 31 it was decided to begin both mobilisation and the evacuation of London. [134] Hitler's speech that evening and Ribbentrop's eventual decision to reveal the German terms[135] indicated to those who wanted to believe it that negotiation was not impossible.[136] The announcement next morning that Danzig had been annexed and Poland invaded seemed to show that it was.

At first, however, it was by no means clear that the invasion was full-scale. It was not until Hitler's Reichstag speech later in the morning that the Chiefs of Staff asked for a declaration of war. Technical reasons were then given for delaying the evacuation of London, [137] and enabling the French to make their declaration first so as to avoid the appearance of being 'dragged into war by us'. [138]

The Cabinet decided not to send an 'ultimatum'. [139] Instead, it approved the text of a 'warning' which had no time-limit attached and was not to be sent until it had been seen by the French government. [140] When the French approved it, it was sent off in the late afternoon.

The warning Hitler received was that Britain intended to 'honour her obligations' unless 'satisfactory assurances' were received that 'the German government had suspended...aggressive action...and was prepared to withdraw...from Polish territory'. [141] At two o'clock that afternoon, one idea was that war would begin at midnight, [142] but it then came to seem likely that the French would not be ready before five o'clock on the afternoon of the 2nd. When he spoke to the House of Commons at six o'clock that evening, Chamberlain explained that a warning was being sent. [143] At 11.30 that night he told Halifax he would do nothing about declaring war until 9.30 next morning. [144]

One reason why the French government was unwilling to

declare war was that it was taking Ciano more seriously than he had been taken in London, where there had been negative responses to his telephone calls on August 31. His first proposal — that Mussolini should approach Hitler on the basis that the Poles would give up Danzig and negotiate on other questions [145] — was turned down, on Chamberlain's instructions, because 'Danzig was the kernel of the matter' and there should be negotiation about that. [146] The second, which arrived while a decision was being made about the first, was that a Five-Power conference should be held to discuss Treaty revision. [147]

Chamberlain's and Halifax's first reaction had been that there could be no conference 'under an open threat of force' but that 'it was undesirable to show any unwillingness to agree to negotiations under more favourable conditions'. [148] In view of Loraine's optimism about Mussolini, Halifax offered the motions of civility (though he attached little importance to them). The Cabinet paid little attention at its meeting on September 1. When Dahlerus telephoned Cadogan after the invasion of Poland had begun, he was told that 'the only way in which a world war can be stopped is...that hostilities be suspended and...German troops...immediately withdrawn from Polish territory'. [149]

On September 1, then, Chamberlain was firm and emphatic. Having asked ministers to resign so as to free him to form a War Cabinet, [150] he had left the impression of waiting only for a German answer in order to convert the warning into an ultimatum.

Waiting for an answer, with German troops in Poland, was an ambiguous position which became more ambiguous the more unwilling the French government seemed to become. Ciano had made approaches in Paris where Bonnet was pressing Daladier to get a conference through an open-ended ultimatum. At about 2.30 p.m. on September 2 Halifax was rung up by Ciano and Loraine, with the result that a statement Simon was scheduled to make in the House of Commons ten minutes later was postponed and the Cabinet called for a quarter past four. [151]

At this meeting Halifax recorded Ciano's claim that Hitler might welcome a Five-Power conference after an armistice, provided the British and French notes were not an ultimatum and so long as he could have until noon next day to make up his mind. After reporting himself as replying that the German army would have to leave Poland before a conference was possible, he laid out the conclusions at which he and Chamberlain had arrived. These were that the note to Germany had been a 'final warning, rather than an ultimatum', that Hitler should be given until noon, or even midnight, on September 3 to reply and that the 'primary conditions for any conference' were the withdrawal of German troops from Poland and the restoration of the *status quo ante* in Danzig.

The Cabinet at once agreed that there could be no conference without a withdrawal, but there was heated discussion about the time-table. The Service ministers gave military reasons in favour of an ultimatum for midnight that night. It slowly became clear that most of the others agreed and that Chamberlain would not be allowed to delay, even if he wanted to. After the meeting had ended with a decision in favour of a midnight 'ultimatum', its members were 'horrified' to find him imposing no time-limit when he spoke in the House of Commons an hour later. [152]

11

THE DECLARATION OF WAR

'Next Thursday Baldwin resigns the Premiership and Neville will become Prime Minister. The latter, two months ago, told me in confidence that he wanted me to succeed him as Chancellor of the Exchequer...I warned him that I had no special knowledge of finance and approached such an office with humbleness'.
Simon diary May 20 1937

'D. Margesson says Simon...hopes he would be considered for the Treasury as if not he would like to consider retiring from politics and writing (all ambitious politicians like to say this at such moments)...He considered his only rival to be Kingsley Wood as Sam [Hoare] had so lost the confidence of the House and country'.
Chamberlain diary February 11 1937

'If only *you* could succeed Baldwin when the time comes'.
Sir Henry Norman to Simon December 16 1936

(i)

In the life of his government, the subject Chamberlain had chosen as the demonstration of his will — relations with Hitler and Mussolini — exploded into being the only subject of importance. It so acutely involved every politician's understanding of the future that even the Cabinet felt the impact.

Between May 1937 and the outbreak of war, twenty-nine ministers served in the Cabinet. Of these Lord Stanley was unwell and rather deaf, mattered very little (except as Derby's favourite son[1]) and was a Cabinet minister for only a short time before he died (young) just after Munich. Others also were of little importance without being deaf, or were so dependent or unwilling to chance their arms that they had the status of backbench voyeurs. Stanhope, for example, after earlier disappointments, had climbed into the Cabinet in 1936 at Chamberlain's insistence, twenty years after first becoming an under-secretary.[2] He had then become President of the Board of Education (in order to develop Chamberlain's interest in physical education) and was First Lord of the Admiralty and Conservative leader in the House of Lords during the period of difficulty over the Coal bill. Almost everything he said was a repetition of the Chamberlain line, just as Burgin's was a repetition of Simon's.[3] Until September 1939, Brown and Colville also said little and, when they spoke, did so in order to ask for firmness which others had asked for already.

In some cases, disagreement was rewarded by dismissal. After thirty years as an MP, including seven as an under-secretary, Winterton had been passed over in 1935 because 'an old stager' without 'enough brains'[4] would be difficult to get rid of. His appointment in Davidson's place outside the Cabinet when Chamberlain became Prime Minister was a gesture of goodwill to an old friend and a way of keeping an important backbencher happy.

Winterton had been an ally of Hoare, a critic of Eden and a collaborator of Churchill and Austen Chamberlain. He had also been a leading opponent of a Colonial deal.[5] His promotion to the Cabinet in March 1938 was designed to keep him quiet after Eden's resignation. When he arrived (at the age of fifty-eight), he became the spokesman of Churchill's attitude to air defence and was 'deeply concerned at our inability to fulfil the [parity] pledges of the late Prime Minister'.[6] In the House of Commons his performance as Swinton's Air spokesman was so appalling that it helped Chamberlain to decide that Swinton should be moved.

During Cabinet discussions in September Winterton was unhelpful in a different way. He made repeated references to the danger of letting down the French,[7] compared the Berchtesgaden meeting with the challenge of 1914 and talked unsuitably about the 'hard fibre of the British people'.[8] He supported the Anglo-French proposals of September 18.[9] But he became extremely critical after Godesberg, presenting the problem as a 'moral' one, taking a favourable view of French determination and claiming that, if Hitler's proposals were accepted 'the government would fall...when parliament reassembled'.[10] Though he approved of Wilson's visit to Berlin[11] and supported the settlement once it was made, he nearly resigned on September 24 and was the only Cabinet minister who did not see Chamberlain off to Munich.

Between Berchtesgaden and Godesberg, Winterton had consulted Duff Cooper and was consulted by de la Warr.[12] But he was of a different outlook or generation and carried little weight with them. In late 1938 he was an object of derision in the House of Commons.[13] Despite continuing regard for Chamberlain,[14] he was turned out of the Cabinet early in the New Year in order to make way when Chatfield succeeded Inskip as Minister for the Co-ordination of Defence.[15]

Ormsby-Gore — a Baldwinian hangover and long-term admirer of Eden[16] — was a Cecilian Christian who discerned an identity of intention between Liberal Imperialism, enlightened Conservatism, the League of Nations and the best sorts of socialism. Before 1935 he had been outspoken — against Vansittart's view of Germany, against Simon for being insufficiently anti-Nazi and against Chamberlain and Norman for being unnecessarily deflationary.[17] He had been Dawson's candidate for the Colonial Office;[18] on succeeding Thomas in 1936, he had compounded a long-standing Zionism by taking up the proposal to build a naval base at Haifa and had opposed a Colonial deal in East Africa in view of the threat that a Black army in hostile hands might present to Imperial communications.[19]

Ormsby-Gore was a Milnerite who had been taught by H.A.L. Fisher. He believed that, though Africans preferred British to other foreign rulers they could no longer be 'hawked about' as 'pawns'.[20] Despite a distinct strategic practicality, his difficulties arose from an Eden-like wish to square the circle between Right and Left, Arabs and Jews, rearmament and disarmament and the ineffectiveness and desirability of the League.

Over Hoare-Laval, Ormsby-Gore had been against Hoare. He had then been a nuisance about Mussolini. In February 1938 he had offered to move on from the Colonial Office if that would enable Eden to stay in the Cabinet.[21] Chamberlain, however, mistrusted his judgment (in which he was not alone). On succeeding to his father's peerage (as Lord Harlech) in May 1938, Ormsby-Gore had his public career cut short without ceremony at the age of fifty-three for being in effect a Cecil.[22]

Hailsham was a thinking die-hard who shared Hankey's views about Spain and classified A.D. Lindsay as a 'bolshy'. In early 1938 he was tired and ill and for this reason moved from the Lord Chancellorship to be Lord President of the

Council. He was armoured against Eden and had a long-standing mistrust of the Nazi régime, which had been greatly accentuated by the Anschluss. [23] On September 24 he gave the Cabinet a long list of Hitler's promises and contradicted Chamberlain's account of his character. [24] A long-standing alliance did not remove doubts which were increased by his son's experience at the Oxford by-election. [25] Having been compelled to make way for Runciman after Munich, he thought seriously about running a national campaign against the return of Tanganyika to Germany. [26]

Not all of Chamberlain's changes were responses to scepticism about Hitler. Swinton, for example, had not been sceptical. But he had been damaged by the Nuffield incident in 1936 [27] and had been gravely ill twice in three years. He was an awkward advocate of air force acceleration after the Anschluss when he failed, despite his undoubted achievement at the Air Ministry, to impose a mass-production system on the aircraft industry. Though consoled as a victim of the 'Press-dogs' and the 'irrational working of the system', his resignation in fact followed his refusal to move elsewhere when the Cadman report made it necessary for the head of a politically-sensitive department to be a member of the House of Commons. [28]

Anderson was brought into the Cabinet in late 1938 because of his knowledge of the administrative machinery; he regarded Munich as a 'humiliation'. [29] Maugham was not made Lord Chancellor because he approved of Chamberlain's foreign policy; once appointed (at seventy-two) he was an articulate supporter.

Before being removed from the Cabinet in 1937, Runciman's Italian position had been much like Chamberlain's. About Germany, however, he had been tougher. After being an advocate of a commercial agreement in 1934, he had reflected a hardening of feeling in the Board of Trade as it came to be assumed that autarky was not really negotiable.

Eden thought Runciman a more significant Liberal than Simon or Hore-Belisha; in 1937 he asked Chamberlain not to drop him. Runciman had also been thought of as a possible prime minister if Chamberlain was not chosen. [30] There is no reason to think that this made Chamberlain remove him from office on Baldwin's retirement, though his standing as a Liberal contributed to his return in October 1938, when his silence made him a doubtful asset and a stroke (together with an unhelpful interest in the Russian alliance[31]) was followed by retirement at the outbreak of war, thirty-four years after he had joined Campbell-Bannerman's government.

Among the fifteen ministers who were in the Cabinet continuously, Chamberlain had a special relationship with Wood; except from him, he had regular support only from Zetland.

Zetland was a Yorkshire landowner and intellectual Curzonian. He had worked with Derby, Amery and Austen Chamberlain in support of the India bill. As both author and politician, however, he was a specialist, having never held office in England and having been an Indian governor in his forties before writing both Curzon's biography and a 'philosophical' book on 'Indian Unrest'. It was this last that enabled him to attribute to Hitler 'the pagan philosophy of Nietzsche', the 'policy of Treitschke' and 'misapplied Darwinism' challenging the mind of Christendom. [32]

Zetland had no illusions about Stalin whom he viewed through the die-hard spectacles of the twenties. Nor did he share the German sympathies of 1936. [33] He not only thought them misguided but regarded Chamberlain and Duff Cooper as the only ministers who would actively resist them. [34] Even when hoping that Hitler and Mussolini might see the futility of an armaments race, it was against hope that he was hoping. [35]

Zetland took an Imperial rather than a League view of the Abyssinian problem, urging strong sanctions if sanctions were to be imposed. [36] But neither then nor later did he pursue Eden's vendettas against Mussolini.

Zetland felt the same detachment as Chamberlain from the ideologies that were dividing Europe. He saw a Bolshevist conspiracy in France, [37] and looked forward with horror to the 'holocaust' towards which the Spanish war was leading. The thought of 'English liberty' being submerged by war showed that 'in theory' there was 'much to be said for the policy of the isolationists'. [38]

In September 1938, Zetland was clear that Hitler would go

on until the Sudeten Germans had joined the Reich. [39] But
Plan Z was 'a stroke of genius' and the Munich invitation a
'miracle'.

> The only people...who...want[ed] war were the communists...and the
> pacifists, [by which he meant the Labour party and the League of Na-
> tions Union; he did] not see why we should plunge into the destruction
> of the present world order...merely to please these peculiarly unpleas-
> ant people. [40]

Zetland supported the Munich agreement, the 'anguish' of
which was worthwhile if it made possible 'a return to sanity'. [41] It was only his willingness to put up with Stalin in
order to prevent him co-operating with Hitler that produced
a period of deviation (which ended with the Russo-German
pact). [42]

There is evidence that, about Italy, [43] Zetland felt more
strongly than he spoke. But he expected no help from the
United States. [44] Whether through lack of interest in the
League (and its political implications) or the unwillingness of a
new minister to express doubts, his acquiescence was unusual.

Elsewhere doubts were expressed frequently. Apart from
Hore-Belisha (who did not form part of their circle) and Duff
Cooper (who did not approve of Eden), the most important
were expressed by Morrison, Elliot, MacDonald, de la Warr
and Stanley who in early 1938 talked each other into the
belief that Eden's resignation would be 'so dreadful an event'
that they ought to be resigning with him.[45] In the end no one
resigned, but the spasms were repeated during the events of
September and recurrently thereafter.

Morrison was a middle-class Scotsman with a good war record, proficiency as an undergraduate politician (at Edinburgh) and experience at the Bar. As a backbencher, he belonged to a parliamentary group which interested itself in
'moral' questions (like Temperance, gambling and the cin-
ema). [46] He played a part in Percy's 'rethinking' of Conservatism, picked up the mantle when Percy faltered and was a
Baldwin man who would have had Lloyd George in the Cabinet if that could have been done without a split. [47] Perhaps
for this reason, Chamberlain had not wanted him as Financial

Secretary to the Treasury. [48] But he recognised that (as chairman of the 1922 Committee) Morrison was 'influential' in the House of Commons [49] and came to accept him when Baldwin insisted. It was Chamberlain's idea, rather than Baldwin's, that Morrison should become Minister of Agriculture when Elliot went stale'. [50]

As Minister of Agriculture Morrison's experience was shattering. A barley crisis in East Anglia, difficulties with sheep farmers and a Conservative revolt over the Milk bill produced public ridicule and the threat of farmers' candidates at by-elections. His removal, a bad period as a Commons spokesman on defence and demotion to the Post Office in April 1940 marked the grave of a future Prime Minister. [51]

About foreign policy Morrison's doubts developed slowly. When Baldwin retired he expected Chamberlain to 'negate' the 'policy of retreat'. [52] In early 1938 he shared Eden's doubts, but ended by defending Chamberlain in the House of Commons. [53] He said virtually nothing, except to agree with Halifax, at the Cabinet of August 30. On September 14 he wanted Hitler told of 'the growing feeling in this country that war was inevitable'. But he approved of the decision to go to Berchtesgaden; [54] the preference he expressed for a delayed plebiscite was not put strongly. It was not until Chamberlain returned that the 'future' became 'dark' as Hitler seemed likely to get what he wanted 'without a plebiscite'. [55]

At this stage Morrison was merely wondering. He distinguished 'intruding...into a quarrel which was not our affair' from the duty to be involved if 'France was drawn in'. But he 'did not feel to the same extent as some of his colleagues that our honour was implicated'. [56] At the Cabinet of September 21, when the objectors were heard, he said nothing. He said nothing at the long Cabinet meetings on the 24th. His only interventions in the week before Munich were made next day when he told the Cabinet that the public did not want war and, while opposing any sort of pressure, wanted the Czechs to be told about the uncertainties of the military situation.

Morrison's few contributions to Cabinet discussion included enquiries about the relationship between Hitler and the rest of the Nazi régime. If his doubts were more extensive, he expressed them discreetly. On September 28 his wife was heard wishing that war had been faced, but there is no direct evidence that he did.

Like Morrison, Elliot was a Scotsman — the son of a wealthy Glasgow auctioneer. After qualifying as a doctor, he had distinguished himself in the war and became a Unionist MP in 1918. In the Lloyd George Coalition, he was a junior minister; he played no part in removing Lloyd George and did not join the Conservative government until 1923. In 1934 he married Asquith's sister-in-law who was a Liberal.

From 1931 onwards he established a reputation as a stimulator of State aid for agriculture, attracting criticism from MacDonald as a soft touch in face of powerful interests [57] but creating an impression — not only in Conservative quarters — that, by honouring the policy of his predecessor, he too had made himself a future Prime Minister. [58] In 1934 he was unusual in thinking that Cecil would be an asset in the Cabinet. [59] He was part of the plot to bring Lloyd George into the government and, like the rest of the plotters, combined 'compassionate' doubts about Chamberlain with intense irritation at the French. [60] Like Morrison, he was thought of as Minister for the Co-ordination of Defence. [61] Over the Rhineland, he was thinking of resigning and beginning to talk about the need for Anglo-French solidarity. [62] Later in 1936 he was moved, unwillingly, at Chamberlain's suggestion, to the Scottish Office. [63]

Elliot was an admirer of Eden, and had been one of the first ministers to demand Hoare's resignation. [64] He also liked Halifax. [65] He did not like the Italian negotiations in 1938 and gave Eden a degree of support. [66] This, however, stopped well short of resignation since two would destroy the government which he would not wish to do 'unless he [saw] his way to another'. [67] When brought back to the Ministry of Health (perhaps in order to keep him quiet), he started talking about a 'Government of National Safety'. [68]

When Swinton resigned, Elliot 'saluted' him as an 'Adventurer'. For him the Runciman mission was a turning-point about which the Cabinet ought to have been consulted. So was Plan Z. On August 30 he had been 'uneasy': on September 14 'expectations' were being raised which would be 'pro-

portionately disappointed'. After Berchtesgaden he refused
to be rushed into self-determination which 'might be' a way
of 'cloaking' a desire to 'surrender'.[69] He recognised that
Chamberlain had prevented an invasion, which nothing could
have been done to resist. But he regarded further negotiations
as a risk[70] and would choose war rather than capitulation.[71]
He told his wife that it would be 'an unjust cause' to go to
war 'because of the Sudeten minorities'. He also told her
that 'a Hoare-Laval feeling' might blow up on the 'moderate
Left' at any suggestion of 'German troops entering Czechoslovakia before the international force had got into position'.[72]
into position'.[72]

While Chamberlain was at Godesberg, Elliot said that the
Anglo-French proposals were 'in the Czechs' own interest'
but that things '[could] not go on and it would be better to
get it over with now'.[73] On his return, he was 'intensely
disturbed at the prospect of delivering another chunk of the
goods...[with] no negotiation...at all, just signing on the dot-
ted line, and once you begin..., no-one can say that you will
ever stop'.[74]

When Halifax turned round after Godesberg, Elliot agreed
with him about the terms and did his best to establish that
the French were willing to fight. He approved of the letter
which Wilson took to Berlin.[75]

During the demolition of the Wilson proposals on the
27th, he said nothing. He was still thinking of resigning but,
though the Munich terms were 'hateful', he had not complained about the rearmament programme in the past and 'in
the present state of our forces — French and British, — could
not say that he would have stopped Chamberlain if he had
been able to.[76] His emphasis, thereafter, was on the need to
restore confidence on the 'Centre-Left' by associating with
the Soviet Union, avoiding enthusiasm whenever it was necessary to associate with Mussolini[77] and having a reconstruction 'on the widest possible basis'.

Despite a half-offer to resign with Duff Cooper,[78] one does
not get the impression that Elliot intended to do so. De la
Warr did. On August 30 he wanted a public commitment to
France and the beginning of mobilization.[79] On September 2
he wanted something done about the Russians.[80] On Sep-

tember 7 he was 'highly agitated'; next day he was 'very distressed'. [81] On September 9 he was hoping for Royal action
to resolve a 'National crisis' and would not stay in office if
the government backed down. [82] On September 10 'world
decency' required tripartite action to stop Hitler before he
was 'firmly established in the East'. [83] At the Cabinet of
September 12 he talked about the 'humiliating position' that
would arise 'if...we were to decide that, in view of our armament position, we could not support the French'. [84]

In 1938 de la Warr was thirty-eight, a year younger than
Malcolm MacDonald. He had, however, been a minor member
of a government as long ago as 1924 and had served continuously since the Labour party took office in 1929. Under
Ramsay MacDonald he had not been in the Cabinet and had
been greatly put out when Baldwin failed to promote him on
Thomas's retirement. [85] He entered the Cabinet the day after
MacDonald left it.

De la Warr had not had to fight; he owed his position to
having been a war-time conscientious objector, a hereditary
Labour peer (immediately after leaving Oxford) and one of
the handful of Labour ministers who joined the National
government in 1931. In a predominantly middle-class Cabinet, he was in some obvious sense, aristocratic, and advanced
socialist opinions in a 'pugnacious' [86] manner which was designed to meet the threat presented by the fact that 'the
younger generation of working class men believe[d] in the
class war'. [87] 'We must', he is said to have said in 1937,
'either have socialism ourselves...or have [it] applied in 1942
by the opposition'. [88]

De la Warr was handsome and energetic, and had run the
National Labour party almost single-handed. When Chamberlain and Margesson threw their weight behind Malcolm Mac
Donald, he became a serious politician. By the beginning of
1938 he was torn between leaving the party when MacDonald
was preferred as leader and rescuing it by leaving the government in order to attack Chamberlain. [89]

In rejecting resignation, de la Warr appears to have taken
Eden's advice. But in thinking of it, and even more in thinking about the party's future, he was on to a real problem.

Even before the 1935 election, it had been difficult to
show what National Labour stood for. [90] When both Mac-

Donalds lost their seats, the difficulty became acute. [91] Disintegration was suggested when Thomas was moved to the Colonial Office, 'screaming and kicking' at having to make way for Malcolm MacDonald at the Dominions Office [92] and when his resignation in advance of the Budget leakage report a few months later was timed to prevent him leaking that as well. [93] The impression had been deepened by the death of King George V (an energetic protector [94]), by the MacDonalds' dependence on Conservative goodwill and by the campaign which the Churchills [95] waged against the attempt to find them new seats. [96]

After his demotion, Ramsay MacDonald's experience had been miserable. He despised Hoare's diplomacy and was at once appalled and gratified by its failure. [97] He had not wanted a 'rushed' election, [98] had resented Baldwin's failure to mention him [99] and had been horrified by the 'ugly' revelation the Seaham campaign gave him of modern ingratitude at its worst. [100] When the election was over, he hung about, cantankerous, dignified and unwanted until becoming MP for the Scottish Universities [101] at the same time as full-scale rearmament heralded a return to the era of 'militarism'. [102]

In his last period of office, MacDonald was 'homesick' for the Labour movement and thought much about human frailty. [103] Except at the Coronation [104] he had no function, his advice was not welcomed and he did not matter — even in his own party. Chamberlain did not want him and encouraged Baldwin to take him when he retired. His resignation — resentful and unwilling — the day before Chamberlain became Prime Minister and his death six months later occurred at least two years after his era had ended. [105]

MacDonald's retirement did not, however, mean the end of the National Labour party which had begun to develop an organisation it had not had before and provided a platform on which de la Warr, Malcolm MacDonald, Denman, Lindsay and Nicolson (along with King-Hall, Elton and Mrs Dugdale) performed in relation to the future.

What they invented was very different from the future that had been invented in 1931. In place of the rhetoric of rescue, they discovered a duty to transcend the selfish conflict of the parties. In face of the reactionary revival of 1936, they were 'pioneers' in thinking about a 'Centre-party' to which liberal

Conservatives could flee. [106] Though overloaded with ministers, they stood for 'social change without revolution' and
'economic equality without sacrifice of political freedom'. In
talking about 'Eden' and 'liberal centrality', they talked a
language which was as acceptable to Stanley and Elliot as to
Sinclair and Macmillan. All four would all have assented to
the pieties de la Warr offered at the National Labour Conference in 1938.

Th[is] generation [he said] was faced with the danger of becoming one
without belief or interest. There were those of the possessing classes
who felt they had a right to their possessions irrespective of the services
they gave while there were those of the working-classes who believed
they had a divine claim on the community, including their fellow workers. We should think a great deal more of duties and services and a great
deal less of our rights...National Labour [should] help to create a new
spirit of belief so that our national life could be something really fine
and that Great Britain and her Empire could so regain her strength not
only of arms but of purpose that she could help both herself and the
world to a better and saner life. [107]

This, though rhetorically elevating, implied nothing about
'appeasement'. Nor was the party united in disliking it. For
this reason de la Warr was conscious of the insignificance of
any action he might take, and was cautious about turning
criticism into resignation.

Nevertheless, after praising the Berchtesgaden visit, he said
what he had to. He objected to the terms as being 'unfair to
the Czechs, dishonourable to ourselves' and the consequence
of 'negotiating with a country which had $1\frac{1}{2}$ million men
under arms'. Neither Hitler nor the Sudeten Germans 'have
yet made any concessions', he told the Cabinet, 'they must
be prepared to make some' since, if they did not, 'it is doubtful whether the government would carry the policy in the
House of Commons or in the country'. [108]

After this statement, which irritated Chamberlain, de la
Warr said very little in Cabinet. But he was hoping that Elliot
would resign (so that he could resign too) and tried to persuade Duff Cooper not to resign so that the dissentients
could all resign together. [109] He was quite clear that, if war
came, Chamberlain would have to go. [110]

De la Warr supported the settlement (which was 'not as
bad as people made out') and persuaded the National Labour
party to support it too. [111] Afterwards he was made Minister

of Education. But his line in the winter of 1938 was that 'in the modern world...right could not prevail without might' and that a League policy should be strengthened by closer relations with Russia.[112] He was upset by Chamberlain's gullibility in Rome. After Prague he talked again about re-signing and wanted Conscription and a Ministry of Sup-ply.[113] In the summer of 1939 he was a coalitionist, was privy (through Astor) to the Churchill press campaign and was willing to think of Halifax as Prime Minister.[114] After the Russo-German pact, he felt no optimism.[115] On Septem-ber 2 he was 'terribly distressed' at the failure to declare war.[116]

De la Warr and MacDonald were rivals for leadership of the National Labour party and did not talk freely to one an-other.[117] But they responded to the same signals and be-longed to the same circle. Though de la Warr first thought of resigning over Abyssinian recognition (in 1937),[118] however, something had always stopped him. It took MacDonald a very long time to decide that Chamberlain's position was untenable.

From Oxford, MacDonald had gone, very early, into Parlia-ment. When he was thirty-four, his father had brought him into the Cabinet where Baldwin kept him when he lost his seat in 1935. He had great difficulty finding a new one and depended on Conservative organisation and Liberal votes when he won Ross and Cromarty in early 1936. After Abyssi-nia and the Rhineland, he preferred the League to Locarno. Like his father, he wanted the rearmament programme kept under review so as to avoid encouraging anything resembling a 'war mentality'.[119]

This sort of position was in no way unusual. The conjunc-tion of reluctant rearmament with an 'active peace diplo-macy'[120] could have described Chamberlain's position, or Eden's. Before Baldwin retired, MacDonald (like Eden) was talking about retiring with him: before Eden's resignation he was Eden's 'best friend in the Cabinet'.[121] He was thought of as a successor[122] and was used as proof of the govern-ment's virtue when Eden had gone.[123] The Anschluss seems to have shocked him.[124]

Like de la Warr's, MacDonald's instinct was to believe that dictators should be resisted. Like other ministers, he knew

that the air defences were such that 'no cabinet could take
a...risk'. As Colonial and, for a time, Dominions Secretary, he
knew how little the Dominions were interested in central
Europe. When pressed to protest, he replied that Eden had
'made a mistake' and that there was a 'national crisis' in
which Chamberlain should be supported. [125]

On August 30 he said firmly that 'we should not go to war'
if Germany invaded Czechoslovakia. [126]   This did not stop
him wanting the Lanark warning repeated next day. [127]   But
he approved of the Berchtesgaden visit and looked forward to
the 'pacifist element in the Labour party' providing 'tremendous support' for a plebiscite. While preferring a plebiscite in
six months' time, he 'prefer[red] an immediate [one] to war
...humiliating though the position might be'. [128]   When Chamberlain returned, the 'overwhelming condition of public feeling' compelled acceptance of the principle of self-determination. [129]

Thereafter, there was anguish. After Berchtesgaden, the
public would not want German troops in Czechoslovakia before the arrival of an international force and, if Hitler pressed
the claims of the Poles and Hungarians, would be showing
that 'his interest lay...in...dominat[ing] Europe'. [130]   After
Godesberg, though Hitler's 'method' was 'outrageous' and his
terms 'shocking' ('through no fault of the Prime Minister'),
war would be so 'disastrous' (not only for relations with the
Dominions) that the Czechs should be allowed to make up
their own minds 'in the light of all the relevant considerations'. [131]

Like everyone else MacDonald approved of the Wilson mission [132]   and accepted the settlement. It was not until the
political disintegration of December that he began to say that
'Munich' had been 'wrong'. [133]

Hankey (who had observed him at close quarters) thought
MacDonald had 'a wise head on young shoulders'. [134]   Until
November 1938 MacDonald's position was unequivocal. Even
when doubts began, his dissent was muted. In any case
neither he nor de la Warr could foresee the future. A similar
uncertainty affected Duff Cooper and Hore-Belisha.

Though Duff Cooper had for long been seen as Eden's rival, [135]   he had other reasons for being sceptical about ap-

peasement in 1936, critical about Italian and Spanish policy in 1937 and negative about resigning at the beginning of 1938.

He had taken a strong line over Abyssinia and associated himself with the belief that the Italians would not win. [136] But he had been critical of Eden's handling of Mussolini and supported the Italian negotiations provided they did not impair relations with France. [137] So far from being an Eden man who would attract the League of Nations Union, he was a Foreign Office Conservative who believed in the French alliance as the lynch-pin of British diplomacy and France and Britain as 'the main supporters of the *status quo*'. [138] At numerous turning-points, and with more hope than accuracy, he had said that the French were willing to fight. He fought a battle about the wording of the statement of March 24 1938 [139] and found it monstrous that anyone could regard Anglo-French staff talks as unnecessary. [140] 'The greatest danger to the peace of Europe', he reported himself as telling the Polish Prime Minister (whom he met on holiday in the summer)

was that Hitler, encouraged by the success of previous adventures, may take a step which, once taken, he could not withdraw...

Germany would not have gone to war in 1914 had she known whom she would be fighting in 1918...The same thing would happen again — but America would come in sooner and the victory would be greater...In fairness to [Hitler] and to Germany, it should be made plain now what forces he would find himself up against. [141]

Duff Cooper believed that Britain and France could afford to take risks. During the Munich crisis, his chief interests were the demands of public feeling, the need to prevent German domination and a sense that an Anglo-French victory was essential. [142] He supported Chamberlain so long as there were 'warnings'. [143] It was the lack of warnings about which he was preparing to complain on September 14 when Chamberlain announced his decision to fly to Germany.

About Plan Z he expressed two reservations. [144] But he 'much preferred' it to mobilising the Fleet and was prepared to see what happened when Chamberlain got there. [145] It was not until the Berchtesgaden interview was described that he raised three major objections.

The first was that Chamberlain had failed to mention any

of the Cabinet's proposals and was asking for 'a complete surrender'. The second was that, in these circumstances, 'the Czechs would probably prefer to fight'. The third was that Hitler was so obviously using the Sudeten problem as a step on the road to European domination that 'there was no chance of peace in Europe as long as there [was] a Nazi régime in Germany'. [146]

These were statements of position rather than of policy. Since the 'prospect of war...was appalling' and the régime might collapse without war, he supported self-determination on September 19. [147]   But the French were to be told that 'we would fight rather than agree to abject surrender' and Hitler that application of the principle must be negotiated. To any further demands Chamberlain was to reply that 'we should go to war...to stop him dominating Europe,' that 'the U.S.A. would come in on our side' and that 'Germany, notwithstanding some initial successes, would be faced with ultimate defeat'. [148]

From September 13 onwards Duff Cooper pressed continually for the mobilisation of the Fleet [149] and objected to Germany occupying the Sudetenland in advance of a plebiscite. [150]   He approved of the decision to withdraw the ban on Czech mobilisation while Chamberlain was at Godesberg and 'was glad to see the terms of the message' which Halifax had sent him on the 23rd. [151]

After Godesberg he spoke often and strongly in Cabinet, contesting the belief that Hitler could be trusted and doubting whether he could be influenced. On September 24 he was 'sure' that the Czechs would 'fight' and demanded general mobilisation 'as a precautionary measure' while they were considering Hitler's proposals. [152]

When Chamberlain brought the Godesberg proposals to the Cabinet, he predicted 'an explosion of public opinion' and defeat in Parliament if they were accepted. 'Great moral issues were at stake', and the Czechs should be told that, if they refused, 'we should stand by them and...we hoped that France would do the same'.

What Duff Cooper was demanding was a stiffer diplomacy and a deterrent which could be made effective by co-operation. He did not trust Chamberlain to handle the French properly or report their feelings truthfully. He told the Cabinet after the Anglo-French meetings on the 25th that he 'appeared to have contested the French point of view on every point...and to have allowed it to appear that [he] disagreed with the French government's suggestions without making any positive suggestions [him]sel[f]'. [153]

When Chamberlain announced Wilson's visit to Berlin, Duff Cooper wanted a promise of intervention if France supported the Czechs: [154] when Wilson returned, he was clear that Chamberlain wanted them to 'surrender'. He could see 'no point' in this 'unless we also told [them] that we should refuse to come to their help'. He found this so 'unjustified' that he 'could not be associated with it'. [155]

Duff Cooper's policy preferences were clear. They were confirmed, he believed, by the public mood and the fate the government would suffer if it ignored it. They were not those of Chamberlain, whose life-style differed from his own and who, after two deviant speeches in December 1937, had sent him a rebuke such as 'in his place' would have brought him 'running' with his 'resignation'. [156] There had been continuous conflict about Chamberlain's emphasis on Air Defence — from a War Office point of view before 1937 and from an Admiralty viewpoint thereafter. Having talked about resigning in early 1938, [157] having twice threatened to resign at Cabinet meetings when the Chamberlain policy seemed likely to collapse and having offered his resignation before Munich, he was refused permission to withdraw it once Munich made Chamberlain impregnable. [158]

By the time Hore-Belisha became an MP in 1923 he had done war service in the Royal Army Service Corps, been President of the Oxford Union and worked as Cecil's assistant in the People's Union for Economy. In the following fourteen years he established a reputation as a flashy, thrusting, but responsible Liberal, whose Radicalism entailed a broadening of the social hierarchy, a regard for administrative efficiency and the effective use of state power. After six years in the National government (including three as a heavily-publicised Minister of Transport), he was suddenly propelled into the highest prominence as the radical reformer of the army.

The introduction of Hart's doctrines and the appointment of Gort as C.I.G.S. both confirmed opinions which Chamber-

lain had long held about the army's rôle in war. [159] Hore-
Belisha was not sent to the War Office in order to democra-
tise its tone, but Chamberlain raised no objection when he
did this as part of a recruitment campaign. After the Anschluss, however, Hore-Belisha began to offer another part of
the Hart doctrine — that since Hitler aimed at dominating
Europe, the French should intervene in Spain. [160] When he
then got involved in Churchill's campaign for a change of
government, Chamberlain began to see through the Radical
energy to the Jewish desire to 'court popularity'. With Hore-
Belisha's over-publicised visit to Mussolini on the way to a
routine engagement in Malta, the period of disenchantment
had begun. [161]

Until Hitler supplied a more attractive issue, Hore-Belisha's
trade mark had been 'modern Radicalism' to replace the su-
perannuated Radicalism of Lloyd George. [162] During the abdication, he had hoped for a new party led by Churchill. [163]
In May 1937 he wanted Churchill in the Cabinet and was
preparing to complain about Runciman's demotion when his
own promotion stopped him. [164] In the summer of 1938 he
quarrelled with Churchill and became the object of personal
attacks about the Court of Enquiry he had proposed for
Churchill's son-in-law, Sandys.

At the end of August his opinion was that Czechoslovakia
should not be defended unless the public demand was 'overwhelming'. [165] He expressed doubts about Plan Z of which
he heard first in Cabinet after the decision had been taken.
On Chamberlain's return he was on the look-out for a 'gust of
public feeling' [166] and wanted the Czechs to express an opinion before Hitler was given a reply. He wrangled with Chamberlain about the extent to which the international guarantee
was likely to be honoured [167] and wrote a letter to establish
that the use of the British army on police duties during a
plebiscite would 'diminish [its] capacity to deal with any
emergency that might arise...in...Egypt and Palestine'. [168]

Departmental difficulties would doubtless have predomi-
nated if Godesberg had not coincided with a marked shift in
public feeling. On September 24 his response (in his diary)
was that 'we are no longer the free agents' in relation to the
Czechs that 'we were before the matter started'. He came to
the conclusion that the Fleet should be mobilised and general

mobilisation considered, adding, in words which look like notes for a resignation speech, that 'we are the trustees of... civilisation which is being abruptly assaulted over ever-widening areas, and it is our bounden duty,...to rearm with vigour, put our industries on a war footing and set up a Ministry of Supply, so that we may never allow this situation to occur again'. [169]

It is probable that Hore-Belisha, while thinking of removing himself from Chamberlain's shadow, was not sure that this was wise. He resented his exclusion from the Anglo-French discussions; [170] on the 25th he was talking about resigning if the Cabinet refused to give the French a 'pledge'. [171] No pledge was given, and he did not resign. But at the Cabinet that day he ridiculed the idea that Chamberlain could 'in-fluence' Hitler and said that the Czechs should be encouraged to refuse his terms. [172] He claimed that the Cabinet, rather than the Cabinet Committee, should meet the French minis-ters and followed this with a request that he and Gort should be present at any conversations they might have with Game-lin. [173] After the Four-Power Agreement, he played down the Cabinet's rôle and claimed — what was wholly untrue — that it 'never had any idea till Neville returned from Berchtes-gaden that there could be any question of asking the Czechs to cede any territory'. [174]

As a Service minister during Munich, Hore-Belisha had felt vulnerable militarily. [175] After Bridgewater he felt vulnerable electorally and tried (unsuccessfully) to get adopted as *Con-servative* candidate for Kingston-upon-Thames. [176] In the fol-lowing months, he developed a public stance as the advocate of the measures necessary to fight a war. At the same time, he was under attack in Whitehall because of defects in the anti-aircraft defences (which may have been why he wanted a Ministry of Supply to relieve him of the burden [177]). Having been widely disliked before this, [178] he was increasingly mis-trusted in the War Office [179] and was the object of a removal operation (conducted by R.S. Hudson [180]). Chamberlain, however, supported him and he survived the Cabinet re-shuffle in the New Year. [181]

At this time Hore-Belisha wanted a large expansion of the army and, probably, conscription, [182] following this, to some extent as an alternative (after Prague) by proposals for doubling the Territorial Army and taking compulsory powers to direct industrial production. [183]   After Albania, he renewed relations with Churchill and came close to resigning when, simultaneously, he was pressing Chamberlain to adopt conscription and Chamberlain was pressing him to provide instant anti-aircraft reaction to air attack. He did not decide to stay in office until Halifax and Simon insisted that Conscription should be adopted. [184]

In these arguments Hore-Belisha was acting, to a certain extent, departmentally as in rasing the question of mobilisation on August 23. [185] He was also preparing for the future in case Chamberlain fell down. [186] He described the draft message to Hitler of August 26 as 'fulsome, obsequious and deferential' [187] and wanted the revised version improved by removing 'any suggestion that we have received with...relief the proposal that Germany should guarantee a...diminished British Empire'. [188] He was unmoved by the Russo-German pact, which he had predicted, [189] and which he interpreted as showing that the Russians had been 'cornered'. [190] He thought the British guarantee to Poland important, whatever was done about Ciano's Four-Power Conference, for 'if an international guarantee [were] given...and [Poland] became dependent upon that for her security...we should...lose our hold on the East and an attack upon us in the West by Germany would be facilitated'. [191]

In saying this to Simon, Hore-Belisha was reflecting the views of Gort, Pownall and Sir James Grigg. A few days later he repeated them to Halifax, adding a blow at the boost Mussolini would be given if Polish-German talks were held in Italy. [192] At the Cabinet on the afternoon of September 2, he opposed any further delay in declaring war which 'might result in breaking the unity of the country'. [193]

That no one resigned of his own volition between February 1938 and the outbreak of war was the result of Halifax's skill in reassuring the dissentients [194] and the difficulty they found in formulating a reason when defence deficiencies were glaring and the real complaint among many of them was that 'this country' could not be 'run' without 'the confidence of the moderate Left'. [195] Elliot's reactions were complicated by his long-standing Zionism (and Hore-Belisha's by his being a Jew). In the cases of Hore-Belisha and de la Warr (as of Bernays outside the Cabinet), there was the added difficulty that they were occupying posts beyond their normal expectation by belonging to the National Liberal or National Labour parties.

For Hore-Belisha, who had few friends on the Eden network, [196] this was restricting. For Bernays (another National Liberal) it may well have been excruciating.

Bernays was the only member of the government who had been a leader-writer on the *News Chronicle*. He had little money [197] and had probably been damaged financially by getting into parliament unexpectedly in 1931. In 1933 he allowed his constituency association to decide whether he should follow Samuel into opposition. [198]

Though Sinclair regarded him as a 'useful link' for the broadened Liberalism of the future, [199] Bernays did his best to recommend himself to Baldwin. When deciding to stand as a 'National' candidate at the 1935 election, however, he refused to become a Simonite because of Simon's foreign policy. [200] When he eventually became one in September 1936, [201] he had already attracted attention for his part in the de la Warr/Nicolson attempt to effect a realignment of 'National' thinking. [202]

At this time he had a low opinion of Chamberlain. [203] This may have risen when Chamberlain made him a junior minister after reading one of his magazine articles. [204] If so, the change did not last. Bernays was in constant touch with Nicolson and agreed, basically, with him. He went with Crookshank to complain about the anti-League tone of the speech Chamberlain made after Eden's resignation. He thought continuously about resigning during Munich (and was cut by Lady Violet Bonham-Carter for failing to do so afterwards). There can be no doubt that he felt that he ought to be resigning and failed to because he lacked a base on which to build a return in the future.

For the National Labour ministers, the problem was acute and each tremor significant. In 1936 Allen left the party because of its failure to defend the League. Before Godesberg, Mrs Dugdale did the same when MacDonald and de la Warr failed to leave the Cabinet.[205] After Munich Nicolson wanted 'a middle party' and 'all-party government designed to organise wealth, industry and manpower' for war against Germany. [206]

They, however, whatever they had said before, [207] were not so certain. Even if they agreed that 'all Left-wing people should fuse' [208] into a foreign-policy based party of the Centre, they needed greater courage, and less intelligence, than they possessed to give themselves up to a future based on a non-existent Liberal party or the dubious friendship of the Labour party. [209]

Chamberlain's opinion of these 'weak-kneed critics' was as low as that of their friends' [210] ; such effect as he allowed them to have was marginal. After the Anschluss, he modified the Italian agreement. After Munich he delayed completion because others might join Duff Cooper if he did not. [211] He was worried by Crookshank, the Under-Secretary for Mines and friend of Macmillan, who had nearly resigned in February 1938, wanted Eden back and had discovered in Baldwin, after he retired, qualities of leadership he had not noticed beforehand.

Crookshank's view of Chamberlain was that he was 'crazy' to go to Germany and had been 'hypnotized' by a 'loony'. When Duff Cooper's resignation was announced, he sent in his. He withdrew it only when Chamberlain promised not to hold an election and, in the Munich debate, made points that Crookshank had asked him to make the day before. [212] In the New Year he was made a Privy Councillor a few weeks after de la Warr had been promoted. Otherwise, the only minister with whom Chamberlain troubled was Oliver Stanley.

Stanley was the second son of that 17th Earl of Derby who, after a military youth, had embodied in the manifest flesh a wealthy, amiable, horse-racing Conservatism which seemed well-fitted to transcend all possible tensions in Liverpool and north-western England. This vast, sly figure had operated in a period of manifest social difficulty when, as associate of Rothermere, Beaverbrook and Birkenhead, and as an ally of Lloyd George, he had created a sybaritic, secular Conservatism which differed markedly from that of his eccentric grandfather.

With Oliver Stanley there was a reversion to that liberal thoughtfulness which so much impressed the intelligentsia of the previous century and a revival of that responsiveness to the 'higher tendencies of contemporary thinking' which was so marked a feature of his great-grandfather's performance. Even when he seemed to be intelligent rather than vigorous, he left an impression of regarding that set of preferences as the best way of relating to mass democracy.

In 1930 he had hoped for co-operation with Mosley. When MacDonald had outlived his usefulness as a Radical, he had wanted Lloyd George. Like Elliot, he thought Chamberlain a liability at the Treasury and that Cunliffe-Lister would be better. Like Cunliffe-Lister and Lloyd George, he mistrusted Chamberlain's interventions in Simon's foreign policy and be-lieved in the paramount importance of taking Hitler at his face value. [213] While lacking Rooseveltian charisma, he shared the yearning of Elliot and Cunliffe-Lister for an ener-getic, smiling Conservatism to replace Chamberlain's mone-tary rigour. [214]

By 1938 Stanley had for long left the impression of being destined for the heights. [215] After his setback at the Ministry of Labour, he had been physically and nervously depressed and had thought of resigning. [216] In the end, he had 'climbed down with admirable grace'. [217] Over the abdication he avoided the Jacobite contamination of Eden, Hoare and Duff Cooper. About the League of Nations Union he registered normal disaffection. [218] His appointment to be President of the Board of Trade at the age of forty-one in May 1937 enabled Chamberlain to put an unquestionably Conservative, low-tariff Lancashire politician into a ministry about which Simonites would be more than usually sensitive once Runci-man had left it. [219]

In office, he was a trial. He played an important part in the argument about the Roosevelt initiative. [220] In the discus-sions which preceded Eden's resignation, he supported Cham-berlain's policy, but announced that resignation 'would have such calamitous results that he must resign too'. [221] After Eden had gone, he made conditions about the Italian agree-ment and, in company with his brother, tried to delay Abys-sinian recognition until Italian troops were out of Spain. [222] Like his brother, too, he needed a rest [223] after an 'evident deterioration' in his health in the spring of 1938, when he was considered for the embassy in Washington in case he could not work hard enough to stay in the Cabinet. [224]

At the end of August Stanley was pointing out that there were deficiencies in Germany as well as Britain. [225] Before Plan Z was announced, 'the need to maintain law and order' was the central feature of the situation. While 'wincing' when 'Russian assistance' was mentioned, [226] he joined Duff Cooper in pressing Halifax to stop *The Times* correspondence about the cession of Czech territory. [227] On September 12 he asked for a Chiefs of Staff statement about the extent to which an immediate war would be more effective than a war in 1939. [228]

In spite of this, he hoped for a way out [229] and 'admired' Chamberlain's decision to fly to Berchtesgaden. Like others, however, he saw a difference between an immediate plebiscite and a plebiscite in five years' time; he was afraid that, whatever happened, 'we' would be accused of 'having betrayed the Czechs or of having encouraged the French to do so'. [230] On September 16 he was 'more dejected than usual' and wanted to know 'what...minimum we could stand upon'. [231]

On Chamberlain's return Stanley refused to be rushed and said flatly that conditions would have to be 'negotiated' if a plebiscite was to be accepted. The Cabinet would have to define these, Hitler to be told what they were and France to be left in no doubt that Britain would support her if he rejected them. [232]

These stipulations were met by the 'Anglo-French proposals' which he more or less welcomed at the Cabinet of September 19. At the same time he added four conditions, two of which [233] he treated as essential. [234] On September 21 he swelled the chorus which said that the public would not accept the proposals if a German occupation was to begin before international supervision had been established. [235]

Thereafter, he was deviant. After Godesberg none of his conditions had been met; they had been refused 'in insolent language' which left him 'under no delusions'. Germany was 'not...prepared for a long war', but if Hitler's terms were accepted, his 'price' would 'rise' and we 'should'...have bartered away many of the strong points in our position'. Britain, he said, ought not to 'act as a Post Office', but should either approve the terms or reject them. [236]

What Stanley wanted was a firm line which left no doubt
that Britain and France would act together. What he found
was a Chamberlain 'plot' to flood the Cabinet with evidence
in favour of 'frighten[ing] the French into ratting'. [237]
Though he helped to establish Cabinet scrutiny of the Anglo-
French conversations, [238] he was far from satisfied with what
was done. Having threatened to resign with Duff Cooper [239]
while Chamberlain was at Godesberg, he would probably
have done so again if Chamberlain had not been overridden at
the Cabinet of the 27th. His view of the final settlement was
that, though 'in many ways...superior to the Godesberg proposals', it had been achieved by methods that were sinister
and objectionable. It was Chamberlain's optimism on his return that made him half-offer to resign in order to educate the
public about the future. [240]

Stanley was not only Derby's son, but was also the son-in-
law of Londonderry who had resumed relations with Chamberlain in 1937 [241] and whose primary belief was that the
extent of German air superiority had been exaggerated. [242]
Stanley also mattered because he had managed to suggest
that there was something as special about his politics in relation to his generation as Halifax had done about his own
generation fifteen years before and, like most dissentients (in
and out of the government), believed in an uncontroversial
Conservatism which he thought that Chamberlain had abandoned. Though Chamberlain thought he never intended to
resign, [243] he spent a good deal of time persuading him to
stay.

In the period of firmness after Munich, he succeeded. In
the winter of 1938 Stanley was an advocate of a Ministry of
Supply. [244] In the New Year he was taking the line that the
Republic would be important if the Spanish war went on
until the German war began. [245] After Prague he wanted a
Russian alliance, and Eden and Churchill in the government. [246] After Albania he was scathing about the agreement
with Italy. [247] In June he was asking for a new Cabinet in
order to make Hitler understand that Britain would 'fulfil
[her] obligations to Poland'. [248]

In asking why he acted as he did, one should impute anxiety rather than ambition. While attaching importance to

Baldwinian centrality, he discouraged the impression that he
wished to 'form a group' of those who shared his point of
view. [249] It is likely that he was thought of, just marginally,
as a successor [250] because his reactions were what they were.
With some of the more senior ministers, the connections may
be reversed.

(ii)

When Chamberlain succeeded Baldwin, it was obvious that
his own successor would have to be found soon. Not as soon
as, in the end, it turned out, and not in the quarter from
which he came. But with a Prime Minister of sixty-eight anything was possible. Simon was often excluded because he was
a Liberal. So, for different reasons, was Churchill. Those
whose business it was asked themselves whether it should be
Hoare, Inskip, Halifax or Eden.

Eden's succession was disputed; his period ended when
Halifax overtook him in the year which followed his resignation. In 1936 Inskip had had a following which was greatly
reduced by his years as Minister for the Co-ordination of
Defence.

Inskip's father was a prosperous Bristol solicitor; as a
young man Inskip was a muscular Christian with a vocation
to become a lay missionary. After Clifton and Cambridge in
the nineties, he had practised at the Bar before becoming a
Unionist candidate in 1906. By the time he became an MP in
1918, he had been in Naval Intelligence during the war. In
1922 he voted with Austen Chamberlain at the Carlton Club
meeting. Thereafter, at the age of forty-six, he became a
regular part of the Baldwin régime.

In the next fourteen years, as Solicitor- and Attorney-
General, he came to embody decent parliamentary reassurance and the Evangelical section of the Church of England.
After the Prayer-Book debates, he could probably have been
Speaker if he had chosen to. During the electoral difficulties
of 1934, he raised flags for a 'National' party against 'Socialism'. In 1935 he was publicly explicit against Lloyd George
and unusually explicit in favour of the Peace Ballot. As
Chamberlain and Hoare gave offence in differing directions,

he emerged as a possible successor if Baldwin had to retire. [251]

What was attributed to Inskip was more physical than intellectual — an ability to look right both in Parliament and
outside. His 'porky truculence' stood 'four square'. [252] He
'batt[ed] all around the wicket' and represented 'something'
which 'the public' would 'understand'. [253] In real-power
terms his period as Minister for the Co-ordination of Defence
was his first test.

In this he was unfortunate. Though he presided at the CID
and picked up the pieces when Swinton quarrelled with Nuffield, his function was mediatory rather than commanding, as
he was at pains to make clear, [254] and would have been hampered in the attempt to be anything else by the conflicts in
which he was enveloped between the Service ministers and
the Treasury. If, as seems certain, the post was established in
order to keep Hankey under control, both Chamberlain's and
Simon's zeal for economy made this unnecessary. [255]

In 1938 Inskip supported Chamberlain's policy in general
and his Italian and German policies in particular. He was
much moved by Britain's weakness, [256] felt no obligation to
encourage Czech resistance [257] and would only do so if
forced to in order to 'save' France [258] or 'check' Hitler. [259]
He had thought Eden wrong in February — because war with
Italy was an imminent possibility [260] — but wanted a *quid
pro quo* from Mussolini before Abyssinian recognition was
initiated at Geneva. [261]

Inskip was unenthusiastic about Plan Z. [262] He sensed
'blackmail' when the Berchtesgaden meeting was described [263] and refused to be rushed after Godesberg. [264] He
did not oppose Chamberlain, even at the meeting of September 27, when war had to be avoided because 'we were in no
condition to fight'. [265] But he did not trust Hitler, [266] had
been under pressure as a churchman to speak out [267] and
would not urge the Czechs to capitulate. There was no question of resignation, but the end of September found him in a
state of Halifax-like doubt.

It is difficult to know whether it was doubt which made
Chamberlain remove him from the Defence post the following January or whether doubt was a consequence of anger at

being made a scapegoat. Inskip certainly thought he was being blamed for defence deficiencies. He resented being moved (even if he had offered to be) and had little need to be reminded that his prospects had been damaged. [268] He still had supporters, [269] but it was tact not accuracy which made Chamberlain say, when offering the Dominions Office, that he would not offer the Lord Chancellorship because that would prevent him being Prime Minister later. [270] Inskip still had supporters when, somewhat resentfully, he became Lord Chancellor in order to enable Eden to return to the Cabinet in September 1939. [271]

Inskip's period as a possible Prime Minister had begun while Hoare was struggling with the India bill. Hoare's expectations rose when he left the India Office and even more (as he thought) when he went to the Home Office in 1937. [272] But they did not really recover from his tenure of the Foreign Office.

Hoare was an important member of the government, but he and Chamberlain were not particularly close. By 1938 Hoare had no more contact than a number of other ministers and felt no obligation to tailor his thinking to Chamberlain's.

Hoare disliked Ormsby-Gore, Stanley and Elliot. [273] He was jealous of Eden who was 'vain' and 'unstable', played to 'left wingers, pressmen and private secretaries' and presided over a Foreign Office which was 'biased against Germany... Italy and Japan'. [274] About Spain and rearmament he was a target for Labour attack and an object of admiration among the Chiefs of Staff. [275]

Otherwise, he responded to whatever feelings were held around him, blowing on Inskip as a strategist, looking for a 'moral basis' in international relations and wondering whether 'the League' could be brought in so as to 'ease things for the opposition'. [276] Once the India bill was passed, he maintained good relations with Churchill. After threatening to join the defence critics if not given the Defence post in order to resist them, [277] he used the Admiralty to acquire a flattering reputation with them.

After the Anschluss, Hoare wanted to avoid action which might make it seem that 'we were on [Germany's] side' in the Sudetenland. [278] From before Munich he was aiming to succeed Chamberlain.[279] Afterwards he was worried about his financial prospects in case the next election was lost.[280]

As a member of the Cabinet Committee Hoare gave general support to Chamberlain's policy. But he emphasised the help to be expected from the Left if a reasonable welcome was given to Russia.[281] Between Berchtesgaden and Godesberg he was firm.[282] During the Godesberg meetings he was firmer. Afterwards he was 'shocked' by the form of Hitler's proposals and would not press the Czechs to accept them. He welcomed the 'guarantee' as a way of easing acceptance, but saw little hope of avoiding war and laid great store by military co-operation with France and Russia.[283]

Hoare played no part in the argument about the Wilson proposals on the 27th. At this time he was 'profoundly gloomy'. After the Munich invitation he was 'with' Chamberlain 'to the end', and defended the settlement once it had been made.[284] But he was tired and depressed and believed that a 'peace policy' could not survive without an election.[285] He wanted Runciman, Chatfield and Geoffrey Lloyd in the Cabinet and was willing to have Eden if he would come. He did not want Churchill or the Labour leaders, since their policies were not those of Chamberlain whose position would become precarious enough without them.[286]

In the winter of 1938 he was rattled by the state of the air defences and managed to pass Anderson the poisoned chalice containing Air Raid Precautions. Until Halifax supported Hore-Belisha, he took the Simon line about air, as opposed to land, rearmament.[287] After the Bridgewater by-election, on the other hand, he had been 'on the prowl, anxious to meet Eden', interested in the sort of policy Cabinet for which Amery had been asking and leaving the impression that Chamberlain was an 'autocrat in the Cabinet'. When a Franco victory seemed imminent, he saw no reason to object if the French insisted on opening the Spanish frontier by themselves.[288]

When the climate changed in February 1939 he was the first to announce the coming era of peace.[289] When Prague showed that the dawn was a false one, he wanted consultation with the Labour and Liberal leaders so as to avoid a government on the lines which Eden was suggesting.[290] In the same spirit, and afraid that the 'patriotic reaction' might

'go too far', he pressed Chamberlain to 'repudiate...encircle-
ment' as likely to 'force the mad dog to bite...with the whole
German people...behind him'. [291]

Hoare's power-base was the Conservative party in the
House of Commons. He was admired in the Admiralty. Elsewhere he seemed a short-tempered trimmer. [292] His attempts
to trim in 1939 produced an 'open mind' about having
Churchill and Sinclair in the Cabinet, [293] a belief that Germany would only be deterred by 'fear' [294] and an impression
(which he conveyed to the Labour leaders [295]) that 'serious
consequences...would follow a breakdown of negotiations'
with Russia. When Chamberlain began listing his War Cabinet
at the end of August, Hoare's was a name he was hoping to
avoid. [296]

Basically Hoare hoped that Hitler would allow the Polish
question to be settled. [297] But when even so multi-purpose a
politician gave Chamberlain flat contradictions [298] and explained that he had 'exhausted...all influence' with him, [299]
Chamberlain had no reason to feel the confidence he had felt
in the past.

(iii)

The Cabinet, then, had never been insulated from the opinions by which it was surrounded. By the late summer of
1939, it was almost an external body. [300] Some of its members had become unfriendly to Chamberlain; the interest of
others lay in 'party' or 'national' unity. At least half a dozen
felt guilty about their failure to resign. Others probably felt
that any decision would be a relief. [301] After Chamberlain's
failure to announce an ultimatum on September 2, there was
not much sympathy.

Before the invasion of Poland, Chamberlain believed that
Hitler had isolated himself internationally, damaged his position internally and miscalculated grievously. After invasion
had been put off once (on August 25), he expected him to
put it off again when the 'decisive' [302] declaration of August 27 established that Britain would declare war if he went
ahead.

Since he believed that this would prevent war happening,

Chamberlain was hoping for negotiations about Poland and eventual discussions about Anglo-German relations. He was not sure of this; he did not feel that he was 'through the jungle'.[303] But he was optimistic. Until the invasion showed that he was wrong, he continued to believe that, in the end, Hitler would *have* to talk.

With the invasion of Poland, he saw that the price had to be paid for the firmness which had been effective in the past. On the morning of September 1, it was only a question of time before the treaty would be honoured. There seems to have been no other thought in his mind until it came to be known in the course of the afternoon that the French government could not mobilise and evacuate for forty-eight hours.

At this point he[304] wanted to put off the decision about an ultimatum in order to synchronise declarations when the decision was made. On the morning of September 2 it was expected that it would be made shortly. That afternoon, after refusing to delay further, the Cabinet insisted on the ultimatum being sent 'after consultation with the French government'.[305] It was the difficulty he had with the French after the Cabinet which made him omit mention of the time-table in speaking to the House of Commons at a quarter to eight that evening.[306]

Chamberlain (and Halifax) may have been hampered by French unwillingness. They may have been trying to persuade the world that they were willing to negotiate (when they were not).[307] Or they may have been hoping for a conference. Whatever they were trying to do, and the last is the least likely, they gave hostages to Churchill, the Edenites and the Labour party.

To the Eden group the Russo-German pact seemed to confirm all that they had said that they expected. Events had shown — as only events could — that Chamberlain was wrong.

Yet, for them, the six weeks before had been a period of anxious uncertainty. Not all of them had liked the newspaper campaign in favour of Churchill. When it died down at the end of July, they could only wait. They waited with apprehension, fearing, on the one hand, that Hitler might do nothing about Danzig and anticipating, on the other, a second

Munich from which 'the Great Appeaser' would 'stigmatize' them as 'war monsters' and drive them out at a general election. [308]

These fears may, or may not, have been reasonable. [309] Whatever the objective situation, they had an effect. The group as a whole behaved cautiously. It behaved with special caution on the adjournment of Parliament. [310] With the signature of the Russo-German pact, expectations rose, even when uncertainty was increased by the prospect of war making Eden and Amery anxious to play a part in running it. [311]

The group met a number of times between July 18 and August 1; it did not meet again until Parliament was recalled on the 24th. At its meeting then, it discussed the handling of Italy. Thereafter its members were subdued. They seem not to have been sure that a crisis was imminent.

When they met on the evening of September 1, they were puzzled by the British warning but reassured by the prospect of Churchill and Eden joining the government. [312] The general attitude was probably that of Duff Cooper, who was so much relieved when he heard that Poland had been invaded that 'his heart felt lighter than it had for a year'. [313] When the group met at five o'clock next day, its information was conflicting. [314] It was not until Chamberlain failed to announce an ultimatum in his statement three hours later that they understood how far he was from their assumptions. [315]

The Edenites were astonished at the extent to which Chamberlain lost the sympathy of the House of Commons during this speech. Some of them urged Eden to speak. Duff Cooper, realising that their own feelings were shared by some of Chamberlain's supporters, persuaded the Chairman of the Foreign Affairs Committee, who was sitting next to him, to speak instead. [316] When Greenwood got up to speak for the Labour party, Amery called out that he should 'speak for England'. Edenites were not the only Conservatives who, fortified by drink, cheered Greenwood when he pressed Chamberlain to go to war. [317]

As it came to seem likely that Hitler would invade Poland, the Labour leaders had asked themselves three questions. Would the government do its duty? Would a united Labour party press it to do so? If war came, should the Labour party enter the government?

About the last question, their position was unequivocal. There was no objection to trade unionists doing administrative work with a low political content. But they had no intention of repeating the mistake Henderson had made in 1915. Since they had already decided not to join a Chamberlain government, they decided that members of the Labour movement — and especially trade union leaders — should be prevented from joining individually. These views were affirmed, sometimes strongly, on August 24 and 25. [318]

So far as policy was concerned, there was little desire, except from the ILP, to hold the government back if Hitler attacked Poland. In Attlee's absence (having an operation), Greenwood was in continuous touch with Chamberlain and the Foreign Office. Such declarations as were made were designed to suggest motion towards evacuation, mobilisation and war. [319]

These declarations registered the realisation that there was a grave situation to which Labour could make a contribution. [320] They also established a position which 'would be on the record for the future'. In general it is safe to say that, behind the dangers and opportunities they anticipated for themselves, the Labour leaders played a 'responsible' rôle in developing the feeling that 'we and the French will certainly be attacked by an even stronger Germany with even fewer allies if we give way now'. [321]

It was in this spirit that Greenwood was acting when he made his appeal to Chamberlain in the House of Commons on September 2. Afterwards he went to Chamberlain's room to explain what he had seen on the benches opposite. This had convinced him that 'unless you present an ultimatum to Germany before 11 o'clock tomorrow morning, neither you nor I nor anyone else will be able to hold the House of Commons'. [322]

It is possible that Greenwood could have destroyed Chamberlain if he had turned his speech in one direction rather than another. [323] In Churchill's flat later that night, Churchill was being told that Chamberlain had 'lost the Conservative party for ever, and it is in your power to go to the House of Commons tomorrow and break him and take his place'. [324]

Like the other Conservative dissentients, Churchill had been
muted and 'quiescent' in the summer of 1939. He had 'done
his best' and 'given his warnings' and awaited the inevitable
'crunch'. The newspaper campaign had petered out. He had
wanted a demonstration on the adjournment of Parliament
but Eden had squashed it. [325] He was afraid that, with Parliament away, Chamberlain would do what he had done the
year before. He did not know whether Hitler would give way
if Chamberlain stood firm, but he thought it likely that Hitler
despised him so much that Chamberlain could not impress
him if he tried to. [326] At the end of July he was saying that
'Hitler was going to make war' and that 'he might even be
Prime Minister'. [327] At the end of August (through Lloyd) he
was in daily contact with the Labour party. [328] When war
became imminent, he prepared to mend his fences.

'I think you are quite right' he wrote to Chamberlain in a letter he did
not send on August 30 'to let things drag on if they will, more especially
because one feels a certain hesitation on the other side as the act approaches. But would it not be helpful to call up the Reserves and mobilise the T.A.? ...The effect would surely add to the force of your exer-
tions to preserve peace...I do not myself see how Hitler can escape from
the pen in which he has put himself, but a victory without bloodshed
would be the best, and this would help not hinder it. [329]

When asked to join the government on the afternoon of
September 1, Churchill expected an early ultimatum to lead
to war and the creation of a War Cabinet. [330] Then, he had
no doubts. On the morning of the 2nd he heard from Paris
the rumours which others had about Bonnet. It also became
clear that Labour had refused to co-operate with Chamberlain and that Sinclair had not been asked to. Having no wish
to join the government in isolation, he wrote Chamberlain a
letter in which he stated that Eden and a Liberal element
were 'important' and that there should be a 'joint Declaration
of War at latest when Parliament meets this afternoon'. [331]
Though no declaration had been made by two-thirty, Churchill did nothing. When Chamberlain announced that evening
that no declaration was in sight, he was inhibited from speaking by the fact that he had agreed to take office.

In his *Second World War* Churchill says that he was visited
that evening by politicians from all parties. When Duff Cooper went to his flat at ten-thirty, he found Eden, Boothby,

Bracken and Sandys 'in a state of bewildered rage', trying to decide whether to save or destroy Chamberlain next morning. [332] At some point in the discussion which went on 'far into the night', Churchill drafted a letter to establish that the basis on which he had accepted office had shifted, that he must know by the time Parliament met at noon next day what Chamberlain intended (especially about Sinclair) and that no announcement should be made about the composition of the Cabinet until he and Chamberlain had had a talk. [333] Having thus freed himself, he sent the letter off, even after hearing by telephone that an ultimatum would be sent. [334]

The Cabinet may not have known that Churchill was hoping to do what he had failed to do in May 1938. But they had no doubt that the government was in danger. When Elliot, Stanley, de la Warr and eight others [335] talked together after Chamberlain's speech, they refused to be cheated as they had been by Munich. They decided that there would have to be a further meeting of the Cabinet. This decision was made in Simon's room in the House of Commons. It was Simon who spoke when they went to see Chamberlain.

Simon was the son of a self-educated Congregationalist minister. He had been President of the Oxford Union, a Fellow of All Souls and a successful barrister before becoming Solicitor-General in 1910. In Asquith's government he was a Little Englander. He nearly resigned in August 1914 and did so over Conscription eighteen months later. After the war, he was a conventional supporter of the League of Nations. His period as Foreign Secretary dented this aspect of his public preferences; in July 1935 he had no faith in the prospect of League action to defend Abyssinia. [336] He had wanted to stay at the Foreign Office, however, [337] was jealous of Hoare [338] and was a searing critic of the Hoare-Laval pact. He hinted at resignation when the condition of Liberal opinion became unmistakable [339] and had the same difficulty as the rest of the Cabinet in knowing what to say when the Italian victory showed that Collective Security was dead.

Simon wanted to make Germany part of the European system. But he did not believe in Eden's plans for appeasement — perhaps because Eden was proposing them. [340] When the Franco-Russian alliance and the Rhineland changed the situation, he was afraid of the French being encouraged to feel 'that they have got us so tied that they can safely wait for the breakdown of discussions with Germany'. [341] He reported, and shared, a public revulsion against Continental entanglements which the 'air factor' had made unacceptable. He believed that 'the British people [did] not really contemplate sending their sons to fight on the Continent' and 'if London was being...bombed' '[would]...not...be despatching regiments of soldiers to the Low Countries'. [342]

During the search for *détente* in late 1936, he said that some sort of colonial deal was inevitable. But he saw no point in trying to make one so long as Hitler kept 'asking for concessions' while giving 'nothing in return'. [343] On succeeding Chamberlain at the Treasury, his foreign-policy assumptions were strengthened by a departmental and backbench concern with the level of public spending and a desire to get Hitler to open up the German economy. But he had few illusions, and knew that economic appeasement was impossible unless Germany became a 'co-operating partner'. [344]

In discussions about defence expenditure after the Anschluss, he advocated restraint. Both then and in the following eighteen months, he was at the centre of disputes with almost all the Foreign Office and Service ministers and departments. [345]

Simon had for long opposed converting Locarno into an alliance. He believed that a forward policy in the Far East could not be combined with a crisis in Europe and that it was impossible to be an air, naval and industrial arsenal under bombardment at the same time as 'fight[ing] with an unlimited army on the Continent'. [346] He was an articulate supporter of the view that 'unorthodox measures', like 'excessive borrowing' and 'currency...inflation', though necessary if war began, should not be adopted in advance [347] and that Britain's 'military efforts' should not 'so far impair [her] economic resources as to render [her] powerless, through incapacity to command vital imports, to bring a long war, or indeed, any war to a successful conclusion'. [348]

Simon assumed that the public was not interested in central Europe. But he did not apply the assumption rigidly. He supported the policy of March 24 1938, while being clear that it was a bluff which depended on Hitler not realising that Britain could not fight. [349] At the same time he wanted Benes to do something for Henlein, while avoiding a British commitment to whatever he might do. [350] Having seen, in the Runciman mission, a slide towards commitment, he made his Lanark speech at least partly in order to halt it. [351] He told the Cabinet on August 30 that 'any idea of going to war' would produce 'a strong body of opinion which would ask whether the Czechs had done all they could to meet the legitimate aims of the Sudeten Germans'. [352]

Simon 'could not understand' how 'a good liberal...could have...sympathy for Czechoslovakia', which in any case could not be saved if war began. [353] He gave warm support to Chamberlain's 'brilliant proposal' of flying to Germany. [354] After supporting the Berchtesgaden terms, [355] he told the Cabinet that the Anglo-French meetings had removed 'any lingering fear he might have had that the attitude of this country might have...prevented the French government from fulfilling their obligations'. [356]

Simon, then, provided valuable help in presenting Chamberlain's policy. It was at his suggestion that the Cabinet turned up to see him off to Munich. He took the lead in congratulating him on his return. Those who disliked him thought that his flattery increased Chamberlain's self-satisfaction. [357]

Nevertheless, his position was double-edged. Whatever its purpose, the Lanark warning was his. After Berchtesgaden, he was unwelcoming about further concessions. He pressed the French ministers with particular brutality on September 18 about what they would do in the event of war. His proposal — for a Sudeten plebiscite in five years' time — was the cause round which the critics rallied when Chamberlain proposed a plebiscite at once. During the Godesberg conference, he was belligerently critical after warning Chamberlain (before he went) of the danger of an 'accusation of unconditional surrender in Parliament or elsewhere...if it is not possible to point to terms having been agreed which distinguished the working-out of the present arrangement from the methods or features of a settlement imposed by a victorious army...'. [358]

When Chamberlain returned, Simon's belligerence receded. The Godesberg memorandum was a 'shocking document'.

But the Czechs could not be allowed the 'final word' about whether Britain should go to war and he would 'not say that [they] would be supported if the terms were rejected'. [359] He agreed that Wilson should go to Berlin [360] and supported Halifax only because of the 'surrender' involved in the proposal Chamberlain made on his return. [361]

Though he willed the decision to go to war, Simon knew how dangerous war was, and was relieved by the Four-Power Agreement. [362] The Agreement, however, did not make him optimistic. He was pessimistic about Anglo-German relations and saw a long haul ahead if public opinion was to face up to rearmament. [363] Despite a compelling speech in the debate of October 5, [364] his doubts persisted throughout the period when he was the only minister on whom Chamberlain could rely for an effective defence in the House of Commons. [365]

In the winter of 1938 Simon felt public opinion drifting away [366] and wanted it brought back. [367] After Albania, he supported Conscription when Hore-Belisha seemed likely to make it a ground for resignation. [368]

In the last year of Baldwin's Prime Ministership, Simon had been technically impressive about the abdication. [369] But he had been anxious about the Liberal rôle in a Chamberlain government and may well have thought of withdrawing. Withdrawal had then been made unnecessary by the generous nature of Chamberlain's reshuffle. [370]

It is difficult to know whether Simon expected war to affect him personally. His claim to the Exchequer had depended on his position as National Liberal leader. His importance would be diminished if a National Liberal resigned. He may not have minded losing Runciman, with whom his relations were bad; [371] the loss of Hore-Belisha would be serious. He wanted to lead a party of 'energy, enterprise and progress' (as well as of 'opposition to Socialism') and knew that Mabane, Bernays and Hore-Belisha had been thinking of foreign-policy disagreement as leading into something more credibly 'democratic'. [372] Though he had kept the party together, he was vulnerable, and had been worried, from Eden's resignation onwards, by the prospect of these feelings being made effective.

As Chancellor, Simon assumed that the sooner a war level of expenditure began, the more difficult victory would be-

come. The restraints he persisted with after Munich [373] implied neither faith in Hitler nor the belief that war would be
avoided. They embodied a departmental husbanding of economic power and a departmental conviction that the pound
must face the deutschmark (and the dollar) in the face.

Simon probably did not expect to become Prime Minister
if Chamberlain was removed. [374] It is much more likely that
he was responding to Hore-Belisha. Whatever he was hoping,
he was acting consistently when he went to Chamberlain's
room in the House of Commons on the evening of Saturday,
September 2 as leader of those who wanted an immediate
declaration of war.

When the ministers arrived, Chamberlain was talking to
Wood; so Simon reminded both of them of the decision that
the ultimatum should expire at midnight. Chamberlain replied at once that he wanted to 'retrieve the impression he
had made in the House' and would get the French to accept
an ultimatum expiring at noon next day. [375] He then returned to Downing Street where, in a disturbed state, he
telephoned Halifax and asked him to come back from his
home to have dinner. Cadogan, Wilson and the French Ambassador were also sent for. After a great deal of telephoning
to Paris, including a direct call to Daladier, a Cabinet meeting
was called for eleven-thirty. [376]

When Chamberlain left them at half-past eight, the ministers had gone back to Simon's room and sent a letter, repeating the points that they were making. [377] After dinner they
met again, and sent Simon and Anderson to find out what
was happening. At about eleven, Anderson came back to tell
them that the French were being worked on. At eleven-
twenty they were called to a meeting of the Cabinet. [378]

At the second Cabinet of the day, Chamberlain explained
that the French wanted their armies in position before war
began because their air force could not defend their lines of
communication. He reported a French proposal for a joint
nine-hour ultimatum to expire at noon next day. But, he
added, Daladier had been left in no doubt that this would not
satisfy the House of Commons and that Britain might have to
declare war by herself.

The subsequent discussion was designed to reconcile the

military requirement (for minimum delay between the ultimatum and the outbreak of war), the diplomatic requirement
(for minimum delay between the British and French declarations) and the political need (expressed forcibly by Mac-
Donald and Stanley) to announce something straightaway so
that the Sunday newspapers might remove the impression
that had been created in the House of Commons. In the
course of discussion, the military requirement was allowed to
override the political desire to announce that Henderson
would be seeing Ribbentrop next morning. In view of the
need to satisfy Parliament at noon next day, the expiry-time
was brought forward to eleven o'clock. When the ultimatum
expired, Chamberlain spoke not to Parliament but through
the BBC. [379]

It is easy to be solemn about this decision. It was the
culmination of the interlude of East European involvement
to which Chamberlain had become committed in 1938. It
marked the end of the policy of *détente* and was a prelude to
the end of the British Empire. Yet it is doubtful whether
Chamberlain, or his critics, knew what they were doing. The
critics who, doubtless, were 'democrats', were responding to
the sort of impulse which Imperialists used to say would kill
the Empire, though many of them thought that they were
honouring it. As for Chamberlain, he saw no need to *fight* a
war, however definitive the declaration.

PART IV

THE POLITICS OF EASY VICTORY

12

CHAMBERLAIN AND THE WAR

'The way to win the war is to convince the Germans that they cannot win'.
Chamberlain to Ida, September 23 1939

'As you know I have always been more afraid of a peace offer than of an air raid'.
Chamberlain to Ida, October 8 1939

'I stick to the view I have always held that Hitler missed the bus in September 1938. He could have dealt France and ourselves a terrible, perhaps a mortal, blow then. The opportunity will not recur'.
Chamberlain to Hilda, December 30 1939

When Chamberlain agreed that war should be declared, he intended to meet any threat Hitler might offer in the air and to take any opportunities that might arise to sink such parts of the German navy as offered themselves to attack. There was no expectation of military victory[1] and no real belief that the state of war need be turned into a war of steel and blood. Fortified by the neutrality of Italy and Japan and unimpressed by the Russo-German alliance, he believed that Hitler's bluff had been called. The French defences presented a deterrent in the West.[2] Anglo-French effort could be directed at producing a collapse of the German home front as the German people came to understand that Hitler could not win.

Nor was this passive conception an aberration. The guarantee to Poland, so far from implying a will to fight, had been intended to make fighting unnecessary. Hitler had not been deterred, but he had had to ally himself with the Soviet Union. He had lost sympathy and support in Italy and Japan. He showed every sign of losing it in Germany, where his difficulties invited a 'war of nerves' to separate him from the forces which had allowed him to come to power in the first place.[3]

Chamberlain conceived himself as fighting a war of feelings rather than force in which his chief assets were past blamelessness, the German fear of unsuccessful war and the hatred of Russia which he supposed to exist in Germany, Italy and Japan. Reversing his rejection of ideological diplomacy, he aimed to show that Britain and France stood for virtue and that the Russo-German alliance was a form of vice.[4]

In this sense the war was an extension of the battle that had been fought in the previous two years with the difference now that he believed himself to be on top. Politically 'the accursed madman'[5] was isolated; 'morally' he had been 'defeated'.[6] He did not have the resources for a long war; the risks would prevent him trying to win a short one. He had, in fact, been cornered, and if the German people did not know this, it would be Britain's business to tell them.

Chamberlain knew that full-scale war would be financially damaging; to that extent his strategy rationalised a disagreeable necessity. In addition, he had moments of doubt. Through all of them he felt necessity coinciding with inclination as the advantage he had gained with the Russo-German pact began to tell. Once it had been announced that the Empire was being mobilised for a three-year war, Hitler would need knock-out victories. Since none would be available in the West, he would look for them in Rumania where the Russians would be as vigilant as they had been in the Baltic.[7] Even before they were settled on his flank, Chamberlain believed that victories would not be forthcoming. After the occupation of eastern Poland,[8] the Russians barred the way.

The belief that Hitler was blocked in the East did not convince Chamberlain that he would attack in the West. Poland had shown that a blitzkrieg was possible, but the German army had fought badly.[9] A direct assault on the Maginot line or a sea-borne invasion of Britain would fail.[10] A flanking attack through the Low Countries (or Switzerland) would be a gamble. Whether successful or not, it would be 'a flagrant...breach of neutrality' which would damage Hitler in the eyes of the world.[11]

Within the framework of a naval blockade of Germany and a German blockade of France and Britain, the war would, therefore, be mainly a matter of giving the air force real striking power, arming possible allies — including Turkey — and preparing to retaliate against an invasion of the Low Countries.[12]

Chamberlain believed that Hitler, too, was fighting a political war and wanted a political way out of his difficulty. [13] Time was not on his side, and it was important to avoid action which would put it there. [14] It was especially important to establish that he had let Germany down by getting 'involved in a world war' after claiming that there would be 'no war because no one dared to go to war' against him. [15] If this was done, Chamberlain said, 'we shall have won...by the spring'. [16] It was in order to let Germans know that the Nazi leaders were piling up fortunes in foreign banks that he preferred leaflets to bombs. [17]

Having formed an estimate, he stuck to it. He was as clear when Intelligence reports predicted an attack after the rejection of Hitler's peace overtures in October as he had been when most of the Cabinet expected one in September. [18] When nothing had happened by the time the November rains made it unlikely that anything would happen before the spring, he knew that he knew more about the politics of war than Gamelin and Ironside.

Chamberlain's governing belief was that Hitler's freedom of manoeuvre had been restricted. He could no longer divert Germans with achievements abroad in order to make up for economic difficulty at home. [19] In a war-time winter, difficulty would be acute. The petrol difficulty would be acutest of all, and occupation of the Rumanian oilfields — if the Russians allowed it — would alienate Italy and Yugoslavia. [20] Since spectacular action in the West would entail a prolonged campaign, 'such frightful losses as to endanger the whole Nazi system' [21] and the 'Bolshevization of Germany', [22] the only thing he could do, short of a 'last...gambler's throw', [23] would be to trick Britain and France into making peace.

Peace, on Hitler's terms, however, was unacceptable. The war had begun because he had used 'force'. It was being fought (as the first war had been) in order to show that states must observe their 'obligations'. [24] It would not be ended until Germany had 'got rid of the gangsters' and was ready to 'co-operate' with 'other civilised peoples'. [25]

Chamberlain's aim, therefore, was 'the elimination of Hitler' and the 'liberation of Europe'. [26] From an early stage, his chief fear was that, after the defeat of the Poles, there would be 'a skilfully timed, carefully planned attack on our home front' in the form of a peace offensive, [27] with support from Roosevelt, the Pope [28] and the Dutch and Belgian monarchs, [29] whose offer to mediate (in order to escape invasion) was picked up by the peace movement in England.

The peace movement was in three parts. From various positions on the Left, it was the work of the Independent Labour party, Lords Arnold, Ponsonby and Noel-Buxton, Lansbury, Stokes and the Peace Pledge Union. On the Right it was the Work of three Conservative MPs (Wilson, Culverwell and Southby), three Conservative peers (Buccleuch, Brocket and Westminster) [30] and (quite separately) Mosley.

The ILP was pacifist about Capitalist wars; the PPU was pacifist in general. Mosley combined anti-semitism with the need for an Anglo-German settlement. The Brocket/Westminster groups and Wilson and his friends were anti-Communist and pro-Nazi. They had not expected war; whether fairly or not, they had been rebuked by Halifax for telling Hitler that it would not happen. When it happened they blamed it on the press, the Opposition and the dissentient Conservatives; for them peace was the only way of destroying 'the seeds of revolution' which Russia was 'anxious to scatter'. [31]

Between the three there was little commerce, and none was very effective. The PPU had some minor effect on the public. Westminster was in touch with Ball, Hankey and Churchill (by whom, as an old friend, he was reminded of MacDonald's experience in 1914). Brocket (an ex-Conservative MP) and Buccleuch (a Household officer) were in touch with Halifax and Chamberlain, though not highly regarded by either. In general, they could all be ignored so long as serious politicians believed that the war could be won.

In fact, in the winter of 1939, no important politician wanted to make peace, apart from Butler, who was too junior, [32] Beaverbrook, who did not matter, [33] and Lloyd, George who was 'a bundle of selfishness and malice'. [34] Nor did Chamberlain feel serious doubts about the public's willingness to face up to war without the drama and death of 1914 to involve them intimately. [35]

In refusing to make peace, [36] Chamberlain aimed to compel Germans who did not want to be defeated to end the war themselves. This was one reason for the cool reception the

Cabinet was persuaded to give to Hitler's peace speech of October 6. It was the chief reason for refusing to define war aims which would have included French statements so extreme as to rally Germans behind him.[37] It was why an interest was developed in alternative German leaders.

The belief that alternatives were available came from sources of varying reliability.[38] Some were distinctly unreliable. But Dahlerus was in close touch with Goering and paid two visits to England in the first three months of the war, conveying offers to guarantee the Low Countries in return for a free hand in central and eastern Europe.[39] Until early November a British Intelligence unit in Holland was in touch with agents of the German army (whether they were double-agents or not). On two separate occasions (on Beck's behalf) von Papen suggested a negotiated settlement, involving the replacement of Hitler and the freeing of Poland and Czechoslovakia.[40] In the new year Thyssen made one approach and Goerdeler another; the Pope, much against his will, conveyed a request from an unnamed general (in fact, Beck) to know on what terms Britain would negotiate if a *coup* or civil war was precipitated by army action in Germany.[41]

Chamberlain had doubts about the genuineness of some of these approaches[42] but was impressed, whether they were genuine or not. It was 'too early' yet to hope that Hitler would be removed. Nor would a settlement be possible until he had been. But these contacts, and the attempt to assassinate him in Munich on November 8, lent weight to the belief that the Germans would soon understand that 'they can't win, and that it isn't worthwhile to go on getting thinner and poorer when they might have instant relief'.[43]

How Hitler was to be pushed was not obvious. The Cabinet, when told about the Intelligence unit, was more cautious than Chamberlain whose major phase of expectation ended when it was dragged, or lured, over the Dutch frontier and shot the day after the assassination attempt failed.[44]

Though the evidence was fragmentary, the idea of a high-level German revolution carried much weight in the higher reaches of the government. Not only Chamberlain, but Halifax, Hankey, Chatfield and Churchill accepted the Foreign Office and Intelligence view that Hitler's 'days' would be 'numbered' unless he repaired the damage which Ribbentrop had done to German influence in northern, eastern and south-eastern Europe. [45]

For a time in November, contact was lost. [46] After a while it was resumed, with results that were not entirely reassuring. Despite 'intense depression' in Germany and the promise of a *coup d'état,* no *coup* was in sight. [47] Yet Chamberlain continued to talk about the Axis 'breaking', Hitler 'getting madder' and the war being over by Christmas 1940. [48] Right up to the invasion of the Low Countries, he repeated that an attack in the West would be so difficult as to be impossible. 'The accumulation of evidence that an attack is imminent is formidable', he wrote on April 13, 'and yet I cannot convince myself that it *is* coming.' [49] 'I am', he wrote a week later, 'firmly convinced' that Hitler's 'basic objectives' are 'iron ore and oil', not an attack on the western front. [50] Even at the beginning of May, when doubting whether 'things' could be 'h[e]ld quiet for the rest of the year', his reason was that Hitler could not 'face a second winter' and might 'exhaust himself in the attack' in order to win before the winter began. [51]

Chamberlain's governing assumption was that victory was certain. By the end of the year, he had begun to believe that German morale had so much improved that Germans would do nothing to help until 'a real hard punch in the stomach' made them. [52]

What this 'punch' could be and where Germany's 'stomach' was to be located was not easy to decide. A Passchendaele was out of the question until Britain and France were stronger. The bombing of Germany was desirable, but was impossible because the British bomber forces were inadequate and the French air defences too weak to withstand retaliation. [53] What, therefore, was wanted was a sideshow which, while not alienating the German public, would remind those who conducted the German war effort that Hitler was destroying Germany. It was in this thought-world that Chamberlain was moving when the decision was made to carry the war into Scandinavia.

The idea of British action in Scandinavia, as distinct from the Balkans or the Black Sea, [54] arose from a coincidence of two events — the Russian attack on Finland in November 1939 and the realisation that Swedish iron-ore was crucial.

Iron ore was 'vital to Germany's prosecution of the War' and would be 'decisive' as to its 'duration'. [55] In the summer months, most of it was sent from northern Sweden across the Gulf of Bothnia. For the rest of the year, it went overland to the Norwegian ports (especially Narvik) and then, by sea, in German ships which, when war started, used the protection of Norwegian waters. [56]

The first proposal to block the Narvik route was made in the form of a mine-laying operation. [57] The War Cabinet approved it in late December in the belief that the Scandinavian governments would not object. [58] It was abandoned after Dominions caution and Swedish objections [59] had so much delayed it that it was no longer worthwhile in view of the reopening of the Bothnian route in May. [60] Attention was concentrated instead on a treble-purpose Anglo-French expedition to help the Finns (via Narvik), [61] occupy the ore mines at Gallivare in northern Sweden en route and support the Swedes if the Germans invaded southern Sweden. [62] It was at this point that Russo-Finnish relations became central.

Nothing the Russians had done since the beginning of the war had altered the opinion Chamberlain had held since 1937 — that they would have at some time to fight Hitler, and that their chief object was to involve Britain and France in softening him up first.

From the signing of the Russo-German pact, British policy had been played both ways. On the one hand, the pact had undermined Poland, which constituted the second front against Germany. On the other, it was assumed that Stalin was as much opposed to German, as Hitler to Russian, expansion and that there was an incompatibility which should be allowed to develop. [63]

About the Russian occupation of Poland, feelings had been mixed. Britain did not have to declare war since the Polish treaty excluded attack by a non-European power. [64] Chamberlain did not want to since Stalin and Hitler were likely, at some stage, to quarrel. [65] Honour, therefore, was satisfied by denunciation which, it was thought, might merge into a campaign to complete Hitler's isolation by succeeding him as leader of the anti-Comintern pact. [66]

While the partition of Poland was thought to have increased the likelihood of Russo-German conflict, it was not assumed that Britain and France should get closer to Russia. On the contrary, a tripartite alliance was expected to do damage. It would increase vulnerability in the Far East, where Japanese eyes were more likely to be kept off the Indian Ocean by keeping the war going in China. It would have a similar effect in Italy where Loraine's view was that the King, Balbo and Ciano were so tired of the Germans that even Mussolini might turn round, provided the Scandinavian operations were successful and the French avoided operations in the Balkans. [67]

Despite trade negotiations with Russia (which continued after the political talks had broken down), it was assumed, therefore, that detachment was essential. This continued to be so even when indirect relations seemed likely via Turco-Soviet and Anglo-Turkish treaties (while the former was under negotiation).

What Chamberlain felt about the Russian attack on Finland was that it was lucky that it was Molotov who had been negotiating in the summer. He was glad that *he* did not have to laugh off the world-wide indignation from which the real sufferer would be Hitler who 'must be in a state of profound depression'. [68] Depression would be induced by the mistrust which Japan and Italy would feel at the spread of Russian power, by the offence caused in the United States, where the Finns were held in special favour, [69] and by the 'consternation' which would result 'among generals and admirals' in Germany as their satellite was assaulted. [70] Though care was taken to avoid war with Russia and consideration given to the Russian threat to Persia and India, [71] it was expected that the Turks, the Japanese, the Italians, the Americans and the German generals — as well as the Scandinavian governments — would all be affected by the right Anglo-French response. All of them were in mind when it was decided to support Russia's expulsion at the special League session which had been summoned in Geneva. [72]

Finnish resistance was expected to subvert Hitler in Germany [73] and to drain Russia of many of the things that he wanted. [74] The Russian failure in the early weeks of the war confirmed the impression, which the speed of action in eastern Poland alone seemed to call in question, that the Russian army was inefficient. [75] It suggested that Britain and France should support Finland by sending arms and encouraging International Brigade-style volunteers, provided the Scandinavian governments would let them through.

From this point onwards, policy was conducted in the belief that a major advantage would be gained if Stalin was defeated and Hitler compelled to intervene, [76] or if Scandinavian entanglements prevented Russo-German advances in the Balkans, where the Russian danger was an aid to keeping Italy neutral [77] and Finnish resistance had made it seem that Britain and France might not be defeated. [78] It was this demonstrative objective, the desire to stop the iron ore traffic and the danger that Germany was preparing to occupy the orefields if Finnish resistance collapsed [79] which made Scandinavia central to British strategy in the first six months of 1940. [80]

The Narvik plan, so far from involving Britain and France in war with Russia, was chosen as an alternative to a French (or Finnish) [81] proposal for an attack via Petsamo which would have done. [82] It was hampered by inadequate preparation and by failures in Anglo-French co-operation. Even more than the mining of Norwegian waters, it depended on the Scandinavian governments who were so reluctant that a decision to land in Norway did not enable the expedition to leave by the time the Finns had to make peace on March 13. [83]

While the operation was being prepared, Chamberlain expected the capture of Gallivere to 'definitely tip the war in our favour'. His attitude to the Finnish capitulation was that the Scandinavian governments had behaved atrociously. He did not deny that the effect would be serious. But he was 'a good deal relieved at not having to send an expedition into Sweden' [84] and the Germans, though 'cock-a-hoop' at Britain's failure, would find Russia freer and more tiresome than she had been before. [85] He was responsible for the decision that the Narvik/Gallivare expedition should be stood down in order to remind the Swedes and Norwegians that the chief lesson they should learn was that 'the only hope of preserving their own independence lies in our victory'. [86]

The Finnish collapse was 'shattering'. [87] Halifax thought of going to Ankara and Rome in order to repair the damage. [88] The chief consequence was the replacement of Daladier by Reynaud, who, like Daladier himself, was then responsible for

recrimination against Chamberlain and requests for joint action to land on the Norwegian coast. He followed this with
proposals for a naval demonstration in the Black Sea, an
amphibious landing in the Caucasus or an air assault on
Batoum and Baku (in order to protect the Rumanian oilfields, deny Russian oil to Germany and prevent Russo-
German advances into the Balkans). [89]

The British answer was a promise of action in early April —
though not in the Black Sea — and decisions to carry out
existing plans to mine the Rhine, Norwegian waters and the
Gulf of Bothnia. [90]

These decisions were proposed as a package at the Supreme War Council of March 28. When the French vetoed the
Rhine project as inviting retaliation on French industry, [91]
the Norwegian project was undertaken, rather reluctantly, by
itself. The mining of Norwegian waters, designed to provoke
sufficient German action to justify a British landing, [92] went
wrong. At the same time as it began, the Germans invaded
Denmark, outwitted the navy and occupied all the main Norwegian ports.

What followed was a rescue operation. Decisions to con-
centrate first on Narvik, [93] and then on Trondheim, [94] to
evacuate Central Norway after the failure there on
April 26 [95] and to make Narvik the seat of the Norwegian
government (and a base for bombing the Bothnian route) [96]
— were taken in the belief that an Anglo-French presence was
essential if Scandinavian resistance was to be effective.

Chamberlain expected success to deter Mussolini from acting in the Balkans. [97] When the decision was made to invest
Trondheim, he could not see how 'the Germans could avoid
ultimate disaster'. Though warned [98] that the operation
would be difficult, he expected it to be over in a week and
that the Germans would be turned out of Narvik 'by at any
rate the week following'. [99]

When expectations collapsed, there were justifications. The
attack on Trondheim had had to be tried because the Norwegians had asked for it, but it was an impossible task. [100]
Chamberlain's hopes had been reflected in the newspapers; [101] when hopes faded, the newspapers were blamed
for the fact that they had had to be disappointed. [102] When
Hitler eventually attacked in the West, it was 'fortunate that

we ha[d] not got large forces of men...guns and planes locked up in Trondheim when we want them so badly here'. [103]

Whatever benefit Chamberlain thought he could discern, the setbacks suffered in Norway were damaging. The Norwegian expedition, however, was a campaign, not the war; when he resigned, ore-ships could not have sailed from Narvik if they had wanted to, and Iceland was about to be occupied. [104] The Low Countries had been invaded. Mussolini seemed about to invade Yugoslavia. But it was not clear why. Nor was it certain that he had decided to attack France or that Britain and France would declare war unless he did. [105] The British army had advanced into Belgium according to plan. The Ruhr was about to be bombed. [106] But there was no sign of the Anglo-French front collapsing and no reason to think that Hitler would break out of the log-jam in which he had been trapped since the previous August. Chamberlain believed that he would fail and that in Germany the effect of failure would be striking. In a month's time the situation had been transformed. It had not been transformed yet. By the time transformation occurred, Chamberlain had been removed.

13

THE FALL OF CHAMBERLAIN

'The government can only be changed if there is a serious breakdown
among their supporters and if, as someone says to me privately,
"Winston is ready to strike" '.
Dalton diary, September 19 1939

'I cannot help feeling that the principles of Liberalism really fulfil what
people want, if they only could realise it'.
Crewe to Lloyd George, April 1 1940

'It is now quite clear that Winston is putting in the jackals and ousting
even those who have done well of what I may call the respectable
Rump of the Tory party'.
Davidson to Baldwin, May 14 1940

Chamberlain's understanding of the war was accepted by
Chatfield — the only professional strategist — and by Halifax
and Hankey, whom he regarded as the most important members of the Cabinet. Chatfield expected the war to be a long
one (unless it was shortened by political collapse in Germany); his ultimate weapons were air power, naval blockade
and economic strangulation. Neither he nor Halifax was an
optimist, and Hankey was positively pessimistic (until Hitler
failed to attack London). All three assumed that the essence
of prudence was Fabian.

Hankey's view before joining the War Cabinet in September was not much different from the views he had expressed
before retiring fourteen months before. Just as Eden's departure had given him a 'strange sense of relief', so Munich had
'laid the foundations of a lasting peace'. But the commitment
of September 18 had renewed the danger of a three-cornered
war. The Polish guarantee had made him 'shiver' as 'a military
commitment to a country that we cannot have safe access to
by sea'. When offered office he was not sure that he wanted
responsibility for a war of which he disapproved.[1]

Nevertheless, he accepted. In the implementation of the
War Book (which he had invented), his rôle was less important than it would have been two years before. His presence
was pivotal in ensuring that Chamberlain had strategic in-

sights independently of both Churchill and the Chiefs of Staff.[2]

If Chamberlain's superiority was to be contested, the most natural critic (apart from. Churchill) would have been Ironside,[3] whose contempt for the politicians who had starved the army was limitless. While over-estimating both the Poles and the Finns and being over-confident about the Scandinavian expedition,[4] Ironside believed that victory was impossible without a land victory in France. But he regarded Chamberlain as an impressive politician and did not dispute his pre-eminence.[5] Though gifted in the manner of Sir Henry Wilson, his instinctive discontent had so little effect that nearly all disagreements concerned incidents in the task of gaining time to repair gaps in case the war became a real one. It was within these limits that Chamberlain's relations with Churchill were conducted.

(i)

As soon as it seemed that war was coming, Churchill was offered office. This was done, not because Chamberlain thought much of him but because he would be a danger if he was kept out. Once war began his presence was a symbol of Chamberlain's determination to go on until Hitler was eliminated.

Nor did Churchill's suitability diminish in the six months that followed. Though suspicious of negotiations with the German opposition, he made no attempt to stop them.[6] About Palestine he allowed himself to be overridden.[7] He was less cautious about challenging the Eire government[8] and wished to be unyielding in India.[9] He was quicker at responding to Belgium's invitation to send in troops[10] and supported the French demand for an active policy in the Balkans and the Black Sea.[11] He treated rationing as a 'slur on the navy'[12] and a 'bureaucratic' interference with both individual liberty[13] and the 'laws of supply and demand'.[14] But he supported the diversion of merchant shipping from the East coast ports which dislocated lines of supply and made rationing more difficult to avoid.[15] Without necessarily believing that the war would have to be won against the German army,[16] he disputed Chamberlain's air priority and questioned his financial scruples about land rearmament. [17]

These differences were marginal. Churchill and Chamberlain both thought that Stalin and Hitler should be entangled in Scandinavia. Both agreed that Mussolini should be handled carefully, that there would be no attack in the West before the spring and that civilian targets in Germany should not be bombed unless Belgium was invaded. Churchill was moved to tears and 'proud to follow' when shown the telegrams in which Chamberlain told Roosevelt that peace talks with Hitler were out of the question. [18]

There was, however, no meeting of minds, and on Chamberlain's side, no desire that meetings should take place. He regarded Churchill as an adult child who neither 'knew his own motives' nor 'where his actions [were] carrying him' [19] and who enjoyed too robustly the wartime descent to the gutter. He talked much, Chamberlain thought, and irrelevantly in Cabinet, gave gratuitous, and unnecessary, advice, [20] and bombarded him with letters which were written for his memoirs. His speeches ignored world opinion and gave undesirable provocations to the Germans when he was supposed to share the collective view that 'time was on our side', not theirs. [21]

When the War Cabinet was first thought of, Chamberlain intended to include Halifax, Hankey, Simon, Chatfield and Churchill, but to exclude the Air and War ministers. They then threatened to resign, so, when formed, it included them (and Churchill) at the Service departments, along with Chatfield who was politically negligible (in spite of being Minister for the Co-ordination of Defence). The difficulty was then compounded when Chatfield was given strategic oversight as chairman of the Military Co-ordination Committee (on its formation in late October). The result was that Churchill, with no overriding responsibility for the conduct of the war, claimed a primacy which Chamberlain rejected. [22]

Although Churchill was a problem, Chamberlain felt confident that he could handle him. He handled him first by failing to answer his letters, replying, when Churchill complained, that they met daily at the War Cabinet. After a press campaign and a Churchill letter in early October, they had 'a frank talk' in the course of which Chamberlain received a promise that the letters (and the 'intriguing') would stop. [23]

Thereafter his attitude was patronising. He was pleased by the poor reception given to Churchill's second broadcast, which he thought would 'do him much good'. He probably thought him 'lucky' to have 'got away' with the sinking of *Royal Oak* in Scapa Flow in October.[24] When he took him to Paris for a meeting of the Supreme War Council, his language was that he had put him 'in his seventh heaven'.[25] When deciding to rule out the mining of Norwegian waters, he felt no apprehension 'for the simple reason that, if I put my foot down, he must either accept my decision or resign...[which he] would just hate to [do] for...he is thoroughly enjoying life and...is much too intelligent to miss the points in the situation that matter'.[26]

It is difficult to measure Churchill's effect on the Cabinet. He played a major part in the decision to make Chamberlain accept a 55-division programme as an ultimate objective at the beginning of the war. He probably initiated discussion of the proposal to intervene in Scandinavia. His presence made Chatfield redundant.[27]

By the time Chamberlain decided to remove Chatfield,[28] he was attracting criticism himself as a result of the failure in Finland which increased the danger from Churchill, who could disclaim special responsibility so long as Chatfield was in the Cabinet. On the other hand, Chamberlain mistrusted Churchill as a strategist and wanted to maintain Cabinet access to the Chiefs of Staff.[29] Instead, therefore, of making him Minister of Defence, he made him deputy chairman of the Military Co-ordination Committee over which he made it clear that he would not himself normally be presiding.[30]

Though the effect once more was to put Churchill into 'his seventh heaven',[31] his handling of the Committee gave Chamberlain a great deal of trouble.[32] He neglected to bring detailed questions to a decision, gave long disquisitions on general questions and 'bullied everyone into sulky silence'. The Service ministers were 'worn out' by argument,[33] the Chiefs of Staff by the vigils they had to keep in making up for the two-hour sleep he had every afternoon. When Stanley conveyed their complaints,[34] Chamberlain was clear that Churchill had 'smashed the machine' that provided professional advice about the conduct of the war.[35]

Churchill not only failed to report what the Chiefs of Staff had decided; he was, Chamberlain thought, at least primarily responsible for two major mistakes — the judgment that the German fleet was sailing to the English Channel, not Narvik on April 8 (with the consequent failure to intercept it) and the decision to divert the rear part of the Narvik force to Trondheim. He changed his mind more than once — four times, according to Chamberlain — in deciding whether Narvik or Trondheim should be the primary object of attention. At the same time as Dill was made Vice-Chief of the Imperial General Staff in order to prepare for the removal of Ironside (whom Churchill had helped Hore-Belisha to appoint), Chamberlain decided that the arrangement should be ended. When Hankey, Simon and Wood asked him to end it, he did so willingly. [36] From April 16 he presided at the Military Co-ordination Committee himself.

At this point Chamberlain believed that Churchill was grateful for being rescued. [37] They then went to Paris together for a meeting of the Supreme War Council on April 23. As soon as they got back, he discovered that Churchill's mood had changed radically.

By the end of 1939 Churchill had regained much of the support he had lost during the abdication. It was not, however, easy to see that he would get very much further [38] unless the war got out of hand. It was not certain that this would happen or that it would even be a long one. Unless it was going to be, he had every reason for avoiding false moves likely to damage his position. Bracken and Lloyd were not so inhibited. [39] He confined himself to urging Chamberlain to promote Hudson and rescue Wood (by making him Minister of Economics after his failure at the Air Ministry), and to bring Croft, Beaverbrook, Amery and Lloyd into the government. [40]

Hardly any of this succeeded; by April 1940 his position was worse than it had been six months before. He had had some of the power that he wanted but Norway had been a disaster which might be hooked onto him like the Dardanelles. After the German occupation of Narvik, the impression he had created in Parliament had been deplorable. [41] Even Keyes quarrelled with him for failing to make the navy attack Trondheim. [42] On April 20 the assault on Trondheim was put off for at least a month. [43] It is not certain whether

Chamberlain's entourage then began to smear him in case he fought back or whether he fought back first. Whatever the sequence, he began to dissociate himself from the government.

Dissociation took the form of 'orations' in Cabinet about returning to the attack or fighting a guerrilla war in the mountains behind Trondheim, [44] and of dark hints about refusing any longer 'to attend the Coordination Committee and give his opinion to be weighed with other opinions'. [45] A disagreeable performance at a Cabinet Committee immediately after the visit to Paris made Chamberlain decide to speak to him. When he did so, he was told what Churchill wanted, 'which was in effect to become Minister of Defence'. [46] In a menacing statement sent in writing later that evening, Churchill added that, though willing to provide support if Chamberlain retained direction of the Military Co-ordination Committee, he would not return to the chair unless given the power to make policy. [47]

Before sending this letter, Churchill had talked to the Labour leaders and to Sinclair. He had also been told what Salisbury and the Watching Committee thought. It was at this point, that his acts of self-defence became a threat to Chamberlain's future. [48]

(ii)

The situation in which Chamberlain's removal became a possibility was the work of five parliamentary groups — the Labour leaders, the Sinclair Liberals, the Eden group under Amery's chairmanship, an inter-party group which Clement Davies had formed at the beginning of the war and a committee of senior Conservatives — 'the Watching Committee' — which Salisbury and Cranborne set up in early 1940. In creating a state of mind, in suggesting responses and in the mechanics of motion, these were the prime agents. In facilitating the positive, and perhaps desperate, action which Churchill took after his failure at the Military Co-ordination Committee, their activities were crucial.

For the Labour leaders the first nine months of the war were a non-event. The Labour organisation was active in the constituencies and Labour local authorities were unhelpful to the government. [49] Labour supporters from universities found their way into government departments. There were outbursts in the House of Commons — over Hore-Belisha's resignation, for example — a great deal of detailed criticism and a stream of public activity by which the Cabinet was greatly worried. [50] Labour spokesmen had regular meetings with relevant ministers who were influenced at many points by a feeling that a price had to be paid for Labour acquiescence. [51] But 'National security' and the electoral truce imposed restraint. [52] Reluctance to repeat the mistake Henderson had made in 1915 and MacDonald in 1931 meant that, unless Chamberlain collapsed physically, there was nothing to do but wait.

Waiting produced problems. There was the problem of Communist defeatism in the Labour movement. There was the shock induced by the Russian attack on Finland and a fear that Conservatives might want to attack the Russians. [53] There was the incompatibility between the demand for a more determined war strategy and the pacifist demand to end the war, which was as strong inside the Labour movement as it was outside.

Support for the war did not involve support for Chamberlain or an increase in cordiality between Chamberlain and Attlee. [54] The Labour party had refused to join the government; it became a policy position that it would not join a government of which Chamberlain was a member. Despite individual backsliding, [55] this prohibition was extended to include Simon, Hoare and Sir Horace Wilson.

The trade union movement was in a position to withhold co-operation from war production. The Labour party could use the party truce to affect policy. What neither could do was to effect a change of government. It was only when action had been taken by Davies, Amery, Salisbury and the Conservative party that this became possible.

Clement Davies played a central part in the events of May 1940 but his group was not established in order to make kings. It began at the outbreak of war as a discussion group of like-minded MPs who 'found action through...party machinery inadequate'. [56] Eleanor Rathbone, its secretary, was an admirer of the Spanish Republic, a supporter of Hailé

Selassie and a Liverpool Liberal authority on a variety of social problems. Nicolson might well have belonged to any of the parties. Grenfell — an admirer of Lloyd George [57] and the Labour MP whom Baldwin liked best — was a self-taught Welsh linguist who had brought from the mines the national sympathies which Hodges had brought in the past. After a period as Baldwin's and Churchill's private secretary, Boothby had been an ally of Macmillan and, from time to time, a Churchill supporter. White had resigned with the Samuelite ministers in 1932 and signed their manifesto in 1935.

In general, the convenors embodied the informed politics of the Liberal Left of which a major exponent was Lloyd George (from whom they failed to get access to the research machinery of the Council of Action). [58] With a few exceptions, this also applied to the regular members. These included one National Labour MP (who happened to be an ex-Liberal), [59] four Sinclairites, [60] an ex-Liberal MP who was Rathbone's Independent colleague for the Combined English Universities, [61] the Labour MP for Ipswich who had tried to get Sinclair on his by-election platform in 1938, [62] and Bellenger, the Labour MP who had had both Conservative and Liberal connections before beating Malcolm MacDonald at Bassetlaw in 1935.

Davies was a Welsh lawyer who had succeeded Lloyd George's benefactor, Lord Davies, as MP for Montgomeryshire in 1929. Despite his predecessor's hostility when he became a Simonite two years later, he had been unopposed since. He had remained a Simonite after the Liberal resignations in 1932 and had declined to join Lloyd George's Welsh opposition. He had not, however, been given office. [63] In 1935 he volunteered to support the New Deal. [64] The leadership of the new group gave him his first opportunity, at the age of fifty-five, to present himself as a significant figure. In the following nine months most of its initiatives were his. [65]

About a negotiated peace, the group had no fixed opinions. Some of its members had long-standing commitments to economic appeasement. [66] For others the alienation of Russia was so serious that a negotiated peace was unavoidable. [67] Despite talk about the need to 'destroy Hitlerism', it was not in these quarters that the most resolute noises were made about fighting on until Hitler was defeated.

Nevertheless, Davies had relations with the Eden group, and was aware of its doubts about the conduct of the war. After the Secret Session had given them an airing,[68] he resigned the Simonite whip on the grounds that the war was not being planned, trade unionists and manufacturers not being involved and the War Cabinet not really operating.[69]

In the next six months he was waiting for an opportunity to move into action whenever Chamberlain was in difficulty. For this reason he took a good deal of trouble with Amery.

When the war began, Amery expected to be given office. He was disappointed. Eden and Churchill had to be accommodated because of their public reputations, but Chamberlain felt free to pay back the intervention of September 2.[70] Despite applications to influential friends, Amery found himself 'spoiling for work' as he had been after the reconstructions of 1935, 1937 and 1938.[71] Consoled by the thought that 'Milner had to wait two years before they used him',[72] he was not consoled when Salter (a League-based Cobdenite) became Under-Secretary for Shipping. He looked on resentfully while Gilmour became Shipping Minister (as though to show that ministers need know nothing about their departments)[73] and Stanley replaced Hore-Belisha (quite 'scandalously')[74] at the War Office. Having declined the chairmanship of a Select Committee,[75] he urged a proper energy in conducting the war (and no early peace) and prepared plans for a 'European Commonwealth based on Western Christendom' as an encouragement 'to superior people in Germany' to face the situation when Hitlerism had been defeated.[76]

In the first six months of the war Amery developed a wider range of allies than he had had before. At meetings of the Davies group, he was acclaimed as the only Conservative fit to be Minister of Economics.[77] At the suggestion of the Finnish embassy, he helped to run the Finnish Aid Committee.[78] In the process of despatching volunteers to fight the Russians, he worked with Cecil's Lytton, with Macmillan and with Lord Davies, who adopted the view (which Amery can hardly have liked) that intervention in Finland was a 'police action' from which a League-based International Police Force would emerge.

In the course of the winter, Amery had a good deal to do

with Sinclair, Greenwood and Attlee. On a French visit with
the Anglo-French Parliamentary Committee, he had agreeable, and extensive, conversation with Grenfell. Over family
allowances — one of his long-term hobby-horses — he had
discussions with Rathbone and Keynes and correspondence with Chamberlain and Ball. After talking to Hicks at a
Davies economic sub-committee meeting, he was encouraged
to work out detailed proposals with an official at Transport
House. Even the young Balogh called to tell him how important it was that Chamberlain should be removed. [79]

Amery was given consideration because he was an obvious
defector who might be used to do Chamberlain down. He
also mattered because, when Eden joined the government, he
became Chairman of the Eden group.

With exceptions, [80] the Eden group agreed that, since there
could be no peace with Hitler, their function was to harass
the government until it conducted the war as though it meant
it. To some extent this was because 'millions of Germans...
w[ould] gladly sabotage Hitler for us if we give them the
chance'. [81] To some extent it was subsidiary to the real aim —
to bring about a change of government — which was important to others besides those who felt under-employed.

Whether 'a change of government' was to mean primarily a
new Prime Minister, coalition with Labour or the removal of
Hoare, Simon and Wilson was not clear. Nor was it obvious
who would be Prime Minister if one had to be found. Eden
had neglected the group and dropped out of consideration
from some time before the war began. [82] In great uncertainty
about the mechanics, many of its members not only favoured
Churchill but were clear sooner than the Davies group that
the government would have to be changed if war was to be
waged seriously. [83]

With this object in mind, [84] they interested themselves in
aid to Finland, the appointment of a Minister of Economics
and the Trenchard policy of bombing Germany to defeat. [85]
Though irritated by the Whips and by Chamberlain's ministerial reshuffles, they were encouraged by the Secret Session
which they had helped to engineer. [86] Law and Macmillan
both made large splashes with first-hand attacks on the government's failure to help the Finns.

Although they could smell blood, they did not begin to be confident until Chamberlain failed to explain Narvik as cleverly as he had explained away Finland. [87] Expectations were raised further when Salisbury set up another group to which some of them belonged.

After the passage of the India bill, Salisbury had phased himself out of day-to-day politics. In 1936 he was a nuisance about defence. [88] His requests for House of Lords reform became a ritual. At the age of seventy-six, he played a part in the abdication. About all these matters, he received the attention which was his due. Otherwise he made the Oxford Group the focus of his attention.

Like many active members of his family, [89] Salisbury looked forward to an inevitable battle between the ideals of Christianity and the 'forces of darkness' and 'infidelity' represented by Hitler, Stalin and Mussolini. He believed that Russia must be avoided, that avoidance would help defeat Germany and that Britain should give 'spiritual leadership' [90] against Hitler who was 'mad dog', 'pagan', 'gangster' and 'anti-Christ incarnate'. [91]

For him, if not for his relatives, the Oxford Group was an instrument in the battle. Hitler and Stalin would not be resisted without rearmament from within. Between military and moral rearmament on the one hand and parliamentary control of foreign policy on the other, as between the League of Nations and the 'Concert of Europe' in his father's version, there was a connection. [92] Through Cecil, his brother, he was in touch with attempts to revive the League. Through Cranborne, his son, he had first-hand knowledge of the House of Commons.

Salisbury was a contemporary of Austen Chamberlain and had admired the stuffed dignity of the converted Radical. He had no sympathy for Neville Chamberlain who was cleverer and stringier and, despite enjoying visits to large houses, did not share his half-brother's consciousness of 'belonging to the middle classes'. [93]

Salisbury approved of Eden's and Cranborne's resignations and took offence at the dismissal of Ormsby-Gore. He was unhappy about Munich which had given Germany 'economic control of Central Europe'. [94] The pogroms were 'outrages'

which made negotiation impossible. [95] The government's conduct suggested 'surrender', [96] 'compromise' [97] or 'the very
dreadful idea' that they had 'no policy at all'. [98]

Salisbury thought Chamberlain had been unreliable about
Poland and expected him to be unreliable about Mussolini. [99]
He did not believe he could conduct a war and wanted a
committee of politicians to investigate and report. Chamberlain's dismissal of the idea did nothing to remove his doubts.
The Watching Committee was his, and Cranborne's, answer. [100]

Unlike his father, Cranborne had no die-hard tendencies.
Before becoming Under-Secretary for League Affairs in 1935,
he had established himself as a modern-minded Cecilian ideal-
ist. Though he had quarrelled with the League of Nations
Union, he believed in the League, [101] did not believe in the
Russian menace [102] and was one of the few ministers whom
Cecil trusted. He shared the dislike, which all Cecils seem to
have felt, for Chamberlain.

As before their resignation, so in the year which followed,
Cranborne was sharper and bitterer than Eden. Then, in the
middle of 1939, he had an illness which made office impossible when the war began. On resuming work in the winter,
he decided that the Eden group needed strengthening if
Chamberlain was to be removed. [103]

The Watching Committee was designed 'to watch the administration of the war and to harass ministers where they
ought to be harassed'. It included six members of the Eden
group and four members of the Cecil family, [104] as well as
Astor, Lloyd, Swinton, Trenchard and Horne. Londonderry
was a member, and also Hailsham. Spens was chairman of the
1922 Committee. Ball had recently retired from being Director of the Conservative Research Department.

Once it got under way, the committee reached much the
same conclusions as the Davies and Amery groups. It too
decided that it wanted a proper War Cabinet and an investigation of Churchill's position. [105] It soon became obvious that
Salisbury was doing to Neville Chamberlain what he had done
eighteen years before to his brother Austen.

(iii)

At the beginning of the war Chamberlain offered office to the Labour leaders but did not expect them to accept it. Nor did he mind either way. Though he had had to abandon one prong of his policy, the policy had had more than one prong to it. Though it had failed, it could be presented in terms which enhanced the 'value of a man who had gone to the limits in trying to secure a peaceful settlement' once the country had, 'in spite of all this, been forced into war'. [106]

Chamberlain began the war, damaged by the policy collapse and unconvincing on September 2. He restored himself because, believing that the Russo-German pact was a defeat for Hitler, he was able to provide the optimism and resolution necessitated by the precariousness of his situation. [107]

Chamberlain felt compulsions to go but, since he intended to stay, needed a government he could control. In this respect his difficulties were considerable. Though Eden was kept out, the War Cabinet had to be bigger than he wanted, because Hoare, Wood and Hore-Belisha would be dangerous if they resigned. Hoare and Simon had developed loose-standing positions. Churchill's position was necessarily loose-standing, and Chatfield's anomalous. Though Halifax's support was politically vital and personally most reassuring, the member of the War Cabinet on whom Chamberlain could rely most confidently was Hankey (who had returned from retirement for a few weeks during Munich and was now brought into the Cabinet in order to 'keep an eye' on Churchill). [108]

Since he expected the war to be a short one, Chamberlain had no wish to disturb the structure of promotion; nor did he want the interlude used in order to get a new Prime Minister. Stanhope paid for a blunder by being moved into a siding so that Churchill could have the Admiralty. Inskip's political career ended when he replaced Maugham as Lord Chancellor in order to make room for Eden. One of the new under-secretaries (Grigg) had been a defence and Munich rebel before being involved in the economic negotiations of 1939. Another (McEwen) was an Edenite who had turned round. But O'Neill — an important back bencher — had never been. Nor had Lloyd George's son. Apart from Hankey, Churchill and Eden, Chamberlain's only important innovation was to give the Ministry of Information to Macmillan, the Conservative Lord of Appeal, who had been Lord Advocate in the first Labour government. [109]

In the subsequent seven months a few changes were made because ministers were inadequate. [110] On the whole, however, Chamberlain's changes reflected the need to sacrifice others in order to save himself. The appointments of Reith and Duncan [111] were responses to the Secret Session of December 13 which was 'very ill-tempered'. [112] The reconstruction of April 3 was a response to the failure in Finland. After the Norwegian vote on May 8, he planned another.

The Finland reconstruction was limited because Chamberlain wanted to keep in the War Cabinet 'one or two people on whom he particularly relie[d]'. [113] He confined himself to making Woolton and Hudson Ministers of Food and Shipping, replacing Wood by Hoare at the Air Ministry (and Hoare by Wood at the Privy Seal) and announcing that Churchill's powers had been increased.

As reassurance, this failed. [114] Though Woolton began well, [115] he was a businessman, not a politician, and was unknown as a public figure. Hoare was too well-known. [116] Churchill's period at the Military Co-ordination Committee was a disaster. When the Norwegian campaign collapsed, it became clear that drastic action would be needed if the régime was to survive.

When disaster broke, Chamberlain's entourage fixed on Churchill as the scapegoat. [117] After the miscalculation of April 8, this seemed plausible. It seemed much less plausible when the whole campaign failed. Even before the decision to evacuate Central Norway three weeks later, Chamberlain's position was being called in question. When the decision was made public at the end of the month, a major crisis was on the way. [118]

Though Chamberlain would probably have liked to remove Churchill from the Admiralty, [119] he did not feel strong enough to do so. When Churchill complained once more about defence arrangements, he decided that he must 'satisfy' him without 'weakening the authority of the Cabinet'. [120] After threatening to resign when the Service Ministers objected, [121] he laid it down that, in his absence, Churchill would preside at the Military Co-ordination Committee, would have authority to call the Chiefs of Staff and would be the channel of communication for Military Co-ordination Committee directives to them. [122]

Under criticism Chamberlain wrote more than once about resigning in face of the 'disappointment at not getting office' of some of the 'smaller fry' who were 'really traitors just as much as Quisling'. [123] He also wrote, with much bitterness, about Sinclair, whose public attack at Edinburgh in early May was treated as a breach of confidence in respect of secret information. [124] There is no doubt that he regarded the Norwegian debate as crucial.

On this occasion, he was less effective than after Finland and annoyed many of his supporters by claiming that the war was being fought according to plan which, in a sense, it was but which it seemed that it was not. [125] In the vote of May 8, at least eight of those who voted with Chamberlain were members of the government who hoped that it would fall. [126] Between fifty and sixty of his supporters abstained. [127] Over forty voted with the Labour party, including Amery, Wolmer, Law, Tree, Spears, Keyes, Hogg, Duff Cooper, Macmillan, Hore-Belisha, Winterton, King-Hall, Patrick, Boothby, Hopkinson, Nicolson, Mrs Tate and Lady Astor.

Among the 280 who supported Chamberlain, some had been preparing for a showdown since the dissentients began to operate in 1938. They had expected a larger abstention than there was and were encouraged to believe that Chamberlain could go on. [128] The difficulty was to see how.

In preparing for the vote, Chamberlain's secretaries had hinted that Hoare and Simon might be sacrificed. [129] In the thirty-six hours after the debate Chamberlain tried three ways of rescuing himself.

First, he let it be known that Hoare and Simon would be removed. [130] Then, he tried to persuade the Labour party to enter a coalition. Finally, after discovering, the day before the German invasion of the Low Countries, that Labour would not enter a coalition under him, he decided that the invasion had made it possible for him to stay. [131] In all these respects he found that the ground had been undermined too thoroughly.

When Chamberlain's removal was under consideration in late 1939, one difficulty was to know what an alternative government would consist of. Little confidence was felt in the second rank of Conservative ministers. Though there was much confidence in Herbert Morrison, Bevin and Alexander, there was none at all in Attlee and Greenwood who were regarded as window-dressing. It was not until Sinclair made a good speech in the Secret Session that he was anything resembling an asset. [132]

Despite uncertainties of this sort, the Davies, Eden and Salisbury groups met continuously between April 25 and May 8 and were in constant touch with one another. They were responsible for there being a division and by their votes contributed to the result. They managed the resistance to Chamberlain's counter-attack and played an important part in creating the climate which made Churchill Prime Minister.

At the end of April it had been by no means certain that he could be. [133] There was little enthusiasm in the Labour party where there was a widespread belief that a Labour government would somehow be the answer. [134] Until late in the day Lloyd George seemed at least as likely. [135]

After the defeat of the Abyssinians Lloyd George had followed the Liberal line about stepping up sanctions against Mussolini. But he had been unimpressed by the German threat. His fellow-feeling for Hitler had increased when he met him. He had played down the air menace and had played up the menace of German communism. [136]

With Baldwin's retirement, he hitched himself on to Chamberlain's deficiencies. He congratulated Eden on resigning and urged him to become the hero of the Left. As an eloquent advocate of alliance with Russia, he was in Paris to stir up the 'war party' after the Anschluss.

In 1939 Lloyd George hovered between wanting to come to terms with Hitler and using Chamberlain's attempts to do so as proof of Chamberlain's inadequacy. When the Russo-German pact convinced Chamberlain that a deal was unnecessary, he adopted the line that a deal was unavoidable. His speech in early October was the only important peace statement between the outbreak of war and the fall of France.

Lloyd George was the only active politician who had dealt at a high level with an adult situation (in March 1918). His claim to the Prime Ministership depended on confidence in his ability to wage war (if he could) or to make peace (if he could not). His advocates were Garvin and the Astor family,[137] Esmond Harmsworth and the *Daily Mail*[138] and Cripps, who wrote for the *Mail* an anonymous letter suggesting that *he* should be Chancellor of the Exchequer in a Lloyd George government.[139]

Although he was seventy-seven, Lloyd George had a certain amount of support in all three parties and, if asked to form a government, might have been able to do so. He, however, let it be known that his object was not to fight the war to the conclusion Chamberlain had indicated but to get out of the 'trap' Chamberlain had fallen into with the Polish guarantee.[140]

How far this was a way of making himself indispensable after further defeats, how far it was his way of adding war-guilt to Chamberlain's other deficiencies is not clear.[141] But, since both the government and its foremost critics had excluded a negotiated peace, this excluded him from consideration.[142]

When Lloyd George ruled himself out, suggesting that Attlee should become Prime Minister instead, the only alternative to Churchill (among the war party) was Halifax who had extensive support among Conservative backbenchers, with the King[143] and from some of the Labour leaders,[144] and who, if he had been asked to form a government, could certainly have done so. It was only the realisation that Churchill would make a great deal of trouble if he did that made him insist on Churchill grasping the nettle at the meeting on May 10.[145]

Until a late stage, however, it was not obvious that there was a nettle to grasp. The decision that there should be a division and vote on May 8 had come slowly. The Labour leaders had not all decided that they wanted to take office.[146] The Davies group, joined (to their irritation) by Hore-Belisha,[147] had decided by May 2 that a Secret Session was the best way of proceeding[148] and that a vote after an ordinary debate might rally waverers behind Chamberlain. The Watching Committee agreed. Until the morning of

May 8, they did not expect much support. At a joint meeting with the Davies group, they had the greatest difficulty in deciding that the time was ripe. [149]

Once the vote had been taken, they acted ruthlessly. Davies tried to abbreviate the Whitsun adjournment and, in company with Beaverbrook, acted as postman between the Labour leaders and the Conservative dissentients. Salisbury was sent to tell Halifax that he or Churchill must form a government and that Chamberlain, Simon and Hoare must be removed. In order to prevent Chamberlain detaching Amery — who had had the (for him) unusual experience of being cheered in the debate on May 7 — Amery was told that he was a possible Prime Minister and made chairman of an expanded amalgamation of the Eden and Davies groups. [150]

At its first meeting on the evening of May 9, the new group agreed to accept any Prime Minister who would 'form a real War Cabinet' and 'truly National Government' chosen on 'merit' and not on the judgment of the Whips. [151] When Chamberlain tried to use the German offensive as a reason for staying, Davies telephoned Greenwood at the Labour Conference at Bournemouth to make sure that he failed. When the Watching Committee met later in the morning, Salisbury was deputed to let it be known that Chamberlain must hand over the Prime Ministership and must not be a member of the new government. [152]

This did not happen. When Amery saw Churchill after Churchill had seen the King, he discovered that Chamberlain was to be Chancellor of the Exchequer and Leader of the House of Commons. When Chamberlain announced, in his resignation broadcast that evening, that he had agreed to take office, Davies and Amery telephoned Cranborne and Salisbury to convey their annoyance. [153] Davies spent next morning conveying it to the Labour leaders who, when they had lunch with Churchill, conveyed it to him. Amery then got Cranborne to ask Salisbury to see Churchill, which he did. By the early evening, the Chancellorship had gone elsewhere. Even after the Labour leaders had agreed that Chamberlain should remain in the Cabinet, Amery telephoned Bracken to say that he should go to the House of Lords. [154] He tried next day, with as little success, to make Gwilym Lloyd George Chief Whip in place of Margesson. [155]

In the week before Chamberlain fell, Amery and Davies had been important figures. Once Churchill had taken his place, they ceased to be. The groups that they led looked to him for advancement, not to them, and disintegrated as soon as advancement was given. Davies received nothing because there was nothing a marginal Liberal of limited experience could be given that he would think good enough; he declined the offer of a peerage. Amery hoped to be Economic Overlord or Churchill's deputy on the defence committees; he was half-offered the Ministry of Supply. When this was withdrawn — perhaps on Chamberlain's advice [156] — he was sent to the India Office, which was not at all what he had expected. The first few days of the new government showed that he would have no more influence over Churchill than he had had over Chamberlain.

The new government included many of the dissentient Conservatives and Sinclairite and Labour contingents. But it was made large enough to retain a large element from the old one. Hoare, Zetland, Colville, Wallace, Stanhope and Burgin all suffered execution a few days before Morrison — the new Home Secretary — had Mosley imprisoned, and Wilson was removed from Downing Street. Stanley refused the Dominions Office, which Churchill offered in insulting terms, [157] and joined Elliot, Winterton and de la Warr [158] in a 'wobblers' ' exile. MacDonald, however, and W.S. Morrison remained. Simon remained, and Inskip returned to the Dominions Office so that Simon could become Lord Chancellor. Wood, the indispensable Judas, was rewarded for abandoning Chamberlain by being made Chancellor of the Exchequer (without membership of the War Cabinet). Halifax remained Foreign Secretary and a member of the War Cabinet (while Eden, at the War Office, remained outside it). Margesson, after offering to resign and declining to become a Secretary of State, [159] was retained as Chief Whip. There was no room for Hore-Belisha who seems by now to have been universally despised. Lloyd George and Astor, for different reasons, declined to go at different levels to the Ministry of Agriculture. [160] But Duff Cooper and Cranborne returned. The new men were Attlee, Bevin, Greenwood, Morrison, Alexander and Dalton (from the Labour party), Sinclair, Johnstone and Dingle Foot (from the Liberals), Nicolson (from the National

Labour party) and Lloyd, Amery, Beaverbrook, Croft, Boothby, Sandys, Law, Bracken and Macmillan from among unbeneficed Conservatives. [161]

During the fortnight since the decision to evacuate central Norway, Churchill had acted with delicacy and tact. He had been as careful to defend the government as Chamberlain had been to associate him in its disasters. [162] When resignation became inevitable, Chamberlain offered to join a government if he formed one. [163]

In accepting the offer on returning from the King, Churchill recognised that he depended on the goodwill of the largest group in the House of Commons. Though nearly a hundred Conservatives had abandoned Chamberlain two days before, some of them had turned round [164] and were shocked by the disloyalty of the previous week. Others looked on Chamberlain as their leader and were not certain that they would take the Whip. [165] Churchill, certainly, was not being chosen as a man of destiny. [166] He would have approved, and perhaps saw, the letter in which the Chairman of the 1922 Committee asked Chamberlain to join his government on the ground that, if he did not 'hold a leading place' in it, 'it would be dissipated in a few weeks'. [167]

CONCLUSION

'If war comes...all forms of property will be taxed nigh to extinction under the delusive name of "Conscription of Wealth" '.
Garvin to Astor, September 21 1938

'Mr Greenwood, when moving the Amendment yesterday, told us that the war would shake many strongly held views. I fear that this war will do very much more than that. The war will bring about changes which may be fundamental and revolutionary in the economic and social life of this country. On that we are all agreed'.
Eden in House of Commons, December 6 1939, reprinted in Eden, *Freedom and Order*, 1947, p. 48.

'It is the beginning of English National Socialism'.
William Mabane, Liberal National MP for Huddersfield talking about Eden's parliamentary speech of November 10 1938, reported in Nicolson diary, same date

The Coalition which arrived in May 1940 appeared at first to be only an arrangement of convenience produced by the alliance system of the previous two years. In fact, it was the beginning of a régime. It had not only a Cabinet but camp followers, among whom were the high-priests of social equality and national regeneration along with a young Mountbatten, a young Maudling, a young Rowse, a young Harrod, a young Gaitskell, a young Heath, a young Balogh and a young Berry (with his bride) who were all doing the new thing, looking to the future and waiting for a ride on Attlee's, Churchill's, Priestley's and Noël Coward's shoulders.[1]

Churchill's shoulders turned out to be broad, but it was not obvious how broad they would become. In May 1940 he was not the saviour of the nation since the nation did not yet need saving. What he had done was creatively opportunistic, uniting hopes and fears which had nothing in common and arriving, through Hitler's instrumentality, where he would have wanted to arrive whether Hitler had shown the way or not. He stood, however, for nothing in particular except the prosecution of a war which was not to be prosecuted and the preservation of an Empire which was not to be preserved.

The Labour arrivals, on the other hand, were the tip of an iceberg or foot in the door for something very much more formidable. They concealed a movement which had been re-born since 1931 around an office-seeking intelligentsia for whom Cole, Laski, Tawney and Strachey provided scriptures. Though few of them were visible at the summits in 1940 (and their mandarinate belongs to the decades following), they had expectations and a ladder which were of major conse-quence for the future.

The future was not to be 'socialist' (in the Crippsian sense). In some respects in intention for a time, it was to absorb 'property' into 'community'. In other respects it was to turn 'socialism' into an élitist radicalism. In all respects its moral merit was attested by the propaganda which the *Chronicle* and *Herald* had established and which Owen, Foot and Howard[2] (as well as Morison's *History of the Times*[3]) developed by using Beaverbrook's methods to denigrate the foreign policy position Beaverbrook had supported.

The Labour leaders were of a generation older than the movement of the thirties; their certainties were flexible and reassuring. Like Priestley, Dalton embodied the jingo egali-tarianism he had invented in the previous four years. Citrine was the first really effective trade union statesman in dis-guise. Bevin had proved that the roughest trade unionist could be educated, imperial and international. Greenwood and Alexander had proved — what Thomas had proved before — that the good things of life were to be enjoyed.[4] Morrison combined a nasty edge,[5] doctrinal integrity and the broad practicality characteristic of a willing coalitionist.[6] Attlee, as surely as Baldwin, was the average embodiment of the ethos he represented.

Attlee was a 'public school and university man' who, having picked up a doctrine when young, had for long held it as the basis for living. After a period as a social worker and as an infantry officer in war, he had spent his forties anticipa-ting in books and lectures the mechanics of its wider imple-mentation.

The doctrine was the doctrine of Green, its basis the belief that 'university men' should help the poor. It was socialist so far as was necessary to bridge the gap and bring them within the framework of the nation. But it was an insular version through which, as councillor, mayor and front bench MP, Attlee had shown forth by his life and works the conscientious hope felt in the Oxford of the nineties for a 'fine collective life' based on a community of freedom between those who had, and those who had not, had the benefits of education.

Though a secular priest, Attlee was in no sense priestly. He was a middle-class gentleman who had seen through his inherited opinions and intended to give effect to decisions about which he had made up his mind a very long time ago. He was a socialist, but his chief objective was an edgeless, egalitarian modesty which, in the Labour party, had found 'typically British' methods of 'adapting' old institutions to 'new...purposes'.[7]

These methods were 'practical'. They depended on 'character' and were nourished by the lives of ordinary party workers who would convert people to socialism 'more by what [they] are than by what they [are] heard to say'.[8]

Like Baldwin, whom he admired and who liked him, Attlee had been an undistinguished undergraduate. Where Baldwin had thought of ordination, he had had some sort of conversion. Both disliked 'intellectuals'. Both felt a shared sense of relationship with 'ordinary' humanity. Both found something safe, or reassuring, in the 'natural dignity' of the genuine leaders of the working-class movement.[9]

Again like Baldwin, Attlee flattered himself on his 'modern outlook'. By this, however, he did not mean that he knew about industrial society (which was not to be found in Oxford, Stanmore or the East End of London). He meant equality, community and a belief that power politics could be moralised. He not only said but evidently believed that nations were members one of another and that a 'world state' was the 'only really effective' way 'of preventing war'.[10] Though sobered by Hitler, he was saying right up to the fall of France that 'power politics' could be avoided. He admired Eden for implying the same (even before he became a minister)[11] and disliked Chamberlain (whom, morally, he much resembled) because, while talking like a pacifist, he thought like an Imperialist, and made war inevitable by piling up armaments.[12]

Attlee was far from charismatic, and his leadership was contested.[13] But he had few illusions about what could be done. All he hoped (and all he did) was to invest the rag-bag

of doctrines that existed on the Left with a deeper analysis
and better purpose than Lloyd George had failed with in
1935, so that it might be said of him in reverse — what had
been said of Baldwin — that 'there [was] no-one half as good
at the business of getting the Middle Class and the Working
Class to vote the same way'. [14]

Before he took office, his position was that 'Socialism'
should not be emasculated. [15] Given his opinions and mode
of expression, and given a certain mute lay spirituality, it is
doubtful whether he could have done more to elevate it if he
had tried to. [16] By the time the war started, he had established for himself a genuine continuity between the 'social
conscience' and charitable energy of earlier generations and
the challenge presented by a chain-store/ribbon-building society to allow 'social reconstruction' to restore the 'individuality' it was destroying. [17]

In these ways he was renewing invitations to the struggle
against Capitalism which, however, he did not expect to collapse [18] and which would be strengthened and transformed
by British Capitalists who were 'the strongest...and...cleverest
in the world'. [19] In these ways, also, he was trying to persuade moderate, decent people to think it as normal to reject
the 'mean ideals' of 'conventional' and 'suburban' homes as
Baldwin had made it to accept them. [20]

In the end Labour arrived rather suddenly, but one should
not exaggerate the difference from what had gone before. On
the other hand, there were differences — about nationalisation, the level of taxation and the importance of Indian and
colonial self-government.

Attlee was conscious of the extent to which his way had
been prepared by the India bill and the Statute of Westminster, by state activity in the first war and the public cor-
porations since, and by the willingness of Conservatives (like
Halifax) to see government as an 'instrument to secure conditions favourable to the fullest possible development of personality'. With rearmament and conscription, moreover,
wealth had had to be taxed; since the beginning of the war it
had been taxed heavily. Eden was not the only 'decent Tory'
(an Attlee conception) who spent the winter of 1939 running
ahead of the consensus and looking forward to 'revolution-

ary...changes...in the economic and social life of the country'. [21]

What a Labour government would have done if it had won
a general election in 1940 is not certain. What is certain is
that post-war Socialism was created when Attlee, Bevin and
Morrison took on post-war reconstruction after Chamberlain's
collapse in 1940.

The reconstruction that was planned thereafter, and the
content of the 1945 platform, were the work of Keynes,
Beveridge and Reith. That they were able to be effective, and
to embody Layton's conception of a régime, was a result of
Attlee's flexibility and the fact that Churchill and Chamberlain between them had destroyed the Conservative party.

Chamberlain had not intended to destroy. He had intended
to hand it over in about 1942 and would probably have done
so if he had not been deposed.

The deposition, however, and the Coalition which followed, upset the Conservative structure. They created a vacuum
in which 'the sacrifices required by the war' suggested an
'advance towards economic equality' [22] and a new range of
leader to replace the leaders who had been rising in the past.

Chamberlain himself had destroyed Morrison and Elliot —
the most obvious guarantors of Conservative liberality. Eden,
to some extent, had destroyed himself. Churchill's contribution was the destruction of some of the others, and the promotion of some of the odd-balls of the thirties. It was not
until Carr and Barrington-Ward had made *The Times* the
home of 'Vital Democracy' and 'liberating truths'[23] that Butler (paradoxically) made it his life's work to show that Churchill's was a new consensus.

If no one knew that a consensus had arrived in May 1940,
it was not for want of looking. Since 1933 it had been looked
for by Malcolm MacDonald, Percy, King-Hall, Hore-Belisha,
Allen of Hurtwood, Boothby, Inskip, de la Warr, Mabane,
Layton, Swinton, Nicolson, Cecil, Cartland, Bernays, Sinclair,
Macmillan, Eden, Elliot, Halifax, the Aclands and Lloyd
George who had all been sowing where Churchill and Attlee
reaped. [24] Whether the remedy was a morally-credible Socialism, Liberal control of the Conservative party or the formation of a Centre party (under Liberal-Conservative or Nation-

al Labour auspices), the object was to lead Labour, Liberal and Conservative opinion towards a 'democratic radicalism' which would come from unsafe hands if safe hands did not bring it first.

This was, of course, a trick. Nor was there a significant difference of intention between the National government and the 'Tory Socialism' which followed, since both were designed to contain class warfare by enveloping it. But there were innumerable differences of scale and generation as the prospect of war and the strength of Labour produced a new version of the situation in which the 'rich' would have to 'sacrifice...money' if 'standards' were to be maintained. [25]

After 1931 the problem had been dealt with through Mac-Donald, Thomas and Snowden. By 1937 they had gone and National Labour was a salon party. Humble pasts were the monopoly of Womersley (an obscure Conservative minister) and of Brown who, having once lived on 'twenty-five shillings a week,...was in a position for meeting Labour attacks' on the Unemployment Assistance bill. [26] Womersley's rags having turned to riches, he had been mayor of Grimsby and a back-bench facilitator of Chamberlain's domestic legislation in the twenties. [27] Brown had been commissioned in the war and was a Liberal convenience who would cease to matter once new faces were needed to replace those which had been serviceable in the past.

The feeling that faces should be changeable was as strong inside the régime as outside it. It followed from the assumption that the chief problem under conditions of universal suffrage was to enable a minority group (the Conservative party) to recommend itself to an electorate which was 'not made up of Eustace Percies'. [28]

Sometimes the problem was approached by propaganda, sometimes by governmental decision, sometimes by alliance with outside groups or interests. In the course of the thirties it issued in the 'national party' of 1934, in the idea of Morrison, Bevin, Addison or Lloyd George as reinforcements and in Chamberlain's alliance with the peace movement. In Halifax's mind it induced acute sensitivity to the war section of the Labour party. In synthetic reverse, it produced Hore-Belisha's attempt to present himself as a class-warrior after his removal from office in January 1940.

Whether the problem was synthetic or real, there was a sense that 'Toryism' and the 'gentle benevolence of the governing class' were 'dead' [29] and that it was necessary to establish a 'Tory Socialism, Red Jingoism [and] Marxian Imperialism' if Conservatives were to compete with the 'great radical-democratic party' which 'democrats of goodwill' hoped for in the future. [30]

This was a renewal, under pressure, of the Conservative 'truth' — that the social structure could only be preserved by talking about something else. [31] It slid slowly, through Eden's agency, from the hope that 'Conservatism' should usually be smiling into the assumption that war required 'real unity... comradeship and...equal opportunity for all...regardless of class or creed'. [32]

Eden may not have meant what he was taken as implying; nor had Chamberlain given offence by his earliest actions as Prime Minister. [33] Indeed, the composition of his Cabinet and the National Defence Contribution had left the impression that he wanted the Baldwinian consensus extended. But the provocations he offered about the League and the victory of February 20 1938 gave his enemies the opportunity to believe that a 'bourgeois shit' could not 'save England'. [34]

The class card was an instrument that came to hand in replacing one generation's Unionism by the revitalised Young Englandism of the next. It registered a fear that the mobilisation of manpower entailed the mobilisation of wealth, and that war would only be supported if a brighter future was promised for afterwards. [35]

These claims escalated when Prague made it uncertain whether Chamberlain could continue to perform the function of a Conservative leader. Whether he was to blame or whether he was the victim of those who had undermined his position, he was then the victim of a fateful collusion between a war policy embarked on in order to restore 'honour' to the 'Conservative cause' and the damage war would do to the structures the 'cause' was intended to protect.

If Chamberlain's pre-Munich policy had not been modified, if it had not been contested, and, even more, if it had succeeded, he would probably have won an election. That he was defeated without one was the result of Halifax's instinct that a difference of outlook had to be resolved.

The difference was about the interlocking options that had dominated analysis since 1934. Where previously Halifax and Chamberlain had agreed (as against the critics) that Imperial security, detachment from Russia, the defence of the Low Countries and a stable economy were of primary importance, Halifax now decided that the Empire should be risked, Russia attached and the economy endangered in order to 'destroy Nazism'.

In the course of 1939 the difference was accentuated by a growing belief that a 'contest was in progress between two theories of life' and that between the 'totalitarian' and the 'democratic', 'compromise' was 'impossible'.[36] This was not Chamberlain's point of view (or Halifax's in 1937); nor was the contest a real one, unless Stalin and Inönü are regarded as democrats. But it united sentiment by implying that the contest was a moral one.

For many of Chamberlain's critics, this became the logic of their *position*. So far as *policy* was concerned, the difference was between priorities. Up to March 1939, and between the following August and May 1940, Chamberlain's policy was not only a high-speed culmination of the policy adopted in 1934. It was also, except at Munich, so much the same as theirs that their criticisms were about the technique of negotiation and the names of the game he should be playing.

The names that were disputed were Peace, Collective Security and Making the World Safe for Democracy; the game was to find words to prevent war. Whether war could have been prevented was, however, a matter of judgment then and is counter-factual now, since all criticism of Chamberlain assumed that events would have been caused by hard words which were not caused by soft one. This is as impossible to verify as it seems to have been to predict that France would collapse. In fact, everyone assumed that France would not collapse.

Given the assumption of French impregnability, it is doubtful whether defence deficiencies had a direct effect on Chamberlain's policy, except in relation to Italy in 1937, in removing Cabinet dissent before Munich and marginally in the summer of 1939. Whatever their effect on Hitler, their effect on him was to confirm aims which would have been pursued even if rearmament had been massive.[37]

Chamberlain's object was to prevent a short-term, knock-out war and to produce conditions in which Hitler would be dissuaded from a long-term one. But he did not really embrace the possibility that a war would be fought out at length. Assured of naval superiority, therefore, he needed only to assume that an air attack on London could not be successful and that the French would not be defeated. In September 1939 air attack was expected, but it was expected also that it could be resisted. Whether the expectation was reasonable cannot be decided, since the Battle of Britain was fought (to a narrow margin) after a further year of preparation. But there can be little doubt that by mid-1939, but for Halifax, Chamberlain would have felt free to pursue the policy he wanted to pursue without restraint from logistical impossibility.

Similarly, the doubts which soldiers and Conservatives alike had felt about French resolution did not envisage the French armistice. Though resistance to blitzkrieg implied a repeat performance of 1914, most doubts about France concerned her ability to attack, not her ability to resist an attack from Germany. Even those who thought otherwise [38] stopped short of assuming that the worst would happen.

The problem of France had been the most awkward of the problems of the thirties. In 1933 it was agreed that the *defensive* interests of France, Britain and Belgium were the same. The problem arose as France's East European and, eventually, Russian commitments gained a new significance in face of German rearmament, and it slowly became clear that a defensive Locarno for western Europe alone was impossible.

This provided scope for disagreement. For, whereas London and Birmingham could be defended from France and Flanders, it was not obvious that France or Flanders would be attacked. So long as an attack seemed unlikely, Chamberlain refused to pay the price his critics wanted, while they moved on from advocating involvement with Russia through the League to direct involvement through an alliance.

After the Polish guarantee there was a military need for alliance, which the Chiefs of Staff put. But the political object had been to prise Chamberlain out of the position in which he could square the circle between the needs of national defence, the preferences of the Conservative party and the feelings of the vast body of peace-loving citizens everywhere.

The argument of 1939 treated Russia as crucial not in defeating Hitler but in deterring him from going to war, and not because the Russians were to be encouraged to resist him in Poland or attack him elsewhere, but because the Poles could not resist unless assured of Russian acquiescence. Even so, and even when Poland collapsed, there was no expectation that France would collapse too.

The assumption that France could fight a defensive land war was demolished within six weeks of Chamberlain's removal. But it was assumed so widely that Churchill's opportunity to be the nation's saviour arose only because he happened to be in office when the common assumption was demolished.

Nor, so far as Germany was concerned, were the contrasts significant. Churchill's belief in the German opposition was greater up to the beginning of the war. But his demands for resistance were almost as cautious as Attlee's. His Russian policy may well have been grounded in gullibilities as great as those he discerned in Roosevelt five years later.

If Hitler's object was to colonise eastern Europe, it is arguable (though Chamberlain did not argue) that Britain had no interest in stopping him. If he had to be stopped (because predominance in the East might entail predominance in the West), it was not obligatory to close options, since Stalin would mistrust Hitler whether there was a Russo-German pact or not. If the British interest was in keeping Hitler out of the Mediterranean and the Middle East, then Mussolini, Metaxas, Inönü, Carol (of Rumania) and Paul (of Yugoslavia) were the crucial figures, not Stalin, who also needed to be kept out, whose battles were not to be fought for him and whose collaboration would divert the Japanese into South-East Asia. If it was dangerous to guarantee Poland without making sure of Russia first, it should nevertheless be said, despite the paradox, that it was Hitler who 'stood alone' after the pact with Russia.

Hitler's abandonment of the anti-Comintern policy — a prime British objective since 1937 — was a direct consequence of the choice he faced after the guarantee to Poland. The choice would not have been made if Halifax had effected the Russian alliance for which the Opposition and the Chiefs of Staff were asking, though it may well have been the case that Stalin interpreted both Opposition pressure and Halifax's search as a concerted attempt to turn Hitler against him. [39] Even if Stalin did not think this, it is far from clear that Russian policy was so much what Maisky said it was that alliance with Russia would have been more valuable to Britain than the political damage Hitler suffered from his.

Even about Roosevelt, where Chamberlain's critics criticised him most emphatically, the contrasts were marginal. He preferred direct rapprochement with Japan to the uncertainties of Anglo-American co-operation and understood, much better than they did, the extent to which American half-commitments might produce an Anglo-Japanese war at the same time as Britain went to war with Germany.

About Japan, the pass had been sold in 1922 when British policy had become subservient to American. It was likely that war would increase subservience, and that the Anglo-American solidarity of Churchill, Eden and Duff Cooper would merely extend the arrangment MacDonald thought he had started by which special relations eased the pain of converting a world Empire into an off-shore debtor. [40]

A special relationship was desirable economically (as in saving the franc in 1936 and in the trade agreement of 1938). But there were three objections — that the United States was a commercial rival, that neutrality legislation made it impossible to rely on American support, [41] and that support, once given, would increase dependence, especially if the accession of strength took Britain, over-confidently, into war with Germany.

The war accelerated dependence. But it was implicit in the linked failures to preserve peace or develop a financial structure for Imperial defence.

For the failure to create an Imperial alliance, there were unavoidable reasons — the sparseness and reluctance of Australia and New Zealand, the Canadian and South African refusals and the difficulty in India. Despite Hankey's Commonwealth tour in 1934 and the Imperial Conferences three and five years later, there was no effective relationship between General Staffs. In London there was no doubt that maritime defence would be conducted by the Royal Navy, that the Middle East would be defended by the Indian and British armies and that the cost would be met by the British tax-payer.

So long as foreign policy could be kept under control, this presented no problem. Once it ran out of control, as a result of political and parliamentary incontinence, insuperable problems were presented.

These were not, as it turned out, the problems of late 1939, since Italy and Japan did not then go to war and it was unnecessary to knock out the Italian fleet (as would have been tried if the war had been fought on the lines that were expected). But the over-stretching of resources in 1938 reduced the plausibility of the deterrent in relation to Germany and made it necessary to pick up whatever reassurance could be picked up elsewhere. The moments of truth of 1942 were anticipated three years earlier when Chamberlain abandoned the two-year-old commitment to send the navy to protect Australasia in the event of war, a few months after Halifax had persuaded Roosevelt to send an American fleet to the Far East after Munich. [42]

There is no evidence that Chamberlain felt constrained by pressure from Dominions politicians. It is much more likely that he shared their assumptions and felt constrained by a fear that war would damage Imperial independence.

Neither Chamberlain nor the Chiefs of Staff wished to accelerate dependence. They wished primarily to keep the peace and keep out of eastern Europe in order to avoid the situation in which it would be America's frontiers that were on the Rhine. [43] After the guarantees of 1939 that situation had come closer, with Italy and Japan lost (by comparison with 1918) and only Turkish neutrality to take their place.

That it arrived was an effect less of strategic decisions than of the propaganda developed by Chamberlain's critics. That the Chiefs of Staff had then to turn against Chamberlain over Russia is a testimony to the critics' effectiveness. That Chamberlain and Stalin thwarted them shows how precarious their influence was.

This is in no way to belittle their achievement, but rather to draw attention to its nature, which consisted less in the establishment of a policy than in the creation of a régime and the achievement for Churchill of the status of a hero.

About the heroism, there was an ambiguity which presented defeat as victory and cushioned 'Imperialism' into decline. During the war the Imperial grip tightened in Delhi, Cairo and Bagdad at the same time as the new régime took a grip in Whitehall. That the declaration of war had narrowed the options became obvious when Singapore fell, when Churchill fell in 1945 and when the United States came into its own as a World Power. More even than after the first' war, debt coincided with domestic demand to compel toothless retreat in the decades following.

In the historical half-light, it is difficult to know whether the death that has been described was the death of Empire or the murder of pre-1914 mentalities. In the long run, the two processes may be the same, since some part of the conflict of the thirties registered transitions (with whatever distortion war casualties had created) from politicians in their sixties to politicians in their forties and thirties. In either case it provided opportunities, which politicians seized, to lock Hitler and Mussolini in hostile embrace and use them to discredit the generation before until compelled (by success) to face up to the crisis which hostility had helped to create.

In relation to the Empire, transitions centred around Europe. Whether from Cobdenite or from Chamberlainite assumptions, the pre-1914 generation had opposed anything more than the most prudent of European connections. For the generation born in the nineties, the salient experience was European war and European commitment. Despite the isolationist undercurrent of the twenties, the consequence was a flight from Little England and Imperial assumptions to the internationalist involvements of 1945.

The involvements of 1945 were not intended to exclude, were, indeed, designed to protect, the Empire, at whose zenith many loyal members of the Attlee government had been born. But the facts of war established an exigency which it is probable that no government could have avoided.

For the Attlee government it was possible, however painful, to reverse the euphoria of victory, since the 'liquidation of Empire' had found a place in the Labour party in the thirties. For Churchill, though possible, this would have been difficult, since he had identified resistance to dictators with its preservation.

It may be that the Empire would not have been preserved

if resistance had been avoided. Even if it would have been, even if Portuguese obstinacy could have been effective, an unedifying story is relieved by the consideration that, of the millions who died in the holocaust which destroyed the peace it needed, comparatively few were its citizens, of whom fewer perished than perished at a stroke in Bengal and the Punjab three years after the holocaust was over.

APPENDIX: THE ACTORS

(Ages in 1936)

(These notes do not normally cover careers after 1936. Where an actor is very well-known or has a bibliography in the text, he is omitted from this Appendix.)

Acland, Rt. Hon. Sir Francis Dyke (62). ed. Rugby and Balliol College, Oxford. 1908-16 Junior office. MP (Lib) Richmond 1906-10, Camborne 1910-22, Tiverton 1923 and N. Cornwall 1932- .

Acland, Richard Dyke (30). ed. Rugby and Balliol. Son of Sir Francis Acland. MP (Lib) Barnstaple 1935- .

Addison, Christopher (67). ed. Trinity College, Harrogate and St Bartholomew's Hospital. ex-Professor Anatomy. MP (Lib) 1910-22. MP (Lab) Swindon 1929-31 and 1934-5. 1914-16 junior minister. 1916-21 Minister of Munitions, etc. 1929-31 Parliamentary Secretary, then Minister of Agriculture.

Aga Khan, The (59). Head of Ismaili Mahometans. President of League of Nations Assembly 1937. Representative of Indian government at international conferences.

Alexander, Albert Victor (51). Elementary School and Technical Classes. Baptist lay preacher. Ex-employee of Somerset Education Committee. Captain in army in World War. Secretary of Parliamentary Committee of Co-operative Congress. MP (Co-op) Hillsborough, Sheffield 1922-31 and 1935- . Told off by Keyes for using Christian names.

Allen of Hurtwood, Reginald Clifford Allen, 1st Baron (47). ed. Berkhamstead, Bristol and Peterhouse, Cambridge. 1911-15 *Daily Citizen*. 1922-6 Chairman of ILP. 1921-6 Chairman of *New Leader*. War-time Conscientious Objector. A MacDonald peer.

Anderson, Sir John (54). ed. George Watson's College, Edinburgh. Edinburgh and Leipzig universities. 1905-32 Civil Servant (inc. Permanent Under-Secretary Home Office). 1932-37 Governor of Bengal. Offered High Commissionership in Palestine in 1937.

Angell, Sir Norman (62). ed. France and Geneva. 1898- Journalist and publicist. Author of *The Great Illusion (1908)* and many other political books. 1929-31 MP (Lab) North Bradford. 1933, Nobel Peace Prize. Ex-Liberal. A MacDonald knighthood.

Arnold, Sydney, 1st Lord. ex-Lib, office holder in 1924 and 1929-31 Governments. Stockbroker, friend of MacDonald. Resigned from Labour party in 1936 over foreign policy.

Astor, Waldorf, 2nd Viscount (57). ed. Eton and New College, Oxford. MP (C) Plymouth 1910-19. 1918-21 Parliamentary Secretary (including PS to Lloyd George 1918). Author of works about agriculture.

Astor, Nancy, Viscountess (57). Wife of 2nd Viscount Astor. American.

MP (U) for Plymouth 1919- . The more she saw of Eden, 'the more certain' she was that he would 'never be a Disraeli'.

Astor, W.W. (29). Son of 2nd Viscount. ed Eton and New College, Oxford. 1932 Secretary to Lord Lytton. 1936-9 PPS to Hoare. MP (U) East Fulham 1935- .

Atholl, Katharine Duchess of (62). Daughter of Scottish baronet. ed. Wimbledon High School and Royal College of Music. MP (U) Kinross 1923-. 1924-29 junior minister. Resigned Conservative Whip over India bill and 'socialist' tendency of government's domestic policy (in 1935) and over Anglo-Italian agreement (in 1937). Supporter of Spanish Republic as 'a government which used Moors could not be a national government'.

Ball, Sir Joseph (51). ed. King's College School, Strand and King's College, London. Called to Bar. Served in war. 1930-9 Director of Conservative Research Department.

Balogh, Thomas (31). ed. Budapest, Berlin and Harvard. Ex-member of League of Nations Staff. Economist in City. 1938- National Institute of Economic Research.

Barry, Gerald Reid (38). ed. Marlborough and Corpus Christi College, Cambridge. Served in war. 1921-34 Assistant editor, then editor of *Saturday Review* and *Week-End Review*. 1936- Managing Editor of *News Chronicle*.

Bartlett, Vernon (42) 1916- Journalist and foreign correspondent; also broadcaster. 1934- staff of *News Chronicle*. Author. First became famous with broadcast in October 1933 and *Nazi Germany Explained* in which basically pro-Hitler and pro-treaty revision position was put with Layton-like touch.

Beaverbrook, William 1st Baron (57). Canadian millionaire. MP (U) 1910-16. 1918 Chancellor of Duchy of Lancaster. Proprietor of *Daily Express* and *Evening Standard*. May possibly have wanted to be Minister of Agriculture in early 1940.

Bernays, Robert H (34). ed. Rossall and Worcester College, Oxford. 1925-31 *News Chronicle* (leader writer, then Special Corr.) Nov. 1931 PPS to Colonial Under-Secretary. 1937- junior office. MP (Lib (Nat) Bristol N. 1931-.

Berry, Michael (25). ed. Eton and Christ Church, Oxford. Younger son of 1st Viscount Camrose. Friend of Randolph Churchill and believed (by Chamberlain) to be responsible for some of the *Telegraph* criticism. Brother of J. Seymour Berry who was in effective control of *Telegraph* after Camrose. Married Birkenhead's daughter.

Betterton, Sir Henry (64). ed. Rugby and Christ Church, Oxford. Bar. MP (U) Rushcliffe 1918-34. 1923-4 and 1924-9 junior minister. 1931-4 Minister of Labour. 1935 Lord Rushcliffe.

Bevan, Aneurin (39). ed. Elementary school. Central Labour College. Coal-miner etc. MP (Lab) Ebbw Vale 1929- .

Bevin, Ernest (56). ed. Elementary school. 1922- Secretary, Transport and General Workers Union. 1937 Chairman of TUC General Council. Euan Wallace thought him 'glib and forthcoming'.

Bonham-Carter, Lady Violet (49). Asquith's daughter. Prominent in

Liberal politics.

Boothby, Robert (36). ed. Eton and Magdalen College, Oxford. 1926-9 PPS to Churchill. MP (C) East Aberdeenshire 1924. Married (briefly) into Cavendish/Cecil families.

Bracken, Brendan (35). ed. Sydney and Sedbergh. Publisher and newspaper director (*Financial News* and *Economist*). MP (U) North Paddington 1929-.

Bridgeman, William Clive 1st Viscount (d 1935). ed. Eton and Trinity College, Cambridge. 1889-99 Assistant to Knutsford and Hicks-Beach. MP (C) Oswestry 1906-29. 1911-29 junior minister and minister in Conservative and Coalition governments. Friend of Baldwin.

Bridges, Edward (44). ed. Eton and Magdalen College, Oxford. 1938-Secretary to the Cabinet after Hankey's retirement.

Brocket, Arthur Ronald Nall-Cain, 2nd Baron (32). ed. Eton and Magdalen College, Oxford. MP (U) Wavertree 1931-4.

Brown, Ernest (55). ed. Torquay. MP (Lib) Rugby 1923, (Lib) Leith 1927-31 and (Lib Nat) Leith 1931-. Baptist lay preacher. Commissioned in War (MC). Ormsby-Gore thought him 'the salt of the earth' and 'the best type of bible-loving nonconformist' who would have 'no use for the neo-paganism of Germany'.

Bryant, Arthur (37). ed. Harrow and Queen's College, Oxford. Bar. Served in War. Further education teacher, journalist and historian (works on *Charles II, Macaulay, Pepys, The National Character, George V* etc.).

Buccleuch, Walter J. Montagu-Douglas-Scott, 8th Duke of (42). ed. Eton and Christ Church, Oxford. MP (U) Roxburgh and Selkirk 1923-35. A prominent visitor to Hitler before 1939.

Burgin, Edward Leslie (49). ed. Christ's College, Finchley and abroad. Solicitor. War (General Staff) in Italy. 1932-7 junior office. 1937-Minister of Transport. MP (Lib) Luton 1929-31 and (Nat Lib) 1931-45.

Butler, Richard Austen (34). ed. Marlborough and Pembroke College, Cambridge (Fellow of Corpus). 1932-7 Under-Secretary at India Office. 1937-8 Parliamentary Secretary to the Ministry of Labour. 1938- Under Secretary at the Foreign Office and chief Foreign Office spokesman in House of Commons. Lloyd George intended a compliment when describing him as 'playing the part of the imperturbable dunce who says nothing with an air of conviction'.

Cadman, Sir John Cadman (1st Baron 1937) (59). ed. Newcastle High School and Armstrong College, Durham. Colliery Manager, then Inspector of Mines. 1908-20 Professor of Mining, University of Birmingham. Chairman of Anglo-Iranian and Iraq Petroleum Companies. Member of Government Commissions.

Cadogan, Sir Alexander (52). ed. Eton and Oxford. Ambassador in Peking. 1936-7 Deputy Under-Secretary at Foreign Office. 1938. Permanent Under-Secretary.

Camrose, William Ewart Berry, 1st Baron (57). Brother of Kemsley, born in Merthyr Tydfil. Journalist and newspaper proprietor. 1928-editor-in-chief of *Daily Telegraph* which both before and after absorbing the *Morning Post* was an expanding, effective and important newspaper.

Cartland, Ronald (29). ed. Charterhouse. 1927-35 Conservative Central Office. MP (U) King's Norton 1935- .

Chamberlain, Ivy Muriel, Lady, wife and then widow of Sir Austen Chamberlain. Had close contact with highest reaches of the Italian government.

Channon, Henry (39). ed. America and Christ Church, Oxford. American who married into Guinness family. Author. MP (U), Southend 1935-.

Chatfield, Admiral of the Fleet Sir Ernle (63). Navy since 1886. 1933-8 1st Sea Lord. 1939-40 Minister for Co-ordination of Defence (Baron 1937).

Churchill, Randolph Frederick Spencer (25). Son of W.S. Churchill. ed. Eton and Christ Church, Oxford. Journalist. Stood as Ind. C. at Wavertree, Toxteth and Ross and Cromarty in 1935-6.

Citrine, Sir Walter (49). ed. Elementary school. 1926- General Secretary of TUC.

Clynes, John Robert (68). 1917-19 Office in Lloyd George Coalition. 1921-2 Chairman parliamentary Labour party. 1924 and 1929-31 Member of Labour Cabinets. MP (Lab), Platting 1906-31 and 1935-.

Cockburn, Claud (32). ed. Berkhamstead School and Keble College, Oxford. 1929-32 Correspondent of *The Times*. 1933-46 editor of *The Week* (where Clivedenism was invented). 1935-46 Diplomatic Correspondent of the *Daily Worker*.

Colville, David John (42). ed. Charterhouse and Trinity College, Cambridge. War. Director of family steel companies. 1931-5 Secretary, Department of Overseas Trade, 1935-6 Parliamentary Under-Secretary for Scotland. 1936-8 Financial Secretary to the Treasury. 1938- Secretary of State for Scotland. A 'good, plodding chap'.

Cooper, Alfred Duff (46). Son of doctor who married the daughter of a duke. ed. Eton and New College, Oxford. War. Foreign Service. 1928-9 and 1931-5 junior minister. 1935-7 Secretary of State for War. 1937-8 1st Lord of Admiralty. MP (U), Oldham 1924-9 and St George's, Westminster 1931-. Author of *Talleyrand* and *Haig*.

Coward, Noël (37). Actor and playwright (*Bitter Sweet*, *Cavalcade* etc. in the thirties).

Crewe, Robert O.A. Crewe-Milnes, 1st Marquis of (78). ed. Harrow and Trinity College, Cambridge. 1892-5 and 1905-16 Minister in Liberal and Asquith Coalition governments. August-October 1931 Secretary of State for War.

Croft, Sir Henry Page (55). ed. Eton, Shrewsbury and Trinity Hall, Cambridge. MP (C), Christchurch 1910-18 and Bournemouth 1918- . Brigadier in war.

Crookshank, Harry F.C. (43). ed. Eton and Magdalen College, Oxford. War, then Diplomatic Service. 1934-5 junior minister. 1935- Secretary for Mines. MP (U) Gainsborough 1924- . Much disliked by Ramsay MacDonald (owing to attacks in 1929 Parliament).

Crossley, Anthony C. (33). ed. Eton and Magdalen College, Oxford. 1932-5 PPS to Under-Secretary at Ministry of Transport. MP (C) for Oldham 1931-5 and Stretford 1935- .

Crozier, William Percival (57). ed. Manchester Grammar School and Trinity College, Oxford. 1903- *Manchester Guardian* (editor 1932-).

Culverwell, Cyril Tom (41). ed. Clifton College and Queens' College, Cambridge. War. Bristol councillor. MP (U) Bristol West 1928-45.

Cummings, Arthur John (54). War. 1920-32, *Daily Chronicle*, then *News Chronicle*. 1932- . Editor and chief commentator in *News Chronicle*.

Cunliffe-Lister (see Swinton).

Dallas, George (68). ed. Elementary school, Technical College, London School of Economics. ILP. MP (Lab), Wellingborough 1929-31.

Dalton, Hugh (49). ed. Eton and King's College, Cambridge. War. Lecturer and Reader (in Economics) at London School of Economics. 1929-31 Parliamentary Under-Secretary at Foreign Office. Author. MP (Lab) Peckham 1924-9 and Bishop Auckland 1929-31 and 1935- .

Davidson, John Colin Campbell (47). ed. Westminster and Pembroke College, Cambridge. 1913-23 Private Secretary and PPS to Crewe, Harcourt, Law, Austen Chamberlain and Baldwin. 1923-4 Chancellor of the Duchy of Lancaster. 1924-7 junior minister. 1927-30 Chairman of Unionist Party. 1931-7 Chancellor of Duchy of Lancaster. MP (U) Hemel Hempstead 1920-3 and 1924-37. Associated with Salisbury in Moral Rearmament.

Davies, David Davies, 1st Baron (56). ed. Merchiston School and King's College, Cambridge. Colliery owner. MP (Lib) Montgomeryshire 1906-29. Cecil thought him 'a bull in a china shop'.

Dawson, Geoffrey (*né* Robinson) (62). ed. Eton and Magdalen College, Oxford (Fellow of All Souls). 1898-1901 Colonial Office. 1901-5 PS to Milner. 1905-10 Editor, *Johannesburg Star*. 1922- Editor of *The Times*.

de la Warr, Herbrand Edward Brassey Sackville, 6th Earl (36). ed. Eton and Magdalen College, Oxford.

Denman, Richard Douglas (60). ed. Westminster and Balliol College, Oxford. 1905-18 Private Secretary/PPS to Lord Buxton, Lord Ernle and H.A.L. Fisher. 1931- Second Church Estates Commissioner. MP (Lib) Carlisle 1910-18, (Lab) Central Leeds 1929-31, (Nat. Lab) 1931- .

Derby, Edward George Stanley, 17th Earl of (71). 1895-1903 junior minister. 1903-5 Postmaster-General. 1915-16 Director-General of Recruiting. 1916-18 and 1922-4 Secretary for War. 1918-20 Ambassador to France.

Devonshire, Edward W. Spencer Cavendish, 10th Duke of (41). Wife a Cecil. ed. Eton and Trinity College, Cambridge. War. 1936- Parliamentary Under-Secretary for Dominions. MP (U) West Derbyshire 1922-38. Vice-President of India Defence League.

Dill, Lieut.-General Sir John (55). ed. Cheltenham College and Sandhurst. 1901- army (1934-6 Director of Military Operations, War Office).

Dorman-Smith, Sir Reginald (Kt 1937) (37). ed. Harrow and Sandhurst. Indian and British armies. 1931-5 Surrey County Alderman. 1936-7 President of National Union of Farmers. 1939-40 Minister of Agriculture. MP (C) Petersfield 1935-.

Drummond, James Eric, 16th Earl of Perth (succeeded 1937) (60). ed. Eton. 1900-19 Foreign Office. 1919-33 Secretary-General to League of Nations. 1933-9 Ambassador to Italy. 1939-40 Ministry of Information. Ivy Chamberlain was not alone in thinking that he had little contact with Mussolini.

Dugdale, Mrs Edgar (Blanche Campbell) (56). 1915-19 Naval Intelligence. 1920-8 Permanent staff of League of Nations Union. 1932 member of British delegation to Geneva. Author of *Life of Arthur James Balfour*.

Duncan, Sir Andrew Rae (52). ed. Canada and Glasgow University. 1919-20 Coal Controller. 1927-35 Chairman Central Electricity Board. 1929-40 Director of Bank of England. 1935-40 Chairman of Executive Committee, Iron and Steel Federation.

Dunglass, Alexander Frederick Douglas-Home, Lord (33). ed. Eton. 1937-9 PPS to Chamberlain. MP (U) South Lanark 1931-.

Elton, Godfrey Elton, 1st Baron (46). ed. Rugby and Balliol College, Oxford. War. 1919-39 Fellow of Queen's College, Oxford. Labour candidate 1924 and 1929; followed MacDonald in 1931. National Labour publicist; author of life of Ramsay MacDonald.

Fisher, Sir Norman Warren (57). ed. Winchester and New College, Oxford. 1903-39 Civil Service (Permanent Secretary to the Treasury 1919-39). 1939 Regional Commissioner for North-West Region.

Foot, Dingle Mackintosh (31). Son of Isaac Foot. ed. Bembridge School and Balliol College, Oxford. Barrister. MP (Lib) Dundee 1931-.

Gaitskell, H.T.N. (30). ed. Winchester and New College, Oxford. Academic Economist (University of London). Contested Chatham (Lab) 1935. Friend and follower of Dalton.

Garnett, J.C. Maxwell (56). ed. St Paul's and Trinity College, Cambridge. Mathematician (Fellow of Trinity, Lecturer in London, School Examiner and Principal of Manchester College of Technology). 1920-38 Secretary of League of Nations Union. League of Nations publicist.

Garvin, James Louis (68). Birkenhead Irishman. ed. Catholic elementary school. *Newcastle Chronicle*. 1912-5 editor of *Pall Mall Gazette*. 1908- editor of the *Observer*.

Gilmour, Sir John Gilmour (60). ed. Glenalmond, Edinburgh University and Trinity College, Cambridge. S. African and World War. 1913-15 and 1919-23 junior whip. 1924-9 Scottish Secretary. 1931-2 Minister of Agriculture. 1932-5 Home Secretary. MP (C) East Renfrewshire, 1910-18 and Pollock 1918-.

Gollancz, Victor (43). ed. St Paul's and New College, Oxford. Schoolmaster and then publisher (Victor Gollancz Ltd). Publicist.

Gort, J.S.S.P.V., 6th Viscount (50). ed. Harrow and Sandhurst. Army
1905- .
Greenwood, Arthur (56). ed. Victoria University, Manchester. Lecturer
in Economics (at Leeds etc.). Wartime Civil Servant (Reconstruction
Committee 1917-19). 1924 junior minister. 1929-31 Minister of
Health. 1935 deputy leader of the Labour party. MP (Lab) Nelson
and Colne 1922-31 and Wakefield 1932- .
Grenfell, David Rhys (55). Coal miner until age of 35, then miners'
agent. MP (Lab) Gower, 1922-.
Grigg, Sir Edward (57). ed. Winchester and New College, Oxford.
1903-13 Times journalist. 1914-21 army etc. 1921-2 Private Secre-
tary to Lloyd George. 1925-31 Governor of Kenya. MP (Nat Lib)
Oldham 1922-5 and for Altrincham 1933- . Author and publicist.
Grigg, Sir Percy James (46). ed. Bournemouth School and St John's
College, Cambridge. 1913-34 civil servant, 1934-9 Finance Member
Govt. of India. 1939- Permanent Under-Secretary at the War Office.
Hadley, William Waite (70). 1892-1923 editor of Merthyr Tydfil Times,
Rochdale Observer and Northampton Mercury. 1924-30 Daily
Chronicle. 1932- editor of Sunday Times.
Hailsham, Douglas McGarel Hogg, 1st Viscount (64). ed. Eton. Worked
for firm of West India merchants. South African war. 1902 Called to
Bar. 1920- (intermittently) director of Insurance company. 1922-4
and 1924-8 Attorney General. 1928-9 Lord Chancellor. 1931-5 Sec-
retary of State for War. 1935-8 Lord Chancellor. May to November
1938 Lord President of the Council. MP (C) St Marylebone 1922-8.
One of the leaders of the more conservative part of the Conservative
party.
Hankey, Sir Maurice (59). ed. Rugby. 1885-1902 Marine. 1902-6 Naval
Intelligence. 1912-38 Secretary to CID. 1919-38 Secretary to Cabinet. Preferred 'plain patriotism and self-protection' to 'high-falutin
principles'. Did not like 'Conchies'.
Hannon, Sir Patrick (62). Company director. ed. Royal College of Science and Royal University of Ireland. Agricultural co-operator (in
Ireland and South Africa), Tariff reformer, Navy Leaguer and arma-
ments manufacturer. MP (U) Moseley 1921- .
Hardinge, Alexander H.L. (42). ed. Harrow and Trinity College, Cam-
bridge. War. 1920-36 Assistant Private Secretary to King George V.
1936 Private Secretary to Edward VIII. 1936 Private Secretary to
King George VI. Neville Chamberlain wanted to send him to Madras
in 1939 because he kept the King aloof from his subjects.
Harmsworth, Esmond (38). ed. Eton. 1919 ADC to Lloyd George. MP
(U) Isle of Thanet 1919-29.
Harris, H. Wilson (54). ed. Plymouth College and St John's College,
Cambridge. For over twenty years a member of the editorial staff of
the Liberal Daily News. Author of political works including two on
the League of Nations. 1932- editor of the Spectator.
Harris, Sir Percy Alfred (60). ed. Harrow and Trinity Hall, Cambridge.
LCC 1907-34 (Progressive Whip 1912-15, Deputy Chairman

1915-16). 1935 Chief Liberal Whip. MP (Lib) Harborough 1916-18 and S.W. Bethnal Green 1922- . Did not like Samuel's leadership.

Hart, Basil H. Liddell (41). ed. St Paul's School and Corpus Christi College, Cambridge. War. 1925-35 Military Correspondent of *Daily Telegraph*. 1935-9 do. for *The Times*. Author of many works of military theory.

Harvey, Oliver Charles (43). ed. Malvern and Trinity College, Cambridge. War. 1919-36 Foreign Service. 1936-9 Principal Private Secretary to Foreign Secretary. 1940 Minister in Paris. Halifax seems to have responded less than Eden to his political advice.

Harvey, Thomas Edmund (61). ed. Bootham School, Yorkshire College, Leeds, Christ Church, Oxford and Berlin and Paris Universities. 1900-4 British Museum. 1906-11 Warden of Toynbee Hall. LCC. MP (Lib) West Leeds 1910-18 and Dewsbury 1923-4, MP (Ind. Progressive) Combined English Universities 1937- . Author of works on religion.

Headlam, Sir Cuthbert (59). ed. King's School, Canterbury and Magdalen College, Oxford. 1897-1924, Permanent official in Parliament. War. MP (Cons) Barnard Castle 1924-9 and 1931-5. 1926-9 and 1931-3 junior office. 'How he disliked Baldwin' after being dismissed in 1933 'no tongue [could] tell'.

Heath, Edward R.G. (20). ed. Chatham House School, Ramsgate and Balliol College, Oxford. 1937 President of Oxford University Conservative Association. 1939 President of Oxford Union. Supported Lindsay at 1938 Oxford by-election against the Conservative candidate.

Henderson, Arthur (died 1935 at age of 72). ed. Elementary school. 1911-34 Secretary of Labour party. 1930-5 Treasurer of Labour party. 1908-10, 1914-7 and 1931-2 Leader of parliamentary Labour party. 1915-17 Minister in Asquith and Lloyd George Coalitions. 1924 Home Secretary, 1929-31 Foreign Secretary. When MacDonald met him at Geneva in 1933, he thought him more and more like 'a stolid iron-moulder who goes to chapel and controls its morals and finances'.

Henderson, Sir Nevile Meyrick (54). ed. Eton. 1905- Diplomatic Service (1932-5 Ambassador in Belgrade, 1935-7 in Buenos Aires, 1937-9 in Berlin).

Herbert, Sir Sidney (Baronet 1936) (46). ed. Eton and Balliol College, Oxford. 1919-20 PPS to Churchill. 1922-3 PPS to Halifax (Wood). August 1923 and 1924-7 PPS to Baldwin. MP (C) Scarborough 1922-31 and Abbey, Westminster 1932- .

Hicks, Ernest George (57) ed. Elementary school and Polytechnic. Bricklayer, then trade union official. 1921-40 Secretary of Amalgamated Union of Building Trade Workers. 1926-7 President of TUC. Member of many TUC and government committees.

Hinsley, Most. Rev. Arthur (71). ed. Ushaw College, Rome (Professor at Ushaw 1893-7). 1898-1917 priest and schoolmaster in England. 1917-28 Rector of the English College in Rome. 1935 Archbishop of Westminster.

Hirst, Francis W. (63). ed. Clifton and Wadham College, Oxford. 1907-16 editor *The Economist.* Ex-Liberal candidate. Author of many Liberal books on politics and economics. Mentioned as a possible Chancellor of the Exchequer on formation of first Labour government.

Hodges, Frank (49). ed. Elementary school, Abertillery, Ruskin and Labour College Oxford and Oxford Labour Colleges. Miner, then miners' agent. The centre of the events which led up to Black Friday in 1921. 1924 junior minister. MP (Lab) Lichfield 1923-4. From 1927 onwards a member of the Central Electricity Authority. Clubs: Bath, Royal Automobile and New, Glasgow.

Hogg, Quintin McGarel (29). ed. Eton and Christ Church, Oxford. Fellow of All Souls College. Barrister. MP (Nat Cons) Oxford City, 1938- .

Hopkinson, Austin (58). South African war. Industrialist. Author of *The Hope of the Workers* and *Religio Militis.* MP (Ind.). Mossley 1918-29 and 1931-45.

Horne, Sir Robert (1st Viscount 1937) (65). ed. George Watson's College, Edinburgh University of Glasgow. Scottish Bar. 1919-20 Minister of Labour. 1920-1 President of Board of Trade. 1921-2 Chancellor of Exchequer. Part of the Austen Chamberlain/Birkenhead group after 1922. Thereafter in City. 1918-37 MP (C) Hillhead.

Hudson, Robert Spear (50). ed. Eton and Magdalen College, Oxford. 1911-23 Foreign Service. 1931-5 Parliamentary Secretary to Ministry of Labour. 1935-6 Minister of Pensions. 1936-7 Parliamentary Secretary to Ministry of Health. 1937-40 Secretary, Department of Overseas Trade. April-May 1940 Minister of Shipping. MP (U) Whitehaven 1924-9 and Southport 1931- . Cadogan claimed to have stopped him becoming Minister of Economic Warfare in 1939.

Ironside, General Sir Edmund (56). ed. Tonbridge and Royal Military Academy. 1899- army. 1936-8 GOC Eastern Command. 1938-9 Governor of Gibraltar. 1939-40 CIGS.

Ismay, Colonel H.L. (49). ed. Charterhouse and Sandhurst. 1905- army. 1926-30 A/Sec. CID. 1931-33 MIlitary Secretary to Viceroy of India. 1933-6 War Office. 1936-8 Deputy Secretary, CID. 1938 Secretary CID.

Johnson, Very Rev. Hewlett (62). ed. King Edward's School, Macclesfield and Victoria University, Manchester. 1905 Ordination. 1931- Dean of Canterbury. Communist author of *The Socialist Sixth of the World* (many editions in many languages).

Johnstone, Harcourt (41). ed. Eton and Balliol College, Oxford. War. MP (Lib) East Willesden 1923-4 and South Shields 1931-5.

Jones, Thomas (66). ed. Pengam County School, University College Aberystwyth and Glasgow University. 1909-10 Professor Economics, Queen's, Belfast. 1912-16 Secretary, National Health Insurance Commissioners (Wales). Brought into Cabinet Secretariat by Lloyd George. After Lloyd George's fall, a close friend of Baldwin. A Fabian. 1930-45 Secretary of Pilgrim Trust. 1934-40 Member of Unemployment Assistance Board. Thought J.H. Thomas had 'fallen a victim to the two weaknesses of his class'.

Kemsley, James Gomer Berry 1st Baron (53). Newspaper proprietor (including many provincial papers and the *Sunday Times*).

Keynes, John Maynard (53). ed. Eton and King's College, Cambridge (Fellow and Bursar). Government adviser and member of commissions. Author of *The Economic Consequences of the Peace, The End of Laissez-Faire, A Treatise on Money* and *The General Theory of Employment, Interest and Money* (1936).

King-Hall, Commander Stephen (43). ed. Lausanne, Osborne and Dartmouth. Retired from navy in 1929. Publicist and commentator on public affairs (1936 *King-Hall News Letter*). Broadcaster. MP (Ind. Nat) Ormskirk 1939. Member of National Labour party.

Laski, Harold J. (43). ed. Manchester Grammar School and New College, Oxford. 1926- Professor of Political Science in University of London. 1922-36 Executive of Fabian Society. 1936- Executive Committee of Labour party. Prolific publicist and journalist.

Law, Richard Kidston (35). ed. Shrewsbury and St John's College, Oxford. Journalist, then MP (U) S.W. Hull, 1931-. Attracted MacDonald's attention as rebel in 1934.

Layton, Sir Walter Thomas (52). ed. King's College School, Westminster City School, King's College, London and Trinity College, Cambridge. 1909- Economics Fellow of Gonville and Caius College, Cambridge. 1922-38 Editor of *The Economist*. Parliamentary candidate (Lib) in the twenties.

Lindemann, Frederick Alexander (50). ed. Blair Lodge, Darmstadt, Berlin and Paris. 1919- Professor of Experimental Philosophy at Oxford.

Lindsay, Alexander Dunlop (57). ed. Glasgow University and University College, Oxford. War. 1924- Master of Balliol College. 1935-8 Vice-Chancellor of Oxford University. Author of works on politics and philosophy. Member of Labour party.

Lindsay, Kenneth (39). ed. St Olave's and Worcester College, Oxford. War. 1923-6 Toynbee Hall and Stepney Guardian and Councillor. 1931-5 General Secretary Political and Economic Planning. 1935-40 junior office. MP (Ind. National) 1933- . Thought 'the brown naked bodies of the Hitler Jugend...different from the bodies produced by the Rt. Hon. Kingsley Wood'. Zionist.

Linlithgow, Victor A.J. Hope, 2nd Marquess of (49). ed. Eton. War. 1922-4 junior minister. 1924-6 Deputy Chairman of Conservative party. 1936-43 Viceroy of India. Never an MP.

Lloyd, Geoffrey William (34). ed. Harrow and Trinity College, Cambridge. 1926-31 Private Secretary to first Hoare and then Baldwin. 1931-5 PPS to Baldwin. 1935-9 junior minister. 1939-40 Secretary for Mines. MP (U) Ladywood 1931-.

Lloyd, George Ambrose 1st Baron (57). ed. Eton and Trinity College, Cambridge. War. 1918-23 Governor of Bombay. 1925-9 High Commissioner in Egypt. MP (C) Stafford 1910-18 and Eastbourne 1924-5.

Lloyd George, Gwilym (42). ed. Eastbourne College and Jesus College,

Cambridge. 1931 and 1939- junior minister. MP (Lib) Pembrokeshire 1922-4 and 1929- .

Londonderry, Charles H. Vane-Tempest-Stewart, 7th Marquess of (58). ed. Sandhurst. War. 1936-7 Mayor of Durham. 1920-21 junior minister. 1921-6 minister in N. Ireland government. 1928-9 and 1931 1st Commisioner of Works. 1931-5 Air Minister. In the four years after his removal in 1935, his resentments were poured out in innumerable and unanswered letters to Baldwin.

Londonderry, Edith, Marchioness of (58), wife of above. Daughter of Henry Chaplin, 1st viscount Chaplin. Close friend of Ramsay MacDonald whom she described (in her *Retrospect*) as admiring 'old families', disliking 'the new with a bitter hatred' and 'expressing opinions that other people...would never dare to express aloud' about 'the system in which money has made all things possible'.

Loraine, Sir Percy (56). ed. Eton and New College, Oxford. 1904-41 Foreign Service. 1933-9 Ambassador in Ankara. 1939-40 Ambassador in Rome.

Lothian, Philip Henry Kerr, 11th Marquess of (54). ed. Oratory, Birmingham and New College, Oxford. 1910-16 editor of *Round Table*. 1916-21 PS to Lloyd George. 1921-2 Director of United Newspapers. Aug.-Nov. 1931 Chancellor of Duchy of Lancaster. 1931-2 Under-Secretary for India. Kipling resigned when he became Secretary of the Rhodes Trustees.

Low, David (45). ed. Christchurch, New Zealand. Cartoonist, mainly in *Evening Standard*.

Lytton, Victor Alexander G.R. Lytton, 2nd Earl of (60). ed. Eton and Trinity College, Cambridge. 1916-22 junior minister. 1922-7 Governor of Bengal. 1932 Chairman of League of Nations Mission to Manchuria.

Mabane, William (41). ed. Woodhouse Grove School and Gonville and Caius College, Cambridge. War. 1920-3 Warden of University settlement, Liverpool. 1921-39 Company Director, 1931-2 and 1939- junior minister. MP (Lib Nat) 1931-.

McEwen, J.H.F. (42). ed. Eton and Trinity College, Cambridge. War. 1920-9 Diplomatic Service. 1938-9 Assistant Whip. 1939- junior minister. Author (inc. *Gallantry* with Sir Arnold Wilson). MP (U) Berwick and Haddington 1931- .

McKenna, Reginald (73). ed. St Malo, Ebersdorf and King's College, Cambridge. Barrister. 1905-7 junior officer. 1907-16 Cabinet (inc. 1915-6 Chancellor of the Exchequer). 1919- Chairman of Midland Bank. MP (Lib) N. Monmouthshire 1895-1918.

Maclean, Sir Donald (died 1932 aged 68). Solicitor. MP (Lib) 1906-18 and 1929-32.

Macmillan, Hugh Pattison, Baron (life peer) (63). ed. Edinburgh University. Scottish Bar. 1918 In Ministry of Information. 1924 Lord Advocate for Scotland. Chairman of Commissions. 1930-9 Lord of Appeal.

Maisky, Ivan (52). ed. Omsk, St Petersburg and Munich universities. 1932- Soviet Ambassador in London.

Mander, Geoffrey Le Mesurier (54). ed. Harrow and Trinity College, Cambridge. Company Chairman. MP (Lib) Wolverhampton East 1929- .

Mann, Arthur (60). Editor of *Yorkshire Post*. Friendly to Lloyd George over New Deal. Hostile to Nazism from an early stage. Formerly editor of *Evening Standard*.

Marchbanks, John (53). Worked as shepherd, then railwayman. 1916-8 Executive Committee of NUR (with subsequent appointments on permanent staff of Union). 1933- General Secretary of NUR (1933 TUC General Council).

Margesson, Henry David Reginald (46). ed. Harrow and Cambridge. War. 1922-3 PPS to Sir C. Montague Barlow. 1924-9 and 1931 junior Whip. 1931- Government Chief Whip. MP (U) West Ham 1922-3 and Rugby 1924- .

Martin, Basil Kingsley (39). ed. Mill Hill School and Magdalene College, Cambridge (bye-fellow). 1927-31 *Manchester Guardian*. 1931- Editor of *New Statesman and Nation*.

Masaryk, Jan (50). Son of Thomas Masaryk. 1925-38 Czech minister to Great Britain.

Maugham, Frederic Herbert, 1st Baron (life peer) (70). ed. Dover College and Trinity Hall, Cambridge. Bar. 1928-34 High Court Judge. 1934-5 Justice of Appeal. 1935-8 and 1939-41 Lord of Appeal. 1938-9 Lord Chancellor (viscount 1939).

Maudling, Reginald (19). ed. Merchant Taylors' and Merton College, Oxford. Visited Harold Nicolson on leaving Oxford. Interested in 'National Labour idea'.

Maurice, Maj-General Sir Frederick (65). 1892-1918 Army. 1922-33 Principal of Working Men's College, St Pancras. 1933- Principal of Queen Mary College, London. 1932- President of British Legion (in which rôle he went to Germany to find a peace-keeping role for the Legion in Czechoslovakia in September 1938). Author.

Meston, James Scorgie, 1st Baron (71). ed. Aberdeen University and Balliol College, Oxford. 1885-1919 Indian Civil Service (Governor of United Provinces and Finance Member of Viceroy's Council).

Midleton, William St John Brodrick, 1st Earl of (80). ed. Eton and Christ Church, Oxford. 1900-5 Cabinet. MP (C) W. Surrey 1880-5 and Guildford 1885-1905.

Monsell, Bolton M. Eyres-Monsell, 1st Viscount (55). ed. *Brittania* 1894-1906 and 1914-7 navy. 1911-4 and 1919-23 junior minister. 1923-31 Conservative Chief Whip. 1931-6 First Lord of Admiralty. 1937- Government director of British Airways Board.

Morrison, Herbert (48) ed. Elementary school. 1920-1. Mayor of Hackney. 1915-40 Secretary of London Labour party. 1928-9 Chairman of Labour party. 1931- LCC Alderman (leader of Council 1939). MP (Lab) for Hackney South 1923-4, 1929-31 and 1935- .

Mosley, Sir Oswald (40). ed. Winchester and RMC Sandhurst. War. 1929-30 Chancellor of Duchy of Lancaster. MP (C.U.) Harrow, 1918-22, (Ind) 1922-4 and (Lab) 1924. MP (Lab) Smethwick 1926-31.

Mountbatten, Lord Louis (36). ed. Lockers' Park, Osborne and Dartmouth; Christ's College, Cambridge. 1913- navy. Quoted as believing that a Communist victory in Spain would be better than Franco and a Fascist triangle.

Muir, Ramsay (64). ed. University College, Liverpool and Balliol College, Oxford. 1913-21 Professor of Modern History at Manchester. 1931-3 Chairman and 1933-6 President of National Liberal Federation. 1923-4 MP (Lib) Rochdale. Author of many works of history, political science and Liberal propaganda.

Murray, George Gilbert (70). Son of president of New South Wales legislative council. ed. Merchant Taylor's and St John's College, Oxford. 1889-99 Professor of Greek at Glasgow. 1908-36 Regius Professor of Greek at Oxford. 1923-38 Chairman, 1938-40 President of League of Nations Union. Prolific author and translator (inc. *Liberalism and the Empire, The Foreign Policy of Sir Edward Grey, The Ordeal of this Generation* and *Liberality and Civilization*).

Nathan, Harry Louis (47). ed. St Paul's School. Solicitor. MP (Lib) 1929-35. MP (Lab) C. Wandsworth 1937-.

Nicolson, Harold (50). ed. Wellington and Balliol College, Oxford. 1909-29 Foreign Service. 1929- Journalist and author (inc. *Peacemaking* and *Curzon*). MP (Nat Lab) Leicester. 'Really' felt that 'the intelligence of the ordinary Leicester businessman' was 'sub-normal'.

Noel-Baker, Philip (47). ed. Bootham School, York, Haverford College and King's College Cambridge. War (Ambulance unit). 1919-22 League of Nations Secretariat. 1929-31 junior minister at Foreign Office. MP (Lab) Coventry 1929-31 and for Derby, 1936- . Thought Eden's Leamington speech in April 1937 should be the 'basic policy of every sane man'.

Noel-Buxton, Noel Edward, 1st Baron (67). ed. Harrow and Trinity College, Cambridge. 1924 and 1929-30 Minister of Agriculture. Author of works about foreign policy (esp. Balkan). MP (Lib) Whitby 1905-6 and North Norfolk 1910-18. MP (Lab) for North Norfolk 1922-30.

Norman, Montagu Collet (65). ed. Eton and King's College, Cambridge. South African War. 1920- Governor of the Bank of England.

Nuffield, William Richard Morris, 1st Baron (59). Chairman of Morris Motors etc. (viscount 1938). Chamberlain believed the Nuffield incident arose out of his 'wounded vanity'.

O'Neill, Sir R.W. Hugh (53). ed. Eton and New College, Oxford. War. 1921-9 Speaker of N. Ireland House of Commons. 1935-9 Chairman of 1922 Committee. 1939-40 junior minister. MP (Northern Ireland) for Antrim 1921-9. MP (U) Mid-Antrim 1915-22 and County Antrim 1922- .

Ormsby-Gore, William Gore Arthur (51). ed. Eton and New College, Oxford. War. 1917-8 Private Secretary to Milner, etc. 1922-4 and 1924-9 junior office. 1931-6 1st Commissioner of Works. 1936-8 Colonial Secretary. MP (U) Denbigh district 1910-18 and for Stafford 1918-38. Like Elliot, he appears to have talked freely about the Cabinet's Palestine discussions.

Patrick, Colin Mark (43). ed. Eton and Christ Church, Oxford. 1919-30 Diplomatic Service. 1933-5 PPS to Hoare. MP (C) Tavistock 1931- .

Petrie, Sir Charles Alexander (41). ed. Corpus Christi College, Oxford. Historian (especially of the Tory party and of Tory politicians).

Phipps, Sir Eric C.E. (61). ed. King's College, Cambridge. 1899-1933 Various posts in Diplomatic Service (chiefly abroad). 1933- Ambassador in Berlin.

Ponsonby, A.A.W.H. 1st Baron (65). ed. Eton and Balliol College, Oxford. 1882-97 Diplomatic Service. 1905-8 Private Secretary to Campbell-Bannerman. 1929-31 junior minister. 1931 Chancellor of Duchy of Lancaster. MP (Lib) Stirling burghs 1908-18 and MP (Lab) for Brightside 1922-30. 1930 Baron. Sankey described the Oxford and Cambridge Club's refusal to elect him as 'separating instead of uniting classes'.

Pownall, Henry Royds (49). ed. Rugby and RMA Woolwich. Army 1906- (1938-9 Director of Military Operations, War Office. 1939-40 CGS, BEF).

Priestley, John Boynton (42). ed. Bradford and Trinity Hall, Cambridge. War. Author of best-selling novels and plays including *The Good Companions, Laburnum Grove, Eden End* in twenties and thirties.

Pritt, Denis Nowell (49). ed. Winchester and London University. Barrister and author. MP (Soc) North Hammersmith 1935-.

Rankeillour, James Fitzalan Hope. 1st Baron (66). ed. Oratory School and Christ Church, Oxford. 1915-21 Household and junior offices. 1921-4 and 1924-9 Chairman of Committees and Deputy Speaker. MP (C) Brightside 1900-6. MP (U) Central Sheffield 1908-29.

Rathbone, Eleanor Florence (64). ed. Kensington High School and Liverpool and Glasgow universities. Author of works on political and social questions. 1929- MP (Ind) Combined English Universities.

Reading, Rufus Daniel Isaacs, 1st Marquess of (died 1935 at age of 75). ed. Brussels, Anglo-Jewish Academy, London and University College, School. 1910-13 Attorney General. 1913-21 Lord Chief Justice. 1918-19 Ambassador to Washington. 1921-6 Viceroy of India. 1931 Foreign Secretary. 1930-5 Leader of Liberal party in the House of Lords.

Reith, John Charles Walsham (1st Baron 1940) (47). ed. Glasgow Academy, Gresham's School, Holt, Royal Technical College, Glasgow. Engineer. War. 1922-38 General Manager etc. BBC. 1938-40 Chairman of Imperial Airways (and then BOAC). MP (Nat) Southampton 1940. In 1933 thought of himself as a possible Ambassador in Washington.

Roberts, Wilfred (36). ed. Gresham's, Holt and Balliol College, Oxford. MP (Lib) North Cumberland 1935- . 'Left-wing' position about India. Johnstone wished he would do less about Spain (where he was an interventionist Republican partisan) and more about agriculture.

Rockley, Evelyn Cecil, 1st Baron (71). ed. Eton and New College, Oxford. Barrister. 1891-2 and 1895-1902 Assistant PS to Salisbury (his uncle). Member of Commissions. MP (C) East Herts 1898-1900,

Aston Manor 1900-18 and Aston 1918-29.

Rothermere, Harold Sydney Harmsworth, 1st Viscount (68). Proprietor of *Daily Mail, Evening News* etc. 1917-18 Air Secretary. 1937 Retired from effective control of newspapers.

Rowse, Alfred Leslie (33). ed. Elementary and County schools, St Austell and Christ Church, Oxford. 1925- Fellow of All Souls, Oxford. Contested Penryn-Falmouth 1931 and 1935. Historian and Labour publicist including *Politics and the Younger Generation*.

Runciman, Sir Walter (Baron 1937, Viscount 1938) (66). ed. Trinity College, Cambridge. 1905-8 junior office. 1908-11 President of Board of Education. 1911-14 President of Board of Agriculture. 1914-6 President of Board of Trade. MP (Lib) Oldham 1899-1900, Dewsbury 1901-18, Swansea 1924-9, and St Ives 1929-31. MP (Lib Nat) St Ives 1931-7.

Rushcliffe, 1st Baron, see Betterton.

Salisbury, James E.H. Gascoyne-Cecil, 4th Marquess of (75). ed. Eton and University College, Oxford. South African war. 1900-3 Under-Secretary, 1903-5 and 1922-9 Cabinet office (1925-9 Leader of House of Lords).

Salter, Sir James Arthur (55). ed. Oxford High School and Brasenose. After 30 years as civil servant (inc. period at League of Nations), became Gladstone Professor of Political Theory at Oxford (1934) and MP (Ind) for Oxford University (1937). Author of works on public affairs, wanted the Republic armed in 1936 and thought Chamberlain was 'doomed' on September 21 1938. Much praised by the Sinclairites. Dawson thought him 'boring'.

Samuel, Sir Herbert Lewis (1st Viscount 1937) (66). ed. University College School and Balliol College Oxford. 1905-9 junior minister. 1909-16 Cabinet. 1920-5 High Commissioner in Palestine. 1927-9 Chairman of Liberal party organisation. 1931-5 Leader of parliamentary Liberal party. MP (Lib) Cleveland 1902-18 and Darwen 1929-35. Author of books on political and philosophical subjects.

Sanderson, H.S. Furniss, 1st Lord (69). Blind since birth. 1916-25 Principal of Ruskin College. Resigned from Labour party in 1936 owing to its foreign policy 'involving so much hatred of other powers'.

Sandys, Duncan (28). ed. Eton and Magdalene College, Cambridge. 1930-4 Foreign Service. MP (Cons) for Norwood 1935- . Churchill's son-in-law (after being opposed by a candidate put up by Randolph Churchill at Norwood by-election in 1935). In May 1935 he was in effect saying that Germany should have a predominant place in central Europe, so as to avoid clashing with British as an Imperial Power (*Hansard* of May 2 1935 cols. 595-598).

Sargent, Sir Orme Garton (52). ed. Radley. 1906- Foreign Office (incl. Assistant Under-Secretary).

Selborne, William W. Palmer, 2nd Earl of Selborne (77). ed. Winchester and University College, Oxford. 1900-5 1st Lord of Admiralty. 1905-10 High Commissioner in South Africa. 1915-16 President of Board of Agriculture. MP (C) Petersfield 1885-92 and Edinburgh W. 1892-5.

Sheppard, Very Rev. Hugh Richard (56). ed. Marlborough and Trinity Hall, Cambridge. 1914-27 Vicar of St Martin-in-the-Fields. 1929-31 Dean of Canterbury. 1934- Canon of St Paul's. Founder of Peace Pledge Union.

Shinwell, Emanuel (52). Of Polish origin. 1924 and 1929-31 junior office. MP (Lab) Linlithgow 1922-4 and 1928-31 and for Seaham (after defeating MacDonald) 1935- . MacDonald believed he had rescued Shinwell's ministerial career when no minister would take him in 1929.

Sidebotham, Herbert (64). ed. Manchester Grammar School and Balliol College, Oxford. 1895-1914 *Manchester Guardian.* 1922-3 *Daily Chronicle.* Scrutator of the *Sunday Times.*

Smuts, Jan Christiaan (66). ed. Victoria College, Stellenbosch and Christ's College, Cambridge. After commanding Republican forces in Cape Colony in Boer War, became Colonial Secretary of the Transvaal in 1907 and commander of troops in East Africa in 1916. 1910-9 Various offices in South African Cabinet. 1919-24 and 1939- Prime Minister. 1933-9 Minister of Justice. A frequent visitor to England, where he behaved as a sort of higher adviser to the Liberal party via Asquith and Lloyd George. In the late thirties became a supporter of Churchill.

Snell, Henry Snell, 1st Baron (71). ed. village school, University College, Nottingham, London School of Economics and Heidelberg University. Son of agricultural worker. LCC 1919-25. MP (Lab) Woolwich East 1922-31. 1935- Labour leader in House of Lords. Described by one Conservative as 'attaining a position of note' in the House of Lords. In 1935 was expecting Baldwin to be succeeded by Mosley.

Southby, Sir Archibald R.J. (50). ed. naval. 1908-20 naval service. 1935-7 Assistant Whip. MP (C) Epsom 1928- .

Spears, Edward Louis (50). 1903-27 army (incl. 1917-20 Head of British Military Mission to Paris). MP (Nat. Lib) Loughborough 1922-4 and MP (U) Carlisle 1931-

Spender, J. Alfred (74). ed. Bath College and Balliol College, Oxford. 1896-1922 editor of *Westminster Gazette.* Liberal publicist and biographer.

Spens, William Patrick (51). ed. Rugby and New College, Oxford. War Barrister. MP (C) Ashford 1933-.

Spier, Eugen. German-Jewish refugee businessman who subsidised a dining and discussion club of which Churchill was a prominent member.

Stanhope, James Richard, 7th Earl (56). ed. Eton and Magdalen College, Oxford. 1901-8 army (inc. S. African war). 1910-13 LCC. 1914-18 War. 1918, 1924-9 and 1931-6 junior minister. 1936-7 1st Commissioner of Works (Cabinet). 1937-8 President of Board of Education. 1938-9 1st Lord of Admiralty. 1939-40 Lord President of the Council. 1938-40 Leader of House of Lords.

Stanley, Edward, Lord (42). ed. Eton and Magdalen College, Oxford. 1924-7 junior Whip. 1927-9 Deputy Chairman of Conservative party.

1931-8 junior office. 1938 Dominions Secretary (until death). MP (C) Fylde 1922-38.

Stanley, Oliver F.G. (40). ed. Eton and Oxford. War. 1931-3 junior minister. 1933-4 Minister of Transport. 1934-5 Minister of Labour. 1935-7 President of Board of Education. 1937-40 President of Board of Trade. 1940 Secretary of State for War. 1923 defeated in Edgehill by-election. MP (C) Westmorland 1924-.

Steed, Henry Wickham (65). ed. Sudbury Grammar School and Jena, Paris and Berlin universities. 1896-1922 *The Times* (editor 1919-22). 1925-8 Lecturer at King's College, London. 1923-30 Editor of *Review of Reviews*. Prolific author on political and foreign policy subjects (incl. *The Habsburg Monarchy, The Real Stanley Baldwin, Hitler Whence and Whither?, A Way to Social Peace, Vital Peace* and *Our War Aims*). Dawson did not much care for his 'Edgar Wallace-like revelations of German villainy'.

Stevenson, Frances (later Countess Lloyd George). 1913- Private Secretary to Lloyd George with whom she lived.

Stokes, Richard Rapier (39). Company chairman. ed. Downside and Trinity College, Cambridge. 1915-18 army. MP (Lab) Ipswich 1938- .

Stonehaven, John Lawrence Baird, 1st Baron (62). ed. Eton and Oxford. 1898-1908 Diplomatic Service. War 1914-5. 1911-6 PPS to Law. 1916-22 junior minister. 1922-4 Minister of Transport. 1925-30 Governor-General of Australia. 1931-6 Chairman of Conservative party. MP (C) Rugby 1910-22 and Ayr Burghs 1922-5. Unwilling to remain party chairman while Greenwood remained Treasurer; removed unwillingly in 1937.

Strauss, George Russell (35). ed. Rugby. Son of Conservative MP. LCC (Lab) 1925-31 and 1932- (Chairman of Committees). MP (Lab) North Lambeth 1929-31 and 1934- .

Swinton, Philip Cunliffe-Lister (formerly Lloyd-Greame), 1st Viscount (52). ed. Winchester and University College, Oxford. 1908 Bar. 1914-7 War. 1917-18 and 1920-2 junior office. 1922-3, 1924-9 and 1931 President of the Board of Trade. 1931-5 Colonial Secretary. 1935-8 Air Minister. MP (U) Hendon 1918-35. 1935 Viscount Swinton. Dill, when asked to find him a job in 1939 declared that he had been treated 'disgracefully'.

Tate, Mrs Mavis Constance. ed. St Paul's Girls School. JP. MP (Nat) West Willesden 1931-5 and (Nat Con) Frome 1935- .

Thomas, James Henry (62). ed. Council schools. From age of nine, errand boy, then railways (engine-driver). 1921 Vice-Chairman of PLP. 1918-24 and 1925-31 General Secretary, National Union of Railwaymen. 1924, 1931 and 1935-6 Colonial Secretary. 1929-30 Lord Privy Seal and Minister for Employment. 1930-5 Dominions Secretary. MP (Lab) Derby 1910-31 and (Nat Lab) 1931-6.

Thomas, James Purdon Lewes (33). ed. Rugby and Oriel College, Oxford. 1931 Assistant PS to Baldwin. 1932-5 PPS to Thomas. 1935-7 PPS to Eden. MP (Cons) Hereford 1931- .

Toynbee, Arnold Joseph (47). ed. Winchester and Balliol College, Oxford (Fellow and Tutor 1912-15). 1915-19 Government departments (incl. Intelligence). 1919-24 Professor of Byzantine and Modern Greek, London University. 1925- Director of Studies and Professor, Royal Institute of International Affairs. Author and writer on politics inc. *Nationality and the War, The New Europe, Turkey, A Study of History* and various Chatham House Surveys.

Tree, Ronald (39). ed. Winchester. War.1936-8 PPS to R.S. Hudson (resigned when Eden resigned). MP (C) Harborough 1933-.

Trenchard, Hugh M. Trenchard, 1st Viscount (63) 1893-1927 army, then air force (1927 Marshal of the RAF). 1931-5 Commissioner of Metropolitan Police. Virtual founder of RAF. Macdonald would not make him Chairman of the Unemployment Assistance Board because Labour identified him with 'Prussian methods'.

Trevelyan, Sir Charles Philips (66). ed. Harrow and Trinity College, Cambridge. 1892-3 Private Secretary to Crewe. 1908-14 junior minister. 1924 and 1929-31 President of Board of Education. MP (Lib) Elland 1899-1918 and (Lab) Newcastle C. 1922-31.

Tyrrell, William George, 1st Baron (70). ed. Balliol College, Oxford. 1889-1928 Foreign Office (inc. Permanent Under-Secretary 1925-8). 1928-34 British Ambassador in Paris, 1935- President of Board of Film Censors.

Vallance, Aylmer (44). ed. Fettes and Balliol College, Oxford. 1914-19 army. 1933-6 Editor of *News Chronicle*. 1933-6 Financial editor, *New Statesman.*

Vansittart, Sir Robert Gilbert (55). ed. Eton. 1902- Diplomatic Service (incl. 1928-30 PPS to Prime Minister). 1930-8 Permanent Under-Secretary. 1938- Chief Diplomatic Adviser to the Government.

Wedgwood, Josiah Clement (64). ed. Clifton and Royal Naval College, Greenwich. Naval architect. South African War. War. 1922-4 Vice Chairman of parliamentary Labour party. 1924 Chancellor of Duchy of Lancaster. MP (first Lib and then Lab), Newcastle-under-Lyme 1906- .

Weir, William Douglas, 1st Viscount (1938). (69). Industrialist. First-war administrator of government munitions directorates (incl. 1918 Secretary of State for Air). Of wide post-war experience. 1936 Brought in to advise about rearmament.

Westminster, Richard A. Grosvenor, 2nd Duke of (57). Served in S. African war. War. Vice-President of India Defence League.

Williams, Francis (33). ed. Queen Elizabeth Grammar School, Middleton. 1929-36 Financial editor, *Daily Herald.* 1936-40 editor *Daily Herald.*

Willink, Henry Urmston (42). ed. Eton and Trinity College, Cambridge. Barrister. Contested Ipswich (C) in 1938.

Wilson, Sir Arnold Talbot (52). ed. Clifton and Sandhurst. 1903-20 Indian Army and Political Service (inc. Mesopotamia 1918-20). 1921-32 Anglo-Iranian Oil Co. Editor of *Nineteenth Century and After* (until removed in 1938 by Voigt and Harold Nicolson after being first anti-Baldwin and then 'fascist' about Spain). Author of *Mesopotamia* and other political works. MP (C) Hitchin 1933- (tried to avoid having a message from Baldwin at by-election).

Wilson, Sir Horace John (54). ed. Kurnella School, Bournemouth and London School of Economics. 1900- Civil Service (incl. 1921-30 Permanent Secretary to Ministry of Labour and 1930-9 Chief Industrial Adviser to the Government). 1935- Seconded to Treasury for service with Prime Minister. 1939- Head of Civil Service and Permanent Secretary to the Treasury.

Winterton, Edward Turnour, 6th Earl (Irish) (53). ed. Eton and New College, Oxford. Landowner. War. 1922-4 and 1924-9 junior office. 1937-9 Chancellor of Duchy of Lancaster (deputy to Air Minister March to May 1938, Cabinet March 1938-January 1939). January to November 1939 Postmaster General. MP (U) Horsham from 1904. Attlee thought him 'clever and far more broad-minded than is realized'.

Wolmer, Roundell Cecil Palmer, Viscount (49). ed. Winchester and University College, Oxford. 1922-4 and 1924-9 junior office. 1934-40 Chairman, Cement Makers Federation. Prominent Anglican layman. MP (C) Newton 1910-18 and Aldershot 1918-40.

Womersley, Sir Walter James (58). ed. Usher Street Board School, Bradford. Started work at 12; senior partner in Womersley and Stamp of Grimsby. 1922-3 Mayor of Grimsby. Chairman of Trade Associations (ind. National Chamber of Trade). 1931 PPS to Sir Kingsley Wood. 1931-9 junior office. 1939- Minister of Pensions. MP (U) Grimsby 1924- . A civic Conservative who upset Harold Nicolson at a by-election in 1937 by making 'a sort of 1912 patriotic speech containing a long recitation from one of Galsworthy's more ghastly poems'.

Woolton, Frederick James Marquis, 1st Baron (53). ed. Manchester Grammar School and Manchester University (Research Fellow). Unitarian. Managing Director of Lewis's etc. Member of Government Committees (inc. Cadman Committee). Dawson described him as 'a cheerful Cove'.

Young, Edward Hilton (1st Lord Kennet 1935) (57). ed. Eton and Trinity College, Cambridge. Bar. War. 1921-2 and 1931 junior office. 1931-5 Minister of Health. Chairman of Commissions. MP (Lib) Norwich 1915-23 and 1924-9 and MP (C) Sevenoaks 1929-35.

BIBLIOGRAPHY

1. *Original Sources*

(a) The private papers (published or unpublished) of:

Vyvyan Adams (London School of Economics)
1st Viscount Alexander of Hills borough (Churchill College, Cambridge)
L.S. Amery (in possession of Rt Hon. Julian Amery, MP)
1st Lord Amulree (Bodleian, Oxford)
1st Viscount Alexander of Hillsborough (Churchill College, Cambridge)
Nancy, Viscountess Astor (Reading University Library)
1st Earl Baldwin (Cambridge University Library)
1st Lord Beaverbrook (Beaverbrook Library)
5th Lord Brabourne (India Office Library)
1st Viscount Bridgeman, diary (Shropshire County Record Office)
Sir Robert Bruce Lockhart (published diary ed. Young vol. I)
Sir Alexander Cadogan (published diary ed. Dilks)
1st Viscount Cecil of Chelwode (British Museum)
Sir Austen Chamberlain (Birmingham University Library)
Neville Chamberlain (Birmingham University Library)
Sir Henry Channon (published extracts from diary ed. Rhodes James)
1st Baron Chatfield (Royal Maritime Museum, Greenwich)
Group-Captain M.G. Christie (Churchill College, Cambridge)
Sir Winston Churchill (Bodleian, Oxford)
1st Marquess of Crewe (Cambridge University Library)
Sir Stafford Cripps (Nuffield College, Oxford)
1st Lord Croft (Churchill College, Cambridge)
1st Viscount Crookshank (Bodleian, Oxford)
W.P. Crozier, interviews with politicians (Beaverbrook Library, since
    published as ed. Taylor, *Off the Record*)
1st Lord Dalton (diary, London School of Economics)
Geoffrey Dawson, diary (in possession of Mr Michael Dawson)
1st Viscount Davidson (Beaverbrook Library)
Alfred Duff Cooper (1st Viscount Norwich) diary (extracts in A. Duff
    Cooper, *Old Men Forget*)
Mrs Blanche Dugdale (published diary ed. Rose)
Walter Elliot (letters in Coote, *Companion of Honour*)
Sir E.M.W. Grigg (1st Lord Altrincham) (in possession of Mr John
    Grigg)
Sir James Grigg (Churchill College, Cambridge)
1st Earl of Halifax (Churchill College, Cambridge)
1st Lord Hankey (Churchill College, Cambridge)
Sir P.J. Hannon (Beaverbrook Library)
Oliver Harvey (1st Lord Harvey) (published diary ed. Harvey)

Sir Cuthbert Headlam, diary (Durham County Record Office)
Sir Samuel Hoare (1st Viscount Templewood) (Cambridge University Library)
L. Hore-Belisha (published letters and diary in Minney, *The Private Papers of Hore-Belisha*)
Ironside, General Sir E. (diary extracts in ed. Macleod and Kelly, *The Ironside Diaries 1937-40*)
Thomas Jones (diary extracts in ed. Middlemass, *A Diary with Letters 1931-50*)
1st Lord Killearn (published extracts from diary ed. Evans)
1st Lord Keyes (Churchill College, Cambridge)
George Lansbury (London School of Economics)
1st Earl Lloyd George (Beaverbrook Library)
2nd Marquess of Linlithgow (India Office Library)
7th Marquess of Londonderry (Durham County Record Office)
J.R. MacDonald (in possession of David Marquand MP)
Gilbert Murray (Bodleian, Oxford)
Harold Nicolson (published diary and letters to V. Sackville-West ed. Nicolson and typescript original, Balliol College, Oxford)
Sir Lewis O'Malley (in the possession of Mrs Zara Steiner)
Sir Eric Phipps (Churchill College, Cambridge)
1st Lord Ponsonby (Bodleian, Oxford)
Sir Henry Pownall (published diary ed. Bond)
1st Viscount Runciman (Newcastle University Library)
1st Viscount Samuel (House of Lords Record Office)
1st Viscount Sankey (Bodleian, Oxford)
3rd Earl of Selborne (Bodleian, Oxford)
1st Viscount Simon (Institute of Historical Research)
Sir Archibald Sinclair (1st Viscount Thurso) (Churchill College, Cambridge)
Sir George Stanley (India Office Library)
Frances Stevenson (published extracts from diary ed. Taylor)
1st Earl of Swinton (Churchill College, Cambridge)
The Times Archive (Printing House Square)
Sir Charles Trevelyan (Newcastle University Library)
Sir Robert Vansittart (1st Lord Vansittart) (Churchill College, Cambridge)
Euan Wallace (diary, Bodleian, Oxford)
1st Lord Weir (Churchill College, Cambridge)
E. Hilton Young (1st Lord Kennet) (Cambridge University Library)
2nd Marquess of Zetland (India Office Library)
1922 Committee Minute-books (in possession of Philip Goodhart MP)

(b) Public Record Office files (referred to as FO, Cab and PREM)

2. *Published works*

The following published works have been quoted or mentioned in the text. Endnote references to an author's name refer to the work listed under his name in this bibliography.

Adam [Colin Forbes, *Life of Lord Lloyd*, 1948]
Addison [C., ed. *Problems of a Socialist Government*, 1933]
Anderson [Mosa, *Noel Buxton, A Life*, 1952]
Angell [Sir Norman, *The Great Illusion*, 1908 (reprinted with new sections in 1933)]
Aster [Sidney, *1939, The Making of the Second World War*, 1973]
Atholl [Katharine, Duchess of, *Working Partnership*, 1958]
Attlee [C.R., *The Labour Party in Perspective*, 1937]
Avon [Earl of, *The Eden Memoirs;*] *Facing the Dictators*[1962]
Barker [Nicholas, *Stanley Morison*, 1972]
Beveridge, Sir William, *Planning Under Socialism and other Addresses*, 1936
Bond [B., ed., *Chief of Staff, The*] *Diaries* [*of Lt-General Sir Henry*] *Pownall* [1973]
Bruce, Lockhart [*The*] *Diaries* [*of Sir Robert Bruce Lockhart* vol. I, 1973]
Bryant [Arthur] *The Turn of the Tide* [1957]
 Triumph in the West [1959]
 The Fire and the Rose [1972]
 ed., *Constructive Democracy* [1938]
Butler, Ewan [*Mason-Mac, The Life of Lt. General Sir Mason Macfarlane*, 1972]
Cameron [Fraser M., *Some Aspects of British Strategy and Diplomacy 1933-9*, Cambridge PhD), 1973]
Cartland [Barbara, *Ronald Cartland*, 1942]
Chatfield [Lord, *It Might Happen Again*, 2 vols., 1947]
Churchill, Randolph [*The Rise and Fall of Sir Anthony Eden*, 1959]
Churchill [W.S.] *Arms and the Covenant* [compelled by Randolph Churchill, 1938] [*The*] *Second World War* [vol. I, 1948]
Churchill [W.S.] *Arms and the Covenant* [compiled by Randolph Churchill, 1938]
 [*The*] *Second World War* [vol. I, 1948]
 Marlborough, His Life and Times 4 vols. 1933-8
 The History of the English Speaking Peoples [4 vols 1956-8]
 Step by Step [*1936-1939*, 1939]
Citrine [Lord, *Men and Work*, 1964]
Collingwood [R.G., *Autobiography*, 1939, 1970 ed.]
Colville [J.R., *Man of Valour*, 1972]
Cook [C.] and Ramsden [J., *By-Elections in British Politics*, 1973]
Cooke [Colin A., *The Life of Richard Stafford Cripps*, 1957]
Coote [Colin, *A Companion of Honour*, 1965]
Cowling, M., *1867, Disraeli, Gladstone and Revolution* [1967]
 [*The Impact of Labour*, 1971]
Cripps [Sir Stafford, in L.A. Fenn *et al. Problems of the Socialist Transition*. 1934]
Dalton, Hugh, *Practical Socialism for Britain*, 1935
Deutsch [H.C. *The Conspiracy Against Hitler in the Twilight War*, 1968]
Dilks [David, ed. *The Diaries of Sir Alexander*] *Cadogan* [*1938-45*, 1971]
D[ocuments on] B[ritish] F[oreign] P[olicy *1919-1939*] second and third series [*1949-*]

D[ocuments on] G[erman] F[oreign] P[olicy] Series D [1949-]
Duff Cooper, Alfred, Talleyrand, 1932.
      Haig 2 vols., 1935-6
      [Old Men Forget, 1953]
Eatwell [R., Journal of Contemporary History, 1971]
Eden, Anthony, Freedom and Order, 1947.
Estorick [E., Strafford Cripps, a biography, 1949]
[Evans, Trefor, The] Killearn Diaries [1934-46, 1972]
Feiling [K., The Life of Neville] Chamberlain [1970]
Gannon [F.R., The British Press and Germany 1936-9, 1971]
Garvin [J.L., The Life of Joseph] Chamberlain [3 vols., 1932-4]
Gilbert [Martin], Plough My Own Furrow [1965]
      The Roots of Appeasement [1966]
Grigg [Sir E.M.W., Britain Looks At Germany, 1938]
Hadley [W.W., Munich, Before and After, 1944]
Halifax [Earl of, Fulness of Days, 1957]
Harvey [J., ed. The diplomatic] diaries [of Oliver Harvey, 1970]
Heuston [R.F.V., Lives of the Lord Chancellors, 1964]
Hollis [Christopher, Foreigners Aren't Fools, 1936]
Howard [Michael, The Continental Commitment, 1972]
Irving [David, ed., Breach of Security, 1968]
Irwin [Lord, John Keble, 1932]
Ismay [The Memoirs of Lord Ismay, 1960]
Jerrold [Douglas, They That Take to the Sword, 1936]
Jerrold [Douglas] Georgian Adventure [1938]
Johnson, Hewlett, The Socialist Sixth of the World, 1939
Elwyn Jones [F.,The Battle for Peace, 1938]
Jones [Thomas, A Diary with Letters 1931-50, 1954]
Keynes [John Maynard, How to Pay for the War, 1939]
Kieft [David Owen, Belgium's Return to Neutrality, 1972]
Kirkpatrick [Sir Ivone, The Inner Circle, 1959]
Lammers [D., Explaining Munich, 1966]
Lammers [Donald] 'From Whitehall After Munich' [Historical Journal,
      XVI, 4 (1973), 831-56] 'Fascism, Communism and the foreign
      Office'
      [Journal of Contemporary History (1971), pp. 66-87]
Langer [W.L.] and Gleason [S.E., The Challenge to Isolation, 1952]
Layton [Lord] Dorothy [1961]
Lee [Bradford A., Britain and the Sino-Japanese War 1937-9, 1973]
Liddell Hart [B.H., The Memoirs of Captain Liddell Hart. vol. II, 1965]
Livingstone [Dame Adelaide, The Peace Ballot, 1935]
Lloyd [Lord[The British Case[1939]
Lloyd George, David, War Memoirs, 6 vols., 1933-6
Londonderry, Edith, Marchioness of, Retrospect 1938
[C.A.] MacDonald ['Economic Appeasement and the German Moderates
      1937-9', Past and Present, 1972]
Maclachlan [Donald, In The Chair: Barrington-Ward of The Times
      1927-48, 1971]
[Macleod, R. and Kelly, D.] The Ironside Diaries, [1937-40,] 1962

Macmillan [Harold, *The Middle Way*, 1938]
McNair [J., *James Maxton, The Beloved Rebel*, 1955]
Macnamara [J.R.J., *The Whistle Blows*, 1938]
Marriott [Sir J.A.R., *Commonwealth or Anarchy*, 1937]
Medlicott, W.N. *Britain and Germany; the search for agreement 1930-7*, 1969
Michaelis [Meir in *Historical Journal* XV (1972), 331-60]
Middlemass [Keith, *Diplomacy of Illusion*, 1972]
Minney, [R.J., *The Private Papers of Hore-Belisha*, 1960]
Mosley [Sir O., *My Life*, 1968]
Mitchison [Gilbert, *The First Workers' Government*, 1934]
Muir [R, *The Liberal Way*, 1934]
Murray, Gilbert, *Liberality and Civilization*, 1934
    Then and Now, 1935
    An Unfinished Autobiography, 1960 (ed. Smith and Toynbee)
Namier [Sir L.B.]*Diplomatic Prelude*, 1948
    Europe in Decay, 1950
    In the Nazi Era, 1952
Newman [A., *The Stanhopes of Chevening*, 1969]
[Nicolson, N. ed., *Harold] Nicolson, Diaries [and Letters 1930-9*, 1966]
    Diaries and Letters 1939-45 [1967]
Noel-Baker [P.J. etc. *Challenge to Death*, 1934]
Parkinson [Roger, *Peace for Our Time: Munich to Dunkirk − the inside story*, 1971]
Percy [Lord Eustace] *Government in Transition* [1934]
    [ed.] Conservatism and the Future [1935]
    [contribution to Adams M., ed.] *The Modern State* [1934]
Petrie [Sir Charles] *Lords of the Inland Sea* [1937]
    The Chamberlain Tradition [1938]
Portsmouth [Earl of, *A Knot of Roots*, 1965]
Reader [W. *Architect of Air Power*, 1968]
Reith [J.C.W., *Into The Wind*, 1949]
[Rhodes James, Robert, ed., *Chips, The] Diaries [of Sir Henry] Channon*, [1967]
Rhodes James [Robert] *Churchill [A Study in Failure*, 1970 (Pelican 1973)]
Robbins [Keith, *Munich 1938*, 1968]
Rose [N.A., ed., *Baffy, The diaries of Mrs Blanche Dugdale 1936-47*, 1973]
Rothermere, 1st Viscount, *My Fight to Rearm* 1939
    My Campaign for Hungary, 1939
Rowland [J.H.S.] and Cadman [Lord, *Ambassador for Oil*, 1960]
Rowse, Arthur Leslie, *The English Spirit*, 1945
    The Early Churchills, 1956
    The Later Churchills, 1958
    All Souls and Appeasement, 1961
    The England of Elizabeth, 1950
Salter, Sir Arthur, *Recovery*, 1932
Samuel [Viscount, *Memoirs*, 1945]

Selby [Sir Walford, *Diplomatic Twilight*, 1953]
Seton-Watson [R.W., *Munich and the Dictators*, 1939]
Spears [Sir E.L., *Assignment to Catastrophe*, vol. I]
Spier [Eugen, *Focus*, 1963]
Stannage [T., 'The British General Election of 1935', Cambridge PhD, 1973]
Strange [Lord, *At Home and Abroad*, 1956]
Tascano [Mario, *Designs in Diplomacy*, 1970]
Taylor, A.J.P., *The Origins of the Second World War*, 1961
    Beaverbrook [1972]
[Taylor, A.J.P., ed., *Lloyd George, A*] *Diary* [*by Frances*] *Stevenson* [*1971*]
    Off the Record. [1972]
Tennant [E.W.D., *True Account*, 1957]
Thompson [Neville, *The Anti-Appeasers*, 1971]
Trevor-Roper [H.R., ed., *Hitler's War Directives 1939-45*, 1966 ed.]
Waterfield [Gordon, *Professional Diplomat*, 1973]
Watkins [K.W., *Britain Divided*, 1963]
Watt [Donald Cameron] *Personalities and Policies* [1965]
    'Appeasement, The Rise of a Revisionist School',*Political Quarterly* [April-June 1965] in *Slavonic and East European Review* [XLIV (1966)]
in *Slavonic and East European Review* [XLIV (1966)]
Wendt [B.J.] *Appeasement 1938* [Hamburg, 1968]
    Economic Appeasment [Dusseldorf, 1971]
Wheeler-Bennett [John] *Munich* [*Prologue to Tragedy*, 1948]
    [*King George VI*, 1958]
    [*John Anderson Viscount*] Waverley [1962]
Williams of Barnsbury [*Digging for Britain*, 1965]
Williams [T.F.D. in *Irish Historical Studies* vol. X]
Wilson [Arnold, *Walks and Talks Abroad*, 1936]
Wingate [Sir Ronald, *Lord Ismay*, 1970]
Zetland [Marquess of, *Essayez*, 1956]
    The Life of Lord Curzon, 1928
    The Heart of Aryavarta, 1925

3. Works of reference that have been used

Dod's Parliamentary Companion
Dictionary of National Biography
Burke's Peerage, Baronetage and Knightage
British Political Facts 1900-1967 by David Butler and Jeannie Freeman

NOTES

NOTES TO INTRODUCTION

1. For Feiling's difficulty with the Cabinet Office, see Feiling to Mrs Chamberlain, March 22 and July 28 1945 and April 14 and May 5 1946. Chamberlain MSS.
2. I.e. Namier, especially *Diplomatic Prelude* (1948), *Europe in Decay* (1950) and *In the Nazi Era* (1952).
3. For 'shrill nonsense', see Collingwood, ch xii and especially pp. 164–7. Rowse, *The English Spirit*, p. 21, *The England of Elizabeth*, p. 1 (dated, ironically, Empire Day). The theme is taken up with barren insistence in *The Early Churchills, The Later Churchills, All Souls and Appeasement* and elsewhere in Rowse's writings.
4. See especially Rowse's *Mr Keynes and the Labour Movement* for an explanation of the relevance of Keynes's *General Theory* (published that year) to the future of the Labour party.
5. Bryant, *The Face and the Rose,* p. 241. For Bryant as defender of the Chiefs of Staff (against Churchill), see *The Turn of the Tide* and *Triumph in the West*. For Bryant as Chamberlain's editor (*In Search of Peace*), see Chamberlain MSS, NC 10/4.
6. For titles see bibliography.
7. Especially in 'Appeasement, The The Rise of a Revisionist-school', *Political Quarterly* (1965).
8. Middlemass, p. 7.
9. Trevor-Roper, p. 14.
10 Michaelis

NOTES TO CHAPTER 1

1. E.g. Baldwin, in Jones, June 12 1934.
2. There are a large number of Labour speeches on the subject in 1933/4, cf. Lord Marley and Ellen Wilkinson speaking of forming an 'anti-Mosley society', in Crozier, interview with Marley January 29 1934. Simon to MacDonald, July 27 1934 FO 800/291. Attlee to Tom Attlee, February 28 1933. Butler to Brabourne, May 2 1934.
3. Cecil to Hankey, October 28 and November 3 1933.
4. Crozier, interview with Cecil, May 5 1934. Cecil to Noel-Baker, April 8 1934, Add. MSS 51108.
5. Cecil to Hankey, October 28 1933.
6. Cecil to Baldwin, February 17 1933.
7. Cecil to Salisbury, January 25 1933, Cecil MSS.
8. Cecil to Halifax (Irwin), March 27, to Salisbury, January 25, to

Baldwin, February 27, to Eden, March 24, to Noel-Baker, May 4, all 1933, Add. MSS 51083 etc. Crozier, interview with Cecil, May 5 1934.

9.   Cecil to Baldwin, March 15 1933.
10. Cecil to Baldwin, October 21 1933 for the secrecy point. Cecil to Halifax, July 18 1932, Add. MSS 51004.
11. Cecil to Halifax, March 27, Cecil MSS, and to Murray, January 5 1933.
12. Cecil to Baldwin, February 17, and to Eden, March 24 1933, Cecil MSS.
13. Crozier, interview with Cecil, May 5 1934.
14. Murray to Austen Chamberlain, October 10 1933.
15. Broadcast by Cecil, October 20 1933. Cecil to Murray, October 31 1933.
16. Crozier, interview with Cecil, May 5 1934.
17. Murray to Austen Chamberlain, May 13 1934.
18. Memo of talk with the Duke of Brunswick including Cecil's suggestions to Eden, Cecil, note of April 24 1934, Add. MSS 51083.
19. Crozier, interview with Cecil, May 5 1934. Cecil to Simon, July 8 1933, FO 800/288.
20. Cecil to Murray, August 29 1934.
21. Cecil to Murray, August 29 and 30 1934.
22. Murray, *Liberality and Civilization*, pp. 57—94 and Cecil, foreword to Noel-Baker et al., pp. viii—ix.
23. N. B[utler], note for P.M., July 20 1935, PREM 1/178. Cecil to Baldwin, February 28 1934. Cecil to Murray, August 29 1934.
24. Austen Chamberlain to Tyrell, February 13 1933, Austen Chamberlain MSS.
25. E.g. Austen Chamberlain to Cecil, December 1 1933, and to Garnett, January 2 1934. Cecil to Murray, March 23 1933 for Austen Chamberlain having an effect.
26. Murray to Austen Chamberlain, November 14 1934.
27. For all this see the large correspondence between Cecil, Austen Chamberlain, Cranborne, Fry, Eden, Baldwin and Murray between May and November 1934 in the Murray, Cecil and Baldwin papers.
28. E.g. Murray *Liberality and Civilization, Then and Now* and *An Unfinished Biography*, pp. 114—15. See also Cecil to Murray, March 13 1934.
29. Cecil to Eden, November 12 1934, Cecil MSS.
30. E.g. G. Herbert to Conservative agents, July 23 1934, Baldwin MSS.
31. Cecil, conversation with Baldwin, November 26 1934. Cecil to Baldwin, November 26, Cecil to Fry, November 27, Fry to Cecil, November 28, all 1934.
32. For report see PREM 1/178 of July 23 1935. For the movement, see Livingstone.
33. E.g. Attlee to Tom Attlee, August 18 1933.
34. Greenwood at Hastings Labour Party Conference, October 3

1933, *Manchester Guardian*, October 4. Lansbury at TUC, September 7 1933, *Manchester Guardian*, September 8.

35. Lansbury to *Daily Herald, Daily Herald*, May 1 1934.

36. Alexander at Manchester, January 14 1933, *Manchester Guardian* January 16.

37. Lansbury at March, June 13 1933, *Daily Herald*, June 14. Lansbury at Brighton TUC, September 7 1933, *Manchester Guardian*, September 8.

38. See e.g. National Executive Committee Report, *Labour and Government*, of September 14 1933, *Manchester Guardian*, September 15. Lansbury at March, June 13 1933, *Daily Herald*, June 14. Cripps, pp. 8 and 35–67 and Attlee in Addison.

39. Alexander at Manchester, January 14 1933, *Manchester Guardian*, January 16, and at Rusholme, November 10 1933, *Manchester Guardian*, November 11. For the American comparison see, e.g., *Manchester Guardian*, September 5 and 6 1933 for TUC agenda and Walkden's presidential address of September 4 and Morison at Walsall, January 13 1933, *Daily Herald*, January 14.

40. Attlee and Cripps at May Day rally, *Daily Herald*, May 8 1933. See also *Daily Herald*, May 12–22 1933, including an attack by Sir Wyndham Childs.

41. Lansbury (foreword to H.V. Morton pamphlet), in *Daily Herald*, April 8 1933.

42. Alexander at Rusholme, November 10 1933, *Manchester Guardian*, November 11.

43. Greenwood, addressing unemployment meetings in Salford and Manchester on February 12 1933, *Manchester Guardian*, February 13.

44. Greenwood, statement of February 8 1933, *Daily Herald*, February 9.

45. In Hungary, Austria and Italy, see Attlee to Tom Attlee, April 3 1933. *Daily Herald* leader, April 18 1933.

46. Henderson, after Clay Cross by-election, *The Times*, September 4 1933.

47. Attlee to Tom Attlee, January 1 and August 18 1933. *Manchester Guardian* (from a correspondent), August 22 1933. Henderson at Labour Party Conference, October 4 1933, *Manchester Guardian*, October 5. See also Dalton describing himself as 'a Socialist and a pacificist', Dalton diary, March 8 1933.

48. Lansbury at West Ham, January 2 1933, *Daily Herald*, January 3.

49. 'A gallant soldier', as Ellen Wilkinson described him, *Daily Herald*, March 27 1933. For Hitler as 'clown', see *Daily Herald*, January 31 1933.

50. 'A Doctor looks at Hitler's Gang', *Daily Herald*, May 24 1933, Citrine, in *Daily Herald*, February 23 1933.

51. National Joint Council declaration of July 18 1933 calling for ban on German goods, *Daily Herald*, July 19.

52. *Daily Herald*, May 22 1933.

53. *Daily Herald*, May 18 1933.

54. For some of the uncertainties and for the varieties of Labour opinion about foreign policy, see Ponsonby, memo of October 22 1933, in Ponsonby to Lansbury, October 22. Cf. Attlee to Tom Attlee, November 6 1933.
55. E.g. Lansbury at Selly Oak, March 19 1933, *Birmingham Post*, March 20.
56. For Henderson's optimism, see e.g. *Manchester Guardian*, August 2 1933.
57. For one of the main debates, see *Hansard* (293) cols. 1293 *et seq.* of November 8 1934.
58. Manifesto issued by TUC, Labour Party and Cooperative Union in preparation for the Peace Campaign of December 1933, *The Times*, December 13. National Joint Council declarations, *Manchester Guardian*, April 26 1934 and in *Daily Herald*, May 16 1934.
59. Memo adopted by the Executives of the TUC, the Labour Party and PLP in *News Chronicle*, June 29 1934.
60. *Ibid.*
61. Attlee to Tom Attlee, February 7 1933.
62. Lansbury to Attlee [? September 5 1934] reporting feelings he did not share. Cf. *Daily Herald*, May 26 1933. Lansbury at Merthyr, July 29 1933, *Daily Herald*, July 31.
63. Morrison to Parmoor, April 12 1929, in Cooke, p. 105.
64. See Cooke, pp. 96—111.
65. Cooke, pp. 126—7.
66. Cripps to Brockway, April 7 1933.
67. Dalton diary, October 21 1937.
68. *The Times*, January 26 1934.
69. Dalton diary, January 19 1934.
70. I.e. *For Socialism and Peace*.
71. See e.g. *Manchester Guardian*, September 17 1934.
72. Cripps's introduction to Mitchison, pp. 12—13.
73. Citrine, pp. 293—301. For 'nationalist passions' see Dalton diary, May 4 1933.
74. Dalton diary, May 11 and July 14 to 16 1933. Citrine at TUC, September 7 1933, *Manchester Guardian* September 8.
75. Dalton diary, entry marked 1934—1935.
76. National Council of Labour declaration of November 12 1934, *News Chronicle* November 13.
77. Dalton diary, March 26—April 25 1935.

NOTES TO CHAPTER 2

1. A junior minister, Graham White.
2. Taylor, p. 335 says from 1931 (i.e. £2,000 p.a.).
3. Snowden in House of Lords, *Hansard* (87) cols. 999—1000 of May 24 1933. Snowden to Grigg, March 18 and July 29 1935.
4. Sinclair to Samuel, July 18 1933.

5.   Crozier, interview with Samuel, November 4 1933.
6.   Eastern Fife by-election result, February 2 1933: Stewart (Lib. Nat.) 15,770, Westwood (Lab.) 6,635, Anderson (Agricultural) 4,404, Keir (Ind.), 2,296, Linklater (Scot. Nat.) 1,083. At the 1931 election the Lib. Nat. candidate had been unopposed. At the 1929 election the result was Liberal 14,329, Conservative 13,748, Labour 5,350.
7.   *Daily Herald*, February 15 1933.
8.   *Daily Herlad*, May 20 1933.
9.   Sinclair to Samucl, July 18 1933.
10. Muir, p. 35. Sinclair to Brock, February 19 1934 and to Johnstone, March 22 1935. Sinclair to Samuel, July 18 and October 14 1933. For the discussions from which *The Liberal Way* emerged, see Sinclair MSS Box 74. See also Sinclair to Rea, October 9 1933 for scepticism about the programme.
11. Brett Young to Baldwin, April 3 1933, quoting Frances Stevenson.
12. For an example of this, see Snowdon to Samuel, November 20 1933 quoting Lloyd George.
13. Stevenson diary, March 25 1934. Lloyd George to Layton, August 29 1934, Lloyd George MSS.
14. Stevenson diary, April 9 1935. Lloyd George to Cecil, April 25 1934 and Stevenson diary, May 31 1934 for the comments on Simon. *War Memoirs*, vol. 3, p. 1074, published in September 1934, contained Kitchener's remarks about Runciman.
15. Stevenson diary, September 25 1934.
16. Hoare to Baldwin, September 8 1933, quoting Lothian quoting Lloyd George, Snowden and Beaverbrook at Churt.
17. Lloyd George to Nathan, January 4 1933, Lloyd George MSS.
18. Stevenson diary, September 25 1934. Lloyd George talking to Wood, in Chamberlain diary, April 14 1935.
19. Stevenson diary, November 22 1934 and April 9 1935. Addison to Lloyd George, October 28 1934, and Lloyd George to Addison, December 12 1934, Lloyd George MSS.
20. Layton, note on policy, December 10 1934 in Lloyd George MSS G/141/26/6.
21. Stevenson diary, November 22 1934. Lansbury at Mitcham, 15 December 1934, *Daily Herald*, December 17.
22. Stevenson diary, February 21, May 14 and September 25 1934, and March 11 1935. Boothby to Lloyd George, March 23 and December 16 1934. Macmillan to Lloyd George, December 12 1934 and January 21 1935. Smuts to Baldwin, November 14 1934. For Astor, see Astor to Lloyd George, December 22 1934. For Macmillan, Elliot, Boothby and Stanley in 1930, see Mosley pp. 273—4.
23. Stevenson diary, March 28 1934.
24. Stevenson diary, November 30 1934. Churchill to Lloyd George, November 24 1934.
25. Stevenson diary, February 18 and November 6 1934. For it being

Goering not Hitler who was responsible for persecution of the Jews see, Lloyd George to Guedalla, March 6 1934 and for the Germans not by temperament being persecutors see Lloyd George to Guedalla, November 6 1934, both Lloyd George MSS.

26. Lloyd George at Bangor, January 17 1935, *Manchester Guardian*, January 18. Lloyd George to Mrs H.A.L. Fisher, January 22 1935 and Lloyd George to Layton, August 29 1934, Lloyd George MSS. Sir Daniel Stevenson to Lloyd George, January 28 1935, refers to Lloyd George's decision 'to use tariffs ruthlessly and to the full'.

27. Stevenson diary, September 28 and October 5 1934. Dawson diary, February 25 1934.

28. Stevenson diary, November 30 1934 and January 29 1935. For some flattering words, see Baldwin at Conservative Women's Advisory Committee, May 11 1934, *The Times*, May 12.

29. Lloyd George to Grigg, January 1 1935, Lloyd George MSS. Grigg to Lloyd George, January 8 1935. Baldwin to Grigg, January 10 1935. Stevenson diary, December 5 1934.

30. I.e. from Putney onwards Lloyd George to Jones, March 16 1935, Lloyd George MSS.

31. Stevenson diary, April 9 and 17 1935.

32. Jones to Baldwin, May 16 1935 (copy) in Lloyd George MSS. Stevenson diary, May 18 1935. Sinclair to Johnstone, May 8 and vice versa, May 9 1935. Sinclair to Samuel, May 4 1935.

33. Stevenson diary, July 17 1935.

34. Gilbert, *Plough My Own Furrow* pp. 304–307.

35. This included luminaries like Layton, Lothian, Snowden, Rathbone, Brown, Crowther, Allen of Hurtwood, Arnold-Forster, Francis Acland, a clutch of Free Church leaders, Sir Basil Blackett, who died in August and Macmillan (rather ambiguously). For all this see Layton to Lloyd George, September 1, Acland to Lloyd George, September 9 and Cummings to Lloyd George, June 2 1935, Lloyd George MSS.

36. Stevenson diary, September 26 1935.

37. For disunity, especially between Lothian and the rest, see Dorothea Layton and W. Arnold-Forster to Lloyd George, August 15 1935 and Layton to Lloyd George, September 1 1935.

38. See Stonehaven memorandum of August 1 1934, Baldwin MSS.

39. Runciman to Shuttleworth, December 1 1933, Runciman MSS.

40. Petrie, *The Chamberlain Tradition* p. 241.

41. De la Warr to MacDonald, November 15 1934, Baldwin MSS, including some of them thinking that the only way to secure their futures was to become Conservatives.

42. Cab 8(34) of March 7 showing Young preparing to negotiate with local authorities. See Stonehaven memorandum of November 21 1934, Baldwin MSS, and Young to Baldwin, October 6 1934 for the non-compensation of slum landowners. For the extensive correspondence about decentralization between Balfour of Burleigh

and Baldwin between February 1934 and February 1935, see
Baldwin MSS vol. 25.
43. Chamberlain diary, December 3 1934. The bill was introduced in
March 1934 after MacDonald had persuaded Gilmour to remove
the police from its purview (Cab 8(34) of March 7).
44. The Betting and Lotteries bill was introduced to the Cabinet on
March 8 1934 (CP 52(34)) pulling together regulations about
betting, lotteries etc. covered by the Royal Commission. It was,
however, introduced 'in order to test parliamentary and public
opinion' (Cab 8(34) of March 7) and was modified by the dropping of football pools (after public and 1922 Committee criticism
(Cab 17(34) of April 25).
45. See below p. 117.
46. See Stannage, p. 92 for TUC converting NEC to demanding abolition of the Means Test instituted by the National government.
(Stannage quotes NJC meeting of February 23 1932 and NEC
meeting of February 24.)
47. Chamberlain to Ida and Hilda, December 9 1934. For the Cabinet
approving them, see Cab 44(34) of November 30.
48. *Hansard* (297) cols. 961—7 of February 5 1935. Chamberlain at
Cab 8 (35) of February 6.
49. Chamberlain to Hilda, December 15 1934.
50. Chamberlain to Ida, February 2 1935.
51. Chamberlain diary, February 13 1935.
52. R.S. Hudson.
53. Chamberlain diary, April 29 and May 3 1935. Chamberlain to
Hilda, March 9 1935.
54. E.g. Salisbury to Baldwin, February 10 1935.
55. Stonehaven to Baldwin, May 14 1933.
56. Hoare to Willingdon, April 20 1934 (Eur.E.240) says only
30 Conservative MPs really wanted it. Cf. Hoare to Sir G. Stanley, May 22 1934, Eur.E.240. For Simon and Hailsham, see
Hoare to Willingdon, January 17 1935, Eur.E.240. For Chamberlain, see Hoare to Willingdon, September 27 1934, Eur.E.240.
57. Cf. Churchill hoping to 'break the bloody "wat" [rat] Hoare's
neck if I risk my own' (during the Privilege Case), in Butler to
Brabourne, April 19 1934.
58. For the dissenting vote in December 1934 being unpleasantly
large, see Chamberlain to Hilda, December 15 1934 and Hoare to
Willingdon, December 13 1934, Eur.E.240. For February, see
Hoare to Willingdon, February 7 1935, Eur.E.240.
59. Stonehaven to Baldwin, May 14 1933.
60. Stonehaven, memorandum of December 12 1933.
61. For House of Lords reform see Chamberlain diary, January 27
1934 and Linlithgow to Baldwin, December 21 1933. For the
Land Tax agitation, see Baldwin to MacDonald, April 7, Mac-
Donald to Baldwin, April 8 and Chamberlain diary, May 9 1934.
See also Courthorpe to MacDonald, May 31 1933 (and for Baldwin holding the land tax agitation in check in 1933).

62. Stonehaven to Baldwin, May 10 1934.
63. Rothermere to Beaverbrook, January 11 1934.
64. Rothermere to Croft, October 28 1934.
65. Rothermere to Lloyd George, January 25 1935. Grigg to Baldwin, January 8 [1935].
66. Rothermere to Beaverbrook, August 2 and October 24 1935 (tel.). For all this, see also Stevenson diary, 1935 *passim*.
67. Hoare to Chamberlain, June 5 and 12 1934 (Templewood MSS) quoting Beaverbrook. Cf. Bruce Lockhart diary, August 6 1934.
68. But for Beaverbrook interceding (successfully) to get Hailsham to introduce Rothermere to the House of Lords on taking up his ten-year-old viscountcy, see Hailsham to Beaverbrook, December 1 1934 and vice versa, December 5.
69. Beaverbrook to Chamberlain, February 15 1934, implies that there were approaches before.
70. Beaverbrook to Chamberlain, February 15 1934.
71. Hoare to Beaverbrook, June 1 1934 etc. and Hoare to Chamberlain, June 12 1934.
72. Beaverbrook to Hoare, June 18 1934.
73. Beaverbrook to Hoare, July 26 and 28 1934.
74. Beaverbrook to Rothermere, January 11 1935.
75. I.e. Margesson sent this request via Sandys, who was the candidate at Norwood, where a Right-wing candidate was standing. Chamberlain diary, March 8 1935 says that Chamberlain had nothing to do with it.
76. At which Randolph Churchill was running a Right-wing Independent Conservative against the official Conservative (in the hope of repeating Wavertree). See e.g. *The Times*, March 14 1935.
77. Chamberlain to Beaverbrook, March 6 1935, Chamberlain MSS. Stevenson diary, March 24 1935.
78. Chamberlain to Hilda, July 28 1935.
79. Chamberlain to Hilda, November 9 1935.
80. This was introduced into the Cabinet on March 21 1934 (CP 75(34)) with the object of simplifying procedures for collection and to some extent in order to mitigate the severity of its incidence on small farmers. But it was opposed on the ground that it made it into a personal debt (Cab 19(34) of May 2). For the desire to refer it to a Select Committee, see Cab 21(34) of May 16. For the eventual decision to abandon the Select Committee and have a Royal Commission, see Cab 23(34) of June 6.
81. Bridgeman to Baldwin, April 12 and 14 1934. Sankey diary, *passim* April 1934.
82. Even when designed also to show that Labour and League of Nations Union propaganda was exaggerated. See Cab 27/508 of October 23 and 30, November 15 1934 and February 11 1935. For Thomas forcing the Cabinet's hand, see Simon to Eden, November 20 1934, FO 800/291. See also Cab 37(34) of October 24 and 38(34) of October 31.
83. I.e. Bayford, Fitzalan, Steel-Maitland and Gretton. Salisbury to

Baldwin, October 23 and November 10 1933. Selborne to Hailsham, May 12 1934, MS Selborne 86. Midleton to Selborne,
April 28 1933, MS Selborne 3.

84. Selborne to Stonehaven, June 8 1934, MS Selborne 86.

85. See e.g. Ball to Chamberlain, October 9 1933 for the subject
being too 'thorny' for the Conservative party to 'touch' unless
'obliged to'. But see Stonehaven to Baldwin, November 1 1933
for the Chairman of the Conservative party thinking it urgent.
(He voted for both the first and second readings of Salisbury's
bill.)

86. See CP 33(2).

87. For the Cabinet Committee see Cab 27/562 (January 29 1934
etc.) and Chamberlain diary, January 29 1934. For Baldwin originally leaving a positive impression, see Midleton to Baldwin,
December 9 1933.

88. See *Hansard*, Lords (90) of December 19 1933 and (92) of
May 10 1934 for the debates and division lists. Cab 19(34) of
May 2. For further evidence of dislike see MacDonald to Steel-
Maitland, August 12 1933.

89. Chamberlain diary, January 22 1934.

90. Midleton to Selborne, November 8 1935, MS Selborne 3, for Baldwin's promise to Midleton in 1933 and Midleton's belief that
Salisbury had made it impossible to carry out. Selborne to Midleton, October 10 1933, MS Selborne 87, for Baldwin promising
Selborne.

91. Baldwin to Salisbury, October 25 1935, PREM 1/223.

92. Chamberlain to Selborne, November 6 1935, MS Selborne 86.

93. See e.g. Amery, Austen Chamberlain, Peto and Herbert Williams
attacking Runciman's Anglo-German, and other, trade treaties for
being insufficiently protectionist, see Amery diary, May 1 and 25
1933 and *Daily Herald*, April 28 and May 2 1933.

94. E.g. Hoare to Willingdon, January 25 1934, Eur.E.240.

95. MacDonald to J. Bromley, November 14 1933, to Londonderry,
December 1 1933, and to Sir William Davison, December 25
1933.

96. MacDonald to Runciman, August 21 1933 and to Davison, December 25 1933.

97. MacDonald to Austen Chamberlain, February 1 & 3 1933. For
MacDonald's long correspondence with Sir Harold Bellman about
a drive to build rented property and clear slums, see MacDonald
MSS 1933–5.

98. MacDonald to J. Richardson, May 30 1933.

99 MacDonald to Steel-Maitland, August 12 1933 for the threat. It is
not clear at what point the threat became unreal.

100. MacDonald to Courthorpe, June 4 1933.

101. De la Warr to MacDonald, November 15 1934, Baldwin MSS. By
August 1934 the National Labour party had been given only
three seats, see Stonehaven, memoranda of December 12 1933
and August 1 1934, Baldwin MSS.

102. Stonehaven memorandum of December 12 1933, Baldwin MSS.
103. Baldwin at Liverpool, March 25 1935, *Liverpool Post*, March 26.
104. Davidson to R.D.F., March 28 1934, Davidson MSS.
105. Astor to Lloyd George, December 22 1934.
106 Baldwin at Culzean Castle, July 21 1935, *Glasgow Herald* July 23. Grigg to Baldwin, January 3 1935. Cf. Namier in Bruce Lockhart diary, December 4 1934.
107. See below Part one.
108. E.g. Grigg to Baldwin, January 11, and to Lloyd George, January 8 1935.
109. Nicolson diary, November 21, December 20 1935, and January 28 1936.
110. Pownall diary, February 10 1936.
111. Percy to Baldwin, November 22 1935.
112. Gilbert, *Plough My Own Furrow*, Ch. 18.
113. *Ibid.* ch. 20.
114. *Ibid.* pp. 309—11 for Allen supporting Mander and Macmillan.
115. For all this, see Chamberlain diary, February and March 1934, *passim*. See also the correspondence between Beechman and Runciman between November 1934 and May 1935 in Runciman MSS and Runciman to Chamberlain, June 4 1935. Cf. Chamberlain to Ida, January 6 1935. See also PREM 1/207 for Coal-mining royalties.
116. For Addison, see Banks to Baldwin, October 14 1933. For Bevin see Jones diary, February 27 1934.
117. Chamberlain diary, March 1 1934 for Hore-Belisha saying that Simon believed that MacDonald was behind it and for Hore-Belisha criticising Simon. Chamberlain diary, February 17 1934 for MacDonald having lunch with Beaverbrook and Rothermere next Thursday. Simon diary, November 22 1934.
118. Chamberlain diary, February 28 and December 3 and 4 1934. Garvin to Astor, March 24, 1934.
119. Chamberlain diary, December 1934, *passim*.
120. Despite the criticisms of a group led by Balfour of Burleigh, see above p. 432 n. 42.
121. Derby to Baldwin, December 21 1934. Cab 43(34) of November 24. Young to his wife, February 5 1934 for Dawson asking MacDonald to get rid of him. For sensitivity to criticism see Young to his wife [February 1934]. Chamberlain diary, February 17 1934.
122. Chamberlain diary, March 1 1934. Sankey diary, March 1 1934.
123. Chamberlain diary, February 19 1934.
124. I.e. Geoffrey Lloyd, Chamberlain diary, February 19 1934.
125. Chamberlain diary, February 24 1934.
126. Chamberlain diary, February 28 1934.
127. Young to his wife, April 5 1934.
128. Stevenson diary, February 21 1934 for Lloyd George saying that 'we should keep a strong hand in India'. But cf. Hoare to Bald-

win, September 8 1933 for Lloyd George's view that India would never be settled until terms were made with Gandhi and the Congress. For another view see Smuts to Baldwin, November 14 1934.

129. See above p. 38, Stevenson diary, April 20 1934. Astor to Garvin, February 23 1934 for Margesson also brooding.
130. Chamberlain to Ida, January 20 1935.
131. Chamberlain diary, March 18 1935.
132. Chamberlain diary, January 28 1935.
133. Chamberlain diary, December 1934, *passim*.
134. Chamberlain diary, December 3, 4, 5 and 11 1934 and January 30 1935. For Cunliffe-Lister as a critic of Chamberlain see Young to his wife, August 22 1933 reporting Irwin (Halifax). For Margesson as a supporter of Lloyd George see Astor to Garvin, February 23 1934.
135. Chamberlain to Baldwin, January 4, and to Ida, January 6 and 28 1935. Chamberlain diary January 28 1935.
136. Chamberlain to Hilda, February 23 1935.
137. Chamberlain to Ida, January 20 1935.
138. Chamberlain to Hilda, February 23 1935.
139. For Simon see speech at Bexhill, January 25 1935, *Manchester Guardian*, January 26 Chamberlain diary, January 30 1935.
140. Ormsby-Gore to Baldwin, Sunday [February 10 or 17] 1935. Butler to Brabourne, March 29 1935.
141. Chamberlain diary, February 5 1935.
142. For Wood reporting that Baldwin was willing to have Lloyd George, see Chamberlain diary, January 28 1935. For Thomas hoping, just possibly, to succeed MacDonald, backed by the support of younger ministers, see Butler to Brabourne, February 1 1935. For Simon congratulating Lloyd George on his speech in the Defence debate, see Stevenson diary, November 30 1934.
143. Chamberlain diary, February 7 1935.
144. Chamberlain to Ida, March 3 1935. Lloyd George in *Daily Mail*, March 1 1935.
145. MacDonald to Lloyd George, March 1 1935.
146. Stevenson diary, March 3 1935. For Lloyd George's immediate reply — an attack upon Chamberlain for rejecting national development based on borrowing — see Lloyd George to MacDonald, March 2 1935, Lloyd George MSS, G/141/29/2.
147. Chamberlain to Ida, March 3 and Chamberlain diary, March 8 1935.
148. Chamberlain to Weir, March 5 1935.
149. Chamberlain to Hilda, March 9 1935.
150. Chamberlain to Ida, March 16 1935. Lloyd George to MacDonald, March 14 1935, for the plans, G/141/29/3.
151. Which had been set up in order to respond to the New Deal, see Chamberlain diary, January 24 1935. Chamberlain to Hilda, January 26 1935, says that it was not: i.e. that it was designed for the general election, but the diary entry leaves the impression that it

was. Cab 6(35) of January 30 and Cabs 17(35) of March 27 and 22(35) of April 10.

152. Apart from Runciman and Baldwin.
153. Chamberlain diary, April 5 1935, and to Hilda, April 6.
154. Stevenson diary, April 18 1935.
155. Chamberlain to Hilda, April 21 and Chamberlain diary, April 18 1935.
156. Stevenson diary, April 18 1935.
157. Chamberlain diary, April 18, and to Hilda, April 21 1935.
158. MacDonald to Hoare, April 30 1935.
159. Chamberlain diary, April 18, and to Hilda, May 18 and June 2 1935.
160. Dawson diary, June 12 1935.
161. Lloyd George to Baldwin, July 9 1935, Lloyd George MSS G/141/4/1. See also the government press statement of July 18 (for publication on July 22) 1935, PREM 1/183.
162. E.g. Butler to Brabourne, February 22 1934, Garvin to Astor, March 14 1934. Hoare to Willingdon, February 7 1935, Eur.E. 240. See also Dawson diary, November 3 and December 3 1934.
163. MacDonald to Thomas, January 2 1933 and to Chamberlain, May 22 1933, both in MacDonald MSS. For inconvenient commitments from the past see *Daily Herald*, May 19 1933 and Alexander at Manchester, March 11 1933 in *Manchester Guardian*, March 13. Chamberlain diary, March 16 1934, Sankey diary, December 31 1934, and MacDonald to Young, November 27 1934.
164. MasDonald to J. Richardson, May 30 1933, to Betterton, August 4 1933 and to Wigram, June 2 1933.
165. MacDonald to Wigram, June 2 1933 and to Usher, June 1 1933. For Kenneth Lindsay being MacDonald's choice and Kilmarnock as a special triumph for MacDonald see Chamberlain to MacDonald, November 3 1933 and Israel Sieff to MacDonald, November 14 1933.
166. Sankey diary, June 19 and 22 1934.
167. Chamberlain dairy, April 26 1934. Hankey diary, March 4 1934.
168. MacDonald to Sankey, July 15 1934.
169. MacDonald to Young, November 27 1934. Sankey diary, November 26 1934. Dawson diary, October 4 1934.
170. Chamberlain to Ida, October 13 1934. Sankey diary, February 11 1935.
171. Chamberlain diary, February 11 1935.
172. Simon diary, February 14 1935. Baldwin at Chelsea, February 21 1935, *The Times*, February 22.
173. Chamberlain to Hilda, May 18 1935. For this change a number of reasons may be suggested. There was Chamberlain's hostility to Lloyd George which was unpopular in parts of the Cabinet and in some Conservative quarters (e.g. Camrose, Astor, Beaverbrook, Garvin) where there would normally be support for a Chamberlain Prime Ministership. There was the reputation he had been given by Labour, by the Liberal newspapers and by Lloyd

George, as the proponent of a narrow Treasury view and the instrument of Norman who was treated as the brain behind the reduction in unemployment benefit. Moreover, in February Baldwin may either have been leading Chamberlain on to believe that he wanted him to be Prime Minister (in the hope that he would be accommodating about Lloyd George) or may just have been obfuscating a situation he did not think he could control. He may, for example, have hoped to take Lloyd George in, even if Chamberlain resigned, provided Chamberlain did not take too many ministers with him. He may have feared that, if relations with Simon went sour when Simon was removed from the Foreign Office, the Simonites would leave a Liberal hole which Lloyd George would be able to fill. Or he may have expected MacDonald to resign and other National Labour ministers to return to the Labour party if he could not remain Prime Minister. Baldwin may also have meant what he said when he (or Margesson) told Chamberlain that Chamberlain was the only person who could lead the party in the condition in which India had left it. For all this there is little evidence. But two things are clear — that Baldwin decided that Lloyd George, however welcome in some Conservative quarters, would be resented more even than MacDonald in others, and that it was not until mid-May that he made up his mind to become Prime Minister.

174. Chamberlain diary, February 13 1935.
175. Hailsham to Baldwin, May 28 1935.
176. Young to Chamberlain, June 25 1935.
177. I.e. with Brown's appointment to the Ministry of Labour, Simon diary, June 4, and Simon to Baldwin, May 20 1935.
178. Simon diary, May 15, and Simon to Baldwin, May 20 1935.
179. Chamberlain diary, May 3 1935, and to Ida, May 4.
180. Chamberlain to Hilda, May 22 1935.
181. Chamberlain diary, May 17 1935.
182. And to get office for Kenneth Lindsay, see Butler to Brabourne, June 20 1935.
183. For Thomas being disliked by Dominions politicians, see Hanworth to Baldwin, May 29 1935, and for being 'the worse for drink' when the Chiefs of Staff came to see the Cabinet, see Pownall diary, May 27 1935.
184. E.g. Butler to Brabourne, February 22 1934.
185. His father was a partner in the firm of Thomas Sankey, 'drapers and, undertakers' in Moreton-in-the-Marsh. After his father's death, Sankey's education was paid for by a vicar in Swansea (where his mother had then moved), see Heuston, ch. on Sankey.
186. Simon diary, June 4 1935.
187. See especially Sankey to Baldwin, January 15 1932 and *passim* in PREM 1/134. *Hansard*, House of Lords (90) cols. 60 *et seq* of November 23 1933 and *Hansard*, House of Lords (95) cols. 366 *et seq* for Supreme Court of Judicature (Amendment) Bill. Sankey diary, December 11–20 1934.

188. See above p. 54.
189. Sankey diary, April 19 and November 14 and 30, 1934. See also Citrine, p. 291 for Middleton as an admirer of MacDonald even after 1931.
190. Baldwin to Sankey, May 31 1935.
191. Sankey to Baldwin, June 1 1935, and Sankey diary, June 3 1935.
192. Sankey memorandum, *'Last Six Months of Lord Chancellorship'*, June 6/7 1935. Sankey diary, May 29 and 30 1935.
193. Dawson diary, July 1 1935.

NOTES TO CHAPTER 3

1. See, e.g., Eden to Baldwin, February 10 and 22 1933, for an arms manufacture agreement.
2. I.e. and especially Hailsham, Monsell and Londonderry.
3. For the British Draft Proposals of January 30 1933, see *DBFP*, Series Two, vol. IV, pp. 492–4. For the British Draft Convention of March 16 1933 see *ibid*. pp. 558–65.
4. Hankey to his wife, July 4 1933.
5. See e.g. Cab 27/505 of January 20 1933.
6. MacDonald to Baldwin, March 12 1933.
7. MacDonald in Cab 27/505 of March 2 and May 12 1933. Simon to Baldwin, May 12 1933.
8. See Cab 27/505 of March 5 1933 (especially Hailsham). Eden at Cab 27/505 of March 3 1933 and MacDonald to Baldwin, March 12 1933.
9. Eden to Baldwin, February 10 and 24, and at Cab 27/505 of February 17 1933. MacDonald at Cab 27/505 of March 2 1933.
10. MacDonald in Cab 27/505 of March 2 1933.
11. For Henderson and the Cabinet, see Simon to Vansittart, December 23 1933. Cab 27/505 of January 20, March 2, May 12, November 7 1933. Ormsby-Gore to Baldwin, Sunday [October 8 1933]. For discussion of the Geneva delegation's Convention see Cab 27/505, March 2, 3 and 5 1933. See also Sargent to Phipps, November 16 1933.
12. Mussolini to MacDonald, April 10 1933 (copy), in Baldwin MSS. Austen Chamberlain to Simon, May 11 1933, FO 800/288.
13. MacDonald to Baldwin, March 12 1933. Baldwin to Cecil, March 12 1933. Eden to Cecil, March 24, and to Baldwin, May 1 and October 13 1933.
14. Cab 27/505 of July 25 1933, fo.402.
15. Simon broadcast, October 17 1933, *The Times*, October 18. Cab 27/505 of November 7 1933.
16. Cab 27/505 of November 7 1933, fo.406.
17. Cab 27/506 of March 6 1934.
18. Eden at Cab 27/506 of March 6 1934. Hoare to Willingdon, January 25 1934, Eur. E. 240.

19. Eden to Baldwin, February 23 1934. Simon at Cab 23(34) of June 6, and to Spender, June 5 1934.
20. E.g. Simon to A—G, November 2 1933, FO 800/288 and Baldwin at Cab 28(34) of July 11.
21. And also French 'corruption', see Chamberlain diary, February 3 1934.
22. See e.g. Davidson, note on E.M.W. Tennant's report of January 19 1934, Davidson MSS.
23. Simon at Cab 27/506 of April 9 1934. Cab 27/506 of March 6 and January 26 1934. Simon and MacDonald at Cab 27/506 of February 26 1934.
24. Eden at Cab 27/506 of March 6 1934.
25. Simon at Cab 27(34) of July 4.
26. Cab 10(34) of March 19.
27. For the unofficial and official economic negotiations of 1934, see Leith-Ross, Wendt and the Tennant correspondence in Davidson MSS. For Baldwin sending Geoffrey Lloyd and Christie to Germany and for Tennant trying to arrange a visit, see Tennant in Davidson MSS. See also Dawson diary, October 18 1933.
28. Eden to Baldwin, February 21 1934.
29. Hankey to Vansittart, January 9 1934, FO 800/291.
30. See e.g. Memorandum on Disarmament, CP 10(34) in Cab 27/510 of January 26 1934.
31. Cab 27/506 of April 19, 20, 24 and May 1 1934. MacDonald, DC(M)(32) 98 of April 6 1934 in Cab 27/510. Simon, draft note of May 2 1934, DC(M)(32) 105 of May 2 in Cab 27/510. See also Chamberlain diary for these weeks.
32. DC(M) (32) 92 in Cab 27/510 of March 23 1934. Cab 27/506 of March 6, 26 and 28, April 9 and May 1 1934.
33. Cab 23(34) of June 6 and Cab 26(34) of June 27. Simon to Spender, June 5 1934.
34. See Cab 28(34) of July 11. Cf. A. L. Kennedy to Daniels, July 10 1934, quoting Simon, *The Times* Archive.
35. Simon at Cab 25(34) of June 19. Vansittart, note of July 3 1934, for the danger of the blood bath being that the Junkers would benefit. Simon at Cab 27(34) of July 4.
36. I.e. the Permanent Secretary to the Treasury, and the Permanent Under-Secretary at the Foreign Office. For the discussions of the Committee see Cab 16/109. The report CP 64 (34) of March is dated February 28 1934.
37. £80—110m. i.e. (p. 33) £82m. plus the items in para. 5 on p. 33.
38. Pownall diary, January 18 1934.
39. Proposing to raise 40½ squadrons over 4 years at a cost of £20m.
40. Cab 31(34) of July 31. The interim report was dated July 19 1934, CP 193(34). The full report is CP 204(34) of July 31 1934.
41. Chamberlain diary, June 6 1934. Fisher to Chamberlain, October 14 1938, for Fisher saying that this was his idea.
42. E.g. the decision not to mention Belgium publicly, Cab 26(34) of June 27.

43. Baldwin and MacDonald at Cab 28(34) of July 11.
44. *Hansard* (295) of November 28 1934, cols. 872–84. See also CP 193(34) in Cab 16/110 of July 19 1934.
45. E.g. Simon in Cab 35(34) of October 17.
46. I.e. because Italy and Yugoslavia might intervene if there was another revolt, Cab 32(34) of September 25.
47. Simon to A–G, November 2 1933, FO 800/288.
48. E.g. MacDonald and Vansittart at Cab 27/506 of February 9 and 15 1934. Simon to Austen Chamberlain, September 7 1933, AC 40/5/85. Simon diary, November 20 1934.
49. E.g. MacDonald at Cab 10(34) of March 19.
50. C.I.D. of November 22 1934 in Cab 2/6(i).
51. For preliminary discussions see Committee on German Rearmament of November 22 1934 in Cab 27/572.
52. *Hansard* (295) cols. 872–85 of November 28 1934.
53. *Ibid.* col. 982. Simon diary, November 28 1934. Cab 27/572 of November 22 1934 (two meetings). Cab 41(34) of November 21 and Cab 42(34) of November 26.
54. Simon in GR (34) 3 of November 29 1934 in Cab 27/572 and at 47(34) of December 19.
55. Simon, GR (34)3 of November 29 1934 and GR(34)4 of December 8, in Cab 27/572. Cab 27/572 of December 11 and 13 1934. Cab 46(34) of December 12 and 2(35) of January 9. Simon diary, December 21 and 23 1934, January 1, 8, 13 and 25 and February 5 1935.
56. For the proposals as they eventually arrived, see CP 33(35) and Cab 7(35) of February 2.
57. Though not in the independence or in the demilitarisation of the Rhineland (on the ground that the latter was covered by Locarno) see Cab 3(35) of January 14.
58. Simon diary, February 9 1935.
59. Cab 27/508 of February 19 1935.
60. I.e. Cmd. 4827, published on March 4 1935. Hankey to Phipps, March 8 1935.
61. Simon diary, March 27 1935. Cab 18(35) of March 27 for Simon's report on the visit. Cf. Cab 16(35) of March 20 for the danger of opposing camps.
62. See especially Cabs 20 and 21 (35) of April 8.
63. *Ibid.* and in Cab 24(35) of April 17.
64. Simon diary, April 11 and 14 1935.
65. See Cab 29(35) of May 21 for acceptance.
66. Even after the Anglo-German naval treaty and Hitler's reversal of support for the Air Pact (Simon diary, May 22 1935. Cab 30(35) of May 22).
67. Cab 30(35) of May 22.
68. E.g. Simon to MacDonald, July 27 1934, FO 800/291.
69. Simon at Cab 10(34) of March 19.
70. Simon diary, March 27 1935. Simon to King George V, March 27 1935, FO/800/290, for 'if Joan of Arc had been born in Austria

and worn a moustache...' Simon to Phipps, April 5 1935, FO 800/290.

71. Butler to Brabourne, July 27 1934, for Ormsby-Gore running down the lobby saying 'in a loud tone...that Simon was the worst Foreign Secretary we had ever had' when he failed to express himself 'more openly' after the assassination of Dollfuss.

72. Cab 27/505 of December 6 and 7 1933 for the Ministerial Committee on Disarmament compelling him to do a somersault in replying to Hitler's peace proposals. Chamberlain diary, October 25/17 1934 and Chamberlain to Hilda, October 21 and November 17 1934.

73. Simon to Baldwin, April 10 1935, for Simon putting it on the record.

74. Chamberlain diary, March 11 1935.

75. E.g. Simon to Murray, January 18 1933, FO 800/288.

76. Butler to Brabourne, July 27 1934.

77. For an example of jealousy, see Chamberlain diary, March 8 1935. Tyrell to Baldwin, September 28 and November 19 1933. Ormsby-Gore to Baldwin, October 1 and Sunday [October 8] 1933 and Monday [c. February 26 1934]. Ormsby-Gore to Baldwin, March 29 1935. Eden to Baldwin, February 10 and 22, 1933 and January 11 1935 [1934 written]. Headlam diary, March 6 1935, for Ormsby-Gore 'shrieking with laughter over the government's messes'.

78. Simon at Stoke-on-Trent, December 18 1933, *The Times*, December 19.

79. Simon at Cleckheaton, November 24 1933, *Manchester Guardian*, November 25.

80. Simon at Liverpool, April 27 1934, *Liverpool Post*, April 28.

81. For an example of Simon squaring the circle, see his presentation of the proposed Locarno Air Pact (designed to edge France towards a disarmament agreement) as involving no new obligations and being a 'deterrent' providing 'immunity' from 'sudden air attacks' (cf. Simon to King George V, February 4 1935, FO 800/290, at Cab 27/508 of February 19 1935, and broadcast of February 3 1935, *Manchester Guardian*, February 4).

82. For an example of detachment from *The Times*'s 'defeatism' see Cabs 20 and 21(35) of April 8.

83. Simon to Chamberlain, March 6 1934 and at Cab 9(34) of March 14. Simon to Vansittart, December 23 1933.

84. E.g. Hailsham to Simon, February 7 1933, FO 800/291.

85. E.g. Cab 27/506 of February 9 1934, fos. 96–7.

86. Selborne to his wife, May 17 1933, MS Selborne 107. Hailsham in *Hansard*, House of Lords (87) col. 897 of May 11 1933. For the speech being singled out as anti-German see *Daily Herald*, May 12 1933. Cf. Cab 27/505 of May 12 1933.

87. E.g. Cab 27/505 of February 17 1933.

88. E.g. Londonderry to MacDonald, February 24 1933 and Cab 27/506 of April 9 1934.

89. Simon to Drummond, February 13 1934, FO 800/291 and Cab 27/506 of February 15 1934. For MacDonald see Cab 27/506 of February 15 1934, fos. 119 and 123.
90. Cab 27/505 of January 10 1934. Cab 27/506 of April 9 1934. Cab 16(35) of March 20. Chamberlain diary, March 8 and 27 and April 2 1935.
91. ' Vansittart talking in Chamberlain diary, April 2 1935.
92. Cab 27/505 of December 6 and 7 1933.
93. Cab 27/506 of January 23 1934, fo.46. Chamberlain diary, January 1934 (recording 'previous two months').
94. Simon diary, April 11–14 1935. Vansittart to Simon, July 31 1934, FO 800/291. Simon to Baldwin, August 2 1934. For Simon being rather against making the Eastern Pact essential, see Cab 27/508 of February 19 1935, fo.111. For Simon not being very pro-Japanese because of his Liberal and Foreign Office China policy see Cab 27/506 of April 20 1934.
95. E.g. A. L. Kennedy to Daniels, July 10 1934, quoting Simon, *The Times* Archive.
96. Simon to MacDonald, October 3 1934, FO 800/291. Simon diary, November 20, December 11 and 21 1934 and February 28 1935. Simon in Cab 27/572 of December 11 1934, fo.42.
97. Sankey diary, March 28 1935.
98. Chamberlain diary, April 8 1935.
99. Austen Chamberlain to Hilda/Ida, April 6 1935. Headlam diary, May 9 1935. Glyn to MacDonald, May 3 1935.
100. MacDonald to Cecil, October 11 1933.
101. Cab 27/506 of February 5 1934, fo.82 and of March 6 1934, fo. 172. For MacDonald saying that he regretted the rejection of the Geneva Protocol in 1924 see Cab 27/506 of March 6 1934. DC(M)(32) 98 of April 6 1934, Cab 27/510. Cab 3(35) of January 14.
102. Cab 27/505 of November 30 1933, fo.442. Cab 26(34) of June 27.
103. Cab 27/506 of April 9 1934.
104. MacDonald to J.G. Braithwaite MP, November 6 1933.
105. E.g. MacDonald to Lord Davies, January 23 1933.
106. MacDonald to Beazley, March 16 1934.
107. MacDonald to Beazley, October 26 and November 19 1934.
108. E.g. Cab 27/508 of May 27 1935. For Thomas objecting to the Chiefs of Staff even being allowed to be present at the Cabinet, see Pownall diary, May 9 1934 and May 27 1935.
109. Cab 16(35) of March 20.
110. Cab 27/508 of February 19 1935.
111. Chamberlain diary, April 2 1935.
112. Jones to Lady Grigg, May 12 1935, quoting Baldwin.
113. Selby, p. 46 for Baldwin saying that Hoare was being sent to clear up differences between pro-French and pro-German positions in the Foreign Office.

114. Cecil to Eden, December 7 1934, Add. MSS 51083, and to Murray, January 14 1935.
115. Cecil to Eden, February 5 1935, Add. MSS 51083.
116. Cecil to Baldwin, March 29 1935.
117. Cecil to Baldwin, May 2 1935.
118. Cecil to Baldwin, May 2 1935.
119. Note by Hoare on talk with Cecil, June 25 1935, FO 800/295.
120. Cecil to Eden, July 11 1935, Add. MSS 51083, and to Murray, August 30 1935.
121. Cecil to Cranborne, October 3 and 17, to Murray, November 1 and August 21, to Walters, August 19 and to Eden, November 14, all 1935.
122. Cecil to Noel-Baker, May 4 and 22 1935, Add. MSS 51108.
123. Cecil to Noel-Baker, May 4 1935.
124. Cecil to Murray, August 30 1935.
125. Cecil, note of luncheon with Lloyd George, June 4 1935, Add. MSS 51076. Cecil to Lloyd George, June 24 1935. Cecil to Eden, May 27, Add. MSS 51083, and to Noel-Baker, May 22 1935, Add. MSS 51108.
126. Cecil to Walters, August 19 and to Murray, August 30 1935. Cecil to Murray, September 5 1935, for Cecil blaming Hoare's restraint on the Cabinet rather than on Hoare.
127. Cecil to Cranborne, September 10 1935.
128. Cecil to Murray, November 6 1935.
129. Cecil to Murray, November 1 1935.
130. Cecil to Lord Stanford, letter for publication, October 28 1935.
131. Lansbury reported in the *Manchester Guardian*, August 23 1935.
132. Hoare's recording of conversation between himself, Eden and Lansbury, August 21 1935, Templewood MSS.
133. Lansbury at Easton Lodge, Dunmow, July 13 1935, *Manchester Guardian*, July 15.
134. Lansbury to Baldwin, May 22 1935.
135. Lansbury at City Temple, August 25 1935, *The Times*, August 26.
136. Lansbury to *The Times*, August 19 1935.
137. Lansbury, statement to the Press Association, *The Times*, August 29 1935.
138. Citrine at TUC, September 5 1935, *Daily Herald*, September 6.
139. Presidential Address to TUC by William Kean, September 2 1935, *Daily Herald*, September 3.
140. Lansbury, note 'A Page of History', October 1935, Lansbury MSS. The speech is reported in the *Daily Herald* of September 7 1935, but not very fully.
141. Lansbury, statement of September 8 1935, *Manchester Guardian*, September 9. Citrine, p. 351.
142. E.g. Lansbury at Swansea, September 20 1935.
143. Morrison at Fulham, September 12 1935, *The Times* September 13, and in *Manchester Guardian*, September 21 1935.

144. McNair, p. 251. *Manchester Guardian*, September 9 1935.
145. Ponsonby to? August 6 1935, Ponsonby MSS, and 'Why I Resigned' of November 4 1935.
146. Lansbury at Labour Party Conference, October 1 1935, *Manchester Guardian* October 2.
147. Daily Herald October 3 1935 gives the vote as 2,168,000 for to 102,000 against. Dalton diary, September 27–October 4 1935.
148. Hoare to Baldwin, September 8 1933.
149. Hoare in Cab 27/572 of November 25 1934, fo.21. Cab 10(34) of March 19 for Hoare believing that the 1906/14 situation had not yet arisen. Cf. Hoare to MacDonald in W.D. Croft to Seymour, September 20 1933, FO 800/291.
150. Hoare to Baldwin, September 8 1933, and in Cab 27/572 of November 25 1934, fo.21 for Hoare statements about the importance of *not* appearing to be reacting to Churchill.
151. See e.g. Chamberlain diary, March 25 1934. Hoare in Cab 27/506 of April 9 1934, fo.246. Hoare to Willingdon, March 22 1935, Eur.E.240.
152. E.g. Simon to A–G, November 2 1933 in FO 800/288.
153. Simon at Cab 27/505 of November 23 1933.
154. Simon in House of Commons, *Hansard* (292) col. 698 of July 13 1934.
155. See e.g. Ormsby-Gore to Baldwin, Tuesday n.d. [1935], in Baldwin MSS.
156. Hoare to Baldwin, May 31 1935.
157. Hoare to Drummond, July 27 1935, FO 800/295.
158. Cab 27(35) of May 15 and 28(35) of May 18. Simon diary, May 27 1935. CP 98(35) of May 11 in Cab 24/255.
159. Cab 33(35) of June 19. Chamberlain to Hilda, June 22 1935. Chamberlain diary, July 5 1935.
160. Cab 36(35) of July 10. Chamberlain to Hilda, July 5 1935.
161. Chamberlain to Hilda, July 14 1935. Hoare in *Hansard* (304) of July 11 1935, cols. 517-20.
162. Cab 40(35) of July 29 and Cab 41(35) of July 31. Chamberlain to Ida, July 6 and Chamberlain diary, July 18 1935.
163. Vansittart to Hoare, August 9 1935, FO 800/295.
164. Avon, *Facing the Dictators*, pp. 245-54.
165. Conference of Ministers on August 21 1935 at 3 p.m. in Cab 23/82.
166. Vansittart to Hoare, August 19 1935, in FO 800/295.
167. Conference of Ministers of August 21 1935 at 5 p.m. in Cab 23/82. Hoare to Chamberlain, August 18 1935.
168. With reservations on Cecil's part.
169. Hoare's reports of conversations with Austen Chamberlain, Lloyd George, Samuel, Churchill and Lansbury and Eden's report of conversation with Cecil on August 20 and 21 in Baldwin and Templewood MSS.
170. And at an informal meeting arranged by Chamberlain and MacDonald after he had left, see Chamberlain to Ida August 25 1935.

171. For Runciman, Londonderry, Hailsham and Cunliffe-Lister objecting, see Hoare to Eden September 17 (Templewood MSS) Runciman to Wigram August 28 (Runciman MSS), Hailsham to Runciman, August 27 and Londonderry to Hoare, October 23, all 1935.
172. See Cab 16/136, meetings 5-16. Runciman to Wigram, July 28 1935, Runciman MSS. Cab 33(35) of June 19 and Cab 36(35) of July 10.
173. Cab 40(35) of July 29.
174. Hoare in Cab 45(35) of September 24. Hoare to Chamberlain, September 17, and Chamberlain to Hilda, September 22 1935.
175. Hoare to Wigram, September 14 1935, FO 800/295.
176. Cf. Cranborne to Cecil, September 16 1935, for Cranborne at Geneva believing this.
177. Conference of Ministers, August 21 1935 at 5 p.m. in Cab 23/82. CID of October 14 1935 in Cab 2/6.
178. For MacDonald having a high opinion of Mussolini's capability and a low opinion of Hoare's, see Chamberlain diary, July 22.
179. Hoare to Clerk, August 24 1935. Chamberlain to Ida, August 25 1935.
180. Chamberlain to Ida, August 25 1935.
181. Hoare to Clerk, August 24 1935.
182. Hoare to Wigram, September 14 1935, FO 800/295.
183. Patrick to Hoare, Tuesday evening [August 27 1935], FO 800/295.
184. Because Hoare himself had gout.
185. Hoare to Baldwin, September 5, and Chamberlain to Hilda, September 7 1935.
186. Drummond to Hoare, August 27 and 28 1935, FO 800/295.
187. Hoare at Geneva, September 11 1935, *The Times* and *Manchester Guardian*, September 12.
188. Channon diary, September 9 1935. Chamberlain to Ida, September 16 1935.
189. Hoare to Eden, September 15 1935. Hoare to Murray, September 16 1935.
190. Chamberlain to Ida, September 16 1935.
191. Hoare to Wigram, September 14 1935, FO 800/295.
192. Hoare to Wigram, September 14 1935, FO 800/295. Chamberlain to Ida, September 16 1935. Eden to Hoare, October 7 1935, FO 800/295.
193. Hoare to Eden, September 24 1935.
194. Hoare to Eden, September 24 1935. Cab 45(35) of September 24.
195. Hoare to Eden, September 24 1935.
196. Eden to Hoare, October 14 1935. Simon diary, October 6 1935 for the view that the French attitude put military sanctions 'out of the question'. Cf. Chamberlain to Ida, October 5 1935, for 'the French are determined not to fight and we are not going to act without them'.

197. Cab 44(35) of October 2.
198. Chamberlain to Ida, August 25, and to Hilda, September 7 1935, for the extreme difficulty of getting an answer when Hoare and Chamberlain saw him in early September about Hoare's anticipated Geneva speech. Also the absolute refusal to face decisions about sanctions until invasion had actually taken place, i.e. ten days before. Cab 45(35) of September 24.
199. Baldwin at National Union Annual Conference, October 4 1935, *The Times*, October 5.
200. Stonehaven to Amery, September 26 1935. For 35 MPs and others signing a letter on the 11th, see Amery and others to the Prime Minister, October 11 1935, Amery MSS. Cf. de Courcy to N.M. Butler, October 14 1935 enclosing Imperial Policy group letter of October 8 1935. Butler to P.M., October 14, and to Wilson, October 15 1935, both PREM 1/177B. Hoare to Eden, October 16 1935. For the Conservative Conference cheering Baldwin's references to friendship with Italy, see Grigg to Amery, October 5 1935. See also R. Wigram to Phipps October 25 [1935], for general Conservative disaffection.
201. R. Wigram to Phipps, October 25 [1935].
202. See e.g. Hoare to Eden, October 9 1935, Templewood MSS.
203. See Hoare to Wigram, October 14 1935, FO 800/295.
204. Hoare to Eden, October 16 1935. Cab 47(35) of October 15.
205. Chamberlain to Ida, October 19 1935.
206. Chamberlain diary, August 2 1935.
207. Chamberlain to Hilda, July 14 1935.
208. Chamberlain diary, August 2 1935.
209. Chamberlain diary, August 2 1935.
210. Ball and Wood for example. Probably also Stonehaven and Margesson, Chamberlain diary, August 2 1935.
211. Pownall diary, May 27 and July 29 1935. Cab 16/136 of July 8 1935. Chamberlain diary, August 2 1935, for Chamberlain being told that de la Warr and Malcolm MacDonald would be welcomed in the Labour party. See Headlam diary, July 1935 for rumours about Thomas and the two MacDonalds thinking of 'ratting' before the general election. Simon diary, of October 22 1935 for MacDonald objecting to a rushed election. See also MacDonald to Baldwin, Wednesday before November 14 1935.
212. Chamberlain diary, August 2 1935.
213. Chamberlain to Ida, August 25 1935.
214. Chamberlain to Hilda, September 7 1935.
215. Chamberlain to Hilda, September 22 1935. For the speech see *The Times*, September 23 1935.
216. Chamberlain diary, October 6 1935.
217. Chamberlain diary, October 6 1935.
218. Chamberlain diary, October 19, and to Hilda, October 15 1935.
219. West Toxteth being regarded as an aberration, Chamberlain to Ida, July 20 1935.
220. Gower to Baldwin, August 1 1935.

221. Gower to Baldwin, August 1 1935.
222. Runciman talking, in Butler to Brabourne, October 15 1935.
223. Wilson, talking to Chamberlain, Chamberlain diary, October 19 1935.

NOTES TO CHAPTER 4

1. E.g. Chamberlain diary, November 20 1935. Dawson diary, November 15 1935.
2. See e.g. Steed to Hoare, November 9 and 13 1935, and Steed to *The Times*, November 8 1935, FO 800/295.
3. Crozier, interview with Hoare, November 21 1935.
4. Hankey diary, November 25 1935 for Hoare talking to Hankey. Eden and probably Ormsby-Gore were on the side of belligerency; Runciman, Baldwin, Hailsham and MacDonald were against it (see Chamberlain diary, November 29 1935, MacDonald to Hoare, November 25 1935, and to Baldwin, November 28 1935).
5. See DPR Committee of November 26 1935 in Cab 24/257.
6. For the discussion see Cab 50(35) of December 2. According to Chamberlain's diary (December 8 1935) Runciman and Baldwin dissented from this decision.
7. Cab 50(35) of December 2, fo.356.
8. Cab 52(35) of December 9, fo. 384 for the meeting. Simon diary, December 11 1935. Chamberlain diary, December 15 1935.
9. See CP 235(35) of December 8 1935 and CP 233(35) of December 9 1935 in Cab 24/257.
10. Cab 52(35) of December 9.
11. Chamberlain diary, December 15 1935.
12. Cab 53(35) of December 10.
13. Chamberlain diary, December 15 1935.
14. I.e. 'an exchange of territory conveying definite advantages to both sides, League assistance to Ethiopia...and special facilities for Italian settlers and companies...in that connection'.
15. Cab 54(35) of December 11. Chamberlain diary, December 15 1935.
16. Jones diary, January 14 1936 quoting W.W. Astor quoting Hoare.
17. Cab 53(35) of December 10, fols. 396-7.
18. For even Hoare's protégé saying that it was no use 'slashing' at 'the collective system', see Butler to Brabourne, December 19 1935.
19. Jones diary, January 14 1936. Hoare to Baldwin, December 14, and Chamberlain diary, December 16 1935.
20. Chamberlain diary, December 17 1935.
21. Chamberlain diary, December 18 1935.
22. Dawson diary, December 18 1935.
23. Which was strengthened at the Cabinet on the 17th by evidence (in fact false) that Hoare had agreed that the Abyssinians should

not be entitled to build a railway to the outlet they would receive on the Red Sea, Cab 55(35) of December 17, fo. 445. Chamberlain diary, December 18 1935.

24. I.e. Austen Chamberlain.

25. For information about the Foreign Policy Committee, I am indebted to Dr Daniel Waley.

26. Cab 56(35) of December 18, Cab 23/90B.

27. He added that Hoare 'embodied all that he stood for', but this was a highly temporary view. (For Ormsby-Gore taking a different view before Hoare became Foreign Secretary, see Ormsby-Gore to Baldwin, Tuesday [n.d. 1935].)

28. For all this see Cab 54(35) in Cab 23/82 and Cab 23/90B, Chamberlain diary, December 18, and Halifax to Chamberlain, December 26 1935.

29. Chamberlain diary, December 18 1935. I have found no direct confirmation of a story, which Bruce Lockhart had from both Boothby and Beaverbrook, that Austen Chamberlain threatened to *vote* against, but Dr Waley's information (see n. 25 above) makes this not inherently incredible, see Bruce Lockhart diary, December 18 and 22 1935.

30. Chamberlain diary, December 21 1935.

31. Chamberlain to Baldwin, December 22 1935.

32. For Baldwin claiming in February that Oliver Locker-Lampson had called that morning to say that Chamberlain's health would not stand the strain, see Baldwin in Chamberlain diary, February 10 1936.

33. Austen to Neville Chamberlain, December 30 1935.

34. Cowling, pp. 270-1.

35. Memorandum, 'Invitation to join Baldwin's government', December 1935, AC 41/1/68, and Austen Chamberlain to Hilda, December 22 1935 (January 22 written).

36. E.g. Tyrrell to Baldwin, September 28 1933 quoting Henderson. Attlee to Tom Attlee, April 20 1935. Lansbury at Fulham, May 17 1935, *Daily Herald*, May 18.

37. Eden in London, May 28 1935, *The Times*, May 29.

38. Eden to Londonderry, May 16 1935, FO 800/290.

39. Eden at Fulham, May 16 1935, *Manchester Guardian*, May 17.

40. Eden at Bristol, November 12 1935, *Western Daily Press*, November 13.

41. See Eden to Baldwin, January 11 1935 [4 *written*] and Chamberlain diary, December 17 1934, for Eden saying he would not go on serving under Simon. For criticism of Hoare see above p. 99.

42. Baldwin at Cab 11(36) of February 26.

43. Baldwin and Eden at Cab 11(36) of February 26 1936.

44. Cab 8(36) of February 19 1936 and CP 53(36) of February 22 in Cab 24/260. Dawson diary, January 2 1936.

45. Cab 11(36) of February 26 1936. For Runciman on the effect of the existing sanctions on British trade, see CP 70(36) of March 5 in Cab 24/260.

46. Cab 11(36) of February 26 1936.
47. Cab 15(36) of March 5.
48. Eden at Geneva, March 2 1936, *The Times*, March 3.
49. For an example, see Barrington-Ward to Dawson, April 14 1936, *The Times* Archive.
50. E.g. Dawson diary, April 21 and 22 and May 6 1936, for Eden being 'tired', 'jumpy' and under 'strain'.
51. Eden to Baldwin, February 24 1934.
52. Eden to Baldwin, June 3 1934.
53. Eden at Cabinet Committee on Germany of February 17 1936, Cab 27/599.
54. CP 217(35) of November 25 in Cab 24/257 enclosing Phipps's despatches.
55. Cab 3(36) of January 29 and CP 13(36) in Cab 24/259.
56. Eden at Cabinet Committee of February 17 1936 in Cab 27/599.
57. Eden, CP 13(36) and 42(36) of February 11 (Cab 24/259) and at Cabinet Committee on Germany, February 17 1936, Cab 27/599.
58. Barrington-Ward to Dawson, January 14 1936, quoting Leeper quoting Eden.
59. Cab 6(36) of February 12 and Cab 3(36) of January 29.
60. Nicolson diary, February 13 1936.
61. Eden at Cabinet Committee on Germany, February 17 1936, Cab 27/599 and Cab 3(36) of January 29 1936.
62. Cab 15(36) March 5 1936.
63. Eden in CP 73(36) of March 7 in Cab 24/261. Dawson diary, March 8 1936.
64. Cab 18(36) of March 11.
65. Chamberlain diary, March 11 1936.
66. Including the proposal to make Britain's future Locarno obligations (to Belgium and France) 'automatic', see Cab 19(36) of March 12.
67. For examples of Flandin's frankness, see Chamberlain diary, March 14 1936.
68. Meeting of Ministers of March 13 1936, Cab 27/603.
69. Meeting of Ministers of March 13 1936, Cab 27/603 fols. 11 *et seq.*
70. I.e., by sending a minister to ask him, provided the French and Belgian governments did not object, Meeting of Ministers of March 13 1936, Cab 27/603.
71. Meeting of Ministers of March 14 1936, Cab 27/603.
72. Chamberlain to Ida, March 14 1936.
73. Meeting of Ministers of March 16 1936, Cab 27/646 and Cab 20(36) of March 16.
74. Chamberlain diary, March 15 1936.
75. Chamberlain diary, March 15 and 17 1936. Cab 20(36) of March 16.
76. Chamberlain to Hilda, March 21 1936.
77. Cab 24(36) of March 25 1936.
78. Cab 24(36) of March 25. Simon· to Baldwin, March 25 1936,

PREM 1/194. Meeting of Ministers, March 30 1936, in Cab 27/646. Cab 25(36) of April 1 1936.

79. For the debate see *Hansard* (310) of March 26 1936, cols. 1435-49 (for Eden) and 1538-49 (for Chamberlain). Cab 30(36) of April 22 1936.

80. See *The Times*, March 9 1936, for Hitler's memorandum and Reichstag speech of March 7 1936.

81. Cab 25(36) of April 1 1936.

82. Cab 30(36) of April 22.

83. Cf. Eden talking, in Nicolson diary, January 6 1940.

84. Chamberlain to Ida, January 16 1937.

85. Cowling, p. 337.

86. Chamberlain to Ida, May 24 1936. Chamberlain to Baldwin, August 21, and to Hilda, August 26 1936. Chamberlain to Ida, September 13 1936. For alternatives see Jones to Lady Grigg, August 3 1936, Jones diary. Dawson diary, August 23 1936.

87. Jones diary, May 25 1936. Chamberlain to Ida, June 20, July 4 and 19, October 24 and November 14, all 1936. Chamberlain diary, February 8 1936. Chamberlain to Hilda, June 27, July 11, September 23, October 17 and October 31 1936. Chamberlain to Margesson, August 2 1936.

88. Chamberlain to Hilda and Ida and diary *passim*, November 1935 onwards, and especially diary of November 20 1935. Chamberlain to Hilda, November 17, and to Ida, December 8 1935.

89. Sinclair to Johnstone, September 11, to Samuel, September 16, and to Harris, September 14 1935, all Sinclair MSS.

90. Stevenson diary, October 23 1935. Samuel to Sinclair, October 11 1935(2).

91. Lothian to Lloyd George, November 25 1935.

92. Sinclair to Lloyd George, November 29 1935.

93. Muir to Samuel, November 17 and 19 1935.

94. Sinclair to Johnstone, November 18 1935.

95. Lothian to Lloyd George, November 25 1935.

96. Lothian to Lloyd George, November 25 1935. Muir to Samuel, November 17 and 19 1935.

97. Snowden to Lloyd George, January 3 1936.

98. Crewe to Baldwin, April 7 1937, for the suggestion coming from Crewe.

99. Sinclair to Johnstone, March 22 1935.

100. Sinclair to Samuel, January 11, 21 and 23 1935 and October 14 1935.

101. Sinclair to Johnstone, November 19 1935, and to F.D. Acland, November 20 1935.

102. Sinclair to Hillman, March 22 1935.

103. Sinclair to Muir, July 24 1935.

104. K. Griffith in *The Times*, May 29 1936.

105. Sinclair at Liverpool, February 1 1936, *Liverpool Post*, February 3, and at Oxford, July 30 1936, *Yorkshire Observer*, July 31.

Cf. Sinclair to Bernays, November 21 1935 and Crewe in *The Times*, June 15 1936.
106. Sinclair in London, June 18 1936, *News Chronicle*, June 19.
107. Sinclair to Johnstone, February 17 1936.
108. Brock to Sinclair, September 15 1936.
109. Sinclair to D. Hatton, April 2 1936. Cf. Roberts to Sinclair, May 9 1936, for Sinclair making just a 'suggestion' of a United Front in a recent speech, 'and no more'.
110. Sinclair at Knutsford, March 28 1936, *Liverpool Post*, March 30.
111. Sinclair to D. Hatton, April 2 1936.
112. Sinclair at Eighty Club, *Manchester Guardian*, February 22 1936.
113. Sinclair at Manchester, *Manchester Guardian*, March 30 1936.
114. *Ibid.*
115. Sinclair in budget broadcast, April 23 1936, *News Chronicle*, April 24, and in London, April 23, *Manchester Guardian*, April 24.
116. Sinclair at Eighty Club, *Manchester Guardian*, February 22 1936.
117. Sinclair at National Liberal Club, February 12 1936, *Manchester Guardian* February 13.
118. Sinclair to Barnett, December 2 1935 and to I.R.M. Davies, May 7 1937. Cf. Johnstone to Sinclair, October 9 1936 and Lady Sinclair to Johnstone, October 12 [1936]. For divisions in the Liberal party, see Sinclair to Johnstone, February 17 1936.
119. Sinclair to Lady Rolleston, April 28 1936, and in London, April 30 1936, *Manchester Guardian*, May 1. Sinclair in London, April 23 1936, *Manchester Guardian*, April 24. Sinclair to Bernays, November 21 1935, to Davies, September 12 1936 and to Samuel, October 7 1935.
120. Sinclair to Principal Martin, June 29 1936.
121. Cecil to Eden, December 10 1935.
122. Cecil talking to Baldwin, League of Nations Union deputation, December 13 1935, PREM 1/195.
123. Cecil to Eden, December 10 1935.
124. Cecil to Baldwin, February 17 1936.
125. Cecil to Murray [January 1936] and Cecil, memo on Oil Sanctions, January 14 1936, Add. MSS. 51087.
126. Cecil to Murray, January 15 1936. Cecil to Murray [January 1936]. Murray to Austen Chamberlain, January 10 1936.
127. Cecil, memo on oil sanctions, January 14 1936, Add. MSS 51087. Murray to Austen Chamberlain, April 4 1936. Cecil in *Daily Herald*, March 25 1936. Cecil to Murray, March 25 and April 6 1936. Cecil to Churchill, April 22 and to Murray, April 15 1936. Cecil to Halifax, March 24 1936.
128. Cecil, memo on oil sanctions, January 14 1936, Add. MSS 51087.
129. Cecil to Eden, March 4 1936.
130. Cecil to Cranborne, April 8 1936. Garnett to Baldwin, April 23 1936 PREM 1/195.
131. Murray to Austen Chamberlain, May 5 1936. Cecil to Murray, May 16 1936.

132. Cecil in *Daily Herald*, May 6 1936. Murray to Austen Chamberlain, May 6 1936.
133. Murray to Austen Chamberlain, June 24 and 26 1936.
134. Cecil to Noel-Baker, June 27 1936.
135. See above pp. 82-4 for an example. See also *Daily Herald*, February 24 1936.
136. *Daily Herald*, February 19 1936.
137. Attlee at Parkstone March 7 1936.
138. At the TUC annual conference, *Daily Herald*, September 11 1936.
139. Of September 18 and October 2, *News Chronicle*, September 19 1936, and *Daily Herald*, October 3 1936.
140. See above p. 147. Cf. Chamberlain to Hilda, November 14 1936, and Morrison at Preston, November 16 1936, *Manchester Guardian*, November 17.
141. Attlee, Broadcast talk of April 22 1936, *Manchester Guardian*, April 23.
142. Passed by a majority of three to one, *Manchester Guardian*, October 7 1936.
143. *Daily Herald*, October 3-7 1936. Attlee to Tom Attlee, October 26 1936.
144. E.g. *Daily Herald*, May 7 1936.
145. Dalton in House of Commons *Hansard* (310) col. 1457 of March 26 1936. *Daily Herald*, March 20 1936, leading article on 'League and Alliances'.
146. Attlee in *Daily Herald*, March 9 1936.
147. Dalton in House of Commons, *Hansard* (310) col. 1453 of March 26 1936. Attlee at Alexandria, Dumbartonshire, March 15 1936, *Daily Herald* March 16.
148. Attlee in London, March 13 1936, *The Times*, March 14, and in *Daily Herald*, March 30 1936.
149. National Council of Labour statement of May 15 1936, *Daily Herald*, May 15.
150. E.g. for Japan, Italy and Germany as capitalist dictatorships which were unable to solve economic problems, see Attlee at Barnsley, June 22 1936, *Daily Herald*, June 23.
151. Attlee in *Daily Herald*, June 15 1936.
152. Meeting of joint council of TUC, National Executive of Labour Party and Executive Committee of parliamentary Labour party, June 23 1937, *Daily Herald*, June 24. Attlee at Carmarthen, July 10 1937, *Western Mail*, July 12, for demand for immediate end of non-intervention.
153. Dalton in *Daily Herald* and *News Chronicle*, June 5 1937.
154. Attlee to Tom Attlee, November 30 1937, and at Rhyl, *Manchester Guardian*, December 13 1937.
155. Attlee in message to R.H.S.C., *Manchester Guardian*, April 21 1937. Attlee at Northampton, September 26 1937, *Manchester Guardian*, September 27. Morrison in *Forward*, September 5 1936, and in *Manchester Guardian*, October 28 1936.

156. Ball to Baldwin, December 8 1935.
157. For *English Review* dinner for Lloyd presided over by Carson, see Amery diary, November 21 1933.
158. Amery diary, October 20, 24, 27 and 30 1933, for fifty or sixty MPs being interested, and also for Douglas Jerrold, Forbes Adam and Arnold Lunn. See also Jerrold, *Georgian Adventure*, pp. 334-48 and Adam, pp. 258-60.
159. Lloyd talking to Amery, Amery diary, October 24 1933.
160. E.g. Winterton reported in *Manchester Guardian*, February 20 1933.
161. Headlam diary, September 15 1935.
162. See Rothermere, *My Campaign for Hungary*, 1939.
163. Rothermere, *My Fight to Rearm*, 1939, p. 134.
164. Rothermere to Croft, October 28 1934.
165. Rothermere to Croft, April 29 and 30 1935, and to Baldwin, April 30 1935.
166. Rothermere to Monsell, November 5 1935 and May 10 1935, FO 800/290. Rothermere to Croft, May 8 1935.
167. See e.g. the importance he attached to the interview Ward Price had with Goering in November 1936 which Rothermere circulated to many leading public men. Cf. Hitler to Rothermere of May 3 1935 which was also circulated by Rothermere among politicians.
168. Beaverbrook to Rothermere, November 29 1934 and April 15 1935.
169. Beaverbrook to Lloyd George, October 6 1936. Bruce Lockhart diary, March 6, July 7 and July 10 1933, July 3 1934 and May 28 1936.
170. Beaverbrook to Amery, April 1 1935.
171. Beaverbrook to Hoare, October 24 and December 27 1935.
172. Beaverbrook to Amery, July 8 and November 10 1936.
173. Amery diary, June 28 1933 and *passim* 1933/4.
174. Amery diary, February 15 1933.
175. Amery diary, March 21 1935.
176. Amery diary, August 15 1933.
177. Amery diary, September 27 1933.
178. Amery diary, April 25 1933.
179. Amery to Bledisloe, May 2 1934.
180. Amery diary, September 18, October 4 and 16 and November 1 1933. Amery to Smuts, January 3 1934.
181. Barrington-Ward to Dawson, September 3 1935, *The Times* Archive.
182. Amery diary, March 28 1935.
183. Amery to Beaverbrook, March 29 1935.
184. Amery diary, April 4 1935.
185. Hoare to Amery, June 8 1935.
186. Cf. Mason, note for N.M. Butler, October 11 1935, for Hoare preferring not to be present when Amery brought his deputation to the Prime Minister on October 15 1935, PREM 1/177B.

187. Amery to Hoare, October 7 1935.
188. Amery to Winterton, September 23, to Garvin, September 23 1935, and to Beaverbrook, November 7 1936.
189. Amery to Beaverbrook, October 7 1935.
190. Amery to Baldwin, October 11 1935, and N.M. Butler to Wilson, October 15 1935, both PREM 1/177B.
191. Amery to Garvin, September 23, and to Bardoux, September 23 1935.
192. Amery to Stonehaven, October 22 1935.
193. Amery to Hoare, December 19 1935, and to Bardoux, March 11 1936.
194. For information about Astor's disappointments in the Garden Suburb, I am indebted to Mr J.A. Turner.
195. *The Times* letter columns of October 1937 for colonies as an economic way to reconciliation. Astor to Garvin, March 26 1936.
196. There is a good deal in the Astor papers about the determined attempt made in 1938 by Lord and Lady Astor to nail the lie about 'the Cliveden set'. See also Astor to Gower, December 21 1938.
197. Garvin to Astor, March 14 1934.
198. Garvin to Astor, August 31 1933.
199. Garvin in the *Observer*, February 5 1933. Garvin to Astor, August 31 1933.
200. Garvin in the *Observer*, March 19, May 19 and September 17 1933.
201. Garvin to Astor, December 18 1933, April 24 and 28 1934.
202. Garvin to Astor, April 24 and 28 1934.
203. Garvin to Hoare, July 18 1935, FO 800/295. Garwin in the *Observer*, August 4 and 25, September 22, October 6 and December 8 1935.
204. Garvin in the *Observer*, October 6 and 20 and September 22 1935.
205. Garvin in the *Observer*, August 25, September 8 and 22 and October 20 1935.
206. Garvin in the *Observer*, December 15 1935.
207. Garvin in the *Observer*, December 22 1935.
208. Garvin in the *Observer*, December 22 1935.
209. Jerrold, p. 163.
210. Lord Phillimore talking to Baldwin, N.M. Butler to Wilson, October 15 1935, PREM 1/177B. Amery to Garvin, September 23 1935. Wilson, p. 273.
211. Garvin talking, in Nicolson diary, April 22 1936. Cf. Gwynne to Amery, October 15 1935.
212. Garvin in the *Observer*, September 22 1935.
213. Lothian to Lloyd George, May 18 1936. Petrie, *Lords of the Inland Sea*, p. 270-1.
214. Astor in *Western Morning News*, December 7 1938.
215. Londonderry to Croft, July 3 1936. Garvin to Amery, June 11

1936. Cf. Astor and Lady Astor in Astor MSS Box 39 File 733. Marriott, p. 217.
216. Wilson to Amery, September 26 1935. Dawson to Lady Astor, March 15 1936.
217. Londonderry to *The Times*, March 12 1936. Wilson, p. 278. Hollis, p. 138.
218. Wilson, p. 277.
219. Arnold Wilson in 1922 Committee Minute-book for February 24 1936.
220. Astor in *Western Daily News*, December 7 1938. For the Aga Khan's opinions see note for Halifax, November 1937 in Halifax MSS (Churchill College), A4.410.3.3. For his importance see Dawson diary, October 28 1937.
221. Wilson, p. 277, and Hollis, p. 139.
222. Londonderry to Lady Milner, March 11 1937, Londonderry MSS.
223. Londonderry in Cab 27/506 of March 6, April 19 and 20 1934. Cab 7(34) of February 28. Londonderry to MacDonald, October 13, 24 and 25 and November 19 and 26 1934, all PREM 1/155. Londonderry to Simon, December 11 1934, FO 800/291.
224. Cab 27/508 of February 19 1935, fo. 115. Londonderry to Simon, February 14 1933 (3 letters, 2 of them in FO 800/291). Londonderry to MacDonald, September 17 1933 and June 11 1934 and to Simon, June 14 1934 (both FO 800/291). Londonderry to MacDonald, February 24, July 4 and 11 1933 (and vice versa, July 13 1933), MacDonald MSS. Cf. Cab 27/506 of February 5 1934.
225. Cecil to Baldwin, July 30 1935.
226. Londonderry to Eden, May 16 1935, FO 800/290.
227. Londonderry to Baldwin, October 17 1935.
228. Londonderry to Baldwin, October 17 1935, and to Ponsonby, September 26 1935.
229. This put an end to Londonderry's eve-of-session receptions, which were not resumed again until 1937. Notes by   and Gower in Baldwin MSS of November 29 1935.
230. Cab 10(34) of March 19. Cab 27/508 of February 19 1935. Londonderry to Simon, December 11 1934, FO 800/291. Cab 16(35) of March 20, fo.242. A.L. Kennedy journal, December 16 1938, *The Times* Archive.
231. Dawson diary, February 26 1934, March 28 and April 10 1935 and February 10 1936.
232. See e.g. Dawson diary, July 3 and 11 and October 22 1935, for slight derogations of Hoare, and May 27 and October 23 1935, for praise of Eden, of whom he had seen more in the previous three years.
233. Dawson diary, February 13, October 15 and November 15 1933, January 23 and 29, February 13 and October 4 1934 and January 29 and March 6 1935.
234. Dawson diary, February 7 and 22 1935 and August 23 1939.

235. *The Times*, May 24 1934.
236. *Ibid.*
237. See among other things *The Times*, November 13 and 29 1934, December 31 1934 and February 11 1935.
238. See *The Times*, January—December 1934 and especially July 26 and 27 1934.
239. *The Times*, February 21 1934.
240. E.g. Dawson diary, November 14 and 15 1933.
241. *The Times*, July 2, 3 and 16 1934.
242. Dawson diary, May 17 1938. *The Times*, February—May 1934 and especially May 7 1934.
243. *The Times*, June 21 1934.
244. *The Times*, March 19 1934, April 9 1934, June 21 1934 and October 9 1934.
245. *The Times*, January 30 1934.
246. E.g. July 8 1936 etc.
247. *The Times*, January 18 1934.
248. *The Times*, July—October 1935.
249. E.g. *The Times*, March 6, April 11 1934, September 12 1935, May 15 and June 4 and 26 1936.
250. *The Times*, May 5 1936.
251. *The Times*, January 21 1935, May 4 1935 and February 11 1936.
252. For the Rhineland see *The Times*, March 9, 12 and 16 1936. For Dawson seeing Eden the day after the occupation, see Maclachlan, p. 114 and Dawson diary, March 8, 22 and 26 1936.
253. *The Times*, May 23 1934 and January 2, 10 and July 9 1936.
254. E.g. *The Times*, February 1, November 1 1936 and June 14 1937.
255. E.g. *The Times*, September 14 and 18 1936.
256. *The Times*, November 26 1936.
257. *The Times*, March 4 1936.
258. See below p. 141. For criticism of Chamberlain see *The Times* of June 13, 19 and 30 1936. For Eden see *The Times*, February 25 and May 4 1936. For Dawson consulting Eden and Baldwin, see Dawson diary, June 12 and 15 1936.
259. *The Times*, March 27 and June 8 1936.
260. Barrington-Ward to H. Brooke, July 28 1936: see also Barrington-Ward memorandum for Dawson, March 19 1936, and to Kennedy, March 24 1936, all *The Times* Archive. See also *The Times*, May 30 1934 and June 30 1935.
261. *The Times*, January 15 1934, July 7 1934 and March 12 1936.
262. Maclachlan, p. 106 and *The Times*, January 31 1935.
263. Maclachlan, p. 103.
264. *The Times*, January 13 1936 etc.
265. E.g. *The Times*, April 14 1937.
266. *The Times*, October 9 1936 and January 28 1937.
267. *The Times*, January 28 1937.
268. In retaliation for the expulsion of four German journalists (who were really spies) from England.
269. E.g. Dawson diary, June 17 and 21 1937.

270. Dawson diary, January 26 and 29 1937.
271. *The Times*, September 3, 6, 8, 19, 13 etc. 1937 and Dawson diary, January 8 and 10 1937.
272. *The Times*, August 4 1937.
273. *The Times*, April 14 1937.
274. *The Times*, September 14, 21 and 22 and October 22 1937.
275. *The Times*, October 28 1937.
276. *The Times*, October 22 1937.
277. *The Times*, November 13 1937.
278. Dawson diary, October 28 1937.
279. Dawson diary, March 15 1938.
280. *Ibid.*
281. Dawson diary, September 6–8 1938.
282. Maclachlan, p. 141. Dawson diary, September 30 1938.
283. For Godesberg see Dawson diary, September 22 1938. Dawson diary, December 29 1938 and January 23 1939. See also Dawson diary, November 15 1938.
284. Dawson diary, April 2 and 3 1939.
285. For Dawson's determination not to give way to e.g. Churchill, see Dawson diary, July 13–17 1939.
286. For Lansbury, Rev. Donald Soper and Rev. Charles Raven signing a letter in company with Astor, Lothian, Grigg and Trenchard (to say that any League-based military sanctions would divide the world into 'two great military alliances' and that the League must use 'peaceful means for peaceful ends'), see *The Times*, April 14 1937.
287. Lothian to Lloyd George, October 11 1935. Lothian, memorandum 'The Crisis in British Policy' in Lothian to Chamberlain June 3 1936 and 'Visit to Berlin May 1937', both in Chamberlain MSS.
288. Lothian to Lloyd George, May 18 1936.
289. Lothian to Lady Astor, February 1 1935 and March 20 1935.
290. Nicolson diary, December 5 1935. Lothian to Lloyd George, May 18 1936.
291. Lothian to Lloyd George, May 23 1936.
292. Lothian memorandum, in Lothian to Chamberlain, June 3 1936.
293. A.L. Kennedy journal for May 18 1937, *The Times* Archive.
294. Lothian, memorandum on 'Visit to Berlin May 1937', Chamberlain MSS.
295. Garvin in the *Observer*, March 29 1936.
296. Garvin in the *Observer*, March 15 1936.
297. Garvin in the *Observer*, November 22 1936. Garvin to Astor, July 9 1936.
298. Garvin to Astor, August 28 1936.
299. Garvin to Astor, August 28 1936.
300. For the 'questionnaire', see below p. 145.
301. Garvin to Amery, October 27 and November 16 1936, and to Astor, January 8 1937.
302. Garvin in the *Observer*, March 14 1937. Garvin to Astor, May 18

1937, for Baldwin being blamed for failing to make Eden resign with him.

303. Garvin in the *Observer*, March 14 1937.
304. *Ibid.*
305. Jones to Lady Grigg, May 3 1936. Amery to Beaverbrook, November 7 1936.
306. Churchill, Winterton, Croft, Horne and Grigg.
307. Butler to Brabourne, October 20 1934.
308. Austen Chamberlain in *Hansard* (309) col. 77 of March 11 1935.
309. *Hansard* (284) cols. 1530-1 of December 21 1933.
310. *Ibid.* col. 1535.
311. *Hansard* (285) cols. 1041-2 of February 6 1934. *Hansard* (284) cols. 1533-5 of December 21 1935.
312. *Hansard* (292) col. 742 of July 13 1934.
313. *Hansard* (299) cols. 73-4 of March 11 1935.
314. *Hansard* (291) cols.2071-2 of July 5 1934.
315. *Hansard* (301) col. 617 of May 2 1935.
316. *Ibid* cols. 620-3.
317. Austen Chamberlain to Hilda/Ida, April 6 1935. For the League of Nations Union see Austen Chamberlain in *Hansard* (301) cols. 617-18 of May 2 1935.
318. See Austen Chamberlain to Hilda/Ida, April 6 1935.
319. *Hansard* (304) col. 566 of July 11 1935 and (307) col. 353 of December 5 1935. Austen Chamberlain to Adams, September 3 1935. For dissuading Mussolini see Chamberlain to Grandi, May 10 1935 (not sent).
320. *Hansard* (307) cols. 2039-42 of December 19 1935.
321. I.e. Winterton, Churchill and Grigg.
322. Note of March 12 1936 in PREM 1/194.
323. Dugdale diary, March 12 1936.
324. TLR (?) March 17 1936 in PREM 1/194. E.g. *Hansard* (311) cols. 1771-3 of May 6 1936 and (315) cols. 1171-8 of July 27 1936.
325. *Hansard* (309) cols. 71-8 of March 11 1936 and (310) col. 1487 of March 26 1936.
326. *Hansard* (311) cols. 1771-3 of May 6 1936.
327. *Hansard* (308) cols. 1360-6 of February 14 1936.
328. Austen Chamberlain to Hilda/Ida, May 16, July 4 and November 14 1936. Neville Chamberlain to Ida, July 4 1936. Austen Chamberlain to Hilda, December 22 1935 (January 22 written).
329. Hoare to Croft, December 22 1935.
330. Hoare to Chamberlain, January 18, and to Beaverbrook, January 13 1936. Beaverbrook to Hoare, January 15 1936. Hoare to Baldwin, December 29 1935. Butler to Brabourne, March 12 1936.
331. Chamberlain diary, February 10 1936. Cf. Hoare talking in Bruce Lockhart diary, February 10 1936.
332. Chamberlain to Ida, February 16 1936.

333. Chamberlain diary, February 19, and Hoare to Chamberlain, February 23 1936.
334. Including Chamberlain, Swinton, Weir, Elliot, Morrison, Wood, Halifax, Churchill and Austen Chamberlain.
335. Chamberlain diary, February 21 1936.
336. Baldwin to Chamberlain March 6, and Chamberlain diary, March 8 1936. Dugdale diary, March 2 1936.
337. Chamberlain diary, March 11, and Chamberlain to Ida, March 14 1936.
338. Baldwin to Hoare, March 13 1936.
339. Hoare to Chamberlain, February 23 1936.
340. Baldwin to Hoare, March 13 1936.
341. Baldwin to Hoare, April 9, and Hoare to Baldwin, April 10 1936.
342. Hoare to Amery, June 4 1936. Hoare in Nicolson diary, June 28 1936.
343. E.g. Hoare to Willingdon, September 27 1934, Eur.E.240.
344. Chamberlain to MacDonald, October 13 1933.
345. Chamberlain to Hilda, December 15 1934 and March 9 1935. Chamberlain to Ida, October 27 1934.
346. Chamberlain to Ida, August 25 1935.
347. Chamberlain to Hilda, November 17 1935.
348. Chamberlain to Ida, December 8 1935.
349. Chamberlain at Cab 23(36) of March 19 and Chamberlain to Hilda, April 19 1936.
350. Eden at Cab 27(36) of April 6 1936.
351. Cab 27(36) of April 6.
352. Cranborne to Cecil, April 8 1936. Halifax to Linlithgow, April 24 1936.
353. Cab 30(36) of April 22.
354. Cab 32(36) of April 30. Chamberlain to Ida, April 25, and to Hilda, May 2 1936.
355. Zetland to Linlithgow, June 22 1938, Eur.609.7.
356. Chamberlain at 1900 Club, June 10 1936, *The Times*, June 11.
357. Chamberlain to Hilda, May 2 1936.
358. Chamberlain diary, June 19, and to Hilda, June 20 1936.
359. E.g. at Manchester on June 27 1936, *The Times*, June 29.
360. Chamberlain diary June 19 1936. Chamberlain to Ida, April 25 1936. Garvin to Chamberlain, June 11 1936.
361. See Stonehaven to Baldwin, October 4 1936. Chamberlain, letter to a constituent, *Birmingham Post*, June 27 1936.
362. Davidson to Baldwin, June 30 1936, for the fear of a Right wing Chamberlain *coup*.

NOTES TO CHAPTER 5

1. Eden at Foreign Policy Committee of April 30 1936, Cab 27/622.
2. See his speeches at League Assembly in Geneva, July 1 1936 and September 25 1936, *The Times* July 2 and September 26.
3. E.g. Cab 20(36) of March 16. Cab 23(36) of March 19. Cranborne to Cecil, March 25, and Cecil to Murray, March 25 1936.
4. Cranborne to Cecil, March 23 1936.
5. From Hankey and the Service ministers.
6. E.g. Cab Committee of March 13 1936, Cab 27/603. CID 2/6(i) of April 13 1936. Cab 25(36) of April 2.
7. Eden at Cab 31(36) of April 29 and at Cab 39(36) of May 27.
8. Which had been reaffirmed by France, Britain and Belgium on March 19.
9. Cabs 36(36) of May 27, 40(36) of May 29, 41(36) of June 10 and 42(36) of June 17. For Chamberlain claiming to have played a part in this, see Chamberlain to Ida, June 6 1936 and Chamberlain diary, June 19 1936.
10. See Cab 42(36) of June 17 for the desirability of a Mediterranean 'understanding' with Greece and Turkey, leading, perhaps, eventually, to a Mediterranean Locarno with France and Italy.
11. CP 100(36) in Cab 24/261.
12. Eden at Cab 26(36) of April 1.
13. Eden in CP 121(36) of April 25 1936 in Cab 24/262.
14. Cabs 32-4(36) of April 30, May 4 and 6. See also Cab 24/262 for successive drafts.
15. See e.g. the exchange between Eden and Baldwin at the end of Cab 32(36) of April 30.
16. Cab 38(36) of May 20.
17. Eden at Cab 32(36) of April 30.
18. Cab 38(36) of May 20.
19. Cab 48(36) of July 1.
20. Cab 52(36) of July 15.
21. Cabs 50(36) of July 6, 52(36) of July 15 and 54(36) of July 22.
22. Cabs 50(36) of July 6 and 53(36) of July 16 for Eden wishing to get away from the questionnaire.
23. Cab 30(36) of April 22.
24. Cab 31(36) of April 29.
25. Cab 50(36) of July 6.
26. Dawson diary, April 22 and May 4 1936. Cab 50(36) of July 6.
27. E.g. Eden talking to Harvey in Harvey to Secretary of State, March 7 1937, Harvey, p. 406.
28. Eden at Cab 50(36) of July 6 and Cab 56(36) of September 2. FP 36(5) of July 13 in Cab 27/626 (circulated by Halifax) and Eden's FP 37(8) of August 20 1936 in Cab 27/626. See also Eden at League Assembly in Geneva, September 25 1936, *The Times* September 26.
29. Cab 57(36) of October 14.
30. Eden at meeting of ministers of January 8 1937 in Cab 23/87.
31. Jones talking to Hitler in Jones diary, May 17 1936.

32. Chamberlain diary, February 8 1936.
33. Halifax to Linlithgow, April 24 1936. Chamberlain to Ida, March 28 and June 20 1936. Jones diary, July 15 1936. Chamberlain to Hilda, July 11 1936.
34. For Baldwin and the midsummer madness speech, see Nicolson diary, June 11 1936, *Spectator*, June 25 and *Hansard* (313) cols. 401-3 of June 11 1936. Baldwin at Cab 18(36) of March 11.
35. Baldwin at Cab 19(36) of March 12.
36. Cab 16(36) of March 9. Eden in *Facing the Dictators*, p. 347 says that *he* asked for Halifax to go. Perhaps he asked Baldwin and Baldwin suggested it to the Cabinet.
37. E.g. Baldwin at Cardiff, July 18 1936, *The Times*, July 20, at Guildhall November 9 1936, *The Times*, November 10, and at Scottish Unionist Conference of November 18 1936, *The Scotsman*, November 19. *Hansard* (317) cols. 1144--5 of November 12 1936. See also Chamberlain to Hilda, November 14 1936.
38. Zetland to Linlithgow, March 22 1937.
39. Chamberlain to Ida, January 16 1937. Eden to Baldwin, December 27 1936. Hankey to Robin Hankey, December 22 1936 and January 31 1937.
40. Chamberlain to Ida, June 20 1936.
41. Chamberlain to Simon, September 23 1936, and to Lothian, January 10 1936.
42. See Cab 58(36) of October 21, Cab 65(36) of November 13 and Cab 67(36) of November 25.
43. Cab 1(37) of January 13. Zetland to Linlithgow, January 18 1937.
44. E.g. Eden at Aberdeen, March 8 1937, *The Times*, March 9.
45. Citrine, p. 323, for Baldwin regarding Stalin as the man who would stop Russia being involved in world revolution.
46. E.g. Barrington-Ward to Dawson, August 26 1936, quoting Eden.
47. Nicolson diary, November 15 1936, for an example. Cf. Eden at Foreign Press Association, January 12 1937, *Manchester Guardian*, January 13.
48. Eden at International Chamber of Commerce luncheon, November 27 1936, *Manchester Guardian*, November 28, at Bradford, December 14 1936, *The Times*, December 15; at Brussels, April 26 1937, *Manchester Guardian*, April 27 and at Foreign Press Association, January 12 1937, *Manchester Guardian*, January 13.
49. Amery diary recording Chamberlain, September 21 1937.
50. Inskip to Chamberlain, May 21 1937.
51. Chamberlain diary, May 3 1937.
52. Chamberlain to Ida, February 6 1937.
53. Hore-Belisha to Chamberlain, December 3 1937, quoting Garvin. For Chamberlain reported as having 'Liberal and radical' views of policy, see Crozier, interview with Hore-Belisha, July 15 1936.
54. Chamberlain to Ida, July 4 1937.
55. Chamberlain to Hilda, August 1, and to Ida, August 8 1937.

56. Chamberlain to Hilda, June 26, August 29, October 24 and November 21, and to Ida, August 8 1937.
57. Chamberlain to Hilda, June 26, July 18 and November 21 1937.
58. Chamberlain to Hilda, June 26 1937.
59. Cab 27/506 of April 19, 20 and 24 and May 1 1934. See also Cab 28(34) of July 11. Cab 27/505 of December 6 1933, fo. 455. Cab 27/505 of November 20 1933, fols. 439—41 and Chamberlain diary, 'January 1934' (recording previous two months). Chamberlain in Cab 27/506 of April 19 1934. Chamberlain to Ida, February 2 1935.
60. Chamberlain diary, March 18 1935.
61. E.g. Chamberlain diary, April 5 1935.
62. Chamberlain diary, March 21 1935.
63. Chamberlain diary, April 14 1935. Cf. *Daily Telegraph*, April 9, 12 and 13.
64. Chamberlain to Hilda, May 26 1935.
65. Chamberlain diary, March 12 1936.
66. Chamberlain to Ida, October 13 1934.
67. E.g. Cab 27/508 of February 19 1935, fo. 95.
68. For all this see Chamberlain to Hilda, May 26 1935. Pownall diary, October 21 1935. DRC 37 of November 21 1935 in Cab 16/123 and Cab 27/508, especially of May 20 and 27 1935.
69. Chamberlain diary, February 27 and to Ida, April 25 1936.
70. Chamberlain to Ida, February 16 1936.
71. PREM 1/196 has a certain amount about this. Cf. Chamberlain diary, February 11 1936. It was first suggested in May 1935 as a way of resolving inter-service conflict for money, see Cab 27/508 especially May 27 1935. It was also the subject of intensive agitation in the House of Commons.
72. Proposed by Baldwin on the understanding that Austen Chamberlain would then become Chancellor, Chamberlain diary, February 16 1936.
73. Chamberlain to Hilda, February 9 1936.
74. For the C.I.G.S. putting this point see Barrington-Ward to Liddell Hart, February 12 1936, *The Times* Archive.
75. Chamberlain at Cab 75(36) of December 16.
76. For the 'Meetings of Principal Delegates' at the Imperial Conference, see Cab 32/130.
77. Chamberlain to Ida, January 16 1937.
78. See above p. 148.
79. Chamberlain at *National Review* luncheon, March 4 1937, *The Times*, March 5.
80. Chamberlain at Cab 1(37) of January 13.
81. Chamberlain to Ida, July 4 1937. Chamberlain at CID, July 1937 fo. 517.
82. Chamberlain to Hilda, June 26 1937. Chamberlain at Cab 29(37) of July 5.
83. Chamberlain to Weir, August 15 1937.
84. Cab 29(37) of July 5.

85. Cab 43(37) of June 23 (for the Chiefs of Staff objecting to Eden's interest in a Turco-Greek commitment as an example of overstretching). Cab 30(37) of July 14. CID of July 2 1937 (Cab 2/6 ii, fols. 511—13. Hankey to Prime Minister, July 19 1937, and memorandum in PREM 1/276. Eden to Chamberlain, July 16, and Inskip to Chamberlain, July 16 1937, both PREM 1/276.

86. Hankey to Robin Hankey, December 22 1936 and January 31 1937.

87. Hankey to Robin Hankey, March 1 1938. Cf. Bruce Lockhart diary, August 16 1936, for the view that Fisher was trying to get rid of Vansittart and give the Foreign Office to Leith-Ross in order to reform it (and that Vansittart refused to go to Paris for this reason).

88. Vansittart minute of May 6 1933 in Vansittart 2/3, of May 26 1933 in Vansittart 2/6 and of August 26 1933 in CP 212 (33) of August 30 1933.

89. Vansittart, notes of September 30 1933 on O'Malley's draft instructions to Phipps, O'Malley MSS.

90. Vansittart memorandum of August 28 1933 in CP 212 (33) of August 30 1933, Vansittart note of July 11 and 28 1934 in Vansittart 2/17 and 2/18.

91. Vansittart note of February 13 1935 in Vansittart 2/29.

92. Vansittart note of July 5 1935 in Vansittart 2/3.

93. Vansittart notes of September 30 1933 on O'Malley, draft instructions to Phipps, O'Malley MSS.

94. Vansittart notes on O'Malley, draft instructions to Phipps, O'Malley MSS.

95. Vansittart to Hoare, September 30 1935 in Vansittart 2/27.

96. Vansittart to Phipps, December 20 and 22 1935 and March 23 1936.

97. Avon, *Facing the Dictators* p. 447—8 and Bruce Lockhart diary, May 26 1936.

98. Vansittart to Phipps, March 5 and December 20 1935, memorandum of June 22 1936, 'Britain, France and Germany' in Vansittart 1/12, and of May 26 1936 in Vansittart 2/26.

99. Vansittart, to Wigram, November 7 1935, and Vansittart memorandum 'A Busman's Holiday' of September 10 1936 in Vansittart 1/17.

100. See e.g. Vansittart on O'Malley draft, 'Collective Security', of December 1 1935, O'Malley MSS.

101. Vansittart, memorandum, 'The World Situation and British Rearmament', December 31 1936 in Vansittart 1/19.

102. *Ibid.*

103. Vansittart memorandum, 'The World Situation and British Rearmament', December 31 1936 in Vansittart 1/19 and Vansittart, notes on O'Malley draft, 'Collective Security', of December 1 1935, O'Malley MSS.

104. For Vansittart's approval of this idea, see Vansittart on O'Malley draft, 'Collective Security', December 1 1935, O'Malley MSS.

105. Vansittart to Chatfield, February 16 1937.
106. Vansittart memorandum of late 1937 in Vansittart 1/21.
107. Dalton diary of November 4 1937.
108. Vansittart memorandum, 'The World Situation and British Rearmament', December 31 1936 in Vansittart 1/19 and memorandum of May 27 1937 in Vansittart 2/31.
109. E.g. Vansittart to Phipps, February 7 1935 and May 26 1937.
110. Dalton diary, November 4 1937 and April 12 1938.
111. Chatfield to Dreyer, June 1 1933 and February 2 1934.
112. E.g. Chatfield to Dreyer, November 3 1933.
113. Chatfield to W.W. Fisher, May 11 1934.
114. Hankey to Robin Hankey, June 6 1936 and October 3 1937.
115. Hankey, note of private visit to Germany in Hankey to Phipps, November 16 1933. For Hankey comparing the English and German versions of *Mein Kampf*, see Hankey to Phipps, October 30 1933. See also *ibid*. of November 24 and December 2 and 8 1933.
116. Hankey to Casey, December 12 1933.
117. Hankey diary, August 9 1934. Hankey to Casey, November 9 1937.
118. Hankey diary, March 4 and 6 1933, January 12 and February 24 1935.
119. E.g. Hankey diary, February 24 1935.
120. Hankey to Robin Hankey, October 20 1938.
121. Hankey to Casey, December 12 1933 and diary, November 25 1935.
122. Hankey to Casey, December 12 1933.
123. Chatfield to Dreyer, May 16 1935 in Cameron, p. 77. Hankey diary, November 25 1935. Hankey to Phipps, January 2 1936.
124. Chatfield, memorandum of December 11 1936 in Cameron, p. 106.
125. Cameron, pp. 123–5.
126. Hankey to Robin Hankey, December 22 1936 and January 31 1937.
127. Chatfield to Backhouse, February 16 1937, and to Pound, November 23 1937.
128. Chatfield to Pound, November 23 1937.
129. Hankey to Robin Hankey, March 1 1938.
130. Chatfield to Dreyer, September 16 1935.
131. Chatfield, notes of January 5 1937 on Vansittart's memorandum on 'The World Situation and Rearmament'.
132. Hankey to Casey, April 20 1936, and to R. Hankey, December 22 1936.
133. As Chamberlain was at pains to let historians know (see Chamberlain, notes of August 26 1937, PREM 1/276).
134. Chamberlain to Weir and to Hilda, both August 1 1937. Chamberlain to Mussolini, July 27 1937 (PREM 1/276).
135. Chamberlain to Halifax, August 7 1937, PREM 1/276.
136. Chamberlain to Ida, August 8, and Chamberlain notes of August 26 1937, in PREM 1/276.

137. Eden to Chamberlain, July 24 and July 26 1937, PREM 1/276.
138. Chamberlain notes of August 26 1937, PREM 1/276.
139. Chamberlain to Ida, October 16 1937.
140. For Ivy Chamberlain, see NC 1/17.
141. Chamberlain to Hilda, May 26 1935.
142. Chamberlain to Hilda, June 22 1935.
143. Chamberlain to Ida, March 28 1936.
144. See Chamberlain to Simon, September 23 1936.
145. Eden to Chamberlain, May 23 1937, for suspicion about Runciman being pushed out. Harvey diary, March 3 1937. See also 'Imperial Conference; Meetings of Imperial Delegates', June 8 and 9 1937, Cab 32/130.
146. However acceptable this was to the Chiefs of Staff (for the Belgian question, see Cabs 58(36) of October 21, 62 and 63(36) of November 4, 69(36) of December 9, 13(37) of March 24 and 19(37) of April 28). See also Eden's FP 36(17) of March 8 1937 in Cab 27/626 and CID of December 10 1936 in Cab 2/6ii. See also Kieft, pp. 85—155.
147. Cab 43(36) of June 23.
148. Nicolson diary, July 15 and 27 1937. Harvey diary, March 31 and October 5 1937.
149. Cab 42(36) of June 17.
150. Austen Chamberlain to Ida/Hilda, November 14 1936.
151. Especially from Hoare, Inskip, MacDonald and Duff Cooper.
152. Cab 62 and 63(36) of November 4, Cab 64(36) of November 11 and Cab 66(36) of November 18. Austen Chamberlain to Ida/Hilda, November 14 1936.
153. E.g. Eden at Cab 57(36) of October 14 and at Cab 58(36) of October 21.
154. Eden to Baldwin, December 27 1936, and at meeting of ministers of January 8 1937 in Cab 23/87. The plan is in CP 6(37). See also Avon, *Facing the Dictators*, p. 435.
155. I.e. by Wood.
156. Cab 5(37) of February 3 and Cab 7(37) of February 10. Cabs 8 and 9(37) of February 17 and 24 and Cab 14(37) of April 7.
157. Harvey diary, March 31 and October 5 1937.
158. Chamberlain to Ida, October 24 and November 22 1936.
159. Eden at Cab 35(37) of September 29.
160. Zetland to Linlithgow, April 19 1937, quoting Eden.
161. I.e. the withdrawal of Italian volunteers, Cab 14(37) of April 7, Cab 15(37) of April 11, Cab 16(37) of April 14, Cab 17(37) of April 19 and Cab 27(37) of June 30.
162. See Chamberlain diary, February 19 1938, for this claim. Chamberlain notes of August 2, memorandum (unsigned) of July 23, Eden to Chamberlain July 24 and 26, and Wilson, note for Prime Minister of July 26, all 1937 (PREM 1/276). Halifax to Chamberlain, August 4 1937. Chamberlain to Hilda, August 1, and to Ida, August 8 1937.

163. 'Record of a meeting held in the Secretary of State's room at 4 p.m. on August 10 to deal with questions arising in connection with the anticipated conservations with the Italian government as proposed in the Prime Minister's letter to Signor Mussolini of July 27', PREM 1/276.

164. Eden to Halifax, August 11 1937 in Avon, *Facing the Dictators*, p. 456.

165. Halifax, note of discussion with Eden, August 18 1937 in Halifax to Chamberlain, August 19 1937, PREM 1/276.

166. Eden, note of telephone conversation with Prime Minister, September 1 1937 in PREM 1/276. Cleverley, note for Prime Minister in PREM 1/276. Halifax to Chamberlain, August 18, and Chamberlain to Hilda, August 29 1937.

167. E.g. Duff Cooper at Cab 24(37) of June 17, Hoare at Cab 19(37) of April 28, Cab 14(37) of April 7, Cab 15(37) of April 11, Cab 16(37) of April 14 and Cab 17(37) of April 19.

168. The *Deutschland* and *Leipzig*.

169. Cab 23(37) of June 2 and Cab 25(37) of June 21.

170. Swinton and Stanley at Cab 25(37) of June 21 and Cab 26(37) of June 23.

171. Hoare in Cab 19(37) of April 28 for the Bilbão case.

172. E.g. Cab 17(37) of April 19 and Cab 25(37) of June 21.

173. Harvey diary, April 19 1937.

174. Eden on May 28 1937 in *Manchester Guardian* May 29.

175. Cleverley note of August 31 1937, in PREM 1/276. See also 'From time to time remarks have been made in the Cabinet, naturally enough in the main by Service ministers, which emphasize that our foreign policy must be dictated by the state of our defences and it is sometimes added that our position in this respect, in particular at sea, is worse than in 1914. While it may be true that our Navy today is not as strong as it was in 1914, that is not, I think, the proper basis of comparison. Our Navy in Europe is today relatively much stronger than in 1914; the German navy of today bears no comparison to that of pre-war days, the French navy is stronger than that of 1914, and relative to the German navy, very much stronger. It is quite true that Italy remains an uncertain factor, but she was that in 1914, in fact she was officially tied by treaty to Germany in those days. Therefore in Europe surely our position is much better than it was in 1914'. (Eden to Chamberlain, September 9 1937, PREM 1/210) For Chamberlain's comment '... the proposition that our foreign policy must be, if not dictated, at least limited by the state of the Nat[ional] Defences remains true') see PREM 1/210 of September 9 1937.

176. For the agreement see Eden to Chamberlain, September 14, and Chamberlain note of September 15 1937, both in PREM 1/360.

177. Eden, broadcast from Nyon, September 14 1937, *The Times*, September 15. Eden to Churchill, September 25 1937.

178. Harvey diary, September 22 1937.
179. Chamberlain to Hilda, September 12, and to Ida, September 19 1937. Cf. Amery diary, October 21 1937, for Eden in the House of Commons 'overemphasising the extent to which Italy had climbed down'.
180. Cab 36(37) of October 6, Cab 37(37) of October 13 and Cab 38(37) of October 20. For Chamberlain supporting Eden under criticism see Cab 40(37) of November 3 and Cab 41(37) of November 10.
181. Wilson, quoted in Harvey diary, November 17 1937.
182. Steward quoting Chamberlain in GFD no. 29 November 18 1937, DGFP Series D.
183. Harvey diary, November 11 1937.
184. Harvey diary, November 16 1937.
185. Eden to Chamberlain, November 16 1937, PREM 1/330.
186. Harvey diary, November 16 1937.
187. Chamberlain to Hilda, November 21 1937.
188. Chamberlain to Halifax, November 25 1937.
189. Chamberlain to Hilda, October 24 1937.
190. Harvey diary, November 14 1937.
191. For Baldwin's failure to remove Vansittart see Eden to Baldwin, December 27 1936, and Vansittart to Baldwin, December 30 1936. Chamberlain to Ida, December 12 1937.
192. Eden at Cab 1(37) of January 13 and to Chamberlain, January 9 1938, PREM 1/276. Cf. Amery diary, October 22, and Dalton diary, October 28, both 1937, and Cab 43(37) of November 24 for further examples of Eden's desire for agreement with Hitler, whatever his doubts about Henderson or *The Times*.
193. Eden to Chamberlain, January 31 1938, PREM 1/276.
194. Eden to Chamberlain, November 16 1937, PREM 1/330, and November 3, PREM 1/210. Harvey diary, November 8 1937.
195. Cab 5(38) of February 16.
196. Chamberlain to Hilda, November 6 1937. Eden to Chamberlain, November 3 1937, PREM 1/210.
197. Cab 42(37) of November 17.
198. See e.g. Cab 8(34) of March 7.
199. E.g. Chamberlain at Cab 36(37) of October 6.
200. Cabs 36 and 37(37) of October 6 and 13.
201. For an account of British policy, see Lee.
202. Hankey to Casey, November 9 1937, and to Robin Hankey, November 21 1937.
203. Hankey to Vansittart, November 3 1937. Cab 21/558 in Cameron, p. 156. Hankey to Robin Hankey, November 21 1937.
204. Chamberlain to Ida, October 30 1937.
205. Chamberlain to Ida, October 30 1937.
206. Chamberlain to Hilda, November 21 1937, quoting Baldwin.
207. See e.g. Chamberlain to Ida, October 30 1937.
208. Steward quoting Chamberlain in GFD no. 29, November 18 1937, DGFP, Series D.

209. Chamberlain to Hilda, November 26 1937.
210. *Ibid.*
211. Dawson diary, January 25 1938.
212. Cab 45(37) of December 1. Foreign Policy Committee of January 24 and February 3 1938 in Cab 27/623.
213. Especially when Germany announced that she would not return to the League (FP (36) 41 of January 1 1938 and FP (36) 43 of January 25 in Cab 27/626). Cf. Eden at Geneva, January 27 1938, *Manchester Guardian*, January 28.
214. Chamberlain at Cab 43(37) of November 24.
215. Chamberlain to Hilda, January 9 and 30 1938.
216. Cab 4(38) of February 9. For the statement see *Hansard* (331) of February 2 1938, cols. 213–16. For its significance see *The Times* of February 3.
217. Eden to Chamberlain, January 9 1938, PREM 1/276, and Chamberlain to Hilda, January 9 1938.
218. Cadogan diary, February 4, 8 and 17 1938. Harvey diary, February 17 1938. Eden to Chamberlain, February 8 1938.
219. Cab 5(38) of February 16. Eden to Chamberlain, February 18 1938, PREM 1/276.
220. Cabs 5 and 6(38) of February 16. Cf. Amery diary, February 7 1938. Chamberlain to Hilda, February 6 1938. Chamberlain diary, February 19 1938.
221. Chamberlain to Eden, February 8 1938.
222. Chamberlain to Hilda, February 13 1938.
223. Eden at Birmingham, February 12 1938, *The Times*, February 14.
224. Eden to Chamberlain, February 10 1938, PREM 1/276.
225. Perth to Eden (telegram), February 17 1938, PREM 1/276. Eden to Chamberlain, February 18, and Wilson to Chamberlain, February 19 1938, both PREM 1/276. Chamberlain diary, February 19 1938. Chamberlain to Hilda, February 27 1938. Cadogan diary, February 17 1938.
226. Chamberlain diary, February 19 1938.
227. Chamberlain diary, February 19 1938.
228. For this coming as a 'bolt from the blue' see Zetland, pp. 234–5.
229. Chamberlain diary, February 19, and Chamberlain to Hilda, February 27 1938. Harvey diary, February 20, and also February 19 1938 reporting Eden saying that Chamberlain snubbed Simon when Simon tried to say that the issue was not one of policy and principle. Zetland to Linlithgow, February 21 1938.
230. Chamberlain to Hilda, February 27 1938.
231. Eden to Chamberlain, February 8 1938, PREM 1/276.
232. Harvey diary, October 20 1937. Eden to Chamberlain, February 8 1938.
233. I.e. by sending 50,000 troops to Spain from last week, Eden to Chamberlain, January 9 1938, PREM 1/276.
234. 'Anglo-American Co-operation, the chances of effectively asserting white race authority in the Far East and relations with Ger-

many', Eden to Chamberlain, January 9 1938, PREM 1/276.

235. Eden to Chamberlain, January 31 1938, PREM 1/276.
236. Cab 5(38) of February 16.
237. Eden to Chamberlain, January 1 and 9 and February 8 1938. Cab 6(38) of February 19.
238. Cab 3(38) of February 2. Eden to Chamberlain, January 9 1938, PREM 1/276.
239. Chamberlain diary, February 19 1938. Eden to Chamberlain, February 8 1938, PREM 1/276. Harvey diary, February 17 1938. Eden at Cab 6(38) of February 19. Avon, *Facing the Dictators*, pp. 579–80.
240. Harvey diary, December 19–23 1937.
241. Harvey diary, April 22 1938.
242. See e.g. Jones to Lady Grigg, October 24 1937. Eden to Chamberlain, November 3 and December 31 1937.
243. For the initiative, see below pp. 174-6.
244. Eden memorandum, 'The Next Steps towards a General Settlement with Germany', FP(36) 41.
245. Eden note for Foreign Policy Committee, February 10 1938, Cab 27/626.
246. See e.g. Eden in Harvey diary, November 2 1937.
247. So important that, until he discovered that Roosevelt objected to recognition of Italian rule in Abyssinia, Eden thought of letting Chamberlain have his way about Abyssinia in return for support about the Roosevelt initiative (Harvey diary, January 18 and 19 1938). See also Harvey diary, December 19–23 1937, and Eden to Chamberlain, January 17 1938 (PREM 1/259).
248. Chamberlain to Hilda, January 9 1938.
249. See e.g. Langer and Gleason, pp. 17–20.
250. E.g. Cab 35(37) of September 29 and Cab 38(37) of October 20.
251. Cab 48(37) of December 22.
252. Eden at Cab 37(37) of October 13.
253. Cab 36(37) of October 6. Chamberlain to Hilda, October 9 1937. Chamberlain diary, February 19 1938. Chamberlain at Cab 48(37) of December 22. For Chamberlain saying that since the USA had 'no intention of taking any decisive action in the Far East', the Nine-Power Conference should be presented in Parliament as 'appeasement', see Cab 38(37) of October 20.
254. Langer and Gleason, pp. 25–6.
255. Cab 1(38) of January 4 and Secret Addendum. Wilson to Prime Minister, January 23 1938, and Eden to Chamberlain, January 17 1938, both PREM 1/259.
256. E.g. Harvey diary, January 21 1938. See also Cab 8(34) of March 7.
257. Cab 7(38) of February 20.
258. For the Cadman report being known about in early February, see Rowland and Cadman, pp. 167–8.

259. 1935 general election result: Conservatives 28,528, Labour 21,278. Result of by-election February 16 1938: R.R. Stokes (Lab) 27,604, H.U. Willink (NC) 24,443.
260. There are many suggestions that he was both over the previous three years (e.g. Jones's conversation with Baldwin, October 26 1937, Harvey diary, December 5 1937, Stanhope to Baldwin, July 6 1936, Simon diary of April 5 1935 and Chamberlain diary, April 2 1935). See, however, the argument Eden had with Simon after the resignation when Simon claimed that illness was a contributory factor, Simon to Eden, February 23 1938, Simon MSS.
261. See e.g. Eden, message to constituency, June 11 1937, *Manchester Guardian*, June 11, and at League Assembly, September 20 1937, *The Times*, September 21.

NOTES TO CHAPTER 6

1.   Chamberlain to Hilda, February 27 1938.
2.   For Butler see GFD no. 750 of April 22 1938.
3.   Amery diary, February 22 1938.
4.   For the speech, see *Hansard* (332) cols. 220—9 of February 22 1938. Nicolson to V. Sackville-West, February 25 1938. Cf. Griffith in *Hansard* (322) col. 234.
5.   Chamberlain to Hilda, December 17 1937.
6.   Chamberlain to Hilda, November 28 1936.
7.   Chamberlain in Cab 49(37) of December 22. Inskip's defence review of late 1937, 'Defence Expenditure in Future Years', is dated December 15 and is in Cab 27/648 (CP 316/37).
8.   Chamberlain diary, February 19 1938. Cab 6(38) of February 19.
9.   Cab 5(38) of February 16 and Cab 9(38) of February 23.
10. Even though Hitler's reply when Nevile Henderson saw him, was that he wanted to get what he wanted in central Europe and 'did not want to tie [his] hands by talks and undertakings', see Halifax at Cab 10(38) of March 2 and Cab 11(38) of March 9.
11. Cab 12(38) of March 12. Chamberlain to Hilda, March 13 1938.
12. Chamberlain at 12(38) of March 12.
13. Chamberlain at Cab 12(38) of March 12 and at Cab 13(38) of March 14. Chamberlain to Hilda, March 13 1938.
14. Chamberlain to Hilda, March 13 1938.
15. Cab 15(38) of March 22. Chamberlain to Ida, March 20 1938.
16. Chamberlain at Cab 16(38) of March 23. Cadogan diary, March 16—18 1938. Chamberlain to Ida, March 20 1938.
17. Cabinet Committees of March 15, 18, 21, 29 and April 7 in Cab 27/623, Cab 16(38) of March 22 and Cab 17(38) of March 30 etc.

18. Chamberlain at Cab 12(38) of March 12. Chamberlain to Hilda, March 13 1938.
19. E.g. Cab 19(38) of April 13.
20. Chamberlain at Cab 15(38) of March 22. Halifax to Chamberlain, March 19 1938, PREM 1/265. Chamberlain in *Hansard*, March 24 1938.
21. Chamberlain in *Hansard* (333) cols. 1399—1413 of March 24 1938.
22. Chamberlain at Cab 15(38) of March 22.
23. Cab 18(38) of April 6. Chamberlain to Ida, April 16 1938.
24. Cab 22(38) of May 4. Chamberlain to Ida, May 1 1938.
25. For apprehension about explaining it to the French, see Cab 19(38) of April 13 and Cab 21(38) of April 27.
26. Halifax to Chamberlain, April 14 1938, PREM 1/308. Cab 22(38) of May 4. For the decision about joint defence preparations see Cab 18(38) of April 6.
27. Cab 22(38) of May 4. Halifax at Cab 18(38) of April 6, at Cabinet Committee of April 7 1938, Cab 27/623 and at Cab 21(38) of April 27.
28. Cab 25(38) of May 22. *DBFP* third series, vol. I, pp. 340—342 and 346—7.
29. Simon and Cadogan diaries, May 22 1938.
30. Chamberlain to Hilda, May 22 1938.
31. Chamberlain to Hilda, May 22 1938.
32. Chamberlain to Ida, May 28 and June 18 1938. For the Turkish request for a loan, see Cab 23(38) of May 11.
33. Cabinet Committee of June 1 1938 in Cab 27/623, Cab 31(38) of July 6 and Cab 32(38) of July 13. Cf. Harvey diary, July 11—16 1938.
34. E.g. Cab 31(38) of July 6.
35. Chamberlain to Daladier, July 8 1938, PREM 1/263. Chamberlain to Hilda, July 9 1938.
36. Chamberlain to Hilda, May 22 1938.
37. Chamberlain to Hannon, June 3 1938.
38. *DGFP* series D, vol. II, no. 247 of June 9 1938.
39. Via W.W. Astor and Halifax, via Snowden's widow and via Elibank, Princess Hohenlohe and Hoare's brother, the banker Oliver Hoare, W.W. Astor to Halifax, June 22 1938, FO 800/309, Harvey diary, July 11 to 16 1938 and FO 800/313.
40. Chamberlain, note of talk to German Ambassador, July 22 1938, PREM 1/330.
41. Wilson, notes for Prime Minister, July 12, 22 and 23 1938. Halifax to Chamberlain, Wednesday afternoon (between July 12 and 15 1938, two letters, PREM 1/330). Harvey diary, July 11 to 16 and 18 1938. Cadogan diary, July 18 and 22 1938. GFD no. 309 of July 22 1938, *DGFP* series D.
42. Halifax at Cab 26(38) of May 25.
43. Which the Germans seemed not to want. Cab 27(38) of June 1, Halifax reporting Strang.

44. Cab 26(38) of May 25.
45. I.e. Strang.
46. See Cabinet Committee of June 16 1938 in Cab 27/624.
47. Cab 29(38) of June 22. Cab 32(38) of July 13.
48. Halifax at Cab 30(38) of June 29, Cab 31(38) of July 6 and Cab 35(38) of July 27. Wilson to Halifax, June 22 1938 FO 800/309 proposing four names and putting Lord Macmillan top. For Runciman's hesitations see Runciman to Halifax, June 30, and to Simon, August 1 1938.
49. Which they sent through Hitler's private office in order to by-pass Ribbentrop.
50. Halifax to Henderson, August 11 1938, *DBFP* third series, vol. II, pp. 76 and 78–80.
51. Henderson, telegram no. 362 in *DBFP* third series, vol. II, pp. 91–2.
52. Kordt to Weizsacker, *DGFP* series D, vol. II, no. 382 of August 23 1938.
53. Cadogan diary, July 28 and September 3 1938.
54. Chamberlain to Ida, September 3 1938.
55. Chamberlain to Halifax, August 19 1938, FO 800/314. Chamberlain at Cab 36(38) of August 30. Chamberlain to Hilda, September 6 1938.
56. Simon at Lanark, August 27 1938, *The Times* August 29. See also Winnifrith to Hoyer-Miller, August 26 1938, for the consultation that went on before Simon spoke.
57. Cab 36(38) of August 30.
58. In the light of other reports from Germany.
59. Halifax at Cab 36(38) of August 30.
60. Halifax at Cab 36(38) of August 30, Halifax to Chamberlain, August 21 [1938].
61. Halifax to Chamberlain, August 21 [1938].
62. Cab 36(38) of August 30.
63. Elliot to his wife, September 12 1938, Coote, p. 164.
64. E.g. Halifax to Phipps, September 12 1938, PREM 1/265.
65. For Halifax's desire to repeat the warning, see below p. 278. For all this see also Chamberlain to the King, September 13 1938, PREM 1/266A.
66. Meeting of Ministers of September 13 1938, Cab 27/646. Chamberlain to Ida, September 19 1938.
67. Chamberlain at Cab 38(38) of September 14. Inskip diary, September 12 and 14, Cadogan diary, September 8, 11, 13, and 14, and Hore-Belisha diary, September 14, all 1938. Chamberlain to Runciman, September 12 1938, PREM 1/266A.
68. On September 2 and, in a modified form, on September 7.
69. Harvey diary, September 11 1938, quoting Halifax.
70. See Seton-Watson, p. 39 for a press conference reported in the *Montreal Daily Star* of May 14.
71. Eden, quoting Halifax, in Harvey diary, September 9 1938.
72. Wilson, note for Prime Minister, August 25 1938, PREM 1/265.

73. But Hitler presumably knew that Chamberlain had given the press conference in May, see above n. 70. So they both knew that cession of territory would be acceptable.
74. Cab 27/646 of September 13 1938.
75. Cab 38(38) of September 14 at 11 a.m.
76. Chamberlain to Runciman, September 12, and Runciman to Chamberlain, September 13 1938, PREM 1/266A. Chamberlain at Cab 38(38) of September 14.
77. I.e. MacDonald, Winterton, Hore-Belisha, Elliot, Hailsham, Stanley and de la Warr.
78. Cab 26(38) of May 25 and Cab 38(38) of September 14.
79. Chamberlain to Ida, September 19 1938. Chamberlain, minute of September 15, PREM 1/266A.
80. Chamberlain, minute of the conversation between the Prime Minister and the Führer, September 15 1938, PREM 1/266A.
81. Schmidt memorandum in *DGFP* series D, vol. II, no. 487 of September 15 1938.
82. Chamberlain, minute of the conversation between the Prime Minister and the Führer, September 15 1938, PREM 1/266A. Chamberlain to Ida, September 19 1938.
83. See above n. 81. Chamberlain to Hitler, September 16 1938, PREM 1/266A.
84. Chamberlain at Cab 39(38) of September 17.
85. Schmidt memorandum in *DGFP* series D, vol. II, no. 487 of September 15 1938.
86. Meeting of Ministers, September 16 1938, Cab 27/646.
87. Inskip, Duff Cooper and Hore-Belisha diaries, September 17 1938. Cab 39(38) of September 17.
88. Meeting of Ministers, September 16 1938, Cab 27/646. Cadogan diary, September 16 1938.
89. Inskip and Duff Cooper diaries, September 17 1938.
90. Hoare at Cab 39(38) of September 17.
91. This was said in various ways by de la Warr, Winterton, Stanley and Eliot.
92. Meeting of Ministers, September 18 1938 in Cab 27/646. The text, dated September 18 is in PREM 1/266A. Cadogan diary, September 18 1938, implies that Chamberlain suggested the guarantee.
93. For the proposals see *DBFP* third series, vol. II, pp. 404–5. Cab 40(38) of September 19. Hore-Belisha diary, September 19 1938. Elliot to his wife, September 19 1938, Coote, p. 166, leaves a slightly different impression.
94. E.g. MacDonald, Stanley, Hailsham, etc.
95. Cab 40(38) of September 19.
96. Halifax to Hitler via Henderson no. 386 of September 19 and Halifax, telephone message for Wilson, September 19 1938, both in PREM 1/266A.
97. Cab 40(38) of September 19. Cadogan diary, September 20 1938. Harvey diary, September 21 1938.

98. Elliot to his wife, September 19 1938.
99. Meeting of Ministers of September 21 1938 in Cab 27/646.
100. See Cab 41(38) of September 21. Harvey diary, September 22 1938. Duff Cooper to Halifax, September 22 1938, FO 800/309. Elliot to his wife, September 22 1938, Coote, pp. 169—70.
101. Cab 41(38) of September 21.
102. According to Wood, see Duff Cooper diary, September 23 1938.
103. *DGFP* series D, vol. II, no. 562, Minute of the conversation between the Führer and Reich Chancellor and Mr. Chamberlain, the British Prime Minister, at Godesberg on the afternoon of September 22 1938. Wilson, telephone message of September 23 1938 10 a.m., PREM 1/266A.
104. Chamberlain to Hitler, September 23 1938, GFD no. 572, *DGFP* series D.
105. Chamberlain to Hitler, September 23 1938, *DGFP* series D, vol. II, no. 572 and Hitler to Chamberlain, September 23 1938, no. 573. Wilson, telephone message, September 23 1938 8.14 p.m. in PREM 1/266A. Hitler to Chamberlain, September 23 1938, no. 573.
106. *DGFP* series D, vol. II, no. 583, memorandum of conversations between the Führer and Reich Chancellor and Mr Chamberlain, the British Prime Minister, at Godesberg on the evening of September 23 1938.
107. Meetings of Ministers, September 22 1938 at 3 p.m. and at 9.30 p.m. (esp. appendix II) in Cab 27/646.
108. See above p. 195.
109. Meeting of Ministers, September 23 1938 at 3 p.m., Cab 27/646. Note the peculiar way in which the chronology of decision in relation to Chamberlain's letter is presented.
110. Elliot to his wife, September 23 1938, Coote p. 171. Meeting of Ministers, September 23 1938 at 3 p.m., Cab 27/646.
111. Meeting of Ministers, September 23 1938 at 9.30 p.m., Cab 27/646.
112. *DBFP* third series, vol. II, p. 497.
113. Meeting of Ministers, September 24 1938 at 3.30 p.m., Cab 27/646.
114. Cab 42(38) of September 24.
115. I.e. Stanley, Winterton, Hore-Belisha, de la Warr, Elliot and Duff Cooper (in addition to R.S. Hudson, who was not in the Cabinet). Amery diary, September 24 1938, reporting Winterton who came to see him that night for a consultation. Elliot to his wife, September 25 1938, Coote, pp. 171—3, Harvey diary, September 25 1938. Cadogan, Duff Cooper and Hore-Belisha diaries, September 24 1938.
116. Cab 42(38) of September 24.
117. For Maugham, Brown, Stanhope and Wood (the latter with evident distaste) supporting Chamberlain, see Cabs 43 and 44(38) of September 25. Duff Cooper diary, September 25 1938. Elliot to his wife, September 25 1938, Coote, pp. 171—3.

118. Duff Cooper diary, September 25 1938.
119. Cab 44(38) of September 25 in PREM 1/266A. Harvey, Duff Cooper and Hore-Belisha diaries, September 25 1938. See also Colville, p. 118.
120. Cab 45(38) of September 26.
121. CID of September 26 1938 (Cab 16/189). Duff Cooper and Hore-Belisha diaries, September 26 1938.
122. Kordt to GFM, *DGFP* series D, vol. II, no. 605 of September 26 1938.
123. Ribbentrop minute of September 25 1938 in *loc. cit.* no. 600.
124. Cab 44(38) of September 25, fols. 241—3.
125. Statement by the British Prime Minister in *DGFP* series D, vol. II, no. 618 of September 26 1938.
126. Minute by Weizsacker in *DGFP* series D, vol. II, no. 611 of September 26 1938, reporting Henderson.
127. Jebb, memorandum of September 26 1938 in PREM 1/266A.
128. Meeting of Ministers of September 26 1938 10 p.m. Cab 27/646. Duff Cooper diary, September 27 1938.
129. For the letter see Chamberlain to Hitler, September 26 1938, PREM 1/266A. *DGFP* series D, vol. II, no. 634 of September 27 1938, memorandum on the conversation between the Führer and Reich Chancellor and Sir Horace Wilson etc.
130. Meeting of Ministers, September 27 1938 at 4.30 p.m., Cab 27/646.
131. Cab 46(38) of September 27.
132. *DBFP* third series, vol. II, pp. 627—9 and 404—6. Cab 47(38) of September 30, fols. 281 *et seq* for the ten conditions.
133. *The Times*, October 1 1938. Chamberlain to Hilda, October 2 1938. For Strang drafting the statement and Chamberlain being very pleased with Hitler's agreement, see Strang, pp. 146—7.
134. Chamberlain to Hilda, October 2 1938.
135. Chamberlain to Hankey, October 2 1938.
136. Garvin to Simon, October 11 1938. Londonderry to Chamberlain, October [September written] 4 1938. Baldwin to Chamberlain, September 15, 26 and 30 1938, NC 13/11. For a survey of the provincial press, see Hadley, pp. 93—110.
137. The phrase is that of Lord Ebbisham, the Chairman of the Primrose League, in a letter to Mrs Chamberlain, October 6 1938. NC 13/8—13 has an immense correspondence and expressions of gratitude from correspondents, known and unknown, in England and elsewhere.
138. In the course of which Baldwin was called a 'guttersnipe' and Churchill, Eden, Greenwood and Duff Cooper attacked as 'warmongers'.
139. Chamberlain to Hilda, November 13 1938. Nicolson diary, December 13 1938.
140. Cabinet Committee of November 14 1938 and of January 23 1939 Cab 27/624. Cadogan diary, December 15 1938 and January 17, 19 and 23 1939. Inskip diary, December 4 1938 and Jan-

uary 23 1939. Harvey diary, January 24 1939. Kirkpatrick, pp. 136–8. Halifax at Cabinet Committee of January 23 1939.

141. Cabinet Committee of November 14 and 21 1938, Cab 27/624.

142. Cab 3(39) of February 1 and Cab 8(39) of February 22.

143. Chamberlain at Cabinet Committee, November 14 1938, in Cab 27/624, but see Chamberlain to Hilda, November 6 1938, for Chamberlain hoping that Mussolini 'might be extraordinarily valuable in making plans for talks with Germany'.

144. Chamberlain to Hilda, November 6 1938.

145. Zetland to Linlithgow, January 24 1939, MSS Eur.D.609.9. Chamberlain to Hilda, January 15 1939.

146. Chamberlain at Cab 1(39) of January 18.

147. Cadogan diary, February 6 1939.

148. Chamberlain to Ida, December 4 1938.

149. Chamberlain to Ida, December 12 1939.

150. Chamberlain to Ida, October 22 1938.

151. Chamberlain at Cabinet Committee, November 14 1938, Cab 27/624.

152. I.e. the importance of avoiding an 'arms race' (Cab 51(38) of October 31) and Chamberlain at Cabinet Committee of November 14 1938, Cab 27/624.

153. Chamberlain at Cab 60(38) of December 21.

154. Chamberlain to Hilda, February 5 1939. Crozier, interview with Wood of February 9 1939. CID of February 9 1939 (Cab 2/7) for Chatfield's announcement of RADAR.

155. Chamberlain at Cab 60(38) of December 21. Chamberlain to Ida, January 8 1939. For Ivy Chamberlain visiting Mussolini 'recently', see Killearn diary, March 8 1939.

156. Chamberlain to Hilda, February 5, and to Ida, February 26 1939. Cab 3(39) of February 1. The Crown Prince of Sweden quoting Chamberlain in Cadogan diary, December 2 1938; Cadogan diary, December 10 and 11 1938, has reports of a Goerdeler plan for an army revolution next month. Harvey diary, December 11 1938. Cf Dawson to Washburn, March 28 1939, *The Times* Archive for 'jealousy'.

157. *Hansard* (340) col. 88 of November 1 1938. Cab 50(38) of October 26.

158. Chamberlain at Cab 59(38) of December 14 and Cab 60(38) of December 21.

159. E.g. Cab 50(38) of October 26.

160. Wilson to Phipps, February 2 1939.

161. *DGFP* series D, vol. IV, GFD no. 300 of January 25 1939. Chamberlain at Birmingham, January 28 1939, *The Times*, January 30.

162. On January 30 1939 (Hitler, speech to the Reichstag, January 30 1939, *The Times*, January 31, for Hitler repeating that he had no demands on Britain). See also Cab 7(39) of February 15.

163. *Hansard* (343) col. 81 of January 31 1939.

164. Chamberlain to Ida, February 12, and to Hilda, February 5 1939.

165. Chamberlain to Halifax, February 19 1939, FO 800/315. Hender-

son to Wilson, March 1, Henderson to Chamberlain, February 23, Chamberlain to Henderson, February 19, all 1939 in PREM 1/330 (the last two are in *DBFP* third series, vol. IV, pp. 591 and 594.)

166. Chamberlain to Hilda, February 19 1939. Cf. Zetland to Linlithgow, February 5 1939, Eur. D. 609.
167. Chamberlain to Hilda, February 19, and to Ida, February 26 1939.
168. Chamberlain at Blackburn, February 22 1939, *Yorkshire Post* February 23.
169. Channon diary, March 7 1939. Chamberlain to Ida, March 12 1939.
170. Cadogan diary, March 10 1939. Chamberlain to Ida, March 12 1939.
171. Gwilym Lloyd George to Lloyd George, March 17 1939. *Hansard* (345) cols. 435–40 of March 15 1939. Cab 11(39) of March 15. Harvey diary, March 16 1939.

NOTES TO CHAPTER 7

1. Greenwood in Lancashire, September 27 1936, *Manchester Guardian*, September 28.
2. Attlee at Oxford, February 25 1938, *The Times*, February 26.
3. Morrison in *Forward*, October 16 1937. Attlee at Labour Party Conference, October 4 1937, *Manchester Guardian*, October 5.
4. Elwyn Jones, p. 306.
5. Morrison at London Political Council of Railway Clerks Association, February 12 1938, *The Times*, February 14, and at Cambridge University Labour and Socialist Club, February 4 1938, *Manchester Guardian*, February 5.
6. E.g. Dalton diary, July 13 1938.
7. E.g. Morrison at Ipswich, February 14 1938, *Manchester Guardian*, February 15.
8. Morrison in London, February 29 1938, *Manchester Guardian*, March 1.
9. Attlee at Langholme, June 12 1938, *Manchester Guardian*, June 13.
10. Attlee in London, February 29 1938, *Manchester Guardian*, March 1.
11. Greenwood at Putney, March 15 1938, *Daily Herald*, March 16. Manifesto by the Three Bodies, February 23 1938, *Daily Herald*, February 24. Attlee at Oxford, February 25 1938, *The Times*, February 26, and at Gosport, February 27 1938, *News Chronicle*, February 28.
12. For Dalton saying some measure of frontier revision in Czechoslovakia was preferable to federalisation, see Dalton diary, November 30 1937. See Dalton diary, May 28 1938, for Dalton rejecting the idea that there should be 'no concessions' from the Czechs.

13. Attlee at Barnsley, June 15 1938, *Manchester Guardian*, June 16, and in *Staffordshire Chronicle*, June 4 1938. Morrison at Bury, Manchester and Barnsley, May 21, 22 and 31 1938, *Manchester Guardian*, May 22 and 23, and June 2. Cf. Harvey diary, May 12 1938, for Ellen Wilkinson talking to Halifax.

14. Morrison in *Forward*, July 9 1938.

15. Citrine at Blackpool, September 6 1938, *Daily Herald*, September 7.

16. Joint declaration of September 7 1938, *Daily Herald*, September 8.

17. Attlee in *Daily Herald*, September 1 1938, at Limehouse, September 18 1938, *The Times*, September 19. Morrison at Hammersmith, September 18, *The Times*, September 19. Greenwood at Swinton, September 17 1938, *Manchester Guardian*, September 19.

18. Attlee in *Daily Herald*, September 1 1938.

19. Halifax, memorandum of September 16 1938, FO 800/309.

20. Dalton, talking to Vansittart, Dalton diary, September 19 1938.

21. Dalton diary, September 19 1938, records the meeting.

22. See National Council of Labour statement in *Manchester Guardian*, September 20 1938.

23. Attlee to Chamberlain, September 20 1938, *The Times*, September 21.

24. Dalton diary, September 21 1938.

25. Joint Labour movement statement of September 22 1938, *Manchester Guardian*, September 22.

26. E.g. Citrine at Bristol, September 25 1938, *Western Daily Press*, September 26.

27. *Ibid.* Greenwood reported in *The Times*, September 26 1938. Attlee in *Daily Herald*, September 23 1938. Morrison at St Austell, September 23 1938, *The Times*, September 24. *Daily Herald*, September 24 1938.

28. The policy referred to being the policy outlined on September 8. Attlee to Chamberlain, September 26 1938, *The Times*, September 27. Dalton diary, September 26 1938.

29. Greenwood at Birmingham, October 8 1938, *Manchester Guardian* October 10. Attlee at Hanley, October 8 1938, *The Times*, October 10, and in London, October 20, *The Times*, October 21. Morrison at Wigan, October 10 1938, *Daily Herald*, October 11. National Executive statement of Labour party policy, *Daily Herald*, October 29 1938. Attlee talking at lunch, in Amery diary, October 21 1938.

30. Attlee at West Hartlepool, October 23 1938, *Manchester Guardian*, October 24.

31. Morrison in *News Chronicle*, July 17 1936, for taking it seriously. Attlee at Blackburn, September 23 1936, *Liverpool Post*, September 24.

32. TUC meeting of September 11 1936, *Daily Herald*, Septem-

ber 12. Labour Party Conference, October 7 1936, *Daily Herald*, October 8.

33. Cripps to R. Dodds, October 10 1939.
34. Cooke, pp. 226–7 quoting Cripps diary, September 28 1938.
35. Cripps to H.R. Williamson, October 6, and to A. Blenkinsop, October 18 1939.
36. E.g. by Morrison, Attlee, Dalton and Alexander in public speeches in early 1939.
37. Middleton to Cripps, December 10 1936. The speech was delivered at Stockport on November 15 1936, *Manchester Guardian*, November 16.
38. *Daily Herald*, October 7 1937.
39. E.g. Cripps to Dallas, April 28, to Miss Forsyth, May 16, and to Lady Mary Murray, May 18 1938.
40. For Russia see Cripps to Trevelyan, March 28 1938.
41. E.g. Dalton diary, October 6 1938.
42. Dalton diary, October 6 1938.
43. Maclean in Cook and Ramsden, p. 150.
44. E.g. Cripps to Middleton, January 9 1939, on Morrison's proposed appearance with Anderson and Brown on a National Register platform at the Albert Hall.
45. Cripps and others to National Executive, n.d. Cripps MSS 572/3.
46. Cripps to Middleton, January 9 1939.
47. Cripps and others to National Executive, n.d. Cripps MSS 572/3.
48. Cripps to Lloyd George, May 9, to Baldwin, June 13, to Churchill, July 5, and to Burton, April 25, all 1939. Cooke, pp. 242–3. Estorick, p. 180.
49. For talk, see Dalton diary, April 7 1938.
50. Maclean, 'Oxford and Bridgewater', in Cook and Ramsden, p. 146.
51. *The Times*, November 25 1938.
52. *The Times*, November 25 1938.
53. Attlee in *Daily Herald*, February 22 1939.
54. Greenwood at Manchester, January 14 1939, *Manchester Guardian*, January 16.
55. Greenwood at Belper, December 4 1938, *Daily Herald*, December 5. Attlee at National Trade Union Club, October 19 1938, *The Times* October 20, and at Walsall, November 11 1938, *The Times*, November 12. Labour Party Executive Committee statement of November 24 1938, *The Times*, November 25.
56. Greenwood at Belper, December 4 1938, *Daily Herald*, December 5.
57. *Ibid.*
58. *Daily Herald*, December 9 1938.
59. Attlee at Oldham, November 13 1938, *Manchester Guardian*, November 14.
60. Attlee in *Daily Herald*, January 31 1939.
61. Greenwood at St Helens, February 3 1939, *Daily Herald*, February 4.

62. *Daily Herald*, May 30 1939.
63. Greenwood at South Beck, April 17 1939, *Manchester Guardian*, April 18. National Council of Labour statement of March 21 1939 *Manchester Guardian* March 22. Dalton diary, March 23 1939. Attlee at Wednesbury, March 24 1939, *Birmingham Post*, March 25, and at Weston-super-Mare, April 7 1939, *The Times*, April 8. Greenwood at Bradford, April 2 1939, *Yorkshire Post*, April 3, and at Wolverhampton, March 19 1939, *The Times*, March 20.
64. *Ibid.*
65. Amery diary, October 11 1938.
66. Attlee at Weston-super-Mare, April 7 1939, *The Times*, April 8.
67. Morrison in *Forward*, April 15 1939.
68. Attlee at Wednesbury, March 24 1939, *Birmingham Post*, March 25.
69. Dalton diary, March 23 and 30, June 28 and 29 and July 5, 10 and 12 1939.
70. Greenwood in *Daily Herald*, April 27 1939. National Council of Labour statement of April 27 in *Manchester Guardian*, April 28 1939. Attlee in *Evening Star*, April 24 1939.
71. Attlee in *Evening Star*, April 24 1939.
72. Labour party statement of policy on the organisation of defence services, *The Times*, May 8 1939. *Daily Herald*, June 1 1939, for party conference debate on statement and on defence.
73. Dallas in presidential address at Labour Party Conference, May 29 1939, *Daily Herald*, May 30.
74. Attlee at Aston, May 15 1939, *Birmingham Post*, May 16.

NOTES TO CHAPTER 8

1. For even loyal Conservatives saying that Baldwin would not have let Eden go, see Geoffrey Lloyd to Davidson, March 8 1938.
2. Chamberlain to Ida, April 10 1937.
3. Chamberlain to Amery, May 30 1937.
4. Amery diary, June 2 1937.
5. Amery diary, May 28 1937.
6. Amery diary, July 13 1937
7. Amery diary, September 21 1937 and October 23 1938 etc.
8. Amery diary, February 10 1938 and October 13 1937 (and *passim* 1937–8).
9. Amery to Londonderry, October 9, and diary, November 15 1937.
10. Amery diary, February 22 1938.
11. Amery diary, February 20 and 21 1938.
12. Amery diary, February 26 1938.
13. Amery diary, March 12 1938.
14. Amery diary, March 24 1938.

15. For all this see Amery diary, between March 20 1938 and May 25 1938.
16. Amery diary, September 11 1938.
17. Amery diary, September 14 1938.
18. Amery diary, September 11 1938.
19. Amery diary, September 13 and 14 1938.
20. Amery diary, September 19 1938, and to Chamberlain, September 17 and 19 1938, PREM 1/249.
21. Amery diary, September 22 1938. Amery to Hannon, September 21 1938.
22. Amery diary, September 23 1938.
23. Amery to Halifax, September 24 1938, FO 800/309.
24. Amery diary, September 25 1938.
25. Amery diary, September 26 1938.
26. Amery diary, October 5 1938.
27. Amery diary, October 5 and 21 1938.
    October 20 1938. Lloyd George to Amery, October 21 1938.
28. Amery to Sinclair, October 19 1938.
29. Amery diary, September 25 1938.
30. Cecil to Halifax, November 20 1936, Add. MSS 51084.
31. Dugdale diary, December 2 1937, for Murray's age telling.
32. Cecil to Murray, November 17 1936.
33. Cecil, memorandum on League policy, May 26 1936, Add. MSS 51083.
34. See e.g. Cecil saying that 'Nazism and Fascism [could not] last', Cecil to Churchill, December 1 1936. Murray to Austen Chamberlain, April 4 1936.
35. Chamberlain to Cecil, February 15, and Cecil to Chamberlain, February 18 1938, for Chamberlain criticising when Cecil was present while Morrison led the singing of the Internationale after a League of Nations Union meeting. See also the decision of Mrs Dugdale (who was virtually a Cecil) to join the National Labour party in 1937, Rose, p. xvi.
36. Murray to ?, November 4 1937.
37. A great deal of the correspondence that passed between Cecil and Murray between 1936 and 1938 refers to this dispute.
38. Cecil to Murray, November 17 1936.
39. Cecil to Halifax, February 26, and to Murray, May 25 1938.
40. Cecil to Murray, May 25 1938.
41. Murray to Eden, June 1 1938. Cecil to Murray, August 26 and 31 1938.
42. There is a large Halifax/Cecil correspondence about the Far East, much of which is in the Cecil papers in the British Museum.
43. Dugdale diary, September 25 1938.
44. A.J. Freshwater to Chamberlain, September 22 1938, conveying a League of Nations Union Executive Committee resolution, PREM 1/249.
45. Cecil to Murray, November 1 1938.
46. Maclean in Cook and Ramsden, p. 146.

47. Cecil to Eden, March 17 1939 (some of it is crossed out), Add. MSS 51083.
48. Cecil to Murray, November 1 1938.
49. Cecil to Noel-Baker, February 16 1939, Add. MSS 51109.
50. Cecil to Murray, September 26 1939.
51. Allen of Hurtwood to Samuel, June 15 1938.
52. Cf. rejection of the Popular Front at the Buxton Conference in 1937, *News Chronicle*, May 31 1937. Cf. Sinclair to A.S. Page, July 25 1936. Sinclair to Macmillan, August 19, and to Dingle Foot, August 27 1936.
53. Muir in *News Chronicle*, September 23 1936.
54. Sinclair at National Liberal Club, November 11 1936, *Manchester Guardian*, November 12.
55. Crewe to Sinclair, September 25 1937.
56. Muir in *Manchester Guardian*, September 18 1936.
57. Muir in *Manchester Guardian*, September 18 and 19 1936.
58. Sinclair to Johnstone, October 30 1936. Cf. Snowden to Grigg, December 26 1935.
59. Sinclair to Johnstone, February 17 1936 and April 27 1937.
60. Mander to Sinclair, June 20 1936. R.W. Black to Lloyd George, July 16 1936. Sinclair to Hirst, June 26 1936, for Sinclair privately hoping Noel-Baker would win.
61. Sinclair to Foot, August 27, and vice versa, September 3 1936. Brock to Miss Mackenzie, February 19 1937, Sinclair MSS. Johnstone to Sinclair, February 17 1937.
62. Sinclair to Johnstone, August 6 1936.
63. Johnstone to Murray, February 3 1937, and to Sinclair, February 5 1937. Sinclair to Johnstone, February 8 1937.
64. Sinclair to Findlay, February 27 1936.
65. Sinclair to Hirst, April 4 and July 24 1936. Cf. Sinclair to Hirst, March 2, 11 and 18 1936, and to F. Acland, March 6 1936.
66. Sinclair at Bradford, April 8 1937, *Yorkshire Observer*, April 9. Sinclair, budget broadcast, April 22 1937, *Manchester Guardian*, April 23. Sinclair at the 80 Club, March 10 1937, *Manchester Guardian*, March 11.
67. Muir in *Manchester Guardian*, September 18 1936.
68. Meston to Sinclair, June 27 1937.
69. Miss Mackenzie to Brock, February 18 1938, Sinclair MSS.
70. Sinclair to Mrs Argenti, February 28 1938, and at Edinburgh, February 25 1937, *Manchester Guardian*, February 26.
71. Sinclair to Johnstone, April 30 1937. Johnstone to Heffer, August 5 1937.
72. Sinclair to Harris, September 8 1937.
73. Sinclair at Leeds, November 15 1937, *Yorkshire Observer*, November 17, *News Chronicle*, December 4 1937 and *Manchester Guardian*, January 27 1938. Sinclair at Edinburgh, February 22 1937, *The Scotsman*, February 23. Muir at Salisbury, February 26 1937, *Manchester Guardian*, February 27. Sinclair at Pontypridd, February 11 1937, *Manchester Guardian*, February 12,

and to Crosfield, April 7 1937. Sinclair to Mrs Argenti, February 28 1938.

74. Sinclair at Cambridge, July 19 1937, *Manchester Guardian*, July 30, and to Mrs Argenti, February 28 1938. Sinclair at Manchester, November 19 1937, *The Times*, November 20.
75. E.g. Wilfred Roberts and Eleanor Rathbone.
76. E.g. Sinclair to Mander, August 31, to Roberts, September 10, and to Rathbone, October 24 1936.
77. Sinclair at Wick, October 1, *Manchester Guardian*, October 2 and, at Berwick-on-Tweed, October 13 1937, *The Scotsman*, October 14. Miss Mackenzie to Brock, October 19 1937.
78. Sinclair at Cambridge, February 14 1938, *Manchester Guardian*, February 15.
79. Sinclair to Allen of Hurtwood, March 22 1938.
80. Liberal party assembly at Bath, May 20 1938, *News Chronicle*, May 21.
81. Sinclair at Barnet, July 16 1938, *Manchester Guardian*, July 18.
82. Sinclair at Middlesborough, March 18 1938, *Manchester Guardian*, March 19, and at Aylesbury, May 16 1938, *News Chronicle*, May 18. Sinclair to Miss Sydney Brown, September 1 1938.
83. Sinclair to Harris, September 6 1938.
84. See e.g. Spender to Harris, April 5 and 9 1938. Meston in *The Times*, May 20 1938. Esher to Samuel, July 4 1938. Cf. 'Notes of discussion at National Liberal Club June 21 1938' for the bad effect of Popular Front on anti-socialist uncommitted voters (especially at Aylesbury by-election).
85. Sinclair to H. Alexander MP, March 17 1938.
86. Samuel at Oxford, July 31 1938, *Yorkshire Post*, August 1.
87. Crewe to Spender, April 30 1938. Esher to Samuel, July 4 1938. Crewe to Sinclair, July 21 1938. Sinclair to Crewe, July 22 1938. Meston at Bath, May 19 1938, *The Times*, May 20. For Muir criticising Samuel's view that the League pace should not be forced, *Yorkshire Post*, August 1 1938.
88. Miss Mackenzie to Thornborough, November 1 1938, Sinclair MSS.
89. Miss Mackenzie to Jones, February 9 1939, Sinclair MSS.
90. Spender to Samuel, July 9 1939. Crewe to Samuel, June 26 and July 11 1939. Spender to Simon, July 24 and October 6 1938. Spender to *The Times*, July 8 1939. Hankey was in fact a friend of Spender.
91. E.g. Harris to Sinclair, August 2 1938.
92. See e.g. Layton, p. 93, for Layton getting printing help from Lord Southwood and the *Daily Herald*.
93. For a judicious Beveridge statement, see *Planning under Socialism and other Addresses*, 1936.
94. Layton to Samuel, January 12 1933, Sinclair MSS.
95. Layton to Lloyd George, January 13 1935.
96. *News Chronicle*, August 7 1934.
97. *News Chronicle*, November 11 and 13 1935.

98. *The Economist*, February 26 1938.
99. *The Economist*, February 26 1938.
100. For all this see *The Economist*, March 19, April 2, May 14, June 11 and September 24 1938.
101. Sinclair to Worsley, December 9 1935.
102. Sinclair to Harris, February 25 1936.
103. Layton to Sinclair, quoted in Sinclair to Davies, September 12 1936.
104. Harris to Sinclair, September 7 1936.
105. Despite Layton's personal involvement at constituency level in Chertsey and his anxiety to get the Liberal party to stand down in favour of Lindsay in Oxford, see Sinclair to Johnstone, February 27 1939, and *vice versa*, February 28 1939, and Harris to Sinclair, October 17 1938.
106. Layton in *News Chronicle*, April 7, 8 and 10 1933 and May 18 1938, and at League of Nations Union, Ilford, November 11 1938, *News Chronicle*, November 12.
107. See Gannon, pp. 38–42 and *passim*. Cf. Layton in *News Chronicle*, March 16 1936, at Chatham House, June 29 1939, *The Times* June 30, and at Kingsway Hall, London, March 30 1939, *News Chronicle*, March 31.
108. For the last two paragraphs, see *News Chronicle* February 21 and 23, March 11 and 14, September 20–22 and September 30 – October 1, all 1938, and March 16 and April 1 1939. See also *The Economist* of October 1 1938 and May 20 and July 1 1939.
109. E.g. Sinclair in Dugdale diary, September 20 1938.
110. Eden to Chamberlain, February 20 1938, resignation letter, PREM 1/276. Eden at Leamington, February 25 1938, *The Times*, February 26.
111. Simon to Eden, February 23 1938, Simon MSS.
112. Chamberlain to Eden, February 26 1938. Hankey to Robin Hankey, March 1 1938.
113. Harvey diary March 12 to 20 1938.
114. Hankey to Robin Hankey, March 1 1938.
115. Eden to Halifax, March 5 1938.
116. Harvey diary, March 12 1938.
117. Jones diary of May 23 1936 seems to imply the opposite.
118. Harvey diary, March 15 1938, quoting Leeper quoting Baldwin. Harvey diary, April 13 and May 31 1938. Cadogan diary, May 7 1938, quoting Leeper probably quoting Eden. Lloyd to Davidson, March 30 1938, for a similar view from a Chamberlainite junior minister who had been Baldwin's private secretary.
119. Baldwin to Swinton, May 18 1938. Dugdale diary, May 22 1938, quoting Boothby quoting Eden.
120. Eden at Grosvenor House, April 26 1938, *The Times*, April 27. Harvey diary, April 22 and 25/6 and September 8 1938.
121. Eden at Leamington, May 6 1938, *The Times* May 7. Eden letter to constituents in *The Times*, June 6 1938. Harvey diary, April 13 and May 20 1938.

122. Nicolson diary, April 11 1938. Harvey diary, June 7 1938.
123. Eden at Grosvenor House, April 26 1938, *The Times*, April 27, and at Haseley Manor, June 11 1938, *Birmingham Post*, June 13.
124. Eden in *Sunday Chronicle*, August 21 1938.
125. Eden at Haseley Manor, June 11 1938, *Birmingham Post*, June 13, and Harvey diary, June 7 1938.
126. Harvey diary, July 2 1938.
127. Eden at Bishop Auckland, July 17 1938, *Yorkshire Post*, July 18, and at Kenilworth, July 23 1938, *Manchester Guardian*, July 25.
128. Eden to Baldwin, August 19 1938.
129. Harvey diary, February 27 1938, for Eden more or less saying this. Cf. Harvey diary, *passim* February–June 1938 (especially February 12 1938), for his entourage saying so. Dugdale diary, February 21 1938, for Elliot thinking it would if he resigned too.
130. The *votes* in a straight fight with Labour on both sides being almost exactly the same as in 1935.
131. Dugdale diary, July 26 1938.
132. Nicolson diary, May 11, and Harvey diary, May 20 1938. See also Boothby in Dugdale diary, May 22 1938.
133. Dugdale diary, July 26 1938.
134. Eden to *The Times*, September 12 1938. Harvey diary, September 9 and 11 1938. Liddell Hart, pp. 162–3.
135. Harvey diary, September 10 1938.
136. Eden at Stratford-upon-Avon, September 21 1938, *Manchester Guardian*, September 22.
137. Eden to Chamberlain, September 28 1938. Nicolson diary, September 29 1938. Coote, p. 173.
138. Harvey diary, September 30 1938.
139. Eden in London, September 30 1938, *The Times*, October 1.
140. Eden to Baldwin, September 30 1938.
141. Amery diary, October 6 1938.
142. Amery to Chamberlain, October 6 1938.
143. Halifax to Chamberlain, October 11 1938. Amery diary, October 6, confirms this.
144. Cecil to Murray, April 6 1936. For the doubts about universal suffrage, see Rhodes James, *Churchill*, pp. 384–6.
145. Not only by standing, e.g. Dawson diary, June 1 1933, for Grigg 'heading off' support from him at the Altrincham by-election by 'wobbling over India'.
146. Butler to Brabourne, November 15 1934.
147. E.g., Crawford to Linlithgow, July 10 1936, Eur.F.125 151/2. Butler to Brabourne, June 20 1935.
148. According to Rhodes James, *Churchill*, p. 317, he did this at Cunliffe-Lister's request and in the teeth of opposition from Chamberlain.
149. Churchill to Baldwin, July 6, July 9 and October 7 1935. Bruce Lockhart diary, September 21 1935.
150. Chamberlain to Ida, October 5 1935.
151. Hoare to Chamberlain, February 23 1936.

152. Chamberlain diary, March 8 1936.
153. Including Horne, Amery, Winterton, Croft, Grigg, Wolmer, Gilmour, O'Neill, Lloyd, Moore-Brabazon, Fitzalan, Trenchard, Milne and Keyes. For these see Hankey to Prime Minister, July 24, Churchill to Baldwin, July 22, Inskip to Austen Chamberlain, November 11, all 1936. All of these, together with reports of the meetings with the deputations of July and November 1936 are in PREM 1/193. Cf. Jones diary, July 31 1936.
154. See *The Spectator*, November 28 1936, p. 886 and Nicolson to Sackville-West, December 9 1936. See also Rhodes James, *Churchill*, p. 294. Churchill to Weir, May 6 1936, for an attempt to get Weir to withhold the use of his name and authority in defence of the defence programme.
155. Chamberlain to Ida, May 22 1937.
156. Churchill to *The Times*, April 20 1936.
157. Nicolson to V. Sackville-West, March 17 1936. *Hansard* (317) col. 313 of November 5 1936. Churchill to Cecil, April 9 1936. Hankey diary, April 20 1936.
158. *Hansard* (317) cols. 318—19 of November 5 1936. Nicolson diary, March 15 1937.
159. *Hansard* (317) cols. 311—12 of November 5 1936. *Hansard* (330) col. 1838 of December 21 1937. Churchill to Linlithgow, November 3 1937.
160. Dugdale diary, November 18 1936.
161. Churchill to Cecil, December 2 1936. But see also Churchill to Cecil, August 22, October 21 and November 13 1936 and April 22 1937, for the caution with which the League position was put.
162. See PREM 1/253.
163. Jones to Lady Grigg, November 3 1936.
164. Lloyd to Murray, July 6 1938. Lloyd to Chamberlain, October 6 1938.
165. D. Davies to Sinclair, April 29 and May 12 1936.
166. Churchill to Crewe, July 19 1937.
167. *Hansard* (326) col. 1839 of July 19 1937 and (330) col. 1831 of December 21 1937. Citrine, p. 328. For Lindsay see Nicolson diary, June 25 1936.
168. I.e. with support from Citrine, Lytton, Noel-Baker, Angell, Steed, Layton, Salter, Sinclair, Clynes and, in a detached way, Lloyd George and Austen Chamberlain. Also Sandys, Oliver Locker-Lampson, A.M. Wall, Mallon, Sir Wyndham Deeds and Guedalla. Cf. Churchill to Cecil, October 21 1936. Steed to Sinclair, February 22 1937.
169. Steed to Sinclair, October 6 and 20 1936 and *passim* 1936/7. Richards to Sinclair, *passim* 1936/7. Angell in *Daily Herald*, April 19 1933. Nicolson diary, April 6 1936, July 16 1936 and June 2 1937. See also Spier.
170. Churchill to Eden, September 9, and Secretary to Secretary, September 29 1937, Lloyd George MSS 9/14/5/22. Eden to Churchill, September 25 1937. Richards to Sinclair, October 16 1937,

for Eden addressing the Defence of Freedom and Peace. Amery diary, February 17 1938. *Hansard* (317) col. 325 of November 6 1936 and (330) cols. 1829–39 of December 21 1937.

171. For Churchill on Vansittart, see Phipps to Hankey, January 9 1938.
172. *Hansard* (332) col. 243 of February 22 1938.
173. *Hansard* (332) col. 241 of February 22 1938.
174. *Hansard* (333) cols. 1444–70 of March 24 1938.
175. Cab 17(38) of March 30 reporting Halifax reporting British Ambassador reporting Churchill's conversation (Cf. FO 800/311).
176. Churchill to Chamberlain, March 12 1938, PREM 1/237. Margesson, memorandum of March 17 1938, NC 7/11/31/188.
177. Cecil to Churchill, May 24 1938. Churchill at Manchester, May 9 1938, *The Times*, May 10, and at Bristol, May 16 1938, *The Times*, May 17.
178. I.e. *Arms and the Covenant*.
179. Churchill to Cecil, May 27 1938. Wilson, note of March 10 1938, PREM 1/238. Astor to Garvin, September 2 1938.
180. See Rhodes James, *Churchill*, pp. 302–03, for MacDonald, Hoare and Neville Chamberlain all allowing him to have special access to defence information (in addition to membership of the Air Defence Sub-Committee).
181. Churchill to Wood, June 9 1938, PREM 1/253.
182. Churchill to Chamberlain, May 15 1938, PREM 1/249. See also the remarks about the possibility of a Sudeten settlement in his Bristol speech of May 16 1938, *The Times*, May 17. Cf. Nicolson diary, March 16 1938.
183. Churchill to Halifax, August 20, and to von Kleist (the agent referred to), August 19 1938, both FO 800/309. Cf. Bruce Lockhart diary, July 10 1938.
184. Churchill to Halifax, August 31 1938, PREM 1/265. Halifax to Churchill, August 3 and 23 1938. Wilson to Prime Minister, August 31 1938, PREM 1/265.
185. Churchill to Halifax, September 3 1938, FO 800/322.
186. Ironside diary, December 6 1937, reporting Churchill. Churchill to Linlithgow, September 23 and November 3 1937. Churchill to Boothby, August 27 1938. Churchill, *Step by Step*, p. 207.
187. Harvey diary, September 15 1938.
188. Dalton diary, September 20 1938.
189. Harvey diary, September 20 and 21 1938.
190. Churchill to Dawson, September 24 1938, *The Times* Archive.
191. Dawson diary, September 26 1938.
192. Nicolson diary, September 22 and 26 1938, Amery diary, September 26.
193. For all this see Cranborne to Cecil, October 16 1938. For Crossley and J.P.L. Thomas see Amery diary, October 11 1938. For Macmillan and Amery see Amery diary, October 6 1938. For Boothby see Boothby to Churchill and vice versa, October 7 and 10 1938. For Cartland see Cartland, pp. 216–17 and 228–9. For

Wolmer (the MP for Chamberlain's sisters) see Chamberlain to
Hilda, November 6 1938 (and also for Gunston). For Duff Cooper
see Thompson, pp. 193-4. For Spears, see Spears, p. 19.

194. Dalton and Amery diaries, October 3 1938.
195. Churchill to Muir, October 18, and to Law, October 18 1938.
196. Churchill to Muir, November 5 1938.
197. Atholl, p. 229.
198. Churchill to Lindsay, October 19 1938. Randolph Churchill,
     however, did (see Rhodes James, *Churchill*, p. 434).
199. Churchill to Bartlett, November 5 1938.
200. E.g. T.L. Horabin to Churchill, May 27 1939.
201. Headlam diary *inter alia* for October 22 1935.
202. Butler to Brabourne, March 6 and December 20 1934.
203. Despite a quarrel with Lloyd George, see Stevenson diary, May 23
     1935.
204. Gilbert, *Plough My Own Furrow*, pp. 315—23.
205. See above p. 53.
206. Thompson, p. 12, n. 16.
207. Macmillan, p. 110—11.
208. Channon diary, July 8 1936. Macmillan memorandum, n.d. after
     election of 1935, Lloyd George MSS G141/30/4. For Macmillan's
     earlier attempts see Macmillan to Lloyd George, August 12, 13,
     18, and 25 1936 and January 16 1937. Cf. Nicolson diary,
     March 2 1936, and Headlam diary *inter alia* for June 6 1935.
209. For a good example, see Amery to *The Times*, October 6 1938.
     See also Dugdale diary, September 28 1938, for Churchill report-
     ed as saying 'By God, you are lucky' after he had announced the
     Munich Conference.
210. *Hansard* (339) cols. 360—73 of October 5 1938.
211. *Hansard* (339) cols. 553 *et seq* of October 6 1938.
212. For Sandys picking up the Percy line see e.g. Nicolson diary,
     July 30 1936. The best accessible account of Bracken's life and
     opinions is in Rhodes James, *Churchill*, pp. 369—74.
213. See e.g. Channon diary, March 21 1938, and Keyes to Chatfield,
     January 6 1937.
214. Sir Terence Keyes to Keyes, July 31 1933, quoting Keyes.
215. Keyes, election address at Portsmouth, February 17 1934.
216. Sir Terence Keyes to Keyes, February 2 1935, quoting Keyes.
217. For the attack and argument (including an argument in the *News
     Chronicle*) see *inter alia* Keyes MSS Box 12/2.
218. For Lloyd's manner, see Zetland to Linlithgow, November 23
     1936 and Dawson diary, January 11 1935. For Keyes as a speaker
     see Amery diary, April 26 1939.
219. For Simon, see Simon to Mrs Chamberlain, October 6 1938. For
     a similar letter, see Boothby to Chamberlain, October 6 1938 (i.e.
     Churchill's speech being 'unworthy of him').
220. Except with Sidney Herbert — one of Baldwin's secretaries in the
     twenties, who offered support (six months before he died) against
     the 'dishonour' involved in the Munich settlement (Herbert to

Churchill, October 8 1938). Cf. Churchill to Duff Cooper, November 22, to Herbert, October 9, to Croft, October 29, and to Londonderry, November 12, all 1938. For Chamberlain as 'the Coroner' see Bracken to Beaverbrook, December 16 1938 and March 16 1939.

221. Amery diary, November 29, December 9 and 15 1938 and January 27 1939.

222. For McKenna as part of *The Focus*, see Nicolson diary, April 25 1939.

223. Cf. Spender to Simon, October 6 1938, for the suspicion that they were.

224. Meston to Sinclair, March 9 1939, and Sinclair to Meston, March 11 1939, for Meston being approached by Wal Hannington of the Unemployed Workers' Movement and for Sinclair encouraging Meston to talk and have lunch etc.

225. Sinclair at National Liberal Club, January 25 1939, *Manchester Guardian*, January 26, at International Peace Campaign meeting, *News Chronicle*, January 25 1939, and at Morecambe, February 5 1939, *Manchester Guardian*, February 6.

226. Sinclair to the Marchioness of Aberdeen, December 12 1938. For Cecil, Dingle Foot, Roberts, Bartlett, Eleanor Rathbone and Josiah Wedgwood speaking for the Duchess while Keynes, Salter, Murray and R.W. Seton-Watson sent letters of support, see Atholl, p. 229.

227. Sinclair to Sir Daniel Stevenson, November 4 1938.

228. Dalton diary, December 9 1938, recording interview with Lord Rea, the Treasurer of the Liberal party. Sinclair to Miss Lakeman, December 9 1938.

229. Angell to Miss Aline Mackinnon, February 2 1939, Sinclair MSS.

230. General election result 1935: Conservative 17,937. Liberal 7,370, Labour 6,240. By-election result November 17 1938: Bartlett (Ind) 19,540, D.G. Heathcote-Amery (C) 17,280.

231. Sinclair to Miss Cooke (Bartlett's secretary), November 16 1938.

232. Johnstone to Sinclair, February 28 1939. Miss Mackenzie to Jones, March 30 1939, Sinclair MSS.

233. Sinclair to Johnstone, December 22 1938, for importance of Johnstone being in touch with and encouraging Hudson's Under-Secretaries' revolt.

234. Sinclair at Broughty Ferry, October 18 1938, *Manchester Guardian*, October 19; at Aberdeen, October 21 1938, *The Scotsman*, October 22; at Leeds, December 7 1938, *Yorkshire Post*, December 8; in London, March 15 1939, *The Times*, March 16; at 80 Club, May 24 1939, *Manchester Guardian*, May 25; at Wadebridge, July 6 1939, *The Times* July 7; at Stonehaven March 27 1939, *Manchester Guardian*, March 28; at Northampton, November 11 1938, *Manchester Guardian*, November 12; and at Scarborough, May 12 1939, *Liverpool Post*, May 13. Muir in 'Westminster Newsletter', *Manchester Guardian*, November 7 1938. Cf. Sinclair to Amery, December 13 1938. Sinclair in House of Com-

mons, *Hansard* (346) cols. 28—9 of April 13 1939. For Churchill's response, see *Hansard* (345) col. 2497 of April 3 1939. For Churchill being satisfied with Halifax see Zetland to Linlithgow, June 27 1939, Eur.D.609. Johnstone to Sinclair, October 17 1938.

235. Nicolson diary, November 24 1938. For Hopkinson as Baldwinian see Hopkinson to Baldwin, October 27 1935. For Spears in Paris see e.g. Phipps to Halifax, November 4 1938, FO 800/311.

236. E.g. Nicolson diary, March 18 1936, and Dugdale diary, May 21 1937.

237. For Tree, see Tree to *The Times* May 17 1934. Nicolson diary, May 19 1935, December 20 1935 and June 17 1937. See also Cartland, pp. 140—7.

238. Dugdale diary, May 21 1937. Duff Cooper to Baldwin, October 4 1938 (September 4 written), and to Halifax, March 22 1939, FO 800/315.

239. Harvey diary, October 16 1938, quoting Eden.

240. Cf. Nicolson diary of April 10 1939 making the same point about Simon and Hore-Belisha being 'middle-class individuals' who were flattered by the anti-German attitude of 'what they suppose with extreme incorrectitude' to be the aristocracy. Crossley, Spears and Nicolson all played a prominent part in the League of Nations Union in 1937/8.

241. Chamberlain to Hilda, November 6 1938. For Eden agreeing to appear at a League of Nations Union meeting, but not on a platform with Attlee and Sinclair, see Cecil talking in Dugdale diary, November 8 1938.

242. E.g. Eden on National Unity, *Sunday Times*, October 9 1938. Eden at International Peace Society, October 18 1938, *The Times*, October 19.

243. For Eden threatening to join with Labour and Liberals in attacking the bringing into force of the Anglo-Italian agreement a week after he had told Halifax that Mussolini no longer mattered, see Harvey diary, October 20 1938. Channon diary, November 2 1938.

244. Baldwin to Linlithgow, MSS Eur.F.125 154/5. Harvey diary, October 11, 12 and 13 1938 and March 9 1939. Harvey diary, October 13 1938, for Baldwin doubting whether Chamberlain could get Labour in but thinking that he might. For Baldwin as the bait to catch Labour see Eden and Tyrrell talking in Cadogan diary, March 28 1939. Cf. Nicolson diary, June 27 1939, for the next election. Bruce Lockhart diary, October 17 1938, quoting Leeper.

245. Harvey diary April 16 1939.

246. 'Our Foreign Policy' by Rt. Hon. Anthony Eden in *Sunday Times*, February 12 1939, and Eden at Warwick, February 24 1939, *Yorkshire Post*, February 25.

247. Chamberlain to Ida, February 12 1939.

248. Eden in House of Commons, *Hansard* (345) cols. 458—62 of

March 15 1939. Eden in London, March 17, *Yorkshire Post*, March 18 1939.

249. Amery diary, March 27 1939.

250. Nicolson diary, June 30 1939.

251. Harvey diary, August 26 and June 5 1939.

252. See e.g. Duff Cooper's buttering-up letter to Chamberlain, December 23 1938, and Amery diary of April 20 1939 for Duff Cooper being very violent against Chamberlain after Burgin had been made Minister of Supply. For Amery's two offers to join the government or do useful work see Chamberlain to Amery, August 22, and Chamberlain to Amery, April 27 1939.

253. Rhodes James, *Churchill*, p. 433. See *Hansard* (341) cols. 1210–14 of November 17 1938.

254. Davidson to Ball, May 9 1939, and to Wilson (same date, not sent).

255. Amery and Nicolson diaries, June 29 1939. For the staff officer talking more widely see *DBFP*, third series, vol. VI, pp. 295–8. For the press campaign (and the staff officer as an Intelligence/Vansittart plot) see Aster, pp. 235–7.

256. Amery and Nicolson diaries July 1 1939, and Amery to Halifax, June 30 1939, FO 800/315.

257. Harvey diary, March 31 and May 5 1939.

258. Harvey diary, June 30 and July 1 1939. Boothby to Churchill, July 6 1939, for Coote failing with *The Times*. Nicolson diary, June 30 1939.

259. For 'Liberal spirit' see Sinclair at Leominster, July 8 1939, *Manchester Guardian*, July 10. See also Jones to Grigg, May 20 1939. Sinclair at Folkstone, July 11 1939, *Manchester Guardian*, July 12, and at Ayr, July 23 1939, *Manchester Guardian*, July 25.

260. Garvin to Astor, March 15 and 16 1939, for Garvin's hysteria at having been bamboozled by Hitler and Ribbentrop. Cf. Garvin to Astor, June 29 1939.

261. Garvin to Astor, March 22, June 1 and 16 1939, and Astor to Mamhead, April 18 1939. Dawson diary, April 12 1939.

262. Dawson diary, June 27 1939.

263. Harvey diary, July 1 and 4 1939. Dalton diary, June 29 1939. Hoare to W.W. Astor, July 11 1939. Astor to Trenchard and vice versa, June 22–8 1939, and Astor to Greenwood and vice versa, June 29 1939. Harvey to Astor, June 27 1939 (and Astor MSS Box 10 File 177 *passim*), Nicolson diary, June 30 1939. For *The Times* insisting on deleting the references to Churchill, see Nicolson diary, July 11 1939, and Eldor to Lady Violet Bonham-Carter, n.d. Sinclair MSS. See also Garvin to Astor, July 10 1939.

264. Channon diary, July 4 and 5 1939.

265. Channon diary, July 6 1939.

266. Dawson diary, July 6 1939, quoting Chamberlain.

267. North Cornwall results 1935: Acland FD (Lib) 16,872, Whitehouse (C) 16,036. July 13 1939: Horabin (Lib) 17,072, Whitehouse (C) 15,608.

NOTES TO CHAPTER 9

1. For the Coal bill, which Chamberlain had put in the 1935 election manifesto and which had been put off during the dilapidation of 1936, see Zetland to Linlithgow, May 23 1936, January 25 1937 and May 1 1938. Amery diary, February 3 1938. For NDC damaging stockbrokers and small businesses see Butler to Brabourne, May 1 and 5 1937, and Garvin to Astor, April 21 1937.

2. Chamberlain to Hilda, July 4 and 9 1938. Amery diary, July 6 1938.

3. Astor to Garvin, July 8 and December 16 1938. Chamberlain to Ida, December 4 and 17 1938 and January 23 1939. Williams of Barnsbury, p. 118. For Runciman describing the Milk bill as 'socialism' see Zetland to Linlithgow, December 6 1938.

4. Barrington-Ward to Dawson, April 26 1938. Chamberlain to Hilda, June 25 1938. Cf. Nicolson diary, May 9 1938, for Margesson and W.S. Morrison being worried by the Liberal vote.

5. Dawson diary, October 4 1938.

6. Chamberlain to Hilda, December 11, and to Ida, December 17 1938. Chamberlain to Simon, December 16 1938. Harvey diary, December 11 1938. Bracken to Beaverbrook, December 16 1938.

7. E.g. Chamberlain to Ida, December 4 and 17 1938.

8. For an explanation see Butler on Mann to Halifax, August 25 1938, FO 800/314. Dawson diary, April 10 1935.

9. Astor to Garvin, July 8 1938, for agriculture.

10. See e.g. Gannon, pp. 53–5 and 218–19.

11. E.g. Chamberlain to Hilda, February 5 1939.

12. Cf. Ball to Chamberlain, June 1 1938.

13. E.g. Austen Chamberlain to Hilda, December 22 1935 (January written).

14. Baldwin in PREM 1/223 of July 14 1936.

15. Chamberlain to Hilda, November 17 1935.

16. E.g. Wilson Harris, editor of *The Spectator*, in *The Spectator*, May 22 1936, and Wedgwood to Baldwin, August 27 1936.

17. Attlee to Tom Attlee, April 3 1933. Laski to Baldwin, March 3 1933. J.J. Lawson to Baldwin, July 17 1935, Williams to Baldwin, April 14 1937. Bevin to Baldwin, January 29 1937, PREM 1/206. Lansbury to Baldwin, May 23 1935. Cf. Grigg to Jones, May 22 1935, for Baldwin 'moving Lansbury to tears'.

18. Tyrrell to Baldwin, May 29 1935.

19. Runciman to Baldwin, November 1 1935.

20. Tyrrell to Baldwin, November 1 1935.

21. Chamberlain to Baldwin, November 2 1935.

22. Baldwin at 1922 Committee dinner, May 21 1936, *The Times*, May 22.

23. Baldwin at the Leys School, June 26 1936, *Methodist Recorder*, July 2.

24. Bryant to Baldwin, September 22 1933.
25. Smithers to Baldwin, March 7 1934. Baldwin to Halifax, September 8 1933.
26. Baldwin to Halifax, September 8 1933.
27. Baldwin to Margesson, October 30 1935.
28. Channon diary, February 24 1936. Nicolson diary, February 20 1936, quoting Winterton.
29. See Foreign Affairs Committee meetings of March 12 and 17 1936 in PREM 1/194.
30. For the wrangling about party funds see the extensive correspondence between Croft, Gretton, Wolmer and Hacking in the Croft papers for May and June 1936. For National Liberal and National Labour fears, see Bernays letter to *The Times* of May 20 1936 and *The Times* leader of the same date. Cf. letters from Nicolson, Markham, Cartland etc. in *The Times* of May 21 and 22 1936. Baldwin at 1922 Committee dinner of May 21 1936, *The Times*, May 22, and at National Labour Group dinner of June 10 1936, *The Times*, June 11. For Simon see Simon to Chamberlain, September 15 1936. For the government's 'humiliation' see Dugdale diary, June 17 1936.
31. For examples, see Hore-Belisha being described as a 'stormy petrel' (Chamberlain to Ida, January 7 1940) and Mussolini behaving like a 'cad and a sneak...thanks possibly to his latest amour' (Chamberlain to Hilda, April 15 1939).
32. Halifax in Harvey diary, June 14 1939. Cf. Citrine, p. 368.
33. Chamberlain to Hilda, September 1 1935.
34. Halifax talking in Reith, p. 357.
35. Chamberlain to Hilda, March 5 1938. For Chamberlain as a Liberal see Reith, p. 352. Citrine, p. 366, for 'veiled sarcasm' towards TUC leaders other than himself. Among the many examples from both sides of the affectation of similarity between the aristocracy and the Labour backbenchers, see Portsmouth, p. 113, for the Marquess of Titchfield and Maxton.
36. Chamberlain diary, January 25 1936, for Chamberlain disliking Kipling's references to 'lesser breeds without the law'.
37. Hankey to Phipps, February 21 1938.
38. Chamberlain to Rankeillour, September 21 1937, PREM 1/223, and Chamberlain to Hilda, November 23 1935 and March 5 1939.
39. Chamberlain diary, March 1 1936. Chamberlain to Hilda, March 5 and April 2 1939. Hankey to Robin Hankey, March 1 1938.
40. Chamberlain to Ida, February 26 1939. Cf. Chamberlain to Hilda, April 25 1937, for Chamberlain regarding the introduction of the NDC as 'the bravest thing' he had 'ever done' as 'I have risked the Premiership just when it was falling into my hands'.
41. For Pitt, see Chamberlain to Petrie, April 11 1939. Hore-Belisha diary, April 13 1938. Cf. Chamberlain to Hilda, July 28 1935, for pride in his own work behind the scenes, even when others take the credit.
42. Hankey diary, March 4 1934.

43. Inskip diary, January 19 1939.
44. Eden in Harvey diary, March 23 1937.
45. Austen Chamberlain to Hilda/Ida, January 13 1935, and Orms-by-Gore to MacDonald, September 23 1933.
46. Chamberlain diary, February 19 1936.
47. Inskip to Chamberlain, May 21 1937.
48. See *The Times*, July 17 1936.
49. Channon diary, September 20 1939. Cf. Crawford to Linlithgow, June 29 1938.
50. Channon diary, October 10 1939.
51. Hore-Belisha diary, January 5 1940.
52. Chamberlain to Ida, November 26 1937, and Amery diary, May 17 1938.
53. See e.g. Dawson diary, October 24 1938.
54. Repeated in Cabinet in June 1936.
55. Simon to Phipps, April 5 1935, FO 800/290. Headlam diary, March 6 and 22 and May 2 1935. Amery diary, March 29 and to Beaverbrook March 29 1935.
56. Margesson to Chamberlain, August 1 [1936], for Margesson hoping for 'a victory for the rebels in Spain and a successful meeting of the Locarno Powers' as something the Conservative party would be pleased by.
57. E.g. Lennox-Boyd in *Hansard* of March 2 1937 (321), cols. 274–5.
58. E.g. Emmott in *Hansard* of March 25 1937 (321) col. 3146. Croft in *Hansard*, March 17 1937 (321) col. 2201. W.W. Astor in *Hansard*, March 25 1937 (321) col. 3134 and Croft in Watkins, p. 118. For further examples from Cazalet, Channon, George Balfour and Sandemann (Conservative MPs) and from Lord Mount Temple (a Conservative ex-minister), see Watkins, pp. 84, 100, 105, 117 and 138–9.
59. Croft in *Hansard* March 17 1937 (321) col. 2201. Cf. Heuston, p. 489.
60. For the rise in public expenditure under the National government and the need to reduce it, see H.G. Williams in 1922 Committee Minute-Book for March 18 1935, December 20 1937, July 25 1938 and November 21 1938.
61. For advice on these lines at the 1922 Committee from Sir H. McGowan, Lord Milne, W. Nunn MP, Sir F. Lindley, Sir Frederic Whyte and G.W. Swire, Chairman of the China Association, see Minute-Book for March 26 1934, May 20 1935, June 3 1935, May 25 1936, June 28 1937, November 8 1937, and April 4 1938. It is notable that the 1922 Committee had no anti-Japanese speakers in these years apart from Sir Bernard Pares (April 27 1936), who was a professional Russophile and described Japan's government as 'Nazi in origin'.
62. Nicolson diary, March 23 1937.
63. E.g. Macnamara, p. 153.
64. For the feeling that there were those who did (including indirect-

ly Eden), see Butler to Brabourne, February 3 and 10 1937.
65.   See H. Morrison in Election broadcast of November 7 1935, *News Chronicle*, November 8.
66.   For the last two paragraphs see Simon to Spen Valley newspapers of March 9 1938, *The Times*, March 11, using Lansbury's (and also Allen's and Ponsonby's) support of Chamberlain in the wake of Eden's resignation. For McGovern in Berlin see Henderson to Halifax, September 20 1938, FO 800/309. For McGovern and Maxton in the Munich debate on October 4 and 5 see *Hansard* (339) cols. 193—7 and 528—34 and Chamberlain to Hilda, October 9 1938. For Lansbury, see *Hansard* (332) of March 7 1938, cols. 1613—19. For Noel-Buxton see Noel-Buxton to Chamberlain, March 18 1938, PREM 1/249, and Noel-Buxton to Halifax, September 27 1938, FO 800/309. Cf. *DGFP* series D, vol. II, no. 351 of August 13 1938, and Allen of Hurtwood to Halifax, August 20 1938, FO 800/309. See also Anderson, p. 132. For Lords Sanderson and Arnold see *Manchester Guardian*, March 9 1938, and Arnold to Chamberlain, February 22 and November 12 1938. For Sanderson supporting Hogg at Oxford by-election, see Eatwell, p. 129. For Citrine, see e.g. Citrine, pp. 366—7, Hankey to Wilson, March 12 1938, and *passim* in PREM/251. Cf. Dalton diary, April 4 1938 and June 28 1939. For disagreement between League of Nations Union and Peace Pledge Union being incapsulated by Cecil and Ponsonby, see *Hansard* House of Lords (112) cols. 329—39.
67.   Allen of Hurtwood to Chamberlain, November 2 1937, PREM 1/213.
68.   Gilbert, *Plough My Own Furrow*, ch. 26.
69.   Lothian to Lady Astor, October 4 1938.
70.   Samuel to Halifax, September 15, to Crewe, September 15, and to Chamberlain, September 30 1938. Cf. Samuel memorandum of November 23 1937.
71.   E.g. Amery diary, January 31 1939.
72.   Selborne to Chamberlain, Lady Day 1938.
73.   W.I. Benson MP to Rushcliffe, October 16 1937, in Rushcliffe to Chamberlain, same date.
74.   Wilson to Phipps, February 2 1939.
75.   G. Lloyd George to Lloyd George, March 17 1939, quoting Conservative MPs. Dawson to Washburn, March 28 1939, *The Times* Archive.
76.   E.g. Lord Lymington who had resigned from Parliament in 1934 in protest against the 'lack of principle' in politics and the government's failure to protect agriculture (see letter to electors of N.W. Hants Parliamentary division, February 14 1934 in Baldwin MSS, and Portsmouth, pp. 124—5) and whom the Cabinet asked Simon to restrain from calling public meetings against going to war for Czechoslovakia in 1938 (Meeting of Ministers of September 13 1938 in Cab 27/646).
77.   Sir Terence O'Connor (the Solicitor-General) to Chamberlain, Oc-

tober 1 1938, quoting Pitt in NC 13/11.

78. Beaverbrook to Winterton, December 6 1938, asking Winterton (as minister in charge of the refugee question) for 'strict limitations' on Jewish immigration.

79. For some of these sentiments (especially those which identified Communism as a Jewish conspiracy) see Cowling, ch. IV.

80. See e.g. H.G. Williams to Beaverbrook, October 1 1938.

81. E.g. Sir Hugh O'Neill to Chamberlain, October 4 1938 in NC 13/11, and Somerset de Chair in *Hansard* (491ff.) of March 15 1939.

82. Bracken to Beaverbrook, March 16 1939.

83. Cecil to Cranborne, October 9 1935, for a good example.

84. Londonderry to Halifax, July 20 1938, FO 800/309, and Dawson to Nigel Law, October 4 1938, *The Times* Archive. For Benes being unhelpful by strengthening French resistance to disarmament plans in early 1934, see Cab 27/506 of March 6 1934. For loyalty see Lennox-Boyd reported in *News Chronicle*, March 21 1938 (shortly after becoming a junior minister). For communism, see J.S. Wedderburn (Under-Secretary at the Scottish Office) to Chamberlain, October 3 1938 in NC 13/11.

85. Gilmour in *Hansard* (339) col. 511 of October 6 1938.

86. Wardlaw-Milne (col. 394) and Croft (col. 374) in *Hansard* (339) of October 5 1938. H.G. Williams to Beaverbrook, October 1 1938.

87. Moore and Fyfe in *Hansard* (339) cols. 238 and 247 of October 4 1938.

88. Croft in *Hansard* (339) col. 374 of October 5 1938.

89. Wardlaw-Milne in *Hansard* (339) col. 394 of October 5 1938. Miss Horsbrough to Mrs Chamberlain, September 28 1938, Beamish to Mrs Chamberlain, September 29 1938, and Ball to Mrs Chamberlain, September 28 1938, all in NC 13/11 (together with other similar letters).

90. *Hansard* (339) col. 49 of October 3 1938.

91. Halifax to Linlithgow, December 5 1937, for Halifax's animadversions on Hore-Belisha's failure as a gentleman.

92. For the last three paras see Irwin (Halifax) pp. 224–7 and ed. Bryant, *Constructive Democracy*, pp. 42–50.

93. Chamberlain diary, October 21 1935, for Halifax disliking this about Churchill.

94. Jones diary, May 23 1936.

95. Halifax to Chamberlain, March 15, and Chamberlain diary, March 16 1934.

96. E.g. Harvey diary, December 5 1937.

97. For a good example of practical idealism see Harvey diary, April 12 1937, reporting Halifax expressing the view that 'on the long view HMG do stand for decency and morality'.

98. Halifax to Linlithgow, April 24 1936. Halifax to Cecil, December 23 1937 and March 1 and 21 1938.

99. Halifax at Cab 1(37) of January 13.

100. Halifax to Chamberlain, November 6 1937 and November 8 1937, PREM 1/330. Halifax to Ormsby-Gore, November 12 1937, Halifax MSS.
101. Halifax in FP (36) 39 of November 26 1937 in Cab 27/626.
102. Samuel, memorandum of conversation with Halifax, November 23 1937. Channon diary, December 5 1937. Halifax to Baldwin, November 15 1937, and to Linlithgow, December 5 1937.
103. Halifax in FP 39(36) of November 26 1937, Cab 27/626. Lady Astor to Lothian, November 27 1937, quoting Halifax.
104. Halifax to Southwood, November 25 and December 1 1937, and to Henderson, December 9 1937, all Halifax MSS.
105. Harvey diary, January 19 1938.
106. E.g. Halifax to Chamberlain, August 18 and 19 1937, PREM 1/276. Halifax to Chamberlain, November 6 and 8 1937, PREM 1/330. Halifax to Eden, October 27 1937, PREM 1/330. Chamberlain to Hilda, October 24 1937. For an example of animosity, see Eden at Cab 5(38) of February 16.
107. Chamberlain diary, February 19 1938. Halifax to Chamberlain, August 11 1937, PREM 1/276.
108. Dawson diary, February 20 1938.
109. Halifax, [A] Record [of Events Connected with Anthony Eden's Resignation February 19th-20th 1938]. Harvey diary, February 20 1938.
110. Halifax, 'Record'.
111. Cadogan diary, February 21 1938, for Halifax seeing all the difficulties and not certain whether to accept if offered.
112. E.g. Cab 11(38) of March 9.
113. Cab 21(38) of April 27.
114. Halifax to Runciman, March 30, Hore-Belisha diary, April 5, and Amery diary March 31, all 1938.
115. Halifax at Cab 31(38) of July 6 and Halifax to Linlithgow, July 1 1937. For Paul-Boncour see Halifax to Phipps, April 3 1938, FO 800/311.
116. Cab 14(38) of March 16 and Harvey diary, July 4 1938.
117. Halifax to Cecil, July 12 1938.
118. Crozier, interview with Halifax, July 12 1938.
119. Halifax to Henderson, March 19 1938, FO 800/313. Harvey diary, March 19 1938. Halifax to Chamberlain, April 14 1938, PREM 1/308. Kordt to F.M. in DGFP series D, vol. II, no. 139 of April 29 1938.
120. For a good example see FO 800/313, fols. 13–28 and 33–4.
121. Cab 11(38) of March 9 1938.
122. Halifax at Cab 5(38) of February 16.
123. Ribbentrop, memorandum of March 11 1938, in GFD no. 150, DGFP series D. Harvey diary, March 19 1938. Halifax to Astor, June 22 1938, FO 800/309.
124. Cadogan diary, March 11 1938.
125. Harvey diary, March 11 1938.
126. Halifax, in CP 67(38) of March 13 (Cab 24/275), at Cab 13(38)

of March 14, to Chamberlain, March 19 (PREM 1/266A) and in 'Possible Measures to Avert German Aggression' for Foreign Policy Committee of March 21 1938 in PREM 1/266A.

127. Harvey diary, April 27 and 28 1938.
128. Halifax at Cab 24(38) of May 18, at Cab 26(38) of May 25 and in CP 127(38) of May 24.
129. Cabinet Committee of June 16 1938 in Cab 27/624. Halifax to Chamberlain, June 9 1938, PREM 1/360. Cadogan diary, May 24, June 8 and 17 1938. For Eden, see Harvey diary, May 31 1938.
130. Burckhardt, the Danzig High Commissioner, in GFD, May 25 1938, *DGFP*, series D.
131. Nicolson diary, May 26 1938.
132. Halifax to Henderson, August 5 1938, FO 800/314.
133. E.g. Halifax at Cab. 21(38) of April 27.
134. E.g. Halifax at Cab 21(38) of April 27 and Cab 22(38) of May 4. Cabinet Committee of April 7 1938 in Cab 27/623.
135. Cab 31(38) of July 6 and Cab 32(38) of July 13 and CP 152(38) of July 1 Cab 24/277.
136. Halifax to Chamberlain, June 2 1938, FO 800/318 and CP 163(38) of July 7.
137. Amery diary, April 16 1938.
138. Cabinet Committee of June 16 1938 in Cab 27/624.
139. Cab 26(38) of May 25. For Halifax insisting on an inter-departmental committee to counter German economic expansion in the Balkans, see Cabinet Committee of June 1 1938 in Cab 27/623 and Cab 28(38) of June 15.
140. Amery diary, April 16 1938.
141. Amery diary, April 16 1938. Halifax to Dawson, June 15 1938, FO 800/309. Cab 26(38) of May 25.
142. Chamberlain to Hilda, March 13, May 22, July 9 and August 13 1938. But see Harvey diary, July 19–24 1938 for Halifax beginning to be annoyed at not being consulted.
143. E.g. Harvey diary, May 19 1938.
144. Cab 13(38) of March 14 and Cab 16(38) of March 23.
145. Harvey diary, May 18 1938.
146. Harvey diary, April 22 1938.
147. Nicolson to V. Sackville-West, May 18 1938, quoting de la Warr quoting Halifax.
148. Harvey diary, February 26 1938.
149. *Hansard* (109) col 215.
150. Cab 39(38) of September 17.
151. Inskip diary, September 12 1938. Halifax talking, in Bruce Lockhart diary, April 4 1938. Halifax to Churchill, August 31 1938. Halifax, memorandum of talk with Attlee and Greenwood, September 16 1938, FO 800/309. Hankey to R. Hankey, April 3 1938.
152. For all this see Meeting of Ministers of August 30 1938 in Cab 23/94 and Cab 37(38) of September 12.
153. And Cadogan.

154. Wilson, notes for Prime Minister, September 1 and 5 1938, PREM 1/265. Harvey diary, September 6 and 8 1938. Inskip diary, September 8 1938.
155. Harvey diary, September 6 and 9, Cadogan diary, September 4, 6, 8 and 10 1938. Wilson to Henderson, September 9, PREM 1/265, and Henderson to Wilson, September 9 and 10 1938, PREM 1/266A. Wilson, note of meeting of September 10 1938, PREM 1/266A.
156. Harvey diary, September 9 1938, quoting Eden quoting Halifax.
157. Chamberlain to Ida, September 3 1938.
158. See e.g. Dawson diary, September 7 1938, for Halifax not objecting to Dawson's advocacy of territorial dismemberment (see above p. 186). This entry should, however, be used cautiously since Halifax knew but did not tell Dawson that Chamberlain was thinking of flying to Germany.
159. See above pp. 192–5.
160. Cab 42(38) of September 24, fols. 182 and 189.
161. Cab 43(38) of September 25, fo. 199. Harvey diary, September 26 1938. Cadogan diary, September 25 1938. Elliot to his wife, September 25 1938.
162. Cab 46(38) of September 27. Cadogan diary, September 27.
163. E.g. Halifax to Phipps, September 27 1938 8.30 p.m., *DBFP* third series, vol. II, pp. 575–6.
164. Elliot to his wife, September 25 1938, says Halifax had lost a stone in weight.
165. Cecil says 'disgustingly good', Harvey diary, October 3 1938.
166. Jones to Fisher, October 5 1938.
167. Harvey diary, October 1 1938.
168. Harvey diary, September 29 1938.
169. Amery diary, September 30 1938.
170. Channon diary, September 30 1938, quoting Lennox-Boyd.
171. E.g. Sargent and Cadogan memoranda of September 20 1938 in PREM 1/266A.
172. E.g. Sinclair at National Liberal Club, September 21 1938 *Manchester Guardian*, September 22. National Council of Labour resolution of September 21 in *Manchester Guardian*, September 22.
173. I.e. Hardinge in Harvey diary, September 19, 20 and 25 1938.
174. Nicolson diary, September 19 and Harvey diary, September 20 1938.
175. Cecil to Halifax, September 20 1938.
176. Lloyd to Halifax, September 12 1938, FO 800/309.
177. Dalton diary, September 21 1938.
178. See e.g. Cadogan diary, October 19 1938. Halifax, *Fullness of Days*, pp. 199–200. Harvey diary, October 11 1938, quoting Eden quoting Halifax. Halifax to Chamberlain, October 11 1938.
179. Halifax and Chamberlain to Runciman, October 20 1938. Samuel memorandum of October 26, and to Crewe, October 27 1938. Crewe to Samuel (telegram and letter), October 26 1938. Chamberlain to Hailsham, October 21 1938.

180. Burgin to Halifax, January 2, and vice versa, January 6 1939, FO 800/315, and Harvey diary, February 17 1939.
181. Halifax to Phipps, October 25 and November 1 1938, FO 800/311.
182. Harvey diary, January 14 1939, quoting Halifax talking in the train on the way back.
183. Halifax at Cab 60(38) of December 21.
184. Cadogan diary, February 6 1939.
185. Halifax to Henderson, February 20 1939, FO 800/315.
186. Cab 53(38) of November 7.
187. Halifax at Cab 57(38) of November 30.
188. See Cab 55(38) of November 16 and Cab 27/624 of January 23 and 26 1939.
189. Halifax at Cabinet Committee of November 14 and 21 1938 in Cab 27/624.
190. Halifax at Cabinet Committee of January 23 1939 in Cab 27/624.
191. Cab 5(39) of February 2. Pownall diary, dated January 30 1939.
192. Halifax to Henderson, February 20 1939, FO 800/315.
193. He is thus described by Admiral Sir Reginald Hall, the Die Hard ex-chairman of the Conservative party in a letter to Keyes on March 12 1940.
194. Cadogan diary, November 28 1938 quoted in Dilks, p. 127. For example of Chamberlain by-passing Halifax over Norman's visit to Germany in January 1939 see Cadogan diary, January 3 and 4 and Harvey diary, January 4 1939. Cf. Chamberlain to Hilda, November 6 1938 (for Chamberlain saying he would 'take Halifax with me to Rome but the important talks would be between Musso and myself') and Chamberlain to Ida, February 26 1939 (for Chamberlain suspecting that Halifax agreed with Eden that Chamberlain had changed *his* policy — which Chamberlain did not believe).
195. Eden in Harvey diary, October 16 1938.
196. Hankey to Phipps, January 11 1938.
197. Bruce Lockhart diary, January 13 1938. Vansittart 4/4 for negotiations with Lord Howard de Walden about Vansittart standing as an independent Conservative in Marylebone in January 1939.
198. Lammers, 'From Whitehall after Munich' pp. 837–8 and 847–9 (for Cadogan) and *passim* for Strang, Collier and Ashton-Gwatkin. Colville, p. 115. Barrington-Ward to Dawson, October 13 1938, *The Times* Archive. Cadogan diary, October/November 1938. Strang, p. 146. Bruce Lockhart diary, October 21 1938.
199. Cadogan, memoranda for Halifax, February 26 1939, FO 800/294.
200. *Ibid.* for Cadogan mentioning that Vansittart was now saying 'as an absolute fact' that Hitler was going to 'engulf Czechoslovakia in May' a few weeks after he had been 'going about London assuring people that Hitler was coming West'. See also Hankey to Robin Hankey, April 3 1938, for Vansittart wanting French intervention in Spain and a British commitment to Czechoslovakia.

For Cadogan's anxiety to show that *he* was in change of the Foreign Office, see Cadogan to Phipps, January 11 1938.

201. For the claim that Halifax got his Intelligence information from Vansittart, see Pownall diary, January 23, February 6 and 13 1939. For Vansittart as Dalton's secret adviser, see Dalton diary, November 4 1937, April 12 1938, May 3 and 7 1939 and *passim*. See Hankey diary, October 2 1938 and 'Notes on Conversation with H. Wilson', October 4 1938, in Hankey MSS 8/32. See also Waterfield, p. 225, and Vansittart to Halifax, September 17 1938, FO 800/311.

202. Phipps to Halifax, April 11 1938.

203. Phipps to Halifax, March 18, 22 and 30 and April 11 and 13 1938 and November 7 1938 in FO 800/311.

204. Phipps to Halifax, April 19, June 23 and November 7 1938, all FO 800/311.

205. Phipps to Halifax, April 19, September 14 and December 5 1938, FO 800/311.

206. Phipps to Halifax, September 16 1938, FO 800/311.

207. Phipps to Halifax September 14 and 17 1938, FO 800/311.

208. Phipps to Halifax, June 16 1938, FO 800/311.

209. Phipps to Halifax, June 23 1938, FO 800/311.

210. Phipps to Halifax, April 28, May 8, June 22 and July 7 1939, FO 800/311.

211. Phipps to Halifax, March 17 1939, FO 800/315.

212. Phipps to Wilson, December 13 1938 and January 27 1939. Wilson to Phipps, November 8 1938 and February 2 1939.

213. Phipps to Halifax, March 18, 22, 27 and 28 FO 800/311, and to Chamberlain, September 30 1938 in NC 13/11.

214. Phipps to Halifax, November 7 1938, FO 800/311.

215. Henderson to Halifax, October 29 1937, Halifax MSS.

216. Cameron, p. 138, quoting Henderson to Lothian, May 25 1937.

217. Henderson to Halifax, November 4 and 23 1937, Halifax MSS, and February 27, March 2 and 16 1938, FO 800/313.

218. Henderson to Halifax, August 23 1938, FO 800/314.

219. Henderson to Halifax, November 23 1937, Halifax MSS.

220. Henderson to Halifax, February 27 1938, FO 800/313, and Irving, p. 49.

221. Henderson to Halifax, April 7 and 13 1938, FO 800/313, and August 12 1938, FO 800/314.

222. Henderson to Halifax, May 19 1938, FO 800/313.

223. Henderson to Halifax, August 3 1938, FO 800/314.

224. Henderson to Halifax, August 22 and 23 1938, FO 800/314.

225. Henderson to Halifax, July 18 and August 6 1938, FO 800/314.

226. Henderson to Halifax, March 29 and May 24 1938, FO 800/313, and September 13 1938, FO 800/314.

227. Henderson to Halifax, August 6 and 8 and 22 and September 9, 1938, FO 800/314.

228. Henderson to Chamberlain, September 30 (Chamberlain MSS) and to Halifax, October 6 1938, FO 800/314.

229. Henderson to Halifax, October 11 and 12 1938, FO 800/314, also Henderson to Halifax, October 6 1938, FO 800/314, and February 1 1939, FO 800/315.
230. Henderson to Halifax, February 15 1939, FO 800/315.
231. Henderson to Halifax, February 22 and 23 and March 15 1939, FO 800/315, and to Cadogan, March 9 1939, FO 800/294.
232. Henderson to Cadogan, May 10 1939, *loc. cit.*
233. Henderson to Halifax, March 15 1939, FO 800/315. Vansittart memoranda of February 17 1939 on Henderson to Halifax, February 15 1939, FO 800/315.
234. Dawson diary, February 11 1939. Henderson to Halifax, April 5 1939, FO 800/313, and February 22 1939, FO 800/315. Henderson to Halifax, March 16 and April 5 1938, FO 800/313, and February 22 1939, FO 800/315.
235. Halifax to Henderson, July 28 1939, FO 800/316. Cadogan note on Henderson to Halifax, May 10 1939, FO 800/294, and Sargent note of June 14 1939 in FO 800/315 and on Henderson to Halifax, February 22 1939, FO 800/315.
236. Henderson to Halifax, July 17 1939, FO 800/316.
237. For all this see Henderson to Cadogan May 14 and 31 and July 4 1939, FO 800/294. Henderson to Halifax April 26, May 28, June 8, 14, 17 and 24 and July 14 and 17 1939, all FO 800/315—16.
238. Henderson to Halifax, July 17 1939, FO 800/316.
239. Henderson to Cadogan, August 7 and 9 1939, FO 800/294.
240. Henderson to Halifax, August 22 and 24 1939, FO 800/316.
241. Henderson to Halifax, August 24 1939, FO 800/316.
242. See Vansittart memoranda of April 23 1938 (Van 2/35) and of March 15 1939 (Van 2/43), to Halifax of August 31 and September 16 1938 (FO 800/314), note on Henderson to Halifax August 6 1938 (FO 800/314) and on *ibid.* of February 15 1939 (FO 800/315). See also Vansittart in FP(36) 74 of January 20 1939 (for Cabinet Committee, Cab 27/627) and Sargent, note on Henderson to Halifax February 22 1939 (FO 800/315). Cf. Aster, p. 202—3.
243. See Halifax memorandum in FP (36) 74 of January 20 1939 (Cab 27/627) for this view and for Vansittart's views being presented to the Foreign Policy Committee of the Cabinet.
244. Channon diary, February 16, Harvey diary, February 17, Amery diary, February 17, all 1939.
245. Harvey diary, January 29, February 17 and March 2 1939. Dalton diary, May 5 1939, for Lady Vansittart reporting Vansittart. Nicolson diary, February 22 and March 9 1939. Cf. Cranborne talking, in Nicolson diary, November 15 1938.
246. *Hansard*, House of Lords (111) cols. 936—42 of February 23 1939. Cadogan diary, *passim* 1939. Harvey diary, February 28 1939. Amery diary, February 17 1939.
247. Cadogan diary, March 10 1939, and Halifax to Chamberlain, March 10 1939, and vice versa, March 11.
248. For Halifax letting it be known that it was Chamberlain who

would not have Eden back, see Lady Astor to Lothian, January 12 1939.

249. Harvey diary, January 14 1939.
250. Harvey diary, February 22 1939, quoting Eden quoting Stanley.

NOTES TO CHAPTER 10

1. Chamberlain to Hilda, February 19 and to Ida, February 26 1939.
2. Chamberlain to Ida, March 12 1939.
3. See e.g. Cab 55(38) of November 16, Cab 57(38) of November 30 and Cab 58(38) of December 7. Cabinet Committee of December 6 1938, Cab 27/624.
4. Halifax at Cab 57(38) of November 30.
5. For the announcement, see Inskip in *Hansard* (339) col. 303. Harvey diary of March 14 1939. Halifax to Selborne, October 18 1938 (MS Selborne 87). See also Chamberlain in Aster, p. 27.
6. Duke of Devonshire, i.e. Macmillan's brother-in-law, who was closely connected with the Cecil family, was an admirer of Inskip (see below pp. 338–40) and had been a vice-president of the India League, at Eastbourne, March 16 1939, quoted in Williams, p. 90.
7. Chamberlain at Birmingham, March 17 1939, *The Times*, March 18.
8. See above p. 206.
9. Cab 11(39) of March 15 and Cab 12(39) of March 18.
10. For the recollections of the Rumanian Minister in London and Foreign Office reactions (but coupled with some possible over-estimate of the significance of the episode) see Aster, pp. 61–74.
11. Cab 12(39) of March 18. COS of March 18 in Cab 53/10.
12. Cab 13(39) of March 20.
13. Halifax at Cab 13(39) of March 20.
14. Halifax at Cab 14(39) of March 22 and Cab 15(39) of March 29. Harvey diary, March 20 1939. Mallet to Rootham of March 26 1939 enclosing Halifax memorandum in PREM 1/321.
15. Cab 15(39) of March 29. Chamberlain to Ida, March 26 1939. Cadogan diary, March 28–31 1939.
16. Harvey diary, March 29 1939. Halifax at Cab 16(39) of March 30. Cadogan diary, March 29–31 1939. Chamberlain to Hilda, April 2 1939, makes it clear that the account given of Hitler's intentions by Ian Colvin, the *News Chronicle* correspondent, seemed so highly coloured when Halifax brought him to see Chamberlain that he did not really believe what he said until his account was confirmed by other (presumably Intelligence) sources.
17. Chamberlain to Hilda, April 2 1939.
18. For a summary of the military situation, see Aster, pp. 115–151.

19. It was primarily with a view to putting the anti-aircraft defences on a regular basis, that he adopted Conscription, which previously he had rejected, see Cab 21(39) of April 19. Wilson to Chatfield, April 9 1939, PREM 1/306. Pownall diary dated April 3 1939. Cab 21(39) of April 19 and Cab 22(39) of April 24. Chamberlain in *Hansard* (339) col. 474 of October 6 1938. Cab 26(39) of May 3.

20. Chamberlain at Cab 12(39) of March 18 1939. Halifax at Cab 16(39) of March 30. Chamberlain to Ida, March 26 and July 23 1939. Chamberlain to Hilda, July 30 1939.

21. The last three not reciprocating very strongly.

22. Chamberlain to Hilda, May 28 1939.

23. E.g. Chamberlain to Hilda, April 29, and Chamberlain diary, May 15 1939, for Chamberlain telling Kemsley to ignore the German Ambassador's claim that Anglo-German friendship was growing, justifying this advice with the claim that British firmness must be starting to bite if Dirksen thought it plausible to persuade a major newspaper owner it was so.

24. Chamberlain to Hilda, May 14 1939.

25. See Chamberlain to Hilda, April 2 1939. For Chamberlain being 'fussed' when the BBC claimed that Poland alone was to be judge of aggression and for the denial he issued when Beaverbrook and *The Times* accurately expressed his own opinion, see Harvey diary, April 3 1939.

26. Channon diary, May 1 1939, Harvey diary, May 3 and Rushcliffe to *The Times*, May 2 1939. Cadogan diary, April 20 and May 22 1939. See also *DBFP* third series, vol. V, pp. 599–600, 653, 682, 690 and 730 and vol. VI, pp. 198–201, 211 and 432–3.

27. Chamberlain to Hilda, May 14 and July 15 1939. For the Foreign Office being hard put to find ways of making sure that Hitler did know, see Aster, pp. 199–201.

28. Chamberlain to Hilda, July 2 1939. Ironside diary, July 10 1939, reporting Chamberlain.

29. See Aster, pp. 203–05.

30. Chamberlain to Ida, July 23, and to Hilda, July 30 1939.

31. Cab 35(39) of July 5.

33. For (usually self-appointed) mediators (e.g. Tennant, Roden Buxton, Mackenzie King and Kemsley), see Aster, pp. 251–6.

34. Conducted by Norman, Stanley, Hudson, Wilson and Ashton-Gwatkin.

35. For the last three paragraphs see Wendt and MacDonald.

36. Hudson, memorandum of July 20 1939 in PREM 1/330.

37. *DGFP* series D, vol. VI, no. 380 of May 14 1939 (Notes on a conversation with Mr Drummond-Wolff).

38. For the Wohltat negotiations see Hudson to Churchill, June 30 1939, and memorandum of July 20 1939 in PREM 1/330. Chamberlain to Ida, July 23, and to Hilda, July 30 1939. Harvey diary, July 23 1939. Butler to Wilson, August 2 1939, PREM 1/330.

Wilson notes of August 4 and 8 1939 in PREM 1/330, and of August 21 1939 in PREM 1/331A. Also GFD *passim* in July and August 1939, *DGFP*, series D.

39. I.e. through the policy imposed by Chamberlain, Malcolm Mac-Donald, Halifax and the Committee on Palestine. For the India Office and Chiefs of Staff views of the importance of the 'Moslem World', see CP 28(39) of January 30 and CP 7(39) of January 16 1939.

40. Chamberlain to Phipps, June 19 1939. Cab 33(39) of June 21. For the Far East see Stanhope to Halifax, May [18] 1939, FO 800/322. CID of May 2 1939. Runciman to Chamberlain, June 19 1939, PREM 1/316. Halifax to Chamberlain, June 19 1939, and PREM 1/316 *passim*. Chamberlain to Ida, June 25 1939. Cadogan diary, June 15, 19 and 20 and August 10 1939.

41. Cab 14(39) of March 22. Wilson note of March 23 1939, PREM 1/329. Chamberlain to Mussolini March 20 and 31 1939 (drafts with comments in PREM 1/327).

42. Chamberlain to Ida, April 9 1939. Harvey diary, April 9 1939. For Foreign Office belligerence, see Cadogan diary, April 7 and 8 1939.

43. Cab 13(39) of March 20, 14(39) of March 22 and 21(39) of April 19. Cadogan diary, April 8, 9, 10 and 11 1939.

44. Chamberlain to Hilda, April 15 1939. Cab 20(39) of April 13 and 24(39) of April 26.

45. Cab 21 (39) of April 19.

46. The new British Ambassador to Italy.

47. Chamberlain to Ida, April 23 1939.

48. Harvey diary, April 29 1939. Chamberlain to Hilda April 29 1939.

49. Halifax at Cab 19(39) of April 10 and at Conference of Ministers, April 8 1939 in Cab 23/98.

50. For this, see the three-cornered correspondence between Phipps, Chamberlain and Daladier in PREM 1/329. Halifax to Chamberlain, August 14 1939, PREM 1/331A and Loraine to Halifax, May 16, July 4, July 8, July 21 and August 1 1939.

51. Cab 50(38) of October 26.

52. Hore-Belisha diary, April 17 to 19 1939. Pownall diary dated April 14 1939. Wilson, note of March 29 1939, PREM 1/296 has Halifax. Wilson, note of April 9 and 11 1939, PREM 1/336.

53. Chamberlain to Hilda, April 29 1939.

54. Chamberlain to Hilda, April 2 1939.

55. I.e. because of the Left in France as well as England see Chamberlain at Foreign Policy Committee of March 27 1939 in Cab 24/284.

56. Chamberlain to Hilda, April 29, and to Ida, March 26 and May 21 1939.

57. Cabinet Committee on Foreign Policy, May 19 1939.

58. Dawson diary, April 27 1939.

59. See Cab 26(39) of May 3, 27(39) of May 10, 28(39) of May 17 and 30(39) of May 24.
60. See Aster, *passim*, for Intelligence predictions of a Russo-German pact.
61. Cab 20(39) of April 13 to Cab 30(39) of May 24. Cabinet Committee of May 19 1939.
62. E.g. Halifax to Colville, May 26 1939, FO 800/311 and Loraine to Halifax, August 1 1939, FO 800/319.
63. Cabinet Committee on Foreign Policy of May 16 1939 and Cab 30(39) of May 24. Chamberlain seems to have been supported only by Zetland and Stanhope in the Cabinet. For the ambiguity of the Dominions position, see CP 193(39) of May 22.
64. Cabinet Committee of June 26 and July 19 1939. Cadogan diary, May 16 1939. Chamberlain to Hilda, May 28, July 2 and 15 1939.
65. For the negotiations in general, see PREM 1/409.
66. Chamberlain to Ida, April 23, and to Hilda, April 15, May 14 and June 17 1939.
67. Chamberlain to Ida, February 26, and to Hilda, April 29 and May 14 1939.
68. E.g. Chamberlain to Hilda, July 30 1939.
69. Chamberlain to Hilda, March 5 and April 15 1939. For Addison (also being a 'miserable cur'), see Chamberlain to Hilda, November 17 1935.
70. Hore-Belisha and Channon diaries, March 28 1939. Wilson, note of March 29 1939, PREM 1/296. Cab 21(39) of April 19, fo. 334. Cab 22(39) of April 24. Chamberlain to Ida, February 26 1938.
71. Chamberlain, talking to German Ambassador, in *DGFP* series D, vol. IV GFD, no. 300 of January 25 1939.
72. Chamberlain to Hilda April 15 1939. Cab 20(39) of April 13.
73. Chamberlain to Hilda, March 5 and August 5 1939, and to Ida, October 22 1938. Cf. Chamberlain to Sinclair, February 6 and 7 1939. For Chamberlain refusing to let Samuel consult Sinclair, see Samuel, p. 279. For Chamberlain's opinion of Samuel, see Chamberlain to Hilda, November 17 1935.
74. Chamberlain to Hilda, April 2 1939.
75. Chamberlain to Ida, February 26 and 12 1939.
76. Chamberlain to Hilda, April 2 and 15, and to Ida, June 10 1939.
77. See above p. 241.
78. Chamberlain to Ida, December 11 1938 and August 5 1939. Cf. Chamberlain to Churchill, October 5 1938.
79. Chamberlain to Ida, April 23 1939.
80. Chamberlain to Hilda, November 6 1938 and April 15 1939. Churchill to Chamberlain, April 9 1939.
81. Churchill to Chamberlain, March 27 1939, PREM 1/345.
82. E.g. Chamberlain to Ida, October 9 1938. Cab 26(39) of May 3.
83. Chamberlain to Ida, April 9, and to Hilda, April 15 1939.
84. Chamberlain to Ida, July 8 1939, for Randolph Churchill,

Michael Berry, Maisky and Camrose all being in it together.
85. Chamberlain to Ida, June 10 1939.
86. See e.g. Chamberlain to Hilda, April 15 1939, for Churchill offering himself after Albania.
87. Chamberlain at Cab 38(39) of July 19. Chamberlain to Ida or Hilda, April 29 1939.
88. Halifax to Chamberlain, August 14, Syres to Chamberlain, August 13 1939, both in PREM 1/331A.
89. Halifax to Chamberlain, August 19 1939, PREM 1/331A (drafted by Cadogan). Halifax, 'Record' in FO 800/317, August 19 1939.
90. Halifax, 'Record', August 21 1939.
91. Chamberlain to Amery, August 22 1939.
92. Cab 41(39) of August 22.
93. See n. 94.
94. But not by Chamberlain or a special ambassador because that would look like a panic-stricken reaction to the agreement or a repetition of Munich, see Halifax to Chamberlain, August 19 1939, PREM 1/331A, and Zetland to Linlithgow, August 27 1939, Eur.D.609.
95. Chamberlain to Hitler, August 22 1939, in *DBFP* third series, vol. VII, pp. 127–8.
96. *DBFP* third series, vol. VII, pp. 161–3.
97. Hitler to Chamberlain, August 23 1939, in *DBFP* third series, vol. VII, pp. 172–3.
98. Inskip diary, August 25 1939. Zetland to Linlithgow, August 27 1939, Eur.D.609.11.
99. *DBFP* third series, vol. VII, p. 195.
100. Cab 42(39) of August 24. Halifax 'Record', August 24. DBFP third series, vol. VII, pp. 146–7 and 185–6.
101. Chatfield, note for Prime Minister of August 24, and Hore-Belisha to Chamberlain, August 23 and 24, all 1939, PREM 1/312.
102. Henderson at Cab 43(39) of August 26.
103. Chamberlain to Hilda, August 27 1939.
104. Henderson telegram nos. 458, 459 and 461 in *DBFP* third series, vol. VII, pp. 227–31 and 235.
105. Cab 43(39) of August 26.
106. Wallace diary of August 26 1939. The drafting committee certainly consisted of Chamberlain, Simon and Halifax. It appears also to have included Cadogan and Butler, and perhaps Wilson. See Pownall diary, August 29 1939, for Chamberlain draft being 'almost cringing in tone'.
107. Postponed from the morning in order to enable Chamberlain to talk to Dahlerus. Inskip and Wallace diaries, August 27 1939.
108. Zetland to Linlithgow, August 27 and 29 Eur.D.609. Harvey, Amery and Wallace diaries, August 27 1939. Cadogan diary, August 27 and 28 1939. Inskip diary, August 25 1939, for the secret nature of Loraine's information. Chamberlain at Cab 45(39) of August 28. Ashton-Gwatkin, note of talk with a confidant of

Goerdeler, August 27 1939, PREM 1/331A. Cab 43(39) of August 26 and 44(39) of August 27. Loraine to Halifax, August 22 1939, FO 800/319.

109. Cab 44(39) of August 27.
110. Halifax at Cab 43(39) of August 26 and Inskip diary of August 26 1939.
111. Cab 44(39) of August 27 1939 Annex F.398 and Cab 45(39) of August 28 Annex F.417. Cadogan diary, August 28 1939. Inskip diary, August 27 1939.
112. Hoare diary notes August 28 1939. Dalton diary, August 28 1939.
113. Harvey diary, August 27 1939.
114. Zetland to Linlithgow, August 23 1939, Eur.D.609. Cab 46(39) of August 30 has the Japanese Ambassador telling Halifax that, if invited to be Japanese Foreign Secretary, he would like to consult Halifax before accepting.
115. Halifax and Hoare at Cab 41(39) of August 22. Zetland to Linlithgow, August 29 1939, Eur.D.609. Chamberlain to Hilda, August 27 1939. Harvey diary, August 27 1939. For the Turks moving the other way, i.e. beginning to demand more money because of German economic pressure, see Cab 42(39) of August 24.
116. Zetland to Linlithgow, August 29 1939, Eur.D.609.
117. Cf. Elliot telling Mrs Dugdale that the delays of Saturday and Sunday were intended as 'insults' to Hitler (Dugdale diary, August 29 1939).
118. Wallace diary, August 22 1939.
119. Pownall diary, August 29 and September 1 1939, for one statement of this view. Killearn diary, August 29 1939, for King George VI taking the view that peace was fairly certain on the basis of the 'tacit view of the advisers that "Hitler's bluff had been called"'. For Halifax saying at lunch on August 31 that we 'had the first view of the beaten fox', see Wallace diary, August 31 1939. See also Hankey diary, August 29 1939.
120. Halifax, 'Record', August 30 1939. Inskip diary, August 26 1939. Cab 45(39) of August 28.
121. Harvey diary, August 25 and 26, and Harvey to Halifax, August 26 1939.
122. Halifax at Cab 44(39) of August 27.
123. The reply is in Halifax to Ogilvie-Forbes of August 26 1938 (*DBFP* third series, vol. VII, pp. 330–2.)
124. *DBFP* third series, vol. VII, p. 374. Cadogan diary, August 29 1939.
125. Henderson telegrams nos. 450, 453 and 498 in *DBFP* third series, vol. VII, pp. 348, 351–4 and 374.
126. Halifax at Cab 46(39) of August 30.
127. *Ibid.* Cf. Halifax; minute in *DBFP* third series, vol. VII, p. 354.
128. Telegram no. 285 to Berlin of August 30 in *DBFP* third series, vol. VII, p. 391. Inskip diary, August 28 1939. Hoare diary, Au-

gust 29 1939. Cadogan diary, August 30 1939.

129. E.g. Chamberlain at Cab 46(39) of August 30, fo. 432. Halifax at Cab 46(39) of August 30. Amery diary, August 30 1939, reporting Chatfield and Inskip in conversation. Cadogan diary, August 30 1939. Zetland to Linlithgow, August 30 1939, Eur.D. 609, for a less categorical view.

130. Halifax at Cab 46(39) of August 30, Cadogan diary, August 30 1939.

131. Halifax at Cab 46(39) of August 30. Cadogan diary, August 29 and 30 1939. For Ismay saying on September 2 that dissension in Germany might avert war see Wingate, p. 39. For Halifax that evening see Dawson diary, August 30 1938.

132. Cab 46(39) of August 30 for discussion about the venue of talks not being in Germany. Harvey diary, August 31 1939, quoting Halifax. Inskip diary, August 30 1939.

133. *DGFP* series D, vol. VII, no. 461 of August 31 1939.

134. Wallace diary, August 30 1939, for the Cabinet putting it off the day before after Chamberlain had told Anderson to start it.

135. *DGFP* series D, vol. VII, no. 461 of August 31 1939.

136. See e.g. Inskip diary, August 31 1939, saying Hitler's terms were 'much more reasonable than I ever thought possible'.

137. Chatfield at Cab 47(39) of September 1.

138. Halifax at Cab 47(39) of September 1.

139. Cadogan diary, September 1 1939, for it not being an 'ultimatum'.

140. Cab 47(39) of September 1.

141. Halifax, telegram no. 311 to Henderson 5.45 p.m. of September 1 1939, *DBFP* third series, vol. VII, p. 488.

142. Harvey diary, September 1 1939.

143. Nicolson diary, September 1 1939. *Hansard* (351) col. 126 of September 1 1939.

144. Harvey diary, September 1 1939.

145. Halifax at Cab 47(39) of September 1. Cadogan diary, August 31 1939.

146. Cab 47(39) of September 1.

147. Cadogan diary, August 31 1939. Inskip, Channon and Hore-Belisha diaries, September 2 1939, referring to August 31. Harvey diary, August 31 1939.

148. Halifax at Cab 47(39) of September 1.

149. Cab 47(39) of September 1. *DBFP* third series, vol. VII, pp. 479–80.

150. Cab 47(39) of September 1.

151 *DBFP* third series, vol. VII, pp. 507–8. Cadogan and Channon diaries September 2 1939. Halifax, 'Record'.

152. Cab 48(39) of September 2 1939 4.15 p.m. Inskip, Cadogan, Channon and Wallace diaries, September 2 1939.

NOTES TO CHAPTER 11

1. See Zetland to Chamberlain, May 23 1937.
2. Stanhope to Chamberlain, November 25 1935. See also Newman, pp. 347–8.
3. For a Simon-like letter, see Burgin to Mrs Chamberlain, September 15 1938, NC 13/11.
4. Chamberlain diary, November 21 1935, quoting Baldwin.
5. E.g. note in PREM 1/190 of backbenchers' meeting with Baldwin on May 20 1936 and Winterton to Beaverbrook, December 17 1935 for Eden.
6. Cab 13(38) of March 14.
7. See Meeting of Ministers of August 30 1938, Cab 23/94. Cab 37(38) of September 12.
8. Cab 39(38) of September 17.
9. Cab 40(38) of September 19.
10. Cab 43(38) of September 25.
11. *Ibid.*
12. Duff Cooper diary, September 16 1938. Dugdale diary, September 18 1938. Inskip diary, September 14 1938. Winterton also consulted Amery (on a Privy Councillor basis) who was much closer to him.
13. R.S. Hudson memorandum of December 12 1938, Halifax MSS.
14. Amery diary, October 8 1938.
15. Chamberlain to Ida, January 28 1939.
16. E.g. Ormsby-Gore to MacDonald, September 23 1933.
17. See e.g. Ormsby-Gore to MacDonald, September 23 1933, and Butler to Brabourne and Ormsby-Gore to Sankey, March 7 1934.
18. Dawson diary, May 24 and 27 1936.
19. Ormsby-Gore to Halifax, November 11 1937, Halifax MSS.
20. *Ibid.*
21. E.g. CID Cab 2/7 of November 18 1937 and the early Cabinet Committees of 1938 in Cab 27/623. Cab 7(38) of February 20.
22. Salisbury to Chamberlain, May 17 1938, for the lack of ceremony. Chamberlain to Ida, March 28 1936, for Ormsby-Gore's lack of judgment.
23. Heuston, p. 489.
24. Cab 43(38) of September 25, fo. 200.
25. Duff Cooper, p. 235.
26. See Heuston, pp. 490–2, but see also Hailsham to Simon, October 31 1938, for Hailsham saying that there was no disagreement about policy.
27. For the incident see Weir MSS 19/15 (and Chamberlain to Hilda, October 24 1936).
28. Chamberlain to Ida, May 13 1938. Halifax to Chamberlain, May 16 [1938]. Wilson, notes of March 15 and of April 22 1938, and Cadman to Chamberlain, April 22 1938 in PREM 1/236. See also PREM 1/252 and Cadman and Rowland, pp. 166–71. Reader, p. 292, says that Weir resigned in sympathy with Swinton. See

also Runciman, Hankey, Inskip, O. Stanley, Lloyd, Ellis and Londonderry etc. to Swinton, May 16–23 1938.

29. Wheeler-Bennett, *Waverley*, pp. 230–1.
30. E.g. Eden to Chamberlain, May 23 1937, and Crookshank diary, May 28 1937.
31. Runciman to Chamberlain, March 31, and to Chamberlain, June 19 1939 (for Runciman against a China alignment).
32. Zetland to Willingdon, February 17 1936.
33. Zetland to Willingdon, February 17, March 29, April 6, July 6 and August 14 in Eur.D.600 and 609, all 1936.
34. Zetland to Linlithgow, August 14 1936, Eur.D.609.
35. E.g. Zetland to Linlithgow, February 21 1937.
36. Zetland to Willingdon, September 27 and October 10 1935, Eur. D.609.
37. Zetland to Linlithgow, June 8 and 15, August 14 and 24 and September 25 1936 and February 8 1937, Eur.D.609.
38. Zetland to Linlithgow, June 8 and 15, August 14 and 24 and September 25 1936 and February 8 and March 22 1937, *loc. cit.*
39. Zetland to Linlithgow, September 2 1938.
40. Zetland to Linlithgow, September 16/20 1938 and to Chamberlain, September 28 1938.
41. Zetland to Linlithgow, October 1 and 4 1938.
42. Zetland to Linlithgow, May 17 and June 13 1939, Eur.D.609.
43. Dugdale diary, September 19 1937.
44. Zetland to Linlithgow, September 9 1938.
45. Harvey and Duff Cooper diaries, February 19 1938, for reports of 100 government supporters being expected to vote against if Eden resigned.
46. R.J. Russell to Runciman, March 28 1934.
47. See his contribution to Percy, *Conservatism and the Future*. For Morrison as a 'friend' of Baldwin see Butler to Brabourne, December 19 1935. See also Brabourne to Butler, March 29 1935. For the effect of a speech in 1936, see Nicolson diary, May 25 1936.
48. Chamberlain diary, November 21 1935.
49. Chamberlain to Hilda, November 23 1935.
50. Chamberlain to Hilda, October 31 1936.
51. Chamberlain to Hilda, March 5 1939. Channon diary, September 12 1937, for Margesson saying so. Dugdale diary, November 3 1936. Zetland to Linlithgow, December 3 and 6 1938. Nicolson to Lothian, September 6 1936 (Balliol MSS) and diary, November 24 1935, May 25 and July 27 1938.
52. Morrison talking in Nicolson diary, June 30 1937.
53. Harvey, Cadogan and Chamberlain diaries, February 19 1938. For the defence, see *Hansard* (332) cols. 314–22 of February 22 1938.
54. Cab 38(38) of September 14.
55. Morrison at Cab 39(38) of September 17.
56. *Ibid.*
57. MacDonald to Baldwin, April 8 1934.

58. Butler to Brabourne, February 22 1934. Jones diary, June 12 1934.
59. Astor to Garvin, February 23 1934.
60. See e.g. Astor to Garvin, February 23 1934, and Chamberlain diary, March 25 1934.
61. Chamberlain diary, February 19 1936.
62. Dugdale diary, March 8, 9 and 27 1936. Coote, p. 151.
63. Chamberlain to Hilda, October 31 1936. Dawson to Lady Astor, November [2 or 7] 1936.
64. See above pp. 99–102.
65. Coote, p. 158.
66. Harvey diary, February 8 1938.
67. Dugdale diary, February 19, 21 and 22 1938. Coote, pp. 151–3.
68. Coote, p. 157.
69. Elliot to Swinton, May 17 1938, and Elliot at Meeting of Ministers of August 30 1938, Cab 23/94. Inskip diary, September 14 1938. Cab 38(38) of September 14. Dugdale diary, July 26 and September 15 1938. Cab 39(38) of September 17 morning session. Cab 39(38) of September 17 afternoon session.
70. Elliot to his wife, September 18 1938, Coote p. 165. Cab 39(38) of September 17.
71. Dugdale diary, September 19 1938.
72. Elliot to his wife, September 19 and 20 1938, Coote, pp. 166–9. Cab 41(38) of September 21.
73. Harvey and Dugdale diaries, September 22 1938.
74. Elliot to his wife, September 23 and 25 1938, Coote, pp. 170–3.
75. Cabs 43 and 44(38) of September 25.
76. Duff Cooper diary, September 30 1938. Elliot to Mrs Dugdale, October 7 1938, Coote, p. 163.
77. Cab 15(39) of March 29. Cab 19(39) of April 10. Elliot to Mrs Dugdale, October 7 1938, Coote, p. 163.
78. Coote, p. 174.
79. Meeting of Ministers of August 30 1938, Cab 23/94.
80. De la Warr to Halifax, September 2 1938, FO 800/314.
81. Dugdale diary, September 7 1938. Duff Cooper diary, September 8 1938.
82. Boothby to Churchill September 10 1938 recording a conversation with de la Warr.
83. De la Warr to Halifax, September 10 1938, FO 800/314.
84. Cab 37(38) of September 12.
85. MacDonald to Baldwin, June 16 1936. Dugdale diary, May 25 1936.
86. Bridgeman to Baldwin, April 12 1934.
87. Nicolson diary, September 10 1937.
88. *Loc. cit.*
89. Nicolson diary, March 4 and May 16 1938.
90. Chamberlain diary, October 21 1935. Butler to Brabourne, June 20 1935.
91. Nicolson diary, February 5 and 24 1936.

92. Chamberlain diary, November 21 1935. Dawson diary, November 24 1935.
93. For timing of publication, see notes of June 2 1936 addressed to Secretary of State in Baldwin MSS.
94. There are many examples (especially in relation to Thomas); for an interesting attempt to persuade Lloyd George not to attack MacDonald in his *War Memoirs* see Stevenson diary, April 24 1934.
95. Or perhaps just Randolph Churchill. See Stevenson diary, April 27 1936, for Churchill wishing to get back into the government and being embarrassed by Randolph Churchill at Ross and Cromarty. But cf. Beaverbrook to Hoare, January 31 1936.
96. Nicolson diary, February 5 and January 28 1936. Malcolm MacDonald to Baldwin, January 5 1936. *Sunday Times*, January 12 1936, for Ross and Cromarty by-election.
97. Chamberlain diary, July 22 1935. MacDonald to Baldwin, November 28, and to Hoare November 25 1935.
98. MacDonald to Baldwin, Wednesday [November1935].
99. MacDonald to Baldwin, November 13 1935.
100. MacDonald to Chamberlain, November 18, and to Amulree, November 16 1935.
101. For the period after the election see Jones to A.F., December 6 1935, and Nicolson diary, November 20 1935.
102. Ramsay MacDonald to Malcolm MacDonald, January 16 1936.
103. E.g. MacDonald to Tillett, July 14 1936. Nicolson diary, July 9 1936.
104. For MacDonald as incompetent chairman of the Privy Councillors' Coronation Committee, see Crawford to Linlithgow, June 10 1936, Eur.F.125 151/2.
105. Baldwin in Jones diary, May 23 1936. Chamberlain to Hilda, November 17, and diary, November 20 1935. Cf. Chamberlain to Hilda, July 25 1936, for Chamberlain trying to stop Baldwin leaving MacDonald in charge while Baldwin was on holiday. For MacDonald's resentment see Nicolson diary, March 22 1937.
106. Marks to MacDonald, October 22 1936, reporting de la Warr. Nicolson diary, July 14 1936, August 1 and November 10 1937.
107. Dugdale diary, November 2 and 9 1937. De la Warr at National Labour Conference, March 18 1938, *The Times* March 19. Cf. Nicolson diary, April 12 1937.
108. Cab 35(38) and 39(38) of September 14 and 17.
109. Dugdale diary, September 18 1938. Nicolson diary, October 2 1938.
110. Nicolson diary, September 28 1938.
111. Nicolson diary, October 3 1938, and Amery diary, September 30 1938.
112. De la Warr to Chamberlain, October 4 1938, PREM 1/266A, and March 21 1939, PREM 1/330, and at Eastbourne, November 4 1938, *The Times*, November 5.
113. De la War to Chamberlain, April 14 1939, PREM 1/336.

114. Based on private information (as are parts of the rest of this paragraph).
115. Based on private information.
116. *Ibid.*
117. Dugdale diary, December 15 1937. Nicolson diary, April 26, May 31, early June *passim* 1937 and August 26 1938.
118. Dugdale diary, September 19 1937.
119. Malcolm MacDonald to Baldwin, February 14 1936, in PREM 1/192 and MacDonald to Baldwin, February 12 1936. Cf. Cab 20(36) of March 16. For by-election see Malcolm to Ramsay MacDonald, January 10 1936 *et seq*, in MacDonald MSS.
120. *Ibid.*
121. Harvey diary, January 19 1938. MacDonald quoted in Nicolson diary, April 8 1937 and February 21 1938.
122. Duff Cooper diary, February 19 1938, quoting Margesson.
123. E.g. Simon to Spen Valley Newspapers, March 9 1938, and Chamberlain diary, February 19 1938.
124. Harvey diary, March 16 1938.
125. Nicolson diary, February 21 and March 29 1938.
126. Meeting of Ministers of August 30 1938, Cab 23/94.
127. Wilson to Prime Minister, September 1 1938, PREM 1/265.
128. MacDonald at Cab 38(38) of September 14.
129. MacDonald at Cab 39(38) of September 17.
130. *Ibid.* MacDonald at Cab 41(38) of September 21.
131. Cab 42(38) of September 24, 43(38) of September 25, 45(38) of September 26 and 46(38) of September 27.
132. Cab 44(38) of September 25.
133. King-Hall reporting him in Nicolson diary, December 13 1938. Cf. MacDonald to Chamberlain, November 26 1938 in PREM 1/247.
134. Hankey to R. Hankey, March 7 1937.
135. For a by no means unique example, see Randolph Churchill, pp. 74–5.
136. See e.g. CP 52(36) of February 24 in Cab 24/260.
137. Duff Cooper diary, January 23 1938. Cab 2(36) of January 22. Duff Cooper to Phipps, April 20 1938.
138. Duff Cooper talking to Beck in Duff Cooper to Halifax, July 8 1938, FO 800/309. Cf. Fergusson talking in Dugdale diary, June 27 1936.
139. Duff Cooper diary, March 23 1938.
140. Duff Cooper to Halifax, April 11 1938, FO 800/309.
141. Duff Cooper to Halifax, August 8 1938, FO 800/309.
142. Cab 38(38) of September 14.
143. Meeting of Ministers of August 30 1938, Cab 23/94.
144. That it might seem to have been done behind the backs of the French and that a British proposal for settling the Sudeten question, if accepted by the Germans and not by the Czechs, might undermine the desire to protect Czechoslovakia.

145. Cab 38(38) of September 14.
146. Duff Cooper at Cab 39(38) of September 17.
147. Cab 40(38) of September 19.
148. Cab 41(38) of September 21.
149. CID of September 13 1938 in Cab 16/189 and e.g. Cab 42(38) of September 24.
150. Duff Cooper to Halifax, September 22 1938, FO 800/309.
151. Duff Cooper to Halifax, September 24 1938, FO 800/309.
152. Cab 42(38) of September 24.
153. For the last two paragraphs, see Cabs 43, 44 and 45(38) of September 25 and 26.
154. Cab 44(38) of September 25.
155. Cab 46(38) of September 27.
156. Chamberlain to Hilda, December 17 1937. Chamberlain to Duff Cooper, December 17, and Duff Cooper to Chamberlain, December 19 1937.
157. Duff Cooper, p. 209.
158. Taylor, pp. 385—6.
159. Liddell Hart, pp. 89 and 100. Colville, pp. 73—83.
160. Cab 12(38) and 14(38) of March 12 and 14 and Cab 24(38) of May 18. Pownall diary, March 14 1938. Hore-Belisha diary, March 13 1938. Colville, p. 92.
161. Hore-Belisha diary, April 13 1938.
162. Crozier, interview with Hore-Belisha, June 19 1935, for Lloyd George as an out-of-date Gladstonian.
163. Channon diary, March 22 1938.
164. Hore-Belisha to Runciman, May 5 1937. For Runciman as Hore-Belisha's mentor see Hore-Belisha diary, February 25 1939. See also Minney, p. 130.
165. Hore-Belisha diary, August 30 1938.
166. Hore-Belisha diary notes of September 17 1938.
167. Hore-Belisha diary, September 19 1938. Cab 40(38) of September 19.
168. Hore-Belisha to Chamberlain, September 21 1938, PREM 1/266A.
169. Colville, p. 112.
170. Hore-Belisha diary notes of September 24 1938. Cab 42(38) of September 24.
171. Pownall diary, September 5 1938 (written on September 25).
172. Cabs 43 and 44(38) of September 25. Harvey diary, September 25 1938.
173. Cabs 43 and 44(38) of September 25. Hore-Belisha diary, September 25 and 26 1938. Hore-Belisha to Chamberlain, September 28 1938, PREM 1/266A. On the other hand a couple of days later, he suggested sending 4 battalions to Czechoslovakia in order to convince Hitler of 'our good faith about the transfer of the Sudeten areas'.
174. Amery diary, October 13 1938.

175. E.g. Ewan Butler, p. 84.
176. Bracken to Beaverbrook, between December 2 and December 16 1938.
177. Pownall diary, October 10 1938 and January 23 1939.
178. E.g. Coote in Pownall diary, June 27 1938. Colville, pp. 93—7.
179. Pownall diary, September 5 1938 (written on September 25) and *passim* in the winter of 1938.
180. In conjunction with one of Hore-Belisha's junior ministers and a couple of younger members of the government. For the Strathcona interview and plot, see Hore-Belisha diary of December 19 1938.
181. Hore-Belisha diary, December 20 1938.
182. Hore-Belisha diary, January 26 1939.
183. Hore-Belisha to Wilson (2 letters), March 28, Wilson, note of March 29, and Hore-Belisha to Chamberlain, April 15, in PREM 1/296 and April 12, in PREM 1/336, all 1939.
184. Hore-Belisha diary, April 11 and 17 1939. Pownall diary, April 3 1939.
185. Hore-Belisha to Chamberlain, August 23 and 24 1939, both in PREM 1/312. Pownall diary, August 23 1939.
186. For example, he had Churchill to lunch on August 28, Hore-Belisha diary, August 28 1939.
187. Hore-Belisha diary, August 26 1939.
188. Hore-Belisha diary, August 27 1939.
189. E.g. at Cabinet Committee on Foreign Policy of May 19 1939, Cab 27/625.
190. Channon diary, August 26 1939.
191. Hore-Belisha to Simon, August 27 1939, in diary September 27.
192. Hore-Belisha diary, August 30 1939.
193. Hore-Belisha diary, September 2 1939.
194. E.g. very early in his prime ministership, Dugdale diary, March 10 1938.
195. Elliot in Dugdale diary, February 21 1938.
196. For Eden's dislike see Dugdale diary, May 22 1938.
197. Nicolson diary, October 7 1936.
198. Bernays to Samuel, Friday night [September 1933].
199. Sinclair to Harris, September 22 1935.
200. Bernays to Baldwin, October 24 1935, and to Sinclair, November 17 1935.
201. Bernays to Simon, September 10 1936.
202. Nicolson diary, May 18 1936. See also *The Times*, May 20 1936, first leader following correspondence.
203. Nicolson diary, September 15 1936.
204. Chamberlain to Hilda, February 13 1937.
205. Dugdale diary, September 20 1938. Allen of Hurtwood to CE Asquith, May 12 1936, MacDonald MSS.
206. Nicolson at Edinburgh, November 7 1938, *The Scotsman*, November 8, and at Caxton Hall, March 25 1939, *Manchester Guardian*, March 27. King-Hall was saying much the same thing after

Prague (e.g. King-Hall to Barrington-Ward, October 15 1938, *The Times* Archive).

207. For Malcolm MacDonald wanting a 'Centre-party' to 'preserve democracy', see Butler to Brabourne, July 8 1937.
208. Mabane in Nicolson diary, April 19 1937.
209. Dugdale diary, September 18 1937.
210. E.g. Harvey diary, March 27 1939, for 'the wobblers wobbling again' (of Stanley, Elliot and de la Warr). Dugdale diary, February 20, 21 and 24 1938. Coote in Dugdale diary, September 21 1938, calls them 'rubber-stamps'.
211. Chamberlain to Ida, October 9 1938. For Samuel making this a ground for not joining the government at this time, see Samuel, p. 279.
212. For Crookshank addressing Baldwin as his 'leader' see Crookshank to Baldwin, August 2 1938. Cf. Crookshank diary, May 29 1937 and February 21, September 17 and 25, 27 and 28 and October 4 and 6, all 1938. For Crookshank's campaign to have a wider circulation of Foreign Office telegrams to junior ministers, see Halifax to Chamberlain, May 7 1938, PREM 1/302 and *passim*. For Crookshank's threats to resign see Chamberlain to Ida, October 9 1938. Harvey diary, March 23 1937, February 21, 25, March 12 and September 17 1938.
213. See e.g. Chamberlain diary, March 25 1934.
214. Butler to Brabourne, December 20 1934.
215. Sankey diary, January 23 1935.
216. Headlam diary, February 6 and 8 1935. Chamberlain diary, February 13 1935.
217. Simon diary, February 13 1935.
218. See Cecil to Murray, May 8 1937, and surrounding correspondence for Stanley echoing Chamberlain's criticisms of the League of Nations Union.
219. See Shuttleworth to Runciman, May 3 1934, for the favourable impression Stanley made on Liberals. See also Margesson memorandum in NC8/24/1 of March 1937.
220. Cadogan diary, January 19 and 21 1938. Harvey diary, January 20 1938.
221. Chamberlain diary, February 19 1938. Cab 7(38) of February 20.
222. Cabinet Committee of March 1 and 15 1938, Cab 27/623.
223. Chamberlain to Stanley, April 11 1938.
224. Harvey diary, June 27 1938, reporting Cadogan.
225. Meeting of Ministers of August 30 1938, Cab 23/94.
226. Nicolson diary, September 11 1938.
227. Duff Cooper diary, September 12 1938.
228. Cab 37(38) of September 12.
229. Nicolson diary, September 11 1938.
230. Cab 38(38) of September 14. Duff Cooper diary, September 14 1938.
231. Duff Cooper diary, September 16 1938.
232. Cab 39(38) of September 17.

233. Reasonable arrangements for 'transferred individuals', German demobilisation on the setting up of a Border Commission and the disbanding of Henlein's Freikorps.
234. Cab 40(38) of September 19.
235. Cab 41(38) of September 21.
236. Cab 43(38) of September 25. Duff Cooper diary, September 26 1938.
237. Duff Cooper diary, September 28 1938.
238. Cab 43(38) of September 25 f.232.
239. Stanley to Halifax, September 22 1938, FO 800/309.
240. Stanley to Chamberlain, October 3 1938, PREM 1/266A. Crookshank diary, October 4 1938.
241. Chamberlain to Lady Londonderry, July 28 1937. In 1938/9, Londonderry was President of the National Union.
242. A.L. Kennedy journal, December 16 1938.
243. Chamberlain to Ida, October 9 1938.
244. Pownall diary, January 23 1939.
245. See Cabinet Committee of January 23 1939, Cab 27/624.
246. Cadogan diary, April 19 and May 16 1939.
247. Cab 19(39) of April 10.
248. Stanley to Chamberlain, June 30 1939.
249. Duff Cooper diary, September 14 1938.
250. E.g. Amery diary, January 26 1939, quoting Godfrey Nicholson MP.
251. For Inskip as advocate of a National party see Inskip at United Club dinner, April 24 1934, *The Times*, April 25. For hostility to Lloyd George see *Manchester Guardian*, February 11 1935. For Inskip as possible leader etc. see Brabourne to Butler, March 29 1935. Channon diary, September 12 1937, quoting Margesson. Chamberlain diary, February 11 1937, Harvey diary, March 23 1937. Garvin to Astor, July 9 1937, for Inskip as a desirable Foreign Secretary. Crookshank diary, March 14 1936.
252. Nicolson diary, July 20 1936.
253. For the qualities see Butler to Brabourne, March 29 1935. See also Heuston, p. 586.
254. See *The Times*, October 29 1936 (for Nuffield), and Inskip at 1936 Club in Nicolson diary, July 5 1937.
255. See e.g. the long discussions of Defence Requirements in the Cabinets of March and April 1938 in Cab 23/92.
256. Cab 43(38) of September 25.
257. *Ibid*.
258. Cab 38(38) of September 14.
259. Cab 39(38) of September 17.
260. Hankey to Robin Hankey, March 1 1938.
261. Inskip at Cabinet Committee of March 15 1938, Cab 27/623.
262. Inskip diary, September 8 1938.
263. Inskip diary, September 17 1938.
264. Cab 42(38) of September 24.
265. Hankey diary, September 27 and 28 1938.

266. Inskip to Hankey, September 12 1938.
267. For an example see Inskip, memorandum of March 11 1938 in FO 800/313.
268. Nicolson diary, November 24 1938. R.S. Hudson, memorandum of December 12 1938, Halifax MSS.
269. E.g. Devonshire to Baldwin, December 21 1938, and Nicolson diary, July 27 1938.
270. Inskip diary, January 17 1939.
271. Inskip diary, September 2 1939, for Chamberlain described as 'faux ami' on this occasion.
272. Dawson diary, May 28 1937.
273. Butler to Brabourne, March 11 1936.
274. Amery diary, February 21 1938, Hoare to Chamberlain, March 17 1937, and Heuston, p. 489.
275. E.g. Greenwood at Edinburgh, October 1 1936, *Manchester Guardian*, October 2; Morrison at Blackburn, September 27 1936, *Manchester Guardian* September 28; and Morrison in *Forward*, October 10 1936. See also Chatfield to Dreyer, May 28 1937.
276. Amery diary, March 20, and Dawson diary, July 14 1938.
277. See Lady Astor in Dawson diary, March 1 1936. Keyes to Chatfield, January 6 1937.
278. Cabinet Committee of April 7 1938, Cab 27/623.
279. Channon diary, June 1 and 2 1938. Cf. Butler to Brabourne, July 8 1937.
280. Lady Maud Hoare to Beaverbrook, November 4 1938.
281. Cab 41(38) of September 21 and Meeting of Ministers of August 30 1938 in Cab 23/94.
282. Cab 39(38) of September 17 and Cab 41(38) of September 21.
283. Cab 43(38) of September 25.
284. Dawson diary, September 27 1938. Hoare to Mrs Neville Chamberlain, September 29 1938.
285. Amery diary, November 21 1938.
286. Hoare to Chamberlain, October 5, and to Linlithgow, November 7 1938.
287. Pownall diary, October 24 and 31 and December 12 1938 and February 20 1939.
288. Amery diary, November 18 and 24 1938. Hoare at Cabinet Committee of January 23 1939 Cab 27/624.
289. I.e. in February 1939. Cf. Jones to A.F., February 19 1939.
290. Hoare to Chamberlain, March 17 [1939].
291. Hoare to Chamberlain, April 2 [1939].
292. Cadogan diary, May 9 1940. Pownall diary, January 23, April 17 and August 23 1939. Killearn diary, p. 77.
293. Hoare to W.W. Astor, May 13 1939 (i.e. a letter to his Private Secretary whose parents were beginning to demand that Churchill should return to office).
294. Cabinet Committee of May 19 1939, Cab 27/625.
295. Dalton diary, May 7 1939.
296. Cab 27(39) of May 10 and Hankey diary, August 23 1939.

297. E.g. Hoare saying at a meeting of editors and newspapers proprietors that there was much to be said on both sides, Francis Williams talking in Dalton diary, August 28 1939.
298. E.g. at Cabinet Committee of May 19 1939, Cab 27/625.
299. Amery diary, June 29 1939.
300. Dawson to Spender, July 14 1939, for lack of Cabinet support.
301. Zetland to Linlithgow, April 4 1939, Eur.D.609.
302. Chamberlain to Hilda, August 27 1939.
303. Chamberlain to Hilda, August 27 1939.
304. And also Halifax.
305. Cab 48(39) of September 2 at 4.15 p.m. Conclusion (2).
306. *Hansard* (351) col. 280 of September 2 1939.
307. Halifax in his introduction to Lloyd, *The British Case*, p. 9, talks about the 'stubborn wish of one man' preventing British efforts to preserve peace.
308. Nicolson diary, July 18 1939. Cf. Harvey to Halifax of August 26 1939.
309. Pritchett to Cartland, August 4 and Chamberlain to Ida, August 5 1939, for evidence that Chamberlain tried to remove Cartland from the King's Norton seat in Birmingham after Cartland made a personal attack on him in the House of Commons at the beginning of August.
310. Amery diary, August 1 and 2 1939. Nicolson diary and Nicolson to V. Sackville-West, August 2 1939.
311. Harvey diary, August 26, and Amery to Chamberlain, August 21 1939.
312. Amery diary, September 1 1939.
313. Duff Cooper diary, September 1 1939. For a similar feeling at the Privy Council, see Wallace diary, September 2 1939.
314. Amery diary, September 2 1939.
315. *Ibid*.
316. *Hansard* (351) col. 286 of September 2 1939 for speech by Wardlaw-Milne who had been appointed in order to keep the Edenites quiet (see Channon diary, May 4 1939).
317. Nicolson, Channon, Wallace, Amery and Duff Cooper diaries of September 2 1939. Hankey to his wife, September 3 1939.
318. I.e. Executive Committee of the PLP, NCL Executive and the National Executive of the Labour party.
319. See Chamberlain at Cab 46(39) of August 30 for Morrison spearheading the demand for the evacuation of London. Cf. National Labour Executive and Labour party declaration of September 2 1939, *Daily Herald*, September 2.
320. See Dalton diary, August 25 etc. 1939, for the Three Executives' decision to send a last message of 'friendship and warning to the German people' and the difficulty they had when the Foreign Office asked the BBC to stop this being done.
321. Dalton diary, August 29 1939.
322. For a junior minister believing that 'a puff would have brought the government down', see Crookshank diary, September 2 1939.

323. Boothby to Churchill, September 3 1939, quoting Greenwood.
324. Boothby in Duff Cooper diary, September 2 1939, Boothby to Churchill, September 3 1939.
325. Nicolson to V. Sackville-West, August 2 1939.
326. Churchill to Rothermere, July 19 1939.
327. Ironside diary, July 25 1939, reporting meeting with Churchill.
328. I.e. through Lloyd who saw Dalton daily, Dalton diary, August 31 1939.
329. Churchill to Chamberlain, August 30 1939 (not sent).
330. Churchill to Chamberlain, September 2 1939, NC 7/9/45.
331. Churchill to Chamberlain, September 2 1939, NC 7/9/45.
332. Duff Cooper diary, September 2 1939.
333. Churchill to Chamberlain, September 2 1939 midnight, NC 7/9/46.
334. *Ibid*. Duff Cooper diary September 2 1939.
335. Hore-Belisha diary, September 2 1939, lists himself, Simon, Elliot, de la Warr, Stanley, Wallace, Anderson, Colville, Burgin and Dorman-Smith. Inskip diary, September 3 1939, adds Brown. Wallace diary, September 2, does not list Burgin.
336. Simon diary, July 7 1935.
337. Hankey diary, February 24 1935.
338. *Ibid*.
339. Chamberlain diary, December 17 1935.
340. Cab 27/599 of February 17 1936. For examples of Simon being sensitive about his own policies by comparison with those of his successors, see Harvey diary, November 17 1937, and Amery diary, November 6 1937 and May 2 1938.
341. Simon to Baldwin, March 25 1936, PREM 1/194.
342. *Ibid*.
343. Simon to Chamberlain, September 23 1936.
344. Simon to Tweedsmuir, November 24 1937.
345. For all this see PREM 1/296, Simon diary and Cabs of 1938--9.
346. Cab 31(38) of July 6. Simon to Baldwin, March 25 1936, PREM 1/194, and to Chamberlain, April 17 1939, PREM 1/296.
347. Simon at Cab 13(38) of March 14.
348. Simon to Chatfield, April 17 1939, PREM 1/296. See also Simon, CP 118(39) of May 18 'Control of Expenditure'.
349. Simon diary, May 22 1938.
350. Cab 21(38) of April 27 and 26(38) of May 25, Cabinet Committee of April 7 1938, Cab 27/623.
351. Nicolson diary, September 1 and 9 1938, reporting Mabane and Bernays. Cf. Halifax to Chamberlain, August 26 [1938], for Simon forcing himself on Halifax's attention.
352. Meeting of Ministers of August 30 1938, Cab 23/94. Simon diary, August 31 1938.
353. Cab 37(38) of September 12.
354. Cab 38(38) of September 14.
355. Cab 39(38) of September 17.

356. Cab 40(38) of September 19.
357. Cf. Inskip diary, September 14 1938.
358. Meeting of Ministers, September 16 1938, Cab 27/646. For Anglo-French meetings, see Cab 27/646. Simon memorandum, n.d. before Godesberg, PREM 1/266A, fo. 137.
359. Cab 45(38) of September 25.
360. Cab 45(38) of September 26.
361. Cab 46(38) of September 27.
362. Hankey diary, September 27 1938.
363. Cf. Simon saying keep the emergency going after September 30 1938 in order to educate the public, CID of September 30 1938, Cab 16/189.
364. Morris-Jones to Simon, October 5 1938.
365. Cf. Chamberlain to Simon, December 16 1938.
366. E.g. Cabinet Committee of November 14 1938, Cab 27/624.
367. Cab 19(39) of April 10 for unilateral guarantees to Turkey and Greece being desirable because facilitating acceptance of the invasion of Albania. For the importance of not seeming to 'condone aggression', see Conference of Ministers of April 8 1939 in Cab 23/98.
368. Hore-Belisha diary, April 18 1939.
369. Hankey to R. Hankey, March 7 1937.
370. I.e. Simon became Chancellor of the Exchequer, Hore-Belisha War Minister and Burgin was brought into the Cabinet as Minister of Transport. Although Runciman was removed (to make way for Burgin), Liberals were greatly reassured when Oliver Stanley, who was in effect a Free Trader, replaced him as President of the Board of Trade.
371. Simon to Runciman, May 7 and 10 1937. There is supposed to have been a coolness between Runciman's and Simon's wives.
372. E.g. Mabane and Bernays, see above pp. 332–3. For Mabane being worried and Bernays agreeing with Crookshank about Eden, see Crookshank diary, February 21 1938.
373. See e.g. CP 118(39) of May 18 in Cab 24/287.
374. Channon diary, September 2 1939, and Crawford to Linlithgow, June 23 1939, for the view that he did. For evidence (second-hand) of Wilson thinking that Simon was thinking of the succession in the summer of 1938 see Bruce Lockhart diary, October 8 1938.
375. Hore-Belisha and Wallace diaries, September 2 1939.
376. *DBFP* third series, vol. VII, pp. 524–6.
377. Simon to Chamberlain [September 2 8.45 p.m. 1939]. Hoare-Belisha diary, September 2 1939.
378. Hore-Belisha and Wallace diaries, September 2 1939. Wheeler-Bennett, *Waverley*, pp. 229–32.
379. Cab 49(39) of September 2 at 11.30 p.m. Halifax MSS, A.410.3.10. has a long discussion in 1942 in which Halifax and Cadogan try to establish with E.L. Woodward and against Dahlerus (for the benefit of American opinion) that the British did try

to avoid war in September 1939 (where Dahlerus was claiming that they did not).

NOTES TO CHAPTER 12

1. Chamberlain to Hilda, September 10 1939.
2. Hankey, war policy memorandum of September 14 1939. But see also Cadogan diary, September 14, and Ironside diary, September 14 1939, for differing opinions.
3. Hankey, war policy memorandum of September 12 1939 for 'war of nerves'.
4. Chamberlain to Hilda, September 10 1939.
5. Chamberlain to Hilda, October 15 1939.
6. Smuts to Amery, October 11 1939. Chamberlain to Hilda, September 10, to Hilda, September 17, and to Ida, September 23 1939.
7. Chamberlain to Hilda, September 17 1939.
8. War Cab 18(39) of September 17.
9. Cadogan diary, September 25 1939, and War Cab 26(39) of September 25.
10. War Cab 66(39) of October 31 for rumours of this.
11. Chamberlain to Ida, September 23 1939.
12. A very great deal of this is to be found in Cab 65(1–6) and especially in War Cab 85(39) of November 17 1939, Cab 65/4. For Turkey see War Cab 2(39) of September 4, 3(39) of September 5, 5(39) of September 6 and 6(39) of September 6. For success with the Turks, see War Cab 22(39) of September 21. For the signature of the Anglo-Turkish treaty see War Cab 52(39) of October 19. See also Zetland to Linlithgow, October 2 1939. Plans were also made, after co-operation with the Rumanian government, to destroy the Rumanian oilfields in the event of invasion there (see especially War Cab 69(39) of November 3 65/4). The object, in pushing ahead with munitions and military preparations and increasing the air force to the point at which it was no longer possible to lose command of the air, was that, when the air defences were complete (with radar), Germans would see that an air offensive could begin (Chamberlain to Churchill, September 16 and to Ida, October 8 1939. War Cab 39(39) of September 19, Cab 65/3. Chamberlain to Hilda, September 17, and to Ida, September 23 and October 8 1939. See also Hankey, War Policy memorandum of September 12 1939).
13. Chamberlain to Ida, September 23, and to Hilda, October 1 1939.
14. War Cab 11(39) of September 11, Cab 65/3. War Cab 47(39) of October 14 Cab 65/3.
15. Chamberlain to Hilda, October 15 1939.
16. Chamberlain to Ida, October 8 1939.
17. Cab 25(39) of September 24. For the decision to drop leaflets and criticism of it see War Cab 1(39) of September 3, 8(39) of September 8 and 17(39) of September 16 1939. Also War Cab

28(39) of September 26, 34(39) of October 2 and 43(39) of October 9.

18. Chamberlain to Hilda, September 17, and to Ida, November 19 1939. Inskip diary, October 5 1939. War Cab 45(39) of October 12 but cf. War Cab 56(39) of October 22 for the Deputy Chief of the Imperial General Staff saying waterlogged terrain making advance unlikely. Cf. War Cab 100(39) of December 1 Cab 65/4.

19. Chamberlain to Ida, November 5 1939.

20. Chamberlain to Hilda, September 17 1939.

21. Chamberlain to Ida, October 22 1939.

22. Chamberlain to Hilda, October 28 1939.

23. Chamberlain to Ida, November 5 1939.

24. Hankey, war policy memorandum of September 12 1939 which, Hankey records, received Chamberlain's approval.

25. Chamberlain to Brocket, February 2 1940, PREM 1/443.

26. Halifax at War Cab 40(39) of October 7. Chamberlain in *Hansard* (351) col. 292 of September 3, and to Ida, November 5 1939.

27. Chamberlain to Hilda, September 10, and to Ida, September 23 1939. War Cab 12(39) of September 11 (also for Chamberlain hoping to get the French to agree that the terms should be as in Halifax's Chatham House speech, i.e. 'respect for international obligations and...the renouncing of force as an instrument of policy'). War Cab 14(39) of September 13 for the French agreeing on the object of 'putting an end to Hitlerism'.

28. For the Pope see War Cab 107(39) of December 7.

29. War Cab 75(39) of November 8, 78(39) of November 10 and 79(39) of November 11.

30. Supported by Mottistone, Sempill, Harmsworth, Rushcliffe, Darnley, Tavistock, Mount Temple, Addington and Sir Philip Gibbs (For Lords Aberconway and Holden and the Bishops of Birmingham, Bristol and Chicester, see Anderson, p. 153). For the peace movement see PREM 1/443, 1/379, 1/249 and 1/380 and FO 800/317, 325, 316, 318, 309 and War Cabs 40(39) of October 7 and 49(39) of October 16. See also Nicolson diary, December 6 1939.

31. For this paragraph, see Sempill to Halifax, October 3 1939, FO 800/317, Culverwell in 1922 Committee Minute-book for October 4 1939 and A.M. Ramsay in *loc. cit.* for October 11 1939. See also FO 800/315, fols. 243—8, and Halifax to Brocket, July 13 1939, FO 800/316, for Halifax's rebuke and their denials.

32. Channon diary, October 11 1939.

33. For Beaverbrook trying to persuade the Duke of Windsor about a peace campaign see Chamberlain to Ida, January 27 1940. For Beaverbrook giving up the peace campaign see Monckton to Rucker, March 25 1940, PREM 1/443. For the remarkable public reaction to Lloyd George's peace speech of October 4, see Lloyd George MSS G/50—G/60.

34. Chamberlain to Ida, October 8 1939.

35. Chamberlain to Ida, September 23 and October 8 1939.

36. See e.g. *Hansard* (352) of October 12 1939, cols. 563–8.

37. For the decisions about the peace speech see War Cab 40(39) of October 7 and for the statement of October 12 1939, see War Cab 45(39) of October 12 Cab 65/3. Chamberlain to Ida, November 5 1939. War Cab 51(39) of October 26. Pownall diary, December 17 1939. For refusal to meet Dominions requests, see War Cab 45(39) of October 12. For the War Cabinet decision to have nothing to do with peace overtures, see War Cab 35(39) of October 3. But for Halifax and the others thinking that a peace aims statement in general terms would reassure moderate Germans, see War Cab 42 and 43(39) of October 9 and 10.

38. For the Swedish minister's reports being based on rumour, see Hankey to Chamberlain, November 21 1939, FO 800/317. For Rauschning's information being out of date, see Dalton diary, November 21 1939. For J.B. Mooney of General Motors reporting that Goering wanted a negotiated peace, see War Cab 61(39) of October 26, Cab 65/3. See also Halifax's anonymous source in War Cab 3(40) of January 4, Cab 65/11. For Darnley, Tavistock, J.L. Bryans and the Duke of Wurtemburg as busybodies or cranks, see Halifax memorandum of January 23 1940, FO 800/318. Cadogan diary December 13 1939, January 23 and February 28 1940.

39. Halifax at War Cab 39(39) of October 6, 43(39) of October 10, 45(39) of October 12, 48(39) of October 15 and 49(39) of October 16, all Cab 65/3.

40. For von Papen making these approaches through the Dutch minister in Ankara (where he was German Ambassador) see Chamberlain to Ida, October 8 1939. Halifax memorandum, December 12 1939, FO 800/317. War Cab 34(39) of October 2, Cab 65/3.

41. Sargent memorandum of February 17 1940, FO 800/318. For doubt about Thyssen's *bona fides*, see War Cab 25(40) of January 27. War Cab 16(40) of January 17 and Cab 65/11. Osborne to Halifax, January 12, February 7 and 19 1940, all FO 800/318. Halifax to Chamberlain, February 13 1940. Cadogan diary, October 28 1939, has Hohenlohe and A.N. Other making approaches via Vansittart which were taken seriously (Halifax to Chamberlain, November 20 [1939] has Hohenlohe being promising. See also Christie MSS 180/1/28 and 30). For all this see also Deutsch, pp. 102–66.

42. For his view of von Papen, whom he had known at Lausanne, as 'hysterical and unreliable', see War Cab 34(39) of October 2, War Cab 35(39) of October 5 and War Cab 38(39) of October 5, Cab 65/3.

43. Chamberlain to Ida, November 5 1939.

44. Cadogan diary, October 23 and November 1, 2, 3, 9 and 15 1939 Chamberlain to Ida, November 5 1939. Cadogan, memorandum of November 16 1939, NC 8/29/2.

45. See e.g. Halifax in War Cab 57(39) of October 23, Cab 65/3 and in War Cab 62(39) of October 27, Cab 65/3. War Cab 79(39) of

November 11, Cab 65/4. War Cab 93(39) of November 24, Cab 65/4. Cf. Cadogan diary, *passim* September/October 1939. Halifax at War Cab 42(39) of October 9. For Churchill see War Cab 108(39) of December 8, etc. etc. etc. See also Dawson diary, September 19 and 24, October 5 and 23 1939, and Chatfield to Lothian, September 26 and November 27 1939.

46. Chamberlain to Ida, December 3 1939.
47. For Halifax taking reports of depression with a pinch of salt see War Cab 97(39) of November 28. But for Hitler as a 'man on the defensive' see Halifax at War Cab 28(40) of January 31. Cf. War Cab 100(39) of December 1, Cab 65/4, and War Cab 1(40) of January 2 65/11 for Benes and Intelligence sources reporting German generals submitting their views on the need for a negotiated settlement. Chamberlain to Hilda, February 9 and 25, and to Ida, March 16 1940.
48. See e.g. report of his interview with Sumner Welles in War Cab 67(40) of March 13. Chamberlain to Archbishop Lang, December 27 1939 and Lady Astor to Lothian, November 23 1939, reporting Chamberlain addressing dinner at Carlton Club.
49. Chamberlain to Ida, April 13 1940.
50. Chamberlain to Hilda, April 20 1940.
51. Chamberlain to Hilda, May 4 1940.
52. Chamberlain to Ida, December 3 1939. For Halifax saying there would be no break unless Germany suffered military reverses, see War Cab 78(39) of November 10.
53. Hankey, war policy memorandum of September 12 1939.
54. Cadogan diary, January 18 1940, for alternatives. See War Cab 66(40) of March 12 for the possibility of bombing the Caucasus oilfields as a way of draining both Russia and Germany of oil and for the danger of Russian approaches towards Afghanistan and consideration being given to the idea of sending a force there to protect India.
55. The quotation is Churchill's. For Thyssen's views about this question being explained to the Cabinet, see War Cab 122(39) of December 22, Cab 65/4. For COS see War Cab 1(40) of January 2, Cab 65/11.
56. For the first Cabinet mention of this by Churchill, See War Cab 31(39) of September 29.
57. War Cab 99(39) of November 30, 116(39) of December 15 and 117(39) of December 17.
58. War Cab 122(39) of December 22.
59. The Norwegians objected too but the dominant fear was of Sweden in view of the opposition the Swedes might raise if upset to the larger object of taking Gallivare (see Chamberlain at War Cab 9(40) of January 11, Cab 65/11 and at War Cab 10(40) of January 12, Cab 65/11). For the Dominions see e.g. Eden to Chamberlain, February 28 1940, PREM 1/408.
60. War Cab 7(40) of January 9, Cab 65/11. War Cab 55(40) of February 29 1940.

61. And perhaps Trondheim, Stavanger and Bergen.
62. See Military Co-ordination Committee of December 20 1939
     (Cab 83/1), and War Cab 122(39) of December 22, Cab 65/4.
     Ironside diary, December 21, 22 and 25 1939 and January 6 and
     12, and February 5 and 18 1940. Cadogan diary, December 22
     1939, January 8, 11 and 12 1940. See also War Cab 18(40) of
     January 19, Cab 65/11 and War Cab 50(40) of February 23.
63. Hankey, war policy memorandum of September 29 1939.
64. Halifax at War Cab 18(39) of September 17.
65. War Cab 43(39) of October 10.
66. Chamberlain at War Cab 19(39) of September 18. Chamberlain to
     Hilda, October 28, to Tweedsmuir, September 25, and to Ida,
     September 23, all 1939. Inskip diary, September 28 1939, for
     Halifax saying the same. Cadogan diary, November 13 1939, for
     Halifax, Cadogan and Sargent describing the anti-Comintern idea
     as Sargent's.
67. War Cab 8(39) of September 8, 12(39) of September 11, 35(39)
     of October 3, 23(39) of September 22, 39(39) of October 6,
     52(39) of October 19, 95(39) of November 26, 99(39) of Novem-
     ber 30, 107(39) of December 7, 115(39) of December 14. War
     Cab 120(39) of December 20 for Chamberlain restraining the
     French at the Supreme War Council. War Cab 62(39) of Octo-
     ber 27, Cab 65/3. War Cab 71(39) of November 5 for Ciano's suc-
     cess in his recent *coup* but not really making a difference to
     foreign policy. Harvey diary, September 6 1939. Cadogan diary
     of September 7 1939. Loraine's letters to Halifax in FO 800/319
     and 320 are the chief source for British estimates of the Italian
     situation. See also Chamberlain to Hilda, September 17 1939.
68. Chamberlain to Ida, December 3 1939. Pownall diary, Decem-
     ber 17 1939 recording Chamberlain talking by the fire and
     smoking pipes at GHQ, BEF.
69. By virtue of Finland being the only state to repay its war debts.
70. War Cab 101(39) of December 2 and 100(39) of December 1.
     Chamberlain to Ida, December 3 and to Hilda, December 10
     1939.
71. For the decision to ask the Chiefs of Staff to report on the
     desirability, or otherwise, of the United Kingdom declaring war
     on Russia in the event of an attack on Finland, see War Cab
     57(39) of October 23. For Chiefs of Staff saying that Britain and
     France could *not* undertake a war against Russia, see War Cab
     67(39) of November 1. War Cab 91(39) of November 22 for the
     impossibility of assisting any of the Scandinavian governments in
     the event of German or Russian invasion. For Halifax saying that
     we have been highly tolerant to Russia but cannot press the Finns
     to make unacceptable concessions see War Cab 85(39) of Novem-
     ber 16. For absolute refusal to go to war, even at Mannerheim's
     request, see War Cab 47(40) of February 20, Cab 65/11. See also
     Zetland to Linlithgow, October 2 and 4 1939, Eur.D.609 11.
72. For military aid see War Cab 103(39) of December 4 and 104(39)

of December 5. For the expulsion of Russia from the League, see *The Times*, December 15 1939.

73. Chamberlain to Ida, December 3 1939.

74. Including especially petrol, see Halifax to Amery, December 11 1939, Chamberlain to Ida, March 2 1940, and Hankey at War Cab 48(40) of February 21.

75. E.g. War Cab 11(40) of January 13.

76. See War Cab 2(40) of January 3, Cab 65/11.

77. See e.g. War Cab 8(40) and 9(40) of January 10 and 11 and War Cab 13(40) and 16(40) of January 14 and 17 for the War Cabinet wanting Ciano encouraged to send Italian volunteers to Finland.

78. Halifax at War Cab 21(40) of January 23. Ironside diary, December 25 1939. Chamberlain to Hilda, December 30 1939. War Cab 3(40) of January 4, 5(40) of January 6 and 10(40) of January 12.

79. See War Cab 6(40) of January 8, Cab 65/11.

80. Perhaps the best example of this belief is Hoare 'almost offer-[ing]' to go as British Minister in Sweden, where he knew the King, in December1939, on the ground that Finland should be helped as soon as possible (Hoare to Chamberlain, December 26 [1939]).

81. War Cab 35(40) of February 7, Cab 65/11.

82. War Cab 31(40) of February 2, Cab 65/11. Cadogan diary, February 5 1940. War Cabinet 26(40) of January 29.

83. Ironside and Cadogan diaries and War Cab (including Confidential Annexes), December 1939–March 1940.

84. Chamberlain to Ida, March 16 1940.

85. Halifax, memorandum of conversation between Chamberlain and Welles, March 13 1940, FO 800/326. Chamberlain to Ida, March 16 1940.

86. Chamberlain to Ida, March 16 1940. War Cab 68(40) of March 14, Cab 65/12.

87. Halifax at War Cab 72(40) of March 19. Hankey, war policy memorandum of March 18 1940.

88. War Cab 72(40) of March 19, but War Cab 78(40) of April 1 for putting it off.

89. War Cab 70(40) of March 16 and 71(40) of March 18. Halifax at War Cab 72(40) of March 19. Cadogan, March 12 1940, and Campbell to Halifax, March 23 1940, FO 800/312. See also Reynaud to Chamberlain and Supreme War Council Agenda of March 28 1940 in PREM 1/437.

90. War Cab 77(40) of March 29, Cab 65/12. War Cab 72(40) of March 19, 76(40) of March 27 and 82(40) of April 5. Cadogan diary, March 28 1940, including a decision to occupy part of Norway if Hitler retaliated. For the Supreme War Cabinet meeting of March 28 see War Cab 77(40) of March 29. For the original decision to mine the Rhine, see War Cab 61(40) of March 6, Cab 65/12.

91. War Cab 84(40) of April 8, Cab 65/12. War Cab 78(40) of April

1. War Cab 82(40) of April 5 showing Churchill going especially to see Daladier to overcome his opposition but being convinced that Daladier was right about the Rhine project. Cf. Cadogan diary, April 1 and 7, and Ironside diary, April 2 1940.

92. War Cab 82(40) of April 5, Cab 65/12, and War Cab 83(40) of April 6.

93. War Cab 84(40) of April 8, Cab 65/12.

94. Chamberlain to Hilda, April 20 1940. Ironside diary, April 12 and 20 1940. Cadogan diary, April 13, 14 and 16 1940. War Cab 90(40) of April 12 and 98(40) of April 20, both Cab 65/12.

95. Cadogan diary, April 20 and 26, and Ironside diary, April 26 1940. Military Co-ordination Committee of April 28 1940, Cab 83. War Cab 106(40) of April 28, Cab 65/12.

96. War Cab 113(40) of May 6, Cab 65/11. Ironside diary, May 6 1940.

97. Chamberlain to Hilda, April 20 1940. War Cab 94(40) of April 16 and 96(40) of April 18.

98. I.e. by Churchill, see War Cab 90(40) of April 12, Cab 65/12, and by the Chiefs of Staff, see Chief of Air Staff at War Cab 95(40) of April 17, Cab 65/12.

99. Chamberlain to Hilda, April 20 1940. See War Cab 102(40) of April 24, Cab 65/12, for the hope that the Germans would find it so difficult to send a land force to relieve Trondheim while it was under siege, that Hitler would facilitate a British advance from Narvik to Gallivare by violating Swedish territory in order to get his forces to Trondheim.

100. War Cab 109(40) of May 1, Cab 65/11. Chamberlain to Ida, April 27, and to Hilda, May 4 1940.

101. See e.g. War Secretary at War Cab 100(40) of April 22, Cab 65/11.

102. Chamberlain to Ida, May 11 1940.

103. *Ibid.*

104. War Cab 113(40) of May 6.

105. For the acute uncertainty about Mussolini's intentions, see War Cab 105–18(40) between April 27 and May 10. See also Loraine to Halifax, May 4 1940, FO 800/320.

106. The decision to bomb the Ruhr on that night was actually abandoned by Chamberlain at his last Cabinet meeting (his third on that day) at 4.30 on May 10. There had however been extensive discussion in the previous two days about the desirability of doing so and the question had been raised and, in principle, virtually decided on April 21 (i.e. the decision to bomb the Ruhr if the Germans invaded Holland or Belgium). For all this see War Cab 99–119(40).

NOTES TO CHAPTER 13

1. For the last two paragraphs, see Hankey diary, August 25 and September 27 1938, to Chamberlain, September 30 1938, and to Phipps, February 21 1938 and April 4 1939. See also Chatfield to Lothian, September 26 and November 27 1939 and March 14 1940.

2. See PREM 1/384 for Hankey's part in constructing the ministerial machine and for the pre-war preparations (which began in late 1938) for a War Cabinet.

3. Ironside diary, *passim* September 1939 onwards, is a good source for Ironside's belief that there was too little interest in the land war and no real determination. Cf. Hore-Belisha diary, especially September 22 1939, for the argument that the war could be lost in France.

4. For Poles see War Cab 2(39) of September 2. For Finns see Lady Astor to Lothian, January 11 or 12 1940. For Scandinavia, see Dawson diary, April 11 1940.

5. E.g. Dawson diary, October 24 1939.

6. Cadogan diary, November 1 and 3 1939.

7. Dugdale diary, January to March 1940.

8. War Cab 58(39) of October 24 and War Cab 68(39) of November 2 in Cab 65/4.

9. War Cab 59 and 60(39) of October 25, 73(39) of November 6 and 30(40) of February 2. Cf. Halifax to Linlithgow, March 31 1940, for Simon being at least as unyielding.

10. Ironside diary, January 2 1940. War Cab 12(40) and 13(40) of January 14 and War Cab 14(40) of January 15, Cab 65/11. For the Keyes mission and Churchill's involvement, see PREM 1/401.

11. War Cab 15(39) of September 14. For British doubts about the French forward strategy in the Balkans, see War Cab 21(39) of September 20.

12. Wallace diary, October 25 1939.

13. War Cab 63(39) of October 25.

14. Wallace diary, October 24 1939.

15. For lines of supply etc. see Wallace diary, October 23 and 25 1939.

16. E.g. as Ironside did, Ironside diary, September 7 1939.

17. War Cab 24(39) of September 23. For the appointment of the Land Forces Committee to investigate the possible size of the Land Forces see War Cab 6(39) of September 6. For Chamberlain urging competing air needs, see War Cab 9(39) of September 9 and *passim* War Cab 1939—40. Chamberlain to Churchill, September 16, and Churchill to Chamberlain, September 15 and 18 1939.

18. Cadogan diary, February 4 1940 and Loraine to Halifax, May 4 1940, FO 800/320, for Churchill (and Chamberlain) wanting to put off any declaration of war against Italy.

19. Chamberlain to Ida, October 8 1939.

20. For a good example see Churchill to Chamberlain, November 18 1939, and vice versa, November 19, PREM 1/330.

21. Chamberlain to Ida, November 19 1939 and January 27 1940. Hore-Belisha diary, September 9 1939.

22. For Churchill suggesting a meeting of War Cabinet ministers without advisers and secretaries, see Churchill to Chamberlain, September 21 1939. For it being held, and for others being held, see Cab 65/1, fo. 154 of September 26 and Cab 65/4. fo. 314 of October 23 1939.

23. Memorandum of October 3 1939, NC 7/9/63, and to Ida, October 8 1939.

24. Inskip diary, October 16 1939. Hoare to Lothian, November 12 1939. There is a lot about this in War Cab (39) especially War Cab 74(39) of November 7, Cab 65/4. Wallace diary, November 8 1939.

25. Chamberlain to Hilda, February 9 1940.

26. For Chamberlain definitely directing the Cabinet, see Cab 55(40) of February 29. Chamberlain to Ida, March 2 1940.

27. Amery diary, October 10 1939, for Chatfield saying so. For relations between Churchill, Chamberlain, Chatfield and the Chiefs of Staff see Chatfield, vol. II, pp. 179–88 and Ismay, pp. 108–15.

28. Chamberlain to Ida, March 2 1940.

29. For an example see War Cabinet 18(40) of January 19.

30. E. Bridges, memorandum of April 25 1940, PREM 1/404.

31. Chamberlain to Hilda, April 6 1940.

32. E.g. his niggling about the disposition of the Expeditionary Force for Norway, as though he was 'a company commander running a small operation to cross a bridge', Ironside diary, April 14 1940. Chamberlain to Ida, April 13 1940.

33. Chamberlain to Ida, April 13 1940.

34. Wilson memo of April 25 1940 (PREM 1/404), also reports Hankey, Simon and Wood complaining.

35. For the setting up of the MCC, see War Cab 66(39) of October 31.

36. Chamberlain to Hilda, April 20 1940. E. Bridges, memo of April 25 1940, PREM 1/404.

37. Chamberlain to Hilda, April 20 1940.

38. E.g. Churchill to Salisbury, December 19 1939.

39. Dalton diary, October 12 1939, for an example of Lloyd buttering up the Labour party.

40. Churchill to Chamberlain, September 29 and November 14 1939 and January 31 and April 1 1940. Cf. Londonderry to Chamberlain, April 1 1940. Churchill seems not to have conveyed Boothby's and Macmillan's offers to serve (for which see Boothby to Churchill, September 7 1939).

41. Nicolson, Channon and Amery diaries, all April 11 1940.

42. See Keyes to Churchill, April 26, 29 and 30, to Chamberlain, May 1, and to his wife, April 16 and 17, all Keyes MSS, all 1940.

43. Cadogan diary, April 20 1940.

44. Cadogan diary, April 24 1940. Ironside diary, April 27 1940. War Cab 105(40) of April 27, Cab 65/12.
45. Ironside diary, April 26 1940, recording Churchill talking to Ironside.
46. Chamberlain to Ida, April 27 1940.
47. Churchill to Chamberlain, April 24 1940.
48. Nicolson diary, April 23 1940. Channon diary, April 25 1940. Salisbury to Swinton, April 20 1940.
49. Hoare to Beaverbrook, October 1 1939. Wallace diary, February 1 1940.
50. Hacking, Conservative Party chairman, in 1922 Committee Minute Book of November 15 1939. Wallace diary, November 15 1939.
51. E.g. the Simon budget, see Channon diary, September 27 1939. Chamberlain to Hilda, October 1 1939.
52. For an example see Wallace diary, February 21 1940.
53. See e.g. Halifax to Chamberlain, February 10 1940, PREM 1/408.
54. Chamberlain to Ida, September 23 1939.
55. Especially from Alexander.
56. Memorandum of All-Party Parliamentary Action Group of September 4 1939.
57. Stevenson diary, March 24 1935.
58. Rathbone to Lloyd George, September 15, and Lloyd George to Rathbone, September 16 1939.
59. R.D. Denman.
60. I.e. Roberts, Mander, Foot and Horabin.
61. T.E. Harvey.
62. R.R. Stokes.
63. See e.g. Rose Rosenberg to MacDonald, February 24 1933, for Clement Davies keeping MacDonald informed.
64. For all this see Clement Davies to Lloyd George, January 25 1935.
65. The Davies Group had three main sub-committees — a foreign policy group under Mander, a home defence group under Mrs Tate and an economics group under Boothby. Of these the economics group seems to have been the most effective, linked as it was through Salter to Keynes, Beveridge and Layton (Boothby to Lloyd George, November 2 1939) and directed at points where government machinery was reckoned to be weakest. Three of them were prominent in the delegation Chamberlain received on the subject in November 1937 (PREM 1/213 October 31 and November 2 1937).
66. E.g. Boothby, Rathbone, Stokes and Salter.
67. For Boothby see Boothby to Lloyd George, September 29 1939. For Salter see Salter to Finney (enclosure) of November 1 1939 (G/141/44/1). For Stokes see R.R. Stokes, Circulated Letter of October 4 1939 (G/19/3/4), Stokes to Halifax, October 19 1939 (FO 800/325) and Stokes memorandum in Stokes to Lloyd George, March 3 1940 (G/19/3/6). For Rathbone see Rathbone letter in *Manchester Guardian*, October 5 1939, and 'Notes on a

possible settlement and war peace aims', October 19 1939 (G/16/7/6 & 7).

68. Nicolson diary, December 14 1939.
69. Davies, interview in *Western Mail*, December 16 1939, for the Davies platform.
70. See above p. 344.
71. Amery diary, September 4 and 5 1939.
72. Amery diary, September 5 1939.
73. Amery diary, October 12 1939.
74. Amery diary, January 5 1940.
75. Chamberlain to Amery, November 30 1939.
76. Amery to Halifax October 9 1939 (Amery MSS) and October 21 1939 (FO 800/325). Amery to Churchill, October 10 1939, and to Croft, December 2 1939.
77. Amery diary, September 30 1939.
78. See War Cab 24(40) of January 26.
79. E.g. George Woodcock. Amery diary, October 29 1939, January 9 and 11 and February 26 1940. See also PREM 1/438.
80. Cartland, for example, at one time, see Nicolson diary, September 20 1939.
81. Wolmer to Churchill, September 6 1939.
82. See e.g. Harvey diary, March 30 1940, for J.P.L. Thomas talking.
83. Cf. Nicolson diary, September 17 1939.
84. It also held meetings at which it entertained, among others, Lloyd, Trenchard, Vansittart, Astor and Hore-Belisha whose dismissal, however, was welcomed. See Nicolson diary, January 7 1940, and J.P.L. Thomas to Baldwin, January 7 1940, for Hore-Belisha having been dismissed because he 'told lies'.
85. See e.g. Trenchard memo of April 13 1940 in Astor MSS, box 43, fol. 824.
86. Nicolson diary, December 14 1939.
87. For Finland see Wallace diary, March 19 1940.
88. Cab 9(36) of February 24.
89. I.e. Cranborne, Ormsby-Gore, Wolmer, Selborne and Cecil of Chewode.
90. Salisbury to Baldwin, August 4 1938.
91. Ormsby-Gore to Baldwin, May 24 1935 and December 19 1938. Cranborne to Halifax, December 10 and 19 1939, FO 800/322. Selborne in Amery diary, December 28 1938. Salisbury to Halifax, October 28 1939, FO 800/325. Selborne to his wife, May 16 1933 (MS Selborne 107) and May 25, May 26 and July 25 1938 (MS Selborne 108). Cecil to Baring, February 8 1935, Add. MSS 51170. Butler to Brabourne, July 27 1934, for Ormsby-Gore after the assassination of Dollfuss.
92. Salisbury to Cecil, August 2 1938.
93. Nicolson diary, April 7 1937.
94. Salisbury to Selborne, December 9 1938, MS Selborne 7.
95. Salisbury to Selborne, November 17 1938, MS Selborne 7.

96. Salisbury to Selborne, November 14 1938, MS Selborne 7.
97. Salisbury to Selborne, November 17 1938, MS Selborne 7.
98. Salisbury to Selborne, December 9 1938, MS Selborne 7.
99. Salisbury to Selborne, September 5 1939, MS Selborne 7.
100. Salisbury to Halifax, September 22, 1939 FO 800/317 and note by Chamberlain. Cf. 'certain sorts of weakness are a form of moral selfishness', Salisbury to Davidson, October 9 1939.
101. For an affirmation of belief in an eventual world state, see Attlee to Tom Attlee, January 11 1933.
102. E.g. Cranborne talking, in Headlam diary, April 30 1935, and Cranborne to Noel-Buxton in Anderson, pp. 152–3.
103. Nicolson diary, January 17 1940.
104. Cranborne, Cecil, Wolmer and Salisbury.
105. Nicolson diary, April 23 1940.
106. Wallace diary, September 25 1939.
107. For a public example see Lady Astor to Lothian, November 23 1939. For another in the House of Commons, see Dawson diary, October 12 1939.
108. Hankey diary, August 23 1939. Hankey to his wife, September 3 1939, and to Robin Hankey, October 15 1938.
109. For Grigg being involved in the East European deal in the summer of 1939 (above pp. 299–300), see Ball to Wilson, September 16 1939, PREM 1/379. For Stanhope's blunder and the newspaper campaign against him, see Hoare to W.W. Astor, June 12 1939. See also Grigg, pp. 54–69, for a statement of the need for economic rapprochement. Avon, *Facing the Dictators*, p. 580. Cf. Nicolson diary, April 22 1939.
110. Macmillan, for example, made way for Reith because he had bungled the Ministry of Information. Morrison made way for Woolton when he bungled the Ministry of Food. Gilmour, who returned to office in October 1939 in order to set up the Ministry of Shipping (four and a half years after he had been removed from the Home Office), would have been removed again if his death in March 1940 had not made this unnecessary (Chamberlain to Ida, March 30 1940. Wallace diary, March 29 and 30 1940).

It is true that Hore-Belisha was removed from the War Office because he had been made a special target of Conservative criticism (Wallace diary says the Secret Session of December 13 was really aimed at the War Office) and had mishandled relations with Gort. But Chamberlain had decided, despite his widespread unpopularity, to send him to the Ministry of Information (which he would have accepted). He would have left him at the War Office, if he had known in advance that he would be compelled, at short notice, to offer him the Board of Trade (which Hore-Belisha refused) after Halifax had been persuaded that a Jew should not have charge of the propaganda machine. Chamberlain says he consulted Wood, Hadley (the editor of the *Sunday Times*), Camrose, Attlee, Hoare, Simon, Churchill and the Ambassador in the United States and that nobody really disapproved until Halifax, who had more or less approved when asked some days before, suddenly said, on Cadogan's advice, two hours before Chamberlain was to tell Hore-Belisha, that he disapproved strongly. Chamberlain then offered Hore-Belisha the Board of Trade, *which Duncan had already accepted*, and was told by Hore-Belisha, after he had consulted newspaper editors and proprietors, that he would not take it unless he had control of some aspects of financial policy (Chamberlain to Ida, January 7 1940 and Chamberlain's comments, NC 8/32/1. Cadogan diary, January 3, 4, 6 and 8 1940).

111. At the Ministry of Information and Board of Trade respectively.
112. Chamberlain to Ida, December 20 1939. Amery diary, December 13, and Nicolson diary, December 14 1939.
113. Margesson talking in Wallace diary, November 30 1940.
114. For Chamberlain offering reassurance in the Finland debate see Nicolson and Channon diaries, March 19 1940.
115. Chamberlain to Hilda, April 6 1940.
116. Cf. Camrose in Pownall diary, April 4 1940. Eden in Nicolson diary, April 3 1940, for this being Chamberlain's way of beginning to edge Hoare out.
117. Channon diary of April 25 1940. Wedgwood (an admirer) to Churchill, April 30 1940. Nicolson diary, April 30 and May 1 1940.
118. Cf. Ironside diary of April 27 1940 for the War Cabinet and public opinion. See also Zetland to Linlithgow, May 2 1940 in Zetland, p. 294.
119. Channon diary, April 25 1940, quoting Dunglass.
120. Chamberlain to Ida, April 27 1940.
121. Chamberlain to Hilda, May 4, and Ironside diary, April 28 1940.
122. Ironside diary, May 1 1940. Chamberlain note of April 30 1940, PREM 1/404.
123. Chamberlain to Hilda, May 4 1940.
124. I.e. given him in virtue of his Privy Councillor's oath, Wallace diary, May 1 1940.
125. Silvester quoting unnamed MP in Lloyd George MSS G/24/1/128. Channon diary, May 8 1940. Dalton diary, May 8 1940 and May 9. Nicolson diary, quoting Hall, May 9 1940. Hailsham to Chamberlain, May 14 1940. For Sir Ralph Glyn 'of all people' see Headlam diary, May 8 1940.
126. E.g. Bracken, Churchill, Crookshank, Eden, O'Neill (see Zetland to Linlithgow, May 2 1940 in Zetland, p. 294), Stanley, Thomas, Grigg (see Amery diary, April 28 1940).
127. For an analysis see *The Times*, May 10 1940.
128. See e.g. W.S. Liddall to Chamberlain, May 13 1940, and P.J. Hannon to Chamberlain, May 7 1940, both in NC 13/17. See also J.S. Crooke to Chamberlain, November1938—May 1940, in NC 13/13/79--84.
129. Amery, Nicolson and Dalton diaries, May 8 1940.
130. Channon diary, May 9 1940 for Dunglass saying so. See also

Churchill, *The Second World War*, I, p. 596.
131. E.g. Reith, p. 382.
132. It was thought likely that Bevin and Morrison would be the most effective members of a war-time government, and there were suggestions, to which Morrison responded, that he might become Prime Minister. For Morrison see Peake's talk with Morrison of December 2 1939, FO 800/325. Crozier, interview with Morrison, March 29 1940, and Harvey diary, April 26 1940. See also Silvester note for Lloyd George, May 5 or 6 1940, Lloyd George MSS G/24/1/128. For Sinclair and the Secret Session see Amery diary, December 13 1939.
133. Amery diary, April 29 1940.
134. Nicolson diary, April 30 1940.
135. For Lloyd George being thought likely at the Salisbury group see Nicolson diary April 30, May 1 and May 3 1940.
136. Rhodes James, p. 292. Lloyd George to *The Times*, April 2 1936.
137. Jones diary, May 7 1940. For Lady Astor being very hostile to the government because Waldorf Astor had not been asked to join see Wallace diary, February 21 1940. For Garvin see Wallace diary, May 6 1940. For David Astor saying Chamberlain must go see Wallace diary, September 25 1939. For Astor see Lady Astor to Lothian, April 11 and May 8 1940.
138. Harmsworth to Lloyd George, April 26 [1940].
139. See Cripps to Lloyd George, May 5 1940, and enclosure. The letter that appeared in the *Mail* on May 6 suggested that Halifax should be Prime Minister and Attlee Chancellor but did not mention Cripps. It was followed on May 7 by a letter from Robert Cary, Unionist MP for Eccles, which suggested Churchill and Halifax as Prime Minister and Deputy Prime Minister and, while including Labour leaders, included neither Attlee nor Cripps. On May 9 the *Mail* demanded Lloyd George as Prime Minister and Churchill as Deputy Prime Minister but did not mention Attlee or Cripps. For Lloyd George's 'high thinking and modest living' see *Daily Mail* of May 10.
140. Lloyd George to Harmsworth, April 30 1940.
141. For Lloyd George expecting more disasters, see Boothby in Dugdale diary, May 7 1940, and *Sunday Pictorial*, April 28 and May 5 1940.
142. Amery diary, May 1 1940, quoting Clement Davies quoting Lloyd George. Boothby to Churchill, May 9 1940. Channon diary, May 9 1940.
143. Wheeler-Bennett, pp. 443–4.
144. E.g. Dalton in Dalton diary, May 8 1940 and Dalton and Morrison in Butler to Halifax May 9 1940, Halifax MSS. But for Greenwood saying that Conservatives must decide between Churchill and Halifax see Amery diary, May 2 1940. Halifax was not supported very strongly by the Watching Committee who found him 'tired and distressed' when they saw him on the 29th. He and Churchill divided the Eden group between them, Amery diary,

May 1 1940. Cf. Lady Astor to Lothian, January 11 or 12 1940.

145. Churchill, *The Second World War*, pp. 596–8. Halifax, p. 220.

146. Attlee had decided by May 1, see Dalton diary, May 1 1940. Amery diary, May 2 1940. Cf. Wallace diary March 19 1940.

147 Who had destroyed what was left of his reputation by attacking the government from which he had been removed.

148. Amery diary, May 2 1940.

149. Amery diary, May 7, and Nicolson diary, May 8 1940.

150. Wallace, Amery and Nicolson diaries, May 9 1940. *Hansard* (360) col. 1435 of May 9 1940. For Amery as a bore, see Dunglass reported in Chamberlain to Hilda, April 10 1937.

151. Nicolson and Amery diaries, May 9, and Boothby to Churchill, May 9 1940.

152. Amery and Nicolson diaries, May 10 1940.

153. Amery diary, May 10 1940.

154. Amery diary, May 11 1940.

155. Amery diary, May 11 and 12 1940.

156. Chamberlain to Churchill, May 11 1940.

157. Dugdale diary, May 14 1940.

158. Whom Chamberlain had already removed from the Cabinet in April.

159. Churchill to Adams, November 16 1940.

160. Astor to Bracken, May 20 1940, and Bracken to Astor, May 24 1940. Lady Astor to Lothian, May 21 1940.

161. They sat with Chamberlain, Halifax, Anderson, Wood, Brown, Inskip, Simon, W.S. Morrison, Duncan, Reith, MacDonald, Woolton, Hudson, Hankey and Tryon from the old.

162. Chamberlain talking in Reith, p. 381.

163. Churchill to Chamberlain, May 10 1940.

164. Channon diary, May 10 1940. Winterton to Hoare, May 9 1940.

165. E.g. E.C. Cobb, Sir George Davies to Chamberlain and James Stuart to Chamberlain, May 10–14 1940 in NC 13/17, together with many other expressions of loyalty and irritation from Chamberlain's supporters.

166. For the cool reception he received at his first appearance in the House of Commons, see Dugdale diary, May 14 1940.

167. Spens to Chamberlain, May 9 1940.

NOTES TO CONCLUSION

1. For J.B. Priestley, whose wartime broadcasts transmuted a contentious Northern radicalism into a central position which the BBC would accept, see *Postscripts*, 1940, and 'Out of the People', 1941. For Noël Coward as laureate of the People's war, see the films *This Happy Breed, In which we Serve* etc.

2. I.e. Michael Foot, Peter Howard and Frank Owen, all Beaverbrook journalists in the thirties and authors of *Tory MP* (1939),

Guilty Men (1940) and *100,000,000 allies — if we choose* (1940), the last two of which helped to create a new outlook after Dunkirk.

3. Stanley Morison being not only the *Times* typographer and its official historian, but also typographer to, and Catholic, Radical, expacifist, friend of Beaverbrook (see Barker, *passim* but especially ch. 15).

4. The case of Greenwood is well-known. For Alexander see e.g. Bruce Lockhart diary, April 26 1934.

5. For Morrison aiming at edgelessness, see Chamberlain to Hilda November 23 1935, but for him being a 'bitter partisan', see Chamberlain to Ida, September 30 1937.

6. For Morrison being thought of as a member of a national government, see Jones to Lady Grigg, November 3 1936 (doubtless in the knowledge that Morrison had wanted to follow MacDonald in 1931). It is one of the few defects of Jones and Donoughue's admirable *Life* that it does not tell us with what degree of self-consciousness Morrison was preparing himself in the late thirties for high (perhaps the highest) office in war.

7. Attlee, pp. 12 and 277.

8. Attlee, pp. 13 and 285.

9. Baldwin to Linlithgow, December 29 1938. Butler to Braborne, March 1 1935.

10. Attlee to Tom Attlee, January 1 1933.

11. Attlee to Tom Attlee, January 1 1933.

12. Attlee to Tom Attlee, April 29 1938.

13. I.e. not only after the 1935 election (when he was elected over Morrison and Greenwood) but also in 1937 (when plans were laid to remove him, chiefly by Dalton).

14. Linlithgow to Lady Salisbury, June 16 1936, Eur.F.125 152.

15. Attlee, p. 279, and Attlee's speeches, *passim*.

16. Attlee, p. 224.

17. Attlee, pp. 154—5.

18   Attlee to Tom Attlee, April 3 1933.

19. Attlee, p. 284.

20. Attlee, pp. 279 and 281—3.

21. Attlee in ed. Bryant, *Constructive Democracy*, p. 113. See also PREM 1/373 for Simon and Chamberlain after Conscription. See also Attlee to Tom Attlee, February 15 1933, and in the *Morning Post*, June 6 1936.

22. Keyes, p. 1.

23. *History of the Times 1921—48*, p. 990.

24. For Francis Acland see Nicolson diary, September 29 1938. For Richard Acland see Nicolson diary, March 14 and December 5 1938. For Mabane see Nicolson diary, April 19 1937. For Cartland see Nicolson diary, July 28 1936. For Wilfred Roberts offering to withdraw Liberal opposition in West Leicester if Nicolson would stop being National Labour see Nicolson diary, April 12 1938.

25. Nicolson diary, September 10 1937.
26. Brown talking in Nicolson diary, July 9 1936.
27. Womersley to Chamberlain, October 1 1938.
28. Butler to Brabourne, June 20 1934.
29. De la Warr in Nicolson diary, September 10 1937, and Titchfield in Nicolson diary, May 20 1936.
30. Sandys talking in Nicolson diary, July 28 1936. Lean in *News Chronicle*, December 14 1938.
31. See Cowling, p. 423.
32. Eden in *Hansard* (341) of November 10 1938, col. 381. Nicolson diary, November 10 1938, and Astor to Garvin, November 17 1938, for two similar views of Eden.
33. Nicolson diary, September 10 1937.
34. Nicolson diary, February 13 and March 8 1939.
35. Astor to Garvin, November 17 1938, and Lady Astor to Lothian, March 23 1939.
36. King-Hall in 1922 Committee minute-book of July 3 1939.
37. In his diary for December 26 1938, Pownall reported himself and Bridges agreeing that rearmament should have started 'a year earlier' but that 'there [was] nothing very much wrong with the scale of our preparations' and that another 'year or eighteen months' would be sufficient to avoid 'defeat in a short war'. Immediately before the war began he believed that, though a 'short war...might have [been] lost...last September, now we shouldn't [lose]...a long war either'. While there can be no doubt about the overriding importance of the 'interlocking options' (see above pp. 159—62), it is interesting that, for example, the Chiefs of Staff 'Appreciation of the Situation in the event of war against Germany' (CP 199(38) of September 14 1938) was written in a moderate tone about German air superiority (paras. 22—7), but was emphatic about the 'three-cornered bogey'.
38. E.g. Hankey, Phipps and Smuts.
39. For the Italian Ambassador in Moscow repeating this to the Italian government, see Toscano, pp. 52—8.
40. To say nothing of e.g. Nicolson (diary, April 15 1939) and Harvey (diary, *passim* in early 1938) for the view that Roosevelt's statements had made America's intervention in war inevitable and that the 'Anglo-Saxons' had therefore 'won'.
41. E.g. Cadogan note on Duff Cooper to Halifax, March 22 1939, FO 800/315.
42. See e.g. Ismay, memorandum for the Prime Minister of June 29 1939 in PREM 1/309. Cf. Dilks, Cadogan diary, p. 172, and Langer and Gleason, p. 104.
43. See Langer and Gleason, p. 49, for a report (denied) that Roosevelt had said this in 1939.

556

bury) 377, (Simon) 349, (Zetland) 318
Murray, Gilbert, 109, 113, 413; and League of Nations Union, 18, 19, 21, 33, 228-9; NC on, 294
Mussolini, B., 51, 72, 78; and Abyssinia, 80-1, 86, 87, 88; Eden and, 102, 103, 132, 162, 164, 169; *Times* and, 129-30, 132; as threat to Egypt and Kenya, 134; Hitler works with, 144, 174; NC and, 155, 180; opinions about, (Baldwin) 147, (Hankey and Chiefs of Staff) 162, (Vansittart) 156, 158; NC opens negotiations with, 162-3, 166; and Spain, 168, 173; NC and 201, 204, 210; 'a good European' (Amery), 225; Churchill and, 239, 242; offensive speech by (May 1938), 277; Halifax and NC visit (Jan. 1939) 281; attempts at appeasement of, 300-1, 306; invited to mediate, 307; Hore-Belisha visits, 330

Narvik: passage of Swedisch iron ore to Germany through, 361; failure of Anglo-French landing at, 363, 364, 371, 377; Germans take, 371
Nathan, H.L., 230, 413
National Council of Labour, and Czechoslovakia, 212
National Defence Contribution, 257, 265, 393
National Economy Act, and judges' salaries, 61
National Government of 1931, 15-16, 46; problem of converting from a coalition into a party, 51
National Government of 1935, 109, 123, 128
National Government of May 1940, 2, 384-6
National Labour Party: (1931-5), 41, 42, 51, 53, 58-9, 60, 92; (from 1935), 249, 322-4, 392; resignations from, 333
National Liberal Party, 112, 251, 333; Simon as leader of, 350
National Register, 226, 351
National Review, 117
National Service, Labour Party and, 214, 220; *see also* conscription
navy: and British Empire, 70; not able

to provide defence against Germany while preparing sanctions against Italy, 144, 155; expansion of, 152; as chief line of defence, 154; proposal for cordon of, round Spanish coast, 165; question of mobilisation of (1938), 200, 328, 330; on manoeuvres in North Sea (Aug. 1939), 293, 298
Nazi regime: opinions about, (Beaverbrook) 119, (Hailsham) 316, (Lothian) 133-4; complains of *News Chronicle*, 235; leaders of, advertised in British airborne leaflets as piling up fortunes in foreign banks (1939), 357
New Commonwealth group (Lord Davies's), 230, 242
New Deal: Lloyd George's, 39, 40, 47, 57, 81, 234, 374; Roosevelt's, 39, 59
New Five Year group, 230
New Outlook, The, 246
New Statesman, 258
News Chronicle, 36, 38, 233-5, 282, 333, 388; and NC, 56, 258, 304; and foreign policy, 109
newspapers: advice to backbenchers from, 5; and NC, 258; Henderson on, 288; and Churchill, 252, 343; *see also individual papers*
Next Five Years group, 40, 52-3, 246
Nicolson, Harold, 323, 333, 413; in opposition to NC, 227, 244, 249, 252, 413; NC on, 294; at fall of NC, 374, 381; in 1940 Government, 385
Nineteenth Century and After, 117
Noel-Baker, P., 82, 229, 413; and League of Nations Union, 18, 21, 33, 115; wins Derby from National Labour, 231
Noel-Buxton, N.E., 1st Baron, 123, 267, 358, 413
Non-Intervention Committee (Spain), 164, 165
Norman, Montagu, 24, 47, 413
North Cornwall by-election (1939), 253
Norway: passage of Swedish iron ore to Germany through, 361; proposed mining of waters of, 361, 370; failure of landing in, 363, 364, 365, 371, 380; Germany occupies,